ICTs for Global Development and Sustainability:
Practice and Applications

Jacques Steyn
Monash University, South Africa

Jean-Paul van Belle
University of Cape Town, South Africa

Eduardo Villanueva Mansilla
Pontificia Universidad Catolica del Peru, Peru

INFORMATION SCIENCE REFERENCE

Hershey · New York

Director of Editorial Content:	Kristin Klinger
Director of Book Publications:	Julia Mosemann
Acquisitions Editor:	Lindsay Johnston
Development Editor:	Julia Mosemann
Publishing Assistant:	Casey Conapitski
Typesetter:	Casey Conapitski
Production Editor:	Jamie Snavely
Cover Design:	Lisa Tosheff

Published in the United States of America by
    Information Science Reference (an imprint of IGI Global)
    701 E. Chocolate Avenue
    Hershey PA 17033
    Tel: 717-533-8845
    Fax: 717-533-8661
    E-mail: cust@igi-global.com
    Web site: http://www.igi-global.com

Library of Congress Cataloging-in-Publication Data

ICTs for global development and sustainability : practice and applications /
Jacques Steyn, Jean-Paul van Belle and Eduardo Villanueva Mansilla, editors.
    p. cm.
 Includes bibliographical references and index.
 Summary: "This book unites the theoretical underpinnings and scientific methodology of an approach of deploying ICT in marginalized communities to bridge the so-called digital divide. This book contains case studies of Asia, Africa, Latin America and the Caribbean that demonstrate which approaches work and which do not in deploying public access to information sources"--Provided by publisher.
 ISBN 978-1-61520-997-2 (hbk) -- ISBN 978-1-61520-998-9 (ebook) 1. Information technology--Developing countries. 2. Digital divide--Developing countries. 3. Economic development--Developing countries. I. Steyn, Jacques. II. Van Belle, Jean-Paul, 1961- III. Villanueva Mansilla, Eduardo, 1965-
  HC59.72.I55I494 2011
  303.48'33091724--dc22
                 2010039758

British Cataloguing in Publication Data
A Cataloguing in Publication record for this book is available from the British Library.

Table of Contents

Section 1
Public Access to ICT and Telecentres

Section 2
Cultural and Social Matters

Section 3
Mixed Media and Localization

Detailed Table of Contents

Section 1
Public Access to ICT and Telecentres

Chapter 1

This chapter highlights the value and limitations of participative development employed in the implementation of an ICT-based research and development project in the Kelabit Highlands of Central Borneo. The first section describes the reasons for e-Bario project and why participative development, with a strong emphasis on the anthropological methods of immersion and Participatory Action Research (PAR), has been adopted as development approach in Bario. In the second section, the author interrogates participatory development as practiced in the e-Bario by bringing to light a number of problematic aspects of the participative technique, in which conflicts have arisen over the development process, and the interpretation of participation itself has been vigorously questioned. Later, a relational view of the participative process is proposed, which suggests a shift of focus from technology to people and social relations. The author argues that a relational perspective of participative process can open up a social space for local people and developers to identify, cultivate and establish social relationships both within and beyond a project's framework. It is these bonds of trust and obligation, developed and sustained over the longer term, that have allowed the Kelabit and the researchers to work out their social relationships to one another in matters concerning e-Bario.

Chapter 2

Malaysia aims to be an information society by the year 2020 can only be achieved if the mass population, that include those who live in the rural area, has the access to use the ICT. This is due to the uneven distribution of the basic telecommunication infostructure between the urban and rural areas in Malaysia that left the rural area to be at the disadvantage to access the ICT. Meanwhile, there are many programs that have been implemented by the government to encourage the rural population to use the Internet, such as 'Kedaikom', a community based telecenter serving the rural population.

Caroline Pade Khene, Rhodes University, South Africa
Ingrid Siebörger, Rhodes University, South Africa
Hannah Thinyane, Rhodes University, South Africa
Lorenzo Dalvit, Rhodes University, South Africa

Rural development and poverty alleviation are a priority for development in South Africa. Information and knowledge are key strategic resources for social and economic development, as they empower rural communities with the ability to expand their choices through knowing what works best in their communities. Information Communication Technologies (ICTs) act as tools which enable existing rural development activities. The Siyakhula living lab (SLL) aims to develop and field-test a distributed, multifunctional community communication platform, using localization through innovation, to deploy in marginalized communities in South Africa. The project exists as research collaboration between the Telkom Centres of Excellence at the University of Fort Hare and Rhodes University. Its current pilot operates in the Mbashe municipal area, which is a deep rural area located along the wild coast of the Eastern Cape province of South Africa. The Dwesa-Cweba Nature Reserve acts as a chief asset in the community, which contributes to tourism development. However, the community is currently not actively involved in tourism development; but potential exists in local arts, crafts, and authentic heritage tourism. Therefore, the SLL aspires to empower the community with appropriate communication technology skills to actively support tourism development and other complementary development activities, such as, education. The lessons learned and applied in the project's current pilot stage identify techniques and approaches that aim to promote the effectiveness and sustainability of the ICT project in a rural context. These approaches and techniques are viewed and described from social-cultural, institutional, economic, and technological perspectives.

Antonio Díaz Andrade, Auckland University of Technology, New Zealand

Using an interpretive case study design, the author analyzes and explains why under circumstances of severe scarcity and geographical isolation computers can do little in helping local people. The findings challenge the sometimes over-optimistic stances on ICT benefits adopted by international development agencies and governments. Conversely, it confirms the need to provide basic infrastructure and stresses the importance of establishing priorities correctly before launching any ICT for development initiative.

The Digital Doorway is a joint initiative between the Meraka Institute of the Council for Scientific and Industrial Research (CSIR) and South Africa's Department of Science and Technology (DST), with a vision of making a fundamental difference to computer literacy and associated skills in the South African population. Underpinning the project is the idea of people's inherent cognitive ability to teach themselves computer skills with minimal external intervention. For this to happen, computers must be easily accessible to potential learners in an environment conducive to experimentation. Given the low percentage of communities in disadvantaged areas in South Africa with access to computer infrastructure, Digital Doorways are installed in communities where the need is greatest. The systems are extremely robust and employ open source content.

This chapter critically examines the role of Information and Communication Technologies (ICTs) in governmental reform processes in development through a case study of the Indian State of Karnataka. This study explores the increasing use of ICTs for property taxation and itsimpact on municipal government reform processes within this developing world context.

Section 2
Cultural and Social Matters

The Northern Territory Library's (NTL) Libraries and Knowledge Centres (LKC) program is one of a number of programs across Australia designed to bring ICTs and Indigenous people together within an appropriate technology / community-networking framework. A center-piece is the use of the Our Story database to hold and display both repatriated and contemporary, including born-digital, cultural material relevant to local communities. The LKC model is distinctive in that it is fully implemented, uses proven technology, has a consistent framework of program delivery, and a clear business case. However there continue to be fundamental questions on striking a balance between technical innovation and sustainability; the capacity of the program to expand while maintaining support in geographically remote areas; and the challenge of maintaining a relationship of trust with local communities. Reviewing the challenges of the Our Story / LKC program sheds light on key reasons why ICT-based community-networking projects succeed or fail.

This chapter summarises the findings of a survey of 74 Chinese migrants living in Prato, Italy, as an example of Chinese migrants in Europe. It was administered in late 2008. Prato as a province has the largest Chinese migrant population in Italy, numbering about 30,000. The research aimed to understand the usefulness of mobile phones to migrant residents who need to keep in touch with their friends and families, in China and Italy, and their other communication needs, and whether mobiles satisfy their expectations. Participants in this study are well-served by mobiles. The typical participant in the study was a recently-arrived young single male from Zhejiang, China, speaking Wenzhouese, but with proficiency in other languages, experiencing the novelty of using a recently-purchased 'Nokia' phone, and who, whilst spending more than 10 Euros a month on the phone for keeping in touch with friends in China, was very aware of mobile running costs. More research is planned to flesh out the findings further.

Chapter 9

There have been many case studies in the literature on telecentres, often seeking to analyse the usage of these facilities via surveys and covering gender issues by "counting women". This chapter presents a more qualitative and ethnographic account, exploring one particular telecentre in a small town in rural Chile and comparing it with the seven local commercial cybercafés.

Section 3
Mixed Media and Localization

This chapter examines the role of People First Network (PFnet) services in enhancing information and communication and contributing to sustainable rural development and poverty reduction in Solomon

Islands. More specifically, it examines two main issues. First, it examines the uptake and appropriation of PFnet services by rural Solomon Islanders. Second, it examines the impact of PFnet services on sustainable rural development and poverty reduction in Solomon Islands. This chapter is based on a empirical research conducted in Solomon Islands between January-May 2004. The chapter is organised as follows: Section one provides an overview of PFnet Project. Section two states the main aims of the study. Section three outlines the methodology used for the research. The Section four reports the main research findings. Section five discusses some problems and finally section six provides the conclusion.

Chapter 11

This case study focuses on a civil society organization called Radio Viva in Asunción, Paraguay. It was found that the interactive use of 'traditional' and 'new' technologies in locally innovative ways was able to meet community needs through the creation of two local products. Specifically, when radio and telephony were integrated with telecentre services (including internet access), new physical and virtual communication spaces were opened up for civic participation. Second, ICT interactivity was found to lead to the creation of locally relevant content production, helping Paraguayan communities to gain access to useful and contextualized information while also turning local 'information recipients' into 'knowledge users'.

Section 4
Managing ICT4D

Chapter 12

This chapter is set against a background of national ICT initiatives implemented in the Vocational and Technical Education (VTE) sectors of developing Asian countries through donor agency funded projects. This research is based on a ten year research study of ICT initiatives implemented in nine VTE sector donor funded projects covering Laos, Sri Lanka and Vietnam. The empirical data was gathered through contextual observations, action research and a review of project documentation. The ICT initiatives studied focussed on MIS (management information systems) aiding strategy formulation and management in the VTE sector and computer based training (CBT). The research reveals that the projects studied were designed by host governments and donor agencies in response to perceived problems in the VTE sector. The research also reveals that process of managing donor projects, which is largely based on hard approaches, is problematic. Soft Systems Methodology (SSM) is based on a learning and enquiring cycle. The research uses SSM to learn about the nature and scope of the selected donor projects in VTE, which can be conceptualised as Project Intervention Processes (PIPs).

Chapter 13

Helena Grunfeld, Victoria University, Australia
Seán Ó Siochrú, NEXUS Research, Ireland
Brian Unger, University of Calgary, Canada
Sarun Im, iREACH Project, Cambodia

Cambodia is for various reasons a challenging environment for ICT development. This did not deter IDRC (Canada) from funding an ambitious and ground-breaking project designed ultimately to influence ICT policy in Cambodia but initially to establish two pilot community-owned networks in poor rural areas. Each comprises both a cluster of local telecentres (10 in each area), and a mini telecoms enterprise run by the communities. Begun in May 2006, with initial funding of USD1.3 million the project runs to May 2010 when the question of sustainability comes to the fore. Additional support is likely to be needed.

Section 5
Informed Planning and Cooperation

Chapter 14

Rajendra Kumar, Ministry of Communications and Information Technology, India

This chapter examines the role of institutional partnerships in making the ICT for development projects more successful and sustainable in developing countries. Employing a regional innovation systems (RIS) perspective, the author examines this issue in the context of lessons drawn from the failure of telecenters in Melur taluka of Tamil Nadu under the Sustainable Access in Rural India (SARI) project.

Chapter 15

Vincent Shaw, University of Oslo, Norway & Health Information Systems Program, South Africa
Jorn Braa, University of Oslo, Norway

This chapter draws on 10 years of experience of the Health Information Systems Programme (HISP), an action research orientated network of public health practitioners and academics who initiated a pilot project in health information systems development in the post-apartheid transformation of South Africa, and which has subsequently had a profound effect on the development of health information systems in Africa and Asia. Through an exploration of health information systems development in numerous countries in Africa, the authors highlight insights into approaches and methodologies that contribute to successful and sustainable health information systems in resource constrained settings.

ICT4D and Development Informatics literature and media reports often use statistics offered by the World Bank, ITU or CIA to make a case for the introduction of ICTs in developing contexts. Arguably the most widely used statistic is the claim of World Bank statistics that a very large proportion of the global population live on less than USD2 per day. When scrutinized, such claims are not based on solid methodology or logic. Such overgeneralized statistics seem to ride on media hype, and appeal to empathy rather than good science. Yet ICT4D evangelists, who present ICT as the holy grail to transform underdeveloped regions into global economic powerhouses, appeal to such statistics for justification of their cases. Here a brief analysis of some problems with statistics, such as ICT4D data, is presented. Claims and policy-making based on such data should be approached critically and interpreted with a large dose of skepticism. A consolidated table of CIA Yearbook data on the global penetration of landline phones, internet access and mobile phones is presented as an appendix.

Foreword

Information and Communication Technologies (ICTs) are increasingly being recognized as constituting a very important and robust engine for sustainable growth and development, especially for economically disadvantaged countries. Consequently, this book and its companion volume *ICTs and Sustainable Solutions for the Digital Divide: Theory and Perspectives* are timely and indeed very relevant for contemporary endeavours that aim to reduce the global digital divide among nations. Contributions for this volume come from all regions of the developing world and which make it very attractive and educative to the international readership. The contents of this book advance our understanding on various aspects of ICTs based on new approaches, research, training and practical applications in the developing world.

There are several chapters from Latin America. A contribution from the remote village in Peruvian Andes tells us that ICT as a tool for development in that area is still new, not well known to many people and hence its utilization very limited. A second chapter from Peru deals with an under-privileged population with a political will striving to connect the poorest communities to the global market economy through utilization of ICT telecentres in the rural areas. This is a very brilliant undertaking to be emulated by many countries. Experience from Chile and Paraguay emphasizes the importance of the convergence of technologies and social services that is necessary to strengthen the execution of developmental projects. The effectiveness of this convergence relies heavily on the availability of sustainable financial and human (i.e. ICT experts) resources. The chapter from Chile underscores the gender-sensitive utilization of ICT in both rural and urban areas. It has been revealed that "men never say that they do not know how to utilize computers". This anathema has a bearing on men's social status whilst female ICT users are willing to be taught new knowledge and skills.

There are chapters on ICT in Africa: one chapter reports on ICT in the health sectors in Ethiopia, Liberia, Nigeria, Sierra Leone, South Africa and Zambia. The main objective of this research work was to produce evidence-based argument for the replacement of paper-based healthcare systems and the introduction of computerized systems in a functional and sustainable manner. ICT research findings from these countries continue to emphasize the need to eliminate the digital divide from the contemporary world and that ICT skills and infrastructure are needed in modern healthcare services in Africa. A chapter from South Africa argues for the need for the deployment of ICT to enhance socio-economic activities of the rural communities in that country. The findings from this research work has demonstrated that information and knowledge are crucial strategic resources for socio-economic development; and that ICTs empower the rural communities to make sound decisions on their expanded choices.

ICT chapters from Asia bring another dimension of the digital divide from that part of the world and report on the continued effort of making ICT a developmental tool to the majority of the people there. The chapter from central Borneo in Malaysia showcases the enhancement of social relationships within the community of the main actors involved in rural development. It has been demonstrated in Laos, Sri Lanka and Vietnam that effective project management and service provision may be attained through the application of ICT. A good example is given in the vocational and technical education sectors in these three countries. Malaysia has recorded tremendous progress in the utilization of ICT and this is mostly due to the country's vision 2020 which includes the desire by that nation moving towards information society by 2020. It has been found that the partnership between the government, the private sector and the communities in question (i.e. rural communities) is obligatory if the digital divide has to be narrowed between the rural and the urban communities of this country. This type of partnership is necessary for all nations. IDRC (Canada) funded an ICT project in Cambodia where the main objective was to make ICT (i.e. local telecentres) a tool for policy-making processes for the poor rural areas. The major challenge experienced here is the sustainability of the project once the injected donor funds dry up at the closure the project. This financial constraint is a salient scenario for most donor-funded projects in developing countries, hence developing countries are today strongly urged to ensure that internal financial and human resources are availed to supplement all their donor-funded projects.

ICT research work on the Solomon Islands has been undertaken with the intention of enhancing the utilization of ICT for sustainable development and poverty reduction from the Islanders. The chapter from India discusses the sustainability of ICT (i.e. telecentres) in rural areas and advocates the presence of an effective regional innovation system (RIS) where the main actors are the user communities, the private sector and institutions of higher learning. The libraries and knowledge centres program introduced in northern Australia with the intention of bringing ICTs and indigenous population (i.e. Aborigines) together, has begun bearing fruit as it negates the classical approach of imposition of inappropriate technologies on the indigenous people.

This book contributes significantly to the magnitude of our understanding of the global digital divide and offers plausible sustainable solutions to this ICT calamity! The chapters presented in this volume give us clear lessons dealing with ICT capacity building (e.g. skills and infrastructure), and involvement of poor communities, especially those in the rural areas, in making decisions for their own development strategies and pathways through deployment of ICTs. Through this book, it has been increasing proven that a partnership between government and its public institutions, private sector and ICT-user communities is obligatory for any meaningful search for sustainable solutions for scaling down the digital divide between nations and within individual nations. However, the need for further work on this subject is still enormous. One should also not forget that our shared understanding of global climate change and its consequences to our lives and national economies requires the availability of functioning ICTs in all nations, and hence this book is another testimony for our shared necessity to drastically narrow down the digital divide between the developing and the developed world.

Sospeter Muhango
Regional Director
ICSU Regional Office for Africa
FAAS, FGSAf, FASSAf, FGIGE, FTWAS, FCAGS, FGS, CGeol, EurGeol

Preface

Development Informatics is the discipline focusing on the development of systems of Information and Communication Technologies (ICT) in constrained or under-developed contexts. Although Development Informatics covers a very wide spectrum of ICT aspects, our interest in this volume is in social computing, covering the experiences and needs of "ordinary" users (or citizens) of technology, as opposed to military, government or corporate and business users. In the first volume of this book set, *ICTs and Sustainable Solutions for the Digital Divide: Theory and Perspectives*, the focus is on the theoretical issues of Development Informatics, or more precisely, the lack of theory, with the contributions in that volume covering aspects that need to be considered for the construction of a theory.

This volume focuses on case studies and covers Development Informatics or ICT4D projects and use of ICT in the geographical regions of Australasia and the Pacific Ocean, Africa, and Latin America. It is hoped that the case studies might inform the goal of eventually developing models and a theory of the use of technology, particularly ICT, among the many diverse cultures on the planet. Most of these cultures are found in economically poor contexts, or geographically remote areas which makes connectivity costly and ICT resources relatively scarce. Although the discipline of Development Informatics is also interested in the technical aspects of ICT (for example, how to provide affordable network access to remote communities), the focus of the chapters in this volume is on the human side of ICT, investigating issues such as the importance of the community, social, cultural and psychological factors and economic sustainability.

The geographical region of Australasia and the Pacific Ocean includes a wide variety of cultures, countries with different levels of economic development, and with different levels of access to Information and Communication Technology networks and devices. It is also the region where the majority of global population lives (3.8 billion, which is about 56%), mainly due to the population sizes of India and China. The many islands in the region require expensive submarine cables or satellite technology for global connectivity. Island populations are also relatively small, with the exception of Indonesia, resulting in a relatively small tax base and the lack of economies of scale, hampering infrastructure development.

Africa is the poorest continent on the planet, the least connected, suffers from numerous problems, and has a population approaching 1 billion. Although there is a trend toward urbanization, the majority of its population (60% - according to Tibaijuka, undated) are still agriculturalists, living in rural areas.

While Latin America is a region with significant similarities among its vast population of almost 600 million (CIA Yearbook - in the Appendix of Steyn, this volume), such as the same language spoken in more than 30 countries, it consists of a diverse collection of cultures, made up of a combination of original communities, mestizaje, an ethnic as well as cultural mixture of European and Aboriginal communities. There is also a clear divide between urban and rural communities, as well as social and economic practices, which are defining factors in the way groups of people relate to the world, being it more localized within the borders of the country or, as it is now more common through technology, the global community. Calculated by using the Gini coefficient, this region shows the most inequality.

The chapters are organized thematically rather than geographically. This organization should not give the impression that the chapters fit neatly into these main themes. On a more detailed level, most chapters touch on the same issues. The notes in the Introduction on the contributions are not intended to be summaries of the chapters. Rather, some aspects are highlighted, and implications for ICT4D projects are noted. The implications are our own interpretations, and not necessarily made explicit as such by the authors of the chapters.

PUBLIC ACCESS TO ICT AND TELECENTRES

The participative research methodology is favored by many researchers in the ICT4D arena, with varying degrees of success. Poline Bala, in her chapter *Re-thinking Methodology through the e-Bario Project. From Participatory Methods to a Relational Approach to ICT for Rural Development in Sarawak, East Malaysia*, relates experiences from the e-Bario ICT project in the Kelabit highlands of Malaysia, and cautions against rushing into communities with technologies without first investigating and understanding the historical, political and social context. Working with complex participants such as humans poses many problems. Even though the participatory method has a set of problems of its own, at least it does not suffer the problems of top-down projects. One implication of the conclusion of Bala's chapter is that ICT4D research and activity within communities cannot be done without project members from many different disciplines - among others cultural studies, psychology and sociology. Such projects should never be attempted by technologists or politicians alone, and with politics is meant outsiders in position of power, including well-meaning NGO's. Another implication is that such projects are time consuming, and thus should be planned for the long-term. There are no quick-fixes.

The Kedaikom project presented in the chapter *Bringing the Internet to the Rural Area: A Case Study of the 'Kedaikom' Project in Malaysia* by Zulkefli bin Ibrahim, Ainin Sulaiman and Tengku M. Faziharudean, documents the Malaysian Government's undertaking to bring Internet access to rural areas in Malaysia. The political vision is to turn Malaysia into an information society by year 2020. To achieve this, the Kedaikom project was launched to offer internet access by means of telecenters in rural communities. The authors document the impact in this study. They conclude that telecentres should serve as public spaces for community interactions. In other words, telecentres should function as one of the activities on the village square. The focus of telecentres may be ICT, but this should fit in with community life. Even in highly developed regions internet cafés often serve coffee and even meals, and as locations to meet friends and "hang out". Public ICT access centres should be designed to fit in with such social places and meet broader community needs than just to serve as access points.

Caroline Pade Khene, Ingrid Siebörger, Hannah Thinyane and Lorenzo Dalvit report in their chapter *The Siyakhula Living Lab: A Holistic Approach to Rural Development through the Development and Deployment of an ICT Communication Platform in Rural South Africa* on their research into a living lab model for ICT projects. The Siyakhula Living Lab involves a holistic approach to bringing modern ICT infrastructures to rural areas. The emphasis is connecting the community by means of a sophisticated communications infrastructure to promote and exploit the tourism potential in the Eastern Cape, one of the most underdeveloped and poorest regions in South Africa. Although sophisticated technologies such as satellite and WiMax were used, the main emphasis on the implementation of the labs was to adhere to 'best ICT4D practices' by using local champions and community-based resources such as schools. Initially focusing on the e-marketing of local crafts and eco-tourism, the possibilities of e-government, e-health and e-learning were later explored and incorporated. Again, the non-technical contexts, the sociocultural and political aspects, are very important. Issues encountered that had impact on the project are such as deliberate misinformation by participants, trust, language, gender and age, and political constraints. It is concluded that the need for public-private partnerships, capacity and local content development are important for the successful deployment of ICT system in rural and poor communities.

In the chapter *Does IT Help or Not? Computers for Development in the Andes*, Antonio Díaz Andrade reviews a telecentre in the small Peruvian village Huanico. This Infocentro, the local name for a telecentre, was financed by foreign donors. Geographical isolation and a harsh environment were just some of the challenges. The outcome of experiences at the Infocentro did not match the expectations of the planners. Díaz Andrade analyzes the disconnection between the expected results and the actual reception of the usage of the Infocentro. He concludes that ICT might be a nice to have, but in communities that lack the basics of human needs (we may add, such as illustrated in Maslow's hierarchy of needs), they are not very useful, especially as local needs are not met. Communication infrastructure is not as important as other infrastructures that deal with lower level needs. Also, if the information supplied by ICT is not locally relevant, a telecentre will not be successful.

In the chapter *Digital Doorways*, Kim Gush, Ruth de Villiers, Ronel Smith and Grant Cambridge report on an initiative of the South African government to introduce robust, kiosk-like computers in rural and poor communities. The Digital Doorways project aims to provide unassisted computer-based computer literacy skills to impoverished communities, an idea which was inspired by Sugata Mithra's hole-in-the-wall concept, adapted to both African circumstances and recent technology evolutions, and based on mesh networking and open source software. The first phase had demonstrated the technical proof-of-concept quite convincingly by using a robust kiosk-based delivery system driven by open source content. However, going beyond the typical 'technical feasibility' stage, this project then expanded its reach and scope. This chapter reports on the current 'mass-roll-out' phase which focuses on the usability and design challenges. The empirical data was based on a roll-out of about two hundred Digital Doorway units across South Africa. The authors use data obtained from observations and user interviews to critically assess the project and which points towards the critical importance of social and contextual conditions (such as full community ownership and participation) for long term sustainability.

The importance of understanding culture before ICTs are implemented is relevant not only for social communication goals, or basic ICT access such as at telecentres. Cultural and psychological issues also influence the failure or success of large-scale e-governance operations. In her chapter, *Information and Communication Technologies in Administrative Reform for Development: Exploring the Case of Property Tax Systems in Karnataka, India,* Shefali Virkar shows why an ICT Property Tax System deployed in India failed. The system was developed to improve tax governance operations, but failed to first analyze the socio-cultural perceptions of tax in India. There was no consideration of plain human psychology or human nature. In this project the administrative process was streamlined by a new ICT system, yet revenue from tax collection itself remained surprisingly unchanged. Prior to the installation of the system, tax officers personally assessed the values of properties and taxes were levied accordingly. The ICT system expected owners to declare the values of their properties objectively and by themselves, but typically of human nature, they undervalued their properties in order to pay less tax. Again, this case demonstrates that a holistic approach is required for the implementation of ICT systems. We are human, after all.

CULTURAL AND SOCIAL MATTERS

Remote and rural communities all over the globe are on the wrong side of the digital divide. This is true not only of the poorer countries, but also in highly developed regions such as Canada and Australia. Most of the Australian population is concentrated on the east and south coasts, with the exception of a few cities, such as Perth and Darwin, while the remainder of this vast country with its land surface larger than that of the USA, is sparsely populated. The Northern Territories is a vast area with little connectivity outside the main centers. There are many remote Aboriginal communities in this area. Community cultures are local, and are not homogeneous, even if a particular culture dominates in a country. A generic European culture may dominate in Australia. But it does not follow that all communities within this economically highly developed region share the values of the dominant culture. If the rights of minorities are to be respected, it means that dominant cultures cannot enforce their own technological and economic views on minorities.

In their chapter *Localisation of Indigenous Content: Libraries and Knowledge Centres and the Our Story Database in the Northern Territory*, Gibson, Lloyd and Richmond demonstrate the importance of distinguishing between the technological aspects of ICT projects and the cultural and community factors. The Our Story database case concerns a more advance use of ICTs for documenting the cultural heritage of an aboriginal community in a variety of physical materials as well as digital multimedia content. Even though strong consideration is given to community inputs, the issues of trust and understanding, sometimes radically different viewpoints from non-Western thinkers on technologies, are brought to the fore. Again, cultural issues cannot be disregarded when ICT is established in communities. What may work in one culture, may not work in another. What works in New York among ICT aficionados is not universal.

In their chapter, *Mobile Phones, Diasporas and Developing Countries; A Case Study of Connectedness Among Chinese in Italy*, Graeme Johanson and Tom Denison report on the use of ICT, specifically mobile phones, by migrant Chinese workers in Prato, Italy. Although some of these 30'000 Chinese, mainly textile workers, have been in Prato for more than a decade, they do not regard the city as their home, and plan to return to China. They work here mainly to support their family back home. It is questionable whether China is to be regarded as a developing or developed country. Whichever way China is perceived, the relevance of the Chinese community in Prato is that they are socially remote from the Italian community in Prato, and geographically remote from their families and real homes. ICT is thus a very important tool for them to maintain their social relationships back in China, and used for their psychological well-being.

One of the social dimensions in culture is gender perceptions and relations which influence interactions with technology. Dorothea Kleine's chapter *"The Men Never Say That They Do Not Know" - Telecentres as Gendered Spaces* investigates the social dimension of gender in the use of ICT in a small village in Chile. Her exploration reveals a very gendered space, where some uses and practices are the realm of males and others of females, bringing into question the current setup of telecentres that assume a gender-neutral perspective. In a heavily-gendered society, as Chile and many other countries of Latin America are, female users of ICT are relegated but at the same time, allowed more leeway in terms of asking questions, while males are supposed to know all that is needed to know, and are not supposed to require assistance, especially if it is to come from a female. Saving their masculine gender faces is very important to males, even if this results in less effective use of ICT. Commercial cybercafes are designed around the demands of male-styled usage and lack floor plans that allow a mother to bring a pram. Understanding human needs and behavior thus has implications even for the design of ICT contexts, such as the spaces in which ICT is used.

MIXED MEDIA AND LOCALIZATION

The importance of human factors is also evident in Anand Chand's chapter, *Reducing Digital Divide. The Case of the 'People First Network' (PFNet) in the Solomon Islands*, which reports on the People First Network (PFnet) in the Solomon Islands, which consists of about a thousand small islands scattered across an area of about 28,400 square kilometers. The total population of all the Pacific islands is only about 15 million. Villages on the islands are small. For example, Sasamunga on the island of Choiseul in the Solomon Islands has a population of only about one hundred people, while it is approximately 1,000 miles away from Honiara, the capital of the Solomon Islands. Distances are immense, and population density sparse, which means that connectivity technologies are expensive to implement. To overcome this, different media (paper, radio, phone and internet) are mixed together in the chain of communication.

The "PFnet model was founded on the three principles of 'community ownership', 'community participation', and 'community management' ". Following a community based operator model, the projects were managed by members of the communities. One finding of this research was that the general perception of community members was that 78% of the managers were not 'doing their work properly', yet to the contrary the project is regarded as a success as, despite these perceived problems, many benefits were obtained through the project. Although this ICT project has some economical benefits, the most important reported result is communication with family members. The implication of this is that the drive of ICT4D to get communities economically active and to join in the global neo-capitalist economy, is misguided. The success of ICT4D projects should not primarily be measured with reference to economics, but to social communication. Quality of life is increased not only by economics, but primarily by social and psychological well-being.

The PFnet system also demonstrates that a mixed media approach can have many benefits. Many activists argue for individual access either through individual network computers or mobile phones. Although such a goal admirable, it is not achievable with the current state of technology and economic disparities. The PFnet system uses a combination of written letters, public email centres and radio (including shortwave radio) for communication. Centre operators act as intermediaries between individuals and other systems, and consequently individuals do not have to be literate, either in language or with devices.

The importance of the integration of media is also evident in the chapter *Stronger Voices? Experiences from Paraguay with Interactive ICTs*, by Claire E. Buré. The operation of a community radio station in the outskirts of Asunción, Paraguay's capital, is investigated. In this case traditional communication technologies such as radio and telephony are integrated with the Internet. Since the production of pertinent information for the immediate needs of the community is important, this chapter shows how a community that creates knowledge and turns their members into knowledge users can use the potential of technology to their collective benefit.

MANAGING ICT4D

Projects need to be managed. Traditional project management theory originated against the backdrop of engineering of particularly large building constructions, and later of military projects. Large business corporations followed this model. Initially software development projects also followed traditional models of Project Management, such as the waterfall approach. The explosion of ICT in the 1990s showed that the traditional models are not efficient in managing projects for the extremely fast pace of

ICT development. Several new methodologies were developed and operate under the banner of agile methodologies. One important characteristic of agile methodologies is the introduction of the human factor. Clients are much more involved, and the focus is often more on relationships than on technology. Managing donor projects (such as those of the ADB, World Bank and IMF) in developing regions also should not follow the classic project management model. Channa Gunawardena and David Brown did research on ICT initiatives implemented in Laos, Sri Lanka and Vietnam, and conclude in their chapter *Donor Project funded ICT Initiatives in the Vocational and Technical Education (VTE) Sector of Asian Developing Countries: A Systems Approach to Managing Project Intervention Processes*, that a soft systems methodology, rather than a traditional method, should be followed in managing donor projects.

The iREACH project in Cambodia involved the target community as active participants. Where ICT was adapted to the local needs of different population segments, the project was deemed to be more effective. Helena Grunfeld, Seán Ó Siochrú, Brian Unger and Sarun Im report in their chapter *iREACH: Lessons from a Community Owned ICT Network in Cambodia* on their experiences with this project, and the lessons learned. Like the PFnet project in the Solomon Islands, a community based operator model was followed, but this aspect requires more research and findings are not conclusive yet whether this model was a success. As with so many other ICT4D projects, the iREACH project has problems with economic sustainability. This leads to the question whether the maintenance of ICT infrastructure should be the responsibility of local communities, or whether they should be centrally funded, along with other government infrastructure responsibilities, such as energy, health and transport.

INFORMED PLANNING AND COOPERATION

Government responsibilities are not restricted to the hardware of infrastructure. Required support involves multiple dimensions such as financial or economic sustainability, cultural or social sustainability, technological sustainability, political or institutional sustainability and environmental sustainability, as Rajendra Kumar points out in the chapter *Why Institutional Partnerships Matter: A Regional Innovation Systems Approach to Making the ICT for Development Projects More Successful and Sustainable*. Stakeholders from all spheres should collaborate to make telecentres a success. Kumar comes to this conclusion based on his research into the failure of Indian telecenters - the SARI (Sustainable Access in Rural India) project in Melur Taluka of Tamil Nadu.

In the chapter by Vincent Shaw and Jørn Braa, *"Developed in the South" – An Evolutionary and Prototyping Approach to Developing Scalable and Sustainable Health Information Systems*, some conclusions of a decade's worth of experience in ICT health information systems in Zambia, Liberia, South Africa, Malawi, Botswana, Nigeria, and Namibia are presented. Important considerations for deploying ICT systems, among others, are participatory development, integration between media (not only computers) and systems, and integrated cooperation between role players. Although some of the issues encountered are technical, such as lack of access to ICTs and reliable power, the case again illustrates the overwhelming impact of social and political practices on projects. The authors concentrate their discussion on the key issues traditionally associated with ICT projects on the continent, namely scalability and sustainability. The former is significantly enhanced by technical "hierarchical clustering" ability and open source approaches while the latter depends crucially on the local human resources and support networks.

Planning and policy are informed by statistics. Planning ICT deployment in developing regions is typically done on the basis of statistics supplied by the World bank, the ITU and the CIA Yearbook. In the chapter *The Role of Statistics in Development Informatics*, Jacques Steyn cautions against the uncritical use of such statistics. An appendix summarizes statistics of the global presence (by country) of landline phones, mobile phones and the Internet.

CONCLUSION

The most important conclusion reached from the contributions to this volume is that the socio-psychological domain of computing is essential in any Development Informatics project. The notion that one size fits all in deploying ICT systems does not work. It does not work consistently across the many different cultures on this planet, and neither does it scale down to projects in small villages, due to factors such as gender roles (as in the case of Chile) or local politics (as in the case of the Solomon Islands). Although not all authors state it explicitly, they all seem to be in agreement that the active participation of targeted communities is essential in the development of ICT systems. An understanding of human nature and values people adhere to is important, as in the case of Indian tax-payers, who understate property values.

The relevance of technological determinism in ICT4D projects is questionable. Technological tools are used within cultural contexts for culturally relevant purposes. There may indeed be a causal feed-back loop between technology and culture, but the causality is never one-directional, linear or simple. The complex whole of humanity needs to be understood in ICT4D circles. And within this complexity, even though there might be common global traits among the peoples on this planet, there is also much diversity. The consideration of pluralism, rather than globalism, seems to be a basic requirement for the field of Development Informatics. The appropriation (or not) of technology cannot be understood without understanding the complex socio-psychological and cultural domains of human plurality.

Jacques Steyn
Monash University, South Africa

Jean-Paul Van Belle
University of Cape Town, South Africa

Eduardo Villanueva Mansilla
Pontificia Universidad Catolica del Peru, Peru

REFERENCE

Tibaijuka, A.K. (n.d.). UN Habitat. Second COASAD General Assembly and Pan-African Congress on Food Security, Trade and Sustainable Development, Nairobi, Kenya. Retrieved 2010 from http://www.unhabitat.org/content.asp?cid=1352&catid=14&typeid=8&subMenuId=0 Last accessed 2010.

Section 1
Public Access to ICT and Telecentres

Chapter 1
Re–Thinking Methodology through the E–Bario Project:
From Participatory Methods to a Relational Approach to ICT for Rural Development in Sarawak, East Malaysia

Poline Bala
University Malaysia Sarawak, Malaysia

ABSTRACT

This chapter highlights the value and limitations of participative development employed in the implementation of an ICT-based research and development project in the Kelabit Highlands of Central Borneo. The first section describes the reasons for e-Bario project and why participative development, with a strong emphasis on the anthropological methods of immersion and Participatory Action Research (PAR), has been adopted as development approach in Bario. In the second section I interrogate participatory development as practiced in the e-Bario by bringing to light a number of problematic aspects of the participative technique, in which conflicts have arisen over the development process, and the interpretation of participation itself has been vigorously questioned. Later, I propose a relational view of the participative process, which suggests a shift of focus from technology to people and social relations. My argument is that a relational perspective of participative process can open up a social space for local people and developers to identify, cultivate and establish social relationships both within and beyond a project's framework. It is these bonds of trust and obligation, developed and sustained over the longer term, that have allowed the Kelabit and the researchers to work out their social relationships to one another in matters concerning e-Bario.

DOI: 10.4018/978-1-61520-997-2.ch001

INTRODUCTION: EMERGENCE AND PROBLEMS OF PARTICIPATIVE DEVELOPMENT

In late 1980s "development" has been criticised and labelled by some as a failed industry especially within the post-structuralist literature as such should be made obsolete (see for instance, Esteva, 1987; Shet, 1987; Fals Borda, 1988). On the contrary, some scholars and practitioners (for example Chambers 1993) who are engaged in a search for better strategies for interventions suggested that taking local culture, context, conditions and participation by local people into account in development process and practices can be one of the solutions to many failures of development projects. This approach is considered important to curtail the negative effects of development interventions and, most importantly to ensure that the economic, social and cultural benefits of technologies reach targeted areas and local communities through efficient and effective deployment of services, (Barr, 1998; Paisley & Richardson, 1998; Anderson et al., 1998).

This raises question why local participation in development process? This is because social and cultural dimensions are crucial to development process. For instance, Porter, Allen, and Thompson (1991) observe and suggest: " a painstaking exegesis of a well-meaning but ill-fated Australian development project in Kenya reveals the reasons for its failure as mainly cultural: past lessons were not learnt, historical local circumstances not examine, indigenous knowledge not harnessed, and the superiority of Western knowledge and experience taken for granted." In this sense, "culture" is fundamental and needs to be taken seriously in development initiatives particularly for ensuring "more effective and beneficial to those people whose lives are being changed" (Schech, S & Haggis, J (2000).

Other international organizations, especially UNESCO, also see culture as intrinsic to development. The agency states that, "...culture has increasingly come to be seen as crucial to human development. We understand better not just that culture can be mechanism for, or an obstacle for development, but that it is intrinsic to sustainable human development itself because it is our cultural values which determine our goals and our sense of fulfillment."[1]

In other words, technologies alone are not sufficient to ensure success, which will depend as much on *how* the technologies are deployed, or adopted and the approach by which they are introduced. In fact, some consider that it is far more important to look beyond the technologies to the social, economic and political systems of the community (Garcia and Gorenflo 1998). This is a shift recommended by the FAO (1998). As pointed out by Anderson, "...in our enthusiasm for ICTs and their potential, we should not forget that the focus should be on people, organization and processes rather than on the technologies themselves" (Anderson et. al.1998).

At the same time, however, there have been severe critiques of participatory techniques to be an antidote to failed development projects. On this front, participative processes have been presented as being increasingly overexposed and even abused, serving as technical and management solutions to what are basically political issues (Gujit and Shah 1998:3). This has resulted in community participation being labelled as a 'sacred cow' (Blackburn and Holland 1998:2) or worse still, as the "new tyranny" in development practice (Cooke and Kothari 2001). In fact, Mosse (2003:5) suggests that community participation is increasingly seen to "advance external interests and agendas, while further concealing the agency of outsiders." All of these arguments suggest that "participation all too easily slips into empty rhetoric, [which] can serve the interest of the status quo and can readily lend itself to the fate of being veneered (Gardner and Lewis 2005:356)."

Drawing on arguments made by these two opposing views of participatory development, this chapter highlights the value and limitations of participative development employed in the introduction of information communication technologies (ICT) such as the computer, Internet, CD ROM and Very Small Aperture Terminals (VSATs) for rural development in Bario of the Kelabit Highlands of Central Borneo. The chapter begins with a brief account of what is e-Bario project and how and why participatory approaches were incorporated in the process of planning and implementation of the project. In doing so I aim to highlight the significance of participation in development for the Kelabit in Bario in historical and cultural context, and what are some of the challenges and issues for participation in development for the Kelabit today. In the next section I bring to light a number of problematic aspects of the participative technique, in which conflicts have arisen over the development process, and the interpretation of participation itself has been vigorously questioned. This will be followed by a proposal for a *relational view* of the participative process in the third and final section. It suggests a shift of focus from technology to people and social relations. My argument is that a relational perspective of participative process can open up a social space for local people and developers to identify, cultivate and establish social relationships both within and beyond a project's framework. It is these bonds of trust and obligation, developed and sustained over the longer term, that have allowed the Kelabit and the researchers to work out their social relationships to one another in matters concerning e-Bario.

WHAT IS AND WHY E-BARIO?

The e-Bario project was conceived in 1999 by a group of researchers from University Malaysia Sarawak (UNIMAS) in partnership with the Kelabit people of Bario. Its main objective is to examine in what ways can the new information communication technologies (ICT) such as the internet, computers, printers, and VSATs can

bring social and economic development for rural communities in Sarawak.

It was initiated within the context of the ICT-hype (Keniston 2002) of 1990s by which the new forms of ICT are seen as new economic and social drivers that can boost further the economic and social development of societies. This has been substantiated by arguments that better telecommunication will induce rapid economic development (Barr, 1998; Omar Abdul Rahman, 1993). As a result many national governments of developing countries have aggressively adopted ICT as developmental tools to propel their societies to greater height of economic prosperity. In Malaysia, for instance, this desire has been translated into a vision of becoming a fully developed nation by year 2020 (Raslan, A. 2000; Goh Beng Lan, 2002). In order to attain this mass development programme, the Malaysian government has outlined specific targets which include to become an Information Society by the year 2005, whereby people would have access to information, and information becomes a commodity; and to be a Knowledge-based-Society by 2010, with a Malaysian society that values the culture of life-long learning and the creation of knowledge-based products and services.

It was partly because of Malaysia's massive ICT development planning that e-Bario was mooted. Its main aim is to explore whether or not the new communication technologies can bring "development" to rural communities in Malaysia. Because of Bario's isolation and inaccessibility in the mountainous region of the Baram and Limbang Rivers in Central Borneo, it is outside the national grid and with very little communication infrastructure. With these situations, Bario represented the disconnected portion of the digital divide and presented a challenging environment to which to test the usefulness and effectiveness of ICT in rural Malaysia (Harris et al., 2001).

All this made Bario an ideal site to explore issues and challenges involved in ICT development in rural areas. This situation has been amplified by the Kelabit own desire for better information and communication infrastructure in Bario. But who are the Kelabit, and why do they need better means of communication in Bario? The Kelabit is a closely-knitted community who traditionally inhabit the Kelabit Highlands of Central Borneo. It is a highland plateau located in north-eastern of Sarawak. It is surrounded by rugged mountains, high peaks and dense jungle, and henceforth is considered isolated from other parts of Sarawak. Nonetheless, due to cultural practices of travelling far and other historical and social processes of the past 50 years, the Kelabit have experienced high level of rural-urban migration. For instance, in 1999 more than 80% of the Kelabit total population of 5,200 have left the Highlands to obtain higher education and find better job opportunities in cities like Miri, Kuching, Bintulu and Kuala Lumpur. This high level of rural-urban migration has led to a geographically-dispersed community, creating communication chasms between the Kelabit who remain in the Highlands (rural Kelabit) and those who have left to live in urban areas (urban Kelabit). It is out of their widespread diaspora that the Kelabit are constantly looking for ways and strategies to foster family relations and community connections.

In 1999 the main means of communication between Bario and the outside world were a radio call centre, locally known as *inan radio call* and the Bario airport (Bala, P., Harris, R.W and Songan, P., (2003). While the radio call centre was equipped with Very High Frequency (VHF) to facilitate communications between Bario and the world outside, the airport in Bario is a meeting point for information exchanges where 'fresh' and important information is received and sent through passengers on the daily flights via verbal exchanges, or in the form of printed material, letters and recordings. But because of the need for faster and flexible services, many local residents in and outside Bario expressed a genuine need for better means of maintaining social relations and links with migrant family members. This is

also considered very important so that the Kelabit can be on par with other Malaysian societies who have embraced these new technologies as means to greater progress.

Yet there was a concern that the technologies introduced through e-Bario would not only function well, but would in reality be a success and bring benefits to the people in Bario. This concern has emerged as a result of two different levels yet interrelated social situations. One is the Kelabit own experiences with failures of development. Of particular relevance was the 1999 Bario mini-hydro dam, which failed to deliver the *benefits* that the Kelabit had anticipated. It did not produce 24 hours electricity supply to the villages as intended at the outset of the initiative. Moreover, not only did the mini-hydro fail to generate power supply, but the way it was implemented has also led to other negative effects, particularly on social relations between villages targeted by the project. It has triggered some violent disputes between members of the community, especially arguments about which villages gained the most financially from the construction of the dam and who was responsible for its failure.

The Bario community's experience has struck a chord with a heightened awareness of poor results and widespread failures of development intervention in different parts of the world. A branch of knowledge which emerged out of this is to transform development by working within, as policy-makers, practitioners, consultants, and not just as critics, analyzers of and commentators on development processes. Henceforth, there have been practitioners and researchers who are in search for strategies that can curtail negative effects of many development interventions and ensure that local communities reap the benefits of development projects (see for instance, Gardner and Lewis, 1997; Doorman, F. 1995; Edelman, M. and Hangerud, A. 2005).

PROJECT FAILURES AND PARTICIPATIVE DEVELOPMENT IN BARIO

It was the amalgam of these two situations described above which paved the way for participative development in the Kelabit Highlands. But, why rely on participatory development in Bario? This is because a principal suggestion which emerged from the comparisons of Bario's experiences and the pursuit for better strategies for intervention was that it was not *what* the team did but *how* it was done that was of greater importance. Since participatory approaches believes that "development is not a process in single direction, but a process of continuous adaptation, problem solving and opportunity...[and] is not movement towards a fixed goal but continuous adaptation to maximize well being in a changing conditions" (Chambers 1993:10), it was adopted as a normative and practical approach in the Kelabit Highlands.

Consequently the following imperatives were placed upon the project: active participation by members of the community in Bario in the process; a good understanding by the implementers from UNIMAS of diverse local perceptions and also of the social and political processes through which the technology would be introduced and used. The overarching objective was to guarantee that the e-Bario technology would not fail like the hydro dam.

Taking all this into consideration, the research team drew from two lessons and experiences in other parts of the world. One was the experiment with Participatory Action Research (PAR) by the M.S. Swaminathan Research Foundation in Madras, India to establish six Village Information Shops that enabled rural families to access and exchange a basket of information using modern communication technologies, (Balaji & Harris, 2000). The second was the academic discipline of Community Informatics, which takes political, cultural and social aspects seriously in the use and deployment of ICT (Gurstein, 1999).

To begin with the anthropological methods of immersion and Participatory Action Research (PAR)[2] were adopted as specific development strategies. At the heart of the approaches is putting "grassroots knowledge" in terms of local knowledge, social arrangements and cultures at the fore front in development practices in Bario. Out of all this, two interrelated concepts were emphasized as guidelines: local context and local participation. These were vital for establishing how and with what aims the technologies would be deployed.

In other words, rather than seeing the technologies as the only source of agency (the perspective of technological determinism), people and communities were seen as the primary agents and mediators of change. Hence key areas of concerns in the implementation process were how opportunities and constraints were considered locally; and how social norms, education, culture, and the way of life in the Highlands could affect the use and application of technologies. These social and cultural factors were seen to have the capacity to enable, shape and influence a development project such as e-Bario, or, equally to resist it (Bala, 2008).

PARTICIPATIVE METHODS IN THE KELABIT HIGHLANDS

But what does this mean for e-Bario implementation in the Kelabit Highlands of Sarawak? To begin with and based on PAR methodologies the following principles were established:

- the researchers should learn about life in Bario from the community;
- the community should learn about ICTs from the researchers;
- community members should perform major portions of the research;
- the researchers should be able to identify with the community;
- as a team, the community-researchers should be capable of critically reflecting

upon iterative cycles of action in order to achieve mutually beneficial outcomes from the project.

- useful information systems will be embedded in the needs of the community;
- specific actions are required by both the researchers and the community in order to articulate those needs;
- methodologies for designing and implementing useful information systems will emerge from participatory action-oriented research activities, and
- data would be obtained using a combination of surveys, direct interviews, workshops and discussion groups.

Guided by these principles and within the context described above, the research team arrived in the Kelabit Highlands in June 1999. First of all, the team had to examine and understand how the Kelabit cope with situations and circumstances in an ever changing environment. Of particular importance, was an understanding not only what meanings the Kelabit assign to situations, but also how they act to solve critical problems of survival when new forms of economic, political and social organization are introduced or imposed upon them. This, it was suggested, would have a bearing on how members of the community would negotiate in interpreting the technology, appropriating the words of Schwarz and Thompson (1990:32) "what meanings would be given to the technology, and how the technologies could become part of the social processes and local contexts."

This understanding was attained through ethnographic practices of immersion, random surveys, and structured interviews and dialogue sessions. Ideally these were organized in an open manner, so that they become important means of airing concerns, perceptions, or suggestions, including disappointments. This range of formal and informal participation observation and dialogue methods were reinforced by a survey of existing social capital among the Kelabit. This was done by using a "need analysis," a research strategy highly recommended by the World Bank as a systematic approach to the application of IT to rural communities (1998). Conducted in October 1999 through a survey, its main purpose is to examine existing communication patterns as a preliminary step towards the effective and successful introduction of ICT to rural areas.

Furthermore, the activities provided glimpses into what values the Kelabit place on peoples, objects and ideas which constantly move between the outside world and the Highlands, and how and why newcomers are integrated into or excluded from social relations at the village level. This is considered crucial since the success of any ICT applications, as suggested by Paisley and Richardson (1998), will largely depend upon their integration within local communication networks.

On top of this, researchers participated in local, communal, social and economic activities in Bario. This included attending Kelabit *iraus,* such as the name changing ceremonies (*irau mekaa ngadan*) in the longhouses, participating in local economic activities like rice planting and harvesting, and involvement in local religious activities, for instance, by attending church services at the weekends.

It was through direct engagement in these local activities the researchers gained insight into the Kelabit's on-going engagement with 'development', and their ability to generate, coordinate and respond to social change. They were conducted to enable consultation between the researchers and Bario people, to provide forum for urban and rural Kelabit to discuss their perceptions and ideas about how ICT could be useful, and how to address possible negative impacts of ICT on Kelabit values. An example of this forum was the Miri Symposium, which was held on 13th March 2000 and was attended by 103 participants. This included Kelabit representatives from Miri, the former Member of Parliament for Ba Kelalan, three members of the Council of Elders, two members of Bario JKKK, representatives of the

Youth Group from Bario and the research team from UNIMAS. In short, these direct engagements become a means for the Kelabit in Bario to participate in making decisions of the potential areas for ICT development in the Highlands, and when encountering problems and challenges generated by development.

Out of these processes of dialogues and interaction, two main practical observations and suggestions were made regarding information use and communication patterns in Bario. These recommendations were:

First, it was suggested that the provision of ICT services, particularly the telephone and Internet at the Telecentre, was a logical extension to existing communication and information infrastructure in Bario. The community displayed a progressive readiness and enthusiasm for technology-induced improvements in their communications resources (for example radio, radio-telephone and the airport). It was therefore suggested that the development of a telecentre in Bario would serve one of the community's basic communication needs, to be able to communicate with friends and family members who had migrated to urban areas or overseas for work, marriage and education. With this, as with the church and airport, it was assumed that the centre would notably link people in Bario with those outside the Highlands, but also become an important place for local people to meet socially and to exchange ideas and news.

Second, since many expressed frustrations over the ineffectiveness of relaying important messages, particularly by the government servants to their bosses and supervisors outside Bario, the development of the telecentre should take into consideration the provision of reliable high capacity communication and information facilities such as email and additional telephones. From this perspective the centre is forseen to link businesses in Bario with bigger businesses in urban areas.

With these considerations and observations the following physical and technological components were gradually introduced in Bario:

1. **Computer Laboratories:** Two computer laboratories were designed and equipped with 16 computers due to demand from students and teachers. The lab was also equipped with 2 printers and a scanner.

2. **Telephonic Equipment:** The new technologies were installed within the existing communications network, the telephones were placed at strategic locations or important meeting places in Bario, such as the airport, the shop area, the school and also the clinic.

3. **Very Small Aperture Terminals and Network Configuration:** To provide access to telephone (voice) and internet networks four internet ground station technologies known as Very Small Aperture Terminals (VSATs) were installed by Telekom Malaysia Berhad. These were located at the shop area, the clinic, the school, and the airport.

4. **Telecentre:** A permanent telecentre, known as Gatuman Bario (Bario Link), was set up in 2001. It is located at Pasar Bario and has 5 rooms: a room for computing services, a visitor's room with table and chairs for meetings and resting, 2 rooms for administration purposes – one for the e-Bario coordinator and the other for technical assistance - and another for staff to monitor and run the day to day management of the telecentre. The telecentre is equipped with 10 computers, an inkjet printer, a laser printer, a laminating machine, a photocopier and internet access.

5. **Power Supply:** Since Bario is outside the national grid, the telecentre was initially powered by diesel run generators. This power supply has evolved into a hybrid diesel (80%) – solar panel (20%) power supply, and more recently a solar panel – diesel system.

6. **Training and Skills:** An Information Technology (IT) Literacy Programme was introduced by the research team from University Malaysia Sarawak in conjunction with COMServe, a local IT company based in Kuching. Training was identified as an ongoing process, and not a one-time or once only activity. The training included word processing, key-board usage, e-mailing, browsing the web, and the management of technologies including trouble shooting.

7. **Website Creation**: Due to web hosting problems this information was incorporated into a web site designed by UNIMAS (www.e-bario.com). The web site contains information on the project, and also on the Kelabit Highlands. It was designed to promote Bario as a tourist destination, and is linked with other web sites developed by or used by Kelabit, such as the Online Kelabit Soceity (OKS).

8. **Storage of Information – Bario Digital Library:** An experiment with recording, documenting and disseminating Kelabit songs and dances on CD ROM has been developed under the project. It is called the Bario Digital Library (BDL). The first record contains 9 lakuh songs by women in Bario with digital images of each singer singing the *lakuh*. Each song has been transcribed in Kelabit, with English translation. It is a step towards the creation of an electronic record of Kelabit oral stories.

9. **Management and Administration:** "Management and Administration" is not a physical or technological component of e-Bario, but rather a management system, which has been put in place in order to manage the project in Bario, and also the community telecentre. To achieve this, a project coordinator-cum-manager has been appointed by the Council of Elders, Authority for Village Protection and Development (Malay, *Jawatankuasa Keselamatan, Kebersihan*

Kampung (JKKK)) and University Malaysia Sarawak to oversee the workings of the initiative in Bario. In addition to the project coordinator, a technical assistant was also trained and appointed to oversee the technical aspects of the project, such as trouble shooting and managing all the equipment and software.

But all this raises the question in what ways the model of participative development made a difference to e-Bario's design and process. That is, whether or not it had a profound effect upon the way on which the project was received and adapted by the community. If yes, why and if not, what lessons can be considered for the future. This is an important issue for the project itself, but also more generally, in the light of previous research and ongoing debates within academia about the value or limitations of community participation in development projects.

To explore these questions in detail, the next section is divided into two parts. The first part will highlight impacts of e-Bario for the people of Bario especially how the technologies above have affected the well being of the people by facilitating information flow in and out of Bario, bridging the communication gaps between urban and rural communities in Sarawak, and also in narrowing the social and economic divide between members of the Kelabit society. Building on the first part, the second part will throw light on certain problematic aspects of participatory techniques encountered during the 10 years experience of e-Bario. I shall highlight these issues in the light of academic inquiry and criticism of participative development. At the same time, I shall detail some positive effects of participative techniques in Bario, and how these can be important pointers for development practices in rural areas and among communities like the Kelabit of the Kelabit Highlands.

ASSESSING E-BARIO AND PARTICIPATIVE DEVELOPMENT IN BARIO

When asked of the impacts of e-Bario, John Tarawe's response is, "it is like a dream." Referring to the payphones, he continues, "We never thought it would come. Although the ultimate goal was to bring in the Internet, the payphones were just as important to the people here. When we saw the payphones, our hearts leapt. This is because we now can communicate with our relatives and friends who are living in cities like Miri, Kuching, Marudi, Kuala Lumpur, and also with those who are currently living overseas. I have asked a shopkeeper this morning the number of phone cards she sells every month. She is selling probably 100 cards and that's just from one shop. There are five shops here. For the older generation the arrival of the telephone is good enough. They tend to think that the Internet is more relevant to their children's future."

John implies that the project has introduced new means for easy communication with diasporic Kelabit. The significance of these information and communication technologies is also reflected in the way that these technologies are perceived and use as means to position the Kelabit within wider networks of interaction that transcend their isolated position in the Highlands. In this way the Kelabit can *continue* to be integrated within (and be part of) the space of global flow of technologies, skills, communication and information. As described, although the Kelabit Highlands are geographically isolated, the Kelabit society has long been connected to the outside world through their geographic mobility, and the dispersal of families. In tandem with their experiences, the Kelabit also see themselves as a part of the wider world of progress and their contemporary acceptance of telephones, the Internet, VSATs and computers in the Highlands is seen as an extension of their existing connections to the rest of the world.

This perception is reflected in the words of 80 years-old Balang Radu, who claimed that e-Bario has enabled further progress (*iyuk*) for those living in Bario by providing the means to forge connections with the rest of the world. He stated, "With these new means of communications, our lives are made much easier, although we live isolated in the headwaters of Baram. We can now liaise with the outside world from our villages, including talking to our children in KL, Kuching and throughout the world. This is progress (*iyuk*) for us. It has made our life easier and we are connected to the rest of the world in a new way. Therefore we are basically very, very pleased with its arrival. We are now on a par with the rest of the world." Balang Radu's remarks demonstrate that the new technologies are being incorporated into the Kelabit ongoing pursuit for connections outside the Highlands. Being connected to the rest of the world through these new technologies is perceived not purely as a means of obtaining better quality information, connectedness and *iyuk*, but also as a symbol that the Kelabit are not being left behind by others.

Furthermore e-Bario has been re-made to negotiate the Kelabit social, economic and political interests in their encounters with ideas, intervention and people from the outside world. A clear example of this is the [new] technologies are being used as new forums for networking, and for acquiring skills, resources and tools for effective organization among the Kelabit. This is especially important in their engagement with the larger issues of development which the Kelabit are currently grappling with in Bario, especially with regard to road access, commercial logging and planning for the future at the state and division levels of governance. The technologies become important forum and stage from which to express compliance and at the same time resistance, and to negotiate, assess and debate the new forms, meanings and practices of 'development'. In other words, e-Bario has been fashioned as a new site to manage the interface of development between the Kelabit and external agencies.

These responses and experiences at the local level suggest that e-Bario initiative has been another milestone in terms of providing equal access to information communication technologies in the Malaysian context. Henceforth, as noted by International Telecommunications Union (ITU, 2003), technologically e Bario is one of Malaysia's most notable of internet development initiatives". At the international arena, the initiative has put Bario and the Kelabit on the world map - a remote community connected with up-to date technologies – thus named as one of the Top Seven Intelligent Communities of 2001 by The World Teleport Association in New York and of one ITU's success stories.

PROBLEMS OF PARTICIPATIVE TECHNIQUES IN BARIO

Nonetheless, reflecting upon experiences of e-Bario as a participative development project, there is no doubt that it reflected a number of problematic aspects of the participative technique as already outlined by its critics. One of the main line of criticisms is that participative development tends to gloss over significant issues of heterogeneity, social division and conflict in favour of consensus, community and locality (Gardner and Lewis, 1996; Wright, 1995). In the context of e-Bario, this situation is obvious at the initial stage of the project. Driven by the emphasis on local participation, the team attempted to reconcile any differences through processes of mediation and informal dialogues. This was partly driven by a need to secure funding from organizations and to make the project a success. The research team worked hard (through the processes I have described) to get the community to make a concerted effort to reach shared interests at the expense of "variation in meanings, experiences, historicities, debates and specificities" (Hoskins 1987:606).

As outlined by other scholars like Gardner and Lewis (1996:76), and also Wright (1995:73-74), this tendency often times creates images of a homogeneous, solid and integrated community, which nonetheless has great implications especially on issues of "balance of power" between the different actors in the e-Bario design and process. This is because, as has been pointed by Abram and Waldren (1998:5), bottom-up approach, active participation and community involvement in the planning and implementation of the development projects often make issues of power complicated between different actors in any planned development like e-Bario.

There had been two parts to this situation in Bario. The first aspect is the asymmetrical relationships and power between those who bring development and those who receive development in the Kelabit Highlands. The other situation is the subtle issue of access to technologies and control over project processes as new symbolic and material resources in the community.

In the nutshell, both situations reflect the asymmetries between the members of the Bario community who were directly involved with e-Bario as a development initiative and those who consider themselves as mere 'by-standers.' This is very apparent between the local manager and other service users, and non-users of the technologies. Often times persons like the manager and his technical assistant were deemed to be empowered more than the other villagers, who did not have access for various reasons. In a sense ICT have introduced a new arena and means for competition among villagers to attain personal benefits. While the local manager and other users with newly acquired skills could somehow affect changes to their social position through the use and application of technologies and project processes, the non-users remained largely unaffected by specific technologies such as the Internet. This has led to tensions concerning empowerment, revealed through criticisms directed at the manager and the courting of his position by others.

At another level are the larger competing political and economic interests of members of the community at the local level, which intersected with the working-out of status and power within the community. This is a result of changes in the local economy as a consequence of the usage and applications of ICT. The Internet has become a useful tool, linking specific businesses in the Highlands to the outside world. This is especially true for the local tourism industry, which has emerged as a major economic activity in recent years. There is a genuine perception that the telecentre serves mostly the interests of the lodge owners and tourist guides. "It enables their business to flourish. They are now competing among themselves," observed a respondent. According to another respondent, the lodge owners, who are also the most frequent users of the telecentre, have now become the new rich in the area. This is translated into their lifestyle: many today possess items such as four wheel drives (in fact ten out of the fourteen cars in Bario are owned by lodge owners), television, motorcycles, and most importantly money.

It was in relation to this imbalance of access and control that the meanings and practice of communal ownership and local participation were challenged and questioned, as individuals such as the manager were perceived as being elevated to a position of power and social status within the community. In a sense, the arrival of e-Bario had triggered a specific local crisis or what Norman Long (2001:1) identifies as "'intertwined battles": different social groups in Bario were locked in disputes over the legitimate control of the telecentre as a new resource, with the meanings of local ownership of e-Bario and, the degree and style of local participation becoming sources of conflict and argument. It has created a new arena for power struggle for some members of the community, in which e-Bario and the telecentre have emerged as a new source of symbolic and material wealth, providing new access to social recognition and skills in the community, creating in the Kelabit Highlands what Preston might consider as the "complexity business of development" (1986:268). The intervention not only exacerbated

the underlying rivalries and struggles for control over limited resources, but also introduced a totally new socio-political space in which the people in Bario have to struggle and negotiate over power, status, reputation and resources.

TRANSFORMING EFFECTS OF PARTICIPATIVE DEVELOPMENT

However, it is important to note that in spite of its apparent shortcomings, the appropriation of participative methods in Bario had a transforming effect upon the project. This is apparent at two levels. The first and most obvious level is that the very manifestations of these issues and problems in the research process suggest that the emphasis on context and local participation have made it possible for the researchers to explore the richness, complexity and interrelatedness of social, cultural life and its vital role in development-induced change such as e-Bario.

The second and more complicated level is the way participatory techniques has led to the emergence of a two-way participation through which both the researchers and local people (and the technologies) were considered as catalysts of social change, with the local population participating in the development process, and the researchers joining in local life in Bario. These forms of community participation and partnership processes, in the words of Marilyn Taylor (2003:121) "have the potential to open up a new public and political space." In Bario, for example, the participative process has opened up public and political space in which negotiations, interactions, the establishing of common interests and a readjustments of social and political relations can all take place effectively within two intertwined arenas of relationships. The first space is between the researchers-cum-developers and the Bario population; and the second arena is between members of the Kelabit community themselves.

Within the first social arena, this was made apparent by the way in which the anthropological method of immersion was appropriated by the implementers, not only as a means of understanding the local context in which they were working, but most importantly as a mechanism for the researchers to join the local population at the same level, as subjects in the project's design and process. In doing so, the immersion process effectively provided a public space, in which both developers and the local population could engage in collaborative work, effective organization and action. It was a framework enabling the researchers not only to take local needs and interests into consideration, but also to enlist the local population themselves as experts on their environment and history, and consequently, appropriate agents of change. This in turn led to a diversity of approach, on-going local modification, and creativity at many levels.

In other words, rather than just attempting to bolt participative processes on to an ICTs-enabled project in Bario, the practice of community participation in e-Bario has involved a deeper approach, to ensure a genuine community empowerment. As pointed out by Michael O'Neill (1992 in Marilyn Taylor 2003:136) these are two different things. While many critics have highlighted the (ab)use of community participation as a technique to mobilize a local population and to monitor their behaviour from the centre or from above, community participation in Bario has taken a different turn. It has promoted a diversity of experiences and usage, which in turn has contributed to a user-centred and a user-owned agenda for ICTs in the Highlands.

In a similar manner, the participative process has allowed the Kelabit to open up a socio-political space for themselves, which is being used to negotiate and come up with solutions for managing the local crises triggered by the project. The participative process in the project design provided a socio-political space for the Kelabit themselves to negotiate what value to attribute to the Internet, computers and telephones, and

how to apply these technologies to their own political, social and economic circumstances. This has been particularly important in the face of the new 'development' being introduced into the area - for example, the over-arching influence of the government in introducing logging as a new industry in the Kelabit Highlands.

All this is reflected through the ways e-Bario has been re-made into a new and active venue to pursue the Kelabit community's own values and interests as they engage with larger issues of development which the Kelabit are currently grappling with in Bario. This is especially with regard to road access, commercial logging and planning for the future at the state and division levels of governance. As they grapple with these issues, participative development introduced through e-Bario have been adopted as a means to nurture cooperation among the village people, and at the same time to renegotiate dialogues or battles with visiting government officials, researchers, corporate interests, and technicians about funding, training and technology options. From this perspective, participative techniques in e-Bario have opened a space to enable collaborative efforts between the villagers and researchers, developers and other agencies to emerge.

Therefore while community participation has triggered competition and tensions at the community level, it has also enabled a strengthening of local institutions for decision making and for conflict management and resolution. One good example of this is the use of the internet, computers and telephone inspire those in Bario to reach out to those that have left the Highlands, but still maintain a strong interest in the affairs of the village. It has become a new means to maintain solidarity, within an increasingly stratified and occupationally mobile population, in the face of the new types of development intervention. The various technologies available at the telecentre, for instance desk tops, associated software and the internet, are being used to strategize the Kelabit position in their contemporary encounters with logging. Examples of this are the documentation of oral histories and the recording of images relating to all the cultural and historical sites found in the Highlands, as well as the marking of their GPS points. All these are uploaded into a GIS database at the telecentre, to allow the construction of a land-use history in the form of a digital map, and spatial and temporal analyses of past land use in the region. These in turn are useful historical and legal documents in negotiations with agencies involved in conservation and logging in the area.

From these experiences it is clear that participative development as a working practice in Bario has caused a multi-level collaborative approach to emerge, which, according to Martin from Padang Pasir, differentiated e-Bario from its predecessor, the 'damned' dam project, which provided Bario with a 45minute electric dream. He says, "It has been very interesting to observe the difference. It has been 8 years now since e-Bario was first introduced to us, and the technologies are still functioning well. Most importantly, together with the team of researchers from UNIMAS, we are still exploring its potential benefits for our interests here in the Highlands. We have faced many challenges and problems. There have been disagreements and arguments among us here in Bario as a result of e-Bario. However, the emphasis on participative processes has provided time and space to discuss and work through our disagreements; something which we did not have with the dam project. It provides flexibility for us to meet and negotiate our different needs and interests. It is also learning by doing, which has made a lot of difference in e-Bario. Unlike the dam project, in which the experts came for a couple of months and left the Highlands never to return, the implementers of e-Bario keep coming back to "walk and talk" through the project process with us. It is not just the technologies that have become part of our life in Bario, but also the researchers themselves have become part of the community. Many people know who they are in the Highlands and vice versa."

CONCLUSION

Martin's comments lead me to my concluding remarks in this chapter. The chapter begins with reasons for participative development as an approach to introduce information communication technologies in the Kelabit Highlands before describing the application of these techniques in Bario. In the final part, it highlights some problematic aspects of the approach, as well as its contributions towards a successful development intervention among the Kelabit.

From narratives and observations illustrated above, several lessons for future considerations are offered. First, while the emphasis on local participation and context is not without issues, it does not mean that participative development has become a new tyranny for researchers to advance their agendas and interests in Bario. On the contrary, the use of participative mechanics approach has been a first step towards a more complete understanding of the richness, complexity and interrelatedness of social, cultural life and its vital role in development-induced change such as e-Bario. But the first step must be considered as an expansion of the idea of context beyond the myopic concerns of computers and internet to include historical, political and social situations. There is no substitute to for the rigour of immersion process to enhance and modify participative development in Bario. Besides enabling the research team to explore individual and collective capacities and abilities of villagers in the Highlands (for instance their technical skills, and computer awareness, their aptitude and ability to manage new technologies), the participative techniques have also opened up a social space for the local population and developers to identify, cultivate and establish social relationships both within and beyond the project's framework.

It is these bonds of trust and obligation, developed and sustained over the longer term, that have allowed the Kelabit and the researchers to work out their social responsibilities to one another in matters concerning e-Bario. In turn, these social contacts and relations between the Kelabit and researchers-cum-developers became the basis for trust and friendship building, or in Tsing's term collaboration (1999), rather than the usual arm's length relations between developer and recipients of development. These established social relations became the very forums for a continuous engagement and negotiations with challenges that emerged in the ongoing process of e-Bario. e-Bario is consequently quite unlike many development projects, which typically do not provide room for the 'community' to discuss and debate the outcomes of an intervention between themselves and outside developers as well as amongst themselves.

Therefore one other major lessons from the e-Bario process is the roles and values of PAR and immersion process in shifting the focus of the research and development process away from national political actions and policies for development " [which] may not coincide with the perspectives of ordinary people" (King, 1999: 33) on to social relations and grassroots organization. From experiences gained in the Kelabit Highlands, it is clear that the mechanics of participatory methods can be used as catalyst to place priority and value on local people which in turn provides space for individual residents, villages and other community groups to use their creativity and skills to negotiate the effects of development and change. This is made clear by how e-Bario as a community-based development project, instead of just creating tension and conflict in Kelabit's internal power and asset struggles, has been largely remodelled by community members to adhere to the ideas of group solidarity and shared benefits. All this is because of local participation and the bottom-up approach employed in the implementation of technologies.

These kinds of emphases and experiences in the e-Bario process resonate well with the call of Amartya Sen (1998 [1987]), an economist and ethicist. He proposes an approach to economics and processes of development that focuses on human agency and social opportunities rather than on mega-structures such as markets or governments. By placing people as main actors at centre-stage, the process of development can empower them to participate in the decisions that shape their lives. As can be seen from the experiences of the Bario community with the e-Bario project, local residents and communities can become agents of development and change, rather than recipients or victims of failed development interventions. Nonetheless, it is important to note, this lesson of putting people and their social relations at the centre of development practices need to be investigated rigorously in other places and social contexts to ensure its replicability as an approach for ICT-enabled rural developments in different parts of the world.

REFERENCES

Abram, S. (1998). Introduction: anthropological perspectives on local development. In Abram, S., & Waldren, J. (Eds.), *Anthropological Perspectives on Local Development: Knowledge and Sentiments in Conflict. The European Association of Social Anthropologist*. London, New York: Routledge. doi:10.4324/9780203451021_chapter_1

Anderson, L., Crowder, L. V., Dion, D., & Truelove, W. (1998). Applying the lessons of participatory communication and training to rural telecentres. In *The first mile of connectivity*. Rome, Italy: Food and Agriculture Organisation of the United Nations. Retrieved May 2007 from http://www.fao.org/WAICENT/FAOINFO/SUSTDEV/Cddirect/Cdre0029.html

Bala, P. (2008). *Desire for progress: The Kelabit experience with information communication technologies (ICTs) for RURAL DEVELOPMENT in Sarawak, East Malaysia*. Unpublished doctoral Dissertation, Cambridge: Christ's College, Cambridge University.

Bala, P., Egay, E., & Datan, E. (2003). *Dynamic Of Cultural Diversity In Everchanging Environment*. Paper Presented at the Simposium Budaya Sarawak IV, 2003 sempena Perayaan Sambutan Jubli Delima Sarawak Merdeka d/a Majlis Adat Istiadat Sarawak, Jabatan Ketua Menteri, Sarawak. Ogos 2-3, 2003.

Bala, P., Harris, R. W., & Songan, P. (2003). E Bario Project: In Search of a Methodology to Provide Access to Information Communication Technologies for Rural Communities in Malaysia. In Marshall, S., Taylor, W., Xinghuo Yu (eds), *Using Community Informatics to Transform Regions*. Hershey, PA: Idea Group.

Balaji, V., & Harris, R. W. (2002). Information Technology Reaching the Unreached - Village Knowledge Centers in Southern India, Second Global Knowledge Conference (GkII), Kuala Lumpur, Malaysia, March 7-10, 2002.

Barr, D. F. (1998). Integrated rural development through telecommunications. In *The first mile of connectivity*. Rome, Italy: Food and Agriculture Organisation of the United Nations. Retrieved December 2002 from http://www.fao.org/WAICENT/FAOINFO/SUSTDEV/Cddirect/Cdre0029.html

Blackburn, J., & Holland, J. (Eds.). (1998). *Who Changes? Institutionalizing participation in development*. London: Intermediate Technology Publication.

Bourdieu, P. (1986). The Forms of Capital. In Richardson, J. G. (Ed.), *Handbook for Theory and Research for the Sociology of Education* (pp. 241–258). Wesport, CT: Greenwood Press.

Chambers, R. (1993). *Rural development: Putting the last first*. Essex, England: Longman Group Limited.

Chambers, R. (1997). *Whose Reality Counts? Putting the Last First*. London: Intermediate Technology Publications.

Cooke, B., & Kothari, U. (2001). *Participation: The New Tyranny?* London, New York: Zed Books.

Doorman, F. (1995). Participation, efficiency and the common good: an essay on participation in development. In Ferks, G., & den Ouden, J. H. B. (Eds.), *In Search of the Middle Ground: Essays on the Sociology of Planned Development*. Wageningen: Agricultural University.

Economic and Social Council, United Nations (2000). Development and international cooperation in the twenty-first century: the role of information technology in the context of a knowledge-based global economy.

Edelman, M., & Hangerud, A. (2005). Introduction: The Anthropology of Development and Globalization. In Edelman, M., & Haugerud, A. (Eds.), *The Anthropology of Development and Globalization: From classical Political Economy to Contemporary Neoliberalism*. Blackwell Publishing.

Esteva, G. (1987). Regenerating people's space. *Alternatives, 10*(3), 125–152.

Fals Borda, O. (1988). *Knowledge and People's Power*. Delhi: Indian Social Institute.

Garcia, D. L., & Gorenflo, N. R. (1998). Rural networking cooperatives: lessons for international development and aid strategies. In *The first mile of connectivity*. Rome, Italy: Food and Agriculture Organisation of the United Nations. http://www.fao.org/WAICENT/FAOINFO/SUSTDEV/Cddirect/Cdre0033.html Last accessed in April 2000

Gardner, K., & Lewis, D. (1996). *Anthropology, Development and the Post-Modern Challenge*. London: Pluto.

Gardner, K., & Lewis, D. (2005). Beyond Development? In Edelman, M., & Haugerud, A. (Eds.), *The Anthropology of Development and Globalization: From classical Political Economy to Contemporary Neoliberalism*. Blackwell Publishing.

Goh, B. L. (2002). Rethinking Modernity: State, Ethnicity, and class in the Forging of a Modern Urban Malaysia.In in C.J.W.-L. Wee (Ed.), *Local Cultures and the New Asia. The Society, Culture and Capitalism in Southeast Asia*. Singapore: Institute of Southeast Asian Studies.

Grillo, R. D. (1997). Discourses of Development: The View from Anthropology. In Grillo, R.D & R.L. Stirrat (Eds.), *Discourses of Development: Anthropological Perspectives* (pp. 1-33). New York: Berg.

Guijt, I., & Shah, M. K. (Eds.). (1998). *The Myth of Community: Gender Issues in Participatory Development*. London: Intermediate Technology Publications.

Gurstein, M. (1999). *Community Informatics: Enabling the Community Use of Information and Communications Technologies*. Hershey, PA: Idea Group Publishing.

Harris, R. W. (1999). Rural Information Technology for Sarawak's Development. *Sarawak Development Journal, 2*(1), 72–84.

Harris, R. W., Bala, P., Songan, P., & Khoo, G. L. (2001). Challenges and Opportunities in Introducing Information and Communication Technologies to the Kelabit Community of North Central Borneo. *New Media & Society, 3*(3), 271–296. doi:10.1177/14614440122226092

Harrisson, T. (1959). *World Within: A Borneo Story*. Singapore: Oxford University Press.

Hoskins, J. (1987). The headhunter as hero: local traditions and their reinterpretation in national history. *American Ethnologist, 14*(4), 605–622. doi:10.1525/ae.1987.14.4.02a00010

Keniston, K. (2002). *IT for the Common Man. Lessons from India. The Second M N Srinivas Memorial Lecture. NIAS Special Publication SP7 – 02*. Bangalore: National Institute of Advanced Studies.

King, V. (1999). *Anthropology and Development in South-east Asia: Theory and Practice*. Kuala Lumpur: Oxford University Press.

Larsen, K. L. (1998). Discourses on development in Malaysia. In Abram, S., & Waldren, J. (Eds.), *Anthropological Perspectives on Local Development: Knowledge and Sentiments in Conflict. The European Association of Social Anthropologist*. London, New York: Routledge. doi:10.4324/9780203451021_chapter_2

Long, N. (2001). *Development Sociology: Actor Perspectives*. London: Routledge. doi:10.4324/9780203398531

Mosse, D. (2003). *Good Policy is Unimplementable? Reflections on the Ethnography of Aid Policy and Practice*. Paper presented at the EIDOS Workshop on 'Order and Disjuncture: the Organisation of Aid and Development', SOAS, London 26-28th September 2003.

O'Neill, M. (1992). Community Participation in Quebec. *International Journal of Health Services, 22*(2), 287–301.

Omar Abdul Rahman. (1993). Industrial targets of Vision 2020: The science and technology perspective. In Ahmad Sarji Abdul hamid (Ed.), *Malaysia's Vision 2020: Understanding the concept, implications and challenges*. Petaling Jaya: Pelanduk Publications.

Paisley, D., & Richardson, D. (1998). Why the first mile and not the last? In The first mile of connectivity. Rome, Italy: Food and Agriculture Organisation of the United Nations. Retrieved January 2004 from http://www.fao.org/WAICENT/FAOINFO/SUSTDEV/Cddirect/Cdre0026.html

Porter, D., Allen, B., & Thompson. G. (1991). *Development in Practice: Paved with Good Intentions*. London: Routlege.

Preston, P. W. (1986). *Making Sense of Development: An Introduction to classical and contemporary theories of Development and their application in Southeast Asia*. London, New York: Routledge & Kegan Paul.

Scheh, S., & Haggis, J. (2000). *Culture, and development: A Critical Introduction*. Oxford: Blackwell.

Schwarz, M., & Thompson, M. (1990). *Divided We Stand: Redefining politics, technology and social choice*. New York: Harvester Wheatsheaf.

Sen, A. (1998). *On Ethics and Economic*. Oxford: Blackwell. (Original work published 1987)

Shet, D. L. (1987). Alternative development as political practice. *Alternatives, 12*(2), 155–171.

Taylor, M. (2003). *Public Policy in the Community*. Palgrave MacMillan.

Tsing, A. L. (1999). Becoming Tribal Leader, and other Green Development Fantasies. In Li, T. M. (Ed.), *Agrarian Transformations in Upland Indonesia* (pp. 159–202). London: Harwood Academic Publications.

Ufford, P. Q. V. (1993). Knowledge and Ignorance in the practices of development. In Hobart, M. (Ed.), *An Anthropological Critique of Development, The Growth of Ignorance* (pp. 135–160). London, New York: Routledge.

World Bank. (1998). *World Bank Development Report, Knowledge for Development*. Washington, DC, USA: The World Bank.

Wright, S. (1995). Anthropology: still the uncomfortable discipline? In Ahmed, A. S., & Shore, C. N. (Eds.), *The future of Anthropology: Its Relevance to the Contemporary World*. London: Athlone.

ENDNOTES

[1] (http://www.unesco.org/culture/development/briefings/html_eng/forword.shtml. Last accessed: 19/4/07 at 5:30 pm)

[2] According to Chambers (1997) PAR is a diverse and loose methodology combining action, reflection and participation as the basis for exploring research and development, with the following ideas as guidelines:

1. professionals should reflect critically on their concepts, values, behaviours and methods;
2. they should learn through engagement and committed action;
3. they have roles as convenors, catalysts and facilitators;
4. the weak and marginalised can and should be empowered;
5. poor people can and should do much of their own investigation, analysis and planning.

APPENDIX

Web Sites

UNESCO. www.unesco.org/culture/development/briefings/html_eng/forword.html. Last accessed on April 2004.

The World Teleport Association. www.worldteleport.org Last accessed July 2007.

International Telecommunications Union (ITU). (1998). World Telecommunications Development Report, Universal Access. http://www.itu.int/ti/publications/WTDR_98/index.htm Last accessed April 2008.

Connecting Malaysia's rural communities to the Information Age: The E-Bario project. www.itu.int/osg/spu/wsis-themes/ict_stories/e-bariocasestudy.html Last accessed October 2002.

Chapter 2

Bringing the Internet to the Rural Area:
A Case Study of the 'Kedaikom' Project in Malaysia

Zulkefli bin Ibrahim
University of Malaya, Malaysia

Ainin Sulaiman
University of Malaya, Malaysia

Tengku M. Faziharudean
University of Malaya, Malaysia

ABSTRACT

Malaysia aims to be an information society by the year 2020 can only be achieved if the mass population, that include those who live in the rural area, has the access to use the ICT. This is due to the uneven distribution of the basic telecommunication infostructure between the urban and rural areas in Malaysia that left the rural area to be at the disadvantage to access the ICT. Meanwhile, there are many programs that have been implemented by the government to encourage the rural population to use the Internet, such as 'Kedaikom', a community based telecenter serving the rural population. A questionnaire survey was conducted to investigate how 'Kedaikom' as a community based telecenter could assist in diffusing the usage of the ICT to the rural population. The result from the survey has indicated that the community telecenter could be used to bridge the digital divide between the underserved rural community and the well-accessed urban community. More of the rural population, especially from the younger generation and those with higher education background (irrespective of age) are using the community telecenter to be connected to the Internet.

DOI: 10.4018/978-1-61520-997-2.ch002

INTRODUCTION

Malaysia is one of the most progressive developing countries in the world and has been promoting the usage of Information and Communication Telecommunication (ICT) to its citizens, both in the public and private sectors. According to an Asian-Pacific Economic Cooperation study, Malaysia's e-readiness level is relatively high compared to other Association of South East Asian Nations (ASEAN) countries except Singapore (Bui, Sebastian, Jones and Naklada., 2002). This indicates that the country is on the right track in the diffusion of ICT to its population at large. Malaysia's achievement in its e-readiness can be credited to the government's dynamic ICT initiative policy, specifically its 'Vision 2020 Agenda' moving the nation towards an information society by the year 2020, Based on figures of 2007, Malaysia's Internet penetration for dial-up connection is 14.3% as compared to only a mere 7.1% in 2000 (Malaysia Communication and Multimedia Commission (MCMC), 2008). As for the penetration rate for broadband connection, there is a considerable increase from only 0.08% in 2002 (when the service was introduced in Malaysia) to 5.0% in 2007 (MCMC, 2008). Data on the Internet penetration shows an increase in the diffusion of ICT to the Malaysia population.

However, there are many challenges that Malaysia has to face in order for the country to be able to fully utilize the usage of ICT by all of its citizens. Malaysia is a developing country with a very large rural population (more than 40%). The physical infrastructure in rural Malaysia differs from that of developed nations. In Malaysia, there is an uneven distribution of the basic amenities, infrastructure and infostructure between the urban and rural area, with the rural area remaining relatively less developed. The rural population also consists of generally less educated people who are involved in an agricultural based economy and have a per capita income less than its urban counterparts. They are also most likely not using ICT as much compared to the urban population.

From the perspective of the government of Malaysia, the issue is how the nation can achieve its main goal to be an information society by the year 2020 if there is a discrepancy between the urban-rural diffusion of ICT. The Malaysia Vision 2020 ICT Agenda could not be materialized if there is digital divide based on the geographical differences where the population live. What is also a pressing issue of the urban-rural digital divide is the fact that most of the rural population who do not use ICT, do so not because of choice, but as a consequence of the lack of access to the ICT facilities. They also do not use ICT because of the lack of Internet content that suits their rural lifestyle or the language and skill that they were not able to acquire. The gap of the digital divide between the urban and rural populations of Malaysia will get wider if government, private sector and the community itself do not intervene with programs encouraging the usage of ICT.

The Government of Malaysia has reacted very actively in order to accelerate the diffusion of ICT to its mass population, especially the rural population. Programs that have been carried out by the government to encourage the usage of ICT by the rural population include 'InfoDesa', 'e-Bario' in the State of Sarawak and 'KedaiKom'. All these programs aim to engage the community to get exposed and to use the ICT.

This chapter will be focusing on the KedaiKom projects that have been implemented in Malaysia as rural telecenters for the underserved rural communities. A questionnaire survey was conducted focusing on how Kedaikom, as a community telecenter, could play a role in encouraging the rural or underserved community to use ICT. The results from that survey will be presented in this chapter so that it can provide a guideline on how the public sector involvement could significantly contribute in narrowing the digital divide between the underserved rural population and the well-accessed urban population in Malaysia.

BACKGROUND OF ICT DIFFUSION AND DIGITAL DIVIDE IN MALAYSIA

Malaysia has already experienced decades of technology transformations impacting the rural community, but the rate of development and adoption of technology are too slow among the underserved rural community as compared to their urban counterparts (MCMC, 2009). Thus, narrowing the gap requires a totally new transformation through an integrated rural development plan, to make the area into more progressive, more attractive, and more profitable. The general well-being of the rural communities must be at least on the same level as what is considered the norm for the whole nation.

The Internet penetration rate in Malaysia is experiencing a rapid increase, and the key reason is because the government's driven initiatives. Other key reasons are because of the introduction of the Asymmetric Digital Subscriber Line (ADSL) and Wireless Local Area Network (LAN) hotspots as well as more competitive pricing for dial-up and broadband services. In 2009 there were 1,378, 000 ADSL subscribers compared to 1,002,000 in 2007 while the wireless application subscribers rose from 96.3 in 2007 to 631.3 in 2009 (MCMC, 2009).

The Household Use of the Internet Survey conducted in 2008 by the Malaysian Communications and Multimedia Commission found 51.9% of Malaysian home users were males; more than 75% are below 39 years old; 73% of them with monthly earnings of between USD300 to USD1500. As expected there were more urban users (85%) compared to the rural areas. The states of Selangor and Wilayah Persekutuan combined consisted of 39% of the total users in Malaysia. These states are economically the more advanced states in the country (MCMC, 2009). The survey suggests that there are differences in the level of readiness according to age, gender, income, and rural-urban regions.

THE ROLE OF KEDAIKOM IN BRIDGING RURAL DIGITAL DIVIDE

Overview of KedaiKom

KedaiKom is one of the government programs designed to encourage the underserved population, specifically the rural population to use ICT in their daily life. As a telecenter, its objective is to build capacity; to introduce and to encourage the usage of ICT; and to create community communication equipped with a range of ICT services to facilitate Internet access, e-commerce and e-learning. The focus is on the areas with an active community base but lack of good infostructure and with village or local area economic activities that can benefit from this access. Every KedaiKom would be provided with hardware by the MCMC as a one-off allocation with a minimum of five computers, a printer and its relevant peripherals. The facilities include satellite access solutions that provide two payphone services and broadband internet access with a dedicated 128kbp for downloading and 64kps for uploading. Internet connection would be supplied by an ISP and the monthly access fee of RM 400 per site is paid by MCMC. The operation hour for the telecenter is from 8.00 am to 6.00 pm on weekdays and would be extended to 10.00 pm on weekends and public holidays. The operators would manage KedaiKom as their own business. The management team consists of a minimum of two staff members: a manager and an assistant manager. Training and courses are provided in the areas of usage of the Internet as a medium of communication for the target groups including KedaiKom operators, local leaders, teachers, students, youth and women. Among the classes offered is basic competency in the use of personal computer, maintenance and Internet awareness programs. By June 2005, 58 KedaiKom projects were implemented and 55 of the sites were in the State of Perak. The study on KedaiKom as a service for the rural community to get access to the ICT was consequently conducted in the State of Perak.

Research on KedaiKom

The research conducted is primarily based on quantitative approach using survey methodology. The research framework is designed to explore and investigate how the community access to ICT would influence the digital inclusion. The role of the telecenter as a medium that has capacity to build, decrease, or supplement the community development outcomes, specifically in diffusion of ICT was to be examined by the survey. The extent to which the KedaiKom implementation objectives have been fulfilled were examined and explored through the analysis of KedaiKom beneficiaries, community technical access, and community social access relating to community technology that lead to the narrowing of the digital divide. The research questions raised are the following:

1. To what extent do demographics influence the characteristics of KedaiKom users?
2. Is the underserved community ready to adopt ICT in their everyday life?
3. What are the objectives of using KedaiKom?
4. Are the beneficiaries satisfied with the facilities and services provided by the KedaiKom?

The developments of hypotheses that are corresponding to the research objective in narrowing the digital divide are as the following:

- **Research Hypothesis 1-H0:** Demographics influence the use of KedaiKom
- **Research Hypothesis 2-H0:** The ICT awareness among community members will influence their ability to adopt ICT in their everyday life.
- **Research Hypothesis 3-H0:** The effective and positive usage of the KedaiKom users will influence their ability to achieve desirable digital inclusion from their KedaiKom.
- **Research Hypothesis 4-H0:** The satisfaction among KedaiKom users will influence

their ability to achieve desirable development outcomes from their KedaiKom.

- **Data Collection:** Primary data was collected through a questionnaire that was distributed throughout the KedaiKom premises in the State of Perak.
- **Data Sampling:** Research Setting and Sample Frame

The research setting is underserved communities in rural areas, located in the state of Perak that comprises of 55 locations or communities - 94.8% of the grand total of 58 nationwide KedaiKom that is operated throughout Malaysia. Perak is also chosen for the study because the of role of government agencies, either at state or federal level that have programs to increase the communities to get wired, by establishing community telecenters, equipped with up-to-date peripherals and connected to the Internet through broadband. These communities, at the forefront of the ICT for development revolution, are the bases for much of the present study fieldwork.

Sample Element and Sample Size

The sample element is a KedaiKom user aged above 15 years old. This cut-off point of the user's age was decided because it is found from the pre-test that users below 15 years old experienced difficulty in answering questions relating to social capital. With an average of 10 to 20 respondents at each KedaiKom, 600 questionnaires were distributed to 55 KedaiKom locations. The location of KedaiKom were distinguished into three zones, the classification of districts according to regions; (1) Zone One, the north region; (2) Zone Two, the south region; and (3) Zone Three, the central region.

Sampling Design

Because of time and cost constraints, this study used nonprobability sampling. The design used was convenience sampling, the collection of information from the KedaiKom users of the underserved community who are conveniently available to answer the questionnaire (Sekaran, 2003).

Questionnaire Design

In phrasing the questions, this self-administered questionnaire included both fixed-choice and open-ended questions. The format of fixed-choice questions included * the fixed-alternative question - a question where the respondent is given specific alternative responses, and asked to choose the nearest to the respondent viewpoint; * the simple-dichotomy question; * a fixed-alternative question which required the respondent to choose between two alternatives, and the * determinant-choice question - a type of fixed-alternative question that requires respondents to choose only one response from among several alternatives. The questionnaire was divided into three parts: first, community technology which consists of ICT and barriers to technology integration in local development awareness; community technical and social access to KedaiKom; and user's satisfaction levels.

QUESTIONNAIRE DISTRIBUTION AND DATA COLLECTION TIMEFRAME

A total of 600 questionnaires were distributed to 27 KedaiKom centres in the state of Perak and 360 (60%) of them were returned Table 1. Although there are 55 KedaiKom in the state of Perak, the questionnaires were distributed to only 27 (49.1%) KedaiKom of the 39 (70.91%) visited. About 25 (95.7%) of the participating KedaiKom returned the distributed questionnaires. The other two KedaiKoms did not return the questionnaires even though they had been approached twice and the operators provided money to return the questionnaires through courier service. Twelve KedaiKom

were visited for a few times, but failed to distribute any of the questionnaire for reasons such as that either they were closed at the time of visit or they did not operate regularly. The remaining 16 (29.09%) KedaiKom were omitted from the sample because they did not operating anymore as envisaged by other KedaiKom operators (i.e. Kampung Bandar Lama, Kampung Ekor Bota, and Kampung Kota Pagar in district of Perak Tengah; Kampung Kota in district of Hilir Perak; and Kampung Senggang in district of Kuala Kangsar) or some of the KedaiKom were located in town area (i.e. Kampung Pengkalan Hulu) or located in a more developed district (i.e. Kampung Manjoi and Kampung Batu 8 in district of Ipoh). KedaiKom located in land settlement areas that include Felda Trolak Utara, Felda Sungai Behrang, Felda Sungai Sekiah in district of Batang Padang; and Felda Ijok in district Larut Matang and Selama. Two of such KedaiKom have been included in the survey: Felda Gunung Besout in district of Batang Padang; and Kampung Ulu Mengkuang in district of Larut, Matang and Selama. Beside the above reasons, certain KedaiKom were ommited from the sample because of distance, time, and cost constraints (i.e. Kampung Lempur Hilir and Kampung Sayung Hulu in district of Kuala Kangsar; and Kampung Parit Haji Hussin and Kampung Semanggol in district of Kerian). The average distance between each KedaiKom is about 50 kilometres and to cover all the KedaiKoms would be very costly.

In order for the survey to be more reliable; at least 50% of the KedaiKom in each district were surveyed. Among the nine districts, only Batang Padang and Perak Tengah accounted for less than 50% of the KedaiKom that were included in the survey. In fact, the total of KedaiKom visited in the Batang Padang district was five (62.5%). Two of them were closed both times attempted at the end of May and in early of June 2006 during the field visit. The situation was different in the district of Perak Tengah where three (60.0%) of the five KedaiKom in that district were not operating anymore, and the other one was closed during two visits.

From the total of 360 returned questionnaires, 326 (90.6%) were useable for analysis. The data collection for the study was carried out over a two month period starting in May and ended in July 2005.

Statistical Data Analysis

The Statistical Program for Social Science (SPSS) Version 12 was used to analyze the data collected through the questionnaire technique, and the SPSS analysis applications that will be used for this study is a descriptive analysis that includes: (1) *frequency analysis* - used to analyze and present the demographic profile of the studied community; (2) *cross tabulation* - used to explore dominant distribution between demographic criterions and independent variables; and (3) *correlation analysis* - employed to explain the association between the independent and dependent variables. In addition, the multivariate analyses that include *Exploratory Factor Analysis (EFA), Stepwise Multiple Regression*, and *Cumulative Factor Score Index"* was used to explore and examine the relationships between independent and dependent variables.

Data Analysis and Findings of the Survey

Based on the questionnaires that have been distributed at the various sites of the Kedaikom in the State of Perak, the findings are described in the following sections.

Table 1. Questionnaire distribution to KedaiKom users in State of Perak

KedaiKom			Site Surveyed				Questionnaire Distribution		
Zone	District	No.	Site Visited	%	Site Surveyed	%	Distributed	Returned	%
One	Kerian	6	4	66.67	3	50.00	60	36	60.00
	Larut, Matang & Selama	8	7	87.50	4	50.00	105	81	77.14
	Hulu Perak	5	4	80.00	5*	60.00	60	18	30.00
Zone One Total		19	15	**78.95**	10	52.63	225	135	60.00
Two	**Batang Padang**	8	5	62.50	3	37.50	85	60	70.59
	Hilir Perak	7	6	85.71	4	57.14	90	45	50.00
	Manjung	5	5	100.00	3	60.00	60	25	41.67
Zone Two Total		20	16	**80.00**	10	50.00	235	130	55.32
Three	**Kinta**	5	3	60.00	3*	60.00	60	15	25.00
	Kuala Kangsar	6	3	50.00	3	50.00	60	33	55.00
	Perak Tengah	5	2	40.00	1	20.00	20	13	65.00
Zone Three Total		16	8	**50.00**	7	43.75	140	61	43.57
Grand Total		55	39**	**70.91**	27	49.09	600	326	54.33

Note: * 1 site each in district of Hulu Perak and Kinta did not return questionnaires
** 12 sites were closed at the time of visit or they did not operate regularly
*** 16 sites were omitted from the sample

Users of the KedaiKom Centers

Most users in (Table 2) use a computer or the Internet at KedaiKom centers (79.1%) compared to cyber cafés (65.6%), workplaces (60.7%) and at home (46.6%).

User Attributes

One way of evaluating and examining whether KedaiKom has fulfilled its objectives in terms of digital inclusion, was to identify the users' attributes.

KedaiKom users were asked a series of questions relating to their demographic characteristics, frequency of visiting KedaiKom, time taken per typical visit, and experience with computers. The gender proportion seems to be balanced, where female users outnumbered the male by only 2.5%, and accounted for 52.5% of the total Table 3. Single users comprised 88.7% of total users, outnumbering the married and divorced users which consisted of 10.4% and 0.9% respectively. The marital status proportion dominance by the single seemed to match the percentage of an age group of less than 25 years (83.1%). The result suggests that most of the users are single and students, either in secondary schools, colleges or universities. The pattern was revealed by the users' education level where 67.8% of the users have secondary school level of education compared to tertiary education 25.1% (Polytechnics, colleges and universities).

The socio-economic pattern of the users illustrates that most of them belong to poor and low-income groups, were either unemployed or self-employed, and a majority of the users were Malays. The study results disclose that 91.4% of the users have a monthly family income of less than RM 2,000, where 66% of them have a monthly family income of less than RM 1,000; lived in their family home (78.5%); and 99.1% were of the Malay ethnicity (as measured by the mother tongue) (Table 4). In terms of occupation, the majority were students (56.1%), while the remainder were self-employed (12.9%), unemployed (12.3%), government employees (4.3%) and private sector employees (9.8%). Hence, the dependence group that includes students and unemployed comprised 68.4% of the total beneficiaries.

Computer Experience

About 45.0% of the users spend at least two hours per typical visit. Furthermore, 37.1% of the users have more than 3 years of computer experience compared to 29.1%, who have less than one year experience (Table 5). Another 33.7% are users who have between one to three years experience using

Table 2. Place of use for the computer and internet

No.	Variable	Percentage Level of Agreement		
		Agree*	**Neutral**	**Disagree ****
1.	**You frequently use the computer at home**	**46.6**	**17.8**	**35.6**
2.	**You frequently use the computer at your work place**	**60.7**	**12.9**	**26.4**
3.	**You frequently use the computer at a cyber café**	**65.6**	**12.3**	**22.1**
4.	**You frequently use the computer at a community telecenter**	**79.1**	**9.2**	**11.7**
n = 326 (based on actual responses) *** Agree includes scales of agree, strongly agree and extremely agree** **** Disagree includes scales of disagree, strongly disagree, and extremely disagree**				

Table 3. KedaiKom users attributes: gender, marital status, age and education

Attribute	Item	Frequency	%	Cumulative %
Gender	**Female**	**171**	**52.5**	**52.5**
	Male	**155**	**47.5**	**100.0**
	Total	326	100.0	
Marital Status	**Single**	**289**	**88.7**	**88.7**
	Married	**34**	**10.4**	**99.1**
	Divorcee	**3**	**0.9**	**100.0**
	Total	326	100.0	
Gender	**Female**	**171**	**52.5**	**52.5**
	Male	**155**	**47.5**	**100.0**
	Total	326	100.0	
Marital Status	**Single**	**289**	**88.7**	**88.7**
	Married	**34**	**10.4**	**99.1**
	Divorcee	**3**	**0.9**	**100.0**
	Total	326	100.0	
Age	**15 – 19 years**	**178**	**54.6**	**54.6**
	20 – 24 years	**93**	**28.5**	**83.1**
	25 – 29 years	**19**	**5.8**	**89.0**
	30 – 34 years	**9**	**2.8**	**91.7**
	35 – 39 years	**8**	**2.5**	**94.2**
	Above 40 years	**19**	**5.8**	**100.0**
	Total	326	100.0	
Level of Education	**Primary School**	**4**	**1.2**	**1.2**
	Secondary School	**221**	**67.8**	**69.0**
	Skilled Institution	**13**	**4.0**	**73.0**
	Polytechnic/College	**46**	**14.1**	**87.1**
	University	**36**	**11.0**	**98.2**
	No Formal Education	**6**	**1.8**	**100.0**
	Total	326	100.0	

computers. Thus, this finding reveals that most of the users are experienced when measured against the frequency of visit per average month and time spent per typical visit in addition to having more than three years' computer experience.

Active and Passive Users

This study divided users into two groups: active and passive users. The division is based on the following: active users were those who visited KedaiKom at least once a week or four times in an average month, and passive users were those who visited KedaiKom less than four times on average per month. Based on this categorisation,

this study found that 230 or 70.5% of the respondents were active users and the other 96 or 29.5% were passive users (Table 6).

Demographic Factors

The first KedaiKom and digital inclusion research hypothesis for influencing personalities of KedaiKom users: *Demographics influence the use of KedaiKom* is against the hypothesised direction as indicated by the Chi-square analysis of results. Through the application of Chi-square analysis, a significant difference (at $p<0.05$) was found between active and passive users in only two different demographic factors: gender and

Table 4. KedaiKom users attributes: Occupation, income, residential and mother tongue

Attribute	Item	Frequency	%	Cummulative %
Occupation	Government Employee	14	4.3	4.3
	Private Sector Employee	32	9.8	14.1
	Self Employee	42	12.9	27.0
	Housewife	8	2.5	29.4
	Unemployed	40	12.3	41.7
	Retiree	5	1.5	43.3
	Students	183	56.1	99.4
	Others	2	0.6	100.0
	Total	326	100.0	
Family Month-ly Income	<RM 1,000	215	66.0	66.0
	RM 1,001 – RM 2,000	83	25.5	91.4
	RM 2,001 – RM 3,000	14	4.3	95.7
	RM 3,001 – RM 4,000	5	1.5	97.2
	RM 4,001 – RM 5,000	4	1.2	98.5
	> RM 5,000	5	1.5	100.0
	Total	326	100.0	
Type of Resi-dential	Rental House	36	11.0	11.0
	Owned House	34	10.4	21.5
	Family House	256	78.5	100.0
	Total	326	100.0	
Mother Tongue	Malay Language	323	99.1	99.1
	Chinese Language	2	0.6	99.7
	Tamil Language	1	0.3	100.0
	Total	326	100.0	

occupation (Table 7). In term of gender, this study found that, in general, male respondents tend to be more active than the female, and in terms of occupation, students tended to be more active than working users and others.

In responding to the issue of KedaiKom and digital inclusion influencing the beneficiaries' ability in achieving desirable digital inclusion from their KedaiKom; *To what extent does demo-*

Table 5. Computer experience

Computer Experience	No. of User	Percentage
Beginner	38	11.7
Less than 1 year	57	17.5
1 to 3 years	110	33.7
3 to 5 years	42	12.9
More than 5 years	79	24.2
Total	326	100.0

graphics influence the use of KedaiKom?. The above findings suggest that the profiles of Kedai-Kom users do not influence their ability to achieve desirable digital inclusion from KedaiKom in the underserved community, particularly as active users, except for male and student users. This showed that the demographic factor has no bearing on the profiles of KedaiKom users, on whether an individual would be an active or passive user. No significant differences were found between the two user groups with respect to age, marital status, education level, and family monthly income.

Community Readiness to Adopt ICT

The second KedaiKom and digital inclusion research hypothesis for influencing community members' ability to adopt ICT; *"The ICT awareness among community members will influence*

Table 6. Active and passive users of KedaiKom

Visit Frequency	No. of Users	%	Type of User	%
First Time User	**12**	**3.7**	**Passive**	29.5
Once a month	**28**	**8.6**	**(96)**	
Two times a month	**33**	**10.1**		
Three times a month	**23**	**7.1**		
Once a week	**31**	**9.5**	**Active**	70.5
Two times a week	**45**	**13.8**	**(230)**	
Three times a week	**67**	**20.6**		
Once a day	**49**	**15.0**		
Many times a day	**38**	**11.7**		
Total	326	100.0	326	100.0

Table 7. Active and passive users: A demographic factor comparison

Demographic Factor	Significance		Active Users		Passive Users		Total
	χ^2	**P**	**n = 230**	**%**	**N = 96**	**%**	**n = 326**
Gender: (a) Female (b) Male	6.707	0.010	**110** **120**	**47.8** **52.2**	**61** **35**	**63.5** **36.5**	**171** **155**
Total			230	100	96	100	326
Age: (a) <25 years (b) 25 to 34 years (c) Above 35 years	4.045	0.132	**185** **23** **22**	**56.7** **7.1** **6.7**	**86** **5** **5**	**26.4** **1.5** **1.5**	**271** **28** **27**
Total			230	100	96	100	326
Marital Status: (a) Single (b)Married/Divorced	2.227	0.136	**200** **30**	**61.3** **9.2**	**89** **7**	**27.3** **2.1**	**289** **37**
Total			230	100	96	100	326
Level of Education: (a)Secondary School / **Skilled Institution** (b)Polytech/College/ **University** (c) Others	2.357	0.970	**166** **57** **7**	**50.9** **17.5** **2.1**	**68** **25** **3**	**20.9** **7.7** **0.9**	**234** **82** **10**
Total			230	100	96	100	326
Occupation: (a)Gov/Private/Self Employee (b) Students (c) Others (Housewife, Unem- ployed/Retiree)	7.394	0.025	**72** **122** **36**	**22.1** **37.4** **11.0**	**16** **61** **19**	**4.9** **18.7** **5.8**	**88** **183** **55**
Total			230	100	96	100	326
Family Monthly Income: (a) Less than RM1,000 (b) RM1,001 to RM2,000 (c) More than RM2,000	1.632	0.443	**156** **54** **20**	**47.9** **16.6** **6.1**	**59** **29** **8**	**18.1** **8.9** **2.5**	**215** **83** **28**
Total			230	100	96	100	326

their ability to adopt ICT in their everyday life" is supported as indicated by the EFA analysis of results in the interrelationship of the measured variables for ICT awareness and technology integration in local development awareness *(*Table 8 and Table 9*)*.

ICT Awareness

The community's readiness to adopt ICT is measured by questions related to user awareness about ICT as well as their knowledge about the integration of technology in the local development. The finding suggests that users are certainly ready and capable to adapt to ICT. Based on the actual responses, more than 70% of users agreed that ICT is important as a tool to develop the local community (Table 8). More than 80% of the respondents agreed that community learning is enhanced by the incorporation of ICT in everyday life; that the rural community adequately supports the implementation of ICT initiatives; and local community leadership are willing to lead ICT development.

Through the deployment of EFA, the variables measuring ICT awareness was split into two fac-

tors: *"ICT Support Awareness"* which consisted of four variables with loadings ranging from 0.50 to 0.74; and *"ICT Knowledge Awareness"* which comprised of three variables with loadings ranging from 0.50 to 0.74 (Table 9). The other five variables are omitted because of low loadings.

Kedaikom and Digital Inclusion

In answering the issue of KedaiKom and digital inclusion for influencing community members' ability to adopt ICT in their everyday life; *Is the underserved community ready to adopt ICT in their everyday life?* the findings showed that for the Factor *"ICT Support Awareness*, the results suggest that rural communities adequately support and are willing to participate in the implementation of ICT initiatives. In addition, rural communities place appropriate emphasis on the integration of ICT, and the local leadership is willing to lead the implementation of ICT development in their local area. For the Factor *"ICT Knowledge Awareness"*, the finding indicates that community evaluation should consider the ICT component as one of the main evaluation criteria. Accordingly, people who have ICT knowledge will be respected by other

Table 8. Level of agreement: ICT awareness

No.	Variable	Percentage Level of Agreement		
		Agree*	Neutral	Disagree **
1.	Community member learning is enhanced by incorporation of ICT in everyday life	89.2	7.4	3.4
2	Rural community adequately supports the implementation of ICT initiatives/ programmes	82.2	13.2	4.6
3.	Local community leadership is willing to lead ICT development	80.7	11.0	8.3
4.	Rural community is willing to participate in ICT initiatives/programmes	79.4	16.0	4.6
5.	Rural community places an appropriate emphasis on the integration of ICT into community development	78.8	14.1	7.1
6.	Community evaluation should include ICT component	76.7	13.5	9.8
7.	People who have ICT knowledge are respected by community at large	73.3	18.1	8.6
n = 326 (based on actual responses) *** Agree includes scales of agree, strongly agree and extremely agree** **** Disagree includes scales of disagree, strongly disagree, and extremely disagree**				

Table 9. Factor loading: ICT awareness variables using PAF

No.	Factor/Variable	Communalities	Loadings
Factor ICT Support Awareness			
1.	Rural community adequately supports the implementation of ICT initiatives/	0.69	0.74
2.	programmes	0.71	0.73
3.	Rural community is willing to participate in ICT initiatives/programmes	0.60	0.68
4.	Rural community places an appropriate emphasis on the integration of ICT into community development	0.43	0.50
	Local community leadership is willing to lead ICT development		
Factor ICT Knowledge Awareness			
1.	Community evaluation should include ICT component	0.68	0.74
2.	People who have ICT Knowledge are respected by community at large	0.54	0.64
3.	Community member learning is enhanced by incorporation of ICT in everyday life	0.53	0.50
Omitted Variable			
1.	Computer literacy or competency should be required of all rural community;		
2.	ICT is important in today's rural community		
3.	Rural community comfortable with the rapid changes in ICT development		
4.	Government places an appropriate emphasis on the implementation of ICT		
5.	development in rural area;		
	Users willingness to share information with other community members		

community members. Users also believed that community learning is enhanced by the incorporation of ICT in everyday life.

In addition, the Factor *"Barriers to Integrate Technology in Local Development* suggests that in order to expand the use of ICT, in particular to bridge the digital divide initiatives in underserved community successful, the combination of community technology and social support is crucial to overcome such barriers. Thus, the result of the EFA is in the hypothesised direction as the high level of ICT awareness and technology integration in local development awareness among community members will influence their ability to adopt ICT in their everyday life. The result indicates that the users as community members are undoubtedly ready and capable to adapt the usage of technology in their everyday life.

The KedaiKom Usage Objectives

To measure the usage objectives, 12 variables were employed. Based on actual responses, for the skills and knowledge usage objectives, more than 70% of users agreed that improving work related skills; improving skills to attain better jobs; and finding employment are important to them. For the social networks usage objective, about 70% of users agreed that keeping them better informed with relevant information; finding mates or friends, making new or keeping existing friendships, encouraging information sharing among users, involvement in entertainment, and increasing interaction among community members are relevant for them.

The third KedaiKom and digital inclusion research hypothesis for influencing users' ability to achieve desirable outcome; *The effective and positive usage of the KedaiKom users will influence their ability to achieve desirable digital inclusion from their KedaiKom* is supported as illustrated by the EFA analysis of results *(*Table 10*)*. Following the application of EFA, the results show that *Skills and Knowledge Usage Objectives* is a solid and clean factor with all eight variables having a loading of more than 0.5. However, for the Factor *Social Networks Usage Objective*, only two of the four variables extracted have a load of

Table 10. Factor loading: Usage objectives variables using PAF

No.	Factor/Variable	Communalities	Loadings
Factor Skills and Knowledge Usage Objective			
1.	Connecting to employer's office	0.65	0.74
2.	Connecting to colleges / universities	0.60	0.69
3.	Saving time in personal transactions	0.62	0.68
4.	Making personal purchases online	0.64	0.66
5.	Finding employment	0.62	0.64
6.	Increasing earnings from farms and businesses	0.50	0.63
7.	Improving skills to get better job	0.57	0.59
8.	Improving work related skills	0.57	0.54
Factor Social Networks Usage Objective			
1.	Finding mate, making new or keeping existing friendships	0.66	0.71
2.	Involving in entertainment	0.61	0.68
3.	Encouraging information sharing	0.52	0.40
4.	Keeping better informed	0.61	0.40
Omitted Variables			
1.	Improving academic studies		
2.	Having more self confidence		
3.	Improving ability to use computer		
4.	Increasing interaction amongst community members		

more than 0.5. Thus, the EFA result as illustrated in Table 10 is in the direction hypothesised as the effective and positive use of KedaiKom will influence their ability to achieve desirable digital inclusion from their KedaiKom.

In responding to the issue of the KedaiKom and digital inclusion for achieving desirable digital inclusion from their KedaiKom; *What is the objective of using KedaiKom?*, the related findings revealed that most of the effective and positive usage objectives are related to improving skills and knowledge including improvement of working skills, increase in earnings, involvement in teleworks, e-commerce and e-learning; and to save personal transaction time. In addition, other effective and positive usage objectives are related to improving social networks that includes finding new friends or keeping existing friendships, involvement in entertainment, encouraging information sharing; and to be better informed with local information. Thus, the effective and positive usage of KedaiKom will further include the community members in the adaptation of ICT in their everyday life.

Users Satisfaction

Based on actual responses, seven variables were used to measure users' satisfaction and indicated that more than 70% of users were satisfied with the services and facilities offered by KedaiKom Table 11.

The fourth KedaiKom and digital inclusion research hypothesis for influencing users' ability to achieve a desirable outcome; *"The satisfaction among KedaiKom users will influence their ability to achieve desirable development outcomes from the KedaiKom* is supported as revealed by the EFA analysis of results. When using EFA, two variables are omitted due to low factor loadings Table 12. "User Satisfaction" is a solid and clean factor when all the seven variables have a loading more than 0.5. In answering the KedaiKom and digital inclusion issue; *Are the beneficiaries satisfied with the facilities and services provided by the KedaiKom?*; the above finding revealed that most of the users are satisfied with the facilities and services offered by the KedaiKom.

Table 11. User satisfaction levels

No.	Variable	Percentage Level of Satisfaction		
		Satisfaction *	**Neutral**	**Dissatisfied** **
1.	**Community telecentre staffs' disposition**	82.8	10.4	6.7
2	**Community telecentre Internet connection**	76.7	12.0	11.3
3.	**Community telecentre hours services open to public**	76.4	12.9	10.7
4.	**Community telecentre charges rate**	75.8	15.0	9.2
5.	**Community telecentre software**	74.8	13.8	11.3
6.	**Community telecentre staffs' technical ability**	73.9	16.9	9.2
7.	**Community telecentre equipments**	73.9	16.0	10.1
n = 326 (based on actual responses)				
* Satisfied includes scales of somewhat satisfied, very satisfied, and extremely very satisfied				
** Dissatisfied includes scales of somewhat dissatisfied, very dissatisfied, and extremely very dissatisfied				

The result reveals that the conditions and the physical outlook of the KedaiKom as well as the availability of courses and training are not significant in attracting users. Instead, the staff disposition, Internet speed, operating time, and rates are more important for the users to consider their likely visit to KedaiKom. Thus, the result is in the hypothesised direction as the satisfaction among KedaiKom users will influence their ability to achieve desirable outcomes from the KedaiKom.

DISCUSSION AND RECOMMENDATIONS ON KEDAIKOM

The present research finding suggests that the implementation of KedaiKom in the underserved community is good and beneficial, even though KedaiKom faces several shortcomings, in terms of meeting its objectives to build capacity, to introduce and encourage growth in the usage of ICT, and to create community communications equipped with a range of ICT services to facilitate Internet access, e-commerce, and e-learning with reference to an active underserved community base but with limited or no access. The survey results also explain that in maximising their usage of Kedaikom, local and relevant contents (even though it is still important) and skilled staffs, are of lesser important in encouraging them to fully use the Kedaikom.

Furthermore, the survey also finds that community members are likely to believe that the usage of the KedaiKom can be extended not just for them to use ICT, but to serve as a public space for community interactions too. This finding is in line with the arguments of Pigg (2003); Kean (2000 cited in Mason and Hacker, 2003), and Davies et al. (2003) who maintain that telecentres are generally established to create public spaces in which to shape the ideas and actions of the community members by providing technical assistance and resources essential to meet the community needs as well as offering a common ground for community members to socialise comfortably. The underserved community is looking forward by considering KedaiKom to serve as new good public spaces that engage diverse group of people and contribute to build local community for creating and sustaining development outcomes.

The finding suggests that most of the users are youth and in a productive cohort which has a relative high education attainment. This group of users also always use KedaiKom in a productive and effective manner. When it comes to family support, even though the family monthly income of the sample locations were relatively low, the

Table 12. Factor loading: User satisfaction variables using PAF

No.	Variable	Communalities	Loadings
1.	**Community telecentre software**	**0.65**	**0.75**
2.	**Community telecentre staff's technical ability**	**0.62**	**0.71**
3.	**Community telecentre staff's disposition**	**0.71**	**0.69**
4.	**Community telecentre Internet connection**	**0.62**	**0.68**
5.	**Community telecentre rates**	**0.54**	**0.68**
6.	**Community telecentre hours open to public**	**0.57**	**0.65**
7.	**Community telecentre equipment**	**0.48**	**0.58**
Omitted Variables			
1.	**Community telecentre ambience**		
2.	**Community telecentre courses and training**		

awareness level in the family was relatively high, thus influencing the frequency of the youth group of users in using KedaiKom. Furthermore, the majority of the users have computer experience of more than three years, visit KedaiKom at least once a week in an average month, and spend at least four hours per typical visit. The finding suggests that most of the users are core users rather than peripheral or excluded users (Murdock, 2002 cited in Selwyn, 2003). The vast experience and the relatively high average time spent per typical visit shows that the usage of KedaiKom is principally productive and effective.

No significant differences were found between active and passive groups of users with regards to age, marital status, education level, and family monthly income, ans indicated by the Chi-square analysis. However, significant differences were found in two demographic factors, gender and occupation.

Male users tend to be more active than females and students tend to be more active than other users. The finding suggests that active users are not influenced by the demographic factors including age, marital status, education attainment, and income. However, the necessity and the need to use KedaiKom are more significant. Job hunting, information seeking and sharing, acquiring work and education related knowledge and skills, keeping and maintaining friendships as well as seeking entertainment are the main forces

encouraging the users to use KedaiKom. Thus, users which are mostly youth, and in a productive cohort with family and community support will frequently visit and use KedaiKom. Students in secondary schools and in community colleges especially need Internet access to seek information for their folios and assignments. However, it is their families that need to bear the costs, but most have limited income. The finding is in agreement with Chen and Wellman (2003) and Warschauer's (2003) argument that social support means the individual and community awareness which can create and sustain social capital capable of supporting the implementation of telecentres in the local community. Males are most active. Except among students, male usage dominated in all user groups. Most of the users seeking and involving entertainment were male; the most frequent users spending more time per typical visit were also male. Females were generally restricted to using KedaiKom during the day because most likely the norms and values of the rural community do not encourage the females visiting public places during certain times especially at night.

Concerning ICT awareness and technology integration among community members to adopt ICT in their everyday life it was found that the underserved communities are certainly ready and capable to adopt ICT. Most of the members of the community are adequately supportive and they are willing to participate in ICT initiatives. The local community places an appropriate emphasis on the integration of ICT, and the local leadership is willing to lead local ICT initiatives. Moreover, the community members are aware that in order for the expansion of ICT, and to bridge the digital divide, the combination of community technology and social support is crucial to overcome the barriers to technology integration in local development. The barriers that need to be overcome include the lack of skilled staff, community support, information sharing, training, planning, infrastructure, funding, and local leadership.

The results from the survey show the effective and positive usage by the KedaiKom users, particularly to improve the user's skills and knowledge, in addition to extending and upholding the user's social networks that will influence their ability to achieve digital inclusion. The most important usage objectives are related to the improvement of the user's skills and knowledge, which include improved working skills, increased earnings, involvement in teleworks, e-commerce, and e-learning, and saving time for personal transactions. The most important effective and positive usage related to the expansion and upholding of the user's social networks include finding new friends, making new or keeping existing friendships, seeking and involving in entertainment, sharing information, and being better informed. Thus, the high, effective, and positive usage of KedaiKom will eventually encourage the community members in the adoption of ICT in their everyday life. The results suggest that the users of KedaiKom are mostly and actively involved in the positive usage of KedaiKom, in particular for improving working and education related skills and knowledge as well as for improving and maintaining social networks. This particular positive usage normally involves students, working users, job seekers and parents who have family outside the community, and tourists in homestays organised by the community. However, certain users who are unemployed and school dropouts comprise mostly of males who are heavily involved in entertainment that is in the category of unproductive usage, explicit games, chatting, movies, and music etc. The involvement in unproductive usage mostly occurred at the unsuccessful KedaiKom where the operators rarely provide a strict supervision on the usage.

The finding is in agreement with Van Dijk (1999, cited in Mason and Hacker, 2003); and De Haan's (2003) who argue that users with limited skills and knowledge will be outpaced. Thus, there is a need for those users to increase their skills in ICT applications. The finding also suggests that most of the KedaiKom users are core users that use telecenters positively and affectively with continuous and comprehensive usage especially for information seeking, communication and origination or production of digital contents which is in accordance with Murdock's (2002, cited in Selwyn, 2003) argument. The finding is in agreement with Warschauer (2002), Pinkett (2001), and Besser's (2003) contention that most of the telecenter projects run into unanticipated complications because these projects persistently neglect positive and effective usage and users are passive and non-producers of local content, which is the stumbling block for realising the expected results.

Harris (2001), Gurstein (2000), Graham (2002) and Cisler (1998, cited in Owen and Darkwa, 1999) propose that a community telecenter will be the typical rural community's first encounter with ICT, and that it would offer delivery of support services, e-commerce, e-learning, telemedicines services, etc. The results from our study clearly show that the rural population is using the facilities at the telecenters as envisaged, especially by the young generations who will shape the country future ICT agenda.

REFERENCES

Bartholomew, D. J. (1987). *Latent Variable Model and Factor Analysis*. Charles Griffin and Company Limited.

Beamish, A. (1995). *Community On-line: Computer-Base Community Networks*. Master of City Planning Thesis, Massachusetts Institute of Technology. Retrieved August 5, 2008 from http://sap.mit.edu/anneb/cn-thesis/

Beamish, A. (1999). Approaches to Community Computing: Bringing Technology to Low-Income Groups. In Schon, D. A., Sanyal, B., & Mitchell, W. J. (Eds.), *High Technology and Low-Income Communities: Prospects for the Positive Use of Advanced Information Technology*. MIT Press.

Besser, H. (2003). *The Next Digital Divide*. Retrieved July 6, 2003 from http://tcla. gseis.ucla. edu/ divide/ politics/besser.html

Breiter, A. (2003). Public Internet Usage Points in Schools for the Local Community – Concept, Implementation and Evaluation of a Project in Bremen, Germany. *Education and Information Technologies*, 8(2), 109–2003. doi:10.1023/A:1024550229787

Brenner, N. (1999). Beyond state-centrism?: Space, Territoriality, and Geographical Scale in Globalization Studies. *Theory and Society*, 28, 39–78. doi:10.1023/A:1006996806674

British Educational Communications and Technology Agency. (2002). *Digital Divide*. ICT Research Network, A Collection of Papers from the Toshiba/Becta Digital Divide Seminar: 19th February 2002. Retrieved on November 23, 2003 from www.becta.org.uk/research

Burt, R. S. (2001). *Bridge Decay*. Retrieved November 6 2003 from http://gsbuwn.uchicago. edu/fac/ronald.burt/research/BD.pdf

Butler, T. (2002). Bridging the Digital Divide Through Educational Initiatives: Problems and Solutions. Special Series on the Digital Divide. *Informing Science*, 5(3).

Charp, S. (2001). Bridging the Digital Divide. [Technological Horizons in Education]. *T.H.E. Journal*, 28.

Chen, W., & Wellman, B. (2003). E-Commerce Development: Charting and Bridging the Digital Divide. *I-Ways. Digest of Electronic Commerce Policy and Regulation*, 26, 155–161.

Coelen, S. P. (1980). *Regression Analysis of Regional Quality of Life*. Dordect, Holland & Boston. MA: D. Reidel Publishing Co.

Costello, A. B., & Osborne, J. W. (2005). Best Practices in Exploratory Factor Analysis: Four Recommendations or Getting the Most from Your Analysis. *Practical Assessment Research and Evaluation*, 10(7), 1–9.

Cullen, R. (2001). Addressing the Digital Divide. *Online Information Review*, 25(5). doi:10.1108/14684520110410517

Daniel, B., Schwler, R. A., & McCalla, G. (2003). Social Capital in Virtual Learning Communities and Distributed Communities of Practice. *Canadian Journal of Learning and Technology*, 29(3).

Davies, S., Schwartz, A. W., Pinkett, R. D., & Servon, L. J. (2003). *A Report to the Ford Foundation: Community Technology Centres as Catalyst for Community Change*. A Report to the Ford Foundation, New School University Retrieved October 25, 2003 from www.bctpartners.com/ resources/ CTCs as Catalysts.pdf

De Haan, J. (2003). IT and Social Inequality in the Netherlands. *IT&Society*, 1(4), 27–45.

Degenne, A., & Forse, M. (1994). *Introducing Social Networks (I. Borges, Trans. 1999)*. Sage Publications.

Denison, T., Stillman, L., Johanson, G., & Schauder, D. (2003). Theory, Practice, Social Capital, and Information and Communication Technologies in Australia. *Many Voices, Many Places – Electronically Enabling Communities for and Information Society: A Colloquium Proceedings*. Monash Prato, Italy, 15-16 September, 2003. Retrieved October 25, 2006 from http:// www.ccnr.net/?q=node/234

Department of Statistic. Malaysia (2006). *Key Statistics*. Retrieved June 16, 2007 from http://www.statistics.gov.my/english/ frameset_keystats.php

Digital Divide Council. *Digital Divide and Underserved Groups*. Retrieved on April 25, 2005 from http://www.digitaldividecouncil. com / digitaldivide/progress_date.html

Donnermeyer, J. F., & Hollifield, C. A. (2003). Digital Divide Evidence in Four Rural Towns. *IT&Society*, *1*(4), 107–117.

Economic Planning Unit. (1999). *Malaysian Quality of Life 1999*. Malaysia: Economic Planning Unit, Prime Minister's Department.

Economic Planning Unit. (2002). *Malaysia Quality of Life 2002*. Prime Minister's Department, Malaysia. Retrieved May 25, 2004 from http://www.epu.jpm.my/ Bi/publi/ mqli2002/content.pdf

Ellen, D. (2000). *Telecentres and the Provision of Community Based Access to Electronic Information in Everyday Life*. PhD. Thesis, Manchester Metropolitan University, United Kingdom. Retrieved May 11, 2003 from http://www.mmu.ac.uk/h-ss/dic/research /ellen/contents.html

Ellen, D. (2003). Telecentres and the Provision of Community Based Access to Electronic Information in Everyday Life in the UK. *Information Research, 8*(2), paper number 146. Retrieved May 11, 2003 from http://informationr.net/ir/8-2/paper146.html

Emory, C. W., & Cooper, D. R. (1991). *Business Research Methods* (4th ed.). Richard D. Irwin, Inc.

Ernberg, J. (1998). *Integrated Rural Development and Universal Access towards a Framework for Evaluation of Multipurpose Telecentres: Pilot Projects Implemented In ITU and Its Partners*. Retrieved August 28, 2004 from http://www.itu.int/ITU-D/univ_access/ telecentres/papers/guelph.html

Ferlander, S. (2003). *The Internet, Social Capital and Local Community*. PhD Thesis, University of Sterling. Retrieved July 23, 2004 from http://www.crdlt.stir.ac.uk /Docs/ SaraFerlanderPhD.pdf

Forrest, R., & Kearns, A. (2001). Social Cohesion, Social Capital and the Neighbourhood. *Urban Studies (Edinburgh, Scotland)*, *38*(12), 2125–2143. doi:10.1080/00420980120087081

Gabe, T. M., & Abel, J. R. (2002). Deployment of Advanced Telecommunications Infrastructure in Rural America: Measuring the Digital Divide. *American Journal of Agricultural Economics*, *84*(5), 1246–1252. doi:10.1111/1467-8276.00385

Government of Malaysia. (1997). *Digital Signature Act 1997 (Act 562)*. Kuala Lumpur, Malaysia: Percetakan Nasional Malaysia Berhad.

Government of Malaysia. (1998). *Communications and Multimedia Act 1998 (Act 588)*. Kuala Lumpur, Malaysia: Percetakan Nasional Malaysia Berhad.

Government of Malaysia. (2001b). *The Third Outline Perspective Plan 2001-2010*. Retrieved May 20, 2004 from www.epu.jpm.my/Bi/dev_plan/opp3.htm

Government of Malaysia. (2006). *The Ninth Malaysia Plan 2006-2010*. Kuala Lumpur, Malaysia: Percetakan Nasional Malaysia Berhad.

Graham, S. (2002). Bridging Urban Divides? Urban Polarisation and Information and Communications Technologies (ICTs). *Urban Studies (Edinburgh, Scotland)*, *39*(1), 33–56. doi:10.1080/00420980220099050

Grootaert, C., Narayanan, D., Jones, V. N., & Woolcock, M. (2003). *Measuring Social Capital: An Integated Questionnaire*. World Bank Working Paper No. 18.

Gurstein, M. (2000). Community Informatics: Enabling Community Use of Information and Communication Technology. In Gurstein, M. (Ed.), *Community Informatics: Enabling Communities with Information and Communications Technologies* (pp. 1–32). Idea Group Publishing.

Habing, B. (2003). *Exploratory Factor Analysis*. Retrieved January 12, 2006 from www.stat. sc.edu/~habing/courses/530EFA.pdf

Hacker, K. L. (2000). *Divide Facts and Fictions Digital*. Retrieved July 6, 2003 from http:// khacker2. freeyellow.com/ddnow6.htm

Hair, J. F., Anderson, R. E., Tatham, R. L., & Black, W. C. (1998). *Multivariate Data Analysis* (5th Ed.). Prentice Hall. Hampton, K.N., & Wellman, B. (2000). Examining Community in the Digital Neighborhood: Early Results from Canada's Wired Suburb. In T. Ishida & K. Isbister (Eds.), *Digital Cities: Technologies, Experiences, and Future Perspectives* (LNCS 1765, pp. 194-208).

Harper, R., & Kelly, M. (2003). *Measuring Social Capital in the United Kingdom*. Retrieved January 19, 2005 from www.statistics.gov.uk/socialcapital/ downloads/ harmonisation_stere_5.pdf

Harris, R. (2001). Telecentres in Rural Asia: Towards a Success Model. *Conference Proceedings of International Conference on Information Technology, Communications and Development* (ITCD 2001), November 23-3-, Katmandu, Nepal. Retrieved May 24, 2006 from http://unpanl.un.org/ introdoc/groups/ public/documents/APCITY/ UNPA C006304.pdf

IDC Market Research. (n.d.). *Malaysia Internet Market*. Retrieved August 12, 2003 from http:// www.idc.com.my/

Institute for Rural Advancement. (1995). *Philosophy and Strategy of Rural Development towards the Year 2020*. Institute for Rural Advancement.

Institute of Strategic and International Studies (ISIS). (2002). *Knowledge-Based Economy Master Plan*. ISIS Malaysia.

International Institute for Management Development (IMD). (2003). *The World Competitiveness Scoreboard 2003*. Retrieved July 21, 2003 from http://www01.imd.ch/documents/ wcy/ content/ ranking.pdf

International Telecommunication Union (ITU). (2003). *World Telecommunication Development Report 2003: Access Indicators for Information Society*. Geneva: World Summit on the Information Society.

Ismawati, N.J., & Ainin, S. (2003). Bridging the Digital Divide in Malaysia: A Review of ICT Programs and Initiatives. *The International Journal of Knowledge, Culture and Change Management, 3*.

Jackson, L. A., Barbatsis, G., von Eye, A., Biocca, F., Zhao, Y., & Fitzgerald, H. (2003). Internet Use in Low-Income Families: Implications for the Digital Divide. *IT&Society, 1*(5), 141–165.

Keeble, L., & Loader, B. D. (2001). *Challenging the Digital Divide? A Preliminary Review of Online Community Support*. CIRA, University of Teesside. Retrieved October 31, 2003 from www.cira.org.uk/downloads/Rowntrees %20 Report.shtml

Kootstra, G. J. (2004). *Exploratory Factor Analysis: Theory and Application. Retrieved January 12, 2006 from odur.let.rug.nl/~nerbonne/teach/ rema_stat s_meth-seminar/Factor_ analysis_ kootrstra_04*. PDF.

Laudon, K. C., & Laudon, J. P. (2004). *Management Information Systems: Managing the Digital Firm* (8th ed.). Prentice Hall.

Lawley, D. N., & Maxwell, A. E. (1971). *Factor Analysis as a Statistical Method*. London: Butterworths.

Lenhart, A., & Horrigan, J. B. (2003). Re-Visualizing the Digital Divide as a Digital Spectrum. *IT&Society, 1*(5), 23–39.

Malaysia Communication and Multimedia Commission (MCMC). (2006). *Facts and Figure – Internet Subsriber 2006*. Retrieved September 26, 2006 from www.mcmc.gov.my /facts_figures/ stats/index.asp

Malaysia Communication and Multimedia Commission (MCMC). (2008). *Facts and Figure 2007*. Retrieved November 10, 2008 from www.mcmc. gov. my/facts_figures/ stats/index.asp

Malaysia Communication and Multimedia Commission (MCMC). (2009). *Facts and Figure – Internet Subsriber 2009*. Retrieved September 14, 2009 from http://www.skmm.gov.my/facts_f igures/stats/index.asp

Malaysia Communications and Multimedia Commission ((MCMC) (2002a). *Communication and Multimedia in Malaysia: Looking Back and Planning Ahead*. Malaysia Communication and Multimedia Commission (2002).

Malaysia Debt Ventures Berhad. (2005). *Perak Launches ICT Blue Print to Become K-State by 2020*. Retrieved June 26, 2006 from http://www. debtventures.com/page.cfm? name=Perak

Malaysian Communication and Multimedia Commission (MCMC). (2001). *Communications and Multimedia Act 1998: Commission Determination on Universal Service Provision – Determination No.2 of 2001*. Retrieved May 26, 2004 from www. mcmc.gov.my

Malaysian Communication and Multimedia Commission (MCMC). (2002b). *Communications and Multimedia Act 1998: Commission Determination on Universal Service Provision (Determination No.6 of 2002) – Variation No.1 of 2003*. Retrieved May 26, 2004 from www.mcmc.gov.my

Malaysian Communication and Multimedia Commission (MCMC). (2004). *Universal Service Provision (USP): Notification of Universal Service Targets (NT/USP/1/04)*. Retrieved May 26, 2004 from www.mcmc.gov.my

Mason, S. M., & Hacker, K. L. (2003). Applying Communication Theory to Digital Divide Research. *IT&Society, 1*(5), 40–55.

Menou, M.J. (2001). The Global Digital Divide: Beyond HICTeri. *Aslib Proceeding: The New Information Perspectives, 53*(4).

Ministry of Energy, Water and Communications (MEWC). (2006). *Industry Introduction: Institutional Arrangement*. Retrieved November 29, 2006 from http://www.ktak.gov.my/bm/ template01.asp? contentid=42

Ministry of Finance. (2003). *Malaysia Budget 2004*. Retrieved May 28, 2004 from http://www. treasury.gov.my/ englishversionbaru/index.htm

Molina, A. (2003). The Digital Divide: The Need of a Global e-Inclusion Movement. *Technology Analysis and Strategic Management, 15*(1). doi:10.1080/0953732032000046105

Morino Institute. (2001). *From Access to Outcomes: Raising the Aspirations for Technology Initiatives in Low-Income Communities*. A Morino Institute Working Paper.

National Information Technology Council. (2000). *Access, Empowerment and Government in the Information Age*. NITC Publication.

National Information Technology Council. *ICT in Malaysia*. Retrieved September, 2003 from www.nitc.org.my/ press/ speeches_ 8jun00.html

National Telecommunication and Information Administration (NTIA). (1999). *Falling Through the Net: Defining the Digital Divide*. Retrieved March 26, 2004 from http://www.ntia.doc.gov/ ntiahome /fttn99/contents.html

O'Neil, D. (2001). *Merging Theory with Practice: Toward an Evaluation Framework for Community Technology*. Paper presented at Internet Research 2.0: INTERconnections: The Second International Conference of the Association of Internet Researchers, October 10-14, 2001 at University of Minnesota, Minneapolis-St. Paul, Minnesota, USA.

Organisation for Economic Co-operation and Development. (2001). *Understanding the Digital Divide*. OECD Publications.

Owen, W. J., & Darkwa, O. (1999). Role of Multipurpose Community Telecentres in Accelerating National Development in Ghana. *First Monday*. Retrieved August 28, 2004 from http://www.firstmonday.dk/ issues/ issue5_1/owen/.

Page, M., & Scott, A. (2001). Change Agency and Women's Learning: New Practices in Community Informatics. *Information Communication and Society*, *4*(4), 528–559. doi:10.1080/13691180110097003

Pejabat Daerah dan Tanah Manjung (2004). *KedaiKom*. Retrieved April 26, 2004 from http://pdt.manjung.perak.gov.my/BM/ dotcom.html

Pigg, K. E. (2003). Applications of Community Informatics for Building Community and Enhancing Civic Society. *Information Communication and Society*, *4*(4), 507–527. doi:10.1080/13691180110096996

Pigg, K. E., & Crank, L. D. (2004). Building Community Social Capital: The Potential and Promise of information and Communications Technologies. *The Journal of Community Informatics*, *1*(1), 58–73.

Pinkett, R. D. (2001). *Integrating Community Technology and Community Building: Early Results form the Camfield Estates-MIT Creating Community Connection Project*. 43rd Annual Conference of the Association of Collegiate Schools of Planning (ACSP), Cleveland, Ohio, Nov. 8-11. Retrieved July 25, 2003 from http://web.media.mit.edu/~rpinkett/ papers/ index.html

Pitkin, B. (2001). Community Informatics: Hope or Hype? In *Proceedings of the 34th Hawaii International Conference on System Sciences, January 3-6, 2001* (pp. 2860-2867).

Preston, P. (2001). *Knowledge or 'Know-less Societies'?* Retrieved January 28, 2007 from www.lirne.net/resources/netknowledge/ preston.pdf

Proenza, F. J., Bastidas-Buch, R., & Montero, G. P. (2001). *Telecentres for Socioeconomics and Rural Development in Latin America and the Caribbean: Investment Opportunities and Design Recommendations, with Special Reference to Central America. FAO, ITU*. Washington, DC: IADB.

Purdue, D. (2001). Neighbourhood Governance: Leadership, Trust and Social Capital. *Urban Studies (Edinburgh, Scotland)*, *38*(12), 2211–2224. doi:10.1080/00420980120087135

Rathswohl, E. J. (2003). Introduction to Special Series on Community Informatics. *Informing Science Journal*, *6*, 101–102.

Reyment, R., & Jöreskog, K. G. (1993). *Applied Factor Analysis in the Natural Science*. Cambridge University Press. doi:10.1017/CBO9780511524882

Robison, L. J., & Flora, J. L. (2003). The Social Capital Paradigm: Bridging Across Disciplines. *American Journal of Agricultural Economics*, *5*, 1187–1193. doi:10.1111/j.0092-5853.2003.00528.x

Rozner, E. (1998). *Haves, Have-Nots, and Have-to-Haves: Net Effects on the Digital Divide.* Retrieved July 6, 2003 from http://cyber.laws. harvard.edu/fallsem98/final_papers/Rozner.html

Russell, N. (2000). *Evaluating and Enhancing the Impact of Community Telecentre: A Companion Project of the InforCauca Initiative to Foster Sustainable Development in Marginalized Regions.* Submitted to the Rockefeller Foundation by the International Center for Tropical Agriculture (CIAT).

Saguaro Seminar. (2000). *Social Capital Community Benchmark Survey.* Retrieved August 10, 2003 from http://www.ksg.harvard.edu/saguaro/ measurement.htm

Schätzl, L. H. (Ed.). (1988). *Growth ad Spatial Equity in West Malaysia.* Singapore: Institute of Southeast Asian Studies.

Sekaran, U. (2003). *Research Methods for Business.* New York: Wiley & Sons, Inc.

Selwyn, N. (2003). *Defining the 'Digital Divide': Developing a Theoretical Understanding of Inequalities in the Information Age.* Occasional Paper 49, 'Adults Learning@Home' – An ESRC Funded Research Project. Retrieved March 23, 2004 from www.cardiff.ac.uk/socsi/ict

Sidorenko, A., & Findlay, C. (2001). The Digital Divide in East Asia. *Asian-Pacific Economic Literature, 8,* 18–30. doi:10.1111/1467-8411.00103

Simpson, L. (2005). Community Informatics and Sustainability: Why Social Capital Matters. *The Journal of Community Informatics, 1*(2), 79–96.

Stones, W. (2001). *Measuring Social Capital: Towards a Theoretically Informed Measurement Framework for Researching Social Capital in Family and Community Life.* Research Paper No. 24, February 2001. Australian Institute of Family Studies.

Strover, S. (2003). Remapping the Digital Divide. *The Information Society, 19,* 275–277. doi:10.1080/01972240309481

Taylor, W., & Marshall, S. (2003). Community Informatics Systems: A Construct for Addressing the Digital Divide. In *Proceedings of the 3rd International Conference on Information Technology in Asia* (CITA '03), Kuching, Sarawak, Malaysia, 17-18 July. Retrieved May 24, 2006 from http:// inforcom.cqu.edu/Research/Research_ Groups/ CIS/Group_Site/CONTENT/ CIS%20a%20 construct%20fa%20DD_WTSM.pdf.

Tipton, F. B. (2002). Bridging the Digital Divide in Southeast Asia: Pilot Agencies and Policy Implementation in Thailand, Malaysia, Vietnam, and the Philippines. *ASEAN Economic Bulletin, 19*(1), 83–99. doi:10.1355/AE19-1F

Tung, X., Sebastian, I. M., Jones, W., & Naklada, S. (2002). *E-Commerce Readiness in East Asian APEC Economies – A Precursor to Determine HRD Requirements and Capacity Building.* Bangkok, Thailand: Asia-Pacific Economic Cooperation, Telecommunications and Information Working Group, Business Facilitation Steering Group, National Electronic and Computer Technology Centre.

United Nation Development Programme. (2003). *MalaysiaICT4D Road Map: Malaysian ICT4D Programmes and the Eight Malaysia Plan (2001-2005).* Retrieved May 26, 2004 from www.undp.org.my/factsheet/docs/ICT4D Roadmap_18Nov03.pdf

United Nation Global E-Government Readiness Report 2005 (2005). *From e-Government to e-Inclusion.* Retrieved April 10, 2009 from http://www.unpan.org/ dpepa-egovernment%20 report.asp

Van Dijk, J., & Hacker, K. (2003). The Digital Divide as a Complex and Dynamic Phenomenon. *The Information Society, 19*, 315–326. doi:10.1080/01972240309487

Warschauer, M. (2002). Reconceptualizing the Digital Divide. *First Monday*. Retrieved October, 16 2003 from www.firstmonday.dk/issues/ issue7_7/warschauer

Warschauer, M. (2003). Dissecting the "Digital Divide": A Case Study in Egypt. *The Information Society, 19*, 297–304. doi:10.1080/01972240309490

World Bank. (2004). *Country Data: Malaysia*. Retrieved April 26, 2004 from http://www. worldbank.org/cgi-bin/sendoff.cgi?page=%2 Fdata%2Fcountrydata%2Fict% 2Fmys_ict. pdf&submit=Go

Chapter 3
The Siyakhula Living Lab:
A Holistic Approach to Rural Development through ICT in Rural South Africa

Caroline Pade Khene
Rhodes University, South Africa

Ingrid Siebörger
Rhodes University, South Africa

Hannah Thinyane
Rhodes University, South Africa

Lorenzo Dalvit
Rhodes University, South Africa

ABSTRACT

Rural development and poverty alleviation are a priority for development in South Africa. Information and knowledge are key strategic resources for social and economic development, as they empower rural communities with the ability to expand their choices through knowing what works best in their communities. Information Communication Technologies (ICTs) act as tools which enable existing rural development activities. The Siyakhula living lab (SLL) aims to develop and field-test a distributed, multifunctional community communication platform, using localization through innovation, to deploy in marginalized communities in South Africa. The project exists as research collaboration between the Telkom Centres of Excellence at the University of Fort Hare and Rhodes University. Its current pilot operates in the Mbashe municipal area, which is a deep rural area located along the wild coast of the Eastern Cape province of South Africa. The Dwesa-Cweba Nature Reserve acts as a chief asset in the community, which contributes to tourism development. However, the community is currently not actively involved in tourism development; but potential exists in local arts, crafts, and authentic heritage tourism. Therefore, the SLL aspires to empower the community with appropriate communication technology skills to actively support tourism development and other complementary development activities, such as, education. The lessons learned and applied in the project's current pilot stage identify techniques

DOI: 10.4018/978-1-61520-997-2.ch003

and approaches that aim to promote the effectiveness and sustainability of the ICT project in a rural context. These approaches and techniques are viewed and described from social-cultural, institutional, economic, and technological perspectives.

INTRODUCTION

Upliftment of rural areas and poverty alleviation are a priority for development in South Africa. Information and knowledge are key strategic resources for social and economic development. Rural communities in South Africa can be empowered by participating in the knowledge society through the use of Information Communication Technologies (ICTs). ICTs act as tools to support existing efforts towards rural development and to enable innovative approaches. In this chapter we describe a holistic ICT-for-development project, which involves developing and field-testing a distributed, multifunctional community communication platform. Such a platform is specifically designed for marginalised communities in South Africa and its distinctive feature is localization through innovation.

A pilot of the project (known as the Siyakhula Living Lab or SSL) is currently running in the Mbashe municipality, a deep rural area located along the wild coast of the Eastern Cape province of South Africa. Like many African rural areas, the Mbashe municipality is characterised by endemic poverty and a lack of infrastructure and services. The Dwesa Nature Reserve (which is adjacent to the five villages in which this project is being piloted) attracts seasonal tourism, although this does not benefit the community directly. The area is also characterised by a rich cultural life and by the production of local music, arts, and crafts. Supporting ecological, heritage and cultural tourism is an example of how the project described in this chapter seeks to empower the local community. The lessons learned and applied in the project's current pilot stage identify techniques and approaches that aim to promote the effective-

ness and sustainability of ICT in a rural context. These approaches and techniques are viewed and described from a social-cultural (political), institutional, economic, and technological perspective.

The chapter is broken down into three broad areas. Firstly, the background to the study introduces the community into which the living lab was field-tested, introduces the concept of a living lab and specifically the SSL together with a description of the purpose of the project and the project's phases. Finally we discuss the theoretical paradigm of the living lab case study. The second part of the chapter describes the Siyakhula project within each of the four perspectives discussed earlier, namely, social-cultural (political), institutional, economic, and technological. The third and final part provides a discussion which relates the work that has been done in the project to the theoretical framework which underpins it and discusses the future directions of the Siyakhula living lab.

BACKGROUND

ICTs can generally be defined as tools that aid in communication between people through electronic means of capturing, processing, storing, and communicating information (Gerster and Zimmermann, 2003; Heeks, 1999). The widespread enthusiasm associated with the use of ICTs in rural development has consequently brought about the misconception in development communities that ICTs are the panacea for all rural development challenges (McNamara, 2003; UN ICT Task Force, 2003). In this sense, the focus has been on increasing the amount of ICTs (specifically infrastructure) in rural areas, without really considering the needs of rural communities, and their capabilities to harness and sustain these technologies. In addressing this misconception, it is important to understand that ICTs are *tools* in rural development, and not necessarily the only solution to combating the challenges of poverty (Gerster & Zimmermann, 2003; Mansell & Wehn, 1998; McNamara, 2003). They are meant to complement ongoing development projects and investments; hence ICTs do not *create* change, but instead *enable* change. The key to understanding the potential of ICTs is to begin an analysis, not considering the absence or presence of ICTs in rural areas, but instead identifying the challenges associated with persistent poverty in a given community, the most effective measures in addressing these challenges, and only then the tools necessary to proceed (McNamara, 2003). In this case, the tools may not only be ICTs, but also other resources, partnerships and development projects. Furthermore, McNamara (2003) indicates that the impact of ICTs in a rural community depend on a complex set of resource endowments, human and institutional capacities, historical legacies and enabling environments. Addressing the deeper economic, social, resource and historical challenges faced by developing countries cannot be substituted by simply providing ICTs where they are not available, but instead identifying how ICTs can act as tools in enhancing development activities with a view to addressing those challenges.

The Mbashe municipality case study, SSL, which operates in the five villages (Mpume, Ngwane, Mthokwane, Nondobo and Nqabara) near the Dwesa Nature Reserve aims to describe the project from a variety of perspectives, to understand how such projects can/do operate in the complex social cultural environments of rural areas. ICTs may have the potential to enhance development activities in combating poverty, as an information, communication or knowledge component of virtually every development challenge can possibly be discerned (McNamara, 2003; Slay, Thinyane, Terzoli, Clayton, 2006).

The SSL attempts to support development in the five villages in the Mbashe municipality (which for simplicity will be referred to as the Mbashe municipality), through initially targeting some development challenges.

Mbashe Municipality Context

The Mbashe municipal area is a deep rural area situated along the wild coast of the Eastern Cape Province of South Africa. The five villages targeted in the SLL are adjacent to the Dwesa-Cwebe area which comprises the nature reserve and frontline communities which are extended over a land area of approximately 15254 hectares (Palmer, Timmermans and Fay, 2002). Both the reserve and the local communities have become involved in a development initiative as the natural environment consisting of the nature reserve and wild coast that they share are assets for the communities (Palmer *et al.*, 2002). The location of the nature reserve and the surrounding communities is indicated by the flag 'A' in Figure 1.

The nature reserve serves to provide income generating activities to support rural development in the area (Palmer *et al.*, 2002). The unspoiled natural scenic beauty and wild beaches significantly promote ecotourism in the region. The area is quite popular for tourism, especially at the Dwesa reserve where at times during the year, all tourist cabins are fully booked in advance. Furthermore, the high levels of rainfall and rich soil in a very dry country area, has potential for controlled agricultural intensification and commercial forestry. Nevertheless, the target of the development vision for the area has been taking advantage of their rich natural asset.

Currently, tourism development in communities surrounding the reserve is hampered by a scarcity of knowledge and experience on how to take advantage of tourism in the community, and hence there is limited community involvement. Development efforts so far rely on the nature reserve.

However, there is potential for authentic cultural and heritage tourism, associated with the area's rich Xhosa tradition and historical significance (Palmer *et al.*, 2002). The Mbashe municipality is also faced with socio-economic challenges associated with poverty and poor development. Some characteristics of poor development in the area include: severe local limitations of a regional road network, limited access to government service and delivery, inadequate education and health care facilities, a lack of national grid electricity, and poor/vandalized telecommunication (landline telephones) infrastructure in some areas. Therefore, this area has recently been a target for development projects. Building communication in rural development can subsequently be supported by ICTs, which can enable the effective operation of existing development activities.

The Siyakhula Living Lab

The *Siyakhula Living Lab* (SLL) commenced in 2005 as a joint collaboration between the University of Fort Hare and Rhodes University. It is run within the Telkom Centres of Excellence in the Computer Science department at both universities. The research from the two universities exists as sub-projects to support the main project objectives (Dalvit, Thinyane, Terzoli, & Muyingi, 2007). Masters and PhD research has developed throughout the years, to build (from lessons learned and applied) and pilot an ICT project in a rural environment. *Siyakhula* means "we are growing" in Xhosa, the African language spoken where the platform is currently being deployed and tested. The name of the project was chosen by the local community itself and encompasses some of the values underlying the project. The project has

Figure 1. Location of the Mbashe municipality on the Eastern Cape Wild Coast of South Africa (© 2009, Google Maps. Used with permission.)

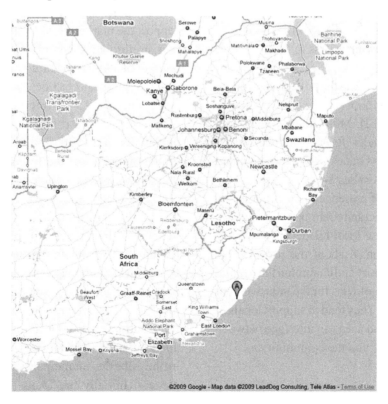

recently adopted the *Living Lab* approach, hence the name, SSL. A Living Lab can be described as "an approach that deals with user driven innovation of products and services that are introduced, tested and validated in real life environments" (Mulder, Bohle, Boshomane, Morris, Tempelman & Velthausz, 2008, pp.8). A user driven approach is essential to understand the local requirements and constraints associated with the rural environment, throughout the progressive development of the ICT project.

In the SLL the local schools in the area have been targeted as venues for the ICT deployments. The schools were chosen as the points of presence within the community for a number of reasons:

- they have the necessary infrastructure for housing computer labs, such as electricity and appropriate venues to contain computer labs,
- schools are educational centres and are thus in a position to be able to train both local learners and local community members, and
- the schools are open to all community members, allowing access to all.

The schools involved in the project are Mpume Junior Secondary school (Grades R-7), Ngwane School (Grades R-12), Mthokwane Junior Secondary school (Grades R-7), Nondobo Junior Secondary school (Grades R-7) and Nqabara Secondary school (Grades 8-12).

The SLL point of presence in the schools and community are project and community *champions*. These champions are local residents, who were identified as passionate about the use of ICTs within their community and champion the use and deployment of technologies for the improvement of their livelihoods. They tend to support locals in their use of ICTs, and act as an interface between the university teams and the community.

The Purpose of the Project

The primary objective of the SLL is to develop and field-test a distributed, multifunctional community communication platform, using localization through innovation, to deploy in marginalized communities in South Africa, where a large number of the South African population live; 42.5% according to the last census conducted in South Africa in 2001 (Statistics South Africa, 2001). These communities, by sheer size and because of current political dynamics, represent a strategic emergent market. The second objective of this project is to build technically skilled human resources in the field of e-commerce, particularly, but by no means only, in the context of supporting e-commerce activities in marginalized and semi-marginalized communities. Accordingly, skills will also be developed through the exposure of university students to the processes of applied research and the experience of real-life rural ICT projects. The second objective forms the basis for the primary objective to be achieved.

The platform was originally designed to support the marketing of local arts craft and eco-tourism through e-commerce. It now includes a number of additional features and links to a set of different sub-projects. Local wireless connectivity and connection to the Internet support e-health, e-government and e-learning. Development of human resources and rural ICT training are integral components of the living lab. Examples of other sub-projects include software engineering of a robust, cost-effective e-Commerce platform for disadvantaged communities; an assessment of adoption barriers to ICT; project management techniques to promote the sustainability of rural ICT projects; language problems in ICT usage; backhaul connectivity options for ICT deployment *etc.* The integration and collaboration of these sub-projects contributes to the vision and goals of the living lab and its supportive role in the Mbashe municipality rural development process. Initially the focus of service delivery has been via desktop computers and fixed line telephony. In the future there will be a move to include service delivery via mobile handsets. As part of this initiative the SSL will pilot the Nokia Siemens Networks Village Connection platform. The Village Connection platform offers affordable voice and sms services specifically targeted at rural communities. The technology provides an addition to GSM networks and extends coverage beyond the point at which a conventional network roll-out would be too expensive.

Phases of the Project

The progressive life of the SSL was undertaken through repeated field trips to the community. On average, a field trip is undertaken by the project team for approximately one week every month. Each field trip focuses on specific aspects of achieving the objective of the project, but was not limited to an individual activity that needed to be implemented. Different field trips therefore portray the life of the project, and present the approach used for implementing and managing the project. However, it is important to note that each field trip was incremental and iterative, in that some activities would be repeated and built on from previous phases. Since the living lab has been extended to other villages in the area, the following phases starting at stage 2 are repeated at different sites. The phases completed and on-going are as follows:

1. **Project Idea Generation and Concept (January – October 2005):** This phase of the project is associated with generating a proposal for the living lab, which defines the needs and concepts that underlie the project.
2. **Project Feasibility (November 2005):** The project feasibility stage focused on determining an appropriate physical location for the Living lab within the Mbashe municipality community.

3. **Technology Introduction and Training (January 2006 – Current):** This phase focused on introducing the technology to the community, and training for its use.
4. **Community Buy-in (April 2006 – Current 2008):** The community buy-in phase relates to the promotion of community participation in driving the sustainability and success of the project.
5. **Technology Implementation and Community Needs Review (May 2006 – Current 2009):** This phase focused on technical infrastructure implementation, further training, and assessing the business operation of local entrepreneurs involved in arts and craft.

A Detailed Technical Timeline

As previously mentioned, schools from five villages nearby to the Dwesa Nature Reserve were targeted for inclusion in the SLL. The schools joined the living lab as follows:

*   Mpume Nov 2005
*   Ngwane June 2006
*   Mthokwane 2007
*   Nondobo 2007
*   Nqabara Oct 2007 (still to be connected to the network)
*   Bafazi 2008 (still to be connected to the network)
*   Zwelenqaba 2008 (still to be connected to the network)
*   KwaNtshunqe 2008 (still to be connected to the network)

Besides equipping the schools with computer lab facilities, work was also done in building the local access network and installing the VSAT link for the shared connection to the Internet. The network installations timeline was as follows:

- The VSAT was installed in early 2006
- WiMAX core network, that is the base station at Ngwane was installed in August 2006
- Additional WiMAX clients were added at the various schools from Sept 2006 (four schools are connected thus far)
- Another tier of three schools have joined the SLL and are connected to each other via WiFi links but are currently not linked to the original five schools in the project
- In July 2009 the network routers were upgraded to make use of lower-powered hardware to conserve power. These routers also run a locally developed network management system, improving upon management and monitoring
- In July 2009 a backup Internet link via the cell phone networks was put in place.

Future technical work includes but is not limited to the following tasks:

- Adding backup local loop links between schools
- Connecting Nqabara to the local loop network and therefore the Internet
- Addition of the Nokia Semens Network Village Connect technology
- Connecting the remote three tier of schools to the original five using WiMAX technologies

The Theoretical Paradigm

The project is situated within the social-constructivist paradigm. Within this paradigm, reality is considered as a product of social interactions. Our emphasis is on the meanings, values and expectations that the people involved (i.e. members of the community and researchers) attach to our intervention (Gergen 2001). This approach has been successfully applied to models of rural development in various fields (see Marsden 2004).

To our knowledge, hardly any research in ICT for development is informed by this paradigm. In this chapter, the social constructivist paradigm serves as an over-arching framework for an approach informed by a social informatics perspective and an action research methodology.

Many ICT for development projects are informed by a technological determinist perspective (Roman and Colle 2003). Authors who subscribe to this perspective see technological innovation as the primary drive for development, independent of the social context (see King 2000). All too often ICT for development interventions are driven by technological innovation rather than the specific needs of the social context in which they are deployed. Although such needs may change partly as a result of the introduction of new technology, one should not forget that ICTs do not *create* change, but rather *enable* it, thus complementing ongoing processes of social transformation (McNamara, 2003). Social informatics emphasises the correlation between technological and social change. King (2000) notes that the influence works in both directions. This bi-directional relationship makes the social informatics perspective particularly suitable for our intervention, in which every step in the development and implementation of technology is informed by the response of the community.

The methodology we use in our intervention can be described as action research. The action research methodology has been applied to a variety of context and is used in different disciplines (see French & Bell, 1978; Elliott & Elliott, 1991; Lewin, 2004). It has been used extensively in the field of Information Systems (see Baskerville & Wood-Harper, 1996) for system development and testing. Avison, Lau, Myeras and Nielsen (1999:94) highlight the focus on 'change and reflection within an immediate problematic situation', which characterises the action research approach and makes it particularly suitable to complex situations. Action research has been used in a variety of studies involving grounded theory, ethnography and case study methodologies. With reference to the latter, Avison *et al* (1999:96) talk about action-research-type case studies, in which 'researchers have large and complicated stories to tell'.

Another distinctive feature of action research is its iterative nature, which makes it suitable for intervention. Research typically follows a cycle of problem diagnosis, action intervention and reflective learning, which can be reiterated for several times if needed. This cycle informed our practice during the project, which involved a symbiotic relationship between technological innovation and social change. The two dimensions of our intervention were harmonized through regular meetings and the constant collection of feedback from the community.

Information and knowledge have become fundamental to the rural development process, given the rapid growth in the information and knowledge society. They both act as key strategic resources in the rural development process as they provide rural people the opportunity to actively participate in the e-Society and to take responsibility for their own development.

Theories, Assumptions and Values

In shaping our theoretical framework, we draw on the input of established scholars in the fields of social informatics and ethno-computing as well as dependency theory. The underlying argument of social informatics is that technological change cannot be considered independent of social change. In an effort to adapt this idea of developmental contexts, the relatively new discipline of ethno-computing emphasises the need for system development to respond to local needs, and for users in developing countries to take part in the process. The latter point deals directly with technological dependency, recognised as hampering the development of marginalised communities within dependency theory.

Within the SLL, active participation of the community is expected to drive the development and implementation of the system and shape the related projects. Through active participation, the community is expected to take ownership of the project rather than depend on external input. In order for the project to become sustainable, both the economic potential of the region and of its human capital needs to be developed. The assumptions informing our project include:

- ICTs do not create change, but instead enable change in rural development
- Community participation and ownership should be encouraged to empower the community to sustain the project
- Sustainability of the project can be viewed either as the sustainability of on-going rural ICT access, independent of specific technologies or projects; and/or the sustainability of rural development results through ICT-enabled development (for example, education, health, empowerment)
- Given the project is driven by tertiary academic research, the sustainability of the project can also be viewed as ongoing tertiary research at Dwesa, from The University of Fort Hare and Rhodes University.

LIVING LAB SETUP

School Deployments

Mpume

Mpume was the first school that was identified as a point of presence for the project. Due to the availability of electricity and being the first school involved it was selected as the ideal site for the installation of the VSAT Internet connection that serves the entire community network. Greater detail regarding the VSAT connection will be covered at a later stage, in the networking section. The school houses a single thin client server, and six thin client computers which connect to the server in order to run software. Refer to the section below for more details on the hardware and software choices. At the targeted schools in the Mbashe municipality we use Edubuntu Linux as our operating system of choice, which comes standard with the Linux Terminal Server Project (LTSP). This allows the applications and environment of Edubuntu to be exported to the thin client computers. Edubuntu Linux is also open source software, and the operating system, together with a number of other applications, such as the OpenOffice Suite and the Firefox web browser, are available in some of the South African local languages, such as isiXhosa, the dominant language in the Mbashe municipality. The school also has a Voice over Internet Protocol (VoIP) phone that allows them to call the other schools on the local network in the area. The school lab also houses the access concentrator (which runs FreeBSD 6.2), which is a router that accepts all the incoming connections from the other local schools in the living lab (more information on the access concentrator will be discussed later in the networking section).

Ngwane

Ngwane was the second point of presence installation for the living lab. Ngwane are a unique school in the living lab as they raised the money and purchased the first thin clients for their school themselves. The school also has a thin client network with one central server and 16 thin client computers, also running the Edubuntu operating system. In addition, the school has a VoIP enabled phone. The school also has a router which allows them to connect back to Mpume and the VSAT. The router runs FreeBSD 6.1. Ngwane is also the host of the WiMAX base station (more detail in the networking section) as the school happens to be at the highest point in the area in which we are working which means that all the other schools in the project have a good line of sight with Ngwane.

Mthokwane

Mthokwane was the third point of presence in the community. Of all the schools in the project, their premise is relatively new and in the best condition. The school has a very small computer lab, consisting of 5 thin clients that boot off a single, central server. The server also runs Edubuntu, which using the LTSP software allows the thin clients to boot off the server. The school also has a router (also running FreeBSD 6.1) together with WiMAX Customer Premises Equipment (CPE) to connect them to Mpume and the VSAT Internet link (via Ngwane). Finally this school also has a VoIP enable phone.

Nondobo

Nondobo was the fourth point of presence in the area and appears to be the poorest of the original five schools. Nondobo has one computer which is kept in the school principal's office, together with a router and WiMAX CPE to connect their computer back to the VSAT Internet link at Mpume. The computer runs Edubuntu Linux while the router runs FreeBSD 6.1. In addition, they also have a VoIP enabled phone. While this school has electricity infrastructure, they seldom have the request funds to pay for electricity and so their limited computing facilities are often switched off.

Nqabara

Nqabara is the fifth and final school currently involved in the SLL. The school has five thick client computers, however, currently no central server and no WiMAX CPE or router and is thus not connected to the community area network or the VSAT Internet connection. Each of the thick client computers runs Edubuntu Linux. The next phase in deployment will be to connect Nqabara to the local network and thus also the Internet and provide them with a VoIP phone.

The Community Area Network

Each of the schools in the project, currently except for Nqabara and the remote tier of three schools (Bafazi, Zwelenqbab and KwaNtshunqe), is linked to one another via a WiMAX network which covers the community-wide area of the project. We will refer to this WiMAX network as the local loop access network. The WiMAX base station is housed at Ngwane as it is the school in the project which is situated at highest point within the geographical area. WiMAX technologies do not require a clear line of sight like WiFi. However, large obstructions, such as mountains will affect the signal path of the wireless communication and disrupt or prevent communication. Thus a relatively high site is still required so that the best path possible is available for wireless communication between the base station and the customer premises equipment (CPE). At each school, Mpume, Nondobo and Mthokwane (later Nqabara, Bafazi, Zwelenqaba and KwaNtshunqe will also be included) there is a CPE unit that connects back to the base station at Ngwane to allow traffic to be transported between schools.

Together with the CPEs, Nondobo and Mthokwane (later Nqabara, Bafazi, Zwelenqaba and KwaNtshunqe) also have a FreeBSD 6.1 router. The router acts as a gateway between the local area networks (LAN) within each school and the bigger local loop access network. The routers run a Point-to-Point Protocol (PPP) client, which contains their school's username and password for authenticating with the access concentrator at Mpume. Once authenticated and the link has been established the router will route all outgoing traffic, intended for one of the other schools (such as local VoIP traffic) or the Internet, onto the next hop which is the access concentrator. At Ngwane, where the base station is housed, is also a router. The image of the Ngwane router is the same as those at Mthokwane and Nondobo, only instead of connecting to a CPE it connects directly to the base station.

Together with the CPE at Mpume, the access concentrator router provides access to the local loop network. This access concentrator is the central router to which all the school routers connect. The router runs FreeBSD 6.2 and provides a Point-to-Point Protocol (PPP) service to the other school sites. The routers at each school use a username and password to authenticate themselves with the PPP service running on the access concentrator (just as one would when connecting to your local Internet Service Provider (ISP)). Once authenticated a PPPoE (PPP over Ethernet) tunnel is created that links the school to the access concentrator at Mpume, via the WiMAX base station at Ngwane. Traffic from the schools intended for another school, or the Internet are then routed to the access concentrator which will in turn route the traffic to either the school in question or onto the next router (which is also the LTSP server at Mpume) which routes all Internet bound traffic out to the VSAT link. A diagram of the network can be seen in the image below (Figure 2). The network design would have been simpler if both the VSAT link and the WiMAX base station were at the same school, but the WiMAX base station had to be at Ngwane as the school is situated at the highest point in the area and had visibility to the other schools. The VSAT was at Mpume for the historical reason of being the first point of presence in the community. Moving the VSAT unit to Ngwane is not viable because of time and costs and so the network configuration is a more complicated.

From the network diagram, it can clearly be seen that each school, Ngwane (even though it houses the base station and doesn't make use of a CPE), Mthokwane, Nondobo connects via a PPPoE tunnel to the access concentrator at Mpume. Once at the access concentrator it will be routed to either one of the other schools (if that is the traffic's intended destination) or out to the Internet via the Mpume router/server and VSAT link. Building the local loop access network allowed us to strategically pool resources across the

Figure 2. The Mbashe municipal area local loop network

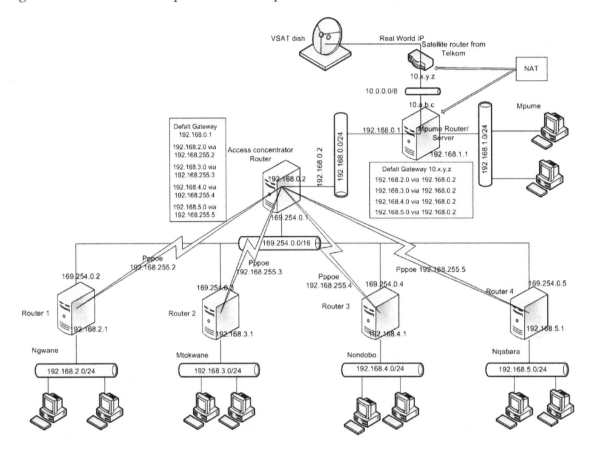

schools, specifically, the Internet connection via the VSAT link. In addition, the local loop network allows us to provide local services to the schools, such as telephony (via VoIP), email, and content sharing (sharing information, lesson plans, rubrics, etc). The network has provided communication channels among the schools and their local communities.

Hardware and Software Choices

Our choice of hardware within the computer labs at each school was to deploy thin client computer laboratories. A thin client computer is one which depends primarily on a central server for all its processing activities. Thin client computers depend on the central server for processing activities and are used to collect input from the user (to the

applications running on the server) and convey the output (from the application on the server) to the users. The thin clients are diskless which means that they have no software installed on them and so using Preboot eXecution Environment (PXE) enabled network cards are able to request the necessary software for booting from the central server. Because the thin clients don't need hard disks and they are not required to do any processing, older and cheaper refurbished computers can be used to act as the thin clients and only the central server requires a significant financial investment. As a result the investment required in setting up a computer lab is reduced when compared to thick client computer laboratory configurations, where thick clients (which are more expensive) and a central server (although this can be omitted) are purchased. As a result of the thin clients being cheaper and that they can be older refurbished computers often means that they are easier to replace, however more time is often needed in providing maintenance (especially where refurbished computers are used) and a good collection of spare parts are necessary for when components break. The collection of spare parts is also necessary when using thick client computers, but perhaps less often and less maintenance is required. The choice of software used in the schools is coupled with the choice of running thin client computer labs. We use Edubuntu Linux. The reasons for this are that firstly, Edubuntu is an operating system aimed at education and the computer labs are in the local schools. Edubuntu is based on the Ubuntu operating system but includes educational applications, tools, content, and themes. In addition to Edubuntu being geared towards education and educational institutions, Edubuntu comes with the Linux Terminal Server project (LTSP) which allows thin clients computers to boot off a central server running the LTSP service.

In terms of the hardware and software that runs the local access network, we initially began by using older computers and servers as the routers (using refurbished computers to reduce costs and extend the lives of PCs). However, we are going to move towards using low-cost and low power consumption hardware such as the Intel Atom processors and boards. These motherboards and processors have been produced for ultra-mobile PCs and other portable low-power applications. However, we are not interested in the portability aspect but rather the low-power and cheap price. The routers run the FreeBSD operating system. FreeBSD is a Unix-like operating system and generally regarded as reliable and robust, which made it an ideal choice for network routers that need to be stable in order to provide a reliable service.

ICT PROJECT SUSTAINABILITY IN RURAL COMMUNITIES

Rural ICT projects tend to be faced with challenges when deploying, implementing and later the use of the technologies in the rural communities. These challenges can lead to either a non-sustainable project or project failure. The sustainability of rural ICT development projects is important for the positive impact and general success of these projects in rural communities (Pade, Mallinson & Sewry, 2006).

Project failure tends to be prevalent in rural communities and thus it is important to understand why these projects tend to fail, so as to avoid repeated mistakes (Heeks, 2002). The key seems to be to work towards making ICT projects sustainable in rural development projects; even though sustainability is not the same as success, it is key and necessary for success. The sustainability of a project should be taken into consideration from the beginning of the project and be part of the project plan, bearing in mind those factors that influence the sustainability of a project (Munyua, 2000). The definition of sustainability is hotly debated, but it can simply be described as: "*Development that meets the needs of the present generation without compromising the ability of future generations to meet their own needs*" (Anand & Sen, 2000: 2033).

Sustainability is concerned with an ICT project that endures. The notion of sustainability takes into consideration whether or not the technology is being put to use to support rural activities. Such activities should benefit the rural population in one particular area such that the project may be replicated and maintained to influence other areas associated with rural development (International Development Research Centre - IDRC, 2005). Often, sustainability is considered in terms of financial sustainability, that is, whether the project is capable of cost recovery in order to continuously operate. However, sustainability encompasses more than just financial or economic sustainability. According to Stoll (2003), in order for a project to reach its goals of community development and sustainability, ICT enabled projects need to integrate social, cultural, institutional, economic, political and technological sustainability as vital elements in the planning and operation of the ICT project. These categories of sustainability strongly relate to the perspectives for describing a project's effectiveness, as discussed in the introduction (grouping social, cultural and political perspectives together), within which we structure the project's description. Each perspective describes the various aspects of the project and highlight issues or challenges faced, together with solutions and recommendations from the SLL experience.

SOCIAL-CULTURAL AND POLITICAL PERSPECTIVE

If a development project is to be lasting and viable, it must take into account the social and cultural context of the community in which it is situated. Stoll (2003) elaborates on this saying that as the ICT project considers these social and cultural aspects of a rural community, the community members themselves feel empowered by the project, increasing their buy-in and motivation to keep the project running. Care must be taken to ensure that no groups are socially excluded, and to maintain social equity within the community (Batchelor * Norrish, 2002; EITO, 2002). Stoll (2003) indicates that men and women, and youth and adults have different needs, interests and possibilities with regard to ICT use. Different social groups in rural areas should therefore be managed differently so that the project team may implement mechanisms that support social or cultural sustainability in a project. The idea of "commons" or shared ownership of resources forms the basis for community based ICT projects to be sustainable. Stoll (2003) defines two different types of commons: social commons, and physical commons. Social commons are expressed as shared community values, and can be analysed and documented using the

following criteria: participation in networks, altruism (rather than egotism), trust, social norms, proactively, and reciprocity. Each of these criteria speak of advancing aims of a community of people rather than an individual, and adhering to a set of unwritten cultural rules. Physical commons on the other hand are public facilities that are given value or worth and on-going support by the community (Stoll 2005). These physical commons can be seen as physical manifestations of the community's social commons. When the community finds strong social commons in a project, it has more chances of being sustainable. It is important to note that project sustainability does not only ensure its success over a number of years. Instead the recipients must understand that they own the project and its related benefits (Etta, 2003). An ICT project may make sense to the implementers, but if the recipients do not own it, its sustainability may be seriously compromised.

Socio-Cultural and Political Perspective: Issues, Controversies and Policies

Some of the community stakeholders of the project have been reluctant to get involved significantly in the ICT project as a result of social and cultural factors. These challenges are highlighted as follows:

Illiteracy and Education: Rural communities are characterized by limited formal education, high illiteracy rates and a low proficiency in English. These factors determine the extent to which an individual may produce, acquire and interpret information through the use of ICTs. According to the IDRC (2003), research findings on ICT projects revealed that users of ICTs in rural areas tend to be those that can at least read and write, especially English. The uneducated and illiterate who make up the majority of the rural population, especially women, have been excluded from access to ICTs, (IDRC, 2003). Norris (2002) maintains that education improves the general capacity for analytical reasoning and information filtering, which assists in coping with the flow of information available online, as well as strengthening numeracy, literacy, English-language and keyboard skills. However, rural people are deprived of the opportunity of a formal education, which limits their ability to use ICTs effectively. The baseline study of a village in the Mbashe municipality indicated that 26% of the population may have not attended school at all, and the highest grade mostly attained in the community is Grade 7 (a primary school education). Currently, training in the SLL is limited to those who can effectively read and write. Furthermore, the project champion stated that most of the community members who attended the training sessions were former students who have finished Grade 10 and are now at home "doing nothing". Most schools in the Mbashe municipality are Junior Secondary schools, meaning the highest grade that can be attained is Grade 9, therefore, students only manage to complete the first year of Secondary/High school. There are only two Secondary/High schools, in the Nqabara community, and Ngwane (which was recently in 2008 upgraded to a high school, although it would only initiate Grade 10 classes in 2009). A number of community members do not study further, either because it is not affordable or because of other social cultural reasons. Less educated community members, specifically in the age groups middle aged to the elderly, are incapable of using ICTs, especially when they consider their low literacy levels. (Refer to '*Reluctance by middle aged to elderly community members to use ICTs*' below).

Content and Language: Access to available ICT content is usually constrained by language, and its relevancy or applicability to the diverse cultures that dwell in rural areas (Warschauer, 2003). Language affects how diverse groups can access and publish information, as well as the extent to which ICT serves as a medium for the expression of their cultural identities. Most ICT content, however, is available in English and often not relevant and responsive to rural user needs and local conditions. According to Pigato (2001), surveys of rural households illustrate that the poor favour and trust information sources close to home and those that are applicable to their existing knowledge base, yet the UNDP (2001) states that the systems and knowledge that arise in poor communities are often ignored. The Open Source Edubuntu operating system used in the SLL, has a Xhosa version for using its applications. However, when the teachers were shown this advantage, they indicated they preferred to use the English version during training. Other community trainers have still not attempted to use the Edubuntu Xhosa version available on the living lab computers. Initially, the teachers indicated language was not too much of an issue during training, as they were able to interpret and train some community members in Xhosa. However, the training material (user manuals) available is in English, which becomes a problem when some trainees would like to refer to the user manuals provided. Furthermore, the teachers hardly used the user manuals developed by the project team to assist with training. A project champion, stated that they only referred to them from time to time, but could not use them in training the community. As a result, they trained the community on topics they knew well, in Xhosa. Two of the community trainers, mentioned that it was difficult to translate continuously to Xhosa, as it was a challenge to translate unfamiliar computer terms. A community trainer pointed out that some community members can read in Xhosa better than English. At this stage of the project, local content development is limited to personal use, such as typing CVs, invitations, programmes etc. Initial research with learners shows initial positive attitudes towards using English. After being exposed to teaching and the use of interfaces in Xhosa, however, Grade 9 to 10 learners appear to appreciate the fact that using their mother tongue *alongside* English can support their learning of computer literacy.

Reluctance by Middle Aged to Elderly Community Members to use ICTs: An interview with older community members revealed that they were under the impression that the ICT project was meant for younger people and they were too old to get involved. A project champion also mentioned that in some cases, the adult population were not encouraging their youth to attend computer literacy training. The project team also felt that the elderly seem quite marginalized in the project, and therefore they held community meetings to make sure everyone felt they were part of the project (they need to be encouraged more to take ownership of the project as they are introduced to new technology). However, it seems that some of the elderly community members are willing to encourage their youth to attend training, but are not interested in attending training themselves. They are often constrained by factors such as eyesight or illiteracy. This presents a challenge for one of the target groups of the project, the arts and crafts people, as they are within the group of middle aged to elderly community members.

Technophobia: is a challenge in rural communities, especially when introducing new technology. The UNDP (2001) postulates that "Technophobia" has acted as a socio-cultural barrier in discouraging the use of ICTs in some developing countries. The elderly may not be the only people reluctant to use ICT, as some community members feel challenged and intimidated by the new technology and its capabilities. In some cases, people feel the children and youth of the community may be more capable of using the new technology. They may also be afraid of appearing inferior, as a result of being asked questions that they cannot answer about the technology or discomfort at the potential difficulties in learning how to use technology. Furthermore, the cultural chasm between oral (word of mouth, physical proximity of object, places and persons) and the virtual nature (files, folders, and windows) of an online society continues to be a challenge in developing countries, especially rural areas (UNDP, 2001). Moving from an oral to a virtual

society has been difficult in most projects, which has made training a slow and complex process.

Reluctance among some Teachers to assist in the Project while the Project Team was Away: During the various trips to Mbashe municipal area it was noted that some teachers could apply their knowledge and skills of the applications they had been trained in, while others were unable to use the applications on the computers. For example, at one of the schools, some teachers knew how to use Wikipedia and integrated its use into their teaching, but other teachers still did not know how to use it. Through interviews and observation, it was evident that they had not asked the other teachers (who are more familiar with the technology) how to use them. The project team therefore had to provide them with refresher courses. Furthermore, the project champions appeared to be the only teachers involved in training the community, with some assistance from community youth. A project champion indicated there were some socio-political reasons possibly associated with 'who takes ownership of the project' and 'who was elected as project champion'. In addition, one of the Headmasters overtly committed to support the project but remained covertly skeptical. Aspects of the project (such as increased electricity use) are an expense to the school. Without constant pressure by members of the community, these considerations might prevail and bring the project to a halt. However, the community is aware of and supported the project. This motivated this particular Headmaster to meet the requirements of the project.

Misinforming the Community: A teacher at one of the participating schools deliberately misinformed the community that the SLL was only meant for those community members who had at least completed their Matric (grade 12). This had a negative impact within the community, discouraging locals from using the computers. The project team and trainers from the community attempted to encourage the community to attend training again. The community trainers indicated that it was difficult to encourage community members to come back for training, and that they are still in the process of encouraging community members to attend.

A Passive Attitude toward Development in the Mbashe Municipality Rural Area: According to one community member, *"People don't want to work"*. This may therefore limit community participation in the SLL. The community has also become heavily dependent on pensions and child grants, which to an extent, has discouraged potential economic activity in the Mbashe municipality. However, there are those who have shown great interest in the project.

Time Limitations: People in the community are often busy during the day and therefore have limited time to attend training. In some cases, people only finish their daily work at 5pm, and have therefore requested that training is provided between 6pm and 8pm, or over weekends. However, the project champions are unavailable at that time for training, as they have responsibilities, such as their homes and families, to attend to after school.

Trust in Community Members as Trainers: The youth of the area have shown great interest in the SLL, and have therefore received the most training in the community. In addition, a number of the youth who are no longer studying or employed have exercised their spare time by assisting with training. As a result, the project champions selected them to assist as community trainers. However, the community is not confident in the youth as trainers because they are not teachers from the school, and hence they undermine their training ability. This discourages the youth from becoming trainers.

Political Constraints: Rural community members are in some cases excluded from freely accessing available ICTs due to political challenges influencing their power to take advantage of those ICTs. The people usually responsible for political influence range from government officials to community leaders, elders and teachers.

Consequently, political conditioning factors at many different levels affect the means in which the development community can promote ICT for development (UNDP, 2001). For instance, the Dwesa Development Board (the director of the Dwesa Nature Reserve and local development initiatives) attempted to skip one of the schools in Mpume, on the development agenda, as they assumed the computers they were provided with were for the exclusive use of the school, and not the community as a whole. Fortunately, the project champion managed to convince the Board otherwise.

Socio-Cultural and Political Perspective: Solutions and Recommendations

Addressing Illiteracy and Education Challenges: The SLL is currently investigating the use of linguistic and cultural localization so community members who are not proficient in English can still utilize the ICTs (in particular targeting isiXhosa, the first language in the Mbashe Municipality). As mentioned earlier, another key concern in rural areas is the high number of illiterate and semi-literate community members. As such, part of localizing interfaces is to ensure that alternatives to purely text interfaces are provided. Currently in the SLL project, work is being undertaken to investigate the use of media wiki's (which use audio files instead of relying solely on text to create, capture, and codify indigenous knowledge) and text free user interfaces for semi literate and illiterate community members. Education in itself is a huge problem, as it is affected by many of the socio-cultural problems mentioned earlier in this section: unfamiliarity with English; lack of value placed in education and in technology by older members of the community; reluctance by some teachers to utilise the technologies that they have been provided with / trained in; and a passive or reluctant attitude to alter from the way "things have always been done". As mentioned in the introduction to the socio-cultural perspectives section, social commons represent shared values that are held by a community. Until education is held as one of these social commons, no amount of new ideas or minor community involvement can make a lasting difference. Only when the majority of the community can see the benefits of education (whether education in this context refers to traditional school education, or new skills being learnt by arts and craft members / teachers / community members) will it be taken up by the community. By including community members in all decision making, and by getting members of the community themselves to show other community members the benefits of particular technologies and solutions, a slow change can be made in the way education is viewed.

Apply Local Language to ICT Training and Use: The living lab team needs to collaborate with community trainers to develop training material in the local language (namely isiXhosa) so that the manuals can be used by trainers and trainees when necessary. In addition, trainers can be encouraged to use the isiXhosa version of the Edubuntu interface and the isiXhosa versions of the available applications to help the local community and learners in the school become more familiar with using the available technologies.

Encourage All Community Members to Use ICTs: Emphasis needs to be placed on encouraging the elderly to attend training courses. Perhaps some courses can be run for their demographic, specifically focusing on skills that are useful and relevant to them and their needs. Members could be encouraged through the avenues of community meetings and also by the local trainers within the community. Also, dispelling fears as a result of technophobia are non-trivial, as fear is not a rational concept that can be controlled by outsiders. In order to aid in dispelling some of these fears, community members can be introduced to technology in a number of "safe" ways. For example, with older community members, have courses that are targeted at their needs and that only older

members can attend. This will help them to see the relevance to technology in their lives and also feel that they are in a safe environment with peers and not have to worry about potentially losing the respect of younger community members.

Changing attitudes is also a non-trivial problem. Hopefully, through the successes of the project and the positive impact it strives to have on the lives of the community members other community members will be encouraged to take part and contribute to the living lab. Over time this will hopefully result in an even greater sense of community ownership of the living lab.

Maintain Communication with Key Local Stakeholders: In order to avoid miscommunication with the local community one of the project team members advised that good, effective communication channels to community members are necessary. Therefore, appropriate agents (target group leaders and project champions) should be elected to disseminate the correct information to the community members. This is important in a rural setting where information dissemination happens via word of mouth. The project team has been advised by the local project champions to maintain communication (when the project team is away) with the other teachers, and not only with the champions, so that they feel that they are a significant part of the project. Likewise, the project team was advised to also maintain communication with the various Headmasters and involve them more in the living lab, in order to show respect and an appreciation of the support they have provided.

Address Time Limitations: In order to alleviate time limitation issues faced by some community members it might be possible for trainers to work in shifts training community members after hours in the evenings or perhaps over the weekends, giving the trainers enough time to train community members and also meet their obligations at home. Training is currently not offered during the weekends because the schools are closed. An arrangement may have to be made with the community and school leadership to provide access to the schools over the weekend. Alternatively, the *community has suggested* a community hall or centre be built, which will allow free weekend access under local supervision.

Promote Trust in the Youth as Essential Trainers: In order to elevate the status of the members of the youth as ICT trainers, the project champions were advised to introduce the youth as community trainers when they attend community meetings and events to market the SLL. This would inform the community of the significant role of these trainers in the project and help to encourage a sense of trust and respect for them as ICT trainers in the living lab.

Address Political Constraints: Unfortunately politics is something that cannot be avoided in any sphere of life. In order to bypass this as much as possible, there needs to be open (and frequent) communication in all areas of rural development projects, from project initiation. Misunderstandings are difficult to entirely avoid, but when the correct information is readily and easily accessible, a solution to these problems can be devised more readily, with positive attitudes toward development. Fortunately, the influence and voice of the local project champions can alleviate the effect of political constraints. It is also important to ensure that those in political power, for instance the local village Headmen are made aware of developmental projects from the beginning. This ensures their support and positive attitude towards development. In some instances, local leaders have been hostile to projects that bypass their authority.

INSTITUTIONAL PERSPECTIVE

The institutional perspective of the ICT project describes the prevailing processes and structures that allow it to have the capacity to perform over the long term (Stoll, 2003). The aspects associated with this perspective include strengthening the empowerment and participation of commu-

nity members. Gerster and Zimmerman (2003) postulate that a key aspect of this perspective is local ownership of the ICT programme, which can be promoted through well-targeted capacity building, local content development, and effective public and private sector organizations that develop a framework in which the livelihoods of rural people can be continuously improved. A community may not be willing to embrace a project if they feel they do not have the capacity to own and operate the project themselves, within their community. Specific processes and structures need to be planned and established throughout the project, with effective local participation and input. This can provide the project team and external stakeholders with a better perspective of the needs of the community, and the necessary structures and processes to ensure ICTs can support the rural development process.

Institutional Perspective: Issues, Controversies and Policies

Institutional aspects can support the foundation of the project in the community, and address the challenges or constraints associated with the use of ICTs in rural communities. Particular challenges typical of rural ICT projects and faced by communities in relation to the institutional perspective include insufficient training and capacity building, limited public and private involvement, and limited local and project evaluation (McNamara, 2003; Pade, Mallinson, & Sewry, 2008; UNDP, 2001). The issues that present a challenge to the SLL are discussed as follows:

Insufficient Training and Capacity Building: Training and capacity building should be central to the whole ICT project process as it creates a critical mass of rural people who can effectively harness ICTs (Munyua, 2000). The Acacia Project in Africa, highlights the following as typical training challenges (IDRC, 2003): limited involvement of rural community members in training programmes which focused on training telecentre management; no technical training in the basic maintenance of ICTs; unavailability of training material especially in relation to appropriate training formats and content for a variety of the needs of target communities and groups (women, youth, and entrepreneurs). These training and capacity building challenges and extreme short supply of skills and human resources in developing countries may be the greatest barrier for the diffusion of ICTs among rural people (Pigato, 2001). As the SLL project has developed, the emphasis on training has gone through ebbs and flows. This is in part due to the cyclic nature of the project, where a technology is introduced and trained and then observations are performed on community member's use of the new technology. Instead of using a fixed structure, the project team trainers use an ad hoc training method where each community member is trained on a one-on-one basis, by simply going through the user manuals that are provided. When a community member shows interest or excitement in a particular part of the course, more information is provided on the next training trip. This ensures that teaching is learner-focused, requiring the community members to be involved in their own learning process (i.e. using the technology between training sessions and asking for help when they need it). At times

this proved difficult for the trainers, and the community members had to be trained over a longer period in order to improve their understanding. When a new pedagogical style is used in any environment (in this instance moving from chalk-and-talk to a more learner oriented environment), teething problems are usually encountered. In this instance, community members were required to reflect on their learning, which was an altogether new and difficult task for some. One of the project champions also indicated that there was a lack of commitment in attending community training sessions. This is illustrated in the graph in Figure 3 which groups the number of times people have received training from 16 March to 4 September 2006 for instance (early stages of the project). The group that has only received training 1 to 3 times shows a lack of commitment. In summary, 48 people have received training 1 to 3 times, 25 received 4 to 10 times, and 10 received training more thatn 10 times. Altogether, 83 community members have been trained at least once.

Some community members requested the introduction of an evaluation system that certifies they have received a level of computer literacy for them to see value in the training. In addition, they are not immediately clear on how to use or integrate the ICT services to support their rural

Figure 3. Bar chart of the number of times people have received training (Pade, 2006)

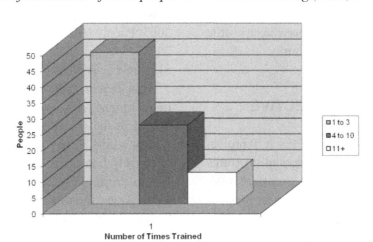

livelihood activities. A project team report indicated that most community members do not know what to accomplish with the information they get from the Internet and as a result some end up playing games on the computers. Some do know how to use computers but they do not know what else to do with the knowledge they attain. This makes it essential for rural ICT projects to target existing development activities, so as to improvise how ICTs can best support and be integrated into these activities.

Limited Public and Private Involvement: Involvement of the public and private sector in a rural ICT project is essential to support existing and potential rural development programmes (McNamara, 2003). Talyarkhan (2004) views the public and private sector as information providers, organisations that promote services and raise awareness, and organisations that offer technological infrastructure and finance to keep the project running. Foreign direct investment needs to be attracted, but developing countries are still associated with fairly inhospitable environments (for example, the difficulty of securing business permits associated with improper discretion, favouritism, and corruption on the part of local officials) for private sector growth and new business development. The SLL attempts to address this issue by involving academic researchers from multiple disciplines, with the Living Lab programme collaborating with both government and the private sector. Significant potential exists in the SLL, for public and private sector involvement in addressing the diverse information and communication needs in the community. However, the project still needs to identify various sectors that can collaborate and support rural development through ICTs. This is important, as the recent baseline study indicated that some of the main problems faced in the community are associated with a lack of commerce and poor or non-existent government service.

The Need for a Comprehensive Evaluation: A number of rural ICT projects tend to be imple-

mented without an adequate understanding of the social, economic, political, and technological readiness of a community (Wagner, Day, James, Kozma, Miller, J. and Unwin, 2005). The SLL has a limited understanding of the local information and communication needs to support rural development and livelihood activities, which can influence community uptake and the sustainable operation of the project in the community. Moodley (2005) emphasizes that governments and development organisations need to understand that the role of ICTs as powerful tools to fight poverty are, at best, a *"working hypothesis"*. Many key questions associated with ICT for development remain largely unanswered, with no concrete or credible data to support a wide range of claims concerning the use of ICT for development (Buré, 2007). The formal evaluation of the SLL is essential as it determines the need, effectiveness, impact, sustainability and extent of the awareness (locally and externally) of the contribution such projects or programmes can make in poverty alleviation and development. The SLL has recently adopted a baseline study (which only forms part of a necessary comprehensive evaluation framework) to assess the status of the community, which has proven to be relevant and instructive for the project team and the community. However, this only forms part of a necessary comprehensive evaluation framework.

The Integration of Projects and Team Dynamics: The SLL's overarching aim is to address the problem of poverty alleviation through the use of ICTs. As this is such a large goal, it is realised through the creation of numerous different research projects, all of which approach it from a different perspective. There are diversified research interests among the project team members, which has resulted in some members focusing on their own projects without assisting each other toward achieving the main goal. In particular this problem occurs when the task to be carried out forms the basis of multiple projects, but is not the *specific* goal of any of them. For example, training the teachers had been the focus of the first phase of the project, but some team members refused to assist in this important process, as they assumed it was not directly linked to their research. The integration of sub-projects needs to be planned appropriately in order to deal with conflicting and differing goals. Ultimately, the sub-projects need to collaborate and be sensitive to the needs of the community, rather than operate individually and create unintended expectations among different target groups in the community. The negative outcomes can spill over onto other sub-projects, hence jeopardizing the overall objective of the SLL.

Institutional Perspective: Solutions and Recommendations

The solutions and recommendations associated with the institutional perspective originate from the successful practices applied, lessons learned and experience in implementing the SLL in Mbashe municipality. They are discussed as follows:

Practices Applied

Promote Participation of the Community in the Project Process: The project team typically consists of people external to the community; therefore, community participation throughout the life of the project is essential. ICT project participation is defined by the IDRC (2003, p. 11) as "an organised effort accomplished by the members themselves with a view to achieving the development objectives that they had assigned to themselves". Participation aims to speed up the project process, as ICTs are appropriately introduced in the rural context, within the expectations of the community, so as to deal with false expectations which inevitably lead to disillusionment and eventually disengagement from the project (TeleCommons Development Group, 2000; UNDP, 2001). The SLL aims to include and empower the community through participation. Initially, project champions were chosen at each

school to inspire, drive and encourage the local community to participate in the project. They effectively communicated the goals and progress of the project to the community, and provided the project team with feedback on the progressive integration of the technology in the community. The project champions organised community meetings to introduce the community to the research group, introduce the technology to the community, and show how they (the champions) used the technology in their everyday lives. As an example of this latter point, it was not until one of the community members told the community that they could use spreadsheets to calculate funeral costs, that the community could see a direct benefit to themselves. The project champions communicated with the project team and took part in making key project discussion through an email list (members of the list consisted of the project team and other external stakeholders of the project). As a result of the SSL deployment being in schools, most of the project champions are teachers at the targeted schools. After initial training was undertaken, community champions were also chosen. As with their teacher counterparts, these community members showed aptitude and excitement to be involved in the project. Continuous communication and feedback through project champions and community meetings provided the project team with direction and awareness of where the project was heading in the community. An approach to measure the level of community participation is through the community's reaction to a particular action in the project (IDRC, 2003). Throughout the three and a half years that the project has been operating, the community, in most cases, has welcomed new and diverse aspects of the project.

Integrate Diverse Research Areas in the Project: The SLL team consists of researchers with diverse research focus areas. Fundamentally, the SLL is a research project which aims to implement an ICT project in a rural context, as well as provide Honours, Masters and PhD students with the real-life experience of such projects.

Researchers include staff and students from African languages, anthropology, communications, computer science, education, and information systems from both the universities. This enables the project to be viewed from diverse perspectives, rather than one focus area which has been typical of a number of ICT projects that focus on the technological aspect of the project. The project is also characterised by continuous field trips by different researchers to build on the project and address any problems affecting the operation of the project. As mentioned in the previous section, key to the operation of these sub-projects is an appropriate approach to integrate these projects toward achieving the overall project objective. There are a number of sub-projects, and therefore cohesion in the project is significantly needed. A more selective approach of projects that can be integrated would also be appropriate, together with a plan/structure to guide the integration of sub-projects throughout the life cycle, to support the main/overall ICT project objective. Project management is therefore crucial to manage and integrate these sub-projects.

Apply an Iterative Approach to the Project Lifecycle: An important aspect of the life cycle of the SLL is that it is iterative and incremental in nature. This enables the project to be flexible enough to adapt to any changes associated with its dynamic rural environment (Pade, 2006). The project does not necessarily follow a formal iterative plan, but rather appreciates and considers the iterative approach of the project, through building up and repeating practices as new aspects are introduced. As the community begins to show an interest in the living lab, local driven needs of the community result in the development of sub-projects that augment the effective use of ICTs for rural development activities. The community could take advantage of typical uses of ICT and reveal the constraints with which they could be faced in using ICTs. The uncertainty and complexity of the rural environment implies that a project

needs to be flexible enough to adapt to changing requirements and constraints of the living lab.

Collaborate with Existing Rural Development Activities: To ensure that community members are effectively supported by ICT, it is fundamental that the project selects existing rural development activities to operate within. It is necessary for the ICT to be part of wider development plans and processes such that broader development issues and goals can be addressed by ICTs, hence providing a more immediate and identifiable development benefit. The aim is to view ICT as an enabler of development, and not a panacea for development. ICTs are most effective when they support existing rural development activities (McNamara, 2003). In the SSL, it is assumed that focusing on the school initially can reveal other development activities, as the schools act as a centre for community meetings. Furthermore, they are viewed as central community places for capacity building and training.

Lessons Learned

Practice Appropriate Training and Capacity Development, and Local Content Development: Training and capacity building are primary in the implementation of ICT projects as they allow a community to directly engage and understand how to use and creatively adapt the technology to their rural development activities (Bridges, 2006). As stated earlier, sufficient training is essential, therefore, the project attempted to continuously understand the existing skills gap in the community by sporadically interviewing the teachers at some schools (Dalvit, Isabiriye, Thinyane, Terzoli 2006). As a result, on-going training (refresher courses) was provided for the community to effectively take advantage of the ICTs available. User training has had to begin from the very basics, how to use a keyboard, how to use a mouse, what the monitor is and what the computer tower is and how to switch it on and off. From there basic computer literacy needed to be taught to the community, such as using word processors, searching the Internet, using e-mail, *etc*. The Edubuntu platform was chosen for the computer labs, as it aims to provide an e-learning environment for schools. The lack of prior technology exposure and computer literacy has made supporting knowledge retention, post training, and the users during use of the computers very challenging, as no locals were already computer literate enough to take on a support role for their peers. Over time and through targeting one teacher per school to be the champion teacher things have improved and now these champion teachers are able to take on the role of support for their colleagues, peers, and the community. In addition, these teachers are able to ensure that the machines in the labs are switched on and running properly as well as identifying problems and reporting faults to members of the two universities' technical team within the SLL.

Project champions and local representatives in Mbashe municipality were in tune with appropriate methods to train the community, as they have closely experienced and observed the local challenges (social-cultural, language, *etc*.) faced. However, local training later became a challenge as they were not provided with a suitable training structure to train the community, nor were they advised on how to effectively conduct training. In some cases, trainers hardly used the provided user manuals in training, because they felt it was too complicated for community members to follow. Therefore, an important recommendation is to involve or delegate to the project champions or community representatives the development of a training structure for community training, after receiving training and guidance from the project team regarding the development such a structure. Recently, an informal training structure has been developed, which was urgently requested by the community. However, the project champions and project team members are yet to collaborate to develop an appropriate structure that is sensitive to the needs and challenges of local training.

Conduct a Baseline Study of the Community: The introduction of the Living Lab aspect in the project instigated the development and application of a baseline study of a sample community in the Mbashe municipality. The baseline study, which was conducted in 2008, aimed to assess the current status of the community by assessing three key areas: the readiness of the community to be or become partners in the operation of the Village Connection Project; the state of the quality of life in the community; and the status of the local economy and the directions of where it could go. The evaluation of the current status of the community provided a foundation for effective consecutive evaluations of the SLL. For instance, it provided direction for the project team in terms of the existing information and communication needs (related to development challenges) that ICTs could support, challenges to ICT use that needed to be addressed, *etc*. Furthermore, during post-implementation, the impact of the living lab in the community (especially in addressing social economic challenges) can be assessed, through a comparison of the initial community status before implementation with the community status post implementation.

Apply Comprehensive On-Going Monitoring and Evaluation throughout the Life of the Project: Evaluation of the project should not only end after a baseline study. It is important that the project is evaluated comprehensively throughout the life of the project, to ensure project objectives are attained and all stakeholders, including the community, are accountable. Therefore, in addition to a baseline study, the SLL needs to conduct evaluations associated with assessing the process, as well as an impact/outcome evaluation. As stipulated in the baseline study proposal, the proposed evaluation and assessment of the SLL is divided into a 3 stage research process which will be implemented throughout the life of the project. The 3 stages are described as follows:

- **Stage 1.** The Baseline Study which assesses the current status of the community.
- **Stage 2.** A Process Assessment which will occur when the Village Connection component of the living lab is operating. It will assess how well the programme is operating, through for instance, its activities, functions, performance, component parts, resources, and stakeholder relationships (the private sector, universities, government and funders).
- **Stage 3.** An Impact/Outcome assessment will occur when the pilot hopefully develops into a sustainable commercial service, or otherwise. Direct and indirect effects of the living lab on people's livelihoods will be assessed. This assessment also aims to identify a "technology adoption" path of least resistance for rural areas and determine from evaluation results, an appropriate approach to implement such projects in rural areas.

Consistent with the multi-disciplinary and exploratory nature of the project, assessment is understood as part of the process of implementation rather than its conclusion. Following an action-research-type methodology, commonly used in research in a variety of fields (e.g. Education, Information Systems *etc.*), there are lessons learnt at any given stage (either through observation, active participation or direct feedback from users) which inform the subsequent phases.

Enable Public and Private Participation: Since inception, the SLL has been run by the two universities, which can be viewed as public/private sector organisations. Their continuous involvement has had a significant impact on the *ongoing* operation of the project, especially through a variety of research perspectives that have built up and developed the project in the community. This has also created a key relationship of trust and collaboration with the community. Recently, the SLL adopted the Living Lab aspect proposed

by COFISA (Cooperation Framework on Innovation Systems between Finland and South Africa). The involvement of COFISA has enabled other private and public stakeholders to participate in the project, namely Nokia-Siemens Networks and the Meraka Institute[1] (a project within the Council for Scientific and Industrial Research (CSIR) of South Africa). Through the collaboration with COFISA the SLL will include a pilot intervention of the COFISA rural component. This component aims at investigating and piloting ICT-based rural innovation mechanisms, supported by training and other interventions aimed at building human capacity, enhancing economic development and promoting poverty alleviation in rural areas. The Village Connection (VC) component, which is one of the projects linked to the SLL, is implemented through collaboration between COFISA, the Universities of Rhodes and Fort Hare, Nokia-Siemens Networks (NSN), and the Meraka Institute. The key responsibilities of each stakeholder group are as follows (COFISA Project Plan: Dwesa Living Lab, 2008):

- The Universities of Rhodes and Fort Hare have a key role in the building of the Living Lab initiative, through providing backbone connectivity between the three Villages for the Village Connection network, coordinating the community relationships, user training, social research and village-level monitoring aspects of the project, and finally interface the GSM component to the e-commerce, e-government, *etc.* sub-systems in Dwesa, to construct a technological ecosystem able to support appropriate and innovative voice- and SMS-based services.
- COFISA is responsible for project development coordination and overall project management, provision of Finnish technical expertise, stakeholder engagement, and evaluation.
- Nokia Siemens Networks will provide the technical network solution, that is,

the Village Connection consisting of one Access Centre and three Access Points including required components and relevant support and documentation for use in the pilot.

- The Meraka Institute is responsible for the technical implementation of the Village Connection solution in the project, including relevant R&D, training monitoring, evaluation and support components. Meraka will also be supporting the project in stakeholder engagement, with a special focus on government and university collaboration.

ECONOMIC PERSPECTIVE

The ability of a rural ICT project to attain a level of expenditure and income for sufficient cost recovery associated with project operation, describes the economic perspective of the project (Stoll, 2003; Batchelor and Norrish, 2002). Naturally, ICT for development projects are initially funded by development organizations; however, in the long-term, appropriate cost recovery mechanisms need to be in place for the local community to manage the self-sustainability of the project. Gerster and Zimmerman (2003) therefore advise that a spirit of entrepreneurship to market ICT services rendered is promoted and an appropriate cost-benefit analysis is implemented to differentiate between priority programmes and wishful thinking that result in unproven business models. Traditionally, ICT projects have focused on non-profitable schemes in the community through positive externalities (social goods) (Cisler, 2002; Heeks, 2005). On the contrary, this can present financial challenges for the project if funding discontinues and there is insufficient income to keep the project running. Furthermore, the aim of rural development is to empower community members to contribute to social and economic activity, therefore, creating a reliance on external funding can cripple their ability to expand their capabilities and actively

sustain the ICT project. Project leaders need to collaborate with the local community to devise activities that enable cost recovery and financial sustainability, as well as conceptualize and implement economic activities and/or business models that support the financial backbone of the ICT programme in the community.

Economic Perspective: Issues, Controversies and Policies

Local Economic and Financial Constraints: The existing economic status of the Dwesa communities' present financial constraints and economic challenges to ICT use, which dispute the financial sustainability of the project. The implementation and use of ICTs in rural areas is obviously associated with costs that require sufficient financial resources that can support the sustainability of the project. Pigato (2001: 7) indicates that the financial resources needed, include those necessary for the supply of technical infrastructure (networks, hardware, software *etc.*) and those necessary to create demand for user technologies, information and communication services. The baseline study of a sample village in the Mbashe Municipality, Mpume, surveyed all members of the community in order to determine the economic characteristics of both existing and potential participants in the SLL. This study found that the percentage of unemployment is extremely high, with 87% of the community surveyed being unemployed (refer to Figure 4). Of this percentage, a significant number are listed as not seeking work. When questioned further about this, community members stated that there is just no work available, or some feel that they are too old to work.

It was also found that there is a high dependency on grants in the community, especially child support grants and old age grants (Figure 5 and Figure 6). Other members of a household also depend significantly on these grants. As a result, the affordability of ICTs may present a challenge to the continuous availability of the ICTs if appropriate business models and entrepreneurial systems are not put in place.

Donor-Dependency of the SLL: At present, the SLL is significantly donor-dependent, where financial costs and ICT resources are provided by the universities through the funding they receive for research, from the Centre of Excellence at each university and COFISA. The Rhodes University Centre of Excellence in Distributed Multimedia is currently supported by Telkom SA, Tellabs, Open Voice, Comverse, Amathole Telecommunications, Mars Technologies, Bright Ideas 39, Stortech, and THRIP (through the NRF), while the Telkom Centre of Excellence in Developmental e-Commerce at University of Fort Hare is currently funded by Telkom SA, Tellabs, Saab Grintek, Amatole Telecommunications, Mars Technologies, DRISA and THRIP (through the NRF).

The equipment costs quoted are the approximate values and not the exact values. Firstly, the costs for purchasing the Alvarion WiMAX equipment that makes up the local loop network: Alvarion micro base station equipment - US$5780 ea; Alvarion Customer Premises Equipment - US$760 ea. The cost of the VSAT unit involves: The VSAT installation - US$380 ea; the VSAT monthly fees - US$188. The cost of the computer

lab facilities: thin client computers - US$500 ea; thin client servers - US$2000 ea; LAN networking - US$180; UPSs - US$1500 ea; Routers -US$500 ea; rack - US$1000 ea; periphery upgrade costs - average of $200. There have been a number of pieces of equipment that have been donated to the project, such as 30 thin client computers, two thin client servers, two switches, and five routers, from a number of different groups. The periphery upgrade costs refer to the costs involved in replacing or fixing faulty components such as network cards, graphics cards and hard disks. Other associated costs include transport, accommodation, food and man hours. On average the project will be visited once a month for the period of one week. The average costs of transport, accommodation and food during this period are US$450. While in terms of people hours, it is an average of five working days per month, per team member.

Economic Perspective: Solutions and Recommendations

Determine an Appropriate Business Model to Keep the Project Economically Sustainable: It is essential that the community is significantly involved in the process of developing a business model as they are more aware of the financial

Figure 4. Unemployment status of Mpume (in percentage)

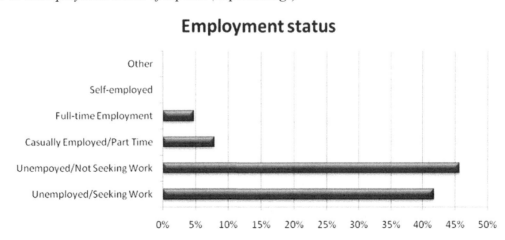

Figure 5. Level of dependency on grants

Receive grant

☐ Yes ■ No

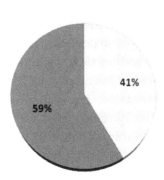

41%

59%

in training, so that the project can have a larger and more sustainable impact on the community. This will also reduce the strain on project champions. The community members have suggested charging for training, not only to pay trainers, but also to account for stationery expenses in the future (paper, printer cartridge *etc.*). The project team has agreed that the community could charge for training, but they would leave the decision to the community to determine when they should start charging and at what price. Because the project champions live in the community they are better positioned to know how much the community can afford.

Apply Social Entrepreneurship to Holistically Support Social (Development) Change in the Community: With respect to the Village Connection project, an entrepreneur needs to be selected in the community to run this component. This person would be able to offer voice and sms services to the community at a price that is affordable to them. An entrepreneur usually aims to make a profit through his/her business. However, the SLL, like many ICT for development projects, aims to support rural development in the community through various services it can provide to the community, for the greater good

constraints of the community. Within the SLL, researchers from the two universities have suggested that the community develop a pricing model (if necessary, in consultation with the universities) for their local costs (electricity, paper, toner, *etc.*). One of the project champions indicated that there are a limited number of trainers available, which is quite challenging as they occasionally have to train many people up to 8pm in the evening. An incentive may need to be introduced to encourage the youth and other community members to assist

Figure 6. Level of dependency on different grant types

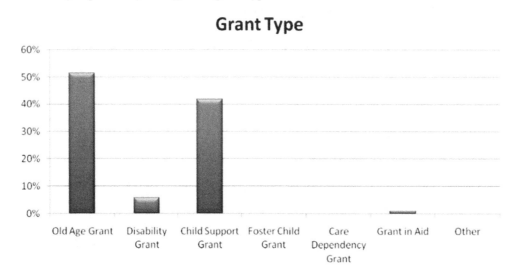

Grant Type

of the community, and not necessarily individual gain. Therefore, it was recommended that social entrepreneurship through the implementation of a Section 21 company (Non-profit) company within the community. Mair and Marti (2005) broadly view social entrepreneurship as "a process involving the innovative use and combination of resources to pursue opportunities to catalyze social change and/or address social needs" (pp. 37). In this case, the village connection centre would be owned jointly by the community and external partners (the universities, Nokia-Siemens Networks, Meraka and COFISA), and revenue from the centre would be used to cover system running costs. Any surplus profits would be used to benefit development programmes and community assets such as infrastructure and education. Furthermore, the centre would be open to research for the universities to build-on and further develop the services offered by the centre.

TECHNOLOGICAL PERSPECTIVE

According to Cisler (2002) the technological sustainability of a project considers the ability to choose technology in an ICT project that can serve satisfactorily for an extended period of time. While rural ICT centres need not have the latest technologies, it is important that they plan for ensuring technological sustainability (Stoll, 2003). Care needs to be taken to ensure that the technological needs are met by the technology present in the project, so that neither a lack of facilities nor technology that is too advanced hampers the users' effective use of the technology. In addition, the availability of spare parts, hardware, software, and supplies (paper, printer toner, and cables) also needs to be maintained in order to keep the ICT facilities usable for long periods, hence preserving the support and interest of community members (Pade et al., 2006a). Cisler (2002) and Pade et al. (2006a) also recommend the use of recycled computers that can save a great

deal of initial costs, however, warning that repair and replacement may become more difficult and expensive later on in the project. Furthermore, the type of software used should be appropriate to local use and offer a community of growing local programmers the facility to customise the programs to local standards, which is the case with open source applications (Cisler, 2002). In addition, open source platforms and applications also allow for language localisation; some ICT projects implemented in rural areas in Africa have failed as a result of the language barrier posed by the use of English (Dalvit, Thinyane, Muyingi & Terzoli, 2007). Within this section we discuss and analyse the issues, controversies and policies affecting the technical deployment, providing solutions and recommendations based on the lessons we have learned (Siebörger, Terzoli, & Hodgkinson-Williams, 2008).

Technical Perspective: Issues, Controversies and Policies

Building a robust network in the environment of the villages in the Mbashe municipality has been challenging. There are a number of things that are taken for granted when working in rural areas with novice users that are perhaps unexpected after working in more urban areas. Even simple things such as not unplugging the electricity from a computer in order to shut it down, something we take for granted as a given in general computer care, but which is not understood or known within the rural communities. In this section we discuss some of the issues and controversies that we encountered during the technology deployment and support in the SLL.

Community Technology Exposure: The level of exposure to technology in the Mbashe municipality is minimal. Results from a base-line study, conducted in August 2008 within one of the villages (Mpume) in the area revealed that 95% of households surveyed have no electricity, while 1.25% of households did have grid electricity from Eskom (the national provider), 3.75% had electricity via solar panels and 1.25% via a generator. When considering regular appliances that people tend to have around the house, 91.25% of the households surveyed do not have a refrigerator, while 95% don't have a television set and 97.5% don't have a Video recorder (VCR) or DVD player. Furthermore, none of the surveyed homes have a computer. However, 60% of houses do have a radio (these are more than likely windup or battery operated) and 66.25% have at least one cell phone in the home. These results accurately depict the lack of technology penetration within the Mbashe municipality and just how little exposure locals have to technology and the use thereof.

Technical Support and Training: Another important necessity in technology deployments is to have technical support for the systems – both the computers that the end users interact with and the computers used in the networking infrastructure. Unfortunately, training an individual with these sets of skills takes a number of years and requires experience. Thus to use someone from the local community will require time to skill them up and obtain the experience necessary to manage on their own. Currently, we do not have anyone with the desire and aptitude to become the local technical expert and so all technical support taking place is currently remote. This poses a number of difficulties in that, should the link to the Internet be damaged in any way we are not able to remotely gain access to the network in order to troubleshoot or fix problems. Furthermore, there are certain failures, such as broken network cards, that prevent remote access and management of systems. These types of errors are not possible to fix remotely and require physical presence. However, the Mbashe municipality where the SLL operates is approximately a 6 hour drive from Rhodes University and a 4.5 hour drive from the University of Fort Hare, so physical presence to solve technical issues can be a logistical challenge and result in systems remaining down for extended periods of

time until a team member can travel to the area and affect repairs.

Electrical, Dust, Heat and Carelessness: Additional problems experienced in the SLL have been surrounding the electricity supply to the schools, equipment exposure to dust and varying temperatures, user-tampering and general lack of understanding and care of technology. With regards to the electricity supply to the schools, the first issue is that the schools are at the 'bottom of the line' with regards to the grid electricity network. Thus the load further up the line has an effect on the quality of electricity that the schools experience. For example if there is a sudden increase in the draw on the electricity further up the line then the schools in the community will experience a dip in power. These surges and dips in electricity can and have caused great damage to equipment within the schools. In addition, the electrical wiring per school can be problematic as schools are not wired in order to support the draw of electricity from a computer lab of 20 computers. This sudden draw often results in tripping the electricity supply. Schools in the rural communities are also exposed to a lot of dust, roads are not tarred and there is loose sand and dust which can get into the computers. In addition, no air-conditioning exposes the computers to temperatures set by the weather, which in South Africa can get very hot. The heat of the weather in the summer, together with the heat generated by a computer can place the hardware at risk of failure due to overheating. Finally, the lack of exposure to technology results in users tampering with equipment. Users of the school labs frequently unplug computers without shutting them down properly in order to gain access to a plug-point for charging cell phones, potentially damaging the computers. In one instance, a user unplugged the router at one school from the UPS, later it was plugged back into the regular electricity supply and a power surge damaged the equipment leaving the school without Internet access for a few weeks until a technical team could be dispatched to repair the damages. While in another of the schools the electricity is disconnected entirely leaving the UPS to run systems each night. As a result of the UPS running on its battery each evening the life-span of the equipment is reduced and will have to be replaced sooner than expected.

Technical Perspective: Solutions and Recommendations

Technological Sustainability and Maintenance of Infrastructure: In order to adequately support ICT development projects such as the SLL the ideal would be to have an on-site technical support team or person who can perform troubleshooting and repairs on some hardware, software and network related errors. Ideally, this individual or group of individuals should come from the community into which the technology is being introduced. Realistically, such individuals require a number of years of experience in order to equip them with the necessary skills. Thus while this takes place, an adequate technological solution is required. The solution to timeous responses to technological faults is to have as much redundancy as possible. In order to ensure that the Internet is always up, a redundant Internet connection is required, so that should the primary link fail the network will automatically fall over to the backup connection. A redundant link of this kind will be implemented in the SLL during the course of 2009 using one of the South African cellular provider's networks. In addition to the redundant Internet connection, additional links are also required throughout the network connecting the various schools such that should the WiMAX local access network fail, the network will fall over to back-up network links between the schools. One of the sub-projects in the living lab is working towards building these back up links in order to improve the reliability of the local network. Furthermore, critical services which run on critical hardware, such as the routers and access concentrator should have redundant spares that can be swapped in should

the originals fail, ensuring a minimum amount of downtime and improving the reliability of the network and services.

Methods for Power Protection and Stability: Uninterrupted power supplies (UPS) can be used to protect critical equipment, such as the servers, switches, routers, CPEs and base stations from power surges. In addition, in order to support the increased power load within schools after the introduction of technology electricians were called in to add an extra circuit breaker (~50A) which is dedicated to the new computer lab in each school. This helps to prevent the power from tripping as a result of the increased load, as repeated sudden loss of power can damage computer equipment. In addition, technical solutions can be implemented to keep the electricity supply to the computers and UPSs always on through wiring directly into the distribution board. Alternative social and financial solutions are to either pay for the school's electricity or to encourage the school to find revenue generating avenues as discussed in the economic perspectives.

Solutions for other Environmental Challenges: In order to compensate for the heat and dust we have placed critical equipment, such as the routers, base stations, switches, servers and CPEs in racks. Racks have additional built in fans which help to keep the equipment cool as well as being a closed cabinet preventing dust from collecting on or inside the equipment. With regards to the client machines in the room, some projects have installed air conditioners in order to keep the room cool. However, in order to keep costs down for financial sustainability we have not taken this route. Rather, rooms with adequate ventilation are chosen that preferably do not face North. In order to help with the dust, schools are encouraged to make cloth covers that can be placed over the computer equipment when it is not in use and not to clean and sweep in the room when the computers are on. Sweeping often lifts dust into the air, and if the computers are on, the chances are higher that computer's fans will draw in air and dust when attempting to cool themselves.

Limiting Damage from the Human Element: In addition to keeping critical equipment cool and dust free the racks also prevent user-tampering by limiting their access to the critical components of their local classroom network and the equipment that provides them with access to the local loop network and ultimately the Internet. This has helped to decrease the number of faults. While users can still access the client computers and cause damage as a result of thoughtless tampering, these machines are less likely to have an impact on the greater network and thus generally do not have as far reaching effects on the ICT facilities.

DISCUSSION

As its Xhosa name suggests, the SLL is still growing so it can neither be categorised as a success nor a failure. Parts of the project have seen success: for example, the community has been afforded the opportunity to acquire new skills, are provided the opportunity to use and experience technology for (for some) the first time, and have access to information that can contribute to their livelihood development. However, there are some challenges, as highlighted before, which threaten the success or sustainability of the project. The iterative nature of the SLL enables the project to be flexible enough to adapt to any changes associated with its dynamic rural environment, and hence address these challenges appropriately, with on-going research and community participation.

As mentioned in the introduction to this chapter, the SLL employs the action research paradigm: diagnose, plan, act, and observe/evaluate (Hopkins, 1985). As illustrated across our discussion of the four perspectives, we first identified key needs in the community such as: lack of communication infrastructure; lack of access to information, government services, health services; lack of employment opportunities. From this point, a plan was developed together with the community (in accordance with our social-constructivist paradigm) regarding how these problems may best be addressed through the use of technology. Next, potential solutions were implemented, deployed and community members were trained in the use of the new systems. This has been followed by both formal observations (such as the baseline study) and informal observations (through the feedback of the champions and community members). This feedback allows us to return back to the planning phase of the action research cycle, where we meet with the community to discuss refinements/alterations to improve the SLL and also allows the community to play an active role in their development.

The SLL case study illustrates that an ICT project can be viewed from four different perspectives: socio-cultural (political), institutional, economic, and technological. The development of these four perspectives is fundamental to the overall sustainability and relevance of the living lab in the rural community. The complex nature of rural contexts requires a multidisciplinary solution. An important factor of the SLL team is that it is multi-disciplinary, therefore consisting of researchers with multiple perspectives, such as, computer science, information systems, anthropology, education, and communications. Given these multiple perspectives, which are all equally important, there should not be a situation where one perspective is sacrificed for another, or one is exchanged for another. In essence, the perspectives are interdependent, where for instance; dealing with social issues becomes essential for technological implementation. The needs, demands and driving forces of these perspectives need to be *harmoniously* developed and applied in the project, as shown in Figure 7, in order to contribute to the overall long-term sustainability and relevance of the project in the rural community (Hietanen, 2002). The SLL is therefore viewed and applied holistically, operating around these four perspectives.

CONCLUSION AND FUTURE TRENDS

Rural areas in Africa are confronted with issues and controversies that limit their ability to use ICTs, resulting in projects that fail at different levels, particularly sustainability failure. Evidently, those issues and controversies associated with the SLL exist and are a challenge to ICT integration in the Mbashe Municipality. Nevertheless, through lessons learned and practices applied, the SLL case offers a valuable contribution to recommendations or solutions for projects that are typically faced with comparable challenges around Africa. These are all viewed in accordance with the different perspectives essentially surrounding the ICT for development framework, namely: socio-cultural and political, institutional, economic, and technological. These perspectives do not operate in isolation, but are interdependent and must be developed harmoniously in order to promote overall ICT project sustainability in rural areas. Using the holistic approach to the implementation of the SLL, we hope to continue refining the implementations of the Living Lab and contribute to the development of the region. Furthermore, through continuous interaction with the community, and perhaps drawing from the results of the recent baseline study that was undertaken, we hope to offer new services in order to meet the communities' needs and contribute to overall developments in their quality of life. As examples, the community currently has limited access to gov-ernance and so services such as e-governance via the ICT platform will allow community members to obtain relevant information and access to vital government services. Furthermore, local health officials like nurses could be provided access to e-Health services, allowing them to be better supported in their work and to provide a better quality of health care.

A new research angle for the SLL is to target the mobile handset, which is more readily available in rural areas than traditional desktop computing. With the help of the Village Connection hardware from Nokia Siemens Network, we hope to extend all of these services to the mobile handset, making important services ubiquitous to the community members. Furthermore, adopting a social entrepreneurship approach through establishing the Village Connection centre as a Section 21 company, can potentially contribute to an economically sustainable business model that benefits the community, as well as promotes needed research in the universities and public/private organisations. It is hoped that through the creation of a Section 21 company community ownership of the living lab will be furthered, allowing them to more actively participate and direct the future of development with their community.

ACKNOWLEDGMENT

The authors would like to thank all the members of the Siyakhula living lab from the University of

Figure 7. A Structure of harmonious development (Adapted from © 2002, Hietanen)

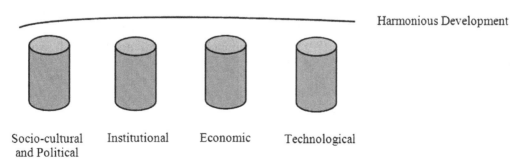

Fort Hare and Rhodes University, as well as the industry sponsors within the Centres of Excellence (CoE). In addition we would also like to thank COFISA for its support to the Siyakhula project. Special thanks must go to Alfredo Terzoli and Hypolite Muyengi as the directors within the two CoEs.

REFERENCES

Anand, S., & Sen, A. (2000). Human Development and Economic Sustainability. *World Development*, *28*(12), 2029–2049. doi:10.1016/S0305-750X(00)00071-1

Avison, D. E., Lau, F., Myers, M. D., & Nielsen, P. A. (1999). Action research. *Communications of the ACM, 42*(1), 94–97. doi:10.1145/291469.291479

Baskerville, R. L., & Wood-Harper, A. T. (1996). A critical perspective on action research as a method for information systems research. *Journal of Information Technology*, *11*, 235–246. doi:10.1080/026839696345289

Batchelor, S., & Norrish, P. (2003). Sustainable Information Communication Technologies (ICT): Sustainability. Retrieved February 7, 2009, from http://www.sustainableicts.org /Sustainable.htm

Buré, C. (2007). *Grounding Gender Evaluation Methodology for Telecentres: The Experiences of Ecuador and the Phillipines*. Ottawa: Telecentre. Org, International Development Research Centre (IDRC).

Cisler, S. (2002). Schools Online Planning for Sustainability: How to keep your ICT project running. *Community Technology Centers' Network*. Retrieved February 7, 2009, from http://www2.ctcnet.org/ctc/Cisler/sustain.doc

COFISA. (2008). *COFISA Project Plan, Dwesa Living Lab: Village Connection Component*. Pretoria: COFISA.

Dalvit, L., Isabiriye, N., Thinyane, M., & Terzoli, A. (2006, July). *A case study on the teaching of computer literacy in a marginalized community*. Paper presented at the Comparative Education Society of Europe Conference, Granada, Spain.

Dalvit, L., Thinyane, M., Muyingi, H., & Terzoli, A. (2007). The Deployment of an e-Commerce Platform and Related Projects in a Rural Area in South Africa. *International Journal of Computing and ICT Research, 1*(1), 9–18.

Elliott, J., & Elliott, J. (1993). *Action research for educational change*. Philadelphia: Open University Press.

Etta, F., & Wamahiu, S. P. (Eds.). (2003). *Information and Communication Technologies for Development in Africa* (Vol. 2). Jointly published by Ottawa, ON: IDRC and Dakar: Council for the Development of Social Science Research in Africa (CODESRIA).

French, W.L., & Bell Jr, C.H. (1978). Action research and organization development. *Organizational Diagnosis: A Workbook of Theory and Practice*, 69.

Gergen, K. J. (2001). *Social construction in context*. London: Sage Publications.

Gerster, R., & Zimmermann, S. (2003). *Information and Communication Technologies and Poverty Reduction in Sub-Saharan Africa*. Richterswil: Gerster Consulting.

Heeks, R. (1999). Information and Communication technologies, Poverty and Development. *Development Informatics, Working Paper Series,* Paper No.5, June 1999. Retrieved February 9, 2009 http://www.sed.manchester.ac.uk/idpm/ research/publications/wp/di /documents/di_wp08.pdf

Heeks, R. (2002). Failure, Success and Improvisation of Information Systems Projects in Developing Countries. *Development Informatics, Working Paper Series - No 11*. Retrieved Feb 2, 2009, from http://www.sed.manchester.ac.uk/idpm/research/publications/ wp/di/di_wp11.htm

Heeks, R. (2005). *Sustainability and the Future of eDevelopment*. Retrieved February 7, 2008, from http://www.sed.manchester. ac.uk/idpm/publications /wp/di/short/DIGBriefing10Sustain.doc.

Hietanen, O. (2002). Indicators of Sustainable Development. Finnish Society for Future Studies. *Futura, 21*(2), 6-7.

Hopkins, D. (1985). *A teacher's guide to classroom research*. Philadelphia: Open University Press.

International Development Research Centre (IDRC) (2003). *Opportunities and Challenges for Community Development: Information and Communication Technologies for Development in Africa* (Vol. 1). Jointly published by Ottawa: IDRC and Dakar: Council for the Development of Social Science Research in Africa (CODESRIA).

International Development Research Centre (IDRC). (2005). Learning from IDRC-Supported Rural ICT Projects in Asia. *International Development Research Centre*. Retrieved Mar 14, 2005, from http://web.idrc.ca/en/ev-67344-201 -1 -DO_TOPIC.html

Kling, R. (2000). Learning about information technologies and social change: The contribution of social informatics. *The Information Society, 16*(3), 217–232. doi:10.1080/01972240050133661

Lewin, K. (2004). Action research and minority problems. *Fundamentals of Action Research, 2*, 19.

Mair, J., & Marti, I. (2005). Social Entrepreneurship Research: A Source of Explanation, Prediction and Delight. *Journal of World Business, 41*, 36–44. doi:10.1016/j.jwb.2005.09.002

Mansell, R., & Wehn, U. (1998). *Knowledge Societies: Information Technology for Sustainable Development*. New York: Oxford University Press.

Marsden, T. (2004). The quest for ecological modernisation: re-spacing rural development and agri-food studies. *Sociologia Ruralis, 44*(2), 129–148. doi:10.1111/j.1467-9523.2004.00267.x

McNamara, K. S. (2003). Information and Communication technologies, Poverty and Development: Learning from Experience. *A Background Paper for the InfoDev Annual Symposium, December 9-10, 2003, Geneva, Switzerland*. Washington DC: The World Bank.

Moodley, S (2005). The Promise of E-Development? A Critical Assessment of the State of ICT for Poverty Reduction Discourse in South Africa. *Perspectives on Global Development, 4*(1).

Mulder, I., Bohle, W., Boshomane, S., Morris, C., Tempelman, H., & Velthausz, D. (2008). Real World Innovation in Rural South Africa. *The Electronic Journal for Virtual Organisations and Networks, 10*, 8–20.

Munyua, H. (2000). Information and Communication Technologies for Rural Development and Food Security: Lessons from Field Experiences in Developing Countries. *Sustainable Development Department, Food and Agriculture Organization of the United Nations*. Retrieved Feb 2, 2009, from http://www.fao.org/sd/CDdirect /CDre0055b.htm

Norris, P. (2002). *Civic Engagement, Information Poverty, and the Internet Worldwide*. Cambridge: Cambridge University Press.

Pade, C. (2006). *An Investigation of ICT Project Management Techniques for Sustainable ICT Projects in Rural Development*. Unpublished Masters thesis, Rhodes University, Grahamstown.

Pade, C., Mallinson, B., & Sewry, D. (2006, October). *An Exploration of the Categories Associated with ICT Project Sustainability in Rural Areas of Developing Countries: A Case Study of the Dwesa Project.* Paper presented at the Annual Conference of the South African Institute of Computer Scientists and Information Technologists (SAICSIT). Gordon's Bay, South Africa.

Pade, C., Mallinson, B., & Sewry, D. (2008). An Elaboration of Critical Success Factors for Rural ICT Project Sustainability in Developing Countries: Exploring the Dwesa Case. [JITCAR]. *Journal of Information Technology Case and Application Research, 10*(4), 32–55.

Palmer, R., Timmermans, H., & Fay, D. (2002). *From Conflict to Negotiation: Nature-based Development on South Africa's Wild Coast.* Pretoria: Human Sciences Research Council.

Pigato, M. A. (2001). Information and Communication Technology, Poverty, and Development in Sub-Saharan Africa and South Asia. *African Region Working Paper Series No. 20. August 2001. The World Bank.* Retrieved February 16, 2009 from http://www.worldbank.org /afr/wps/wp20.pdf

Roman, R., & Colle, R.D. (2003). Content creation for ICT development projects: Integrating normative approaches and community demand. *Information technology for Development, 10*(2), 85-94.

Sieborger, I., Terzoli, A., & Hodgkinson-Williams, C. (2008). *The development of ICT networks for South African schools: Two pilot studies in disadvantaged areas. Learning to live in the knowledge society.* Boston: Springer.

Slay, H., Thinyane, M., Terzoli, A., & Clayton, P. (2006). *A preliminary investigation into the implementation of ICTs in marginalized communities.* Paper presented at the Southern African Telecommunications Networks and Applications Conference (SAICSIT), Spier - Western Cape, South Africa.

Statistics South Africa. (2001). Census 2001: Investigation into appropriate definitions of urban and rural areas for South Africa. Discussion document. Report no. 03-03-20 (2001), 2001, Retrieved February 26, 2009, from http://www.statssa.gov.za/ census01 /html/UrbanRural.pdf

Stoll, K. (2003). Telecentres sustainability: What does it mean? *ICT for development, Development Gateway.* Retrieved February 14, 2006, from http://topics.developmentgateway.org /ict /sdm/previewDocument.do~activeDocumentId=442773

Stoll, K. (2005). Basic Principles of Community Public Internet Access Point's Sustainability. In Badshah, A., Khan, S., & Garrido, M. (Eds.), *Connected for Development: Information Kiosks and Sustainability* (pp. 61–66). New York: United Nations Publications.

Talyarkhan, S. (2004). Connecting the first mile: a framework for best practice in ICT projects for knowledge sharing in development. *Intermediate Technology Development Group (ITDG).* Retrieved February 16, 2009 from http://www.itdg.org/ docs/icts/ ict_best_practice_framework.pdf.

Telecommons Development Group. (2000). Rural Access to Information and Communication Technologies (ICTs): The Challenge of Africa. *Prepared for African Connection Initiative of the African Connection Secretariat. Department for International Development (DFID), The World Bank, InfoDev.* Retrieved March 18, 2006 from http://www.unbotswana.org.bw/ undp/docs/bhdr2002/ rural%20access%20to%20ICT%20the%20challenge%20of%20Africa.pdf

United Nations Development Programme (UNDP). (2001) Essentials: Information Communication Technology for Development. Synthesis of Lessons Learnt, *Evaluation Office No. 5, September 2001.* New York: United Nations Development Program. Retrieved February 16, 2009 from http://www.undp.org/eo/documents /essentials_5.PDF.

Wagner, D. A., Day, B., James, T., Kozma, R. B., Miller, J., & Unwin, T. (2005). *Monitoring and Evaluation of ICT in Education Projects: A Handbook for Developing Countries.* Washington DC: The World Bank (InfoDev).

Warschauer, M. (2003). *Technology and Social Inclusion: Rethinking the Digital Divide*. Cambridge: Massachusetts Institute of Technology (MIT).

ENDNOTE

[1] For more information on the Meraka Institute, their website is http://www.meraka. org.za/. The CSIR website is http://www. csir.co.za

Chapter 4
Does IT Help or Not?
Computers for Development in the Andes

Antonio Díaz Andrade
Auckland University of Technology, New Zealand

ABSTRACT

The number of initiatives aiming at improving people's living conditions through the provision of information and communication technology (ICT) has been increasing around the globe during the last decade. However, the mere provision of ICT tools is not enough to achieve such goals as this chapter illustrates through the examination of the existent conditions in Huanico, a remote village in the northern Peruvian Andes. Using an interpretive case study design, the author analyzes and explains why under circumstances of severe scarcity and geographical isolation computers can do little in helping local people. The findings challenge the sometimes over-optimistic stances on ICT benefits adopted by international development agencies and governments. Conversely, it confirms the need to provide basic infrastructure and stresses the importance of establishing priorities correctly before launching any ICT for development initiative.

INTRODUCTION

This chapter echoes pretty much my reflections during the last ten years or so, which Walsham (2001) summarized in one immense question "Are we making a better world with information technology?" (2001: 251). The increased wave of hope and enthusiasm in the circles of international development agencies, national governments, non-governmental organizations and donors has prompted a debate in the academic community about the effective contribution computers can do to improving people's living conditions (see Walsham, Robey, & Sahay, 2007).

Going into a large research project, which is partially documented here, I had a strong belief that ICT can help in creating better conditions for undeserved communities and that belief has not been diminished. But we must admit that ICT is neither a one-size-fit-all artifact nor an end by

DOI: 10.4018/978-1-61520-997-2.ch004

itself. As this chapter demonstrates, we should look first for the conditions where ICT tools are to be deployed.

This chapter's title paraphrases Carr's (2003) challenging question to remind us the importance of going back to the fundamentals when deciding ICT investments. Unlike Carr's (2003) reflection, which is in the for-profit sector and highlights the relevance of corporate strategy with reference to information technology spending, mine is well-positioned in the ICT for development debate and emphasizes the importance of essential physical infrastructure vis-à-vis the provision of techno-logical tools in a rural Peruvian community.

The Call of ICT for Development

The concept of development has evolved, from its original association with economic growth and modernization according to the Western standards, to an integrative view that entails health, educa-tion and quality of life (Mchombu, 2004) while recognizing local cultural differences (Walsham, 2001). The Nobel laureate Amartya Sen (1999) declares that development aims at bringing so-cial opportunities, that is "the arrangements that society makes for education, health care and so on, which influence the individual's substantive freedom to live better" (1999: 39). Access to information is one of these arrangements and it is widely accepted that ICT tools facilitate such access to information (Avgerou, 1998; Heeks, 2002; Kenny, 2003; Lewin, 2000).

If the idea of social opportunities brings to mind a positive connotation, it is reasonable to recog-nize that the lack of social opportunities leads to social exclusion. Social exclusion is a "process by which certain individuals and groups are systemi-cally barred from access to positions that would enable them to an autonomous livelihood within the social standards framed by institutions and values in a given context" (Castells, 2000a: 71). Those excluded from the social networks are also excluded from the information available within

the networks and get involved in a perverse circle that exacerbates their exclusion (Slater & Tacchi, 2004; Walsham, 2001).

It is against this background that a number of agencies called for granting access to the new ICT tools to those previously excluded. Some of them bestow to these tools a superlative role in the process of social inclusion.

Just to illustrate this point, I mention three statements that reflect how the potential benefits of ICT were – or are – perceived by these agen-cies. The first one comes from the World Bank's Development Report (1998), *Knowledge for De-velopment*, which advocates for the use of ICT as a means to spread knowledge and, consequently, improve living conditions of poor people in poor countries. I found the second one in the *Human Development Report 2001, Making New Technolo-gies Work for Human Development*, which praises the qualities of the ICT tools:

"Linking computing devices and allowing them to communicate with each other creates networked information systems based on a common protocol. Individuals, households and institutions are linked in processing and executing a huge number of instructions in imperceptible time spans. This radi-cally alters access to information and the structure of communication – extending the networked reach to all corners of the world". (UNDP, 2001: 30)

This report continues, claiming that new infor-mation technology enhances political participa-tion, achieves greater transparency, creates new sources of income and contributes to improved people's health. The third statement is even more forceful and comes from the exclusive club of the most powerful countries:

"Information and Communications Technology… is fast becoming a vital engine of growth for the world economy. It is also enabling many enter-prising individuals, firms and communities, in all parts of the globe, to address economic and social

challenges with greater efficiency and imagination. Enormous opportunities are there to be seized and shared by us all". (G8, 2000)

These optimistic – even maybe over-optimistic – statements have the implicit assumption that technology is advantageous per se. Their proponents might be reasoning in the following terms: If we recognize, as Castells (2000b) affirms, that information generation, processing and transmission are the sources of productivity and power in the so-called networked society, those currently non-valuable people and locales could get better if we provide to them the ICT tools to generate, process and transmit information. It hints that if ICT is provided we are contributing to solving the developmental problems.

This view, however, is flawed in two accounts. On the one hand, even though the evidence linking access to ICT and development is increasing, it is still largely anecdotal (Bhatnagar, 2003; Kenny, 2003). One the other hand, it assumes a naive stance and grants a rather universalistic role to computers. Computer technology is a neutral element; its consequences will depend on how we use it. The dilemma, "[Computer] has become a symbol for all that is good and that is evil in modern society" (Taviss, 1970: 3 cited by Holvast, Duquenoy, & Whitehouse, 2005: 137), expressed in the precursor work *The Computer Impact*, is non-existent. Computer technology, like any other technology, can help in development efforts but we must avoid taking a technological deterministic standpoint.

The Real Problem

Technological infrastructure is not enough to achieve a successful deployment; it is not just a matter of ICT provision. Empirical evidence suggests that the digital divide is not a completely new phenomenon at all; it simply mirrors other long-term and pre-existing forms of economic and social divisions. Warschauer (2003) calls to leave behind the digital divide issue and move forward

onto an "examination of social structures, social problems, social organization, and social relations" (2003; 211). We should take into consideration the needs of the intended beneficiaries of the ICT intervention while observing the whole context in which this intervention would take place. The belief of importing "best practices" and assuming that they can fit into any particular situation in their entirety needs to be challenged.

To be successful, the ICT intervention needs to take into consideration the context of where it is going to be deployed. And by context I mean both social and physical contexts. As regards the social context, it is recognized that individual abilities are indispensable in order to benefit from the new available technological tools from an individualistic perspective; people with the essential skills for interpreting contents and being ready for adopting, adapting and exploiting the provided technology (Lee, 2001). However, individual abilities are of little use if they are not utilized to some extent in a community; if we have talented but isolated individuals, the information cannot have any value for a community. Social structures are needed in order to exploit the technological potential (Avgerou, 1998). Still, these social structures do not develop in a vacuum; they are organized within definite space and time limits – cf. Giddens's (1984) structuration theory.

The physical context deserves to be equally and thoroughly analyzed before the ICT deployment takes place. It may be the case that poor existing physical infrastructure (e.g., no clean water and lack of electric supply) and remoteness do not provide the necessary conditions for triggering the process of accessing and distributing information; rather to the contrary they may hinder people from using ICT.

In this chapter, I present the case of the village of Huanico, which was part of a large research project I conducted in five other communities in the Cajamarca region in the northern Peruvian Andes between July and November 2005. Although the social context seemed to be promising for the widespread distribution of computer-mediated information, Huanico's poor existing physical infrastructure and extreme isolation demonstrated to be overwhelming obstacles. The reflections expressed in this chapter explain why the ICT deployment in a village like Huanico was eventually impracticable.

AN INITIATIVE FOR THE CAJAMARCA REGION

Cajamarca region is the third most populated area with more than 1.5 million inhabitants and encompasses the largest rural proportion among all the regions in Peru; 75.3% of its population lives in the countryside (INEI, 2006b). Cajamarca is one of the largest producers of dairy products in the country and in its territory is Minera Yanacocha's site, one of the world's top five gold mines. Paradoxically, Cajamarca lacks an adequate road infrastructure and only 36.3% of its population enjoys electric power (Reyes, 2005). It ranks 21ˢᵗ among the 24 Peruvian regions on human development index and its population is regarded among the five poorest in the nation (PNUD, 2002).

Given that in the Peruvian countryside the small entrepreneurs and local authorities do not have enough information for making timely and correct decisions, a European non-governmental organization launched the *Infodes* project in the Cajamarca region. It proposed to provide information in order to increase the productive capacity and improve local governance. The project was implemented over two and a half years until 2001 in six communities: Chanta Alta, Combayo, Huanico, La Encañada, Llacanora and Puruay Alto. As a result, these communities had available a number of information services, for the first time, at the recently installed local "infocentros" – rural information centers, which resembled local libraries.

Since the local infocentros lacked Internet access and even telephone service at that time, two additional projects were initiated. One of them resulted in an AM broadcasting station for the region; the other one was the rural telephony pilot project named *Conectando los Andes*, which was totally funded by the Fund for Investment in Telecommunications (FITEL), a government agency. By then, the necessity to interconnect the local infocentros was apparent. The idea of creating a rural telecommunication system, which would integrate and provide instant access to the database produced by the *Infodes* project, came up.

So, the *Rural-Urban Information System* project (*Sistema de Información Rural-Urbano – SIRU*, as it is known) was planned to continue upon the platforms established by both *Infodes* and *Conectando los Andes* projects. It entailed the implementation of a rural system of information in the Cajamarca region aiming at providing "timely and useful information to local farmers, businessmen and government agencies in order to build capabilities for local development" (my translation, Pereyra Romo, 2002, p. 5) through the diffusion of contents and interactive communication among the infocentros.

In August 2003, the SIRU Project got underway when the Llacanora infocentro was equipped with four computers connected to the Internet. It materialized a conjoint effort of a number of non-governmental organizations and international agencies aiming to improve people's living conditions in the Cajamarca region. Following the introduction of ICT to Llacanora, the infocentros at Chanta Alta, Combayo, Huanico, La Encañada and Puruay Alto were provided with Internet access, too. Since then, the infocentros have been offering for a fee the following services: Internet access, phone calls and phone messages as well as document printing, scanning and typewriting.

The Village of Huanico

Santa Rosa de Huanico is by far the most isolated village and endures the hardest living conditions of all the recipient communities of the SIRU Project. It lacks the basic public services. Electricity, public sewage, landline and mobile phones are not available at all. At the time of the fieldwork, drinkable water was not available either due to the dry season. Just to illustrate this point, it serves to say that I could not even brush my teeth during my stay there. One of the teachers at the local school complained, *"We have to share the water with cattle at the diminishing [nearby] pond"*.

There are two institutions on their own right that make it easier for local people to face their harsh living conditions. The Peasant Organization is a communal association that provides the intangible structure for coordinated actions and unites villagers around common goals. The practice of minga is another expression of the existing strong communal links. Minga (or minka) is a Quechua word that defines the voluntary communal work since the Inca times. It is not uncommon in Huanico to see people working together in maintaining the track that connects the village to Cajamarca City – the chief city of the region – or helping each other with the harvest or putting up corrugated roofs on their adobe houses.

The population of Huanico is barely 300 (INEI, 2006a). According to the local mayor there are around 78 households in Huanico. Many of the houses in the village are locked with padlocks from outside; their owners come back during the Friday open-air markets only. Most of the time, they are in the neighboring areas looking after their cattle or cultivating potatoes. Certainly, if Huanico looks like a ghost town for six days a week, on Fridays the picture is completely different. It is customary that kids do not go to school on Fridays because they help their parents during the active open-air market in trading their produce.

Huanico is at 3,700 meters above sea level and 78 kilometers east from Cajamarca City. The only transportation available to get there is the "milk truck", which collects milk along the way from several scattered hamlets on a daily basis. However, on Fridays there are additional trucks and buses crammed full of people heading to Huanico to participate in the open-air market.

The trip from Cajamarca City to Huanico takes 14 hours; the milk truck usually departs around 19:00 every day and arrives next day around 09:00. Passengers travel on the wagon, very well sheltered to bear the freezing temperatures. During the journey I observed that the truck driver operates as a postman. *"Please, tell my godfather at Malat [one of the stopover hamlets] that I am going to visit him next Wednesday"* and *"Take this rucksack of potatoes to my friend in Bella Unión"* are typical of the messages I heard. And the truck driver delivers. It is a clear indication that people know one another in a relatively large area. This observation is an instantiation of the widespread network of contacts and how local people use the available resources to keep in touch.

Since Huanico lacks electric power, the infocentro is equipped with solar panels. This solution imposes a restriction: the unique computer at the infocentro can only operate for two hours a day. That is because the agreement between the company that provides satellite communication and FITEL stipulates that the telephones must be accessible between 08:00 and 20:00 everyday; if they are not, the former is to be fined. Consequently, the company prioritizes the operation of the telephones and imposes severe restrictions on the functioning time of the computers.

METHODOLOGY

Huanico is one of the cases analyzed under a holistic-multiple case study design. The other five aforementioned communities constituted the other cases – interested readers may refer to Díaz Andrade (2009) for more details on the entire research project. Huanico was somewhat the odd one compared to the other five communities in terms of physical infrastructure and remoteness. These unique conditions provide exceptional analytical opportunities to understand the factors that hampered the deployment of ICT.

The case study research is useful for building theoretical models to understand the phenomena existing in specific backgrounds because it is a methodology that follows "an empirical inquiry that investigates a contemporary phenomenon within its real-life context" (Yin, 2003: 13). The resulting theoretical models are expected to be strongly attached to empirical reality (Eisenhardt, 1989; Eisenhardt & Graebner, 2007). In particular, field studies are appropriate to generate a well-founded interpretive comprehension of human-technology interaction in the natural social setting (Orlikowski & Baroudi, 1991).

The analysis of textual data took an exploratory interpretive approach. The analysis was carried out according to the Glaserian (1992) version of grounded theory (Glaser & Strauss, 1967) concrete pieces of data were analyzed in an inductive fashion grouping them together around ever-increasing abstract categories. While the case study design guided the data collection procedure in a well-defined unit of analysis, grounded theory principles provided the framework for the interpretive analysis (Charmaz, 2006).

During the analysis, special attention has been paid to the context. The existing context at the time of the fieldwork is described with much detail as possible in the next pages to share with the reader my experience during the fieldwork – cf. Klein & Myers's (1999) principle of contextualization.

Engaging with the Fieldwork

I have to admit that before getting into the field I thought I would find reasonably a well-equipped infocentro crowded with villagers keen on receiving computer-mediated information with the assistance of a fully committed infocentro manager. However, my experience in Huanico threw up a completely different picture for the reasons that I will explain later on.

The data collection process took place between the last week of August and the first week of September 2005. Focused in-depth interviews were key elements for this research, which assisted me to uncover participants' understandings, meanings, stories and experiences, feelings and motivations (Collis & Hussey, 2003; Tacchi, Slater, & Hearn, 2003; Walsham, 1995) about the use, or not, of computers. The interviews were audio taped and transcribed for their subsequent analysis. In addition, I produced hand-written annotations containing detailed descriptions and explanations of the observed phenomenon during the fieldwork. The field notes proved to be twofold useful. On the one hand, they contain not only an account of the facts I observed but also a preliminary interpretive analysis of what was going on in Huanico, which assisted me to conduct a deeper examination of the events once I was back to my office thousands of kilometers away from and with no opportunity to go back to the field. On the other hand, the field notes became an excellent complement when one of the participants, who was very expressive on his thoughts about the meaning of computers in his everyday life during our informal conversations, turned monosyllabic in his answers when the audio tape recorder was turned on.

I conducted in-depth interviews with the only three local people who were able to use computers in Huanico at the time of the fieldwork: Abelardo, Ramón and Manuel. I also interacted with many others, mainly with Francisco, who provided me accommodation. In addition, I held long conversations with the primary school principal and some schoolteachers, who were not locals; they spend the weekdays in Huanico during school time – other than that, their usual place of residency is Cajamarca City. In order to protect participants' confidentiality, the names used in this chapter are fictitious.

Abelardo – 28 years old – is a high school teacher and the infocentro manager at Huanico. The main reason to be appointed as the infocentro manager – after the solar panels were stolen from the previous infocentro manager's place – was "the central location of his house", just in front of the site where the open-air market takes place every

Friday. Indeed, he skipped the two-step process the other infocentro managers followed. The standard process for appointing an infocentro manager entailed the SIRU Project officials offering computer training to those who volunteered, first and then, presenting the shortlist to the community for consideration. It was up to the community to make the final decision based on the candidates' leadership and reputation qualities. The fact that Abelardo, being a schoolteacher, was recognized as one of the most educated and respected persons in the village – and, to some extent, the urgency for filling the vacant position – made possible his appointment without observing the standard process. In practice, however, the infocentro is in the hands of Abelardo's wife. Abelardo works as a full-time teacher at the nearby Bella Unión hamlet's school and looks after his in-law's farm, juggling with the operation of the infocentro.

Ramón – 32 years old – is a father of four children and a villager who was trained in using computers by the SIRU Project along with the previous infocentro manager as part of the selection process for appointing the infocentro manager. Eventually, he was not successful in the application and continues with his usual farming and stockbreeding activities. During my time in Huanico, he was particularly concerned about his wife's health who was suffering from persistent headaches. She was present during the interview, and her strong and painful headaches became apparent; more than once he made reference to his interest in finding a doctor to help her.

Manuel is a 16 years old boy who has been boarding at his grandparents' place in Huanico since the beginning of 2005 after his family experienced economic hardship in Cajamarca City. He looked very well adapted to a rural environment, but his city-dweller style was evident.

It was an unexpected happy event that during my time in Huanico, villagers were celebrating Santa Rosa – the village's patron saint – festivity on the 30th of August. It allowed me to be a first hand observer of Huanico's social life. People

from surrounding hamlets got together to participate at the party with local live bands; there was a display of thunderous fireworks, a quick soccer tournament, a christening mass – under the Catholic tradition – and a small procession around the local church. It was clear to me that despite their degree of deprivation, Huanico villagers take time to celebrate.

FINDINGS

In this section, I present the conceptual categories that were produced as a result of the inductive thinking process described above. The categories emerged from the analysis of the interview transcripts and field notes. The sub-headings below represent the conceptual categories the concrete data – i.e., transcripts and field notes – were grouped around. Participants' expressions are presented in italics within quotation marks.

Individual Capacities: Education, Reading and Computers

The only existing high school for Huanico teenagers is not actually within Huanico jurisdiction; it is in the neighboring Bella Unión hamlet – two kilometers away. Most of the teachers only arrive in Huanico (from Cajamarca City) on mid-morning Mondays by the milk truck and leave the village every Friday at mid-morning by the same means.

Ramón complains about teachers' poor performance and puts forward an explanation, *"Education is poor here because teachers have to travel for many hours [to get here]"*. Moreover, it is a habit for the students to have Fridays off because their parents make them work during the open-air market day. Francisco justifies, *"My children have to learn [how to run] the business"*. These expressions illustrate the low priority formal education has for local people.

I could verify that reading in a remote village like Huanico is an almost impossible activity.

There is no public library, while the few books available at the infocentro are irrelevant and inappropriate for the local people who are hardly able to read and write – e.g., a collection of research articles on agricultural economy seems more appropriate for a university environment than for a village whose inhabitants struggle to put food on their tables. Not surprisingly, those books are new and are sitting on the shelves covered of dust. If the peasants could afford it, they would still be able to receive by mid-morning yesterday's newspaper.

Another aspect that deserves attention is the fact that girls seldom complete high school. There were five students in the final year at the secondary school; all of them were boys. The girls simply gave up school to help at home or on their parents' farms. Although none of the people I talked to denied the importance of education for women, I observed a contradiction between what they said and what they did.

As regards the use of computers, Abelardo learned to use them as part of his teaching training and Ramón did during the training workshops when he was one of the candidates for the infocentro manager position during the previous selection process. Manuel had learned to use computers in Cajamarca City at an Internet café before he moved to Huanico. According to Abelardo and Manuel's own account the latter's friends always ask him for assistance in using computers – *"Come on, open an e-mail account for me"*, they say. Abelardo affirms, *"When there were no computers at all, nobody in the village knew what a computer was and what its purpose was"*. My observation indicates that the situation has not changed even after the introduction of the infocentro. When I shared my opinion with Abelardo, he grumbled, *"Certainly, local people seldom use the computer"*. This is an ironic expression in view of the fact that Abelardo has not offered any computer-training workshop for local people since taking the responsibility of the infocentro in 2003; that is supposed to be one of the infocentro manager duties. He admits, *"Well, this year, a student from*

Cajamarca City has come [to town] and, since he knows better than me, he teaches his friends". That student turned out to be Manuel.

Individual Attitudes: Personal Dreams in the Middle of Harsh Living Conditions

Lacking a basic infrastructure and suffering from an extreme state of isolation mean that most of local people are peasants living in a subsistence economy. The only people that I found having some degree of urban exposure are Manuel – as he lived in Cajamarca City until 2005, Abelardo – who did his teaching training in San Marcos – and the schoolteachers – who are from and spend the weekends in Cajamarca City. The rest of the villagers have hardly visited other places beyond the surrounding area.

I have already explained the difficulty of getting to Huanico. And that is probably the reason why local people have only a limited degree of exposure beyond the village. The time-consuming and fatiguing trip to Cajamarca City keeps Huanico villagers isolated. Abelardo regrets, *"It is very difficult for us to go to Cajamarca City"*. Indeed, there are many difficulties; they are not only barriers for traveling but could also turn a wearying trip into a dangerous adventure. Manuel explains, *"I do not use the milk truck. I had a bad experience; my uncle was in the truck when an accident happened and he ended badly injured… The driver went asleep; the truck turned over"*. Certainly, Manuel prefers to hike across the hills rather than using the milk truck when he needs to go to the city.

Without doubt, people in Huanico have a harsh life. My impression as a foreigner is that things go very slow and most of the local people have simply accepted things as they are. Ramón shows resignation, *"We do not have any other option; so, we have to accept it"*. He hints that people in Huanico are doomed; he projects the blame to the natural environment – i.e., cold weather and high altitude. However, Manuel shows an enthusiastic and heartening view, *"I want to see how we can improve all this mess"* when he talks about Huanico's state of backwardness. On the personal strand, he not only brings aspiration closer to someone who has been exposed to a more diverse environment but also goes beyond when clearly affirms, *"My personal goal is to reach NASA"*.

The earlier discussion suggests that Huanico's people are not prone to catch up with progress. Indeed, Manuel is very critical about Huanico villagers' view of life, *"If you do something different according to their conventional parameters, you are judged as a rebel, as a very, very liberal person... They are very concerned about what people would say"*. He laments that the villagers reject anything that is not according to their values: *"It is difficult to talk to local people... They are less open than people in the city... They do not understand me"*. It is clear the role Manuel is intending to play in bringing to the village his city-dweller views, which are in conflict with the locals' more traditional way of life. The harsh living conditions they face seem to have imposed on them a glass ceiling that makes them hard to break.

Communal Life: The Strong Social Links

Strong presence of a communal organization and face-to-face contacts where everybody knows each other are visible characteristics of Huanico life. Ramón expresses his satisfaction of being part of Huanico's life, *"I feel very well integrated [in this community]... Because we know one another; neighbors, fellow countrymen, and so on"*. Similarly, the communal assemblies summoned by the Peasant Organization, provides the opportunity for people to contact one another. Abelardo confidently says, *"I know everybody in Huanico. Since the village is not big at all, I got acquainted with everyone"*. I corroborated this fact. My presence was immediately noticed by local people. Some of them approached me to inquire what the reason of my visit to the village

was; some others went even further and invited me to participate at the festivities for the patron saint. They demonstrated their interest in showing me what Huanico had to offer.

Being Huanico a tiny village, everybody has to look after the community because they know that the village is not among the provincial, regional or, even less, the national authorities' priorities. A communal identity sense prevails where all the inhabitants are interested and participate collectively in the affairs concerning the village. Clearly, the Peasant Organization is the one that represents villagers' expressions. Abelardo explains the mechanisms under which the Peasant Organization works, *"The community assembly takes place once a month... Everybody attends the meeting. Everybody!... They all make agreements about communal works among others"*. Abelardo recalls when he was chosen to be the new infocentro manager in a Peasant Organization assembly, *"[The SIRU Project officials] had to respect community's decision"*. As has been explained earlier, he did not undergo the competitive selection process that the other infocentros managers did; his appointment was merely a communication to the SIRU Project officials about a de facto local decision. Ramón also recognizes that the Peasant Organization is the collective entity where the decisions are taken based on communal consensus. He also mentions minga – the traditional communal and voluntary work – as an important institution in Huanico.

Unsurprisingly, the most popular way for sharing information is through face-to-face interactions both at casual encounters and at the prearranged assemblies. With regard to the former, Manuel affirms, *"Here people give notice immediately [for any event]"*. Regarding the latter, Abelardo states, *"During the communal meetings, everybody knows about what is going on in the village"*.

At this point, the raising question was about the role the unique computer available at the infocentro played in the distribution of information from and to the village.

Restricted Use of Computers: Preparing Documents but not Accessing Information

None of the people I talked to in Huanico denies the advantage that computers represent. One of the villagers said that computers represent a *"huge benefit"*. Ironically, using computers seems not to be a widespread activity in the village. For instance, Ramón foresees computer benefit and affirms, *"It is useful for preparing documents, for example"*. Paradoxically, he has never used it to prepare a document. That role seems to be reserved to Abelardo who contributes preparing documents to the Peasant Organization when they require it once in a while. People naturally recognize he is the most educated among the villagers and put him in charge of that.

As might have been expected, the only available computer would ideally be used for seeking information; however, the hardly any time it has been used was for preparing the documents Abelardo does for the Peasant Organization. During my interaction with local people, they expressed potential benefits rather than actual experiences. For instance, Manuel complains, *"If people used the computer, we would see progress [in this village], but that is not the case"*. He links using computers and getting information that might boost village's progress, *"Because if you learn [how to use] computers you have the information you need to confront the authorities"*. His interpretation of the local scene is that people cannot take action against authorities at the district and provincial levels, who according to his account do not do enough for the village, because the villagers do not have the right information. Manuel grants computers an empowerment capacity.

In addition, Manuel says he is recording his experiences of living in the village: *"I am writing a diary about Huanico's life… how things are in here"*. It must be said, however, that Manuel's progress on his diary is made from an Internet café in Cajamarca City during his sporadic and short visits to town. After some bad experiences, which are going to be explained next, he decided not to use the infocentro's computer.

This piece of evidence led me to investigate what the infocentro and its computer meant for local people.

Perceptions of the Infocentro: The Telephone is Fine but the Computer is Useless

I observed that if it were not for the telephone, the infocentro presence would have been unnoticed in Huanico. Once again, I heard expressions of good intentions from the infocentro manager and the other two who are computer literate in the village. They foresee computer's advantages, but the computer available at the infocentro has been hardly ever used.

Phone communication is by far the main contribution people perceive from the infocentro. In fact, I saw many people making and receiving calls. Abelardo affirms, *"Telephone's demand is higher than the computer's"*. He proudly recalls the most important contribution from the infocentro, *"On one occasion, a girl was seriously ill. Thanks to the phone we could communicate and evacuate her to Cajamarca City. If it were not for the telephone, she would have died"*. To mark the contrast, he recounts the case of a pregnant woman who died since she could not be evacuated due to the lack of communication before the installation of the infocentro and its telephone.

Similarly, Ramón appreciates the phone communication available at the infocentro. He strongly affirms, *"The only benefit I get [from the infocentro] is that it makes the communication easier"*. Even Manuel, who seems to be only real computer enthusiast in Huanico, bitterly declares, *"The infocentro did not bring any benefit, except for the phone communication"*.

The other characteristic that contributes to make the infocentro a distinguishable place in Huanico is its loudspeaker, mainly during Fridays' open-air market. Abelardo uses the infocentro's loudspeaker for *"announcing the phone calls and also for communicating authorities' messages"*. Manuel adds, *"Local authorities summon in people using the infocentro's loudspeaker"*.

Surprisingly, neither the interviewees nor the other people I interacted with mentioned any positive contribution from the infocentro's computer. Quite the opposite, when they were prompted to recall benefits they received from the computer, I only heard expressions of frustration.

Huanico infocentro technical restrictions are indeed disappointing. Abelardo starts admitting, *"The problem we have is that we can only access to the Internet for a maximum of two hours per day due to energy restrictions"*. Then he adds, *"Our computer is a little bit slow [for accessing to the Internet]"*. The Internet access speed is 9.6 kbps and saying *"a little bit slow"* is a euphemism. I had a first-hand experience that confirmed it is extremely and painfully slow. One day, I spent more than one hour just to get to my e-mail inbox; I could read no one of the incoming messages because the slot of energy allocated had finished before I could open the first one. In other words, it took me two hours just to see my e-mail inbox, without being able to open a single message. Manuel – the only person I identified in Huanico who was really interested and active in using computers – had a similar experience. He recalls, *"I tried to search for information only once; never ever again! My allocated time elapsed and the website [I was accessing to] had not been downloaded yet... [The computer] is extremely slow!"* Now, when he needs to access computer-mediated information, he does on his occasional visits to Cajamarca City.

DISCUSSION

The categories explained in the previous section present a picture of Huanico's social life: the degree of social cohesion among Huanico inhabit-

ants is high. This high degree of social cohesion facilitates the distribution among local people through their frequent face-to-face interactions and should also facilitate the dissemination of computer-mediated information. As regards the use of computers for accessing information, the findings demonstrate that the infocentro has not achieved the SIRU Project's declared objective: the provision of timely information through the diffusion of contents. There is no content generated by the project and generic content available on the Internet is not accessible due to technical limitations. Moreover, in Huanico, people suffering from a lack of basic public services are busy finding solutions to immediate problems. The conditions are so extreme that it seems that Huanico inhabitants – Manuel appears to be the only exception – are either almost unable or not motivated to get information from virtual contacts or searching on the Internet. If there were anyone who embraces the action of looking for information using computers, the transmission of that piece of information to their country fellows may be neutralized by the burden of the issues that must be addressed straight away, even though the high degree of social cohesion.

Indeed, I observed a strong sense of being part of the community in Huanico. It is epitomized in people's motivation to play a part in communal issues, like being members of the Peasant Organization and participating in mingas. These two institutions have established social frameworks accepted and instantiated by norms, habits and rules both explicit and implicit (Bloor, 1997; North, 1990). Their involvement in collective activities "give[s] rise to profits, both material and symbolic" (Field, 2003, p. 17) by establishing and reinforcing rules of reciprocity. Huanico inhabitants constitute a group largely homogeneous where everybody is socially accountable for their acts and omissions before the rest of the community because individual acts or omissions are immediately visible and cannot be hidden. In this way, they harmonize collective actions (Coleman, 1988;

Putnam, Leonardi & Nonetti, 1993). The level of communication and trust among the inhabitants is apparent; they participate in mingas and share information through a word-of-mouth scheme – transacting favors symmetrically (Adler & Kwon, 2002). Their interpersonal interactions are characterized by what Granovetter (1973) called strong ties: "[the] combination of the amount of time, the emotional intensity, the intimacy (mutual confiding), and the reciprocal services" (p. 1361).

However, since Huanico suffers from extreme isolation and backwardness, its inhabitants simply have to satisfy first their basic needs, i.e. food and water, relegating their cognitive ones to the last – cf. Maslow's (1943) hierarchy of needs. The solutions they might find in computers may be unworkable, at least in the short term, in such hostile environment. Manuel, the most computer-enthusiast person in Huanico, makes apparent his frustration on villagers' lack of interest in using computers. What he seems not to comprehend is that peasants' worldview and needs are quite different from the ones of a person like him, who comes from an urban background where he had the opportunity to enjoy certain level of comfort that for a Huanico dweller – who hardly had the chance to have an experience outside the village – would be an unimaginable extravagance. Being convinced that his future is not in Huanico, Manuel knows that the inconvenience and lacks he is experiencing there are temporary – he is almost certain that sooner or later will go back to Cajamarca City, or even maybe to a larger city. That is not the case for the other villagers, whose options are more limited than Manuel's. Their emotional and functional links to Huanico are so strong and their real opportunities to make their lives outside the village so limited that it is almost unimaginable for them to explore the possibility to move out. The promise of improving their living conditions by means of computer-mediated information never realized not only because the technical restrictions explained earlier but also,

and most importantly, because they must address urgent needs before start using computers.

I argue the conditions to install computer technology were not only inadequate but also – in the event of overcoming technical problems – people would still have urgent issues to solve before start using computers.

A Hostile Environment for the Infocentro and Its Computer

While still in the field, I started reflecting on what the infocentro's computer meant for local people and the viability for the infocentro itself.

As regards the infocentro manager, Abelardo is in an extremely difficult situation. On top of striving for his subsistence, which is even harder because he is married and has one daughter with the everyday responsibilities they entail, he has to look after the infocentro on a volunteer basis. The source of income he would receive as an infocentro manager was planned to come from service fees. When he realized local people were not using the infocentro as was supposed to happen, and consequently, not receiving the expected income, he naturally started losing interest in the infocentro operation. As one of the SIRU Project officials regretfully acknowledges, *"The problem is in [Huanico], with only one computer and just two hours [of energy] per day. That is terrible... A suicide!"* And Abelardo himself casts doubts about the infocentro future, *"Definitely, we have not reached self-sustainability yet"*. His tone indicates that he is not very sure if the infocentro will reach self-sustainability at some time in the future. The financial viability infocentro was, without doubt, in jeopardy at the time of the fieldwork.

The premise of the group of non-governmental organizations funding the SIRU Project was that the services offered at the infocentro would yield the source of income for its manager. So far, this assumption proved to be erroneous. They assumed an unsatisfied demand for information that villagers were willing to pay for. They reasoned that after solving the computer illiteracy problem by the delivery of computer training workshops, in an area where just a few had seen a computer before, the infocentro would work reasonably smoothly – it must be noted that, unlike the other communities beneficiaries of the SIRU Project, no computer training workshop has ever been offered in Huanico. The fact is that the income from service fees is almost nothing. It is made mainly from the overpriced sale of phone cards at S/. 3.50 instead of the marked S/. 3.00 – a fact that have irritated phone users, especially the schoolteachers. Schoolteachers are aware that in the city they can have access to much better communication services at a considerably lower price. Local people have no other option than pay the 17% overprice if they need to make a phone call. Abelardo's justification for this overcharge is that it is the only way his work for looking after the infocentro and the space it occupies at his place can be compensated.

As I explained earlier, only a few people – exactly three – are able to use computers in the village. Among those three who became computer literates, the only one who demonstrated eagerness in using computers is Manuel. But Manuel accesses computers from Internet cafés in Cajamarca City, where he pays less money for a significantly better service. In Cajamarca City he only pays S/. 1.00 compared to S/. 1.50 per hour of computer use in Huanico and enjoys broadband access and the MS Office® suite – which is not available at the infocentro in Huanico. In order to put things in perspective, S/. 1.00 is enough money to have lunch in Huanico. At least, Manuel can afford spending a weekend or the school holiday at his parents' place in Cajamarca City. Going to the city is an indulgence Huanico peasants simply cannot afford. They should stay in the village or its surroundings because their livelihoods depend on their farms and a handful of livestock that needs to be looked after.

In light of this reality, using a computer with an extremely slow Internet connection speed that can operate two hours per day only at a price that represents a significant portion of their income becomes another unaffordable extravagance in Huanico. Even assuming an ideal scenario with a fast Internet connection available 24/7, Huanico villagers would still have urgent issues to address. It is not hard to figure out now why local people lack interest in computers: it does not help them in their immediate needs.

CONCLUSION

Grounded on the evidence presented above and the previous discussion, the idea of generating revenues from fees to make the infocentro sustainable is not realistic. It has been demonstrated that charging a fee for using the computer is not a solution at all in Huanico. In addition to user fees, other revenue sources have been also proposed to make financially viable the telecenters operation in the developing world: e-commerce for the informal and small agricultural sector, e-government services, entertainment, education and health applications, computer training workshops and back-office activities (Best & Maclay, 2002). I explain why none of these are viable options either in an impoverished and remote community like Huanico.

Providing e-commerce services for the informal and small agricultural sector at the infocentro is unrealistic under the current circumstances. On the technical side, the current limitations make it inconceivable to tender proposals or process payments online. On the commercial side, the goods produced in Huanico have low commercial value. It is necessary to improve the quality of local produce, mainly potatoes and milk, in order to attract demand before thinking in providing ICT tools to facilitate e-commerce.

E-government services in Peru are still in an early stage of development and the few already available are oriented to credit card holders only, who are mostly located in the urban conglomerates.

Credit cards in Huanico are non-existent; there is no a bank office there not even a post office – the closest bank and post office are around five-hour driving from Huanico. And cash is scarcely available in the villagers' pockets.

An attempt to generate revenues from entertainment – like equipping the infocentro with a TV set and a DVD player – is meaningless in a village like Huanico that lacks of electricity. Even assuming that people use battery-powered TV sets, the free-to-air aerial signal is not strong to reach the village. Generating an income by renting DVD movies is also unworkable because of two reasons. First, the infocentro manager is not willing to invest in a collection of DVDs. The second one is that the few locals – around 300 – could not afford the price of renting a movie. It is worth mentioning here that the idea of generating revenues from renting DVDs has proven to be an unsuccessful one in the other infocentros were electricity is available. Rather to the contrary, it has created tensions among the infocentro managers and villagers because of the perceived unfair use of the provided technology.

Education and health applications are heavily dependent on government initiatives. So far, there are no e-health government projects and the Huascarán Program – an educational government initiative in Peru – requires other associated services, which are not currently available in rural areas. The health office in Huanico is poorly equipped and the person in charge of it struggles to keep local people reasonable healthy in an area where malnutrition is common currency. Although computer training courses could be offered at the infocentro, the infocentro manager has not offered them because he simply *"has to deal with other issues"* and local people, too. There is weak evidence that only young people are willing to learn how to use computers. Nevertheless this interest cannot be translated into a possible source of income for the infocentro. Young people cannot afford it – and even if they could, it would be a one-off income not a regular one.

Back-office activities, like transcription services or inputting data, are highly unlikely because they depend on an external demand for these activities. Unfortunately, Huanico is not a node in what Castells (2000b) called the "networked society". Its inhabitants' low level of literacy make them improbable players in the market of outsourcing services – even assuming the technical issues have been addressed.

The above discussion has pointed out why the infocentro cannot be self-sustainable in Huanico. Indeed, after the fieldwork was completed, the SIRU Project managers shared with me their plans to phase out the Huanico infocentro. However, focusing the discussion on the infocentro viability can only render a low explanatory power of the underlying causes for the apparent failure of this initiative.

The Real Causes

The real causes for the failure of the Huanico infocentro can be found in Maslow's (1943) classical work on human motivation. He declares that humans have to meet their deficiency needs – which include physiological, safety, love and esteem needs in that order – first before moving up in the hierarchy to the growth needs, like creative and problem solving activities. In Huanico, people are still striving to secure their physiological and safety needs in a very hostile environment. More than fifty years after Maslow's (1943) theory of motivation, when the World Wide Web was still in its beginnings, a precursor report from PANOS presaged: "In countries where access to the basic needs of food, water, shelter and health care are still major problems, providing access to the Internet will have to work hard to justify a high prioritization" (Pruett and Deane, 1998:4).

The empirical evidence from this study confirms PANOS's assertion. Huanico villagers quickly realized that they could not find effective solutions to their life-threatening problems on computers or the Internet. However, they did not adopt a negative stance against the offered technology. It is revealing that no one opposed to the installation of the infocentro in 2003 and no one wanted the computer to be taken out at the time of the fieldwork. Rather to the contrary, everyone I talked to recognized that the infocentro's computer could be helpful at some point in the future. The problem is that local people did not see any benefit on using computers when I was there – cf. Rogers's (2003) relative advantage. There is a temporal dimension that should be factored in; the temporal component reflects the underlying causes of not using computers. While ICT tools have added momentum to human progress, they can be effective only after basic human needs have been satisfied. As Avgerou and Madon (2005) state, policy makers, donors and non-governmental organizations should determine first if ICT initiatives are "necessary or sufficient for solving developmental problems" (p. 212).

Launching ICT initiatives for development without paying attention to the essential infrastructure – like drinkable water, roads, just to mention a couple – could result in a waste of resources. Alas, Huanico, which enjoys a well-built social texture that might support the distribution of ICT-mediated information, provides the best example of the failure of an ICT initiative for development.

ACKNOWLEDGMENT

I would like to thank the SIRU Project officials for allowing me to conduct this research. Special thanks go to the three folks who agreed to be interviewed and to numerous anonymous people who shared their views on computers with me. Their open-handedness and their traditional wisdom in the middle of much deprivation were a great lesson of life for me.

REFERENCES

G8. (2000). Okinawa Charter on Global Information Society. Retrieved on the 5th of August 2004 from http://www.mofa.go.jp/policy/economy / summit/2000/documents/charter.html.

Adler, P. S., & Kwon, S.-W. (2002). Social Capital: Prospects for a New Concept. *Academy of Management Review, 27*(1), 17–40. doi:10.2307/4134367

Avgerou, C. (1998). How Can IT Enable Economic Growth in Developing Countries? *Information Technology for Development, 8*(1), 15–28. doi:10.1080/02681102.1998.9525288

Avgerou, C., & Madon, S. (2005). Information Society and the Digital Divide Problem in Developing Countries. In Berleur, J., & Avgerou, C. (Eds.), *Perspectives and Policies on ICT in Society* (pp. 205–217). New York: Springer. doi:10.1007/0-387-25588-5_15

Best, M. L., & Maclay, C. M. (2002). Community Internet Access in Rural Areas: Solving the Economic Sustainability Puzzle. In Kirkman, G. S., Cornelius, P. K., Sachs, J. D., & Schawb, K. (Eds.), *The Global Information Technology Report 2001-2002: Readiness for the Networked World* (pp. 76–89). Oxford, UK: Oxford University Press.

Bhatnagar, S. (2003). Development and Telecommunications Access: Cases from South Asia. In Avgerou, C., & Rovere, R. L. L. (Eds.), *Information Systems and the Economics of Innovation* (pp. 33–52). Northampton, MA: Edward Elgar Pub.

Bloor, D. (1997). *Wittgenstein, Rules and Institutions*. London, UK: Routledge.

Carr, N. G. (2003, May). IT Doesn't Matter. *Harvard Business Review*, 41–49.

Castells, M. (2000a). *End of Millennium - The Information Age: Economy, Society and Culture* (2nd ed., *Vol. 3*). Malden, MA: Blackwell Publishers.

Castells, M. (2000b). *The Rise of the Network Society - The Information Age: Economy, Society and Culture* (2nd ed., *Vol. 1*). Malden, MA: Blackwell Publishers.

Charmaz, K. (2006). *Constructing Grounded Theory: A Practical Guide through Qualitative Analysis*. London, UK: Sage Publications.

Coleman, J. S. (1988). Social Capital in the Creation of Human Capital. *American Journal of Sociology*, *94*, 95–120. doi:10.1086/228943

Collis, J., & Hussey, R. (2003). *Business Research: A Practical Guide for Undergraduate and Postgraduate Students* (2nd ed.). Basinstoke, Hampshire, UK: Palgrave Macmillan.

Díaz Andrade, A. (2009). Interpretive Research Aiming at Theory Building: Adopting and Adapting the Case Study Design. *The Qualitative Report, 14*(1), 42-60. Retrieved on April 7, 2009 from http://www.nova.edu/ssss/QR/ QR-14-1/diaz-andrade.pdf

Eisenhardt, K. M. (1989). Building Theories from Case Study Research. *Academy of Management Review, 14*(4), 532–550. doi:10.2307/258557

Eisenhardt, K. M., & Graebner, M. E. (2007). Theory Building from Cases: Opportunities and Challenges. *Academy of Management Journal, 50*(1), 25–32.

Field, J. (2003). *Social Capital*. London, UK: Routledge.

Giddens, A. (1984). *The Constitution of Society: Outline of the Theory of Structuration*. Cambridgeshire, UK: Polity Press.

Glaser, B. G. (1992). *Basics of Grounded Theory Analysis*. Mill Valley, CA: Sociology Press.

Glaser, B. G., & Strauss, A. L. (1967). *The Discovery of Grounded Theory: Strategies for Qualitative Research*. Chicago, IL: Aldine Pub.

Granovetter, M. S. (1973). The Strength of Weak Ties. *American Journal of Sociology, 78*(6), 1360–1380. doi:10.1086/225469

Heeks, R. (2002). i-Development not e-Development: Special Issue on ICTs and Development. *Journal of International Development, 14*, 1–11. doi:10.1002/jid.861

Holvast, J., Duquenoy, P., & Whitehouse, D. (2005). The Information Society and its Consequences: Lessons from the Past. In Berleur, J., & Avgerou, C. (Eds.), *Perspectives and Policies on ICT in Society* (pp. 135–152). New York: Springer. doi:10.1007/0-387-25588-5_10

INEI. (2006a). Banco de Información Distrital. Retrieved June 30, 2006 from http://www.inei.gob.pe

INEI. (2006b). Perú en Cifras. Retrieved on June 20, 2006 from http://www.inei.gob.pe.

Kenny, C. (2003). The Internet and Economic Growth in Less-Developed Countries: A Case of Managing Expectations? *Oxford Development Studies, 31*(1), 99–113. doi:10.1080/1360081032000047212

Klein, H. K., & Myers, M. D. (1999). A Set of Principles for Conducting and Evaluating Interpretive Field Studies in Information Systems. *Management Information Systems Quarterly, 23*(1), 67–88. doi:10.2307/249410

Lee, J.-W. (2001). Education for Technology Readiness: Prospects for Developing Countries. *Journal of Human Development, 2*(1), 115–151. doi:10.1080/14649880120050

Lewin, K. M. (2000). New Technologies and Knowledge Acquisition and Use in Developing Countries. *Compare, 30*(3), 313–321. doi:10.1080/713657464

Maslow, A. H. (1943). A Theory of Human Motivation. *Psychological Review, 50*, 370–396. doi:10.1037/h0054346

Mchombu, K. J. (2004). Sharing Knowledge for Community Development and Transformation: A Handbook. Retrieved on September 12, 2004 from http://www.oxfam.ca/publications/ downloads/ Sharing%20Knowledge%202%20Inside%20 Pages.pdf

North, D. C. (1990). *Institutions, Institutional Change, and Economic Performance.* Cambridge, NY: Cambridge University Press.

Orlikowski, W. J., & Baroudi, J. J. (1991). Studying Information Technology in Organizations: Research Approaches and Assumptions. *Information Systems Research, 2*(1), 1–28. doi:10.1287/ isre.2.1.1

Pereyra Romo, A. (2002). *Sistematización Fase Piloto: Proyecto Sistema de Información Rural Urbano (SIRU) - Socializando Nuestra Experiencia.* Cajamarca, Perú: ITDG.

PNUD. (2002). *Informe sobre Desarrollo Humano - Perú 2002: Aprovechando las Potencialidades.* Lima, Perú: Programa de las Naciones Unidas para el Desarrollo - Oficina del Perú.

Pruett, D., & Deane, J. (1998). The Internet and Poverty: Real Help or Real Hype? *Panos Briefing.* Retrieved on June 3, 2006 from http://www. panos.org.uk/resources /reportdetails.asp

Putnam, R. D., Leonardi, R., & Nonetti, R. Y. (1993). *Making Democracy Work: Civic Traditions in Modern Italy.* Princeton, NJ: Princeton University Press.

Reyes, J. C. (2005, 12 September). Siete Millones sin Electricidad. *La República,* p. 9.

Rogers, E. M. (2003). *Diffusion of Innovations* (5th ed.). New York: Free Press.

Sen, A. K. (1999). *Development as Freedom.* New York: Alfred A. Knopf.

Slater, D., & Tacchi, J. (2004). ICT's at Works in the Hands of the Poor: Innovation and Research in South Asia. *i4d online.* Retrieved on July 6, 2004, from http://www.i4donline.net/issue/ may04/innovation_research_full.htm

Tacchi, J., Slater, D., & Hearn, G. (2003). Ethnographic Action Research. Retrieved on May 19, 2004 from http://unescodelhi.nic.in/ publications/ ear.pdf.

UNDP. (2001). *Human Development Report 2001: Making New Technologies Work for Human Development.* New York: United Nations Development Programme.

Walsham, G. (1995). Interpretive Case Studies in IS Research: Nature and Method. *European Journal of Information Systems, 4*(2), 74–81. doi:10.1057/ejis.1995.9

Walsham, G. (2001). *Making a World of Difference: IT in a Global Context.* Chichester, UK: Wiley.

Walsham, G., Robey, D., & Sahay, S. (2007). Foreword: Special Issue on Information Systems in Developing Countries. *Management Information Systems Quarterly, 31*(2), 317–326.

Warschauer, M. (2003). *Technology and Social Inclusion: Rethinking the Digital Divide.* Cambridge, MA: The MIT Press.

World Bank. (1998). Knowledge for Development. *World Development Report.* Retrieved on November 15, 2001 from http://www.worldbank. org/wdr /wdr98/contents.htm

Yin, R. K. (2003). *Case Study Research: Design and Methods* (3rd ed., *Vol. 5*). Thousand Oaks, CA: Sage Publications.

KEY TERMS AND DEFINITIONS

Digital Divide: An expression that reflects the gap between the 'haves' and 'have-nots' in terms of access to information and communication technology.

Grounded Theory: A method of analysis that builds theory from data in an inductive fashion without imposing any theoretical preconception.

Human Capital: Skills and abilities acquired by the individual that allow her/him to incorporate new information and knowledge.

Institutions: Both formal and informal habits that have been accepted by the collective group.

Networked Society: A social configuration that is characterized by the existing links among its constitutive nodes. These links are facilitated by information and communication technology.

Social Capital: The rules of reciprocity and trust existing among actors in a social group.

Chapter 5
Digital Doorways

Kim Gush
Meraka Institute, South Africa

Ruth de Villiers
University of South Africa

Ronel Smith
Meraka Institute, South Africa

Grant Cambridge
Meraka Institute, South Africa

ABSTRACT

The Digital Doorway is a joint initiative between the Meraka Institute of the Council for Scientific and Industrial Research (CSIR) and South Africa's Department of Science and Technology (DST), with a vision of making a fundamental difference to computer literacy and associated skills in the South African population. Underpinning the project is the idea of people's inherent cognitive ability to teach themselves computer skills with minimal external intervention. For this to happen, computers must be easily accessible to potential learners in an environment conducive to experimentation. Given the low percentage of communities in disadvantaged areas in South Africa with access to computer infrastructure, Digital Doorways are installed in communities where the need is greatest. The systems are extremely robust and employ open source content. The project team has moved from an action research to a design-based research paradigm, simultaneously deploying and improving the systems over the past six years. The novel method of instruction (unassisted learning) and the challenging operating environment call for both innovation and careful engineering of all aspects of the system. User interaction at the sites has been carefully observed. Numerous challenges, complexities and controversies, both social and technological, have surfaced and continue to surface as the project progresses. Valuable learning has been acquired around community engagement, ownership and site acquisition and numerous 'soft' issues that ultimately determine a project's success or failure. Both qualitative and quantitative research have been conducted. Feedback from users has been mostly positive and there is a demand both from government and private sector companies for many more Digital Doorways to be deployed throughout South Africa

DOI: 10.4018/978-1-61520-997-2.ch005

and worldwide. Sustainability, community ownership and maintenance remain the greatest challenges to the long-term success of the project. Despite the challenges, unassisted learning can be effectively used to provide basic computer literacy training in rural and impoverished communities in South Africa.

INTRODUCTION

On the outskirts of Kei Mouth in the Eastern Cape province of South Africa, lies the impoverished township of Cwili. The residents of this area were the first recipients of a public computer terminal (see Figure 2) designed by the Council for Scientific and Industrial Research (CSIR) to provide an alternative means of ICT literacy delivery, where the focus was specifically on learning without formal teacher intervention. The novel ICT education project was named the 'Digital Doorway' (DD) and from its humble beginnings in 2002, grew to a large multi-provincial drive to increase computer literacy in South Africa.

This chapter will provide an overview of the DD project, highlighting some of the technical aspects of the design, the research philosophy, various social issues encountered, and some of the lessons learned during its six years of implementation. The mix of theory, technical challenges and social aspects reflects the complexities that are encountered in projects of this nature.

BACKGROUND AND OBJECTIVES

There is a great need for increased access to computer infrastructure in South Africa and Africa. Table 1 tabulates the extent of schools with computers for five African countries.

In 2000, Dr Sugata Mitra of NIIT, India began his innovative 'Hole In The Wall' experiment by placing a computer into a recess cut in a wall. Via a video camera in a tree, he observed how members of the community interacted with this high tech device, even though they had never before used a computer (Mitra, 2000). After some months of observation Dr Mitra concluded that unassisted learning through trial and error is indeed an effective mechanism for supporting the acquisition of basic ICT literacy skills. NIIT proceeded to deploy similar devices around India (see Figure 2).

The CSIR in South Africa exists to promote basic research and to find mechanisms for that research to be turned into beneficial implementations. One of the CSIR's goals is to find ways of making a tangible improvement to the lives

Figure 1. Users, both young and old, of the first Digital Doorway (a single-terminal), in Cwili, Eastern Cape, South Africa. This DD was the first public computer in the area that was both available and accessible to the entire community and not under lock and key within a school laboratory.

Figure 2. A remote Hole in the Wall site, 40 mins drive from Jaisalmer, visited by two of the authors in December 2005

of the poorest of South African people. In 2002, the Meraka Institute of the CSIR, in conjunction with the South African Department of Science and Technology (DST), made a decision to implement a South African version of 'Hole In The Wall' in order to investigate the value of unassisted learning in a South African rural context. This marked the beginning of an extended and notable developmental project, the history of which is traced in the time line later in the chapter (Table 2).

The aim of the Digital Doorway project is, consequently, to better understand the issues behind using technology for the promotion of computer and information literacy in South Af-

rica, specifically in the context of remote, unsupervised kiosks in various impoverished areas of the country, where target users have had little or no previous exposure to computers. What began as a purely investigative research project, developed into a combination of contractual implementation and on-going research. However, sufficient flexibility is permitted within the project for the contractual side not to 'dictate' the outcomes of the research, which can be a problem where funding for a project is provided by a body outside of the research organisation (Oates, 2006:160).

Table 1. Computer penetration ratios at schools in selected African Countries, 2006. From InfoDev 'Survey of ICT Education in Africa'

Country	No of Schools	Schools with Computers	Percentage of schools with computers
Egypt	26,000	26,000	100%*
Ghana	32,000	800	2.5%
Mozambique	7,000	80	1.1%
Namibia	1,519	350	22.1%
South Africa	25,582	6,651	22.6%

*Based on figures obtained from the Ministry of Education in Egypt, 2006.

Specific Objectives

The objectives of the South African Digital Doorway initiative can be described in terms of its initial research objectives and ongoing high-level objectives.

The initial research objectives (Smith et al., 2005) were to:

- Test the viability of unassisted learning as an alternative mechanism for attaining large-scale computer literacy in South Africa
- Determine the efficiency of the DD concept as a mechanism to enable computer literacy as well as information and service delivery in South Africa
- Determine whether potential users in a rural community in South Africa would use a PC-based outdoor kiosk without any instruction (unassisted learning)
- Determine whether a PC-based kiosk could operate without supervision in an outdoor location in South Africa

- Provide a platform for the evaluation of appropriate technology solutions and open-source applications

The ongoing high-level objectives are to:

- Narrow the 'digital divide'
- Provide technology for social inclusion (Warschauer, 2002)
- Prepare users, both young and old, for the information society
- Expose users in previously disadvantaged areas to computer technology
- Provide meaningful software and content to underprivileged communities

Research Method Overview

From the outset, the project employed a dual thrust of research and implementation. The designers were concerned not only with the development of a system, but also with an understanding of how that system was being employed in its context of use. The research goal was the creation of new knowledge particularly with respect to

Table 2. Digital doorway time line

1999	Dr Sugata Mitra of NIIT, India trials a mechanism to observe 'unassisted learning' of a computer system in his 'Hole In The Wall' (HOITW) project
2000-2001	Mitra's MIE concept proven to be successful in India (Mitra 2000)
2002	Digital Doorway project commences in South Africa with introduction of single-terminal device (Gush, Smith & Cambridge, 2004)
2002-2004	Similar findings on the success of unassisted learning validated in South Africa
2003	Migration to fully open source software begins with the introduction of the Debian operating system
2004	4-terminal DD housings introduced, together with improved open source based operating system
2005	Project expanded to 24 diverse sites around South Africa for comparison purposes
2006	Xubuntu 3-terminal diskless fat client solution developed
2007	Project expansion to 100+ three-terminal sites, software refinement, initial MESH network integration prototypes
2008	Further massification (deployment of over 200 units) and system refinement. Additional single-terminal desktop system designed. Protoype solar-powered standalone container system developed
2009	Five solar powered container systems to be deployed in rural locations. Formulation of an independent entity to manage installation and maintenance of DDs commences.

unassisted learning and technology deployment in impoverished communities in South Africa. Various research strategies and data generation methods were utilized with an underlying design-based research strategy. In the iterative research and development process, further insight was provided by consultation, surveys and community case studies. Data was generated through the use of questionnaires, interviews and observation.

Researchers chose an initial site based on high poverty levels and low computer penetration in the area. Site visits were performed in order to engage with the community and assess installation requirements. A prototype system was designed, constructed and installed on site. Software containing activity-logging functionality was installed. Researchers set up video monitoring equipment to record user activity at the site.

Data gathered from the application logging and video monitoring was analysed in combination with reports from field workers appointed to observe and interview community-based users. System designers performed post-installation site visits in order to assess the effectiveness of the hardware and software from a technology perspective. The team used the analysis and assessment data to improve the design of subsequent systems, as well as to inform upgrade decisions on the existing system.

Subsequent installations employed an 'on-line' user feedback mechanism to gather qualitative data from users. In addition to this, application-usage tracking tools were designed and implemented in order to gather quantitative data of broad trends in software usage. Field workers carried out further questionnaire-based and interview-based research.

Installation deployment was extended to cover a diverse range of sites, so that comparisons could be made between urban and rural installations, as well as between sites at varying locations (schools, community centres, police stations and so on). At a certain stage of the project, an external consultation company was tasked with performing case study research and system evaluation of a number of existing sites. Qualitative and quantitative data analysis from these case studies was used to further inform the design of subsequent systems.

Evaluation was also done in conjunction with comments, suggestions and requests from community stakeholders including users, teachers and municipal officials involved at the site. Many suggestions such as the final placement of the unit and possible design modifications (e.g. the addition of an external USB port) originated from the community.

Digital Doorway Time Line

Table 2 highlights the key milestones of the DD project from initial catalyst to current deployment status.

Table 3 shows the number of DDs installed in each province, and their type of location, as of January 2009.

THE DIGITAL DOORWAY UNWRAPPED

This section briefly describes the main components of the DD innovation, in particular the hardware, software and content.

While the 'One Laptop Per Child' (OLPC) project (Negroponte et al, 2006) aims to equip each child with their own laptop, DD terminals are designed to be social entities where a number of users congregate around a central device. Users benefit from peer learning (with users physically showing other users what to do) and individual interaction with the system. The design is based around a rugged, centralized hub of activity rather than individually distributed laptops (although collaborative peer learning is possible in both instances). Rather than individual ownership of a computing device, the DD emphasizes the need for community ownership of the equipment, the rationale being that 'a little needs to go a long

Table 3. Digital doorway distribution per province (July 2009)

Location: Province:	School	MPCC	Community Centre	Library	Fablab	FET College	Other*		Total
Eastern Cape	28	1	3	1			9		42
Freestate		1			1		1		3
Gauteng	4	1			2		1		8
Kwazulu Natal	6	6					4		16
Limpopo	27	6	7	2		4	5		51
Mpumalanga	27	1	4	2			2		36
North West	8	1		1	1				11
Northern Cape	22	1		2	1		2		28
Western Cape					1		2		3
Lesotho							1		1
Total	122	18	14	8	6	4	27		199

*Church, Post Office, Police Station, Mall, Butchery, Farm, Hospice

way', with higher utilisation when the computer is shared amongst members of that community.

Hardware

From the outset the team realised the necessity of building a computer housing that was rugged, robust and vandal-proof. From an initial single terminal unit, the housing developed into a 4-terminal arrangement for greater standing capacity, and finally a space-saving 3-terminal arrangement. The current 3-terminal configuration consists of a client/file-server PC and two diskless clients ('fat clients') connected via an Ethernet switch. The system includes a separate educational content server (containing 100 Gigabytes of additional educational content), a satellite dish (for downloads only) and GPRS (cellular network) modem back-haul (for status reports and log file uploads to a central server). Other hardware designs include the Desktop DD (single terminal designed for classrooms), DD for disabled users and Solar-Container DD.

The development of the various DD housings is illustrated in Figure 4, which highlights how innovation in a real-world context led to refinement and improvement of the initial design.

The single terminal was limited in terms of the number of users, hence the move to the 4-terminal unit in 2004. This unit contained an HP441 server with multiple graphics cards and a customised operating system that could support four clients from one server, using Universal Serial Bus (USB) connections for the client mice and keyboards.

In 2005, there was a move towards accessibility, as the team designed a DD housing for use by the physically disabled. The housing had two low-level screens for wheelchair access, grab-handles to enable unsteady users to stabilise themselves, and large joysticks and oversized buttons rather than the usual touch-pad configuration.

A 3-terminal server/fat-client configuration was designed in 2006 following the withdrawal from the market of the HP441 units. There was also a requirement to reduce the cost of installed

Figure 3. Digital doorway housings

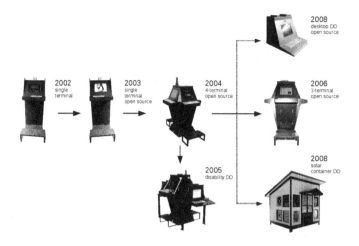

equipment while maintaining the multi-terminal functionality. This configuration is the one being used currently. A 3-terminal configuration is viewed as optimal to reduce the floor-space required, while still allowing more users to access the machine compared to the single-terminal model. In a server/client setup, the clients can be low cost machines, without hard drives. The server acts as a file server for all terminals, with associated cost savings. See the appendices for more details of the hardware. A desktop single terminal version was, however, developed for use within a classroom where extra protection was required for the PC equipment.

Figure 4. Simple representation of the research and implementation process

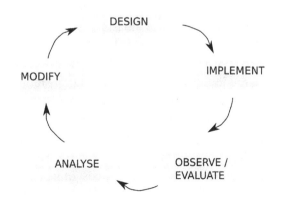

In 2008, following the requirement by the main funding agent (the Department of Science and Technology) to install DDs in the most remote areas of South Africa, a prototype self-contained solar-powered container DD unit has been developed. This unit eliminates the requirements for both power and covered floor-space at the installation site.

Software and Content

In order to stimulate users to return to the DD, and in order to support the development of information literacy skills (through return visits to the computer), there is a need for relevant and engaging software and content that stimulates curiosity. Alessi and Trollip (2001) mention two aspects of curiosity identified by Malone (1980), namely sensory and cognitive curiosity, sensory curiosity being related to images and sounds encountered, while cognitive curiosity is 'curiosity about information' (Alessi & Trollip, 2001:288). According to Alessi and Trollip, frequent renewal of what is seen on the screen helps to maintain the user's attention, stimulating sensory curiosity. A game such as Tuxmaths that is installed on the DD embodies audio and dynamic graphics to maintain attention, while simultaneously promoting the drill of solving mathematics tables.

Content and software on the DD is accessed either via icons on the desktop (high visibility) or via a customised Xfce XML menu structure / taskbar menu system (lower visibility). The menu is divided into two chief groupings, namely, 'Programs' and 'Resources'. The 'Programs' menu is subdivided into the categories of: Edutainment, Office, Internet, Games, Sounds and Miscellaneous. The 'Resources' menu is subdivided into: Simulations, Wikipedia, Agriculture, AudioBooks, Computers, Crafts, Fun, Heath and Safety, Literature, Realworld and Science. Content is stored in the form of binary applications, PDF documents, html pages, Java applications, and audio and video content files.

The Mamelodi DD (version 2) and subsequent models (4-terminal and 3-terminal) all employed one flavour or another of open source Linux software. The latest 3-terminal DD PCs employ a modified Ubuntu Linux OS with the Xfce display manager and a distributed client system, where each client becomes an independent terminal, but content is shared among all terminals. The inherent security of Linux is employed to prevent unauthorized modification of system-critical files. User-generated content saved within a home directory is modifiable by the owner of that directory only.

Prevention of desktop degradation is crucial in remote unmanaged projects of this nature. Scripts are run each evening to clean up guest (non user-generated) accounts, restore the look of the desktops, and clean up the guest directories of all extraneous files.

Various kiosk mode options were implemented in the windows manager. The options also prevented the starting up of shell scripts, locking of the screen, moving of toolbars, execution of the command line 'run' command, and the starting of a new session. This was necessary to keep the system usable.

For all the 3-terminal systems, scripts were developed to wrap each application in code that could detect when that application was accessed (see later section on application usage). Other scripts manage the compression and transmission of the log files to a centralised server accessible by the researchers.

As in the case of the hardware design, the software went through various iterations and refinements, in line with an action research or design-based research paradigm (see next section). As illustrated in Figure 9, the DD is addressing a real need in a natural setting and, as such, the content has the potential not only to inform, but also to transform the community of users.

DESIGN-BASED RESEARCH

What is the underlying research design of the Digital Doorway? The answer to this question is intrinsically related to the DD's main purpose. Is it an implementation of the emergent discipline of community informatics (CI) or is it first and foremost an educational system? If the former, then its research design requires a theoretical foundation that integrates and directs CI's double agenda of information systems (IS) problem solving and practical community problem solving (Stillman & Linger, 2009). If, on the other hand, it is primarily a technology to support learning, then it requires grounding in a research methodology that emanates from the educational sciences. A study by de Villiers (2007) on interpretive research models for informatics takes cognisance of Walsham's (1995) work on interpretivism and addresses design-research and development-research which, de Villiers posits, are implemented in IS as design-science research and in educational technology as design-based research.

That said, one returns to the issue of the DD's main vision. Although it has potential for community-based add-ons, such as community bulletin boards and community specific content generation facilities, its prime purpose was, and still is, the support of learning. Hence an educational technology research design is more appropriate than a CI- and IS- based conceptual grounding.

The concept of unassisted learning in rural South Africa as set out earlier in the section on objectives, i.e. learning without any external instruction whatsoever, is a new and challenging research area. Critics such as Warschauer (2002), have reacted against Mitra's concept of 'minimally invasive education' by calling it 'minimally effective education' due to the fact that it does not deal with important factors that play a role in acquisition of access to ICT, such as social resources (e.g community support). These aspects had to be included in the research.

The DD project has a dual thrust, involving both a research focus and an implementation drive, as in action research with its action outcomes and research outcomes (Bjerknes, Ehn, & Kyng, 1987; de Villiers, 2007; Sandberg, 1979). Through real-world experience, the developers of the DD learned the value of explicating a research design. This section highlights some of the key aspects in the research side.

The project followed an iterative process of *design, implement, observe/evaluate, analyse, modify, redesign, implement, observe* as shown in Figure 4.

As the practices of the DD progressed further to meet real-world needs, the iterative research processes became a series of cycles. The underlying research paradigm moved beyond classic action research to become an example of design-based research (DBR), an emerging and maturing research design increasingly used for studies involving the development of innovative educational technology (Barab and Squire, 2004; Design-Based Research Collective, 2003; Wang and Hannafin, 2005).

Design research owes its origin to Herbert Simon, the Nobel laureate (Simon, 1981), who distinguished between the *natural sciences* and the so-called *design sciences*. Natural sciences relate to natural phenomena such as those described in physics, astronomy and anatomy, where descrip-

tive theories and formulas explain phenomena in terms of laws and relationships. Design sciences or 'sciences of the artificial' relate to man-made objects and phenomena, where prescriptive theories and models represent goals to be achieved and procedures to achieve them. They are applied sciences, characterized by problem-solving processes, invention, construction, and evaluation of artifacts or interventions. Examples are medical technology, engineering, architecture, product design, and education with its theories and procedures. Design science led to *design research*, which in the context of e-learning and educational technology, is termed design-based research (de Villiers, 2005).

Education and learning are characterized by complex problems, which call for inventive solutions, and the associated construction and evaluation of artefacts or interventions. DBR terminology evolved from the 'design experiments' of educational practice conducted by Brown (1992) and Collins (1992), through 'development research' (Reeves, 2000; van den Akker, 1999) and 'developmental research' (Richey, Klein and Nelson, 2004) to consolidate at 'design-based'.

Features of Design-Based Research

Barab and Squire (2004:2) define DBR as an iterative 'series of approaches with the intent of producing new theories, artefacts and practices that account for and potentially impact learning and teaching in naturalistic settings'. It is suitable for problems in ill-structured environments with complex interactions. The experimental generation of new prototypes highlights the roles of cognition, intuition, creativity, inquiry and teamwork in solving problems and generating new knowledge. Claims about the functionality of a design are evidence-based, emanating from natural settings. Knowledge about an artefact thus evolves in context, and even by trial and error. In the context of e-learning technologies, Wang and Hannafin (2005) describe DBR as being:

- *Pragmatic and theoretical*: extending and generating theory while producing principles to inform and improve practice.
- *Grounded*: design of 'interventions' in real-world contexts; ideally, theory-driven, based on appropriate learning or instructional theory/ies.
- *Interactive, iterative and flexible*: designer-researcher-participant teamwork; iterative cycles; formative evaluation and usability analysis; generation of evidence to guide revision and improve design; initial prototypes.
- *Integrative*: hybrid research methods using data from multiple sources.
- *Contextualised outputs*: results connected to research setting; the design principles generated are contextually-sensitive.
- *An extension of existing methodologies:* e.g. an extension of action research

Dede (2005) expresses an intriguing concern about combining designs from the 'skills of creative designers' with research by 'rigorous scholars'. Where designers have free reign, there may be design creep as exploratory interventions evolve into full-scale initiatives instead of being bounded research. Driven by technology and not by need, a technological guru might champion a particular solution and look for situations to apply it. Pure researchers have a contrasting weaknesses called 'design constipation', as they look for designs that offer straightforward data collection and analysis, so they can retain analytic and methodological frameworks at the expense of effective, scalable and sustainable innovations (Dede, 2005). DBR can bridge this gap.

DBR fosters cross-disciplinary work - for example, in the DD project, engineers, educational researchers and sociologists were involved. This collaborative approach leads to insights in unpredictable real-world settings (Kelly (2003). In complex and ill-structured environments, the design of artefacts and the development of theories proceed concurrently, informing each other. DBR aims to influence practice with real changes at local level and to develop tangible applications that can be adopted elsewhere, although caution must be exercised in transferring context-specific claims.

Figure 5 shows the features and themes of a DBR research design. The central model in the oval with iterative processes and evaluative feedback loops, represents development research which preceded DBR (Reeves, 2000; de Villiers, 2007). The surrounding infrastructure shows how DBR has developed further. The surround depicts

Figure 5. Model of design-based research (de Villiers, 2007)

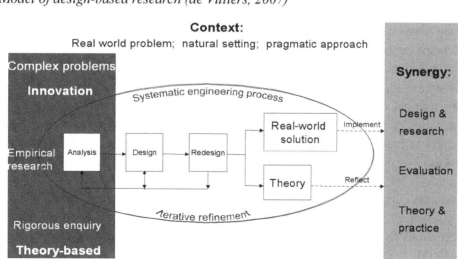

the real-world setting and its complex problems (left side) that can be addressed by innovation, empirical research and experimentation. Synergistic consequences of the reflective processes of the model (right side) are the joint advancement of design and research, and similarly of theory and practice as DBR – implemented here by the DD - sets out to change situations.

Features and Themes of DBR as Applied to the Digital Doorway

Features from the meta-analyses and reflective studies of Cobb, Confrey, diSessa, Lehrer, and Schauble (2003), the Design-Based Collective (2003), Barab and Squire (2004) and Wang and Hannafin (2005) are tabulated in Table 4 against their implementations in the DD. The right-hand column also refers to community contributions, indicating the role of users in participative research.

DATA COLLECTION AND ANALYSIS: QUALITATIVE AND QUANTITATIVE

As mentioned earlier, research data is gathered in multiple ways:

- Observation and interviewing of participants by the core DD team
- Appointment of sociologists and dedicated teams (out-sourced) to observe and interview participants, both orally and through the use of questionnaires / surveys
- Implementation of software mechanisms to capture user activity and demographics
- Implementation of software mechanism to enable users to provide feedback on their experiences.
- Video analysis of data captured via installed security cameras
- Initial assessment and evaluation of the DD installations focused on the following (Smith, 2005)

- Who used the DD, e.g. what age groups and genders?
- How many participants were present at a specific time?
- How long did they stay?
- What activities did each participant or collaborative group of participants do?
- What were the reactions of spectators?
- In each case, was there evidence that learning occurred?

Results from Observations at the Cwili Site

The following observations, taken from Smith (2003) are important in providing a general impression of activity at the very first DD. This DD kiosk in Cwili was installed and became operational without any announcement or instruction in November 2002. It was officially opened by the Minister of Science and Technology in December 2002. Initial observations commenced on 22 November 2003, and were performed by Prof. Denzil Russel, professor emeritus of Adult Education at the University of the Witwatersrand. Prof. Russell, who was staying within a few kilometres of the site, was well positioned to carry out this observational research, which included informal interviews, analysis of computer captured data, group discussions with users and non-users and systematic debriefings of the community champion and others informants. Prof. Russel made the following observations:

- Once installed the kiosk was used immediately – even during installation the interest of children, in particular, was intense.
- The kiosk was used almost continuously from as early as 4:15am to around midnight and even later.
- Group size varied: normally from 4 to 12.
- There was intense vocal activity, music and constant jostling for position.

Table 4. Summary of design-based research models and associated digital doorway features

Features of DBR models	Elaboration	As implemented in Digital Doorway
Real-world complex problems	Design theory addresses complex problems in collaboration with practitioners/ educators.	Complexities: remote and rural locations; lack of infrastructure; school teachers not computer literate. DD enthuses some of them and they in turn encourage learners to use it.
Problem solutions grounded in pre-existing theories,	Where appropriate theories/principles pre-exist, design should be theory-driven, along with technological affordances, to propose solutions to the problems.	Minimally invasive education / unassisted learning in India through the hole-in-the-wall experiment has been shown to be successful (Mitra, 2000). Children's natural curiosity motivates learning. Peer learning is a valid form of learning (Boud, D. 1999). Both curiosity and peer learning are clearly in evidence in the use of DD. Requests by users have contributed to extensions to DD features, making the users co-researchers and 'co-developers'.
Innovation	Underlying innovative approach (Kelly, 2003). DBR should investigate less-common practices and generate technological support; design of innovations, novelty, interventionist approaches.	Solution unique to Africa in terms of rugged, vandal-proof computer housing when compared to typical lab-based computers. Multi-terminal – social interaction occurs alongside learning. Fully Open Source Operating System and Content. HW and SW innovations as detailed elsewhere.
Engineering	Systematic methodology that involves designing and studying means or artefacts of learning.	Usage tracking tools used to study learning that has taken place. Statistics gathered on a site by site basis, hard data available. Subjective, qualitative data accumulated through interviews and observation.
Iterative design	Cycles of design, enactment, analysis, redesign.	Following on from first installation in Cwili, hardware and software underwent numerous design changes and improvements based on user co-participation via interviews. Further feedback obtained from observation of user interaction. Sites upgraded when major software releases are available.
Context and environment	Research studies in context, i.e. in naturalistic settings; use of artefacts/ interventions in the real-world; theories also to be contextualized; Responsive to emergent features of the setting (Kelly, 2003).	DDs are located in designated communities where a need is identified. Data gathered on site. Participative workshops involve community-based stakeholders, who offer suggestions. Authentic use in real communities.
Empirical research	Studying tangible, real-world products, which ideally, should be usable elsewhere, i.e. influence on teaching, learning and training practice. Data collection and analysis.	Data collection through observation of learners and video data, interviews and surveys. Instruments: automated logging/ recording of usage statistics. Knowledge obtained from these systems transferable to similar installations elsewhere.
Participants as collaborators	Participants are not merely subjects, but can be co-participants in the research.	In day- or half day workshops, community leaders and, in some cases, other community members joined Meraka researchers as co-participants to discuss aspects of DD implementation and usage.
Refining the artefact / system	Using formative evaluation to derive research findings; design and explore artifacts, environments, etc. with rigorous inquiry methods to refine them and define new design principles.	Hardware progression from single terminal to 4-terminal to space-saving 3-terminal. Further work led to a DD for disabled users and a desktop variety. Software refined based on experience gained from previous versions. Content increased to better meet the needs of the users.
Output products: 1.Useful real-world products 2.Development of theory	Real-world products: technical and methodological tools; frameworks; interventions; even curricula. These offer immediate value in the environment of use. Theories that are generated, evaluated and refined in a reflective cycle. They provide a set of theoretical constructs that can be transferred and adapted beyond the initial environment.	Success of initial prototypes led to rollout of more DDs. Poor electricity supply at some sites and unsuitable venues led to solar-powered DD Container. Desktop single-terminal DD. Production of a DD Software DVD. Teachers (e.g. Gatang high school) realised the value of the DD as an information resource, sending pupils there to do homework research. Theories developed around effective and ineffective systems (deployment strategies) and dealing with the rural context in the design of technology.

continued on following page

Table 4. Continued

Pragmatic	The theories developed should do real work and be supported by evidence-based claims about learning.	The success of the DD in teaching basic ICT literacy has resulted in the deployment of multiple machines, nation-wide. Evidence seen in the feedback received, and social assessment of users.
Synergy	Design and research; theory and practice; are advanced concurrently.	Project has a deployment and research phase, mutually feeding into and affecting each other.

- Random exploration was initially very prominent but this rapidly progressed to confident deliberate application.
- Peer learning was evidenced, as township children taught each other basic computer functions, including the ability to drag icons, re-arrange windows, open applications and access the Internet (available for a limited period on the Cwili and Mamelodi DDs).
- The relevant touch pad computer skills were rapidly acquired by the 7-16 age groups.
- The 7-16 age groups also acquired some general knowledge and competence in English.
- Estimated 8,300 user-visits in 3,3 months (regular user-visits 60%; occasional 40%).
- Ages of users ranged from 7 to 56 (most in the range of 10-19). (see later section for similar results from other sites)
- Gender distribution about equal, but more girls amongst regular users. (Note that in other communities, male:female ration was approximately 3:1)
- The majority of users during daylight hours were school children. Young adults (20-30 years) tended to use the computer very early in the morning and in the evening.
- A small group of users determined how to keep the computer to themselves by using a piece of wire to switch it off through a concealed hole at the side of the kiosk.

Results from Observations at the Mamelodi Site

The Mamelodi DD, installed in 2003 was the closest to the researchers' base at CSIR, and therefore the easiest to visit. This was a single terminal machine. It took a while for the news to circulate that the DD machine was for the use of anyone in the area. This is understandable, as very little was done in the way of promotion other than by word of mouth. The terminal was initially installed at the council offices, and later moved to a high school.

On average, between 15 and 30 users accessed the kiosk per day. The ages of users ranged from approximately ten years old to 40 or 50 years old (as noted from video observation). Predominantly young adults and boys seemed the most interested. Typically there were from one to three users at any one time, although on occasions there had been as many as eight users at the same time.

Initially, many users were curious to look at the machine and perhaps touch a few keys. About one in five of the people who entered the room where the terminal stood, stayed to really explore the computer system. Within a few weeks, most of the applications had been accessed, with users playing the educational games, typing words using the text editor, using the Tux Paint drawing application, accessing the Internet and capturing their image from the webcam onto file.

Much of the activity observed, involved navigating the cursor around the screen, clicking on various icons, and scrolling through the menus. It was obvious from the erratic nature of this behavior that most of these activities were new to the users. Most users had a tendency to minimize rather than close a particular application when they lost interest in it. This resulted in the system eventually becoming overloaded with open applications, and on more than one occasion KDE - the desktop environment - became unusable. It became necessary to remotely close the applications, and instigate a daily forced system reboot.

Further Observations from Early Sites

- The younger children were the most spontaneous participants. Their groups were generally larger than those of young adults and older adults, generally up to twelve in size. When children used the DD they were excited and noisy, interacting with each other much more than the older users. They were much more comfortable squeezing in front of a single terminal to work together.

- The time users spent at the DD depended to a large extent on the total number of users at a single time; whether they could use a terminal on their own; their specific purpose for using the DD; as well as their age. Users who had a workstation to themselves, older users, and users with a specific objective seemed to stay longer than children or those just exploring. Users typically stayed at the DD for 30 minutes to an hour at a time.

- Spectators also participated actively in the proceedings. Many of them moved from one workstation to another to see what the various participants were doing. They made comments and gave inputs, based on what they observed at the other workstations.

- Peer learning was evident in that especially children showed one another what to do. Young and older adults were also comfortable learning from each other and asking

for assistance, albeit less frequently than the younger users. Researchers concluded that it was clear that the users were learning without, or with minimal, help from the outside. Co-operative learning took place most of the time, usually because some of the participants had previous experience with computers. Less confident users would watch while other users interacted with the DD.

- Peer learning amongst the younger children was more a matter of competition than collaboration, whereas collaboration seemed to be the learning method of choice for young adults and older adults. All participants rapidly acquired the relevant keyboard and touch-pad skills. Children, especially, seemed content to explore until they achieved the desired outcome, rather than ask for assistance.

The Collection and Analysis of User Feedback, Demographic Data and Application Usage Statistics

In order to analyse user feedback, demographics and usage at the sites more accurately in the subsequent 3-terminal installations, two mechanisms for collecting this data and transmitting it back to a central server were designed. The first involves a simple form accessible inside a web browser on the DD where users are encouraged to provide feedback about their experiences of using the DD. Users type a message into the text window, optionally enter their name and contact details, and the message is stored locally for transmission back to a central server once a day. Secondly, for the collection of empirical demographic and usage data, the following sequence of events occurs:

- User chooses between guest account login, own login or 'new user' creation
- If new user creation is chosen, user takes action to create own user space

- User enters details (age, gender etc.) on form
- Details are added to user registration file on DD server
- File is updated once a day to communications server
- Applications on DD are launched from menu using a wrapper script (tracker)
- Wrapper script writes start time, application name and arguments to user-specific log file
- Log files are compressed together and copied to communications server once a day
- GPRS modem is used to transmit compressed log files and registration files back to central ftp server for download and analysis.

Feedback from Users

Qualitative feedback received from users has been categorised into positive, negative and suggestions. Encouragingly, when this feedback was reviewed, 49% (66 responses) comprised positive comments, 46% (63 responses) suggestions or requests and only 5% (7 responses) comprised negative comments. Examples from each category are given below.

Positive:

'Dear people of Location. Do not mass [authors: 'mess'] with this computer because it can work it help us to find important things that we don't do anything that make this computer stop to work. Please people do something best for your children. MR. Nothoriuos.' - (Cwili, 2002 – written in an electronic note saved on the Digital Doorway itself)

'hi i'm enjoying it a lot coz there are many things i''ve learn. and i'using it to find info.about how people were living long time ago.&finding out about what happening around us "ya" oh! i nealy fogort your science is absolutely great there are

many things i can say about your computers thnx a lot'"Duma" - (Ntshongweni School, May, 2007)

Suggestions:

'The learning contents that make it easy for learners to doassignments, the health contents messages to the youth about HIV and Aids. However it is very difficult for people to seek contents and transfer them into books standing. We therefore recommend that this DDW be fitted with a USB slot for esy transferance of learning contents since this DDW IS getting to be more and utelised for games.' - (Elandskraal MPCC, February 2007)

Negative:

'I am using this Digital Doorway for playing games and many other things which this machine does have. The only problem is it is stationed at a place which we usually do our home-work during free periods and many students make a lot of noise. So please may you change place?' - (Letaba College, February 2007)

Results from Quantitative Data Analysis

The results below (Gush, 2008) are based on data gathered from 75 sites around South Africa. Given that data is being collected from so many sites, each consisting of three DD terminals and multiple users per terminal, the amount of data is extensive. Numerous social insights and conclusions can be drawn from the analysis of this data. Some broad results have emerged from this process and are highlighted in the ensuing discussion.

- Sites analysed: 75
- Time period: January 2007 to January 2008
- ***Registered users***
  - Total self-registered users: 3,896
  - Average number of self-registered users per site: 52

- *Registered user versus guest user application launches (number of times a program is run)*
  - Registered users: 52,409 recorded application launches
  - Guest users: 468,433 recorded application launches

Thus, only 11.2% of activity is generated by logged in, self-registered users. Either most users have not registered their own user names or they do not log in with them or use them. Reasons for this may be the added level of complexity and computer skill required to create one's own user name, or the desire for anonymity. Logging in as a guest user is a one-step process (entering the guest login as indicated on the screen), whereas logging in as a registered user for the first time is a three-step process (typing 'new' to reach the user creation screen, entering details, logging in with the newly created user name and password). No benefits of creating a user name are indicated on the login screen, further encouraging the user merely to log in with a guest account.

Registered User Demographics

The following results were generated from 75 sites with data up to January 2008.

- **Gender:** Sixty-nine percent of all registered users indicated their gender; 31% did not. Of this 69% who specified gender, the following results emerged: Male: 75%, Female: 25%. These results vary from site to site. At a DD located in a high school exclusively for girls, feedback was mostly positive and utilisation was high, therefore the high percentage of males reflected in these general statistics is unlikely to be as a result of disinterest by females. No research was conducted to ascertain why the discrepancy exists, but it could be due to males being physically stronger than females, thus pushing them out at congested terminals (see Figure 6).
- **Age Distribution:** Plotting a graph of age (in years) on the x-axis versus number of registered users on the y-axis, yields the results shown in Figure 7.

The high percentage of registered users in the 10 – 25 age range can be attributed to the following factors:

- a number of DDs are located in schools and higher education facilities.

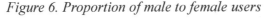

Figure 6. Proportion of male to female users

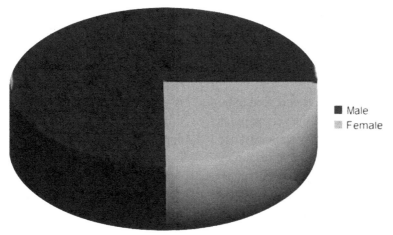

Male
Female

Figure 7. Age distribution of registered user

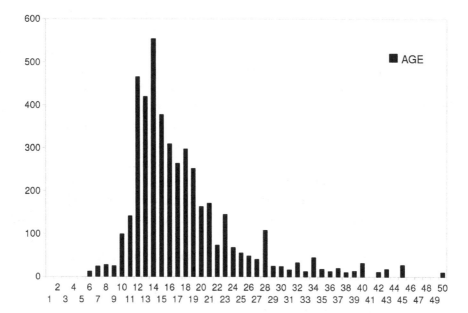

- young people are not afraid of new technology
- young people have more spare time to spend at the DD
- details of the self-registration process (the source of these results) are shared between youngsters more than adults, as the youngsters are generally more sociable and keen to share their experiences

Application Usage

Application usage data was collected from 165 sites and reflected user activity from the various installation dates until July 2009. The fifty most popular applications on the DD were identified. Grouping these results into broad categories gave the results shown in Figure 8.

While much application usage was seen to be the launching of games (such as the very popular Gnibbles), there was also a healthy amount of use of the educational applications and resources provided, such as Gcompris (an educational suite), Wikipedia and the science simulations. The platform needs to be seen as entertaining as well as educational, and not just another classroom resource, hence the pragmatic decision to retain games as part of the content.

For examples of typical user sessions at the DD, please refer to 'Snapshots of user activity' in the appendices.

FINDINGS FROM PARTICULAR SITES

Mamelodi

One of the earlier Digital Doorway sites that illustrated both the good and the bad aspects of an urban site was the one located in Mamelodi, just north of the city of Tshwane (Pretoria). Mamelodi is a residential area inhabited by close to one million people, with an unemployment figure of approximately 55% (Revised Tshwane Integrated Development Plan 2020, 2009) and many others earning very low wages. The DD terminal was housed inside a small room with a single entrance from the street, adjacent to the municipal offices.

Figure 8. Categorised application usage

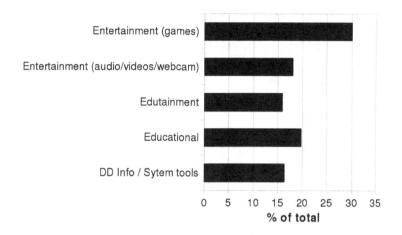

The room was modified by blocking up the door facing the municipal site and breaking out a new outward-facing door. A small roof was constructed over this door, and an antenna mounted on the roof of the building to allow connectivity with the nearby CSIR campus in Pretoria. Inside the room a security camera was mounted in one corner to record live video data of the activity at the DD. This footage could be analysed at the CSIR.

The site location was favourable in the following aspects: first, it was located in a busy street with a high density of pedestrian traffic passing by, either on their way to the municipal offices, nearby train and taxi station, or to the local street vendor selling various items. Second, parents could leave their children at the DD while they visited the municipal offices

A few months after installation however, some undesirable aspects of the site emerged: The closed room with single door entry meant that some users, especially girls, did not feel safe using the computer inside. Furthermore, the room became a shelter during rain and from time to time the home for the homeless who unfortunately left it looking and smelling bad. The provision of a trial Internet connection (via a wireless link back to the CSIR campus) resulted in the terminal regularly being used exclusively by young adults and older teenagers who used it solely as a 'free Internet

cafe', often searching for content of questionable value. From the logs it became evident that when the Internet was down, the system was used by a much wider range of ages who accessed the wealth of content cached locally on the DD. Finally, an incident was caught on film where a certain user found his way to the back of the computer and cut the cable leading to the security camera. After this point, no further video data could be gathered!

Subsequently the DD was relocated to a high school elsewhere in Mamelodi where further research could be conducted in a different context.

Pampierstad

The rural town of Pampierstad in the North West Province has a population of between 10,000 and 20,000 people (depending on radius). The DD here was an example of a successful location from a site champion perspective. The site champion (a local librarian) took ownership of the device, demonstrating his willingness to make the project a success by ensuring that a protective cage was built around the DD and by organising that plants be used to decorate the area inside the cage (see Figure 9). The librarian also requested that the DD be connected to the library printer, and would occasionally complain that he had to chase people out of the cage and library complex at 5pm when

Figure 9. Children at the Pampierstad digital doorway

the library gates were locked, an indication of the popularity of the DD.

The Pampierstad DD helped highlight the need for an enthusiastic site champion at each site.

FURTHER DISCUSSION AND FINDINGS

Hardware and Maintenance

The long-term success and sustainability of each Digital Doorway installation depends on many factors.

System ruggedness is a key requirement for unsupervised installations such as these. Only after a number of iterations did the degree to which this was true become apparent. The choice of keyboard is a good example of the many hardware aspects that underwent scrutiny, research and refinement as the project progressed. The initial choice of plastic keyboard, installed in Cwili, at the first site, did not last more than a week as enthusiastic children repeatedly plucked off the keys of the keyboard to play with them and take home as souvenirs. A second imported 'industrial' keyboard did not last more than a month or two, before the waterproof silicon coating over the keys literally disintegrated due to repeated use. The next version was a metal keyboard with metal trackball. The keyboard proved to be fine, however one enthusiastic user managed to insert a ten cent piece between the trackball and trackball housing, a feat the designers claimed was impossible until they saw the actual keyboard. Only after installing an expensive ($400-$500) metal keyboard with reinforced touch-pad, did the keyboard woes subside. The cost of the keyboard had to be weighed against the even higher cost (and effort) of repeated visits to replace a cheap keyboard.

On installation, a particular person, a 'champion', in the community must assume responsibility and accountability for ensuring the success of that DD. This responsibility must be maintained either through a paid incentive or due to the passion and commitment of this particular stakeholder. Where a community has been identified to receive a machine (top down approach), a paid incentive may be necessary. Where a DD has been requested by a particular school or community (bottom up approach), there is usually an enthusiastic person behind this request, who will ensure its ongoing success.

System failure or downtime must be reported immediately to one central call centre, rather than to the individual cell phone numbers of maintainers. In the latter case, staff may leave or change job responsibility or go on leave, and the fault is not picked up. Fault reports must be maintained so that trends can be analysed and preventative measures implemented.

In the areas of greatest poverty, the cost of the electricity to supply the DD can become an issue. Units get switched off to save electricity. This problem needs to be dealt with in a structured way upfront, as part of the installation process for each site. Where the installations are largely driven by national government, the local municipalities need to be mandated to provide an electricity budget for the machines. In schools, provision should be made for this increased cost, in the running budget of that school.

The answers to the following questions should be determined before equipment installations:

- Who owns the equipment?
- Who is responsible for its continued success?
- Who is responsible for electricity costs?
- Who will provide maintenance?
- For how long is the equipment expected to run?
- What procedure should be followed in the case of a system failure?

Community Stakeholders

For leaders and stakeholders in the community, it is important that the perceived value of the device is understood. Without this, there will not be the motivation to ensure its continued operation. In order to achieve this, time needs to be spent with community leaders before each installation. Although time consuming, this will be time well spent, as it will save money in the longer term. The machine is then perceived as a valuable asset

to the area, and is consequently better managed and cared for, reducing maintenance costs.

One potential solution to some of the above-mentioned problems is to ensure that the local municipality or local government is involved right from the outset. The municipality can then take responsibility for ensuring electricity supply and promoting the DD. This will 'institutionalize' the DD, and allow local authorities to allocate a portion of their budget to looking after the DD.

Instead of having a 'Community Champion' who has been trained merely to monitor indicators and provide feedback, it may be preferable to empower several local residents to do more detailed first-line fault finding, training them in the diagnosis and rectifying of basic errors (such as the need at times to reboot the uninterrupted power supply (UPS) after a lengthy power failure).

In regard to conducting research in similar community-based projects, it is important to ensure that community members become 'co-researchers' in the exercise, rather than mere data sources. This can be achieved through the following mechanisms:

- ensure that there is communication with the community leaders from the outset of the project
- allow typical user comments, suggestions and criticisms to inform both the design and implementation of the technologies
- use interviews, questionnaires and meetings to engage with the community and ascertain their expectations and needs; and
- be sensitive to cultural differences between those conducting the research and those in the community

Holistic and Tangible Solutions

Theory needs to be applied in real life situations. Unless words and ideas are transformed into actions, they remain powerless to change people's lives. A successful project will invariably lead to an increase in sites, and this presents its own challenges, requiring an enthusiastic core team, and partnerships with all the necessary human resource elements (communities, hardware suppliers, installation and maintenance contractors, funders and social researchers). In order to deal with the many complexities and challenges that arose, the DD team had to address problems holistically, addressing both social and technical issues. Solutions in a social context were often site specific, while technical challenges remained fairly consistent from site to site.

A critical success factor in this project was the iterative construction and installation of tangible solutions. From the very beginning, the physical DD prototypes provided a concrete object that served as a catalyst for healthy discussion. Somehow, being able to demonstrate a real model, and talk around that, rather than having to rely on documents and words only, produced enthusiasm in potential stakeholders that would have been absent otherwise. These discussions were supplemented by photographic and video presentations that further brought home the realities both of the needs in the communities and the potential of the DD to meet those needs.

Controversies

Invariably, when dealing with people, certain controversies arise as to the correct course of action. We highlight some of these issues.

Politics and Language

The impact of politics was unavoidable – community politics, regional politics and national politics. What hindered on the one hand, helped on the other. Although community engagement slowed the process down, community buy-in ensured a more successful site. Securing a suitable site often involves lengthy discussions with a number of different leaders in a community,

however, if there is full support for the project, the long term success is ensured.

While national politics added red tape, the availability of funds to install more DDs was crucial. However, issues arose around the boundaries of responsibilities. It is important, right from the outset, to define where the national government's involvement ends, and where the local or municipal government would be expected to take responsibility for the site. This is more important in installations such as community centres and recreation sites than schools (where the school typically takes ownership and responsibility for the unit).

The availability of content in all official languages of South Africa is often a contentious issue. The reality is that most content is available in English only, and translation is a lengthy and costly process. Where possible, content is made available in other languages besides English. For example, the DD on-site tutorial front page was translated into Afrikaans, Zulu, SeSotho and Venda.

Provision of Free Internet Access

Another controversial issue is the provision of free Internet access. This was tested at the Mamelodi site, with interesting results, as mentioned earlier. The high cost of Internet access in rural South Africa also made it unsustainable (the South African government does not sponsor Internet connectivity) and thus the decision was made to cache as much content as possible on site and not provide Internet access. As a consequence, the user is not able to experience the full power of social networking sites, email and access to on-line search engines, educational sites and other websites. Various ideas for overcoming the undesirable surfing activities and the high cost of Internet access have been proposed. One feasible alternative is to provide user-paid GPRS Internet access with a content filter.

Housing Colour

Seemingly innocuous design decisions and aspects of the human-computer interface often proved to be controversial, for example the choice of colour of the DD units. The point has been raised that the colours should be chosen to appeal to both boys and girls. From another perspective, funding parties preferred a colour scheme that reflected the colours of their organisation. No research was conducted to help determine the most suitable choice of colour for the housing. It has been noted that the original royal blue seems to show less dirt than the later rescue orange.

Challenge: Ensuring an Effective Installation

This section proposes two possible outcomes for an installation based on our experiences to date. The first is the 'Ineffective System' and the second is the 'Effective System', with effectiveness being defined as the ability of the DD to deliver on the expected goals of the project, namely: basic ICT literacy training; information literacy training and provision of information; and community enabling. Effectiveness can be measured more by qualitative than by quantitative means, for example, observing how users without any prior knowledge of computing, learn to navigate their way around a computer system and perform basic operations; access information; maintain attention and engagement; and eventually gain the expertise to track down information on a particular topic.

Ineffective System

In an ineffective system, see Figure 10, the device is installed in the community and, possibly following some apprehension from some of the community members about the purpose of this strange new box, excitement builds up about having access to a computer for the first time. In the weeks and months after installation, the community becomes familiar with the device and if there is no updating of content - possible via a satellite download - then users become bored and interest wanes. If there is no hardware maintenance, eventually a component will fail and the community is left with a white elephant. The resulting disillusionment of community members leaves the community in a state worse than before the device was installed.

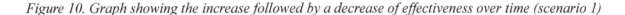

Figure 10. Graph showing the increase followed by a decrease of effectiveness over time (scenario 1)

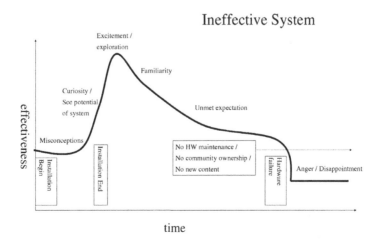

Effective System

In an effective system, see Figure 11, the content is updated regularly, and proper system maintenance is carried out. Failing components are repaired or replaced within a few days of failure. The community is involved from the outset and users take ownership of the equipment (cleaning the device and surrounding area, advertising the fact that the DD exists, informing maintenance teams of failures). The level of computer literacy of users increases. Users regularly use the device both for learning and fact finding. Peer learning takes place as knowledge is transferred between users. Proficient users are eventually able to generate their own content and the device is an undisputed boon to the community.

Experience has shown that the DD sites which become ineffective over time do so due to two main reasons: firstly, hardware failure - due to a lack of adequate system maintenance and a lack of community 'ownership' of the unit - and secondly, lack of new and stimulating content. On the other hand, where community ownership, proper system maintenance and relevant content updates are present, the site grows in popularity and becomes effective in terms of ICT literacy and community engagement. This confirms the important role of social resources in the acquisition of access to ICT as stressed by Warschauer (2002).

Due to the extremely remote locations of many sites, proper system maintenance is possible only where the status of the system can be ascertained. This is achieved either by the presence of a community champion who provides feedback to the maintainers, or by the installation of a technical mechanism for automatic site status reporting.

The Future

In the quest for improving the lives of the poorest of the poor, there is no finish line. The DD team will continue to install terminals throughout South Africa. Interest from other countries on the continent and abroad has already resulted in several DDs being installed beyond the boundaries of South Africa, including Lesotho and Ethiopia. As the challenges around installation and maintenance are resolved, an even greater focus will be given to long-term sustainability of each site through various means including sponsorship, advertising

Figure 11. Graph showing the increase and maintaining of effectiveness over time (scenario 2)

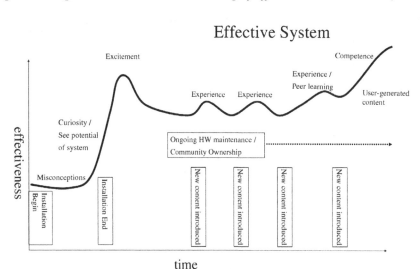

revenue, linked service provision (for example income-generating printing services) and other community-inspired initiatives aimed at sustaining equipment life. An installation and maintenance entity - separate from the research side - is currently being set up to handle the repetitive day to day aspects that occur. The issues of suitable Internet provision and user-generated content will be given greater attention, offering users more active participation. More robust clustered DD mesh networks will be created to enable communities to communicate and share information between themselves at no cost to the user. Research will continue to investigate and evaluate the long-term impact of the introduction of DDs into communities, aiming for optimal hardware and software design to serve the ICT learning needs of people in impoverished parts of the world.

CONCLUSION

ICT will continue to play an increasingly important role in the lives of people and in society in general. The development of computer literacy is a necessity, not a luxury, and developing countries are missing out on many of the advantages afforded by ICT, largely due to a lack of computer facilities as well as trained ICT teachers. Unsupervised learning, such as that afforded by the DDs provides a mechanism to promote mass computer literacy in developing countries.

From both a technical and social standpoint, this project has proved to be an interesting challenge. The team learnt a lot about the innovative use of technology in rural South Africa, but even more about the social and cultural aspects that accompany the introduction of ICTs in such communities. We were also encouraged by the quantity of positive feedback received from users of the machines and external observers of the project.

A design-based research approach has been extremely valuable in merging research with actual on-site installations. Through the introduction of equipment into real-world communities, careful observation of the use of this equipment and cyclical refinement and redesign of the equipment, the team has produced an innovative, powerful and popular device that is making a real impact in communities.

The results of open source based multi-terminal DD configuration are very satisfying. Compared to the two sites where single-terminal DDs were installed, the sites with multi-terminal DDs experienced considerably less competition for access. The various participants also had more time to interact with the DD and to consolidate their learning.

The DD initiative is feasible as a means of providing supplementary ICT literacy training, provided there is sufficient funding for both ongoing installations and maintenance of the equipment, as well as community buy-in. Community members themselves have expressed a need for more DDs. Users in underprivileged and rural parts of South Africa can now join the growing digital community. This initiative could truly open a Digital Doorway for people who have not previously had access to computing, enabling them to become computer literate.

Despite the many challenges to be faced in this daunting task of education and poverty alleviation, the excitement of community members, grateful thanks and appreciative smiles of users of Digital Doorways makes the effort worthwhile.

REFERENCES

Alessi, S. M., & Trollip, S. R. (2001). *Multimedia For Learning* (3rd ed.). Allyn & Bacon.

Balkcom, S. (1992). Cooperative learning [Online]. *The Education Research Consumer Guide*. Retrieved January 2004 from http://www.ed.gov/pubs/OR/ConsumerGuides/cooplear.html

Barab, S. A., & Squire, K. (2004). Design-based Research: Putting a Stake in the Ground. *The Journal of the Learning Sciences.*

Boud, D., Cohen, R., & Sampson, J. (1999). Peer Learning and Assessment. *Assessment & Evaluation in Higher Education,* 24(4), 413–426. doi:10.1080/0260293990240405

Brown, A. L. (1992). Design experiments: Theoretical and methodological challenges in creating complex interventions in classroom settings. *Journal of the Learning Sciences,* 2(2), 141–178. doi:10.1207/s15327809jls0202_2

Cobb, P., Confrey, J., Disessa, A., Lehrer, R., & Schauble, L. (2003). Design experiments in educational research. *Educational Researcher,* 32(1), 9–13. doi:10.3102/0013189X032001009

Collins, A. (1992). Toward a design science of Education. In Scanlon, E., & O'Shea, T. (Eds.), *New Directions in Educational Technology.* Berlin: Springer-Verlag.

Collins, A., Joseph, D., & Bielaczyc, K. (2004). Design research: Theoretical and methodological issues. *Journal of the Learning Sciences,* 13(1), 15–42. doi:10.1207/s15327809jls1301_2

de Villiers, MR (Ruth). (2007). Interpretive research models for Informatics: action research, grounded theory, and the family of design- and development research *Alternation,* 12(2), 10-52. (Dated 2005, appeared 2007).

Dede, C. (2005). Why design-based research is both important and difficult. *Educational Technology,* 45(1), 5–8.

(2002). *Department of Science and Technology.* Pretoria: South Africa's National Research and Development Strategy.

Fox, N. (1998). How to use observation in a research project [Online]. *Trend Focus Group.* Retrieved November 2003 from http://www.trent-focus.org.uk/resources/ how%20to%20use%20 observations.pdf

Gush, K. (2004). *Open Source and the Digital Doorway.* Paper presented at the Idlelo Conference, Cape Town, January 2004.

Gush, K. (2008). Towards a more personalised user experience and better demographic data on the Digital Doorway public computer terminals. *5th Prato Community Informatics & Development Informatics Conference 2008: ICTs for Social Inclusion: What is the Reality?* Conference CD. 27 October-30 October, Monash Centre, Prato Italy. December 2008. Editors: Larry Stillman, Graeme Johanson

Gush, K., Smith, R., & Cambridge, G. (2004). *The Digital Doorway, Minimally Invasive Education in Africa.* Paper presented at the ICT In Education Conference, Cape Town, March 2004.

Herron, R. E., & Sutton-Smith, B. (Eds.). (1971). *Child's Play.* New York: John Wiley and Sons.

Homer-Dixon, T. (2000). *The ingenuity gap.* New York: Knopf.

InfoDev Survey of ICT Education in Africa. (2006). Retrieved January 2009 from http://www.infodev.org/en/Project.7.html

Intel Teach Program – South Africa Case Study, (2006). Retrieved January 2009 from http://download.intel.com/ pressroom/kits/education/teach/ SouthAfrica-IntelTeachProgram.pdf

Kelly, A. E. (2003). Research as design. *Educational Researcher,* 32(1), 3–5, 35–37. doi:10.3102/0013189X032001003

Kirby, J. R., Knapper, C. K., Maki, S. A., Egnatoff, W. J., & Van Melle, E. (2002). Computers and Students' Conceptions of Learning: The Transition from Post-Secondary Education to the Workplace. *Journal of Educational Technology & Society*, *5*(5), 47–55.

Mbeki, T. (2002). State of the nation address. Retrieved 2008 from http://www.info.gov.za/ speeches /2002/0202281146a1001.htm

Mitra, S. (2000). *Minimally Invasive Education for mass computer literacy*. Paper presented at the CRIDALA 2000 Conference, 21-25 June 2000, Hong Kong.

Mitra, S. (2002). Experiments in Bangalore, Karnataka. Retrieved November 2003 from http:// niitholeinthewall.com/home

Negroponte, N., Bender, W., Battro, A., & Cavallo, D. (2006). One Laptop per Child. Retrieved August 2009 from http://olpcnews.com/presentations/ olpc-nov-2006t.pdf

Reeves, T. C. (2000). Socially Responsible Educational Technology Research. *Educational Technology*, *40*(6), 19–28.

Revised Tshwane Integrated Development Plan 2020 (2009). Retrieved Julyk 2009 from http:// www.tshwane.gov.za/ documents/idp2020/

Richey, R. C., Klein, J., & Nelson, W. (2004). Developmental research: Studies of instructional design and development. In Jonassen, D. (Ed.), *Handbook of Research for Educational Communications and Technology* (2nd ed., pp. 1099–1130). Mahwah, NJ: Lawrence Erlbaum Associates, Inc.

Russel, D. (2003). *Minimally Invasive Education pilot project: Cwili Village. Interim evaluation report on the Digital Doorway pilot site in Cwili Village* (pp. 1–12). Eastern Cape.

Rysavy, S. D. M. & Sales, G. C. (1991). *Cooperative Learning in Computer-based Instruction Educational Technology Research and Development*. Lecture notes distributed in 'The teacher as a competent professional educator' at Southeast Missouri State University, Spring 1998.

Sampson, D., Karagiannidis, C., Schenone, A., & Cardinali, F. (2002). Knowledge-on-Demand in e-Learning and e-Working Settings. *Journal of Educational Technology & Society*, *5*(5), 107–112.

SearchEnterpriseLinux.com. TechTarget (2008). Retrieved January 2009 from http://searchenterpriselinux.techtarget.com /sDefinition/0,sid39_ gci212709,00.html

Simon, H. A. (1981). *The sciences of the artificial* (2nd ed.). Cambridge, MA: MIT Press.

Smith, R., Cambridge, G., & Gush, K. (2003). *Curiosity cures the knowledge gap - Cwili township Digital Doorway project: a case study*. CSIR.

Smith, R., Cambridge, G., & Gush, K. (2005). *Unassisted Learning – Promoting Computer Literacy in Previously Disadvantaged areas of South Africa*. Paper presented at the WSIS Conference, 2005.

Stillman, L., & Linger, H. (2009). Community Informatics and Information Systems: Can They Be Better Connected? *The Information Society: An International Journal*, *25*(4), 255–264.

Tapscott, D. (2003). *Future Leaders*. McGraw-Hill. Retrieved February 2004 from http://www. growingupdigital.com

The Design-Based Research Collective. (2003). Design-based research: An emerging paradigm for educational inquiry. *Educational Researcher*, *32*(1), 5–8. doi:10.3102/0013189X032001005

Van den Akker, J. (1999). Principles & Methods of Development Research. In van den Akker, J., Branch, R. M., Gustafson, K. L., Nieveen, N., & Plomp, T. (Eds.), *Design Approaches and Tools in Education and Training*. Dordrecht: Kluwer Academic Publishers.

Van den Akker, J. (2002). The Added Value of Development Research for Educational Development in Developing Countries. In K. Osaki, W. Ottevanger C. Uiso & J. van den Akker (Eds), *Science Education Research and Teacher Development in Tanzania*. Amsterdam: Vrije Universiteit, International Cooperation Center.

Walsham, G. (1995). The emergence of interpretivism in IS research. *Information Systems Research*, 6(4), 376–394. doi:10.1287/isre.6.4.376

Wang, F., & Hannafin, M. J. (2005). Design-based research and technology-enhanced learning environments. *Educational Technology Research and Development*, 53(4), 5–23. doi:10.1007/BF02504682

Warschauer, M. (2002). Reconceptualizing the Digital Divide. [Online]. Retrieved July 2009 from http://firstmonday.org/htbin/cgiwrap/bin / ojs/index.php/fm/article/view/967/888

APPENDIX

Hardware

Figure 12 indicates the various hardware elements contained inside the 3-terminal DD housing (square box) as well as the network elements that make up the entire system.

In addition to the hardware displayed in the diagram, the server is connected to a bluetooth dongle, and the GPRS antenna is housed inside a custom-constructed radome that allows the signal to propagate outwards while the antenna remains protected inside the radome. Each terminal has its own webcam.

As mentioned earlier, it is critical that the maintenance team be informed when a remote system stops functioning. A mechanism for providing update status information of each site has been included in the design. The GPRS modem is employed to transmit a 'sign of life' signal back to a central server which keeps a record of all sites and their current status.

The existence of actual machines in the field served to inform the research side of the project at all stages, providing good synergy between design and research as the project matured.

Specialised Content

What-What Mzansi (quiz game)

This game was developed for the DD to provide content matter specifically relevant to South Africa. The game takes the form of a question and answer session, with correct answers increasing the participant's score. A locally developed musical score and local voice talent ensure that the game is engaging and contextual.

Figure 12. Digital Doorway hardware and network components

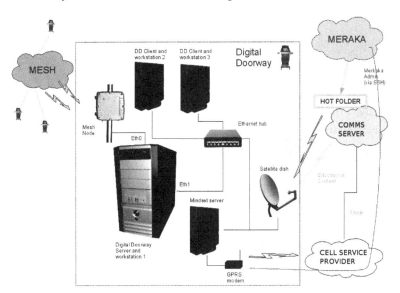

Figure 13. Screen shot of the What-What Mzansi quiz game

Themba's Journey (Life Skills Game)

This game is multi-lingual, custom-designed and implemented to teach basic life skills in the context of a journey from the countryside into the city. It is authentic, situated in the real world, as the main character is faced with choices (e.g. whether or not to take drugs). The user decides on a course of actions, with each action having direct consequences, favourable or unfavourable.

Snapshots of User Activity

The following three snapshots were generated using data received via satellite and illustrate typical user activity at a site.

Snapshot 1:

Location: Multi purpose community center - MPCC
Participant: 12 year old male
Logged in at: Thursday, 17h57
Last recorded activity: 18h46
Analysis period: 49 mins, 17h57 - 18h46
17h57 – 18h00: Webcam application
18h00 – 18h01: Digital Doorway Homepage
18h01 – 18h04: 'Potato Guy' graphical application
18h04 – 18h05: Inkscape vector illustrator
18h05 – 18h06: 'Little Miss Spider' movie
18h06 – 18h08: Electricity document
18h06 – 18h32: Wikipedia (open encyclopedia)

Figure 14. Screen shot of Themba's Journey game

18h32 – 18h40: Science of rollercoasters
18h40 – 18h41: Beginner's guide to electronics
18h41 – 18h45: NASA videos
18h45 – 18h46: Theory of relativity document

It is notable that, although the user tended to application hop, he spent 26 minutes (more than half his time) on Wikipedia, followed by 14 minutes on scientific applications.

Snapshot 2:

Location: Rural High School
Participant: 14 year old male student
Logged in: Saturday, 15h30
Analysis period: 1 hour 20 mins, 15h30 - 16h50
15h30 – 15h50: Mindset (curriculum based educational content)
15h50 – 15h57: File manager navigation
15h57 – 16h22: Mindset (curriculum based educational content)
16h22 – 16h27: 'Little Miss Spider' fun movie
16h27 – 16h41: Webcam application
16h41 – 16h43: 'Sol' game
16h43 – 16h43: 'Gcompris' educational activities
16h43 – 16h44: 'Kmplot' plotting application
16h44 – 16h45: 'Kasteroids' game
16h45 – 16h50: 'Potato Guy' graphical application

This user must have decided to come in on a Saturday to use the computer. The initial 20 minutes were spent on the Mindset educational material initially. Thereafter his activities turned to less serious pursuits.

Snapshot 3:

Location: Public library
Participant: 19 year old female
Logged in at: Thursday, 15h25
Last recorded activity: 17h05
Analysis period: 1 hour 40 mins, 15h25 - 17h05
15h25 – 16h29: Wikipedia (open encyclopedia)
16h29 – 16h30: NASA video clip
16h30 – 16h33: 'Electricity and magnetism' document
16h33 – 16h36: 'Health and Safety – electricity' document
16h36 – 16h40: 'HIV Aids facts' document
16h40 – 16h42: 'Beef – cattle castration' document
16h42 – 16h43: 'Are my pigs healthy' document
16h43 – 16h44: 'Alice in wonderland' story
16h44 – 16h47: Science simulations application
16h47 – 16h48: 'Lowfat cookbook' document
16h48 – 16h51: Wikipedia (open encyclopaedia)
16h51 – 17h05: Science simulations

This user spent the first hour and 5 minutes browsing the on-line encyclopaedia (Wikipedia). It is interesting to note that the science simulation applications were visited briefly at 16h44 (for three minutes) and then again at 16h51 (for thirteen minutes), a good indication that she had become aware of that particular application and actively sought it again at a later stage.

Chapter 6

Information and Communication Technologies in Administrative Reform for Development:
Exploring the Case of Property Tax Systems in Karnataka, India

Shefali Virkar
University of Oxford, UK

ABSTRACT

This chapter critically examines the role of Information and Communication Technologies (ICTs) in governmental reform processes in development through a case study of the Indian State of Karnataka. This study explores the increasing use of ICTs for property taxation and its impact on municipal government reform processes within this developing world context. The case study is focused on a collaboration between the government of the Indian state of Karnataka and the eGovernments Foundation (a non-profit private sector organisation) between 2002 and 2006. This collaboration was designed to reform existing methods of property tax collection by establishing an online system across the municipalities of 56 towns and cities within the state. The case study describes the interactions between new technologies and changing information flows in the complexities of public administration reform. In doing so, this paper examines the interplay of local and external factors shaping the project's implementation. On the basis of this analysis, this case study suggests that disjunctions in these local and external relationships have inhibited more effective exploitation of ICTs in this development context.

INTRODUCTION

Technology, twentieth century modernists prophesied, would dramatically alter the landscape of local, national and international politics. Although the idea of a communications network spanning the globe is not new, the past decade has witnessed the burgeoning growth of new Information and Communications Technologies (ICTs), such as the Internet, which reached nearly one-quarter

DOI: 10.4018/978-1-61520-997-2.ch006

of the world by 2009. The diffusion of ICTs has enabled the electronic production, transmission, processing, communication, and consumption of increasingly vast quantities of information. What effect will technological change have on the political and governmental arena? Historically, developments in communication technologies have resulted in changes in the way in how governments function, altering existing administrative processes and challenging public agencies to find new ways in which to communicate and interact with their citizens. Today, ICTs are seen to possess the potential to change institutions as well as the mechanisms of service delivery, bringing about fundamental changes in the way governments operate and transforming the relationships between governments and citizens (Misra, 2005).

This chapter engages with issues related to the use of ICTs in the governmental process through a case study of the use and impact of the Internet and Internet-related technologies on municipal government within a developing world context. Given the paucity of empirical research on the interaction between the context of development administration and the process of technology adoption, this paper attempts to trace a collaboration between the government of the Indian state of Karnataka and the eGovernments Foundation (a not-for-profit private sector organisation) between 2002 and 2006. This collaboration was targeted at reforming existing methods of property tax administration within the state and, in the process, establishing a system of online property tax collection across its 57 towns and cities. The case study examines the interplay of local contingencies and external influences, finding them to play a key role in the project's implementation and eventual impact.

GOVERNANCE, GOVERNMENT AND ICTs: A CONCEPTUAL EXPLORATION

Since the 1980s, the accelerating pace of globalisation has prompted the growth of literature on how globalisation affects governance. This literature is comprised of a number of disparate "islands of theory" that focus on small parts of the larger question of the impact of globalization. Three domains of thinking have emerged as the most popular within development discourse over the past few years.

The first is that of the 'race to the bottom'; where national governments, locked in fierce competition to keep highly mobile capital within their borders, are forced into lowering labour and environmental regulatory standards and reducing spending on social welfare (Legrain, 2002). Another cluster of literature focuses on the growing importance of non-state actors such as Multinational Corporations (MNCs), non-governmental organisations (NGOs), and transnational activist networks. A third cluster focuses on the ability of international institutions to effectively support global governance (Drezner, 2004). While distinct, these different strands of thinking share one basic conclusion: rapid development is leading national and international actors to place tremendous demands on the state and its institutions, such as demands for increased accountability and transparency in political decision-making and bureaucratic functioning.

During the same period, discourse and scholarly activity, both in academic and policy circles, has shifted its focus away from a more centralised, top-down conceptions of 'government' – those formal institutions and processes which operate at the level of the nation state to maintain public order and facilitate collective action (Stoker, 1998) – towards the more bottom-up notion of 'governance' and its reshaping and improvement. The idea of governance, while traditionally a synonym for government, has been captured in recent theoretical work as signifying 'a change in the meaning of government referring to a new process of governing; or a changed condition of ordered rule; or the new method by which society is governed' (Rhodes, 1996, pp. 652-53) by a set of relationships between the state, the market and society. Governance is thus seen to be concerned with crafting the *conditions* for ordered rule and collective action, comprised by those "…complex mechanisms, processes, relationships and institutions through which citizens and groups articulate their interests, exercise their rights and obligations and mediate their differences" (Cheema, 2005, p.5). Governance may be said to consist of two distinct but complementary elements: that of *government* – which encompasses all the formal institutional and legal structures of a country, and *democracy* – which can be said to refer to the participative and deliberative processes which operate within those structures.

The idea of 'good governance' has become, in recent years, an important criterion to determine a country's credibility and respect on the international stage. This is particularly true for developing countries with respect to the flows of aid and international investments, where there has been a growing trend to link measures of the quality of governance with the amount of aid and investment provided to them. Increasingly, evolving assumptions in development communities, as reflected in trade agreements and the conditions demanded by donors, such as industrialised countries and international donor organisations, suggest that the quality of a country's governance can be judged by the degree to which its institutions and processes are transparent, accountable to its citizens, and participatory, allowing citizens to participate in decisions that affect their lives.

Good or democratic governance, to paraphrase Cheema (2005), is in evidence when the authority of the government is based on the will of the people and is responsive to them, when open democratic institutions allow full participation in political affairs and when human rights protections guarantee citizens the right to speak, assemble and dissent (Cheema, 2005). Good governance thus addresses the allocation and management of resources to respond to collective problems, and is characterised by the principles of participation, transparency, accountability, the effective rule of law, equity and strategic vision (Cheema, 2005).

In the parlance of the development community, *accountability*, *transparency* and *integrity* are billed as essential elements for the effective functioning of democratic institutions and processes and the attainment of good governance. While these principles are not limited to the public sector alone, and impact the operations of both private organisations and civil society bodies, their application to the assessment of public institutions is critical as these bodies are responsible for the generation and allocation of public funds and the provision of public goods and services in the economy (Cheema, 2005). This idea is gradually gaining a foothold in the developing world, where a major development strategy since the 1980s has been to reshape and improve governance (Misra 2005), chiefly through an active agenda of slimming down the state, increasing the efficiency of public services, and extending the range of public-private working relationships (Minogue, 2002), but also focusing on making government participatory, accountable and transparent, and ensuring that the voices of the poorest and most vulnerable are heard.

Worldwide enthusiasm for the potential of ICTs has made its mark on the concept of good governance. The promise has led to conceptions of electronic-governance or 'e-Governance', a concept that may cover the use of all Information and Communication Technology platforms and applications by the public sector (Ronaghan, 2002). For the purposes of this chapter, e-Governance will be defined as: "the use of ICTs by government, civil society and political institutions to engage citizens through dialogue to promote greater participation of citizens in the process of institutional governance" (Bhatnagar, 2003c, p.1). This may be achieved through the use of ICTs to improve information and service delivery and in encouraging citizen participation in the decision-making process, thereby making government more transparent, accountable and efficient (Misra, 2005), and involves the governing or management of a system using electronic tools and techniques, wherever government offers services or information. Therefore, the essential aims of e-governance are:

- To initiate a process of reform in the way Governments work, share information and deliver services to external and internal clients.
- To produce greater transparency in the functioning of government machinery.
- To help achieve greater efficiency in the public sector.
- To deliver services to citizens and businesses on-line targeting tangible benefits such as convenient and universal access (time and place) to such services, and lowering transaction time and costs (Bhatnagar, 2005).

The term e-governance thus encompasses both the installation of computers and computer operations in public organisations, and the creation of systems wherein electronic technologies are integrated with administrative processes, human resources and the desire of public sector employees to dispense services and information to people fast and accurately. It consists of the political but also the technical aspects related to the improvement of public sector management capacity and citizen participation (Bhatnagar, 2003c).

Conceptually, e-Governance may be divided into e-Democracy (defined by an express intent to increase the participation of citizens in decision-making through the use of digital media) and e-Government (the use of Information and Communication Technologies by government departments and agencies to improve internal functioning and public service provision). Some have also used the term e-Government for Development, underscoring its potential for developing nations [This term is used by the e-Government programme of the United Nations University International Institute for Software Technology.] e-Government is hence not just about the Internet and the use of Internet- and web-based systems with government and citizen interfaces (Heeks, 2006); instead it includes office automation, internal management, and the management of information systems and expert systems (Margetts, 2006). In short, it is a process of reform in the way governments work, share information and deliver services to internal and external clients by harnessing the use of digital information and communication technologies – primarily computers and networks – in the public sector to deliver information and services to citizens and businesses (Bhatnagar, 2003a). Broadly speaking, e-government may be further divided into 2 distinct areas: (1) e-Administration, which refers to the improvement of government processes and to the streamlining of the internal working the public sector using ICT-based information systems; and (2) e-Services, which refers to the improved delivery of public services to citizens through ICT-based platforms.

e-Government has become an influential concept for the reform of public administration, and is increasingly being seen as the answer to a plethora of problems that country governments at all levels face in serving their citizens effectively (Heeks, 2000). Information and communication technologies have the potential to bring about rapid changes in management patterns such as the breakdown of traditional administration hierarchies and the streamlining of decision-making within and across agencies. The use of information technology in government is thus generally rolled out as part of a broader reform or change-management agenda whereby new technology is introduced to solve existing problems. The reengineering of administrative processes is possibly the most important step for implementing an application (Bhatnagar, 2004), as it requires that an agency implements substantial reform in its organisational structure since using ICTs with out-dated or inappropriate processes has a tendency to increase inherent inefficiencies and corruption by providing opportunities for officials to perform corrupt activities faster and avoid detection (Pathak & Prasad, 2005). In particular, reengineering includes changing the mindset and culture of the organisation's employees, training employees and improving skill sets, and the implementation of appropriate supporting ICT infrastructure to enable online processes that are useful to both the user and the implementing organisation. It begins with the mapping of existing methods and procedures, usually followed by the simplification of these procedures in such a way that the overall task can be completed in as few steps as possible (Misra 2005). The outcome of such an exercise is thus usually the modification of processes resulting in fewer steps, a reduction in the number of people needed to perform tasks, and the automation of certain operations; particularly as a result of complete back-end computerisation.

From a citizen perspective, services can be delivered more rapidly, with shorter processing and information retrieval times increasing the quality and efficiency of service delivery. Waiting times may be reduced, as routine cases are dispensed with quickly and access to different databases allows civil servants to cut down processing times. Citizens also have easier access to service agencies through, for example, information kiosks and have access to public information at the click of a button. Increased access to services can stimulate the openness of government, enhancing organisational transparency, increasing accountability and reducing corruption by taking away discretion, curbing opportunities for arbitrary action and increasing chances for disclosure (Bhatnagar, 2003c). Indeed, e-government pilots in some developing countries have demonstrated a marked positive impact on corruption, transparency and quality of service (Bhatnagar, 2003a). Thus, although the term e-government is primarily used to refer to the usage of ICTs to improve administrative efficiency, it arguably produces other effects that would give rise to increased transparency and accountability, reflect on the relationship between government and citizens and help build new spaces for citizens to participate in their overall development (Gasco, 2003).

URBAN PUBLIC ADMINISTRATION REFORM AND ICTs: THE INDIAN EXPERIENCE

India, according to the 2001 national census, has a population of 1.2 billion people – 1/6 of the world's population – living in 5000 towns and cities and 581,000 villages across the country (Misra, 2005). By 2025, it is estimated that the population will touch 1.5 billion people, living in 10,000 towns and 700,000 villages. The country faces the enormous and unenviable challenge of managing and improving the quality of life of its people living in fast growing and changing local communities – both urban and local.

In India, public administration has been evolving ever since its initial inception during the British colonial period (Huque, 1994), and in more recent times there have been calls from many quarters for a more comprehensive reform of the system. The development of urban governance structures has its roots well after Independence when, in 1954, The Central Council of Local Self-Government was created to coordinate urban development issues between the centre and states under Article 263 of the Indian Constitution (Rao, 1986). In 1991, two separate Constitutional amendment bills were introduced, covering *Panchayats* (rural local bodies) and municipalities respectively. These were passed by both houses of parliament towards the end of 1992, ratified by more than half the state assemblies, and brought into force as the 73rd and 74th amendments to the Constitution of India in 1993. The 74th Amendment, known as the *Nagarpalika Act* (Singh & Misra, 1993), is particularly relevant to this paper as it provided a parallel set of reforms for urban and transitional areas. Under the Amendment, the composition of municipalities remained under the guidelines of the states, subject to the population categories outlined (5,000 to 10,000 for a *nagar panchayat*, 10,000 to 20,000 for a municipal council, etc.). *Nagar panchayats* (half-way urban/rural governance structures) were to be constituted for areas in transition from rural to urban, and, for most purposes, were combined with existing municipalities. An important feature was the legislative creation of tiers within larger municipalities, in the form of wards and zones, each with their own committees.

The emphasis of reform programmes which deal with both urban and rural local government structures has thus been on the devolution of responsibilities for district planning to locally elected representatives (Madon & Bhatnagar, 2000), with the central goal of all these initiatives being to improve access to information leading to more informed, better-reasoned decision-making. As municipal or other urban governments in India derive their status and powers solely from state level legislation, laws and practice have varied substantially across states, and in some respects – as is the case with rural local government bodies – urban local government bodies are relatively restricted in the scope of their activities. Urban bodies are, however, relatively more fiscally self-reliant than rural government agencies (cf. Bhagwan, 1983; Datta, 1984; Rao, 1986; Sachdeva, 1991 and Singh, 1996), and derive most of their revenue through the levying of various localised taxes including Octroi and other transport duties and – more recently – Property Tax.

Following the abolition of transport taxes in most parts of the country, property tax has become a major source of revenue for local government bodies; particularly those located in urban areas (Urban Local Bodies or Municipalities), and oftentimes constitutes more than 50% of the overall revenue generated. However the levying of property tax, whilst making significant contributions to municipality coffers, has been subject to its own problems. On the one hand, tax collection systems across states usually lack uniformity and are generally characterised by the presence of outdated procedures for assessment and collection (Datta, 1984), and on the other, municipal authorities are often beset by procedural inadequacies, with administrative problems, legal issues and corrupt practices eroding the tax

yield from within (cf. Datta 1984, Rao 1986). In particular, a distinct lack of accountability, political interference, poor information collection and disorganisation, all discourage the efficient enforcement and use of such taxes effectively, and tend to result in a large proportion of city properties escaping the tax net, to the extent that an annual average collection efficiency of more that 60% is rarely achieved (NIUA, 2004). Ineffective revenue collection ensures that, even in the relatively prosperous parts of Indian cities, constraints are imposed on the quality of local public goods and services like as water, electricity, garbage collection, and roads in such a manner that their level of provision is strikingly low and that existing inefficiencies inherent in public service provision are even further compounded. A quick back-of-the-envelope calculation indicates that current tax revenue figures are a definite cause for national concern, as while urban area revenues constitute over 55% of the national gross domestic product (GDP), urban municipal revenues make up only a paltry 0.6% and grow at a slower rate than central or state revenues (NIUA, 2004). This implies that – even at the best of times there are not enough funds for good roads, clean water and 24-hour electricity for consumption by urban residents across the country.

Parallel with these developments has been the advent of the 'Information Age' in India, and the increasing recognition of the great potential of ICTs to contribute to the public reform process. India has been at the forefront of Asia's information technology boom for some time now, and has recently emerged as one of the largest investors in e-government initiatives in the Asia-Pacific region. While the Indian government has in the last decade widely acknowledged that the expanded use of ICT in the public sector can offer important benefits such as improved planning and monitoring mechanisms, cost savings through rationalisation and more effective administration and delivery of certain public services (Madon, 2004). Overall, however, progress is still slow, with just a handful of Indian states - such as Andhra Pradesh, Karnataka, Kerala and Gujarat - having built a few service delivery applications which aim to cover the delivery of specific services to a large proportion of their population (Bhatnagar, 2003a).

In order to further the analysis of issues affecting the impact of ICTs on administrative reform in India, this chapter sets out a four-fold categorisation of existing e-government projects in India. Case studies may be discussed along different axes depending on the level of the participating government agency, the geographic focus of the project (rural or urban), the nature of the initiating agency, and the central relationship impacted by the project. The four categories which may be derived from this author's research are explored briefly below:

Level of Government: Case studies may be classified according to the level of government at which they are implemented; more specifically as projects implemented by local government agencies, at the level of the state government, or at the national government level.

a. **Local Government:** includes those e-governance projects of note which are initiated at the level of local government.

b. **State Government:** covers those e-governance projects initiated by state government departments and agencies.

c. **National Government:** Those e-governance initiatives begun by or within national government ministries and other national-level agencies and institutions.

Geographic Focus: Projects may also be categorised and discussed according to the location of their target audience or in terms of the section of the population from whom feedback is sought – namely rural or urban populations.

a. **Rural:** Those projects whose target population or target audience is primarily based in rural areas.

b. **Urban:** Those projects that impact people living primarily in urban areas.

Nature of Collaborative Process: e-Governance projects may also be classified according to nature of the initiating agency or according to the context of the political dynamic between the public and private sectors within which the project was conceived and implemented. More specifically, they may be discussed as government-led initiatives, civil society-led projects, or collaborative ventures.

a. **Government-led Initiatives:** are projects initiated either wholly by government departments and agencies or those in which the government take a leading role.

b. **Civil Society-led Projects:** include those projects initiated within the broader sphere of governance, involving efforts initiated wholly or primarily by civil society bodies and Non-Governmental Organisations.

c. **Collaborative Ventures:** cover those projects initiated across sectors, generally conceived as a joint venture between a government agency and a private sector/ civil society entity, and having a variety of different stakeholders.

Central Relationship Impacted: The final axis against which case studies may be classified is based on the central relationship impacted by the project under study. Existing projects deal with improving government-to-government functioning, government-to-citizen interactions or government-to-business dealings.

a. **Government to Government:** Electronic service delivery can result in productivity gains within government organisations. Data may be easily shared across government agencies electronically, resulting in a tighter monitoring of employee productivity, the identification of bottle-necks in service delivery, and the accumulation of historical data which may be mined for policymaking purposes.

b. **Government to Citizen:** A number of States across India have developed online systems for the delivery of municipal services to their citizens. Citizens benefit from shorter processing times, the availability of a plethora of services in one place, fewer visits to government departments, greater government accountability and reduced corruption through the elimination of intermediaries.

c. **Government to Business:** These projects involve the online delivery of public services to businesses and industry and include systems such as tax collection and e-procurement, thus providing businesses with an easier channel through which they may interact with government.

PROPERTY TAX AND E-GOVERNMENT IN INDIA: THE CASE OF KARNATAKA STATE

The state of Karnataka is particularly interesting when studying the various initiatives related to the introduction of information technology in different Indian government departments as the ongoing processes of change in the state have the use of ICTs deeply implicated in them. Karnataka is the eighth largest state in India both in area and in population (Centre for Policy Research, 2001), and is the fourth most industrialised state in India after Maharashtra, Gujarat and Tamil Nadu. According to the 2001 National Census Report, the population of Karnataka is 17.62 million people (Third State Finance Commission, 2007), of which over one-third live in urban areas (Directorate of Municipal Administration, 2003). Most of the urban population lives in Class I cities – cities with a population of over a 100,000 people.

Urban Local Bodies (ULBs) in Karnataka were recently reconstituted into a four tier system:

City Corporations, administering cities with a population of more than 300,000; City Municipal Councils, which govern those cities that have a population of between 50,000-300,000 people; Town Municipal Councils, which oversee the running of towns that have a population of between 20,000-50,000 people; and Town Panchayats, which administer those towns that have a population of not less than 10,000 people. There are currently 211 urban local bodies in the state, comprising 8 City Corporations, 37 City Municipal Corporations, 93 Town Municipal Corporations, and 68 Town Panchayats plus 5 Notified Area Committees (Third State Finance Commission, 2007) - which together are run and administered by a total of 6,896 elected representatives. The ULBs in Karnataka are governed chiefly by three Acts of Parliament: the Karnataka Municipal Corporations Act (KMCA) of 1976 (which governs City Corporations), the Karnataka Municipalities Act (KMA) of 1964 (which governs the other ULBs) and the Amended KMC Act of 1994 (Centre for Policy Research, 2001). Both the KMCA and the KMA require ULBs to perform obligatory and discretionary functions, in addition to which they also perform additional functions laid down in the 74th Constitutional Amendment Act (Third State Finance Commission, 2007). Major obligatory functions include the maintenance of roads, street lights, sanitation, water supply, registration of births and deaths, public immunisation and regulation of residential and non-residential construction, whilst discretionary functions include the formation and maintenance of parks, schools, libraries and hospitals.

Under the manual system, first laid down by the British in the latter half of the 19th century, the collection of property tax in Karnataka centred around three registers: the Assessment Register or the MAR 19 which contained information on all properties in a municipality, and included details such as the location of the property, plot size and built-up area; the Demand, Collection and Balance or DCB Register which contained information about property tax payments; and the Mutation Register (Directorate of Municipal Administration, 2007). Prior to 2000, property tax was assessed and recovered by a tax officer, who paid annual visits to all the properties in the area allocated to him and was expected to correctly assess and collect property tax, noting property details and payments made into a handbook which was then used to update the tax registers. This method for assessing and recovering taxes remained in operation until the late 1990s, when property tax in Karnataka was calculated according to its expected annual rental value (ARV) – i.e. the estimated value of rent a property might bring in for the coming year. The problems with this system, however, were many as the amount of tax which could be levied was often calculated at the discretion of the tax collector. Thus in some instances anecdotal evidence suggests that some collectors were either paid bribes or harassed by influential citizens who sought to use their political clout to have their properties undervalued or ignored completely. In other instances, owners were put under pressure from local tax officials and were being regularly charged excess tax. In response to numerous complaints, the government introduced a self-assessment system (SAS), by which citizens were made responsible for filing their own tax returns according to set parameters (Directorate of Municipal Administration, 2008). The provisions of the SAS were simple:

- **Certainty:** Tax would be calculated according to a specified rateable value across the city, which was valid for 5 years
- **Safeguards on Assessments:** A maximum and minimum cap on taxes was fixed.
- **Enforcement:** The scheme provided for a 5% random scrutiny of tax returns documents
- **Appeals:** An appeals process was available to those citizens who wished to challenge decisions (adapted from Rao, 2003)

The chief goal of the SAS was straightforward: to get property owners to voluntarily declare their property tax liability and pay their taxes within a set time to avail of the benefits of the scheme. The scheme was made optional to avoid any legal challenges, with a proviso that those who chose to opt out of it would be assessed according to a similar yardstick by an assessor after he made a visit to the property (Rao, 2003).

It is interesting to note that whilst Karnataka (and more particularly its capital city Bangalore) has become a centre of global software development and is experiencing rapid growth in demand for civic services, its municipal bodies have been hard-pressed to find the resources and capabilities to provide the services required to cater for the growth in population and associated demands on infrastructure. Physical infrastructure is generally inadequate and often poorly maintained. As cities grow there is a continuous migration of people into them from the rural areas in search of work, and a continual increase in the number of urban poor, with over a quarter of the urban population not having access to proper sanitation. Bureaucracies are often under-funded and unable to mobilise adequate resources needed for their effective functioning. They are often overstaffed and their employees underpaid. Record keeping and other bureaucratic functions tend to suffer as they are generally manually carried out, with little attention paid to maintaining proper standards, often hampered by antiquated rules and procedures and rarely open to citizen scrutiny.

Revenue collection is thus often poor: for instance, a look through existing documents for nominal figures of property tax collection indicates that, when adjusted to take into account inflation, revenue from property tax has been stagnant over recent years (Madon et. Al 2004). In Bangalore alone, one survey estimated that for the year 2002-2003, of the 720,000 properties in the city, only two-thirds of that number (around 530,000 properties) had been taxed, with the estimated loss to the Revenue Department being close to

Rupees 3 billion (approximately US $68.3 million) (eGovernments Foundation, 2004) – a poor reflection on the efficiency of the city's municipal corporation to extract essential revenue to meet the infrastructural demands of Bangalore's rapidly growing population. Consequently, there has been growing pressure from citizen groups, international agencies and the local media on the city corporation and the state government's Urban Development Department to rationalise the existing revenue collection structures, and particularly improve the collection of property tax, within the state.

COMPUTERISING PROPERTY TAX: THE NIRMALA NAGARA PROJECT

In recognising the need to turn property tax in to a productive tax instrument, Bangalore-based technology non-profit eGovernments Foundation developed the eGov Property Tax Information System (PTIS) to aid in the establishment of a rigorous and efficient revenue system. The Foundation collaborated with the Directorate of Municipal Administration (the state government coordinator for Karnataka's municipalities) and the Survey of India (the apex central government mapping authority) in a partnership that aimed to improve tax collections using Geographical Information Systems (GIS)-based property mapping. The project, reckoned by some to be among the most ambitious municipal e-government projects in the country, included the digital mapping of over 3000 square kilometres of urban area, and involved the improvement of property tax record-keeping through the filling out over 7 million property register forms for an estimated 2.5 million properties across 57 municipalities.

The key aim of the project was to streamline municipal systems in Karnataka through government process reengineering, better record keeping and the use of IT tools and technologies, thus improving tax revenues and payment compliance.

The implementation of the software was taken up by the Karnataka State Urban Development Department as part of their 'Nirmala Nagara' (or 'Clean City') initiative, which was funded in part by the Asian Development Bank (ADB) to the tune of US $5 million, and whose ultimate aim was to bring about greater transparency, accountability and increased efficiency within the municipalities, and the smoother delivery of services to the citizens living in urban centres. The eGovernments Foundation provided the software and IT consulting free to the government, and was paid for service costs only. The Survey of India (which conducted the street-level surveys) footed half the cost of the project, while the other half was paid for by the state government.

The aim of the project designers was to create an internet-based 'back-office' database for monitoring all aspects of property taxation – property identification, tax dues assessment and revenue collection. Property records for an entire city were to be contained on a central server, accessible over the internet on secure networks to designated payment centres in each of the participating towns and cities. The back-end technology ultimately consisted of an Oracle database built on an open-source software platform, with the architects using J2E and Java technology to build the back-end application servers. In some cities, Personal Digital Assistant (PDA) devices were to be integrated into the system so that revenue officers could go out in the field to collect taxes, and use them to upload data back into the system in real time to keep records up to date. The immediate users of the system were thus senior state revenue officials, municipal tax administrators and local tax collectors, who would use the system to assess taxes, monitor tax compliance and issue tax certificates. Citizens would eventually become indirect users by being able to have access to their property records online.

The unique feature of the system was to be its use of Geographic Information Systems (GIS) or online virtual mapping, to visually aid the revamping of the addressing system and to help tax officials bring as many properties as possible under the tax net. The use of geographic information systems has become a fairly widespread developmental practice (Odendaal, 2002), and as a system it is a powerful tool for facilitating visual decision-making: by capturing, storing, and analysing all forms of spatially referenced information digital maps enable the end-user to monitor and manage the logistics of the development process. Creating such a database is, however, a time consuming process as it requires an extensive survey in order to get a detailed idea of not only the property being surveyed but also the geography of the surrounding area. It was therefore decided that while the property tax application would go live in all 57 Nirmala Nagara cities and towns, the GIS component would be deployed in only 18 selected cities: first in the 7 municipalities of Hubli-Dharwad, Belgaum, Gulbarga, Mysore, Byatrayanapura, Tumkur and Hassan, and then in the remaining 11 municipalities of Mangalore, Bijapur, Udupi, Mandya, Bommannahalli, Dasarahalli, Mahadevpura, R.R. Nagara, Yelahanka, K.R Puram, and Kengeri.

From July to August 2003 the eGovernments Foundation, in collaboration with the Urban Development Department, set up a pilot project using the PTIS with the GIS mapping application in Bytrayanapura City Municipal Corporation. In conjunction with the Survey of India (SoI) and the Directorate of Municipal Administration (DMA), details of property tax records for selected wards of Byatrayanapura were collected and a total station survey of the area was done. Based on the experiences of the pilot, potential barriers – relating to *data, people* and *technology* - were identified, and a workflow was designed to overcome them and proceed with the implementation of the computerised property tax system with GIS in the remaining areas of the state.

CHALLENGES TO EFFECTIVE IMPLEMENTATION

The first challenge encountered was a serious lack of good data, with the non-uniformity of data collection structures in existing government systems posing initial problems for system designers. The absence of a robust process of data validation, issues of poor data integrity and accuracy and incomplete/missing data were found to further compound issues during the implementation of the system. Difficulties arose chiefly from haphazard addressing systems and poor record keeping, and the consequent inability of government agencies to uniquely identify properties within cities and towns for tax purposes (The eGovernments Foundation 2003). The need for a standardised method for property numbering and street naming was thus essential, with each property needing to be assigned a unique Property Identification (PID) Number, based on its municipal number, street, and administrative location so that it might be identified on the database.

In the case of the PTIS a two-pronged approach was used in order to improve the quality of data. First, to rectify the lack of standardisation in addressing systems across the state, the eGovernments Foundation put together a comprehensive set of street naming and property numbering guidelines for use by local government agencies across the board. The data format was designed to be both compatible with the existing record-keeping system as well as the proposed computerised database. Second, it was decided that a new property register had to be put together for each municipal authority before computerisation could be undertaken. The new register would contain comprehensive information on each property within the municipal district, which would be gathered in stages through the use of 3 forms – known as Form A, Form B and Form C. These three forms would not only collate existing information gleaned from current registers but integrate it with details obtained from a ground survey of the properties. The PTIS would be considered ready for use once the combined data was uploaded to the digital database.

The next set of challenges faced by the project designers related to change management, in particular dealing with personnel issues. Government staff – especially those who worked in smaller municipalities – were often found to be low on core competencies required to work with and maintain a computerised system. Further, anecdotal evidence gained from discussions with senior government administrators suggested that officials within the civil service (particularly those in the lower ranks of the cadre directly involved with the collection of taxes) and government I.T staff (especially those posted to smaller municipalities) were extremely suspicious of the new system and were altogether resistant to the proposed changes. Training and capacity building thus became central to the successful implementation of the computerised system, with the eGovernments Foundation holding a number of training sessions and workshops for government employees ranging from established state Revenue Department officials (Bill Collectors, Revenue Inspectors, Revenue Officers and Commissioners/Chief Officers) to newly hired software engineers. In one instance, for example, more than 200 survey engineers were given field survey training for a month on the renaming of roads, the renumbering of properties, collecting data using Forms A, B, and C, and the detailing and sketching of properties for use in the compiling of the new register. These trained engineers were then used to train a further 600 hired engineers recruited to maintain the system. Additionally, 45 government employees were trained on the GIS software in order that they might liaise with people at the Survey of India, and at least 2 people from each municipality (1 engineer and 1 member of the IT staff) were trained to run the software and analyse GIS data (Directorate of Municipal Administration, 2008).

Thirdly, there were challenges relating to the technology itself and the implementation and use

of the system. Based on the results of the pilot, the user interface was also redesigned to make the system as user-friendly as possible, and the programme itself was coded to automatically generate daily reports. Both featured required users to possess only a basic level of training on the system. With such a wide distribution of municipalities, project management was a complex affair, and keeping on top of details a necessary but time-consuming process. In order to monitor the implementation process and increase accountability, the eGovernments Foundation devised a ranking system whereby the performance of the municipalities was ranked weekly according to a set series of weighted parameters. The rankings were reviewed by the Urban Development Department, and an average monthly rank for each municipality was generated. In order to ensure official commitment to the project, the outcome of the each local commissioner's Career Progress Report (the report which determines transfers, promotions and pay) was affected by ranking of their municipality. Commissioners of municipalities located in the top half of the table (Ranks 1-29) were given incentives to carry on with their good work, while the commissioners of those in the bottom half (Rank 30 and below) were summoned to Bangalore each month to explain their poor progress.

RUBBER HITS ROAD: A DISCUSSION OF RESULTS

In order to determine the success or failure of the project, this chapter analyses Property Tax data for 56 Nirmala Nagara cities under the Self Assessment Scheme (SAS) for the tax years 2002/03 – 2005/06, obtained by this author from the Directorate of Municipal Administration (Vijayadev, 2008). Data analysed included the total annual revenue accrued from property tax under the Self Assessment Scheme for the years covered, total number of properties assessed annually for the same period, and the annual average revenue per property. Separate analysis was also conducted to compare the performance of those cities where GIS mapping had been implemented with those where GIS mapping was not implemented.

Figure 1 illustrates the total property tax revenue collected from 2002/03 to 2005/06. It may be seen that from 2002/03 to 2004/05, property tax revenue collections rose overall from Rs. 826 million to Rs. 962 million. However, in 2004/05 revenue accruing from property tax remained virtually unchanged, with collections totalling Rs.956 million, before falling sharply to Rs. 633 million for the tax year 2005/06. A closer look at the figures reveals that whilst on the one hand, for cities in which GIS mapping was implemented, tax revenues rose during the period 2002/03 – 2004/05 from Rs. 549 million to Rs. 721 million, revenues *fell* in those towns and cities where GIS was not implemented, from Rs. 276 million to Rs. 235 million during that same period. Both sets of cities experienced a drop in revenue for the tax year 2005/06. It must be noted that the drop in 2005/06 was unexpected and large (particularly for those cities in which GIS was implemented) and for which a robust explanation could not be deduced. Further, the sharp drop in total revenues

for that year was largely the result of the inexplicable drop in revenue collections for GIS cities.

Figure 2 shows the number of properties (both land and buildings) brought under the tax net for the period 2002/03 to 2005/06. Overall, the number of properties assessed for tax in the Nirmala Nagara towns and cities increased from 1,736,995 properties in 2002/03 to 2,345,671 in 2005/06 (an increase of 35%). Cities where GIS mapping was implemented experienced a consistent rise in the number of properties brought under the tax net – from 876,416 property units in 2002/03 to 1,316,994 in 2005/06 (a 50% increase); as did cities where GIS was not implemented, which saw the number of properties rise from 860,579 properties to 1,028,677 properties (an increase of 19.5%) during that same period. As in the case of total revenue collected, the increase in the total number of properties was largely driven by the increase in the number of GIS properties, where out of a total increase of 608,676 properties, GIS properties accounted for 440,578 properties (72.4%).

Figure 3 indicates the change in the average revenue per property during the period 2002/03 to 2005/06. Overall for Nirmala Nagara towns and cities, the average revenue per property fluc-

Figure 1. Total property tax revenue collected under the self assessment scheme from 2002/03 – 2005/06 (Source: Author analysis of data on Property Tax: figures issued by the Government of Karnataka)

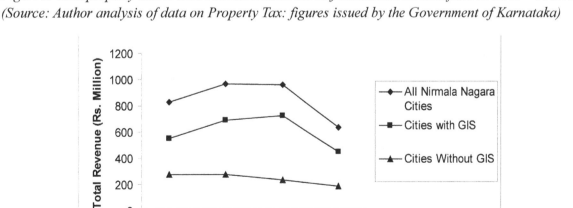

Figure 2. Total number of properties assessed under the self assessment scheme from 2002/03 – 2005/06 (Source: Author analysis of data on Property Tax: figures issued by the Government of Karnataka)

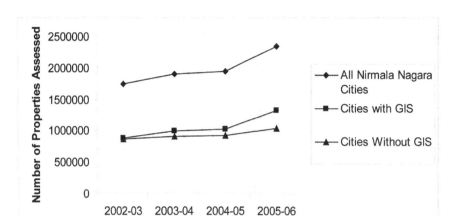

tuated over the given time period, first rising from Rs. 475 per property in 2002/03 to Rs. 506 in 2003/04, remaining virtually unchanged at Rs. 491 in 2004/05 and then falling to Rs. 270 per property in 2005/06. A similar trend holds true for properties in those towns and cities where GIS was implemented – the average revenue per property first rose from Rs. 627 per property in 2002/03 to Rs. 703 per property in 2004/05, and then inexplicably fell sharply to Rs. 340 per property in 2005/06. For those cities and towns which did not implement the GIS component, the Average Annual Revenue per Property declined continuously from Rs. 321 in 2002/03 to Rs.180 in 2005/06.

Thus overall, for the 56 Nirmala Nagara towns and cities analysed, the data shows while the number of properties brought under the tax net

Figure 3. Changes in average revenue per property from 2002/03 to 2005/06 (Source: Author analysis of data on Property Tax: figures issued by the Government of Karnataka)

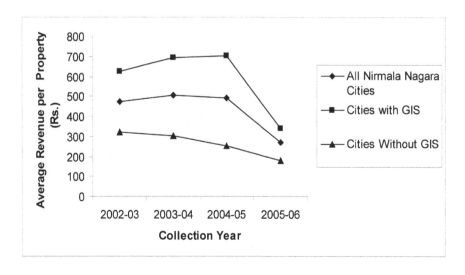

steadily increased from 2002/03 to 2005/06, revenue collected under the Self Assessment Scheme system fluctuated – rising significantly from the first to the second year, before falling marginally in the third year and then dramatically reducing in the fourth year. One may conjecture, therefore, that the SAS allows for the undervaluation of the declared tax per property, possibly in collusion with tax assessors, and that such a fluctuation in revenue is indicative of poor compliance, as a steadily increasing number of properties brought under the tax net should otherwise logically result in an increase in revenues for the government. Poor compliance appears to be a direct cause of the dramatic fall in revenue in 2005/06, with figures indicating a compliance percentage of as low as 3% in some towns and cities (Vijayadev, 2008).

A deeper analysis brings to light an interesting difference between those cities and towns where GIS mapping was implemented and those where it was not. Revenues in GIS towns and cities rose steadily from 2002/03 to 2004/05, with the number of properties brought under the tax net increasing at the same time. The average revenue per property also rose, as is to be expected. However, for the same period, cities and towns where GIS mapping was not implemented experienced a steady decline in revenue, despite an annual increase in the number of properties assessed. One may conclude that the implementation of the Property Tax Information System marginally improves compliance (and consequently revenues) in those cities which have used GIS mapping techniques, as these maps help to better identify properties and their characteristics, allowing for a more accurate calculation and collection of tax and a resultant reduction in instances of tax evasion. However, relatively low average revenue per property, even in those cities where GIS has been implemented indicates that there are still loopholes in the assessment and collection processes, and that while people are declaring their properties they appear to be undervaluing them, either on their own or

in collusion with the local tax officials. This is particularly so because GIS mapping has been rolled out in some of the larger cities and towns in Karnataka and the average value per property should be rising sharply as these cities grow.

CONCLUSION

The PTIS uses automation to improve data management, reduce the use of discretion by manual operators, and to make collection processes transparent. Project designers sought to ensure top-level commitment by not only tying in the implementation process with each municipal commissioner's career progress report and transfers, but also regularly taking to task those commissioners whose municipalities failed to meet implementation targets. In order to circumvent the inevitable opposition from those lower level staff who stood to lose the most from these changes, the project did not dramatically alter the old system, but instead worked within existing legal and administrative frameworks to digitise (and thereby streamline) existing methods of tax assessment and collection.

Therein, however, lies the problem. While the system has improved back-office processes significantly it does not, in its current form, possess any mechanism to improve compliance and aid enforcement. Accountability is currently very low – there is currently no way to completely prevent arbitrary assessments and it is difficult for the state government agencies based in Bangalore to monitor the accuracy of tax calculation and collection, particularly in remote corners of Karnataka. In other words, the introduction of a computerised database is not enough to close existing loopholes in the self assessment process. People are still able to undervalue their properties (either on their own or in collusion with tax officials), resulting in low revenue collections despite more properties being brought under the tax net, and do not seem to be aware of the importance of property tax revenue to the well being of the common good. Thus, whilst the process of tax administration has been successfully streamlined, simplified even, the system has only partially succeeded in achieving its other stated aim of improving tax collections in the state and calls into question the overall viability of such a top-down approach

This chapter sets out three suggestions to help bolster the functioning of the PTIS and improve revenues:

1. An online property tax calculator, accessible to both government officials and citizens, may help reduce arbitrary assessments and allow for accurate calculation and collection of tax. On one hand, citizens would be able to accurately calculate property tax online prior to filing their returns, thereby making them aware of exactly how much tax they owe the government and reducing instances of erroneous assessments. On the other, tax officials would be able to accurately compute how much tax they ought to be receiving, thus aiding enforcement by thwarting attempts by citizens to undervalue their properties. An online property tax calculator is currently being piloted in Bangalore city, and is reported to have been popular with citizens and tax officials alike (Times of India, 2009a, 2009b). While an online calculator alone would not completely stop officials from overcharging citizens or prevent citizens from making false declarations, its presence might serve to act as a deterrent for those tempted to undervalue properties by making transparent (available to all, at the click of a button) the process by which property tax is computed and the precise amount of money that is owed to the tax authority. Further, by simplifying the process of tax assessment, an online calculator could make the prospect of filing taxes less daunting (and consequently more attractive) for the average citizen.

2. While the use of GIS mapping technologies is the right way forward, an analysis of the data reveals that monitoring processes need to be made more robust. Another way in which revenues may be increased is through the institution of independent tax audits to bolster the tracking currently done through the use of GIS maps. Currently, audits are carried out in-house by municipalities, but the results may be manipulated by people who have vested interests. An option would be to have a department in State Government audit municipal tax collection in order to reduce the effects of those vested interests.

3. A final possibility would be to introduce graded levels of scrutiny to help tax enforcement. As mentioned earlier, the SAS provides for the random scrutiny of 5% of all returns filed. However, this chapter proposes that the number of declarations scrutinised should increase depending on size of property, with more returns from bigger properties being scrutinised as that is where the bulk of the property tax revenue comes from. Further, information of property transactions should be available to the monitoring authority, in order to help them verify that the correct data is being used.

At the beginning of the 21st century, countries across the world are preparing for e-government. India, too, is experiencing dramatic changes in its development agenda. Technology and high-calibre professionalism are available for municipalities and state governments to use in ways previously not thought possible, and new crop of responsive, technology-savvy politicians seems to be emerging within governments and government agencies to take advantage of such opportunities. As more and more national, state, and local bodies sign up to the Indian e-government agenda, it is important to note that a number of major issues remain unresolved.

The eGovernments Property Tax Information System is unique in that, not only is it one of the few e-government applications rolled out in India to reform the municipal government processes, but also it is a striking example of a working partnership between federal and state government agencies, municipal government bodies and a private not-for-profit software development firm. However, its full impact is yet to be determined, and while on first examination project indicators point to it having the potential to be a successful example of e-government in India, a measure of its success or failure will only be gained after a slightly longer period of time.

Secondly, should the system flourish, there are still uncertainties as to whether it would be possible to repeat such success elsewhere – whilst it is clear that there are currently a number of reform-minded individuals willing to push e-government projects from both within and outside the government, the use of information technology is only gaining ground in a few key states like Karnataka, and the rare combination of political vision and political will is still missing in most parts of the country.

And finally, the broader debate surrounding prioritisation of issues in India's development agenda still rages. While it is recognised that ICTs are strategically important to the country (Schware, 2000), and the need for investment in e-government is widely accepted, questions relating to the balancing of investment in ICTs with the need to give priority to investment targeting other basic needs still need to be answered, and there is apprehension in some quarters that money used for e-government will absorb scarce developmental resources whilst not delivering on potential benefits. This fear is not without reason – India accounts for close to 26% of the world's poor (Roy, 2005), and it is still unclear whether administrative reforms stimulated by e-government will in the long run feed into India's other development goals, or simply divert resources away from areas where they are needed. Only time and further research will be able to tell.

REFERENCES

Agarwal, A. (Ed.). (2007). *eGovernance Case Studies*. Hyderabad: Universities Press.

Aluko, B. T. (2005). Building Urban Local Governance Fiscal Autonomy through Property Taxation Financing Option. *International Journal of Strategic Property Management*, 9, 201–214.

Avgerou, C., & Walsham, G. (2000). Introduction: IT in Developing Countries. In Avgerou, C., & Walsham, G. (Eds.), *Information Technology in Context: Studies from the Perspective of Developing Countries* (pp. 1–8). Aldershot: Ashgate.

Bahl, R. W., & Linn, J. F. (1992). *Urban Public Finance in Developing Countries*. New York: Oxford University Press.

Bangalore Mahanagara Palike. (2000). *Property Tax Self-Assessment Scheme Handbook: Golden Jubilee Year 2000*. Bangalore: BBMP.

Bangalore Mahanagara Palike. (2007). *Assessment and Calculation of Property Tax Under the Capital Value System (New SAS): 2007- 2008*. Unpublished Handbook.

Bhagat, R. B. (2005). Rural-Urban Classification and Municipal Governance in India. *Singapore Journal of Tropical Geography*, 26(1), 61–73. doi:10.1111/j.0129-7619.2005.00204.x

Bhagwan, J. (1983). *Municipal Finance in the Metropolitan Cities of India: A Case Study of Delhi Municipal Corporation*. New Delhi: Concept Publishing.

Bhatnagar, S. (2003a). E-Government: Building a SMART Administration for India's States. In Howes, S., Lahiri, A., & Stern, N. (Eds.), *State-level Reform in India: Towards More Effective Government* (pp. 257–267). New Delhi: Macmillan India Ltd.

Bhatnagar, S. (2003b). Public Service Delivery: Does E-Government Help? In S. Ahmed & S. Bery (Eds.), *The Annual Bank Conference on Development Economics 2003* (pp. 11-20). New Delhi: The World Bank and National Conference of Applied Economic Research.

Bhatnagar, S. (2003c). *Transparency and Corruption: Does E-Government Help?* Draft paper for the compilation of the Commonwealth Human Rights Initiative 2003 Report 'Open Sesame: looking for the Right to Information in the Commonwealth.

Bhatnagar, S. (2004). *E-Government: From Vision to Implementation.* New Delhi: Sage Publications.

Bhatnagar, S. (2005). *E-Government: Opportunities and Challenges.* World Bank Presentation Retrieved June 22, 2005 from http://siteresources. worldbank.org/ INTEDEVELOPMENT/ Resources/ 559323-1114798035525/1055531-1114798256329/10555556-11 14798371392/ Bhatnagar1.ppt

Bresciani, P., Donzelli, P., & Forte, A. (2003). Requirements Engineering for Knowledge Management in eGovernment (LNAI 2645, pp. 48-59).

Budhiraja, R. (2003) *Electronic Governance: a Key Issue in the 21ˢᵗ Century*. Additional Director, Electronic Governance Division, Ministry of Information Technology, Government of India. Retrieved June 14, 2008 from http://www.mit. gov.in/eg/ article2.htm

Centre for Policy Research (2001, June). *The Future of Urbanisation: Spread and Shape in Selected States*. New Delhi: Centre for Policy Research.

Cheema, G. S. (2005). *Building Democratic Institutions: Governance Reform in Developing Countries*. Bloomfield: Kumarian Press, Inc.

Colby, S.-S. (2001). *Anti-Corruption and ICT for Good Governance*. Deputy Secretary-General, OECD in Anti-Corruption Symposium 2001: The Role of Online Procedures in Promoting and Good Governance.

Datta, A. (1984). *Municipal Finances in India*. New Delhi: Indian Institute of Public Administration.

Datta, A. (1999). Institutional Aspects of Urban Governance in India. In S.N. Jha & P.C. Mathur (Eds.), *Decentralization and Local Politics* (pp. 191-211). New Delhi: Sage Publications.

De'. R. (2007). *Antecedents of Corruption and the Role of E-Government Systems in Developing Countries*. Paper presented at the Electronic Government 6th International Conference, EGOV 2007, Proceedings of Ongoing Research, Regensburg, Germany, September 3-7, 2007.

Dillinger, W. (1988). *Urban Property Taxation in Developing Countries*. World Bank Policy Research Working Paper Series, Number 41.

Directorate of Municipal Administration. (2007). Retrieved from http://municipaladmn.kar. nic.in

Directorate of Municipal Administration. (2008). The Intention of Self Assessment of Property Tax: Part 1. Retrieved November 10, 2008 from http:// municipaladmn.kar. nic.in/SASe1.htm

Drezner, D. W. (2004). The Global Governance of the Internet: Bringing the State Back In. *Political Science Quarterly, 119*(3), 477–498. doi:10.2307/20202392

Dutton, W. H. (1999). *Society on the Line: Information Politics in the Digital Age*. Oxford: Oxford University Press.

Flatters, F., & MacLeod, W. B. (1995). Administrative Corruption and Taxation. *International Tax and Public Finance, 2*, 397–417. doi:10.1007/ BF00872774

Gasco, M. (2003). New Technologies and Institutional Change in Public Administration. *Social Science Computer Review*, *21*(1), 6–14. doi:10.1177/0894439302238967

Gupta, P., & Bagga, R. K. (Eds.). (2008). *Compendium of eGovernance Initiatives in India*. Hyderabad: Universities Press.

Hammond, A. L. (2001). Digitally Empowered Development. *Foreign Affairs (Council on Foreign Relations)*, *80*(2), 96–106.

Heeks, R. (1998a). *Information Technology and Public Sector Corruption* (Working Paper 4). Institute for Development Policy Management, University of Manchester.

Heeks, R. (1998b). *Information Age Reform of the Public Sector: The Potential and Problems of IT for India* (Information Systems for Public Sector Management Working Paper Series Paper No. 6). IDPM, University of Manchester.

Heeks, R. (2000). The Approach of Senior Public Officials to Information Technology Related Reform: Lessons from India. *Public Administration and Development*, *20*(3), 197–205. doi:10.1002/1099-162X(200008)20:3<197::AID-PAD109>3.0.CO;2-6

Heeks, R. (2002a). i-Development not e-Development: Special Issue on ICTs and Development. *Journal of International Development*, *14*(1), 1–11. doi:10.1002/jid.861

Heeks, R. (2002b). Information Systems and Developing Countries: Failure, Success and Local Improvisations. *The Information Society*, *18*, 101–112. doi:10.1080/01972240290075039

Heeks, R. (2003). *Most eGovernment-for-Development Projects Fail: How Can the Risks be Reduced?* (iGovernment Working Paper Series – Paper No. 14), University of Manchester.

Heeks, R. (2005). eGovernment as a Carrier of Context. *Journal of Public Policy*, *25*(1), 51–74. doi:10.1017/S0143814X05000206

Heeks, R. (2006). *Implementing and Managing eGovernment – An International Text*. New Delhi: Vistar Publications.

Hindriks, J., Keen, M., & Muthoo, A. (1999). Corruption, Extortion and Evasion. *Journal of Public Economics*, *74*, 395–430. doi:10.1016/S0047-2727(99)00030-4

Huque, A. S. (1994). Public Administration in India: Evolution, Change and Reform. *Asian Journal of Public Administration*, *16*(2), 249–259.

Jalal, J. (2005). Good Practices in Public Sector Reform: A Few Examples from Two Indian Cities. In Singh, A. (Ed.), *Administrative Reforms: Towards Sustainable Practices* (pp. 96–116). New Delhi: Sage Publications.

Keohane, R. O., & Nye, J. S. (2002). Power and Interdependence in the Information Age. In Kamarck, E. C., & Nye, J. S. Jr., (Eds.), *Governance.com: Democracy in the Information Age* (pp. 161–177). Washington, D.C.: Brookings Institution Press.

Kumar, R., & Best, M. L. (2006). Impact and Sustainability of E-Government Services in Developing Countries: Lessons Learned from Tamil Nadu, India. *The Information Society*, *22*, 1–12. doi:10.1080/01972240500388149

Legrain, P. (2002). *Open World: The Truth About Globalisation*. London: Abacus.

Lewis, A. (1982). *The Psychology of Taxation*. Oxford: Martin Robertson & Company.

Madon, S. (1993). Introducing Administrative Reform through the Application of Computer-Based Information Systems: A Case Study in India. *Public Administration and Development*, *13*, 37–48. doi:10.1002/pad.4230130104

Madon, S. (2004). Evaluating the Developmental Impact of E-Governance Initiatives: An Exploratory Framework. *Electronic Journal of Information Systems in Developing Countries, 20*(5), 1–13.

Madon, S., & Bhatnagar, B. (2000). Institutional Decentralised Information Systems for Local Level Planning: Comparing Approaches Across Two States in India. *Journal of Global Information Technology Management, 3*(4), 45–59.

Madon, S., Sahay, S., & Sahay, J. (2004). Implementing Property Tax Reforms in Bangalore: An Actor-Network Perspective. *Information and Organization, 14*, 269–295. doi:10.1016/j.infoandorg.2004.07.002

Maheswari, S. R. (1993). *Administrative Reform in India*. New Delhi: Jawahar Publishers and Distributors.

Margetts, H. (1998). *Information Technology in Government: Britain and America*. London: Routledge.

Margetts, H. (2006). Transparency and Digital Government. In Hood, C., & Heald, D. (Eds.), *Transparency: the Key to Better Governance?* (pp. 197–210). London: The British Academy.

Mathew, G. (2006). A New Deal for Municipalities. In *Proceedings of the National Seminar on Urban Governance in the Context of the Jawaharlal Nehru National Urban Renewal Mission* (pp. 102-116). India Habitat Centre, New Delhi 24th – 25th November 2006.

Mechling, J. (2002). Information Age Governance. In Kamarck, E., & Nye, J. S. Jr., (Eds.), *Governance.com: Democracy in the Information Age* (pp. 171–189). New York: Brookings Institution.

Meijer, A. (2002). Geographical Information Systems and Public Accountability. *Information Policy, 7*, 39–47.

Minogue, M. (2002). Power to the People? Good Governance and the Reshaping of the State. In Kothari, U., & Minogue, M. (Eds.), *Development Theory and Practice* (pp. 117–135). Basingstoke: Palgrave.

Misra, S. (2005). eGovernance: Responsive and Transparent Service Delivery Mechanism. In A. Singh (Ed.), *Administrative Reforms: Towards Sustainable Practices* (pp. 283-302), New Delhi: Sage Publications.

Mitra, R. (2000). Emerging State-level ICT Development Strategies. In Bhatnagar, S., & Schware, R. (Eds.), *Information and Communication Technology in Development: Cases from India* (pp. 195–205). New Delhi: Sage Publications.

National Institute of Urban Affairs (NIUA). (2004). *Reforming the Property Tax System. Research Study Series No. 94*. New Delhi: NIUA Press.

Newman, J. (Ed.). (2005). *Remaking Governance: Peoples Politics and the Public Sphere*. Bristol: The Policy Press.

Nilekani, N. (2004, October 25). Redemption in this World, this Land. *The Economic Times*. Retrieved June 31, 2008 from http://economictimes.indiatimes. com /articleshow/897648.cms

Odendaal, N. (2002). ICTs *In* Development – Who Benefits? Use of Geographic Information Systems on the Cato Manor Development Project, South Africa. *Journal of International Development, 14*, 89–100. doi:10.1002/jid.867

Olowu, D. (2004). Property Taxation and Democratic Decentralisation in Developing Countries (Working Paper Series No. 401). Institute of Social Studies, The Hague.

Parks, T. (2005). A Few Misconceptions about eGovernment. Retrieved November 10, 2008 from http://www.asiafoundation.org/ pdf/ICT_eGov.pdf

Pathak, R. D., & Prasad, R. S. (2005). The Role of eGovernment in Tackling Corruption: the Indian Experience. In R. Ahmad (Ed.) *The Role of Public Administration in Building a Harmonious Society, Selected Proceedings from the Annual Conference of the Network of Asia-Pacific Schools and Institutes of Public Administration and Governance (NAPSIPAG)*, December 5-7, 2005 (pp. 343-463).

Paul, S., & Shah, M. (1997). Corruption in Public Service Delivery. In Guhan, S., & Paul, S. (Eds.), *Corruption in India: Agenda for Action*. New Delhi: Vision Books.

Pratchett, L. (1999). New Technologies and the Modernization of Local Government: An Analysis of Biases and Constraints. *Public Administration*, 77(4), 731–750. doi:10.1111/1467-9299.00177

Rao, N. R. (1986). *Municipal Finances in India (Theory and Practice)*. New Delhi: Inter-India Publications.

Rao, V. (2003). *Property Tax Reforms in Bangalore*. Paper presented to the Innovations in Local Revenue Mobilisation Seminar. Retrieved December 10, 2008 from http://www1.worldbank.org/publicsector/decentralization/June2003 SeminarPresentations/VasanthRao.ppt

Rhodes, R. A. W. (1996). The New Governance: Governing without Government. *Political Studies*, 44, 652–667. doi:10.1111/j.1467-9248.1996.tb01747.x

Ribeiro, E. F. N. (2006). Urban Growth and Transformations in India: Issues and Challenges. In *Proceedings of the National Seminar on Urban Governance in the Context of the Jawaharlal Nehru National Urban Renewal Mission, India Habitat Centre, New Delhi 24th – 25th November 2006* (pp. 1-11).

Ronaghan, S. A. (2002). *Benchmarking E-Government: A Global Perspective*. The United Nations Division for Public Economics and Public Administration (DPEPA) Report.

Rosengard, J. K. (1998). *Property Tax Reform in Developing Countries*. Boston: Kluwer Academic Publications.

Roy, S. (2005). *Globalisation, ICT and Developing Nations: Challenges in the Information Age*. New Delhi: Sage Publications.

Sachdeva, P. (1993). *Urban Local Government and Administration in India*. Allahabad: Kitab Mahal.

Sarangamath, S. (2007). BangaloreOne: Integrated Citizen Service Centre. In Agarwal, A. (Ed.), *eGovernance Case Studies* (pp. 148–152). Hyderabad: Universities Press.

Schware, R. (2000). Useful Starting Points for Future Projects. In Bhatnagar, S., & Schware, R. (Eds.), *Information and Communication Technology in Development: Cases from India* (pp. 206–213). Delhi: Sage Publications.

Singh, A. (1990). Computerisation of the Indian Income Tax Department. *Information Technology for Development*, 5(3), 235–251. doi:10.1080/02681102.1990.9627198

Singh, N. (1996). *Governance and Reform in India*. Paper presented at Indian National Economic Policy in an Era of Global Reform: An Assessment, Cornell University, March 29-30 1996

Singh, S. S., & Misra, S. (1993). *Legislative Framework of Panchayati Raj in India*. New Delhi: Intellectual Publishing House.

Stoker, G. (1998). Governance as Theory: Five Propositions. *International Social Science Journal*, 50(155), 17–28. doi:10.1111/1468-2451.00106

Taylor, J., & Williams, H. (1988). *Information and Communication Technologies and the Transformation of Local Government* (Working Paper 9), Centre for Urban and Regional Development Studies (Newcastle).

The Economic Times. (2008). Urban India Gets Under the Digital Mapping Radar. 8th June (p. 14).

The eGovernments Foundation (2003). *Street Naming and Property Numbering Guide*. The eGovernments Foundation, Bangalore, India.

The eGovernments Foundation (2004). *The Property Tax Information System with GIS*. Presentation document.

The Government of India. (2003) Electronic Governance – A Concept Paper. Retrieved November 12, 2008 from http://egov.mit.gov.in

The Government of Karnataka. (2005, Unpublished). A Note on the Process of Implementation of Computerisation etc – Guidance Notes.

The Times of India. (2006, July 22). E-governance, GIS: New Face of BMP (p.1).

The Times of India. (2008, December 15). Hiding Property Tax Info? Face Checks, Pay Fine: Revenue Officials Can Now Come Calling (p.1).

The Times of India. (2009a, January 8). Popular Debut for Online Tax Calculator: Applicable for Residential Properties, Citizens Rue Increase in Net Amount (p. 2).

The Times of India. (2009b, January 10). E-Calculator Spreads its Wings (p. 2).

The World Bank (2004). *Building Blocks of eGovernment: Lessons from Developing Countries* (PREM Notes No. 91), August 2004.

Third State Finance Commission (Government of Karnataka) (2007) *Decentralisation in Karnataka: A Status Report*, October 2007.

United Nations Development Programme (UNDP). (1997). *Corruption and Good Governance: Discussion Paper 3*. New York: UNDP

Vijayadev, V. (2008). 'SAS 02-03 to 06-07 Excel Spreadsheet', State Nodal Officer, Municipal Reforms Cell, Directorate of Municipal Administration; Private Communication.

Vincent, S. (2004). A New Property Map for Karnataka, *IndiaTogether.org*. Retrieved September 12, 2008 from http://www.indiatogether.org/2004/mar/gov-karmapgis.htm

Wade, R. H. (1985). The Market for Public Office: Why the Indian State Is Not Better at Development. *World Development, 13*(4), 467–497. doi:10.1016/0305-750X(85)90052-X

ENDNOTES

[1] For example beginning with Norman Angell in 1910 right up to Peter Drucker, Alvin and Heidi Toffler and Esther Dyson in the 1980s and 1990s. For greater detail see Robert O. Keohane and Joseph S. Nye (2002) Power and Interdependence in the Information Age' in Elaine C. Kamarck and Joseph S. Nye Jr. (eds.), *Governance.com: Democracy in the Information Age*, p. 161

[2] There is currently a fierce debate raging in development circles as to the efficacy of such conditionalities and their impact on development. Some aid donors argue that the linking of conditionalities such as internal political and economic reform to development assistance such as debt relief is a trend in the right direction, while others worry about such a system creating a divide between "winners" and "losers" and leaving behind those countries most in need of help. For a detailed discussion of this debate, see G. Shabbir Cheema (2005)*Building Democratic Institutions: Governance Reform in Developing Countries*, pp. 5–6

[3] The term 'online' need not necessarily imply a connection to the Internet. It implies

that transactions access/ update databases immediately to minimize errors and speed up processing. If applications are submitted electronically, the movement and processing of documents is also subsequently electronic. The resulting benefits could be more transparency, empowerment, greater convenience, less corruption, revenue growth, and cost reduction.

4 Octroi: A tax levied by a local authority on certain categories of goods entering its jurisdiction.

5 This could be for a number of reasons: a fear of redundancy, loss of bribes or 'pocket money', or a simple lack of exposure to technology.

6 No data was available for the 57th city, Mangalore

Section 2
Cultural and Social Matters

Chapter 7

Localisation of Indigenous Content:
Libraries and Knowledge Centres and the Our Story Database in the Northern Territory

Jason Gibson
Independent Researcher, Australia

Brian Lloyd
Researcher, Australia

Cate Richmond
Northern Territory Library, Australia

ABSTRACT

The Northern Territory Library's (NTL) Libraries and Knowledge Centres (LKC) program is one of a number of programs across Australia designed to bring ICTs and Indigenous people together within an appropriate technology / community-networking framework. A center-piece is the use of the Our Story database to hold and display both repatriated and contemporary, including born-digital, cultural material relevant to local communities. The LKC model is distinctive in that it is fully implemented, uses proven technology, has a consistent framework of program delivery, and a clear business case. However there continue to be fundamental questions on striking a balance between technical innovation and sustainability; the capacity of the program to expand while maintaining support in geographically remote areas; and the challenge of maintaining a relationship of trust with local communities. Reviewing the challenges of the Our Story / LKC program sheds light on key reasons why ICT-based community-networking projects succeed or fail.

DOI: 10.4018/978-1-61520-997-2.ch007

INTRODUCTION

Sustainability in ICT projects relies on a combination of 'doing enough' while not 'doing too much': giving the project something to live for, to communicate and share with its stakeholders, without over-extending the supply-lines and capacities. For ICT projects, there are inherent questions over the possibility of extending the project in a technical sense while protecting both sustainability and usability. It is generally accepted within the technical community that progressive technical development is necessary to maintain currency, but too much emphasis can lead to a loss of focus on other key aspects of program health. The ability of the program to support its installations, to frame its service in such a way that it meets and responds to local demand, is no less important, and achieving a balance essential. This chapter's description of the *Our Story* database, and the Libraries and Knowledge Centres (LKC) program, of which it is a key component, across 16 remote Indigenous communities across the Northern Territory, demonstrates that this is so. We believe that the implementation of *Our Story* / LKC model, as form of 'elaborated library' that spans the digital and physical domains, has significant implications for other projects operating in similar territory.

It is now four years since the first *Our Story* / LKC installation. The program's owner, Northern Territory Library (NTL), is currently engaged in planning and development for a second generation of software for *Our Story*. Taking stock of progress to date, and given the findings of an evaluation of the program conducted by researchers from the University of Technology of Sydney (Nakata et al, 2006), we characterize *Our Story* / LKC as a successful program. We argue that it does indeed fulfill its objectives and that this is confirmed by consistent patterns of use by its intended user-base, and by signs of growth and development in the ways it is being used[1]. However, we also acknowledge that it must be considered successful in the qualified sense that any continuing program must be. There are risks and challenges ahead that are inherent in the area of operation of the *Our Story* / LKC program. These are inherent in the innovative scope of the program. In identifying them we also identify areas of future growth and development, through which the project can continue to fulfill its promise.

THE PROGRAM

Our Story is a File Maker Pro software application originally developed in the mid-1990s for use in the Aboriginal communities of northern South Australia. Originally named *Ara Irititja* by its creators, the Pitjantjatjara Council, the system allowed for local access to historical and cultural documents taken by non-indigenous researchers or people who had worked in their remote communities in the past. The software went through gradual and incremental change over a fifteen-year period and has since become a popular tool for community-based archiving projects in a remote Aboriginal context. Receiving similar requests for local access to information and knowledge resources from Aboriginal communities in the Northern Territory, the Northern Territory Library began to implement the system across many of its remote community libraries. As is described in detail later on in this chapter, the *Ara Irititja* software was rebranded the '*Our Story*' database and quickly became the focal point of the Northern Territory Libraries Indigenous library program, known as 'Libraries and Knowledge Centres'.

Background

The *Our Story* / LKC model is one expression of a broader enterprise on the development of culturally-attuned knowledge and information services in areas of disadvantage. This is now an established subject of discussion at the global level. Recommendations from the World Summit on the Information Society (WSIS) in 2004 for example stated that:

"Equitable access [to information services] has to be contextualised and as far as possible based on local linguistic/cultural, economic and technological imperatives of communities so as to bolster their local knowledge content and its ownership and management." (Weigel and Waldburger, 2004: 56).

In Indigenous Australia though, the notion that Aboriginal 'communities should have the possibility to store and keep their own information resources in digital format' and that the sharing of knowledge may help to 'improve livelihoods', has been relatively slow to take hold (Weigel & Waldburger, 2004: 163). The reasons for this protracted introduction are not difficult to adduce: the dearth of technical support and training in remote areas, the lack of accessibility to digital archive materials, low income and employment opportunities, low rates of literacy and a relatively unreliable telecommunications infrastructure are just some of the reasons for this.

Rationale

The notion of a new mode of library service for remote Indigenous clients in the Northern Territory (NT) dates from the early 2000's. It was decided that a new program was required to better meet the information needs of all people living in the Territory's remote areas, with a particular focus upon the disadvantaged Aboriginal populations living in small communities across tropical and desert regions. This new approach, the LKC model, combined traditional library services with a greater emphasis on electronic resources and new media tools to assist communities to care for, and cultivate, local knowledge.

Consistent with this, a distinctive feature of the LKC program has been to place, within a semi-traditional library context, a fully-supported database facility – *Our Story* - that allows local material, such as still and moving images, scanned documents, and audio to be added and then made available for display. The material, some of which requires sensitive handling due to cultural protocols, must be managed in such a way as to provide a requisite level of cultural security.

To appreciate the significance of this process, the reader should be aware of two relatively recent socio-cultural developments in remote Indigenous communities. The first is a move towards increased local Indigenous access to and management of knowledge, often embodied in processes of 'cultural repatriation'. Many Australian Indigenous communities have been subjected to extraordinary levels of research and documentation. The collecting of physical artifacts, documentary records — and later audio-visual documentation — originally began under the auspices of church missions and agents of government, and of anthropological projects in the late 19th and early 20th century. Attitudes towards these collections and the cultural institutions that hold them have undergone significant change in the last thirty years. Just as Greece seeks the Elgin/Parthenon Marbles, so too do Indigenous people in Australia — as they do internationally — seek access to, and the right to hold and administer, a range of materials pertinent to their own past and present (Hendry, 2005). Non-Indigenous sentiment, at least in specialist circles, has also changed to support this different way of viewing objects and records, hitherto seen as best kept under lock and key in the custodianship of non-Indigenous professionals.

Many remote Indigenous communities have enjoyed access to only a tiny fraction of the materials collected about them, in contrast to the substantial collections held in the museums and other institutions of the non-Indigenous world. Awareness that this requires redress has been underscored by the wider acknowledgement that policies of successive Australian governments have very significantly disturbed the family and cultural life of Indigenous people in Australia. This has had the effect of making cultural knowledge and connection less available to many members of the Indigenous community, and with negative consequences for well-being.

However, the movement toward improving access to these records, or even handing over ownership of the original materials to a 'community', begs the question as to how those materials may best be dealt with and made accessible to and by local communities. Differences in cultural attitudes to material things are as different as can be imagined from the 'scientific fetishism' of the modern museum. Also, physical environments in a number of remote communities can exercise a less-than-benign influence on objects that have been preserved in controlled environments for quite some time. Similar conditions are most often not provided on-site in many of these locations, and efforts in the past to establish local 'keeping places' or museums for repatriated physical collections have met with varied success (Batty, 2005; Campbell, 2006: 76).

The second major influence has been the advent of ubiquity for digital media texts and technologies in remote communities. This provides new avenues for holding and sharing cultural information — as opposed to cultural objects in a physical sense. There is also a more contemporary aspect to this. Indigenous people in remote communities are familiar with and have access to many of the tools and expertise with which they can create digital objects that record the present-day life of the community. This time, the narrative is in their hands. Hence, alongside archival materials now newly-accessible to Indigenous communities are a range of born-digital objects in a variety of formats, notably audio, still and moving-picture materials. A number of programs have emerged to support this process in remote communities, particularly those making equipment available and offering skill transfers in relation to the use of that equipment.

Considering these two influences together, we can see that debate regarding improved access to, and in some cases the repatriation of, cultural materials has been ignited by the expectations placed on emerging digital technologies. Most of the archive so far remains in analogue form, yet to be digitized, but there are new horizons on the scope of what could be done in terms of restoring access to cultural information.

The confluence of these two streams results in what is, clearly, a complex environment, bristling with questions over the management of physical and digital objects, materials from the archive and those created in the digital present. Some choices are inescapable for a program wishing to meet demand created by these conditions: program *niche* and purpose needs to be clearly defined to allow its scope of action to be defined and objectives formed. The LKC program supports digital repatriation only, in a sense simplifying its scope of action. However, some matters retain an inherent complexity whether they inhabit the digital or physical domain: some materials bring with them sensitivities over who has the cultural authority, within the community, to view and control access to materials. There are other serious challenges regarding digital objects that need constant monitoring. Standards for digital formats for moving pictures, for example, remain quite fluid, and may necessitate software development/hardware upgrades to ensure the continuance of security and access for digital objects: dilemmas also faced by much larger institutions.

It will be seen, if we return to our original concept (what might be termed the 'elaborated library'), that there is far more at stake here than simply a change of modes and materials. Libraries are in the midst of an intense process of self-questioning: how best to use emerging technologies, and how to process and absorb, in the most positive way, their consequences for libraries' sense of mission (Greenhill, 2009; Jaeger et al, 2007). The *Our Story* / LKC model should contribute to these discussions, for there is something quite novel in the way this model works regarding the control, management and creation of information in this system. The community not only controls access and contributes new material, but adds further layers of information when the material in the *Our Story* database — current and archival — is viewed within the community, and elicited responses from community members are added to the database record by community 'operators' employed to work within the LKC. Typical scenarios are that viewers identify people pictured in images, and identify cultural activities. In this way, local people re-contextualise cultural information which, hitherto, may have existed in isolation within an external archive. This process leads to considerable enriching of the collection, providing a dynamic and pattern of use that is distinctive when compared with mainstream library practice.

The true magnitude of the shift in the 'library model', then, is this: that local people are actively involved as contributors rather than cast in the passive role, which the traditional library has often scripted for its users (Nakata et al, 2006: 35-53). In this particular setting, Indigenous library clients review and 'speak back' to the historical records made by non-Indigenous people in the past, opening up a unique avenue of contemporary cultural practice. Of course, there is nothing inherently 'Indigenous' or indeed non-Indigenous about an opportunity for 'users' to add layers of information to a digital object. But the LKCs, and the contextual setting so-far described, have provided a driver for this kind of interaction with shared materials that has brought the model together, and made a 'business case', for it.

We have considered some reasons why this is particularly important in Indigenous remote communities, but there are others. While the process of government-sponsored dislocation of Indigenous communities has apparently ended, the results of earlier practice have not. Indigenous knowledge has relied on oral transmission, and there have been severe disruptions to this process. Elders are concerned that the cultural knowledge they embody

may not get handed on to subsequent generations, particularly in view of current challenges with their younger contemporaries. So, here too there are compelling reasons to support the local retention of Indigenous culture, its importance voiced by an authoritative and yet vulnerable component of the Northern Territory's Aboriginal populations.

Demographic and Geographic Context

To grasp the context in which library and information services are provided in the Northern Territory one must appreciate the uniqueness of its demography and geography. The Northern Territory, constituting approximately 1% of the Australian population, in one-sixth of the total land area, is the most sparsely populated region of Australia. By almost every measure available the Northern Territory's population differs greatly from that of other Australian jurisdictions. This includes the fact that over 31% of Territorians are Aboriginal[2] (Australian Bureau of Statistics, 2006). Indeed, over two thirds of Aboriginal Territorians live in remote communities some up to a 9-hour drive away from the major centres and often only accessible by 4 wheel drive or alternatively light aircraft. Many of the communities are poorly serviced and in many cases material goods - clothing, food, building supplies etc - must be brought in by barge, road-trains or air.

The Northern Territory Library is guided by two primary responsibilities, firstly, to collect, preserve and make accessible the Territory's documentary heritage; and secondly, to provide public library services in partnership with local government authorities in remote areas. Northern Territory Library works with Shire councils to ensure library services are of a reasonable standard and relevant to the community. In all there are 33 public libraries in the Territory, with 22 of these situated in isolated and remote Aboriginal communities. In 2004 the current Libraries and Knowledge Centers (LKC) Program was developed to provide access to local content and to respond to the immediate need to preserve Aboriginal cultural heritage.

ICTs in these regions still lag behind connections speeds and technologies available in the metropolitan areas of Australia. Infrastructure covers vast distances and links between regional hubs to remote locations or outstations are hindered by the geographic isolation. Many remote communities continue to use 2-Way Satellite connections in order to access the internet and although this is generally effective, many of these services suffer from periodic outages and services are not properly maintained. To put issues of the digital divide into further perspective, home ownership of personal computers in the Northern Territory's remote communities is extremely rare and in 2005 was as low as 4 per cent amongst the Aboriginal population outside of the capital city of Darwin (Department of Corporate and Information Services, 2005: 11). National figures have also shown that 78.4 per cent of Indigenous people in remote areas of Australia do not use the Internet (Radoll, 2006: 15). Indeed, for the most part Internet access in remote Indigenous communities is either non-existent or only available via community service organisations such as community councils, schools or libraries. However, as Radoll (2006: 12) has identified in many of these circumstances access is often restricted or inhibited in some way; meaning that people have less opportunity to explore or freely develop aptitude in computing and/or online technologies.

With these challenges in mind the Northern Territory Library; in partnership with newly formed Shire councils (replacing now defunct Community Government Councils) provide public library services to 22 isolated and remote communities. Understanding that equitable access to ICTs is a critical component to the effective operation of these library services the Northern Territory Library provides online resources, a Library Management System for the entire library network and access to reliable and effective information management tools. NTL also provide technical

skills and support necessary to maintain these systems which are often difficult to obtain given the remoteness of these libraries in both tropical (around Darwin and the Top End) and desert Australia (around Alice Springs and Tennant Creek).

Planning for effective information or communications services is even more difficult, given the high cultural and linguistic diversity the Territory's small and diffuse population. Indigenous clients in these areas combine high levels of Indigenous knowledge with often-lower levels of English-language literacy, income-earning capacity, and (non-Indigenous) educational achievement. Although it is now widely understood that library and information services operating in similar regions across Australia must accommodate Indigenous culture, the NT presents a particular challenge. The Territory boasts approximately 60 Indigenous languages and dialects, and in many communities, English is spoken as a second or third language. In the Central Australian region alone (surrounding the main township of Alice Springs) there are five cultural and linguistic regions consisting of approximately 20 Indigenous languages/dialects and English literacy is generally very poor. (IAD, 2002; Ramsey, 2003: xi). Designing programs that intend to connect people in remote locations to information resources must therefore first acknowledge and then work with the high levels of linguistic and cultural heterogeneity unique to the region.

Digital Knowledge Management

The persistence of Aboriginal cultures in the Northern Territory has meant that it is necessary for any library or information service handling their materials to observe traditional rules and protocols governing information exchange. The anthropological literature has shown that while the details of these protocols may differ across Australia, in the Northern Territory they are typically shaped by overarching 'laws' relating to a person's relationship to particular 'estates' of land

and their ritual status (Michaels, 1985; Thorley, 2002). Given the disjunction between Indigenous and Western ways of processing and transmitting information, the question needs to be asked as to exactly how much a library service can truly assist communities in the management of their own information resources. Indeed, the usefulness of digital technology in the management of Indigenous knowledge has been the subject of a number of research projects across Australia. (Christie, 2003; Christen, 2005; Cohen, 2005).

Around the same time as the LKC program was being implemented Charles Darwin University's School of Australian Indigenous Knowledge Systems (SAIKS) had begun working with communities in Arnhem Land to assess the role of digital media in the maintenance of traditional Indigenous knowledge. Together, SAIKS and the Northern Territory Library were able to organise a number of seminars exploring the best ways of managing Indigenous information in digital formats and what technologies could be applied to this end. Contributions from the SAIKS project, between 2003 and 2006, were persistently critical of many of these databases and their inability to provide an 'ontologically flat' structure. (Christie, 2004) Michael Christie and his team have provided an essential check on the move towards digital archives by forming a critique of database structures and the recording of Indigenous histories, knowledge and practices:

"In processes of setting up a database, we make decisions about how the data is to be structured [...] Whichever way these political and technical decisions go – who makes them and why, and which features are excluded, none of them will remain apparent after the interfaces are developed and put in place. They will be obscured by the illusion of objectivity the interfaces convey. Not only does the information architecture reflect a particular politics of knowledge but it also somehow enacts it." (Christie, 2003: 4).

As people begin to enter their information into database systems they ultimately submit to the logic of the dominant system of a pre-developed digital collection. This is true even where the technology has been used for cultural preservation purposes, and its use may signal a strategically crucial loss. That is, the technology itself may embody the logic of another culture which Indigenous society would in time yield to. In this view utilization of electronic database technology is at its *worst* a threat to traditional culture, and at *best* could only ever be used to compliment cultural practice. Nevertheless, as the library is charged with the task of assisting communities to preserve their documentary heritage, the Northern Territory Library must work within their ambit of expertise. Databases were identified as one practical way that a library and information service could assist communities in their expressed desire to preserve local stories. Provision of these services would also encourage new digital literacies that are now common to social and economic life in mainstream Australia.

The issue of how database collections might assist the transfer of knowledge between generations of people was also high on the agenda of discussions between SAIKS and NTL (and others). The context for inter-generational transfer of knowledge is particularly grim in some regions and, as mentioned above many communities were actively requesting assistance in documenting the knowledge of the elders. Current Indigenous population statistics showing that the Australian Indigenous population is characterised by a very young age composition combined with high a mortality rate amongst adults, explain this sense of urgency (Taylor, 2006). To be succinct: less and less 'old people' remain to hand on their knowledge to a growing population of young people, and this brings a special urgency.

The usefulness of databases in helping people retain their knowledge remains largely untested and will require closer examination over the next few years. But this is not to suggest that these systems are not without already recognisable benefit. Regarded as one element 'in a wider system of Indigenous knowledge management', it is commonly asserted that while the value of active knowledge use should not be overlooked, database collections may serve as an effective means to secure recognition of community rights over Indigenous Knowledge and offers a degree of protection against theft of Intellectual and cultural property. As Langton et al (2003) have stated in their report on 'traditional lifestyles and biodiversity' to the United Nations Environment Programme, documentation of knowledge and linked education initiatives can boost local community capacity in the promotion, protection and facilitation of their knowledge.

There are now multiple projects across Australia and the globe working on a range of technologies to better accommodate Indigenous cultural information (Christen, 2005; Cohen, 2005; Hughes & Dallwitz, 2007; Hunter et al, 2003). As many of the devices are portable, increasingly affordable and do not require advanced literacy to operate, their popularity and ubiquity in these communities is on the increase. Furthermore they utilise audio-visual material far more engaging to people with low-literacy. Manggarai weavers of Flores, Indonesia, use digital cameras to document their age-old designs (Threads of Life, 2006); the San hunter-gatherers of the Kalahari of southern Africa use 'cyber-tracker' palm pilots to record information about species on their land (Bazilchuk, 2004); and more and more Australian Indigenous peoples are using databases to access and document their social and cultural histories.

In early 2008 the Commonwealth Government of Australia hosted the 'Australia 2020 Summit'. Bringing together Australia's 'best and brightest', the summit charged participants with the task of envisioning a long-term strategy for the nation in key policy areas. The notion of 'a national Indigenous Knowledge Centre network' provid-

ing 'support to regional knowledge centres', was listed as a 'Top Idea' in the initial report:

"Regional [knowledge] centres reflect that each Indigenous group is different and has different knowledge to preserve and to develop. These need to be linked to the development of community hubs, and would utilise existing facilities." (Commonwealth of Australia 2008a: 26).

It was proposed that a National Indigenous Knowledge centre be established to give support to regional knowledge centres and that 'hub' knowledge centres would document, record, keep and tell local Indigenous stories using digital media technology (Commonwealth of Australia, 2008b: 229, 246). According to this vision the knowledge centres would improve local employment options, focus on supporting and capturing regional knowledge, provide a location for Aboriginal knowledge production and research by Aboriginal people, and provide a social and cultural context and increase value and self-esteem. Although neither the Northern Territory Library's LKC program nor the State Library of Queensland's Knowledge Centre initiative were referred to in this document, any further development of these ideas would surely entail an assessment of existing Knowledge Centre programs.

The LKC Program Model

Nine years ago, after being approached by a number of communities looking to explore alternative library services, the Northern Territory library began devising its Indigenous Knowledge Centre concept. As the first library organisation to begin using the 'Knowledge Centre' suffix, the experience of the Northern Territory Library is particularly interesting. The remote communities of Wadeye (Port Keats), Aleyaw (Ti Tree) and Galiwinku (Elcho Island) were chosen as sites to initially pilot what was then described as the 'Indigenous Knowledge Centres' concept. Initial consultations with the Galiwinku community revealed that their thinking around the knowledge centre dated back to the 1970s. They imagined a physical space that would combine various information and cultural services, thus challenging the well defined boundaries between various cultural institutions (Personal communication, P. Webb, August 14th 2008). The Knowledge Centre was to be a meeting place for the community and combine a range of services such as an interpretative centre, a keeping place, a museum and a library.

The overarching purpose of the Knowledge Centre would be to improve access to collections of relevance to the community, enable the creation of new documents / recordings and give people a measure of ownership and control over these collections. Very early on in their development a resident of Galiwinku, Richard Gandhuwuy Garrawurra, described the Knowledge Centres as:

"...breathing places...they keep our culture strong for our children...look after our traditions, songs, language, stories and artwork...bring back the things that guide us today for the future...combining a meeting place for traditional business with modern library services." (Taylor 2004: 1).

After a two-year study involving a number of remote Aboriginal communities in the Top End, the community of Galiwinku (Elcho Island) was chosen as the site of the first Indigenous Knowledge Centre in 2002 (Australian Broadcasting Commission, 2003; Northern Land Council, 2002). At the locus of the Galiwinku Knowledge Centre plan was a '42 level relational database' that aimed to preserve local knowledge and represent the way the Yolgnu people understand the natural world (Rothwell, 2003). This ambitious task was, according researchers at the School of Indigenous Knowledge Systems at Charles Darwin University, 'impossible to achieve and in fact unnecessary

to attempt' (Christie, 2005) and, as far as can be ascertained, has since fallen into disuse.

In 2003 NTL sketched a 'Community Knowledge Centre Road Map' outlining the Library's response to 'increased demand' from communities to assist in managing their 'traditional Indigenous knowledge'. Under this proposed model a 'hub' community with a functioning library service, would manage a digital collection that could then be distributed – potentially via the web - to other communities within a regional network of linked databases. Just prior to the implementation of the remodeled Libraries and Knowledge Centres program in 2004, the National Indigenous Languages Survey Report indicated that 'In many instances' the fledgling Knowledge Centres suffered from 'a lack of ongoing resources and some poorly developed policy guidelines' (Australia Institute of Aboriginal and Torres Strait Islander Studies, 2005:94). Despite this the report went on to recommend that the NT Government ensure that links are made between education services in remote communities and the newly devised 'Indigenous Knowledge Centre initiative' (NILS, 2005: 100). A few years earlier the Territory Government's own report into secondary education commented that the Knowledge Centres could potentially become sites for further nurturing 'language and tradition', via documentation and archiving as well as community events. In hindsight it appears that the report pre-empted NTL's decision to implement software and digital media equipment tailored to Indigenous needs stating that:

"There may also be benefit in investigating and building on the Ara Irititja project in South Australia and the initiatives being undertaken through the Cape York Partnerships in relation to digital holdings of Indigenous knowledge and enabling contemporary avenues for cultural transmission. The Indigenous Knowledge Centre Initiative [...] could be linked to the smaller Language Nests [in schools] and become the places for the holding, renewal and creation of traditional practices that

could be accessed and utilised by education and other services [...] the digital medium presents great opportunity for education, enterprise and cultural maintenance." (Ramsey, 2003: 174-175).

The following year a comprehensive review was conducted into the 'readiness' of communities in the West MacDonnell's region of Central Australia for the LKC program. The numerous recommendations made centered around the need for the program to develop an ICT training initiative that would build upon existing library programs, infrastructure and local skills. The report (Northern Territory Library, 2005) emphasised the need for a well considered implementation, training and support regime and the relatively low standard of ICT skills in each of the studied communities.

Without access to seeding monies, new funding or project funding the LKC program was first implemented using re-directed Northern Territory Library operational funds. A training methodology was trialed and supporting manuals created for the *Our Story* database. A common set of scanner, digital camera, digital audio-recording gear and supporting software was recommended to each library and a small grant to cover this initial setup cost was provided from NTL.

NTL provided – and continues to provide under the LKC model – training, and support through visits by program staff based in Darwin and Alice Springs, annual operational funds and funds for library materials. A small team of Northern Territory Library staff provides ongoing training and support to Community Library Officers (CLOs) and their Councils. This involves onsite visits and regular, often weekly contact by telephone and email. The community library, supported by Northern Territory Library, provides a solid foundation for sustainable library services, and a permanent presence in the community. In remote communities this long-term, annual support is critical, as many services and programs can be unreliable and short-term.

Each library is staffed by one or two CLOs and is open from between 10-30 hours per week, Monday through Saturday. Community Library Officers (CLOs) are employed by local Councils to operate the library. In all cases, CLOs are local residents of their communities. The program has created meaningful jobs for some community members, who are motivated to increase their own skills through employment at the library and involvement in important cultural work. One CLO on the Tiwi Islands community of Pirlangimpi has been employed in the library for 7 years. Over that time she has developed expertise in using a range of computer programs, gained skills in use of the internet, digital cameras, scanners etc., and now she is passing on these skills to others in the community through her work at the library.

Technology is a key component of the LKC model and each LKC has free public access computers which are connected to the Internet (although outages are not uncommon in many communities). In Indigenous communities, the library is often the only public space where people can come to read, interact with other community members, find information, access computers or use the Internet. Access to the Internet is becoming increasingly important to remote users particularly for online banking and web browsing (Papandrea et al, 2006: 61). The Library is also often a place where those who have had little or no contact with information and communications technology can begin to develop familiarity with various systems.

The Our Story Database

In this section we describe the principal ICT tool used in the LKC program, the *Our Story* database. Embedded within the LKC Model, *Our Story* is being used to provide communities with a further resource in sustaining culture, and to develop and extend local engagements with literacy and ICTs. This often means providing access to materials featuring local Indigenous languages and dialects as well as local cultural practices.

Our Story uses the *Ara Irititja* database platform, a *File Maker Pro* application originally developed by the Social History Unit of the Anangu Pitjantjatjara Yankunyjatjara Council (APY Council) in north-western South Australia in the mid-1990s (Hughes & Dallwitz, 2007).[3] The *Ara Irititja* database came about in response to senior Anangu[4] requests for improved access to the records of past anthropologists, missionaries, and others who had so fervently documented their lives in a period of cultural change. Following a 15-year period of software development, user testing and interface refinement the *Ara Irititja* project devised an appropriate database template for community-based archiving projects for Indigenous Australia. The creation of a digital archive specifically designed for residents in remote desert communities began to transform peoples' thinking about the delivery of information and heritage services to remote Indigenous Australians.

Recognising the suitability of this system for use across its network of remote libraries, the Northern Territory Library purchased a Territory-wide license to *Ara Irititja* in 2004. While the interface and functionality of the system was regarded as proven in the Indigenous community context some necessary modifications were nonetheless required before implementation could occur. The system required superior import/export functionality, additional scope for customisation of the interface by each community and a PC version of the system was needed for those sites not running Mac OS X; the preferred environment of the original software designers. While enhanced import/export functionality was essential, so that all of the metadata could be moved into a new system in the future, the requirement of community customisation was deemed equally critical. Without this front-end flexibility, community/user acceptance and ownership of each database may have been jeopardised.

Despite the fact that *Ara Irititja* had been using the software for many years across the Anangu Pitjantjatjara (AP) Lands, Northern Territory Li-

brary's model of delivery was going to be quite different. NTL's version of the software was embedded in the Libraries and Knowledge Centres program with all of its associated support, training employment opportunities, and furthermore, the system would be implemented across numerous Indigenous communities covering approximately fifteen distinct cultural and linguistic regions. (See Table 1) Conversely, the *Ara Irititja* system had originally been designed for use within a relatively homogenous cultural and linguistic region on the AP lands - where a series of mutually-intelligible western desert dialects and languages are spoken - and was set to display Pitjantjatjara names only. *Our Story*, on the other hand, needed to be flexible enough to ensure that each of the relevant local Indigenous languages could feature not only in the database title-name but also throughout the interface; icons, buttons etc. With this flexibility enabled, the program could meet the high priority that most communities place on the continuance of local Indigenous knowledge and language.

The *Our Story* database has been a cornerstone of the LKC model. The wider LKC model is intended to support Our Story installations, and to expose and develop the engagement of Indigenous communities with literacy practices in hard-copy and electronic formats. Each community was then able to create a database, unique to their region, and administered by a locally employed Community Library Officer (CLO). Populating the system with newly digitised or born-digital material would therefore be the responsibility of the CLO, with support from NTL project staff.[5] During these initial implementation stages, NTL provided intensive training to local CLOs in order to install, set-up and populate the system with local content. Each of the participating communities received additional financial support to purchase suitable digitisation equipment and software, following recommendations from Northern Territory Library's IT staff and appropriate, simple English documentation was also created. The *Our Story procedures manual* included advice on

Table 1. Northern Territory databases currently supported under the LKC model [6]

Community	Language/s	Database Name	No. of Items
Lajamanu	Warlpiri, Gurindji	*Nganju* ('Roots')	111
Ti Tree (Aleyaw)	Anmatyerr	*Anmatyerr Angkety* ('Anmatyerr Talking')	1,550
Ltyentye Apurte	Central and Eastern Arrernte	*Anwernekenhe Ayeye* ('Our Story')	1,438
Milingimbi	Grupapungu, Djambarrpuyngu	*Limurrung Dhawu*	6,943
Elliott	Jingulu, Mudburra	*Our Story*	432
Wadeye	Murrinh-patha,	*Murrinh Nekinigme*	21,031
Peppimenarti	Ngan'gikurunggurr	*Ngan'gi Ngagurr*	2,314
Ngukurr	Ngalakgan, Yugul	*Melabat Stori*	1,959
Umbakumba	Anindilyakwa	*Yirrilangwa Alawudawarra*	3,139
Angurugu	Anindilyakwa	*Groote Eylandt Story*	5,237
Milikapiti	Tiwi	*Ngini Tiwi*	2,409
Barunga	Jawoyn, Mayali	*Bla Mibala Stori*	1,095
Pirlangimpi	Tiwi	*Ngini Tiwi*	2,409
Galiwin'ku	Nhangu	*Our Story*	792
Borroloola	Mara	*Our Story*	215
Ramingining	Djinang	*Our Story*	747

digital standards and step by step guides to importing items and adding new metadata into the system.

Finding content for the databases was in most cases not difficult, as many of the community libraries had already begun to store hard copies of important local historical and cultural materials. The Library and Knowledge Centre in Wadeye for example had already received hundreds of repatriated photographs and sound recordings from anthropologists and missionaries, ready for inclusion in their *Murrinh Nekinigme* (*Our Story*) system. *Our Story* databases in most communities have been quickly populated with similar material and now contain a mixture of repatriated digital content (photos, film, sound etc) from cultural institutions and private collections, as well as born digital materials deposited by local schools, researchers, community members and visitors.

These database systems have allowed for materials from a range of different and distinct collections to come together for the first time as a unique compilation in their own right. In *Our Story*

for example, each item in the database is associated with its original catalogue information as well as enriched with annotations added dynamically by local library staff and other interested community members. With the diversity of archived materials and the emphasis on community directed population of the *Our Story* databases, these systems have become 'organic' in the way that they expand and change over time. This combination of content and descriptive data has meant that each database is a valuable resource of not only local historical materials but also perspectives on these histories. Researchers and visitors to these communities are beginning to show interest in gaining access to these collections and the library is in the process of advising each Shire of the issues associated with access to Indigenous digital collections. Cognisant of the principles that underlie the success of the *Our Story* databases – acknowledging local control and ownership of the collections - the library have not pursued making these collections available to a wider-audience online. The Northern Territory Library has instead started a consultative process regarding what material communities might consider making available for publication on Northern Territory Library's online digital repository, *Territory Stories*.

THEORETICAL DIMENSIONS

The Program Paradigm

The overarching objectives of the LKC Program can be reduced to two core elements: to assist with Indigenous knowledge management and to introduce and develop digital and other literacies amongst this clientele. The program hopes to achieve these objectives by (a) supporting remote Indigenous communities with access to and use of recorded Indigenous knowledge, (b) providing an elaborated library model to meet indigenous needs, (c) utilising emergent digital technologies to order to achieve the above and keep library services relevant, and (d) assisting in the development of remote communities via the provision of relevant and engaging literacy and information resources.

In practice, the *Our Story* / LKC paradigm operates at a number of levels. At one level, we can distinguish between those of *Our Story* itself and, spreading over and containing it, the Libraries and Knowledge Centres paradigm. Between these two paradigms, there is an interdependency that is critical to their continued viability, and to the 'success' that is considered in a later section of this chapter.

As described earlier in this chapter, *Our Story*'s paradigm is predicated on the idea of cultural repatriation. This gave the project its initial impetus by creating a "need" which the project could seek to fulfill: that is, to take materials originating from a community, yet alienated from it, and make them accessible to that community. As pointed out by those working with Indigenous collections in the library sector, the technology of digitisation has enabled the repatriation of heritage materials

without 'institutional relinquishment' (Nakata et al, 2008 p.226). Within this proposal of repatriation lies a broader imperative that has had implications for the project: the idea of the community sitting in the driver's seat in the management of those materials.

This bigger idea, this sense of agency on the part of the "clients" of the service, has influenced the project in a number of dimensions, made manifest for example in the born-digital content that has been generated by local people and ingested into the database. The productive role of community members within by this process is underscored through the process of community annotation of digital records, through an operator, to reinstate information about people and cultural activities that are pictured in repatriated objects — a process akin to the tested ethnographic method of 'photo elicitation' without the influence of a researcher (Hurworth, 2003). A further dimension is added by community members working within the service as LKC managers and operators, and in the consistent process of in-service training and professional development in which they participate by virtue of their role in the LKC program.

This amounts to a consistent thread of focus on empowerment, expressed in a number of ways. It is this that makes the broader LKC paradigm, which provides the context for the *Our Story* service, such an interesting elaboration of the library model. The traditional library, as it has developed in its most recent historical manifestation, has implied a kind of passivity on the part of its clientele: content is created elsewhere, and provided to clients, who are often described as "users".

When we consider the LKC model, however, this now-traditional paradigm stands on its head. For now we do have "players": people engaging with the service are far from being consumers alone: they are either creating new material for addition to this community-level digital library, or are intimately involved in providing successive layers of additional information to a degree that it could, quite reasonably, be seen as transforming the nature and status of the object in question: for context is everything, and a new informational context produces something that must, at times, be considered quite different and distinct.

This is an exciting elaboration of the library paradigm: 'users' become 'players'. However, the suggestion that this is substantially and significantly new could be challenged: is this not similar to a wiki where, just as in the *Our Story* setting, participants can add edit and add layers of information — in this case through a form of moderator? And, clearly, this kind of service is anything but new: suggestions that a new internet-based 'participatory culture' is developing, through wikis, blogs and other web services, are hardly novel statements within the now-emergent world of Web 2.0.

To recapture and defend the significant novelty of the *Our Story* / LKC paradigm, we must return to context. In the first instance, we are obliged to remember the local focus of these services. Content held in *Our Story* databases is 'personal' to that community. Communities are not comfortable with the material being accessible through networks, and the prospect of cultural information being stored on, and accessible from, an internet-accessible server represents an unacceptable level of cultural safety and control. There can be acute sensitivities: as noted, in many communities it is culturally offensive to display images of persons who are deceased and there are other important intra-communal prohibitions around access to cultural knowledge.

As a consequence, it is a priority for communities to be in control of the material, determining access rights according to traditionally-determined constraints. Another significant component of local context lies in the varying levels of literacy which community members bring to their interaction with the *Our Story* service. This makes the presence of the operator, when annotations are to be added to database records, imperative. This also provides for a level of control and consistency as the database collection grows and develops as it is used by the community.

A third, very significant, component of context in this regard is one which brings the two paradigms together: the active, participatory, self-managed but non-web environment of the *Our Story* databases and the elaborated library paradigm of the LKC itself. This is the physical presence and persistence of the LKC within the community. The 'genius' of the contemporary, developing library model, the thing that libraries can uniquely provide, comes into being as a result of this physical presence and its ability to host a broad variety of information modes and media. An early evaluation of the program (Northern Territory Government, 2006 p.4) stated that the LKC program was an 'innovative approach to engaging with changing community needs for knowledge and information, and that it could become a leading example for the ways such services can be delivered to Indigenous.'

LKCs show that this amounts to more than a passive response, on the part of libraries, to a simple increase in availability and demand of new media. Present-day libraries operate to maximise engagement with the materials they present to their communities through a process of overlap. A community member might move into the library space to access one kind of object, and then segue to another, or combine the use of a number of objects and types of object. The pulling-power of the *Our Story* database means that community members move into an environment where ink-on-paper literacy materials are also present, increasing the likelihood of use for those materials as well. These opportunities are reflected in the increasing use of LKCs as the physical setting for early childhood literacy programs mounted by Northern Territory Library.

In this way, the Library has been able to make a case, as it were, to the members of remote communities: that the library space is relevant and responsive to their interests. While mainstream libraries strive to provide their clients with access to information across the globe, the LKC program is using computer and digital media technology to focus in on the local. As recent research conducted by Kimberley Christen in Warumungu communities has shown (2007), the adoption of new technology can fit comfortably alongside the cultural imperatives of Aboriginal peoples, such as the retention of local narratives and the affirmation of local identity. Proceeding from this understanding the fundamental message of good faith in this sense is that the LKC takes, manages, and makes accessible the very significant local knowledge in a way that does not, in contrast to earlier non-Indigenous practices, then proceed to alienate that material from the community to which it belongs.

It should be obvious that these two paradigms have implications beyond Indigenous communities alone. Contemporary libraries sometimes struggle to find a role which they, uniquely, can fill in the lives of their would-be clienteles. LKCs show one way in which a traditional library paradigm, where relevancy was in doubt and at risk, by changing the relationship between "providers" and "clients" of such a service into one where clients are providers or producers of content and, in a certain sense, managers of the material.

But the key impact of the *Our Story* / LKC model continues to register, most effectively, in view of the conditions faced by Indigenous people in Australia. Indigenous people have been objectified, controlled, and their social fabric, at times, has come close to being destroyed. So much of that has been implicit in models of Indigenous / non-Indigenous interaction that have portrayed first nations in a situation of passivity. In a small way, the *Our Story* / LKC model engages with and pushes back against this back-drop, both because of the direct support it provides for participatory heritage management, and thus for cultural memory and identity, but also because the paradigm itself operates on the basis of counting-in Indigenous people rather than counting them out.

Theories, Values and Assumptions

The paradigms so described rest on a number of theoretical and value judgements, and on certain assumptions about the relationship between the Northern Territory Library, as funder and provider of the *Our Story* / LKC service, and the communities it is designed to support.

We have argued that the *Our Story* / LKC package amounts, essentially, to an 'elaborated library model'. Similarly, the underlying values that inform the service have taken an elaborated form, building on traditional library concerns and broadening them so that they are capable of encompassing a particular environment.

A thread of continuity centres on the continued emphasis on literacy. As argued above, the *Our Story* / LKC environment presents a series of overlapping opportunities to engage with words-on-the-page materials, audio and video, internet access and, of course, a combination of media in the *Our Story* database. However, left at that such an approach could have the appearance of "build it and they will come" mentality, which is not always a productive way to engage a community. Again, thoughts go back to the traditional library model, where materials are provided, but the drivers for their use come from other quarters. For centuries libraries have contributed to this process by holding the physical collections and providing the social spaces for interactions between readers and knowledge (Anderson, 1994). Knowledge does not exist 'out there' – in books and libraries, records, movies and archives – but is created in social environments.

In this elaborated model, drivers stem from two sources. First, the cultural imperatives associated with the *Our Story* database, where demand is created by community members who wish to view and add to objects in the database, and by community elders who see an opportunity to pass on cultural information in this "assisted" way (in addition to more traditional oral pathways). A second driver consists of the early childhood literacy program put into place by NTL (Northern Territory Library, 2008). In this, local library staff are supported to offer regular and appropriate reading, storytelling, music making and arts activities to young children and their parents and carers. This program is informed by a body of international research on the efficacy of early-childhood literacy programs, which has been added to by locally-specific research commissioned by NTL, to identify methods and resources suitable to the program's real-world context.

Of course, a third driver is generated by conditions of remoteness. As for all isolated communities, entertainment is relatively scarce, and this must account for a component of visitation to the service. Under the implicit "overlap" doctrine described for the *Our Story* / LKC paradigm, it is anticipated that, given a sufficient diversity and relevance of objects available, that this type of contact with the service would, again, result in opportunistic engagements with other materials. This scenario, again, supports the importance of the persistent, physical space of the LKC, with its consistent hours of opening so that community members can plan and assume their contact with the service. This level of expectation keeps the service alive: there have been examples where a stand-alone *Our Story*-style database service has withered simply due to varying hours of access and loss of the inadvertent and opportunistic engagement made possible by a mixed-use facility.

But, for all of these forms of engagement, it is with a form of 'literacy' that is, itself, elaborated. The *Our Story* database provides not only contact with traditional marks-on-the-page style literacy, but also with the controls and functionalities that, together, make up a literacy conceived in terms of ICTs. In terms of *Our Story*, opportunities for engagement with this form of literacy come — in order of increasing sophistication — from accessing the product in user mode; contributing metadata with an operator; determining viewing rights with an operator; developing digital content for addition to the database; and being an opera-

tor, managing, editing and adding to objects in the collection. In a service that is predicated on a vision of local content provision and management, these contacts all stand to contribute to experiential assets within the community. Other contacts with ICTs, either in the context of training or use, could leverage these as, indeed, contacts with ICTs outside of the *Our Story* / LKC context stand to raise levels of capability when community members return to the service.

Within the *Our Story* / LKC service, as well, and as for 'marks on the page' literacy, an implicit concept of overlap is important. There are broad levels of commonality in the commands and functionality encountered in *Our Story* and in the other electronic modalities made available within the LKC, such as those provided through open and subscription-based internet services. Papandrea observed engagement with new media technology via the LKC program while conducting research on Phone and Internet usage in the Anmatyerr community:

"There was an interesting and relatively advanced use of computers and Internet by two young men in the community who were engaged as research assistants on a water culture research project being conducted by Charles Darwin University. They were engaged in identifying and mapping of water resources, including the recording of digital photographs in an electronic database [Our Story]. They were very proud of their work and keen to demonstrate what was being included in the database. Their relatively high level of computer skills had been acquired through intensive, practical training." (Papandrea, 2006: 32).

So again, even staying within the electronic domain, the unique possibilities of the physical mixed-mode library are critical. Again, the disadvantage of remoteness and poor socio-economic conditions which has meant that private computer and internet access in these communities is very low compared with urban Australia. Factoring this into an appreciation of the LKCs context again gives a better fix on the significance of the service they provide to their communities.

INSIGHTS, CHALLENGES AND THE FUTURE

Lessons Learned

There have been numerous research projects over the past decade investigating the prospects of database technology in the retention of Aboriginal knowledge. Some of these projects have created prototypes of databases but few have been able to concentrate on or implement a system with the required levels of support and maintenance. As referred to above, the Charles Darwin University projects had a significant theoretical component, particularly in relation to the ontologies and structures of Indigenous knowledge and went as far as offering a design concept of what a more appropriate system might look like. Since this time an American researcher working with Warramungu people in Tennant Creek has created the *Mukurtu* database (Christen, 2005) and a prototype system, *Memory Place*, has been created to hold the ethno-biological documentation of a long-term researcher on Groote Eylandt.

But amongst these many projects there was nothing quite like the *Our Story* / LKC project, in that it was in full production; adding to its collections; being annotated and accessed by local people; competently supported; and gradually growing outward to meet demand from local people. Whilst not ignoring questions of ontology and knowledge structure the LKC program has not allowed this to take precedence over getting *Our Story* implemented. Regular visits from support staff based in Darwin, installing and maintaining equipment, refreshing physical collections, providing training and support for local LKC managers, provided a layer of practical investment that has led, over time, to a sustained and growing network of *Our Story* / LKC installations. The

Our Story / LKC combination was emerging as a hardened ICT program improved, cycle by cycle, by confronting practical challenges and solving them. In the meantime, others involved in similar projects in other parts of Australia continued to explore the implications of ontological differences and, on some occasions, to look askance at the lack of technical sophistication attributed to the *Our Story* platform.

From our perspective, it has been a wise decision to maintain a central focus on the nuts-and-bolts of rolling-out and sustaining the network of *Our Story* / LKC installations. Comparable programs have some similar elements, not least the program put in place by the Pitjantjatjara people, at whose behest the *Ara Irititja* / *Our Story* software has been developed over more than a decade ago. But there appear not to be any other programs that have kept their promise to deliver such facilities in remote Indigenous communities, and to sustain and develop them over time with recurring funding and staff commitments.

The program has been part of substantial discussions on developing a successor to the current production version of *Our Story*, and has made considerable investments toward software development in this regard. The technical challenges, seen across all dimensions, are surprisingly similar to digital services operating on a larger scale and in metropolitan settings: where digital moving-picture objects are involved, back-up alone poses questions from a technical perspective.

However, as flagged in the opening sections of this chapter, it is notable that critical dimensions of the effort to put the *Our Story* / LKC program into full production are not, strictly speaking, technical alone. A significant component has hinged on the commitment to an elaborated model of a service that was struggling to engage its intended population, and that has involved significant ongoing investment in terms of funding, support staff, and regular training and in-service for the locally-based people, the majority of whom are Indigenous.

The importance of these logistical components of the project is highlighted by the everyday challenges of mounting these services in remote locations. The result is that technical equipment is subject to variations in operating environment, and is situated far from any other source of technical support: there are few computer maintenance services willing and able to attend, and costs for so doing are incredibly high. As with most projects and programs in remote areas, there are also considerable challenges with maintaining staffing. Where local staff decide not to stay with the LKC, there can be difficulties replacing them, and the program as a whole must cultivate, as best it can, certain levels of redundancy to anticipate these predicaments.

Success

As in so many cases, then, the full scope of a successful ICT project depends on more than the technical component. To the extent that the *Our Story* / LKC program has been a success, much is owed to the levels of focus and tenacity applied to making sure these bases are covered. However, before we make any claims for the program's success, we should offer some criteria on which it can be judged. As noted at the opening of the chapter, any 'success' must necessarily be considered as contingent, since in any ongoing program, risks can always emerge.

In June 2005 Professor Martin Nakata and a team of academic researchers conducted an evaluation of the model in its fledgling stages of implementation (Nakata et al, 2006). The evaluation provided an external perspective of the programs fundamentals, and delivered baseline information to guide future developments. A cross-disciplinary team of Indigenous and non-Indigenous academics and specialists, was assembled, including specialists on Indigenous literacy, programs policy, Information and Communications Technology, and intellectual property, under the leadership of Professor Martin Nakata from the Jumbunna

House of Indigenous Learning at the University of Technology Sydney. The team visited a number of LKC sites in 2005 and reviewed the policy settings and other documentation associated with the program. The team provided a substantial report, with specific recommendations, to which NTL responded in 2006.

The LKC program is at the cutting-edge of library services to Indigenous communities. NTL sought confirmation that its model was robust and sustainable and was meeting current needs. Independent evaluation of the program would demonstrate its value to communities and as a contribution to broader government goals, and might also provide evidence for future funding applications. Since then the Program has received a Northern Territory Chief Minister's award (2006) and the Bill and Melinda Gates Foundation 'Access to Learning Award' (2007). Visitor statistics have increased in all cases once the program was introduced.

With the findings of the evaluation report in mind, the present section further identifies some of the fundamental risks associated with the LKC model, and asks if the present program is in a position successfully to anticipate and respond to them. Here, we describe a number of parameters that provide an appropriate test of success for such a program. We propose that such a program would fail if:

- NTL were not able to implement and maintain installations;
- The installations did not result in appropriate results from measures of use;
- The program was not able to build on and develop from the initial foothold established with an installation;
- The instances were seen by local communities as irrelevant to their interests and concerns;
- There were too great a level of un-met demand, with no prospect of gradual progress toward meeting that demand;

- Technical development of the Our Story platform over-reached, or under-reached, providing either an insufficiently reliable user experience, or was demonstrably under specification in comparison with other services available to communities;
- NTL's theories and assumptions about the connection between library-style facilities, the database product, literacy activities and levels of literacy in communities, and other anticipated positive results, proved not to be reliable; and,
- There were areas of NTL's responsibility that it failed to manage, resulting in a break-down of trust and good-faith between NTL and local communities.

As demonstrated above, the first two criteria are satisfied by the program as it currently stands. From initial pilot installations in 2004/2005, the *Our Story* / LKC program has flourished across the Northern Territory, and covers communities in Central Australia and the Top End. Technical and other forms of support have indeed been successfully maintained, and statistical records of visitation to these sites form a basis for claims that *Our Story* / LKC instances are generating, and meeting, demand. Literacy programs are a palpable sign of NTL building on the basic *Our Story* / LKC model, leveraging the physical base the LKCs provide as a stepping-off point for further services. Each time such a service is added, so long as it is sustainable, the program recommends itself, as it were, more and more to the community it seeks to serve, and builds a strong case for its relevancy to community life.

There are positive indicators on the other criteria proposed for the program's success. Feedback on levels of relevancy in this sense is positive. Indigenous elders are, as they have been from the start in connection with the project, passionate about the possibilities it represents for transmitting their cultural knowledge to young people. A resident of the Nthwerey community explained

to a group of men - while providing annotations for the database - the importance of maintaining these historical records in the community:

"Our family connections are a big mess. All of these photos help explain to family members who they are related to. People living today might be family of these old people. Today's grandchildren want to look. People who have [recently] passed away, we leave them alone. We look at these pictures to help us remember our families. By showing our community what's in these books - this is true. This person here [young Anmatyerr trainee] shows everybody these photos. This is true. They can put it in the library." (Personal communication with Aleyaw community member 1st November 2006, translated from Anmatyerr and Warlpiri by Sebastian Walker and Hamilton Morris).

Further visual observation and anecdotal evidence bears out expectations that local people are extremely interested in accessing, viewing and annotating material held in database collections relating to their local area and community. Each Community Library Officer at the Anmatyerr Library and Knowledge Centre in Ti Tree has used the database to not only enter data for the community collections but enter their own 'story' into the database. The following entry into the system serves as a good example:

"[This woman] was a Kaytety woman who lived at Phillip Creek and Alekareng. This photo is taken from Peter and Jay Reads book 'Long Time Olden Time' (page 97) See Audio/Sound files 5000/5 (in the Anmatyerr Angkety Database). Anthropologist Dianne Bell worked with [her] for many years. See 'Daughters of the Dreaming' book for more information and pictures. [She] is featured on a Coloured Stone song.... song name unknown. This is [my] Grandfather's sister. Grandfather is Jupurrula... [She] passed away in 1999 in Tennant Creek." (From the Anmatyerr Angkety database, item p2/107. Names withheld).

In addition to the image of her grandmother, an oral history, digitised from a now out of print series of cassettes, was also included in the database system to provide further context for anyone perusing the database.

At a Territory-wide level, there would seem to be few grounds for a perception by communities that demand for new *Our Story* / LKC instances would not be met. The expansion of the network provides a basis to suggest that instances can be put in place where demand is high and other conditions, such as the provision of a building by the local community council or other local government body, are met. Similarly, on its present record, given its record of focus on implementation and support rather than abstract technical challenges, and NTL's evident commitment to the development of a successor to the current *Our Story* software platform, it appears that over- or under-reaching in a technical sense is less likely, given NTL's record to date and stable organisational settings.

Challenges

This leaves us with a handful of areas where there are potential risks. Above, we identified a set of assumptions which had motivated NTL to view the elaborated mixed-media library as a platform on which to take a more active role in enhancing literacy competency than has traditionally been the case in a library setting. It will be remembered that the traditional model has been confined to providing materials, and training people to access them, rather than providing a further focus on such core skills as those involved in literacy. It will also be remembered that the implicit approach in this instance has been to provide an overlapping environment which provides opportunities — and, in some instances, demand — for the use and development of these competencies, and that this extends beyond print/text literacy to more composite forms of digital literacy.

However, checks of this process based on the anecdotal information and visual inspection performed to date are less compelling than a more systematic approach might provide. Such an approach would also be likely to offer important pointers to how the process, if it does prove significant, could be enhanced. Of course, such data, were it to be generated, could be used by NTL as a tool to advocate on behalf of the program, as it was able to do with the Gates Foundation. A similarly higher level of systemization would also be beneficial for metrics of the dimensions and character of more general use within the elaborated library environment.

Risk to trust and good-will between NTL and local communities represents a more persistent dilemma for the program. In a 2005 NTL internal paper it was argued that NTL's management of Indigenous materials was, due to modest coverage of Indigenous rights within a European legal framework, more likely to result in damage to relationships with Indigenous people who had provided content than exposure to risks in a (non-Indigenous) legal sense. As the program expands NTL will need to find ways of managing Indigenous Intellectual and Cultural Property Rights within a non-indigenous legal and institutional framework that can be at odds with Aboriginal knowledge management protocols. Following on from the success of the program and subsequent publicity of the 'Access to Learning Award' a number of Aboriginal organisations have approached NTL with requests that they become a 'trusted repository' for community-made content. Difficulties in articulating between Indigenous and non-Indigenous law mean that this will continue to be a risk for all organisations adopting a stewardship role in relation to Indigenous material.

An associated, yet distinct issue arises in relation to the potential for political division to impact on accessibility to materials in collections. As collections develop, they become inherently more valuable, even if that value were only to be perceived within the immediate community that has given rise to it. Remote communities are not strangers to political and social division, and some *Our Story* collections have become subject to political contest. In a worst-case scenario, this has resulted in a freeze in the process of accessing, viewing, up-loading and annotating objects in the database. Similarly, in communities where ownership of the database and/or individual items has not been well documented or explained the viability of the collection has been brought into question. This scenario eventuated in one Central Australian community where photographs from the collection of a past, and controversial anthropologist where added into their local database. A community member began documenting detailed stories related to each photographic until he discovered that the copyright of the images were retained by an institution which he regarded as antagonistic to his communities interests. Despite that fact that the *information* entered by this person would legally be the property of the local governing body and not the institution that donated the photographs, all information was withdrawn and trust in the LKC was negatively affected.

The current NTL position on ownership of the collections is that they are owned by the relevant Shires in which the collections are held, but this has never been tested. Until recently this mean that (now defunct) Community Government Councils could nominally take responsibility for the collections via a decision making process involving locally appointed, an most often Indigenous, councilors. Local Government reform in 2008 has meant that 'ownership' of the database collections now resides with larger Shire Councils incorporating many communities, covering multiple linguistic and cultural boundaries and including non-indigenous residents. Naturally, there is some concern that this new model of local government might lack both the legal authority to 'own' these databases and the cultural authority to make decisions on collections developed within a particular sub-region of the Shire.

One of the key successes of the Libraries and Knowledge Centres program has been in its ability to improve access to collections of relevance to Indigenous communities, and as such give people a measure of ownership and control over these collections. As stated in the aforementioned 'Road Map', the LKC program was in part a response to 'increased demand' from communities to assist in managing their 'traditional indigenous knowledge'. As many of these databases contain or will begin to collect information regarded as the intellectual and cultural property of Aboriginal people and their communities NTL needs to ensure that these interests are not neglected. In any case, it is imperative that trust is maintained between the organisation and its Indigenous constituents, who provide all of the material, and therefore the key driver, for the *Our Story* / LKC program. The position of NTL to date has been that Indigenous rights over this material is sacrosanct, and it is critical that this continues to be the case if information flows are to be maintained into the *Our Story* instances, so that they can be enjoyed and extended within the context of the communities which have given rise to them.

Future Trends and Recommendations for Future Projects

While there were minor changes made to the software during initial deployment of *Our Story*, there are a number of technical shortfalls within the current system and there is general consensus regarding the need for a browser-based solution. The new system is intended to build upon the existing, and successful features of the system including its interface design and functionality. The growth of Indigenous land management programs across the Northern Territory has meant that documentation of geospatial data and database tools to capture Indigenous ecological knowledge have become key requirements of future systems. There is already considerable interest from existing *Our*

Story users to use popular web-mapping applications (such as Google Maps) to register and record important places in a storied landscape. As one Community Library Officer described, navigating through a 'glass map' of peoples traditional lands is a more intuitive way of searching for data, more intuitive than typing a place name in a text box. As one CLO reflected:

"Many people in our communities have connections all across the Territory. We've all grown up and moved around to many different places. Our old people used to live in the bush and this technology lets us see places that are hard to visit by car. This is a new way of learning about country." (*Bill and Melinda Gates Foundation, 2007*)

Using software that has avoided any attempt to mirror, or reflect an Indigenous knowledge system has been a tremendous strength of the LKC Program to date. The database schema of the *Our Story* software is relatively 'flat' – in that it does not privilege different hierarchies of knowledge – and has been shaped much more by a concern to replicate the structures of a physical archive than an Indigenous episteme. While future developments of the software will necessarily become more advanced and intend to accommodate greater scope for 'Indigenous Knowledge' – such as new database fields for ecological and cultural information, the ability to create audio and video annotations – the developers need be extremely careful not to over-extend in functionality.

With the certainty provided by annual funding from NTL grants, planning can occur for future developments of the program. This has been a major strength of the program and permitted a staged approach to implementation and program growth:

- Increase in training / staffing capacity for CLOs;

- Increased participation by Indigenous people as staff in the program;
- Greater direct role for technical / database management by Indigenous people;
- Development of suitable modes through which communities can use material to generate a presence;
- Development of more accurate and appropriate methodologies for service evaluation;
- Clarification of 'ownership' rights / responsibilities over databases;
- Continued monitoring / development of Indigenous Intellectual Property protocols;
- Further ways to leverage service to support ICT and language literacies; and
- Further ways to make LKCs central to, responsive to, remote communities.

CONCLUSION

By listening to the needs of Northern Territory Indigenous communities, and learning from similar programs across Australia, the Northern Territory Library has been able to implement a distinctive information technology service with some success. The creation of these digital collections has enabled marginalized and isolated communities to access and preserve materials extremely important to the cultural and historical identity of the user base. Unlike other 'database' projects that administer a collection on behalf of the community, or present short-term project-based solutions, the LKC model places responsibility with locally employed Community Library Officers who act on behalf of their communities. This is particularly important in that many are Indigenous members of the local community. Even so, issues regarding ownership of the collections and the inescapable need to upgrade the database system will continue to challenge - and provoke - future developments in the program.

REFERENCES

Anderson, G. T. (1994). Dimensions, Context and Freedom: The Library in the Social Creation of Knowledge. In Barrett, E. (Ed.), *Sociomedia: multimedia, hypermedia and the social construction of knowledge* (pp. 107–124). London: MIR Press.

Australia Institute of Aboriginal and Torres Strait Islander Studies. (2005). *The National Indigenous Languages Survey Report. Report submitted to the Department of Communications, Information Technology and the Arts by the Australian Institute of Aboriginal and Torres Strait Islander Studies in association with the Federation of Aboriginal and Torres Strait Islander Languages.* Canberra: Department of Communications, Information Technology and the Arts.

Australian Bureau of Statistics. (2006). *Population Characteristics, Aboriginal and Torres Strait Islander Australians.* (No. 4713.7.55.001). Canberra.

Batty, P. (2005). White Redemption Rituals: Reflections on the Repatriation of Aboriginal Secret-Sacred Objects. In Lea, T., Kowal, E., & Cowlishaw, G. (Eds.), *Moving Anthropology: Critical Indigenous Studies.* Darwin: Darwin University Press.

Bill and Melinda Gates Foundation. Remote Australian Library System Receives Award for Teaching Technology Literacy Skills Through Preservation of Culture. (2007) Retrieved December 12, 2008, from http://www.gatesfoundation.org/press-releases/Pages/northern-mn territory-library-atla-winner-070820.aspx

Christen, K. (2005). Gone Digital: Culture as Interface in Aboriginal Collaborations. *International Journal of Cultural Property, 12*(3), 315–345.

Christen, K. (2007) The Politics of Search: Archival Accountability in Aboriginal Australia. Presented at the MIT5: Media in Transition 5 Conference Technological Translations and Digital Dilemmas Panel. April 28th, 2007. Retrieved January 12, 2008 http://web.mit.edu/comm-forum/mit5/papers/Christen.pdf.

Christie, M. (2003). Computer Databases and Aboriginal Knowledge. Learning Communities. Retrieved December 13, 2008, from: http://www.cdu.edu.au/centres/ik/pdf/CompDatAbKnow.pdf

Christie, M. (2004) Words, Ontologies and Aboriginal databases. Retrieved December 13, 2008, from: http://www.cdu.edu.au/centres/ik/pdf/ WordsOntologiesAbDB.pdf

Cohen, H. (2005). The visual mediation of a complex narrative: T.G.H. Strehlow's Journey to Horseshoe Bend. *Media International Australia, 116,* 36–51.

Commonwealth of Australia. (2008a). Australia 2020: Initial Summit Report. Retrieved May 1, 2008 http://www.australia2020.gov.au/docs/2020_Summit_initial_report.pdf.

Commonwealth of Australia. (2008b). *Australia 2020 Summit Final Report.* Canberra: Department of Prime Minister and Cabinet.

Department of Corporate and Information Services. (2005). *Telecommunications in Remote NT Indigenous Communities: assessing the economic and social impact of upgraded telecommunications services in remote Indigenous communities in the NT.* Darwin: ACIL Tasman.

Greenhill, K. (2009). Why Learning about Emerging Technologies is Part of Every Librarian's Job. Peer reviewed paper presented at Educause Australiasia. Retrieved 22 August 2008 from http://librariansmatter.com/published/EducauseAustralia09/ GreenhillEmergingTechReasonsRevised.doc.

Hendry, J. (2005). *Reclaiming Culture: Indigenous People and Self-Representation*. New York: Palgrave MacMillan.

Hudson, E. (2006). Cultural Institutions, Law and Indigenous Knowledge: A Legal Primer on the Management of Australian Indigenous Collections. Intellectual Property Research Institute of Australia, the University of Melbourne, Melbourne.

Hudson, E., & Kenyon, A. T. (2005). *Copyright and Cultural Institutions: Short Guidelines for Digitisation*. Melbourne: Centre for Media and Communications Law, University of Melbourne Faculty of Law and the Intellectual Property Research Institute of Australia.

Hughes, M., & Dallwitz, J. (2007). Towards Culturally Appropriate IT Best Practice in Remote Indigenous Australia. In Dyson, Henriks, & Grant, (Eds.), *Information technology and Indigenous people*. University of Technology Sydney, Sydney.

Hurworth, R. (2003). *Photo-interviewing for research. Social Research Update, 40*. Department of Sociology University of Surrey.

IAD. (2002). *Central Australian Aboriginal Languages – current distribution. Map produced by the Institute for Aboriginal Development Press.* Alice Springs.

Jaeger, P.T., Bertot, J.C., McClure, C., & Rodriguez, M. (2007). Public Libraries and Internet Access across the United States: A Comparison by State, 2004-2006. *Information technology and Libraries, 26*(2), 4-14.

Kral, I. (2008, November). *Literacy and remote Indigenous youth: Why social practice matters.* Presented at ANU seminar, Canberra.

Langton, M., & Ma Rhea, Z. (2003). *Traditional lifestyles and biodiversity use regional report: Australia, Asia and the middle east. Composite report on the status and trends regarding the knowledge, innovations and practices of indigenous and local communities relevant to the conservation and sustainable use of biodiversity. Prepared for the secretariat of the convention on biological diversity.* Geneva: UNEP.

Michaels, E. (1985). Constraints on Knowledge in an Economy of Oral Information. *Current Anthropology, 26*(4), 505–510. doi:10.1086/203312

Nakata, M., Gibson, J., Nakata, V., Byrne, A., & McKeough, J. (2008). Indigenous digital collections: an early look at the organisation and culture interface. *Australian Academic & Research Libraries, 39*(4), 223–236.

Nakata, M., Nakata, V., Anderson, J., Hart, V., Hunter, J., Smallacombe, S., et al. (2006). Evaluation of the Northern Territory Library's Libraries and Knowledge Centres Model Darwin Northern Territory Library. Retrieved January 1, 2009 from http://www.ntl.nt.gov.au/_data/assets/pdf_file/0018/4680/nakata_finalreport.pdf

Nakata, M., Nakata, V., Anderson, J., Hunter, J., Hart, V., Smallacombe, S., McGill, J., Lloyd, B., Richmond, C., & Maynard, G. (2007). Libraries and Knowledge Centres: Implementing public library services in remote Indigenous communities in the Northern Territory of Australia. *Australian Academic & Research Libraries, 38*(3).

Northern Territory Library. (2005). Comprehensive Review of the 'Readiness' of Communities in the West MacDonnell's Region for the Libraries and Knowledge Centre's Program. Unpublished report. Northern Territory Government, Darwin: Jason Gibson.

Northern Territory Library. (2008). *The Walk to School: an indigenous early years literacy strategy for northern territory public libraries and knowledge centres. Northern Territory Library.* Darwin: Cate Richmond.

Papandrea, F., Daly, A., & McCallum, K. (2006). *Telephone and Internet Use in Remote Indigenous Communities.* Canberra: University of Canberra, Communication and Media Policy Institute.

Radoll, P. (2006). Information Communication Technology. In Hunter, B. H. (Ed.), *Assessing the evidence on Indigenous socioeconomic outcomes: A focus on the 2002 NATSISS Research Monograph 26* (pp. 197–212). Canberra: Australian National University, Centre For Aboriginal Economic Policy Research.

Ramsey, G. (2003). Future Directions for Secondary Education in the Northern Territory. Report submitted to the Northern Territory Government. Northern Territory Government, Darwin. Retrieved December 12, 2008 from http://www.betterschools.nt.gov.au/history/sec_ed_report.shtml.

Taylor, J. (2006). Population Diversity: Policy Implications of Emerging Indigenous Demographic Trends. (CAEPR Discussion Paper No.283/2006). Canberra: Australian National University, Centre For Aboriginal Economic Policy Research.

Taylor, S. (2004). Indigenous knowledge centres - the Queensland experience. ALIA Biennial Conference, Challenging Ideas. Gold Coast, QLD. Retrieved August 2, 2008 from http://conferences.alia.org.au/alia2004/pdfs /taylor.s.paper.pdf.

Thorley, P. (2002). Current Realities, Idealized Pasts: Archaeology, Values and Indigenous Heritage Management in Central Australia. *Oceania, 73,* 110–124.

Weigel, G., & Waldburger, D. (Eds.). (2004). ICT4D: Connecting People for a Better World. Berne: Swiss Agency of Development and Cooperation and the Global Knowledge Partnership.

ENDNOTES

[1] It should be noted that two of the authors of this paper have been thoroughly involved in the design and implementation of the LKC program, while the remaining author was employed as a project officer for the program for a short time and contributed to the programs evaluation in 2005.

[2] In comparison the percentage of the State or Territory's total population that is Indigenous in New South Wales is 2.1, in Queensland 3.5 and in Victoria 0.6.

[3] The platform is under further development by the Pitjantjatjara Council and the Northern Territory Library.

[4] A generic term used across the Western Desert to refer to Aboriginal people.

[5] The Pitjantjatjara Council initially developed three databases – a community collection, a collection for Anangu men only and a collection for Anangu women only – with the community version being distributed throughout the Pitjantjatjara and Yankunyjatjara lands in northern South Australia. The majority of content populating the database is entered in by staff in at a central location with corrections or annotations being contributed at each of the community sites and then synchronised with the main database in the capital city of Adelaide. A new version of the database is then re-distributed to each of the participating sites.

[6] Figures accurate as of October 2008.

Chapter 8

Mobile Phones, Diasporas and Developing Countries:
A Case Study of Connectedness among Chinese in Italy

Graeme Johanson
Monash University, Australia

Tom Denison
Monash University, Australia

ABSTRACT

It is no coincidence that the mobile phone suits the lifestyle and needs of the mobile migrant worker well. Research into the role of mobile or cell phones by Chinese migrant labourers, migrating within and outside China, show that the phones are a survival device, a means to perpetuate an important sense of belonging to a community in virtual form, and a method of transferring resources back to poor parts of the homeland. Mobiles help to cope in a foreign culture and to find work and ethnic solidarity. Above all, they provide connectedness. This chapter summarises the findings of a survey of 74 Chinese migrants living in Prato, Italy, as an example of Chinese migrants in Europe. It was administered in late 2008. Prato as a province has the largest Chinese migrant population in Italy, numbering about 30,000. The research aimed to understand the usefulness of mobile phones to migrant residents who need to keep in touch with their friends and families, in China and Italy, and their other communication needs, and whether mobiles satisfy their expectations. Participants in this study are well-served by mobiles. The typical participant in the study was a recently-arrived young single male from Zhejiang, China, speaking Wenzhouese, but with proficiency in other languages, experiencing the novelty of using a recently-purchased 'Nokia' phone, and who, whilst spending more than 10 Euros a month on the phone for keeping in touch with friends in China, was very aware of mobile running costs. More research is planned to flesh out the findings further.

DOI: 10.4018/978-1-61520-997-2.ch008

CHINESE MIGRANTS AND DEVELOPMENT

It is a moot point as to whether China is a 'developing' or 'developed' country. There is certainly no doubt that Chinese migrants play an essential role in its development. The 50 million or so Chinese migrants who live outside their country (IOM 2008), and the 225 million migrants who work in Chinese cities, separated from their rural villages (PRC 2009), are attracted to new places of work by higher wages. In Italy a local worker in 2006 was paid more on average per hour than a Chinese urban worker in China received in a week (Finfacts 2009). The number of emigrant workers from China around the globe is enormous; there is a Chinese saying that 'there are Chinese people wherever the ocean waves touch.' (Fullilove 2008: vii, 18). The International Office of Migration points out that

The Government of China has ... creat[ed] an enabling environment for the overseas Chinese to get involved in the economic development of China. Mobile or cell phones follow the trajectory of the massive migrations. China is the largest consumer in the world of mobiles (Donner 2008:145).

Mobile phones support a two-way synchronous communication channel for the Chinese diaspora to keep in touch with its homelands, whilst at the same time enabling negotiation of survival in host countries, and assisting migrants to exchange personal messages, photos and funds (Zhang 2009: 261) with their kith and kin all over the world. In a study of disoriented migrant workers in China, Chu and Yang wrote:

The use of cell phones somewhat bolsters their self-esteem. After all, there is no other consumer durable than the cell phone that can be held in the hand and that will allow them to demonstrate their feelings, confirm their sense of freedom, and

assure their existence as [an agent] in a rootless time-space (Chu 2006:230).

Large quantities of remittances are sent from migrant labourers to hometowns. Each year China receives more than any other developing country with billions of dollars from its overseas migrants (Page 2005:10,57), for altruistic reasons, as a form of family insurance, and as an investment (migration life-cycle planning) (Page 2005:15). These various fund transfers benefit the local economy of the developing country in multiple ways (Page 2005: 18). In addition to remittances, there are a large number of direct donations (often undocumented officially) to home communities (Xiaolv 2009:261-262).

The benefits which derive from the use of the mobile phone are not simply economic. The power of mobile communication to reduce isolation and loneliness cannot be overestimated, as indicated by a report derived from thorough fieldwork among female migrant workers in Beijing:

Social capital ... has been strongly connected to mobile phone use ... Understand the role of the mobile phone in migrant women's sociality ... They work[ed] extremely long hours ... some without ever having a day off ... Work schedules are frequently extended by the constant pressure to work overtime ... Contributing to this small social world is the fact that most ... tend[ed] to live in tiny apartments or dormitories with as many as 18 to a room ... The mobile was a key to enriching their social relationships. Many friendships were maintained strictly through a mobile phone (Wallis 2007:11-12).

A sense of belonging to a community (whether virtual or real) and concomitant improvement of quality of life are reinforced by mobile phone use. A study of the role of Information and Communications Technologies in the quality of life of people in Beijing, Taipei and Hong Kong concluded that the mobile phone was classed by poorer Chinese as the most important medium for them (Lee 2007:467). They believed that their lives were greatly improved because the mobile helped with interaction, keeping in touch, instant communication, and entertainment (Lee 2007:470).

CHINESE MIGRANTS AND MOBILE PHONES; FACTS AND THEORIES

A recent review of research about mobile communication found that there have been surprisingly few fine-grained, or theorized, studies about mobiles' role in connecting diasporic communities, although there are studies about the role of the Internet, television, and video for migrants (Goggan 2008:357). This chapter aims to help to fill the gap, by exploring the use of mobile phones by the large uprooted community of Chinese in Prato, Tuscany, in northern Italy (Denison 2009:2).

Emigration from China began long ago (Fitzgerald, 2007), and substantial numbers came to Prato in the 1980s. The actual number of Chinese in Prato today is contested (Comune di Prato, 2008), partly because of the reputedly large number of illegal migrants (Dinmore 2010). An estimate of 30,000 is often quoted. Official Wenzhou records indicate that about half a million Wenzhouese are overseas, and that 98% of these are in Europe. Italy is their most popular migration destination (Wu, 2008:248).

As an object of recent study, the social role of the mobile phone in daily life in China shows that it provides the most 'personal, convenient, synchronous and asynchronous communication' that has ever been available (Cui 2007:483), and remarkably, its primary virtues are embraced worldwide, with little variation from place to place (Donner, 2008:151; Katz, 2002:316). Some time ago, the sociologist, Anthony Giddens, named this type of spread 'co-presence', that is, the ability to 'be' in more than one place at the same time. He saw co-presence as 'the main anchoring feature of social integration' based on communicative encounters and reflexive monitoring (Giddens, 1987:132,186). More recently researchers write of 'the spirit of the machine that influences both the designs of the technology as well as the … significance accorded them by users' (Katz, 2002:305); 'a form of absent presence' or a 'floating cyber presence' that is promoted by mobile communications (Law 2006:250-251); and of 'timeless time' and the 'space of flows' created by mobile communications (Castells, 2008:449).

Most researchers into the use of mobiles by Chinese migrants adopt as strong an interest in the social benefits and the impacts of mobiles, as they do in the actual spread of the technological artefact itself (Chu, 2006:223). This co-constructivist approach has an impressive lineage (Donner, 2008:143,147). The main identified value of the mobile to migrants is its invitation to 'keep in touch':

Apart from interacting with other people, humans want to be in touch with others whenever they want to, regardless of time and place … Instantaneous interaction without the restriction of space is a unique feature of mobile phone[s]. It is more instantaneous than the Internet because it is ubiquitous, personal and mobile (Lee 2007:471).

Yet, although space is shrunk mentally by the extensive use of mobiles, there is still a very real sense of the ongoing effects of diasporic distance. As an example, caregiving at a distance can require special attributes which Baldassar calls 'distant thinking':

A distant thinker is someone who does not view distance as an impediment to functioning kin relationships and who has a view of distance as 'malleable' … [This way of thinking] is largely dependent on family histories, negotiated commitments, capacity, and sense of obligation (Baldassar 2007:217).

Mobiles provide a platform to facilitate distant thinking.

There is a strong theme about Chinese cultural values and mobiles to note, because it permeates the evidence collected in our survey. Chinese researchers into the use of mobile phones by internal migrants in China itself point to the interests of the individual in society as being subsumed beneath collective needs and binding Confucian values about relationships. For instance, we are told that

responding to SMS messages is not just for the sake of killing time; there is a deeper meaning behind these activities: responding to an SMS message is one way of maintaining a relationship, an act of bao (reciprocity) full of Chinese cultural wisdom ... To the workers ... one can barely survive without an appropriate guanxiwang (relationship network) ... The closer the relationship between two persons, the more frequent the SMS exchange between them (Chu, 2006:232-233).

Another project reported that marriage of older internal migrant workers was primarily a functional arrangement for the overall benefit of the family unit, and that individual emotional commitments were unlikely to be expressed by voice in telephone communications. Emotions are carefully concealed. Values are observed to be changing from traditional functional objectives to wider acceptance and dissemination of individual romantic feelings among younger Chinese migrants.. Mobiles facilitated ephemeral and 'floating relationships' to an unprecedented extent (Law, 2006:251,255). Whether for functionality or romance, therefore, the mobile cements personal relationships.

A commentator on Habermas alludes to a relevant paradox by questioning the power of the agency of the individual:

You have the peculiar fusion of opposites that makes the mobile vision of the world. On the one hand you have the supremely individualistic

view, you might almost call it atomistic. There's no real gathering at all. Instead there are only isolated individuals, each locked in his or her own world, making contact sporadically and for purely functional purposes. On the other hand, there is a system of messages, and at that level there are no humans agents at all, because they are overwhelmed by the sheer exuberance of the messages as they multiply ... Instead of a group, there is on one level just the individual, and another level just the pure system (Myerson 2001:38).

This chapter argues that mobile users and their systems are not divorced from each other in the minds of the migrant users, as suggested, but are linked by highly significant social content consisting of daily interactions of friends and family, and much other meaningful discourse.

RESEARCH DESIGN

Not all Chinese emigrants are the same, of course, and many factors influence the decisions of migrants as to whether they should to try to integrate into a host community at all, and if so, by what means. From the perspective of the individual, the factors include: the duration of the actual migration, the period for which the migrant intends to remain, how voluntary the migration is, any prior migrations, any prior experience of major cultural change, any existing network in the new country (whether personal or national), age, employability, language skills, educational level, shared interests, political tradition, the degree of physical isolation of the homeland, ability to remain fully in touch with the home community, strength of prior social ties, and others (Maya-Jariego, 2007).

With these factors in mind, we developed and pilot-tested a brief 3-page survey for distribution among a sample of 74 Chinese residents in Prato. We realise that the results may not be typical, but only indicative, and that they should be investigated more rigorously, but that is unlikely to occur in the near future.

The authors called on colleagues from Wenzhou University because of their facility with the Chinese language and the fact that the bulk of Chinese in Prato come from Wenzhou, Zhejiang. They undertook preliminary groundwork in Wenzhou before the survey, by speaking to the Department of Overseas Chinese Affairs in Wenzhou. Once in Prato, it became very obvious that the survey would prove hard to administer because of local resistance; potential respondents were repulsed by 'excessive interviews from different researchers in recent years'. In brief, unfortunately Wenzhouese in Prato have been subjected to excessive scrutiny, and they expressed 'disgust' at surveillance, however well-meaning it may be (Yang, 2010).

Although our sample was by no means random, in a sense it was purposive, because we aimed to understand only Chinese migrants with mobile phones. By far the majority were from Zhejiang (86%), the bulk of these from Wenzhou (69%). Commune figures indicate that in 2002 83% of the Chinese in Prato were from Zhejiang (Denison 2009:5). The rest (14%) were from other parts of China.

In addition, our two emissaries were extremely assiduous in using the snowballing technique for identifying and acquiring participants, by spending several days in October 2008 speaking with Chinese leaders in Prato from the Chamber of Commerce, with entrepreneurs, managers of businesses (restaurants, supermarkets, food cafes), newspaper staff, customers in hair salons, Internet cafes, computer shops, pharmacies, and bookstores, and teachers and students in Chinese schools in Prato, all the time handing out and explaining the survey. Thus the sample was based on a selection of organisations with core social functions in the community, and individuals 'off the street'. The employment profile of our respondents reinforces the spread of the sample: 36% were students, 36% were 'workers', 15% managed businesses, and 3% were unemployed.

This is probably a fairly typical composition of a migrant group in Europe.

The survey covered three broad topics: personal demographic data, information about the actual phones in use, and the purposes behind mobile use. If a profile of the typical participant can be posited at this point, it is of a recently-arrived young single male from Zhejiang, speaking Wenzhouese, with proficiency in other languages, experiencing the novelty of using a recently-purchased 'Nokia' phone, and who, whilst spending more than 10 Euros a month on the phone for keeping in touch with friends in China, is very aware of mobile running costs.

Findings: Demographic Data

Demographic data from our survey provided understanding of the mobile phone community, but also some insights into features of the community of Wenzhou migrants in Prato as a whole. Our sample bore a reasonably close resemblance to features of the Chinese community overall. How the magical new communication devices serve the needs of the Wenzhouese migrants is of as much interest as what it is capable of (Donner, 2006:147).

Unfortunately there are no city-wide figures of the ages of Chinese in Prato. Younger survey participants (18 and less) were slightly more common (at 25%) than those in the age groups in their 20s and 30s, but were about the same in size as those aged more than 35 years (22%). The youngest group of participants (25% of all respondents) were all students, presumably children of migrants. All but one of them spoke Italian and/or English, as well as Chinese, suggesting a high level of linguistic skills and the possibility of social integration. Age is related to other variables further on.

There were many more males than females (45:29), and about the same ratio of single individuals to married participants (48:26). Thus 35% in our survey were married. National government figures suggest that 48% of Chinese in Italy are women (our survey figure for Prato is just 35%) (Dipartimento, 2008:97). A slight majority of the singles were males (57%). Of those who were married, only 15% had a spouse back in China (that is, 85% lived with their spouses in Prato). Commune figures indicated that in 2002 30% of the Chinese spouses in Prato did not have their partners with them (Denison, 2009:5).

An analysis of the use of the mobile for keeping in touch with family showed that there was little difference between these two groups; spouses in Prato and spouses in China were contacted in roughly equal amounts. This suggests that physical proximity bears no relationship to frequency of family contact, reinforcing the Giddens' concept of co-presence.

A survey question about the length of stay in Prato produced noteworthy results. The length of time that many of the respondents had lived in Prato was a surprise: although 41% arrived less than 2 years ago, 46% had resided for between 2 and 10 years, and a group of stayers (13%) for more than 10 years. Although 18% of Chinese in Prato were born there (Denison 2009:4), it has often been assumed that Wenzhou migrants stay in Prato only a short time (Wu 2008:248), enough to save (stereotypically) to support family in the homeland for a developmental period (Fladrich 2008: 98), or for the purchase of land and a home back in Wenzhou (Denison 2009:11; Xiao 2009:199). Those who lived in Italy for longest (longer than 10 years) were primarily the oldest respondents, aged over 35 (13%), or between 25 and 34 (3%). The cementing of the physical connection with Prato is supported by the finding that 70% of the older long-term residents spoke Italian, as well as Chinese.

Second-generation Chinese break the pressure of the poverty link to the homeland, and are normally better educated, more settled, and more integrated into the local environment (Chu, 2006: 226). Heavier mobile usage is associated with better education, urban living, and higher income (Fortunati, 2008:26).

Many studies indicate that the mobile phone is not only a communication device, but a strong status symbol among migrants, especially if it is a non-Chinese brand. For most migrants, a new 'Western' phone is an important symbol of urbanity and modern sophistication (Portus 2008:114; Wallis 2007:8-9). Not surprisingly, our survey found that newly-arrived migrants – of less than one year of residence (18%)—were more likely to own a Chinese brand of phone than a Western one. The most popular brand of phone amongst the rest, some form of a 'Nokia', was owned by 76% of participants, along with 'Samsung', 'Micky', 'Motorola', and 'Sony Ericsson' phones. It is remarkable that precisely the same brands were found in a study of migrant workers in Dongguan city, in Guangdong, in 2005 (Law, 2006: 247). Just 8% of our Prato participants used a cheaper Chinese-made phone with fewer features (such as 'K-touch', 'XiaXin', or 'SOAI').

Fladrich (2010) has noted that it would be worth investigating whether the Chinese purchase their phones in Prato, or back in China, i.e., during visits back to China. Or do newly-arrived Chinese bring the Chinese brands with them?

Several factual observations from other studies about brands can be related to our findings:

- Ownership of any mobile phone by a migrant from Wenzhou would show that he or she had better communications than compatriots at home (where in 2004 only 37% of the population had mobiles). (Chu, 2006:239).
- In China too internal migrants are heavy consumers of Western brands for design, look, functionality, and reliability of servicing (Law, 2006: 247).
- For factory workers in Dongguan, 'the more advanced the model [of phone that the worker carries], the more "face" (*mianzi*) he gains' (Chu, 2006:232).

- Of the Chinese who had been in Prato for more than 10 years, 89% were male. This group had owned mobiles for longer than the average. Of the overall 14% of participants who possessed their first mobile phone, 70% of them were female; women migrant workers in China acquire mobiles more slowly than men (Wallis, 2007:3). There is a hint in the research literature that women in the textile manufacturing businesses are less likely to use technologies (or to manage businesses) than males (Ceccagno, 2008:56; Fladrich, 2008:122; Wallis, 2007:15). Much more research is needed into use of mobiles by women for family and work.

Findings: Phone Ownership

The second part of the survey collated more information about mobile ownership.

Recent ownership was the norm: 61% had a phone for less than 2 years, and only 39% owned their mobile for more than 2 years. Just 4% had a phone for more than 10 years. There was a strong relationship between length of migrant residence in Prato, and length of ownership of a mobile, suggesting that owning a mobile is a normal part of diaspora life. Of the 39% of all participants who owned mobiles for more than 2 years, 74% of them had lived in Italy for more than 2 years. Of the 13% of all mobile owners who owned them for 5 or more years, 56% had lived in Italy for 5 or more years. Yet ownership of phones for many years was very common: 86% had a mobile phone before their current phone; 39% were on their second phone; 15% had used more than 4 phones.

The survey did not investigate many aspects of the cost of purchase or servicing mobile phones. It was clearly important, however. One survey question asked what additional services would be valued by phone owners, and most answers related to value for money: unlimited free phone access, good Internet access, accessible QQ chat

(with over 300 million Chinese users), online shopping, and a better mobile signal.

There is considerable discussion of the initial purchase cost in published research about mobile phones for development. Prices are relative to so many variables that it is impossible to generalise about what proportion of their income migrants might outlay on a phone. It was obvious that some of our respondents were not parsimonious – one played online Internet games, and two others sent photographs, using their mobiles. Three aimed to use the Internet on mobiles. Still, another source shows that the average monthly wage of a hard-working migrant factory labourer in Prato at this time was 600 Euros (Kynge 2006:73), which an Italian on the median wage earned in 15 hours (Finfacts 2009). One Prato migrant worker said:

We get 600 euro a month. That is about what you need to survive here. If you can really cut down on food, maybe you can save 50 to 100 Euros a month on that wage. But it is exhausting (Kynge 2006:73).

Other researchers suggest that Chinese migrants spend extraordinarily wide-ranging amounts (from one to 7 months of their salaries) on the purchase of mobiles because they are such an important lifeline – for friendship, finding work and shelter (Chu, 2006:225; Law, 2006:247; Wallis, 2007:7):

The fetish for mobile communications among migrant workers has caused them to contribute a large part of their salaries to both the mobile phone manufacturers and network providers (Law 2006:250).

Most respondents (73%) did not have a mobile phone contract. Not knowing how many Euros would be spent monthly on phones by migrants in Prato, we assumed that 10 Euros might be a defining expenditure. It represents 2% of average income. It was not a watershed; 78% spent more than 10 Euros a month on mobile usage. Only 20% spent between 5 and 10 Euros per month.

The survey did not investigate multiple phone ownership, which is growing in popularity. Fladrich (2010) observes:

There is a 'trend' to have different and multiple mobile phones in Prato as in China in general. [Apart from] prestige and status, two or more phones may be used for local calls and international calls and/or private and business phones -- to benefit from different plans and rates offered by phone providers ... Maybe also the market for second-hand phones is worth exploring.

Findings: Mobile Use

The final section of the survey assessed usage.

Was one mode of communicating—voice communication or texting—more important to migrants in Prato than the other? Texting is cheaper than calling in most countries (Law 2006:249). Cultural preferences are also involved. When offered a choice, Italians will speak on a mobile more readily than use text, whereas Chinese use both enthusiastically, especially where 'QQ' chat is an available message medium (Johanson 2008:123; Baron 2008:336,342). One study of 4 countries indicated that the most important consideration for any user of a mobile phone is the cost of messages and voice (Baron 2008:338). Prior research of other migrant use of mobiles suggested that SMS was likely to be their first choice. In our study the ratio of calls to SMS messages overall was very close at 1:0.94.

Chinese researchers suggest that SMS is ideal for a society which perceives the other not as an individual but as a relationship with the self, and which eschews public displays of emotion. Strong personal expressions are not shared face-to-face with ease, not even romantic feelings (Law, 2006:251-252; Chu, 2006:231). A relationship network, or *guanxiwang,* is essential for survival

(Chu 2006:233) and for the maintenance of distant family support (Baldassar, 2007:222).

In our survey friends were the most common beneficiaries of mobile communication. Among Beijing mobile phone users, social communication was regarded as the most important function of the mobile (Fortunati, 2008:24). Both voice and SMS communications with friends involved the following numbers in Prato:

- 38% of users phoned friends more than 10 times per week; 7% of users phoned friends more than 100 times per week.
- 20% of users sent SMS texts to friends more than 10 times per week; 200 SMS texts per week were sent to friends by 4% of users.

Without wishing to make too strong a comparison between migrant groups, it is worth noting that these figures are consistent with the findings of a study in Dongguan in 2004, where the average number of SMS messages per migrant user per week was 163 (Chu, 2006:243).

The next most common recipient of mobile calls and the SMS was family members: 15% phoned family more than 10 times per week; 12% used SMS for this purpose more than 10 times per week. A small group (12%) used phones for work. Contacting family was the main motivation for purchasers of mobiles by internal migrant labourers in Dongguan (Chu, 2006:228). Kinship is fundamental to the fabric of Chinese social relationships (Law, 2006:250). It is difficult to argue on the basis of one survey alone that mobiles expand supportive social networks, but at least it is clear from a range of studies in China and elsewhere that networks are enriched (Fortunati, 2008:22; Katz, 2008:436; Wallis, 2007:12).

As expected, the primary language of communications was Wenzhouese, with 76% as regular users. In addition, 47% of users spoke in Italian, and 23% spoke in English. Those who spoke more languages used the mobile more frequently, and remarkably, half of the respondents spoke more than one language.

Communication with China using mobiles was almost twice as common as communication with family or acquaintances in Italy (1:5.7). Nevertheless, in addition to mobile contact with China (73%), contact was made regularly with Italy (42%), as well as France and Spain. The Chinese diaspora in Europe is well connected internally, regardless of its external relationships to local groups. Often Chinese migrants have little initial intention to put down local roots, but rather to roam Europe 'as a chessboard' seeking any work prospects (Smith 2004).

In Prato 36% of survey respondents were 'workers'. Many of them lead very brutish lives, as witnessed by another researcher:

The [textile] workshops are closed to outsiders and are mostly situated in basements far removed from crowds. For the labourers, workshops are their working premises and [only] living space ... The subjects [of the study] kept reminding me of their rural origins ... [They] still identified themselves as 'peasants' ... They suffered double disadvantage – they had lost their identity as rural workers [in China], but were still unqualified as industrial workers [in Prato] (Xiao, 2009:195, 196).

The mobile phone is a social lifeline.

For job-seekers and micro-entrepreneurs, Fladrich (2010), who has visited Prato and Wenzhou several times in the past 3 years, makes the following observations about the Chinese use of mobiles:

The mobile phone is playing an important role in employment attainment ... Job seekers and/or job leavers in the market square outside Xiaolin Supermarket [in Prato] often view new job ads with their mobile phones readily in hand to call an employer. In a competitive labour market access to a mobile phone can be seen as a critical time advantage, as well as [providing] the ability for employers to contact employees 24/7, also when orders come in unexpectedly and staff are needed at short notice. The majority of job ads and company ads of micro-entrepreneurs also include mobile numbers which allow for better availability for current and prospective customers, including for massage services and the like.

In order to try to capture other aspects of 'use' of a mobile, the survey asked about users other than the phone owner, and the use of other phones. Not a lot of data was volunteered. A minority (22%) lent their mobile phones to a few other people each month (1.5 people on average). An exceptional respondent lent the phone 5 times per month. Half of the mobile users surveyed had no regular access to an alternative fixed-line phone. Sharing phones seems to be a more common practice in poor communities, but it has not been researched to any great extent (Donner 2008:150).

CONCLUSION

Migrants and mobiles play an important role in all aspects of development, by assisting with finding work in new countries, by helping with social improvement, by encouraging the transfer of essential funds, and by permitting the maintenance of established and fresh social networks whilst enduring miserable working conditions. Keeping in touch and creating a sense of community were identified by migrants as the key roles of the mobile phone. Quality of life issues were as important to the mobile migrant as economic improvement. Living in factories is harshly degrading, and the mobile provides a small window onto other worlds. It is argued that, in the context of migrants, large-scale development can only be achieved with the prop of the mobile.

Before this survey was undertaken, there was little available knowledge about the relationship between migration, mobile phones, and development. The chapter has shown that the mobile enables migrants to defy the dislocation associated with space-and-time distance by using voice and text communication as often as they want. Friends and family benefit, and the recent migrant acquires modern status and a symbol of affluence by means of ownership of Western phone brands. Costs seem of less significance to them than to have the ability to maintain instant communication.

There are special cultural advantages of the mobile as a form of communication to the Chinese, and it is notable that a growing second generation of multilingual Chinese in Italy have removed many of the socio-economic barriers that the mobile has been used to bridge.

A consideration of the concepts of co-presence, floating cyber presence, and timeless time, are not preoccupations of the Chinese themselves in Prato. They are anchored firmly in their daily reality, wherein mobiles help them to function effectively and purposefully. The medium and the message are equally important (Katz 2002: 309). The ideas of parallel communities – of intense interest to researchers and policy-makers -- are tied to the thorny issue as to whether mobiles promote integration into a host community, such as Prato, or tend to encourage continuing close links with Wenzhou, perhaps thereby diminishing genuine connection with the Italian experience.

This chapter shows that the mobile phone promotes development socially and in the home country, by enabling virtual and real communities to function independently at times, to overlap at times, and to interconnect at times. Mobiles breed further mobility – in terms of job, personal relationships, language use, and cultural baggage. Migrants have more control over their mobility and self-direction than in the past. Research needs to focus on 'connectedness' (Fullilove 2008:2,39) as an arm of development. Increased 'connectivity' is appreciated by mobile users in many contexts (Fortunati 2008:22). As Maya-Jariego points out:

Physical presence is no longer necessary or a guarantee of participation ... While as individuals we give meaning to our realities across a complexity of communities, our relationships are continuously situated in time and space (Maya-Jariego 2007:743).

Connectedness to each other is a primary concern of the migrant. Mobiles infuse relationships in and with the here-and-now. Based on pressing ephemeral needs -- work, friends, and family -- the real and virtual networks (enabled by mobile phones) become the main modus operandi for migrants, rather than embedding them in any particular geographical community, developed or developing, or compelling them to devise a long-term strategy to move on to other communities for study or work.

ACKNOWLEDGMENT

The authors are glad to acknowledge that the research reported in this chapter was supported by funds from the Strategic Initiative Fund of the Office of the Deputy Vice-Chancellor, Monash University.

REFERENCES

Baldassar, L., Baldock, C. V., & Wilding, R. (2007). *Families Caring Across Borders; Migration, Ageing, and Transnational Caregiving.* Basingstoke, UK: Palgrave Macmillan.

Baron, N. S. (2008). Text, Talk, or View: How Much of Ourselves do We Reveal? In *The Role of New Technologies in Global Societies; Theoretical Reflections, Practical Concerns, and Its Implications for China. Conference Proceedings 30–31 July 2008 Department of Applied Social Sciences, Hong Kong Polytechnic University* (pp. 330-347).

Castells, M. (2008). Afterword. In Katz, J. E. (Ed.), *Handbook of Mobile Communication Studies* (pp. 447–451). Cambridge, MA: MIT Press.

Ceccagno, A. (2008). Chinese Migrants as Apparel Manufacturers in an Era of Perishable Global Fashion: New Fashion Scenarios in Prato, Italy. In Johanson, G., Smyth, R., & French, R. (Eds.), *Living Outside the Walls: The Chinese in Prato* (pp. 42–74). Newcastle upon Tyne: Cambridge Scholars Publishing.

Chu, W.-C., & Yang, S. (2006). Mobile phones and new migrant workers in a South China village: an initial analysis of the interplay between the 'social' and the 'technological. In Law, P., Fortunati, L., & Yang, S. (Eds.), *New Technologies in Global Societies. Part 3* (pp. 221–244). doi:10.1142/9789812773555_0010

Comune di Prato. (2008). Stranieri residenti a Prato divisi per cittadinanza. Retrieved April 20, 2010 from http://www.comune.prato.it/prato/htm/strwrld.htm

Cui, Y., Chipchase, J., & Ichikawa, F. (2007). A Cross Culture Study on Phone Carrying and Physical Personalisation. In Aykin, N. (Ed.), *Usability and Internationalisation, Part I, HCII 2007* (LNCS 4559, pp. 483-492).

Denison, T., Arunachalam, D., Johanson, G., & Smyth, R. (2009). The Chinese Community in Prato. In Johanson, G., Smyth, R., & French, R. (Eds.), *Living Outside the Walls: The Chinese in Prato* (pp. 2–24). Newcastle upon Tyne: Cambridge Scholars Publishing.

Dinmore, G. (2010). Tuscan town turns against Chinese migrants. Financial Times. Retrieved April 20, 2010 from http://www.ft.com/cms/s/0/a2ff28f6-1 4df-11df-8f1d-00144feab49a.html

Dipartimento per le Liberta Civili e l'Immigrazione Organizzazione Internazionale per le Migranzioni (2008). Analisi ed Elaborazione Date Sull'Immigrazione Cinese in Italia. Dipartimento per le Liberta Civili e l'Immigrazione Organizzazione Internazionale per le Migranzioni.

Donner, J. (2008). Research Approaches to Mobile Use in the Developing World: A Review of the Literature. *The Information Society, 24*(3), 140–159. doi:10.1080/01972240802019970

Finfacts; Ireland's Business and Financial Portal (2009). Pay in Europe in 2006 – The Gap in European Pay. Retrieved April 20, 2010 from http://www.finfacts.ie/Private/isl/Payin Europe.htm

Fitzgerald, J. (2007). *Big White Lie. Chinese Australians in White Australia.* Sydney: University of New South Wales Press.

Fladrich, A. (2009). The Chinese Labour Market and Job Mobility in Prato. In Johanson, G., Smyth, R., & French, R. (Eds.), *Living Outside the Walls: The Chinese in Prato* (pp. 96–128). Newcastle upon Tyne: Cambridge Scholars Publishing.

Fladrich, A. (2010). Email communication with G. Johanson. 26 March.

Fortunati, L., Manganelli, A. M., & Law, P. L. (2008). Beijing Calling… Mobile Communication in Contemporary China. *Knowledge Technology and Policy, 21*, 19–27. doi:10.1007/s12130-008-9040-1

Fullilove, M. (2008) *World wide webs: diasporas and the international system.* Lowy Institute Paper 22. Retrieved April 20, 2010 from http://www.lowyinstitute.org/ Publication.asp?pid=753

Giddens, A. (1987). *Social theory and modern sociology.* Stanford University Press.

Goggan, G. (2008). Cultural Studies of mobile Communication. In Katz, J. E. (Ed.), *Handbook of Mobile Communication Studies* (pp. 353–366). Cambridge, MA: MIT Press.

IOM (International Office of Migration). (2008). *Developing Migration Policy; Diaspora and Development.* Retrieved April 20, 2010 from http://www.iom.int/jahia/Jahia/pid/539.

Jarus, O. (2010). 'Ambassador or slave? Researchers Mystified by East Asian Skeleton Discovered in Vagnari Cemetery'. *The Independent.* Retrieved April 20, 2010 from http://www.independent.co.uk/news/ science/archaeology/news/ambassador-or-slave-east-asian-skeleton-discovered-in-vagnari-roman-cemetery-1879551.htm.

Johanson, G. (2008). Flicking the Switch: Social Networks and the Role of Information and Communications Technologies in Social Cohesion among Chinese and Italians in Melbourne, Australia. In The *Role of New Technologies in Global Societies; Theoretical Reflections, Practical Concerns, and Its Implications for China. Conference Proceedings 30–31 July 2008* (pp. 118-127). Department of Applied Social Sciences, Hong Kong Polytechnic University.

Katz, J. E. (2006). *Magic in the Air: Mobile Communication and the Transformation of Social Life.* New Brunswick, NJ: Transaction Publishers.

Katz, J. E. (2008). Mainstreamed Mobiles in Daily Life: Perspective and Prospects. In Katz, J. E. (Ed.), *Handbook of Mobile Communication Studies* (pp. 433–445). Cambridge, MA: MIT Press.

Katz, J. E., & Aakhus, M. A. (2002). Conclusion: making meaning of mobiles – a theory of Apparatgeist. In Katz, J. E., & Aaakhus, M. A. (Eds.), *Perpetual Contact: Mobile Communication, Private Talk, Public Performance* (pp. 301–318). New York: Cambridge University Press. doi:10.1017/CBO9780511489471.023

Kynge, J. (2006). *China Shakes the World; the Rise of a Hungry Nation.* London: Weidenfeld & Nicolson.

Law, P., & Peng, Y. (2006). The Use of Mobile Phones among Migrant Workers in Southern China. In Law, P., Fortunati, L., & Yang, S. (Eds.), *New technologies in global societies* (pp. 245–258). Singapore: World Scientific. doi:10.1142/9789812773555_0011

Lee, P. S. N., Leung, L., Lo, V., & Xiong, C. (2007). The Perceived Role of ICTs in Quality of Life in Three Chinese Cities. *Social Indicators Research, 88*(3), 457–476. doi:10.1007/s11205-007-9214-3

Lin, A., & Tong, A. (2008). Mobile cultures of migrant workers in southern China: informal literacies in the negotiation of (new) social relations of the new working women'. *Knowledge. Technology and Policy, 21*(2), 73–81. doi:10.1007/s12130-008-9045-9

Maya-Jariego, I., & Armitage, N. (2007). Multiple senses of community in migration and commuting. *International Sociology, 22*(6), 743–766. doi:10.1177/0268580907082259

Myerson, G. (2001). *Heidegger, Habermas and the Mobile Phone.* Cambridge, UK: Icon Books.

Page, J., & Plaza, S. (2005). *Migration Remittances and Development: A Review of Global Evidence.* World Bank.

Portus, L. M. (2008). How the Urban Poor Acquire and Give Meaning to the Mobile Phone. In Katz, J. E. (Ed.), *Handbook of Mobile Communication Studies* (pp. 106–118). Cambridge, MA: MIT Press.

PRC (People's Republic of China), National Bureau of Statistics. (2009). Chinese Migrant Workers Totaled [sic] 225.42 Million at the End of 2008. China News, 25 March. Retrieved April 20, 2010 from http://www.boxun.us/news/publish/chinanews/ Chinese_Peasant_Workers_Totaled_225_42_Million_at_the_End_of_2008.shtml

Smith, T. (2004, February 19). Crisis in Tuscany's Chinatown. *BBC News*. Retrieved from http://news.bbc.co.uk/2/hi/europe/ 3500285.stm.

Wallis, C. (2007). *Techno-mobility and Translocal Migration: Mobile Phone Use among Female Migrant Workers in Beijing*. Paper presented at Female Labor Migration in Globalising Asia: Translocal/Transnational Identities and Agencies, 13-14 September, Asia Research Institute. Retrieved April 20, 2010 from http://arnic.info/Papers/Techno-Mobility%20and%20Translocal%20Migration_CaraWallis.pdf

Wu, B. (2009). International Migration and Wenzhou's Development. In Johanson, G., Smyth, R., & French, R. (Eds.), *Living Outside the Walls: The Chinese in Prato* (pp. 238–260). Newcastle upon Tyne: Cambridge Scholars Publishing.

Xiao, C., & Ochsmann, R. (2009). Lost in Alien Surroundings: the Identity Crises Among Chinese Labourers in Prato. In Johanson, G., Smyth, R., & French, R. (Eds.), *Living Outside the Walls: The Chinese in Prato* (pp. 192–201). Newcastle upon Tyne: Cambridge Scholars Publishing.

Xiaolv, Z., Yi, C., & Smyth, R. (2009). The contribution of donations of overseas Chinese to Wenzhou development. In G. Johanson, R. Smyth, & R. French (Eds.), *Living Outside the Walls: The Chinese in Prato* (pp. 261-273). Newcastle upon Tyne, Cambridge Scholars Publishing. 261-273.

Yang, X-Y., & Hua-bing, X. (2010). Collecting survey responses in Prato in October 2008. In e-mail communication to the first-named author on 13 March 2010.

Chapter 9

"The Men Never Say that They do not Know":
Telecentres as Gendered Spaces

Dorothea Kleine
University of London, UK

ABSTRACT

There have been many case studies in the literature on telecentres, often seeking to analyse the usage of these facilities via surveys and covering gender issues by "counting women". This chapter presents a more qualitative and ethnographic account, exploring one particular telecentre in a small town in rural Chile and comparing it with the seven local commercial cybercafés. This local reality is situated in the context of Chile's national ICT strategy, the Agenda Digital, and linked to interviews with policy makers at the national level. The chapter examines the Chilean telecentre strategy, in particular the Biblioredes programme. The primary research included a short survey at the telecentre, on users' age, gender, occupation, education, access habits and usages, but even more revealing is six months' participant observation and interviews with users. The analysis confirmed availability, affordability and skills as important factors in determining internet usage, but also uncovered two other key issues: social norms around the use of time and of space. These social norms are heavily gendered. Social norms around time usage mean that married women struggle to fit in IT trainings with household duties. As far as space is concerned, it is far more socially acceptable for women to spend time in the telecentre than in cybercafés. In the commercial cybercafés, computers are placed in narrow cabins and screens are not publicly visible. There is little interaction between users, who are almost exclusively young men. The telecentre is situated in the local library, run by a female librarian and used as a social space by women of different ages. The space is wide enough for prams and wheelchairs and the screens are publicly visible. Users, often less affluent members of the community and/or women, are socially in a position to ask the staff questions, while men's higher social status makes it harder for them to seek help with their IT skills learning. The

DOI: 10.4018/978-1-61520-997-2.ch009

chapter concludes with some practical recommendations for designing access spaces and IT training courses in a gender-sensitive way which may apply to rural Chile and other heavily gendered societies. It also calls for a more nuanced analysis of gender aspects in ICT4D research, one that goes beyond simply "counting women".

INTRODUCTION

Telecentres are among the best documented aspects of the growing field of information and communication technologies for development (ICT4D). These public access points to the internet, which offer computer and internet use free of cost to the user, have become part of many national ICT strategies in Latin America. In many cases, months or years after the telecentres' installation, studies have been carried out to see what kind of users were taking advantage of the facility and what kind of use they made of it. The majority of these studies have been based on quantitative surveys of users. From a gender perspective, the key concern in such studies has been the gender balance among users – "counting women". This chapter reports the findings of a much more qualitative, ethnographic study of a telecentre in rural Chile. The study is part of a larger piece of research (Kleine, 2007) which included six months of qualitative social research comparing the intentions of policy makers in the Chilean capital with the daily realities of people in some of the poorest municipalities in Chile. Based on a subset of observations and interview data, the chapter offers a holistic understanding of the way informal social norms affect men and women's usage of the telecentre. The chapter works with a wider conceptualisation of access, which recognises not only the three dimensions of access as outlined by Gerster & Zimmermann (2003) as availability, affordability and capabilities necessary to use ICTs. It argues that if men and women are to have equal access to ICTs, the gender-based norms around the use of time and the use of space also need to be addressed.

After explaining the situation of Chile as one of the leaders in e-readiness and active state ICT policy in Latin America in general, this chapter will take the reader to the small town in one of the poorest areas of Chile where the research was conducted. Dimensions of access and the effects of public ICT agendas are explored from a gender-aware point of view. The case study of one particular female microentrepreneur will be used to see ICTs in the broader context of women's lives in the small town. The conclusion will offer some aspects to consider, in regards to gender, in further enquiry and policy making around telecentres in Latin America and beyond.

BACKGROUND TO ICTS IN CHILE

Chile was among the first countries in Latin America to formulate a broad national strategy with regard to ICT, a move instigated by successive centre-left governments. The *Agenda Digital* was intended to support both the government's neoliberal macroeconomic agenda and its more social-democratic aims to ensure that the benefits of ICTs would be shared by all Chileans.

Chile was arguably the first experiment of neoliberal reform (Harvey 2005) when, after the military coup in 1973, the Pinochet regime, guided by economists from the Chicago School, deregulated the national economy and sought to integrate the country into global trade (Cademártori, 2001). The same macroeconomic ideology saw investment in research, development and innovation as primarily the domain of the private sector, so technological change was not state-induced (Díaz & Rivas, 2005). The democratic centre-left governments that followed after 1990, on the other hand, decided to fund research, development and innovation initiatives much more directly. This decision coincided with a realisation that Chile, relatively integrated into the global economy and one of the most free-market oriented economies in the world (Kane et al., 2007), was in a difficult position in terms of global competitiveness. Its productivity and innovation indicators lagged behind those of North American and many European countries (Pollack, 2003), while wage levels were much higher than in other emerging economies such as China and India. Choosing the 'high road' to competitiveness (Schmitz & Musyck, 1993), the Chilean government decided to invest in human resources and innovation. The first important ICT-related initiative was in the early 90s, the establishment of REUNA (*Red Universitaria Nacional*), a network which connected universities and research centres. In 1998, President Frei founded a Presidential Commission on the Information Society and from 2000 onwards, President Lagos launched components of the national IT strategy, the *Agenda Digital* (Díaz and Rivas 2005). When analysing the process of drawing up and implementing the *Agenda Digital*, the following section draws on existing literature as well as six expert interviews conducted in 2005/6 with key senior civil servants involved in aspects of the *Agenda,* each lasting about an hour.

When President Lagos came into power, he used a key speech to the nation on 21 May 2001 to lay out how Chile needed to integrate into a globalised world and how ICTs would be instrumental in this process. From the start, the strategic focus was on ICT-enabled development, rather than on ICT-based development: in other words, on the mass diffusion of internet usage by individuals, companies and the public sector, rather than building development around a national software industry, a focus which governments such as India had adopted (Díaz & Rivas, 2005). The idea was to improve ICT infrastructure through public-private partnerships, provide free universal skills training and free universal access via

telecentres, to offer a maximum of government services online, and to adopt e-government policies which would force the public sector to work more efficiently and transparently and improve coordination (Díaz & Rivas, 2005).

In 2003 a presidential working group on the digital economy, the *Grupo de Acción Digital* (GAD), was formed. Coordinated by a senior civil servant (Executive Secretary) in the Economic Ministry and his team of four people, it brought together the senior civil servants in charge of the different action lines of the national ICT strategy, the *Agenda Digital,* as well as politicians, business leaders from the IT sector and the representative of the Santiago Chamber of Commerce, academics and representatives of ICT4D-related charities.

The *Agenda Digital* explicitly endorsed the principles set out at the World Summit on the Information Society in 2003 and stated as its objectives:

To contribute to the development of Chile by using information and communication technologies to increase competitiveness, equal opportunities, individual freedoms, quality of life and the efficiency and transparency of the public sector, while at the same time enriching the cultural identity of the nation and its indigenous peoples. ICTs are not an end in themselves. They are an instrument in the modernisation of the state, increasing productivity and reducing the differences between large and small enterprises, improving the efficiency of social policies, reducing the development disparities between regions and increasing equality.(Grupo de Acción Digital 2004, p.3, translation DK).

This wide-ranging and ambitious set of goals seems to reflect the concerns of various actors from across the political spectrum. The GAD formulated the *Agenda Digital 2004-2006* which consisted of six work areas: mass access, education and training, e-government, use of ICTs in enterprises, development of an ICT industry and regulatory framework. Amongst the lines of work set up was the network of *Infocentros*, free public internet access points, and a Campaign for Digital Literacy (*Campaña Nacional de Alfabetización Digital*), which was intended to offer free basic IT training to 500,000 Chilean adults who were outside formal education. The IT courses consisted of 18 hours of training, at the end of which participants were supposed to be able to search for information on the internet, communicate via email, produce and register information while using word processors and spreadsheets and be able to conduct specific electronic transactions. The Campaign was rolled out between 2003 and 2005 across around 2000 internet access points, including schools and *Infocentros*.

The Campaign for Digital Literacy was only made possible by the fact that Chile has implemented a strong infrastructure providing free public access to the internet. The free access points, termed *telecentros* or *Infocentros*, were set up according to different models. The first model, *Biblioredes*, relied on the pre-existing networks of the public libraries which were then equipped with computers and internet access; the second embedded computers with access to the internet in local authorities; the third offered licenses to private chains to supply *Infocentro* services; and the fourth model was one of *Infocentros* run as social projects. The GAD Executive Secretary, Jaime Gré, stated that the model which had proved most institutionally sustainable had been the *Biblioredes* model, based in public libraries. The following section draws on two interviews, one with the National Coordinator of all *Infocentro* initiatives and one with the Director of *Biblioredes*.

The National Network of *Infocentros* had an appointed Coordinator, a senior civil servant within the Ministry of Telecommunication who originally headed a team of two and from 2005 a team of four. In addition to this, there was one designated liaison person in each region. The Coordinator oversaw an annual budget for the *Infocentros* of 267 million pesos (504,000 USD) (2005). Her role was to co-ordinate the efforts

towards public non-commercial internet access to make sure *Infocentros* were appropriately geographically diffused. The original government target was to have 1,400 *Infocentros* across the country; in March 2006 an estimated 800 had been set up.

Biblioredes was launched in November 2002, in cooperation with the Bill and Melinda Gates Foundation which donated 9.2 million USD to equip the libraries with hardware and standardised software on each computer. The libraries had internet connections ranging from terrestrial broadband to, in some cases, satellite connections. In 2005, *Biblioredes* accounted for 385 of Chile's *Infocentros*, equipped with 2,114 computers in total. While it was up to the municipalities running the libraries to decide whether to fund additional full-time staff as directors of the local *Infocentros*, 54 people worked directly for the *Biblioredes* programme. One to three staff per region coordinated the efforts and oversaw the computer laboratories used to train staff of local *Infocentros*. Staff at the central office in Santiago numbered 20 and the overall annual budget was 2,500 million pesos (4.7 million USD) (2005).

The National Coordinator of *Infocentros* believed that the *Infocentros* were predominantly a social, not economic, policy initiative. She was particularly concerned to ensure a good gender balance among the participants, recognising that the *Infocentros'* opening times did not extend long enough in the evenings. In her view, this was particularly problematic for the men, since, according to her, the women "have more time to come" (ID 52, F3).

Similarly, the Director of *Biblioredes* explained how the model of *Biblioredes* had been imported from the US, where the Gates Foundation had been setting up public access points targeted at income-poor sections of the population. *Biblioredes*, in turn, explicitly stated in its successful entry to the Stockholm Challenge award that "women, young adults have preferential access to *Biblioredes* services" (Stockholm Challenge 2006). In line with this, the Director of *Biblioredes* was also concerned with the gender balance among her target group: their internal data showed that the gender balance in the free IT courses taken in their *Infocentros* overall was 65% women versus 35% men, while later on the gender balance among users of the *Infocentro* was 49% women versus 51% men, suggesting possibly that either men were more likely to have other ways of acquiring IT skills or that women were less likely to continue practicing their skills in the *Infocentro*.

Without reference to the gender issue, the Director of *Biblioredes* stressed the role of the library as a communal space, a space for interaction and a space for information gathering, whether from printed or from digital media, and she pointed out that, ideally, there would be no spatial division between the library of books and the *Infocentro* with the computers. As far as usage was concerned, the management team of *Biblioredes* did not feel that using email or playing games on the computer was of less value than other usages. Their aim was to give all users total freedom to do whatever they wanted to during the hour of usage they were entitled to.

Overall, the *Biblioredes* team was very satisfied with what they had achieved in widening access to ICTs in Chile via the *Biblioredes* centres:

"The general target for this year is 150,000 newly registered users. And in terms of training courses it's in the order of 72,000 basic training courses and 28,000 advanced level training courses. And further, in the websites with local content it's more or less 1,450 local content sites per year. This is divided by region. There are indicators per computer, which is more or less the methodology we apply, but regionally they adapt these [targets] based on the number of staff, number of people who normally come and the problems they might have." (Director of Biblioredes, ID 53, F3, all quotes translated by DK).

It is worth noting the Director's fluency in these figures and that three out of four of the targets she mentioned were input targets. All of these targets were achieved in the year 2005, and *Biblioredes* gained national and international recognition, by winning the ACTI prize from the Association of Chilean Technology Companies and the Stockholm Challenge Award 2006. The *Biblioredes* managers were convinced that they were having a positive impact. They were encouraged by their overall success of synthesising the local libraries and the *Infocentro* idea and were winning prizes for it. In cooperation with the Gates Foundation, they were exporting their model of running telecentres to other countries such as Botswana, Latvia and Estonia. Focusing on just the Chilean context for now, the next section will explore the local reality into which the state ICT policies were inserted.

INTRODUCING ALGUN, A RURAL TOWN IN CHILE

The research findings presented in the following section are based on a subset of data from a larger study involving three field visits in 2005 and 2006, each lasting between six and ten weeks. Combining policy analysis with an ethnographic approach (Geertz, 1973), the methodology focused on participant observation and in-depth interviews with policy makers at the national and regional level on the one hand and on the other hand with users at the local level. The qualitative research design was based loosely on a grounded theory approach (Strauss & Corbin, 1990), moving cyclically between defining the research interest and phenomena, fieldwork, gathering observation and interview data, data analysis, development of theory, theory-testing during fieldwork and then further analysis in an ongoing inductive-deductive dialectic. 99 interviews and follow-up interviews were conducted with 68 interviewees, mainly microentrepreneurs and public servants, men and women. Returning to the same places and people for follow-up interviews allowed for prolonged engagement with the local community (Lincoln & Guba, 1985) as well as the development of rapport with local people (Baxter & Eyles, 1997). Theoretical sampling (Flowerdew & Martin, 1997) was used in recruiting interviewees and interviews were semi-structured. Different data sources and methods of data gathering were compared in a constant process of triangulation (Denzin, 1989) to test the validity of the findings. Analysis of interview data followed an open coding approach (Flick, 2006) and was assisted by Atlas.ti software. A comprehensive account of the methodology can be found in the full study (Kleine 2007).

Algun (name changed) is a small town of around 13,000 inhabitants, located in the Araucanía Region in Chile, one of the poorest regions in a country characterised by high regional inequality. It is about 500km, or eight hours by bus, from the capital Santiago. The regional capital, Temuco, is about 150km away, but the bus trip takes three hours because of the road conditions and the frequent stops. Algun is situated in a fertile valley between sparsely populated, wooded hills. There were 172 registered businesses in town (Municipio, 2005) and hundreds of informal ventures, but productive activity was limited to the large timber companies, carpentry, honey making and weaving. Official unemployment stood at 12.8% (CASEN 2000) and between 1992 and 2002, the population had shrunk by 7.5% (Censo, 2002), as young people left the town in search for work or to pursue further study. Meanwhile, the illiteracy rate was 9.9%, more than twice the national average (CASEN, 2000).

Despite the economically depressed situation, the telecommunication infrastructure in town was expanding. In 2000, 18.7% of households had a private landline telephone, and 23.9% had a mobile phone (CASEN, 2000). There were 28 public access telephones in the urban part of Algun and 13 in the rural area surrounding the town. 4.8% of households had a computer and only 1.6% had private internet access at home (CASEN,

2000). Shared access was common, with 26.7% of households reporting access to a computer and 8.2% access to the internet. The local *Infocentro* had been established in the local library as early as 1998 and by 2006 offered 9 computers to access the internet. By 2006, there were, in addition to the *Infocentro* in the local library, seven privately-run cybercafés in Algun.

Gender norms were very strict in Algun, particularly among the older generation. For example, non-indigenous men wore short and unmarried women long hair, women and men sat in separate areas in church, married women would often identify themselves as 'housewives' (*dueñas de casa*) and older women would never be seen wearing trousers or ride bicycles. It was considered inappropriate for unmarried women to walk around unaccompanied after dark, while this was also the time that less religious men congregated in the all-male bars of the town. Women also traditionally had fewer educational opportunities. In the families, women (maids, housewives, professional women) tended to do practically all of the housework, and also waited on the men at table. Divorce had only become legal in Chile in 2004, but there were several women in Algun whose husbands had left them and who had to raise the children on their own while the fathers refused to pay for their children's upkeep. From the mayor to the priest and pastors, the president of the sport club, the director of the school to the indigenous leaders, all local leaders, with the exception of one female local councillor, were men. The terms *machismo* and *machista*, common throughout Latin America, are used to describe gender inequalities and often misogynist attitudes – in Algun, when spoken by a woman, these were frequently accompanied by a resigned shrug of the shoulders.

After this short introduction to the realities in Algun, the next section will analyse how state ICT policies, specifically the Campaign for Digital Literacy and the *Infocentro* impacted on people's access to ICTs.

ANALYSIS OF THE THREE DIMENSIONS OF ACCESS

Gerster and Zimmermann (2003) identified three dimensions of access to ICTs: the availability and affordability of ICTs and the capability to use them, each of which may be influenced by axes of exclusion such as gender, age, disability etc.

Availability

Availability, according to Gerster & Zimmermann (2003), relates to the physical presence of ICTs and the opportunity to connect to these. Given that some authors have posited the "death of distance" (e.g. Cairncross, 1997) as a consequence of the introduction of ICTs, it is worth stressing the need to conceptualise digital divides not only in connection with social, but also spatial, inequalities.

In the context of this case study, a number of different ways emerged by which space influenced the way microentrepreneurs used ICTs. Firstly, space could act as a barrier to infrastructure development and, secondly, access opportunities followed a spatially concentrated pattern.

ICT infrastructure is never simply 'rolled out' evenly across countries; the spatial pattern of ICT infrastructure is a product of feasibility assessments and planning decisions based on geomorphological characteristics, population patterns and, to a large degree, political considerations. All over the global South, connecting "the last mile" (Talyarkhan et al., 2005) in the rural parts of the countries remains a challenge. Different kinds of wireless technologies are being piloted and used to improve connectivity where no cables exist. In the Araucanía Region of Chile, it is particularly the rural, thinly populated areas in the mountains and hills which still are largely disconnected from internet or mobile phone coverage.

In addition, ICTs and their related network effects carry an institutional and economic logic which favours connecting the largest number of people in the shortest possible time, thus focusing on connecting centres before (if at all) connecting people living in so-called peripheral regions. Many countries, like Chile, have opted to establish a strong internet backbone architecture which runs between national centres. As a result, peripheral regions located along the backbone gain, while other peripheral regions' communication infrastructure remains less developed, thus further weakening their competitive position as locations of economic activity.

Algun was not on Chile's internet backbone, but in the urban part of Algun, internet access via cable was physically possible, and the *Infocentro* and most of the cybercafés were located either close to schools or as centrally as possible, to take advantage of this. By contrast, phone lines, internet cables, wireless internet access and even mobile phone coverage were not universally available in the vast 465km² of hilly terrain that belonged to Algun. There were many rural settlements in the area which had no electricity. The cybercafés and the *Infocentro* in the urban part of town could be difficult to reach from the rural areas, especially for those who did not have a car or bicycle or who could not walk. Thus, for the 41% of Algun's population who lived in the rural sector (CASEN 2000), choice of ICT was limited by the availability of infrastructure, as mediated by the physical distance and time required to reach it.

However, even people living in the centre of Algun might have difficulty with the availability of internet access. Here the constraining factor was not one of distance but of time: if they did not have private internet access and were unable or unwilling to pay for access in a cybercafé, they had to adhere to the limited opening hours offered by the *Infocentro*: Monday to Friday from 10am to 6pm.

This in turn shows how the factors of availability and affordability are linked: the cybercafés were open in the evenings (some up until midnight) and at weekends, so those people able and willing to pay for the cybercafé had a much wider choice of times when computers were available.

195

Affordability

When examining affordability as a dimension and possible limitation to access, it is important to assess not only the absolute affordability of access, say the 600 pesos (1.13 USD) it cost to use the internet in a local cybercafé for an hour, but to see this in the context of other living costs in Algun.

Firstly, it is important to see how this cost related to the affordability of other kinds of communication and possibly, transport (see Table 1). Secondly, comparing this figure with the relative costs incurred for the same service in the national and regional capital allows an assessment of whether or not microentrepreneurs in the rural towns were disadvantaged in terms of access costs.

As to the first point, the choice of comparison points above reflects the fact that the internet as a medium can fulfill different functions, among them gathering information and communicating with other users. For the informational role of the internet the relevant medium for comparison in Algun was the regional newspaper, which cost 250 pesos (0.47 USD), slightly cheaper than the 300 pesos (0.57 USD) for half an hour in a cybercafé (the shortest timeslot available).

As far as the communicative function is concerned, the price of internet access has to be seen in the context of the cost of other communication media. One key point of comparison was the cost of phoning from a public call centre, versus the

Table 1. Comparison of costs of different media in Algun (1 USD = 530 Chilean pesos)

Medium or Vehicle	Cost (in Chilean Pesos)
1 hour internet access (cyber-café)	600
1 minute local call (call centre)	40
1 minute national call (call centre)	80
1 minute call on pre-paid mobile	350
local newspaper	250
return bus fare to regional capital	4,400

cost of using the internet from a cybercafé. The travel and opportunity costs of reaching a call centre would be similar to those involved in using a cybercafé since their spatial distribution was similar, so the costs are directly comparable. In a call centre, landlines are 40 pesos (0.08 USD) locally and 80 pesos (0.16 USD) nationally, while calls to mobile phones cost 100 pesos (0.19 USD) a minute. Thus half an hour online costs slightly less than a 4-minute national call to a landline.

A more expensive option for those people who did not have private phone access was a mobile phone. A mobile handset cost 19,900 pesos (37.55 USD), and prepaid calls cost 350 pesos (0.66 USD) a minute. Thus one minute on a mobile cost slightly more than thirty minutes online. However this direct comparison was not representative of the genuine costs that many people living further away would face in using a cybercafé, since the travel and opportunity costs of reaching a cyber-café might be very high (travel was expensive, for instance, 2,200 pesos (4.15 USD) to reach the regional capital from Algun). Thus a mobile phone call might ultimately be the relatively cheaper option for those living in rural areas.

The comparatively high cost of communication in Algun becomes clear when one compares the relative costs of an hour of internet usage to other key living expenses, such as rent levels. According to estimates by a local social worker (ID 66, F2), renting a room in Algun cost about 30,000 pesos (57 USD) per month; renting a similar room in Temuco cost 80,000 pesos (151 USD) and in the centre of Santiago 150,000 pesos (283 USD). The cheapest price for an hour of internet usage was 600 pesos (1.13 USD) in Algun, 400 (0.75 USD) in Temuco and 350 (0.66 USD) in the centre of Santiago. According to these figures, an hour of internet in a cybercafé cost 2% of monthly rent in Algun, 0.5% of monthly rent in Temuco and 0.23% in Santiago. By this measure, an hour of internet use in a cybercafé was not just, in absolute terms, 71% more expensive in Algun than in Santiago, but in relative terms, it can be estimated that the cost was over eight times higher in the rural town than in the capital.

While the comparative costs of using a cybercafé were high, these comparisons between the cost of communicating online or offline suggest that in many cases, for people who did not own a fixed line phone or internet connection, it might be cheaper for someone living close to a cybercafé to communicate by email than by phone. However, the crucial factor which is not reflected in the cost was the relative penetration of the different media: interviews indicated that far fewer people had email accounts or regularly accessed a computer than had some sort of access to a phone. The comparative cheapness of online communication was outweighed by the fact that it could be used to contact far fewer people.

People who were able to afford home phone or internet access were in a very different position. Interestingly, the cost comparison between renting a private phone line or private internet access shows that the running costs were very similar. A private phone line cost around 12,000 pesos (23 USD) a month (including 250 to 500 minutes in local calls). This was the same price as renting a 128Mb home internet connection which could be used from 8pm at night to 8am in the morning. Thus a home internet connection cost the same per month as renting a phone line, 34 minutes' call time on a mobile, or 150 minutes on national calls from a call centre.

The major difference between the cost of having a home phone line or home internet access, however, was the upfront cost of buying a home computer, which was prohibitive for many people in Algun. During the time of the research, the Chilean government under President Lagos had asked private companies to develop a cheap PC that could be mass produced. A consortium made up of Microsoft, Intel, VTR and Olidata designed four basic computer packages – three desktop PCs and one Notebook – in a line called *Mi primer PC* (My first PC), the cheapest package starting at 219,000 pesos (413 USD). These machines

had very basic features[1], came in a package with four hours of computer training, and could be paid for in installments over 36 months, at 9,990 pesos (19 USD) per month. All major department stores and electrical stores sold them after they were formally launched by President Lagos on 11 August 2005 (Mouse 2005).

In Algun, in families where the head of the household was male, the family budget would often be controlled by him. Women who worked as "housewives" tended to receive a set weekly allowance to use for shopping and even women in paid employment often shared their bank accounts (if they had one) with their husband. Thus, spending money on information or communication services was a much more difficult proposition for the women who often did not control their own budget. Given the lack of affordable alternatives, the *Infocentro*, which was the only place providing free internet access, thus had a vital role to play in opening up Internet access to the poorer members of the community, especially to women. The following sections will explore some barriers to access which were even more powerful than lack of financial resources.

Capability

The third barrier to access that Gerster and Zimmermann (2003) identify is capability, which was found to be a serious problem for many people in Algun. Using the internet in Algun required literacy at least in Spanish, an opportunity to learn basic IT skills, and a certain degree of mental agility and confidence.

Literacy was an issue for a number of people in Algun, 9.9% of Algun's population being illiterate (CASEN 2000). Most indigenous Mapuche people spoke Spanish as their second language and few people knew enough English to read websites in that language. Access to training in IT skills was a major national policy issue, and in Algun, the director of the *Infocentro* estimated that 2,500 people out of the ca. 13 000 inhabitants had taken part in free IT courses at basic level and 2,000 had taken part in a free advanced IT course.

However, the existence of training courses alone was not enough to guarantee that people would be able to learn.

"They have tried to do this campaign of [digital] literacy. But what happened was that they delivered the modules but nobody came to see whether the people had actually learnt and whether they had learnt it well."(Director of the Infocentro, ID 20, F3)

With the ambitious target of 500,000 trained participants nationwide to reach, the monitoring of the success of the Campaign for Digital Literacy had been neglected. One of the factors which influenced individuals' learning was education. In interviews, respondents claimed that education levels co-determined who took the courses, how well they learned and whether they had the ability to use the skills they learned in the long run. The director of the *Infocentro* also saw a reflection of the relative educational backgrounds of men and women:

"The women are more detail-focused. They are more dedicated. They come and come again, several times. Here [at the Infocentro, learning] has been more difficult for the women. I don't know why. Because they have been at home or have been out selling things, but they have not done other things. But it has been hard for them. Generally, women here have less formal education."(Director of the Infocentro, ID 20, F3)

An important dimension in people's capability to learn to use computers was their own confidence in their abilities. Interviews showed that low self-confidence was often connected with low levels of education. Lack of formal education made people learn more slowly, and in addition many felt that the technology was not for them, the courses were not intended for them, or that

successful learning was not within their reach. Thus a lack of educational resources might erode psychological resources. On the other hand, psychological resources could play an important role in overcoming practical restrictions on access to and use of ICTs, an aspect which will be explored further below.

ADDITIONAL ASPECTS: NORMS RELATED TO TIME

As indicated above, Gerster and Zimmermann (2003) identify three main barriers to access to ICTs: availability, affordability, and capability. Research in Algun indicated that availability of ICTs was not limited to the issue of whether the ICTs existed in a certain geographical area, but also whether individuals had the time to access them, and how social norms around the spaces in which ICTs were available influenced people's behaviour.

Time was a particularly central issue for the people of Algun, for learning and using ICTs had not only monetary costs, but also time costs attached to it. At the most basic level, the question of time related to whether individuals were able to access ICT facilities at a time that suited them. People who did not have access to computers at home, and who could not afford cybercafés, were restricted to using computers during the opening hours of the *Infocentro*. However, the question of time-related access was far more complex and nuanced than this.

In Algun, social norms related to, for example, age, occupation and gender, imposed different time-commitments on people. School children had more free time than most adults to spend at the *Infocentro*. Among adults, pensioners and unemployed people had more time at their disposal, employees had set working hours, and microentrepreneurs regulated their own hours of work but might face high opportunity costs when spending time online. Full-time carers and "housewives" juggled various commitments, often fitted around the schedules of other family members. Those running their own shops often could not leave them unattended, except during the lunch break, between 1 and 3 pm, when most shops closed but the *Infocentro* remained open.

Beyond these constraints, which were imposed by age or occupation, a strong gendered element was uncovered in the time budgets available to individuals. For example, while male microentrepreneurs could use the lunch break to access the *Infocentro*, female microentrepreneurs often did not have this option. In Algun, lunch was the main meal of the day and women were expected to cook it for their families. This was just one of the cultural norms affecting men and women's time budget. According to the director of the *Infocentro*, the rather incomplete user statistics showed that more men than women used the computers. On the day of a one-day survey we conducted, 60 per cent of the users were indeed male. This was in the summer. According to the director, user statistics fluctuate between the seasons:

"[In winter], the women do not leave the house because there is more to do. The clothes get wet more often. They get muddy, with the rain, the mud, so there is more work. The woman always has more roles to fulfill. So for her this [going to the Infocentro] is something additional. For them it is like a present that they have to earn because they have other things to do. […] Always when I invite people to come to courses I try, without paying any less attention to the men, but try to be more enthusiastic with them [the women]. […] In the beginning it was difficult because the men come home in the evening and when things [at the Infocentro] take a bit more time, the men come home and the food is not ready. So experience taught us and we told the women: you go and do all the housework first and leave it ready and then you come here. And this has gone on and there has been hardly any change [in attitudes]. The years go by, new technologies arrive, everything

becomes more modern, but that does not change." (Director of the Infocentro, ID 20, F1)

In Molyneux's (1985) terms, the *Infocentro* may have helped women with their practical gender interests (allowing them access to ICTs while still enabling them to balance their traditional household roles) but key strategic interests (questioning the intra-household division of labour which ties women to the house more than men) were not raised.

ADDITIONAL ASPECTS: NORMS RELATED TO SPACE

In Algun, there were social norms surrounding not only norms related to time, but also related to space. This section takes the notion of space beyond the physical into the realm of space as socially constructed and negotiated, demonstrating how space can be delineated by physical as well as socially explicit and implicit barriers.

On the local level, there were, for example, the physical characteristics of the cybercafés in Algun which influenced who had access to them. Officially, other than the opening times, there were no written rules in the cybercafé around who could use it: anyone who could pay seemed to be welcome. However, the physical space imposed its own constraints. For example, all of the cybercafés were crammed with computer desks. None of the cybercafés provided a space in which a wheelchair could be easily turned or a seated wheelchair user could fit behind a screen; for similar reasons, it was difficult to bring a pram into a cybercafé. Throughout the observation period, there were never any mothers or fathers with young children to be seen in any of the cybercafés.

In addition to the obvious physical barriers to access, the space imposed other social constraints on the users of the cybercafés. All of the cybercafés were set up with headphones and partitions between the different computers (see Figure 1), and one offered cubicles with doors. These cabins provided privacy (accentuated by the fact that the majority of cybercafés only had space for one chair to fit comfortably in front of each computer), but they also presupposed users who could be largely left to their own devices, thus requiring a certain degree of IT literacy. The attendants usually sat at their own desk, and would not approach any of the computers unless fetched to come and help. All of this emphasis on the individual user working alone meant that the user could move in the online space in almost complete privacy and free from social control, but also that there was little support for anyone who might need help.

The cybercafés also appeared to be coded largely as male spaces: all of the attendants of the cybercafés in Algun were male, with the exception of the two young women running the two smaller phone-focused cybercafés. On regular visits to the five larger cybercafés in Algun the majority of the users tended to be students or adults in their 20s, the majority male. The décor in three of the cybercafés included posters of scantily-clad women. After 9 pm, there were very few women there, and those that were there tended to be with their boyfriends. So the clientele of the cybercafés was disproportionately young, accustomed to using computers, mainly male, and without children. Attending a cybercafé signified youth, the ability to deal with male assertiveness, having some disposable income and a degree of IT knowledge, although it also indicated that the users were not rich enough to have internet at home. Users who lacked these qualities, while they were not formally barred from accessing the cybercafés, might very well feel unable to enter.

The *Infocentro*, on the other hand, offered a very different space. It was physically more inclusive, with good access for wheelchairs and prams. During the period of the fieldwork, a young woman in a wheelchair visited the *Infocentro* almost every day, as did several mothers with babies and small children in prams. Rather than being placed in small individual cubicles, the computers were laid out in a circle, with the screens facing towards the centre of the room, and no partitions between the screens (see Figure 2). This enabled users to talk to each other, as well as ensuring that the assistants in the *Infocentro* were constantly available to help with problems or queries. As a result users needed little to no previous IT knowledge to go there and it was the norm to ask questions (see Figure 3).

Figure 1. Cybercafé in Algun

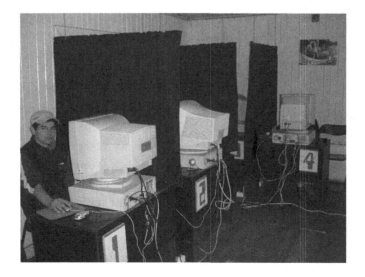

Figure 2. Infocentro in Algun

However, the physical layout of the *Infocentro* also ensured that users had far less privacy than people using the cybercafés. The lack of partitions between the screens meant that people could read their neighbour's screen, as could the people standing in line to use the computers. Some sites, such as pornography, were blocked, and certain usages, which were considered frivolous (such as playing games), could lead to people being asked to leave the computers before their 30-minute slot was up. In such an environment, it would, for example, not be advisable for a microentrepreneur to research a business idea he intended to keep secret, or for a woman or man to research sexual health issues. Private or emotional emails or chats could also not be exchanged in such a public environment without the risk that other users would notice. Men in particular were expected to appear strong in public and so could not freely respond to distressing news. One male interview partner explained that when talking about his unemployment via email, he sometimes cried and

Figure 3. The Infocentro director explaining how to print an email

therefore preferred to use the cybercafé with the cabins. The physical layout of the *Infocentro* thus placed constraints not so much on who was able to access ICTs, but on what they were used for.

Situated next to the library, a space of learning, the *Infocentro* was more like a communal meeting point than a quiet space for study. The director, Julia (name changed), who led both the library and the *Infocentro*, explained:

J: Many libraries are very pretty, very orderly and everything in its place. But for me the idea is not that everything is clean and orderly. Rather that the people when they come they feel in a communal space, a meeting place. That people come and ask. Sometimes talk about their problems. Those are the things that a woman can do but a man doesn't do.

DK: Do you think it is a feminine space?

J: I would just say it is a space. Because also many young people come to the Infocentro and ask things, which guide us when we order new things, books, software and so on. But I would say that it has turned itself into a meeting place especially for the women. Sometimes they simply come and sit down opposite me, grab a chair and then we simply have a conversation. Afterwards they go and don't use the computers, rather they have just come to have a chat. So I would say that we have created this and it's beautiful. [...] What we are trying to do here is that every person feels that they are unique and they are special. [...] For me this is not what I am trying to do but simply what I feel. I try to make them feel that. (Director of the Infocentro, ID 20, F3).

As this comment suggests, the *Infocentro* was at times a female-coded space, "a meeting place especially for the women", in contrast with the male-dominated cybercafés. Both attendants were female and, in the mornings, the majority of visitors was also female.

Observations indicated the ways in which the space of the *Infocentro* was coded differently at particular times of the day. During the morning, the focus was on women, particularly women with children (see Figure 4). At lunchtime, when the women left to prepare lunch, various users stopped by on their lunch break, including occasionally some microentrepreneurs. In the afternoons, when students came after school to do assignments, the space's character changed again to be dominated by school children.

It was precisely its inclusiveness which characterised the *Infocentro* as a social space, for better or for worse. Going to the *Infocentro* not only meant that one did not have internet access at home, it also meant that one would be interacting with women, children, and disabled, unemployed and indigenous people, some of the lower-status groups in the town. On the one hand, the fact that the *Infocentro* was free of charge and was accessible for those with no IT skills was clearly valued by its users. On the other hand, this combination of factors meant that going to the *Infocentro* had very little status. This in itself placed different restraints around who would be willing to access ICTs via the *Infocentro*: just as social construction of space in the cybercafé came with one set of social codings, the *Infocentro* came with another, and both had an impact on who would be able or willing to access ICTs via these different routes.

OVERCOMING LIMITS: SOCIAL AND PSYCHOLOGICAL RESOURCES

So far, it has been shown how access to ICTs, and the choices that they open up, is restricted by five factors: availability, affordability, capability, norms related to time and norms related to space. The next section considers some of the general strategies individual men and women used to overcome these limits, particularly their use of social and psychological resources.

Figure 4. Female user and her son with the Infocentro director

People feeling able and confident enough to use ICTs was of vital importance. The case study identified a number of individuals who, due to traditional axes of exclusion, had limited financial, material or geographical resources, but who were able to overcome these barriers through a combination of personal qualities which I have called psychological resources (Kleine 2007).

Psychological resources are closely linked with other resources, particularly educational resources, in a society in which levels of formal education are equated with power and the right to speak. One quotation from a female microentrepreneur indicates the wider implications that low educational resources could have for psychological resources such as personal confidence:

No, no, I could never be president [of the association of microentrepreneurs]. I only have elementary school education. The others in the group have more education. Not that much, but more. (Female carpenter, ID 11, F3).

It is therefore important to recognise how individuals who have been traditionally disadvantaged in the formal education system – such as women,

indigenous and poor people – have found other ways to build psychological resources. One female microentrepreneur spoke of the "university of life" (1D 19, F2) which she had attended and which gave her confidence.

Another mechanism which the inhabitants of Algun used to overcome limits in their own educational and financial resources was social resources, often termed "the capital of the poor" (Woolcock and Narayan 2000). Social resources can be described as links to other individuals or groups which provide a person with access to opportunities, facilities, assets or services. In Algun, some individuals were able to use social resources to increase their access to ICTs, and particularly the internet. Interestingly, there was a significant gender bias in the ability to exploit social resources in the context of the *Infocentro*. Most women in Algun had not had the same educational opportunities as their male counterparts, but gendered social norms allowed women to ask questions, to ask each other for help or to ask Julia, the female director of the *Infocentro*, for assistance, in a way that men did not seem comfortable doing, particularly not in a public space. Women often came to the *Infocentro* in pairs, or would ask Julia to sit next to them to show them something. One would often see small groups of children or two women sharing a machine, but male youths or men always sat alone in front of the computers. Julia expressed her experience as director of the *Infocentro* thus:

The [women] help each other more than the men. They show more solidarity. They accept what they don't know. They are able to say when they have made a mistake or they do not know something. The men, no. [...] They never say that they do not know [...]. (Director of the Infocentro, ID 20, F3).

The men who used the *Infocentro* appeared to have far more difficulty in using their social resources in their access and use of the internet. The fact that the director of the *Infocentro* was a university educated woman made it hard for the men with elementary or incomplete secondary education to place her in the social hierarchy. She was treated with respect and typical Chilean politeness, but socio-cultural norms meant that it would have been embarrassing for a man to admit not knowing something in front of a woman who would traditionally be considered his social inferior.

Thus, in the context of the *Infocentro* the women's educational resources might be fewer, but by making use of their social resources they were able to increase their resource portfolios. Paradoxically, here it was their lower status within the *machista* cultural norms governing behaviour in public spaces which allowed women to behave in a way more conducive to learning. As a result, under the same (availability, affordability, capability) or worse access conditions (time), once they were in the space of the *Infocentro*, women could make more use of ICTs. They also further accumulated psychological resources though learning successes and social resources through repeated interaction amongst each other.

CASE STUDY: MARTA CASTILLO

The following example will introduce a female entrepreneur, Marta Castillo (name changed) who did not have the financial resources to buy her own hardware, but did try to make the most of existing ICT access opportunities. To understand her situation, this section describes the things that mattered most to her (her family and her livelihood), before exploring the role ICTs played in her life.

Marta Castillo (55) was the female head of a household and operated a diverse livelihood portfolio to ensure her family's survival while developing ideas for future business development. She sold cookies, cakes and pastry, either door to door or at special occasions, and produced jams and fruit conserves. On Fridays, she cooked lunches at the local school and on other days she served lunch for the local teachers in her kitchen. She also resold liquid gas bottles in her neighbourhood. After her husband left her she had raised their three children alone, taking different jobs, including, when they were older, working for four years as a *nana* (cook and housemaid) in Santiago. In 2003 she had returned to Algun to take care of her elderly mother and in 2005 and 2006 she lived in a modest house outside the town centre with her two daughters, one of whom was in her 30s and a kindergarten assistant, and the other who was in her 20s and studying to be a teacher. Her 28-year old son had almost finished technical studies and was traveling around the country, doing jobs such as working as a day labourer on the fruit harvest in central Chile.

While Marta herself had left secondary school early to marry, it was important to her that her children finished school and went on to tertiary education. She had paid for part of the education of the two older children while each of them also worked to co-finance their studies. The tuition fees (52,000 pesos (98 USD) a term), travel costs and living expenses (52,000 pesos (98 USD) monthly) of the youngest daughter had to be paid alongside the normal household expenses, while the wages of the older daughter (130,000 pesos (245 USD) per month), the mother's pension (70,000 pesos (132 USD) per month) and the profits from the small business constituted the joint household income. Since Marta's turnover in her jams and cakes fluctuated from month to month and she had no consistent bookkeeping, she had no clear idea of her turnover or profit.

Given that Marta had worked for rich families in Santiago, her cooking skills were well-respected in the community. She had also taken another two state-funded courses in baking and making preserves. Her latest product innovations included letting housewives in Algun order specific kinds of dough from her which they then collected to make cookies or pastries at home. She was also trying to persuade a friend of hers, a Mapuche school teacher, to jointly produce traditional Mapuche meals.

Marta was an extremely determined and resilient individual, with a strong sense of pride in what she had achieved:

People listen to me and it is funny because my husband used to say to me "you are worth nothing, you are nothing" and now I see how they congratulate me and say, "Senora [Marta], your husband has no idea what he has lost". So this is what lifts one's ego up. Because they have seen how I have worked and got myself out of the dirt, as one says, doing a thousand things. […] There are many female heads of households. […] And on their own they have to face being mama and papa, send the kids to school, feed them, dress them and everything. And one promises oneself: "This month I will manage to put this much aside". And one keeps one's promise, with tears running down, but one keeps one's promise. I have kept going for ten years now, getting up at 6 and going to bed at 12. With the alarm clock in my hand because otherwise I would sleep through it. And I have not rested a single day. (Marta, ID 13, F1).

When I first met Marta in summer 2005, she had, with a loan of 1.5 million pesos (2,830 USD) from a faith-based NGO, just set up a separate kitchen-building next to her dilapidated old house. Equipped with a professional oven, cooking stove and chairs with little tables it was planned as a small cooking school. She had hoped to be able to give cooking courses there, but soon realised that the women had no budget to pay for the lessons and the state would not normally pay for courses that would teach skills that were mostly associated with non-paid labour. The NGO started to exert pressure on her to make a profit so she could start repaying the loan and Marta was in desperate search for a way to raise money. One limiting factor was that she did not have the money to pay for fruit and conserve glasses as primary materials upfront in order to produce larger numbers of jams. So she invited the 23 women who had taken the one-off state-funded baking course with her to found an association so that they could buy ingredients and produce cakes and jams in bulk, but nothing ever came of this initiative, partly because there was never a large order.

The women get demoralised when they see no possibility and then they don't have time. (Marta, ID 13, F2).

Marta explained that many women's time budgets were limited by their household duties, except the single mothers who like her were desperate for sources of income, willing to invest their time and did not have to ask their husbands' permission to do so.

In winter (August) 2005, Marta caught a serious bronchitis from working between the steam of the kitchen and the wet and cold old house. But in summer 2006, things were looking brighter. She had gathered an informal group of women with whom she was offering party services at weddings and functions in the local municipality and in the schools. She had registered the party service as a formal business with the local administration and was thinking of producing business cards, a leaflet and a catalogue with different cakes to choose from. She had also taken a trip to a bakery in a neighbouring town to see and write down which machines were being used in the large-scale production of dough, hoping to ask for a state subsidy to buy such a machine.

Marta's media usage (Figure 5) is represented in the star diagram and was generated from her answers on a media usage survey, asking how frequently she used each medium. Each full line represents 365 days, or daily usage. The family had a radio and a black-and-white television at home. She used a mobile phone to receive calls from clients, but spent less than a single prepaid card (3,500 pesos (6.60 USD)) on it per month.

All this however, was enhanced by her knowledge of ICTs and frequent visits to the *Infocentro*. Marta had participated in a competition for seed funding from the government for which she had had to apply online. By then, she had already taken three free computer courses in the *Infocentro*:

DK: Why do you go to the Infocentro?

MC: To get oneself more up to date. Because now wherever you go you need it. If you need to pay taxes you can do it via the internet. You can do whatever payments via the internet. But what if one has no idea of any of this? So, what are we trying to do? To bring ourselves up to date, to modernise ourselves. (Marta, ID 13, F1).

Marta had the advantage of living comparatively close to the *Infocentro*, only a 20-minute walk away. She used a Hotmail email account to communicate with her son, her friends and occasionally clients in other cities. For her email name, she had chosen her middle name which she intended to use as her company's name. Via Google, she researched recipes online, including how to make jam for diabetics since, as she explained, there were more and more older people

with diabetes in Algun and in the region. Since she only spoke a few words of English, she, like most other microentrepreneurs, only used pages that were in Spanish.

Marta went to the *Infocentro* on a regular basis and had enjoyed the computer courses, but would have liked to have been given better course documentation:

And at my age, I am 55 years old, it takes effort to retain the information because the hard drive up here is already pretty scratched. So it does not have the capacity to retain all the information. (Marta, ID 13, F1).

The language of this quote reflects her enthusiasm for the technology which she shared with two other women from her evangelical Christian church. For some months, the three "sisters" would meet once a week to go to the *Infocentro* together, to "learn computers" as they put it:

DK: Do you help each other?

MC: Yes, at least I always forget things. I always walk around with something to write and my materials to help me. Because if I have a doubt I have my material and I check it. I work with a folder in my hand. I don't trust myself. I also ask Carmen and Isabella. So if we have doubts we ask each other. [...] I think for the men the act of asking someone else is like feeling inferior. Or it makes them feel less sure of themselves. But for us, asking each other is to be sure that we are not making a mistake. (Marta, ID 13, F1).

Marta did not have a computer at home and, therefore, had no chance to practice her computer skills there. For her university studies, Marta's youngest daughter used the internet access in the *Infocentro* or went to a friend's house.

I would like to have a computer at home. But of course, with what? My little ones always asked me when I went to work: "Mummy, buy me a computer". Oh yes, and I came back and brought

Figure 5. Marta's media usage

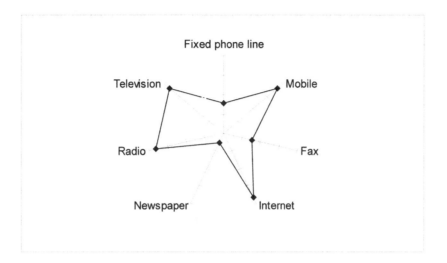

them a paper cut-out of a computer. "There, here is a computer." (Marta, ID 13, F1).

Summary of Marta Castillo

Key points which can be drawn from Marta's case include, firstly, that Marta had benefited from the free courses and free access at the local *Infocentro* more than other users because she was free, as a single mother, to invest more time. While she had similar household duties to other married women in Algun, without a husband, she was free to set her own priorities in her use of time and so could prioritise practicing her IT skills. Despite her limited formal education and her age she had continued using her basic IT skills and could later use them for personal and business reasons. Going to "learn computers" gave her a chance to get out of her kitchen to meet other women in the pro-women space that was the *Infocentro*, especially in the mornings. In such a space, she was free to ask and receive help with her IT skills. The *Infocentro* programme had had an empowering effect by strengthening her access to information as well as her social and psychological resources. The verbal abuse she had suffered from her husband also seemed to have helped her build up psychological resources based on resilience, perseverance and seeking out solidarity.

CONCLUSION

This chapter has brought together the ambitious goals of policy makers trying to create an inclusive ICT strategy for Chile with the complex realities at the local level, in one of the poorest municipalities in the country. There are many inequalities at the local level, running along age, ethnicity, education, occupation and gender lines. In this chapter, we have focused particularly on the way access to ICTs is mediated by the largely informal social norms that regulate the behaviour of women and men. While dimensions of access such as availability and affordability affect men and women in similar ways, the fact that men in Algun often have benefited from more years of formal education puts them at an advantage in relation to the capability dimension of ICT access. Norms related to time usage are another framing dimension of ICT access, and here women's time is more regulated by household responsibilities than that of men. Most significantly, it is important to recognise how gendered social norms related to the usage of space represent an important framing dimension to access to ICTs. While cybercafés in Algun are coded as young, male spaces, the *Infocentro* is coded differently. While in the afternoon the *Infocentro* becomes an extension of the classroom with many school children coming in to work on assignments, in the morning the *Infocentro* is heavily frequented by women. The female staff, their availability for questions, and the open spatial set-up make the *Infocentro* a space where women can go, access the Internet and receive help if their knowledge of IT is not sufficient. Since in this traditional community their gender already classes them in a lower-status group than men, they have less status to lose in asking for help in front of other people than the men.

The men, however, "never say that they do not know", a response which may well be connected with the idea that they must not be seen to be somehow weak in public. Furthermore, with staff at the *Infocentro* being female, they would have to admit this to a woman in order to get help from them.

The research shows that technology is situated in framing institutions (Wajcman 2004) and that such framing institutions can be heavily gendered. The *Infocentro* as a space has an empowering effect for some of Algun's women who come there. It also fits well to the collaborative learning style of these women. As for the men, the set-up is not conducive to their learning new things within the confines of the social roles they have learnt to play.

What does this mean for the telecentre debate in ICT4D? There are three broad points to be made. Firstly, often when gender is introduced as an aspect in ICT4D research, it is limited to "counting women" among the participants or beneficiaries. This study has shown that research needs to move beyond that, to a more nuanced, holistic analysis of the social norms framing the relationship between ICT and an organisation, community or group. Some of these social norms,

like those governing the use of space and time, will be related to gender. Gender-aware analysis is a powerful tool in explaining patterns of technology adoption.

Secondly, while many of us may wish that patriarchal societies such as Algun would become more egalitarian and allow both women and men full self-expression rather than confining them to strict gender norms, we must recognise that this process will take longer than the current rapid process of technological change towards ICTs. A change in attitude especially from men as the dominant group will be very welcome, but in the meantime, policy makers and practitioners will need to work, at least to a degree, with the existing social norms. If men and women have profoundly different styles of learning ICT skills, due to the way they have been socialised, then it may be that both men and women would benefit if they were taught in gender-specific groups. Men might perform better in an all-male group with a male instructor who they feel they can ask questions, while women may feel less under the oversight of men in a women-only group with a female instructor. Further research in this direction should also consider age as a variable, as older participants may find it easier to relate to an older person, or may find it stimulating to be taught by a younger instructor.

Thirdly and lastly, ever so often in the literature on telecentres the question arises about the long term financial sustainability of such centres. This is an important debate, but as this chapter has shown, telecentres can become important offline social spaces as well as access points to the Internet. In this case, the *Infocentro* was particularly important as an intellectually stimulating and empowering place for women, that is citizens who had often not been given the same access to formal education. In the cost-benefit analysis preceding decisions over whether funding for such telecentres should be continued, this aspect is worth taking into account.

ACKNOWLEDGMENT

I would like to thank the people who contributed their time to this research, particularly my interview partners. Thanks also to Alexandra Norrish, Diane Perrons, Robin Mansell, Jacques Steyn, Jean-Paul Van Belle and Eduardo Villanueva Mansilla for their comments on this chapter and earlier versions. The Instituto de Informática Educativa, Universidad de La Frontera in Chile extended a warm welcome during the fieldwork. The research was made possible with a grant from the Dr. Heinz Dürr Stiftung (Studienstiftung).

REFERENCES

Baxter, J., & Eyles, J. (1997). Evaluating qualitative research in social geography: Establishing 'rigour' in interview analysis. *Transactions of the Institute of British Geographers*, *22*, 505–552. doi:10.1111/j.0020-2754.1997.00505.x

Cademártori, J. (2001). *Chile - El Modelo Neoliberal*. Santiago: Ediciones ChileAmérica CESOC.

Cairncross, F. (1997). *The Death of Distance. How the Communications Revolution will Change our Lives*. London: Orion Publishing.

CASEN. (2000). Encuesta de Caracterización Socioeconómica Nacional. Retrieved August 26, 2006, from http://www.mideplan.cl/casen/modulo_demografia.html.

CENSO. (2002). *Instituto National de Estadísticas. Censo 2002*. Retrieved May 5, 2006, from http://alerce.ine.cl/ine/canales/chile_estadistico/demografia_y_vitales/indicecenso02.php.

Denzin, N. K. (1989). *The Research Act*. Englewood Cliffs, NJ: Prentice Hall.

Díaz, À., & Rivas, G. (2005). Innovación tecnológica y desarrollo digital: el aporte de los gobiernos de la Concertación. In Meller, P. (Ed.), *La Paradoja Aparente - Equidad y Eficiencia: Resolviendo el Dilema* (pp. 473–528). Santiago: Aguilar Chilena de Ediciones.

Flick, U. (2006). *An Introduction to Qualitative Research*. London: Sage.

Geertz, C. (1973). *Description of Cultures*. New York: Springer.

Gerster, R., & Zimmermann, S. (2003). *Information and communication technologies (ICTs) for poverty reduction?* Bern: Swiss Agency for Development Cooperation.

Grupo de Accíon Digital. (2004). *Agenda Digital - Chile 2004-2006. Te Acerca el Futuro*. Santiago: Report by the Grupo de Acción Digital.

Harvey, D. (2005). *A Brief History of Neoliberalism*. Oxford: Oxford University Press.

Jaramillo, O., & Castellon, L. (2002). *Telecentros, Usuarios y Apropriación de las TICs*. Santiago: Universidad Diego Portales.

Kane, T., Holmes, K. R., & O'Grady, M. A. (2007). *2007 Index of Economic Freedom*. Washington, D.C.: The Heritage Foundation.

Kleine, D. (2007). *Empowerment and the Limits of Choice: Microentrepreneurs, Information and Communication Technologies and State Policies in Chile*. Unpublished PhD thesis, Department of Geography and Environment. London: London School of Economics and Political Science.

Lincoln, Y. S., & Guba, E. (1985). *Naturalistic Enquiry*. London: Sage.

Molyneux, M. (1985). Mobilisation without emancipation? Women's interests, states and revolution in Nicaragua. *Feminist Studies*, *11*(2), 227–254. doi:10.2307/3177922

Municipio (2005). *Informe de Patentes Industriales, Patentes Comerciales, Patentes Profesionales, Patentes Alcohólicas*, Municipio de [Algun].

Pollack, M. (2003). Más y mejor capacitación para una economía competitiva. In Gomá, O. M. (Ed.), *Hacia un Chile Competitivo: Instituciones y Políticas* (pp. 193–238). Santiago: Editorial Universitaria.

Schmitz, H., & Musyck, B. (1993). Industrial districts in Europe: policy lessons for developing countries. *Institute of Development Studies, Discussion Paper No. 324*. Brighton: University of Sussex.

Stockholm Challenge. (2006). Biblioredes: Nosotros en Internet (us on the Internet), a window to local culture. Retrieved October 3, 2006, from http://www.stockholmchallenge.se/ projectdata.asp?id=1&projectid=1134.

Strauss, A. L., & Corbin, J. (1990). *Basics of Qualitative Research: Grounded Theory Procedures and Techniques*. London: Sage.

Talyarkhan, S., Grimshaw, D. J., & Lowe, L. (2005). *Connecting the First Mile. Investigating Best Practice for ICTs and Information Sharing for Development*. Rugby: ITDG.

Wajcman, J. (2004). *Technofeminism*. Oxford: Polity Press.

Woolcock, M., & Narayan, D. (2000). Social capital: implications for development theory, research and policy. *The World Bank Research Observer*, *15*(2), 225–249.

ENDNOTE

[1]   Windows XP Starter Edition; Intel Celeron de 2.0 MHz processor; 40Gb hard drive; 128Mb memory; 15 inch monitor; CD reader; Software: Encarta Standard 2005, Works 8.0, Picture It 1.0; includes keyboard, mouse and speakers.

Section 3
Mixed Media and Localization

Chapter 10

Reducing Digital Divide:
The Case of the 'People First Network' (PFNet) in the Solomon Islands

Anand Chand
University of the South Pacific, Fiji

ABSTRACT

This chapter examines the role of People First Network (PFnet) services in enhancing information and communication and contributing to sustainable rural development and poverty reduction in Solomon Islands. More specifically, it examines two main issues. First, it examines the uptake and appropriation of PFnet services by rural Solomon Islanders. Second, it examines the impact of PFnet services on sustainable rural development and poverty reduction in Solomon Islands. This chapter is based on a empirical research conducted in Solomon Islands between January-May 2004. The chapter is organised as follows: Section one provides an overview of PFnet Project. Section two states the main aims of the study. Section three outlines the methodology used for the research. The Section four reports the main research findings. Section five discusses some problems and finally section six provides the conclusion.

INTRODUCTION

In the South Pacific Region, deployment of ICT and it's usage is still in an infant stage. Only Fiji and Solomon Islands has attempted to use ICT and these initiatives have come about as a result of encouragement and funding from overseas countries. In Fiji the ICT programme started in 1995 and is funded by Republic of China and Japanese International Cooperation Agency (JICA). In Solo-

mon Islands the ICT programme (PFnet) started in 2001. This chapter examines the role of PFnet services play in reducing digital divide between urban and rural people in Solomon Islands. More specifically, it examines two main issues. First, it reviews and examines the usage of PFnet services by rural Solomon Islanders. Second, it examines the benefits of PFnet services for rural people. The chapter is organised as follows: Section one provides an overview of PFnet Project. Section two states the main aims of the study. Section three outlines the methodology used for the research.

DOI: 10.4018/978-1-61520-997-2.ch010

Section four reports and analyses the main research findings. Section five discusses some problems and finally section six provides the conclusion.

BACKGROUND INFORMATION ON PFNET

The PFnet ICT System

The PFnet is basically an example of ICT 'email system'. It was established as a joint venture between an NGO called the 'Rural Development Volunteer Association' (RDVA) and the Ministry for Rural Development in Solomon Islands. It has a Headquarters in Honiara (capital of Solomon Islands) and is connected to eleven sub-email centres in small remote islands. Each email centre was setup by officials of RDVA. Each sub-email centre is housed in a small room, usually in a provincial health clinic, community school, or some other publically accessible building. Out of the eleven email centres, six are 'commercially oriented' email centres because they were set up for commercial purposes, mainly fishing businesses. The remaining five are 'community-based' email centres to provide communication channel for people in remote islands.

Origin and Funding

The PFnet project was established in 2001 as part of a UNDP-UNOPS project. Between 2001 and 2005, major funding came from Japan, NZODA, Britain, the Republic of China, AusAID and the EU. Since 2006, the PFnet project has been self-sufficient and only the salary of the Manager is paid by the RDVA.

System Configuration / Type of Technology Used

In each rural email centre, there are four technical equipments: a computer laptop; a High Frequency (HF) short-wave radio operating in 3-22 MHz range; a modem which connects the laptop to radio; a solar power panel on the roof of a building which provides power to laptop. At the PFnet Headquarters in Honiara, there is a large radio receiver and computers as part of internet café.

In each email centre, the laptop computer is linked via a modem to a High Frequency (HF) short-wave radio which transmits the email message to the main radio receiver in Honiara where operators receive and forward the emails to the relevant addresses. The main radio system receives, stores and forwards emails several times daily between each of the thirteen emails and PFnet Headquarters in Honiara.

The Operation of the PFnet System

Sasamunga is a small village in the island of Choiseul with around hundred people and is approximately 1,000 miles away from Honiara. The village does not have electricity nor is it connected via telephone line. Prior to PFnet, the only two means of communication from Sasamunga village to Honiara and overseas was through letters or by short wave radio. But since 2001, villages in Sasamunga have been able to communicate to their family members, friends, schools and government departments in Honiara via email. How this is possible without electricity and telephone connection? The PFnet email centre addresses this question.

The way an email message is sent and received at each email centre operates as follows:

- A villager brings in a handwritten note on a piece of paper (usually in *Pidgin* language) or verbally dictates the message to the centre operator;
- The centre operator types the message and then sends it to the main radio receiver at the Headquarters in Honiara. Since the operators perform the functions on behalf of the customers, literacy in English does

not impact on the usage of PFnet services. Only a few customers who are literate in English and can afford a private email account are allowed to send and receive their own emails.

Cost of Setting Up of PFnet System

The total initial cost of setting up the PFnet project was around USD20,000 and initially partly funded by the UNDP under the UNDP-UNOPS project and some funds came from the Solomon island government. The USD20,000 amount was used for buying the technical equipment and laptops.

Project Scope-Types of Services Provided by PFnet

Primarily, the PFnet project provides email, news, typing and printing services. With the exception of the internet café at PFnet Headquarters in capital city Honiara, the eleven email centres in the remote islands do not provide live Web access due to lack of sophisticated technology.

Basically, PFnet provides the following services:

- Sending and receiving emails;
- Receiving local and overseas news from Headquarters and the operator informs the people in the villages
- Sending local news to officials at PFnet Headquarters in Honiara who then distributes it to local newspapers and national radio,
- Typing services. For example, operators at the centres type letters for people and test papers for school teachers.
- Printing services.
- Browse the Internet. This service is only available in the Headquarters in Honiara.

PFnet's service of sending and receiving emails is reliable, but it takes around one hour to send and receive messages. The reason why it takes one hour to send and an hour to receive emails is because of the indirect method of transmitting messages via radio frequency and in the delay in the process downloading and uploading by the operators in Honiara. Despite this delay, rural people in remote islands regard this to be a quick method of communicating.

Cost of Using PFnet Services

The cost of using PFnet services is as follows:

- Sending an email message – SBD2.00 (USD 0.26 cents)
- Receiving an email message – Free. In most centres, receiving email messages is free because PFnet Management wants to encourage people use emails. However, some centres (especially the well established ones) charge USD 0.7 cents for the printing cost of email messages.
- Sending news items via email – SBD3.00 (USD 0.39)
- Typing service (per page) – SBD5.00 (USD 0.65)
- Printing cost per page – SBD0.50 (USD 0.07)

Main Reason for Establishment of PFnet

The PFnet project was set up to improve communication and information flows for rural remote and largely subsistence communities throughout the Solomon Islands archipelago, which spreads over more than one million square kilometres in the South Pacific, with a population of less than half a million. The project was designed, with the limitations of resources, infrastructure, technology appropriateness and sustainability in mind. PFnet was set up on a trial basis so that, if successful, it could be replicated in other Pacific Island countries.

Structure of PFnet

The organisational structure of PFnet consists of three partners:

- The PFnet Management (based in PFnet Headquarters in Honiara),
- PFnet committees (based in each email centre in rural areas).
- Operators at each centre.

Ownership

PFnet is a community-owned project operated by the Rural Development Volunteer Association (RDVA). A model of community ownership, leadership and operation was formulated and piloted to ensure grassroots ownership, community empowerment, and the security of facilities and equipment. The location of the email centres was decided on in consultation with community and PFnet Management working with each email centre committee.

The model is founded on community ownership, management and participation and operates as follows:

- A three-way agreement is signed between the committee, operators and PFnet, defining the roles of each party (including technical support, maintenance, security, and ownership), as well as the sharing of revenue.
- The Committee chooses the location where the email centre will be housed, hire the centre operators and are responsible for the effective operation of the PFnet centres.
- Awareness of an email centre project is raised among the community and a village management Committee is established.
- Local experts such as village chiefs, graduates and semi-professionals are identified among potential users with email awareness and needs, and are expected to initiate

other members of the community into the use of email services, and provide locally available technical support. Their support is rewarded with a free email account.

EMPIRICAL RESEARCH ON PFNET MODEL

This chapter is based on an empirical research conducted in Solomon Islands between May 2004 and June 2009. Research was conducted to critically evaluate the success or failure of PFnet model. This research was funded by Japanese International Cooperation Agency (JICA) through the University of the South Pacific in Fiji.

Aims of Research

There were two main aims of the research. The first main aim was to find out the extent of access and utilization of PFnet services in Solomon Islands. Within this broad aim the following research questions were asked:

The first broad aim was to find out what are the main issues affecting community uptake of PFnet services? Within this broad aim the following research questions were asked:

1. What are the principal factors underlying differences in utilization amongst the email centres?
2. Why are approximately only 20-25% of the users of the email centres women? What can be made to increase women's participation?
3. What are the information needs of differing groups (women, the elderly, farmers, students, entrepreneurs and business people, etc.) using the email centres?
4. Why do certain email centres generate more revenue than others?
5. What are the significant descriptors (and primary interactions) of an email centre and a user community?

6. What is the optimum spread of the network and where can additional sites be located to best effect?

7. The second broad aim was to find out the impact of PFnet services on the lives of the grass-roots people. Within this broad aim the following research questions were asked:

8. Has the PFnet project improved the livelihoods of people in PFnet project communities? If so how?

9. Which groups in these communities have benefited most? Which groups have benefited the least?

10. Has the PFnet project in PFnet project communities contributed to:

11. environmental awareness and sustainable resource management;

12. improved gender equality in PFnet project communities;

13. improved well-being (including health and security) for people in PFnet project communities; and

14. peace-building and reconciliation.

15. In what ways have any improvements to livelihoods, environmental awareness, gender equality and well-being been sustained?

16. Has the PFnet project been able to increase awareness of the use of ICT as enablers for development at policy- and decision-making levels in Solomon Islands? If so how? Has the PFnet project stimulated activity at the policy level in Solomon Islands?

RESEARCH METHODS

Three research methods were used to conduct this study: survey interviews, focus group interviews and an analysis of existing PFnet data. Details are given below.

Survey Interviews

Questionnaires were designed and face-to-face interviews with different sets of stakeholders were conducted. The main reason for selecting the interview method was to gather in-depth data from the various stakeholders. In addition to the villages at the email centres, interviews with key informants were also conducted. The key informants included: staff of PFnet, national and provincial government officials, rural development officers, policy-makers, and village leaders.

Focus Group Interviews

A total of twenty focus group interviews were conducted in the five PFnet centres (four in each centre). The reason for selecting focus group interviews was to get a comprehensive understanding of the complex issues that are operating in a village. More focus group meeting were conducted in between January and July 2009 with the USP students using PFnet services.

Use of Existing PFnet Quantitative Data

User-Log Data
Data was gathered on 'users' of PFnet services in each of the five centres. The operators of each centre maintain a user log book with details of each 'emails users'.

User-Log Data from PFnet Monitoring System
PFnet's existing Monitoring System Data kept at each centre were used. The monitoring data were taken from the reports from the five centres studied.

Data from Socio-Economic Profile of each Centre
A socio-economic profile of each centre was compiled during the research and this information in conjunction with survey data to compare and contrast email usage.

Sample

Sample of PFnet Centres Researched
Five PFnet centres out of a total of eleven were selected for this study. The five PFnet centres

that were chosen were: Hutuna centre, Pirupiru centre, Sasamungga centre, Sigana centre, and Silolo centre.

Sample Size

A sample of 538 respondents was interviewed from the five email centres. The sample involved members from all relevant groups in the community: women, young people, and the elderly and key respondents such as community leaders.

RESEARCH FINDINGS

Utilisation of PFnet Services

Table 2 shows the data on 'email traffic' from the five email centres.

Table 2 reveals that, relative to their population size, four centres (Hutuna, Sasamungga, Pirupiru and Sigana) are high performers while Silolo email centre is relatively lower in performance. It is noteworthy, that Silolo centre is situated in

the most densely populated area (by far) and one would have expected correspondingly higher usage, but this is not the case. There are a few explanations for this. Firstly, Silolo Centre was established as a partnership between CPRF and the *Kastom Gaden Association* (an NGO) and hence a factor contributing to the low usage is that people see it as a private organisation and not for public use. Such a perception has an impact on usage. Secondly, KGA and CPRF have their own private accounts and this is not included in the daily reports and hence there is under-reporting. Thirdly, Silolo has a stronger link to Honiara and Auki townships through regular shipping and road transportation and this may undercut communication needs.

More specifically, Sasamungga has the highest number of users, monthly email traffic and revenue. Pirupiru has the second highest number of users and monthly revenue, but the third highest monthly email traffic (explained by more use of other services such as secretarial and printing services and this is probably due to the presence of a large secondary school). Hutuna has the third highest number of users and the second highest average monthly email traffic, but less revenue than Pirupiru. Sigana has the lowest number of users and female utilization, monthly email traffic and revenue. The email traffic is between 4 and 8 times less than the three best-performing centres. Silolo has good revenue but the fourth-least utilization in email traffic.

Table 1. Sample size for survey

Types of respondents	Number
People who currently use or ever used PFnet services	251
People who never used PFnet services	261
Committee members of PFnet centres	21
Operators at PFnet centres	5
Total	**538**

Table 2. Summary of the utilization by each email centre

	Number of logged users	Total Population (including infants)	Users as % of Total Population	% Female users	Average email traffic per month
Sasamungga	121	2,824	4.3%	31%	397
Hutuna	89	3,124	2.9%	42%	271
Pirupiru	107	2,788	3.9%	35%	228
Sigana	43	1,767	2.5%	16%	50
Silolo	79	12,638	0.006%	19%	161

The study examined a number of factors affecting utilization of PFnet services. The discussion below examines each factor and the evidence for any linkage to utilization and appropriation.

Environment Factors
Affecting Utilization

Population density, population distribution and centre accessibility have an effect on the utilization of PFnet services. In order to understand the relative utilization, an examination of both the population distribution and access to the centres is important. Sasamungga email centre is situated on Choiseul Island in the centre of a large cluster of conterminous villages along the coast, with a gravel road providing easy access on foot, and there is also easy access from nearly all the villages by canoe. Choiseul is one of the largest islands, and is very mountainous with nearly all the population on the coast. The Sasamungga population cluster is isolated from the rest of Choiseul, with access only by expensive motor-driven canoes.

Hutuna is situated by Lake Tenggano on Rennell Island, a raised atoll with all of its population inland. A long coral road connects west and central Rennell to the lake. There are four main villages along the lakeside, joined together and connected to the road by a 15km bush trail. This is fairly flat and easy to follow, although time-consuming. The lake villages can also be accessed easily by canoe, although the cost of petrol is a major hindrance. Hutuna is the furthest village and thus the remotest of villages on Rennell. The village next to Hutuna is Tenggano, which is about 6km or 45 minutes walk along the bush trail. The distance between Hutuna and the other villages is the major inconvenience, and the cost of canoe transport. Villagers from the west of the island have to travel by infrequent truck traffic to the lake (a two-hour journey) and then take a canoe to Hutuna.

Pirupiru is situated on Ulawa Island, which is about 30km long with a circular coral road connecting all the villages. Canoes are not generally used. Access on foot is possible from the entire island, even though it is a full day's journey from the furthest villages. In addition, truck transport provides affordable, if irregular, access.

Sigana is situated in a bay on mountainous Isabel Island, which has no connecting roads and only some very rough bush trails. The main means of access from surrounding villages is by motor canoe. The canoe traffic between villages is quite heavy, but the price of petrol is a real problem for people. Thus, the people living beyond a few kilometers from the centre have quite a difficult and expensive journey to access the centre.

Silolo is situated in North Malaita (constituency), the most densely populated of the country's main islands. There is a good road network joining the villages along the coast, some inland areas and adjacent constituencies. Villages across the bay from Silolo have easy access by canoe. Access is good for a large area of northern Malaita.

In summary, the user log data show that most of the users live within a few kilometers of the email centres. The distribution of (a) the logged users, (b) the population, and (c) the percentage of the population using the email centre is shown in the three tables below.

The data in the tables show that the community living near the centre gets most benefit. In the three locations where the email centre is situated inside a village, about two thirds of the logged users live within 2km of the email centre. All centres, however, recorded a significant number of users from well beyond the local village community. In fact, in the case of Pirupiru (Ulawa Island), Sigana (Isabel Island) and Hutuna (Rennell Island) there is significant usage from villages over the entire island. For example, in Ulawa, as many as 30% of users live more than 10km away from the email centre. On Isabel Island, 21% users live more than 10km away by road. On Rennell, 12% of users came from over 12km away and as far away as the provincial centre Tingoa (40km). In these communities, the entire

Table 3. Distance and utilization of services

Percentage of users living at different distances from email centre (from user log)			
	<=2km	2-10km	>=10km
Sasamungga	67%	31%	2%
Hutuna	63%	25%	12%
Pirupiru	33%	39%	30%
Sigana	65%	14%	21%
Silolo	17%	76%	6%

Note: "Distance from email centre" is measured along the most convenient route.

Table 4. Estimated population within zones

Estimated population within zones centered on the email centre (from Census data)			
	<=2km	2-10km	>=10km
Sasamungga	731	831	1262
Hutuna	210	609	2305
Pirupiru	306	1020	1462
Sigana	490	1009	> 268
Silolo	380	7340	> 4918

island would appear to benefit from the PFnet facilities.

More specifically, within the 2km zone, the population has good access to the facility in all the five locations. Sasamungga has, significantly, the highest total population within this zone (731 people- see Table 4), and has the second highest (11%) number of users per resident (see Table 5). Hutuna, with only one third (210 people — see Table 4) of the population of Sasamungga (within 2km), has more than twice the utilization per resident (26% compared to 11%). On the other hand, Sigana, which has more than twice the resident population of Hutuna, has the lowest utilization with only 6% of residents logged as users. Silolo recorded only 4% of these people as users. Silolo is not situated within a large village, although the general density of population in North Malaita is by far the highest of the five areas, resulting in a higher than average total population in the 2km zone.

In the 2-10km zone, the effect of access problems was expected to become apparent. The results show that Sasamungga and Pirupiru, both with good utilization figures and easy road access, show only a small drop in the percentage of the population using the email centre in this zone compared to the 2km zone (both showing 9% of users compared to 11% – see Table 5). But Hutuna, which is isolated from the next village by a 6km bush trail, shows a more significant drop from 26% down to 4%. However, the other two centres (Sigana and Silolo) seem to counter the trend found in Hutuna. Sigana has difficult access for people in the 2-10km zone but shows a relatively small drop in usage (from 6% to 5% of the population in the two zones), whereas Silolo with its large population with easy road access, shows very poor usage in the 2-10km zone (2.4%). If Silolo experienced the same level of utilization as Sasamungga, one would see almost 400 users (compared to the 79 recorded).

Table 5. Percent of utilization per resident

Percentage of estimated population within each zone logged as email centre users			
	<=2km	2-10km	>=10km
Sasamungga	11%	9%	0.2%
Hutuna	26%	4%	0.5%
Pirupiru	11%	9%	2%
Sigana	6%	5%	0%
Silolo	4%	2.4%	< 0.1%

Similarly, the survey results also show that distance was a factor when using PFnet services. Table 6 shows that around 32% of the user's live less than one kilometer from their respective PFnet centres.

Location and Sense of Ownership of EMail Centres Affecting Utilization

The location of the email centre and sense of ownership (whether it is privately or community-owned) has an effect on the utilization of the PFnet facilities.

The locations of the five centres are as follows: Sasamungga centre is located in a clinic of a major rural hospital. The hospital board donated the use of a room that opens onto the main road through the village, and it is also centrally located. Hutuna centre is located in a room in a community hall financed by AusAID (CPRF), and shared by a kindergarten. It is centrally located in the village.

Pirupiru centre is sited in a special building on the campus of a large secondary school. The building has three rooms, and a large sign: Pirupiru Email Centre. The centre is not located in a village, although there are villages close by and the school community is large in its own right. Sigana centre is in a specially constructed building provided by the village community, situated in the middle of the village. Silolo centre is situated not in a village but in the offices of the *Kastom Gaden Association*, a rural farmers' advice centre. The centre was established in partnership with this NGO, financed by AusAID (CPRF). The email centre is next to a private house.

The results show that the utilization of Silolo centre (relative to the population with access) is less than one fifth of that in the other centres. The setting of the centre away from a population centre may be one reason for this. Furthermore, the lack of a sense of community ownership of the facility at Silolo was mentioned by the operator.

Table 6. Users vs. distance to each PFnet centre

Distance from centre	Sigana	Sasamungga	Hutuna	Pirupiru	Silolo	Total	%
less than 1 km	17	16	27	19	1	80	31.9
1 km	6	20	2	5	2	35	13.9
2 km	2	4	1	6	2	15	6.0
3 km	1	8	1	7	5	22	8.8
more than 3 km	13	2	18	12	8	53	21.1
not sure	14	2	2	1	27	46	18.3
Total	53	52	51	50	45	251	100.0

In the case of Silolo centre, the lack of a sense of community ownership caused by the setting of the email centre away from a village seems to be connected with poor awareness of the email centre and what it can offer.

The other four centres are all situated in the centre of villages (or, in the case of Pirupiru, a large school community with conterminous villages nearby). Sasamungga and Pirupiru are situated in a clinic and a community school, respectively, but in this case these institutions are neutral and have no negative associations for the general community. No unfavorable comments were recorded about their locations during the fieldwork.

It is concluded that the location of an email centre is quite critical to its appropriation and utilization by the targeted communities. The centres will be most utilized if they are located in the centre of villages and in buildings that are regarded as being owned by the community. No matter how much awareness-raising is conducted, if an email centre is housed within private premises people will not regard it as available for public utilization.

Isolation, Ease of Transport and Alternative Communications Affecting Utilization

There is an apparent correlation between the degree of isolation and the utilization of the facilities. The survey results show that 44% of the 'never used' group indicated that the PFnet centres were too far from their village. In particular, the very-well utilized centre of Hutuna is very isolated. Rennell and Bellona province has no regular shipping. Typically several months pass before a chartered vessel calls at the nearest 'port', Lavanagu Bay, where all cargo has to be ferried ashore by canoe. The provincial capital Tingoa is 50km by canoe and road from Hutuna, and this is not an easy or affordable journey to make. Alternative communications between Hutuna and Honiara consist of hand-delivered letters couriered by air passengers, and short-wave radio calls. Due to the distance of

Hutuna from Tingoa airstrip, hand-delivered letters are not easy to arrange, nor are they reliable. Radio owners in Hutuna charge SBD5 – SBD10 for voice calls to Honiara. As few Rennellese in Honiara have access to a short-wave radio, people have to rely on such messages being passed to the intended recipient - not a very reliable or confidential system.

In this case, it is obvious how convenient email will appear to Hutuna residents, and to their Honiara-based relatives and contacts. The survey data and the user data show that basic communications are the main service used by Hutuna people.

Sasamungga and Pirupiru are also remote and isolated, although they have slightly better transport options. In the case of Pirupiru, which is situated in a large school, teachers have a need to communicate with their provincial headquarters and with the nearest bank in the provincial centre Kirakira, which means an expensive and dangerous open-sea canoe crossing. This isolation and resulting need is obviously a factor driving up utilization.

The two least-used centres, Silolo and Sigana, are the best connected with Honiara. Sigana is only a six-hour sea crossing from Honiara, with often more than one ship calling each week. This constitutes an excellent transport service in Solomon Islands. Silolo is also quite near Honiara and has weekly shipping. It also has a road connection with the provincial capital Auki, and the large population makes transport quite easy. Villagers catch a ride with their relatives, or pay a small fee to ride on the back of a public truck. One of the reasons quoted by Silolo people about why some did not use the services was that there were short-wave radios available for voice calls.

It can be concluded that isolation and lack of alternative means of communication drive up utilization. However, the benefits of Internet-based communications are perhaps not being made clear enough to the potential users. More training and demonstration of information access should be planned by PFnet to address this, especially for special interest groups and in the less isolated centres.

Migrants Affecting Utilization

There is an apparent correlation between the degree of dispersion of people within and outside Solomon Islands and the utilization of the facilities. Although in most rural parts of Solomon Islands the communities are very ethnically homogenous, most ethnic groups have relatives living away from their home islands in Honiara and other urban centers and close to sources of employment such as plantations. They also have students attending university overseas and secondary students pursuing their education in schools away from their home islands. There are Solomon Islanders married to foreigners and professionals residing overseas.

The proportion of emails sent from each centre is broken down into domestic and international in Table 7. This data is taken from the daily reports of user data collected over 15 months.

This data shows that the populations of all communities have a need to communicate with their overseas contacts. In particular, Silolo and Hutuna email centres have a high proportion of overseas communication, 44% and 42% respectively. People from the village told the researcher that many families in that community have family members who are studying or resident overseas such as New Zealand and Australia. In summary the results show that communication between the remote communities and their dispersed populations, in particular those based in Honiara, is obviously a prime mover for utiliza-

tion. PFnet should encourage such communications traffic through open days, training and by any other means. This can then be expected to stimulate increased utilization.

Personal Income Affecting Utilization

In order to find out if there was an apparent correlation between the village economy and the utilization of the facilities; data was collected on the average incomes of PFnet users in each community. This is summarized in Table 8.

Table 8 shows that the average income of a PFnet user in these five communities is SBD187 (about USD25 per month or less than USD1 per day). It varies quite significantly, with Sasamungga users income averaging SBD297 a month and Hutuna users income averaging SBD107 a month.

This is interesting because income does not correlate with utilization. Although Sasamungga is the most utilized of the five centres, in fact Hutuna is consistently the second-most utilized, and in Silo, where the number of users is lowest compared with the total population, the users reported the second highest monthly incomes.

Awareness of the Existence of the PFnet Centre and its Services

Awareness of the PFnet services has an impact on utilization. Most people are aware of the existence of a PFnet centre in their area. Rather than asking this obvious question, the researchers wanted to find out if the people (both users and 'never used' knew how the email centres worked and if they

Table 7. Percentage of emails sent by each centre by destination

	Sasamungga	Hutuna	Pirupiru	Sigana	Silolo
Domestic	88%	58%	87%	84%	54%
International	12%	42%	13%	15%	44%
Unknown	0%	0%	0%	1%	2%

Table 8. Average monthly incomes of PFnet users by centre

Monthly income	Users of PFnet						
	Sigana	Sasamungga	Hutuna	Pirupiru	Silolo	Total	%
$5- $50	22	13	34	25	14	108	43.0
$51- $100	7	10	3	5	7	32	12.7
$101- $200	13	6	4	2	10	35	13.9
$201- $300	1	5	0	6	9	21	8.4
$301- $500	4	4	4	3	4	19	7.6
$501- $1000	1	7	0	2	1	11	4.4
$2,500	1	0	0	0	0	1	0.4
NR	4	7	6	7		24	9.6
Total	**53**	**52**	**51**	**50**	**45**	**251**	**100.0**
Average max income	**$157**	**$297**	**$107**	**$173**	**$258**	**$187**	

were aware of all the types of services provided. Hence, in the survey, the first set of questions asked whether they knew about the types of services provided by the PFnet centres. Amongst the 'users' a high proportion (94%) indicated email, typing, and printing services (see Table 9). These are the core services provided by PFnet centres. In contrast, amongst the 'never used' only 18% indicated that they knew that the PFnet centre provided email, typing, and printing services.

A further question was asked on how users knew about PFnet services. The results are shown in Figure 1.

The results varied with around one third (32%) indicating that they knew via friends, close to one third (31%) knew it through family and kinship, a quarter (24%) though PFnet committee members, 21% through village meetings, 10% via radio, and 5% through newspaper. In other words, 63% of all the respondents knew of the PFnet centres through friends, family and wider kinship. This finding is similar to the 'non-user' group in which 72% indicated they knew of the PFnet centres through friends, family and wider kinship. This trend is understandable because in Solomon Islands communities are close-knit and information is usually exchanged during informal gatherings. This information is very useful for the centre committee for their awareness promotion programmes.

Table 9. Services known to respondents by centre amongst the 'user' group

Specify known services	Sigana	Sasamungga	Hutuna	Pirupiru	Silolo	Total	%
Email, typing, printing	44	52	46	50	45	237	94.4
News	3	0	0	0	0	3	1.2
Email only	0	0	3	0	0	3	1.2
Typing	2	0	0	0	0	2	0.8
Radio	0	0	1	0	0	1	0.4
No response	4	0	1	0	0	5	2.0
Total	**53**	**52**	**51**	**50**	**45**	**251**	**100**

Figure 1. Source of knowledge about PFnet (user group)

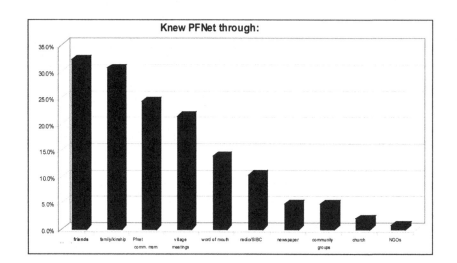

Reasons for Use and Non-Use of PFnet Services

The 'user group' respondents were asked the main reasons why they use PFnet services (Table 10). The results show that for a high proportion (88%) their first ranked reason was to communicate with family and friends; next came educational purposes (36%); and then business purposes (around 22%).

For their second ranked reason, around 40% indicated education purposes, 25% indicated communication with family and friends, and 24% indicated business purposes. For their third

Table 10. Main purpose of using PFnet services (user group)

Main purpose of using PFnet	Sigana	Sasamungga	Hutuna	Pirupiru	Silolo	Total	%
Communication with family and friends	43	44	49	46	37	219	87.3
Education	16	30	16	16	13	91	36.3
Business purposes	13	14	8	8	13	30	22.4
Church	8	1	7	5	3	24	9.6
Remittance of money		14	1		4	19	7.6
Project/NGO	2	3	5	1	4	15	6.0
Health/medical	1	11			2	14	5.6
Government administration	1	2	3		3	9	3.6
Travel	4	1	1			6	2.4
Women's issues		3		1		4	1.6
Sports		3			1	4	1.6
Police/law and order					3	3	1.2%
Agriculture		2				2	0.8%
Other	1		1		1	3	1.2%

ranked reason, around 27% indicated education purposes, 19% indicated business purposes and 11% remittance of money.

The 'user group' was then asked how many of them were not currently using the PFnet services and the reasons for it (Table 11). The results show that 11% of them were not currently using PFnet services. Of these, 41% said they had no urgent need to use emails; 26% said they had no message to send; 19% said they had no money and 8% used other means of communication. The 'other means of communication' are traditional *wantok* courier service (by word of mouth or hand written notes), messages read on Solomon Islands Broadcasting Corporation radio centre and short-wave telephone (where available).

Amongst those that are currently using PFnet services, we further asked about their frequency of use of PFnet services (Table 12). The results show that 3% use the services every day, 15% use it 2 or 3 times a week, 21% use it once a week, 13% use it once fortnightly, 20% use it once a month, and 28% use it rarely.

The 'user group' was also asked to indicate the types of services that they use and the results are shown in Table 13. A very high proportion of the respondents (99%) indicated that they use email services, 29% use it for news and 27% use it for typing services. As the results show that the majority of the respondents use the centres to send and receive emails, we can conclude that PFnet centres are fulfilling their objective in providing the villagers with contact with the outside world via email. This is important because in the absence of other forms of communications, the PFnet email centres are the only link with the outside world,

Table 11. Reasons for 'user group' for not currently using PFnet services by centre

Why are you not using now?	Sigana	Hutuna	Silolo	Total	%
No urgent need	2	7	2	11	40.7
No message to send	6	1	0	7	25.9
No money	2	2	1	5	18.5
Have other means of communication	1	0	0	1	3.7%
The person to contact has no email	1	0	0	1	3.7
Send messages through SPBEA	1	0	0	1	3.7
No Response	1	0	0	1	3.7
Total	**14**	**10**	**3**	**27**	**100.0**

Table 12. Frequency of PFnet services use by centre

How frequently do you use PFnet?	Sigana	Sasamungga	Hutuna	Pirupiru	Silolo	Total	%
Every day	1	1	4	1	1	8	3.2
2 – 3 times a week	5	13	11	2	6	37	14.7
once a week	8	10	14	6	14	52	20.7
once fortnightly	6	7	5	5	9	32	12.7
once a month	10	16	4	11	9	50	19.9
Rarely	23	5	11	25	6	70	27.9
No response			2			2	0.8
Total	**53**	**52**	**51**	**50**	**45**	**251**	**100.0**

Table 13. Types of services used by centre

What services do you use?	Sigana	Sasamungga	Hutuna	Pirupiru	Silolo	Total	%
Send and receive emails	52	52	51	49	44	248	98.8
Send and receive news reports	9	21	22	5	16	73	29.1
Typing	10	18	11	18	11	68	27.1
Search for information	1	5	5	2	3	16	6.4
Other	1			1	3	5	2.0

either to ensure essential contacts with family, health security, public services, and education.

Around 42% of people use the PFnet services to send and receive news reports and majority of them find the news very useful. Once again these results indicate that to some extent one of the objectives of PFnet — to disseminate news to rural areas — is being met. However, more awareness work needs to be carried out to promote the news service, as 58% of the respondents do not use PFnet for news.

It should be noted that there is no Web Internet facility at the rural email centres. Only the Internet Café in Honiara provides Internet services. Hence in the rural centres customers cannot browse the Internet for local or overseas news. The news service operates three ways. Firstly, village people can pass news of events to other areas by going to the email centre and asking the operator to type the news and send it to the PFnet Headquarters in Honiara for dissemination. The operator in Honiara does the editing and releases the news

to the Solomon Islands Broadcasting Corporation (SIBC) (main radio centre) or Radio New Zealand, or to the local newspaper (the Solomon Star). Secondly, the staff at the PFnet Headquarters compiles national news and sends news (via email) to all centres. In each centre, the operator prints the news on demand and charges them a small fee (SBD1) for the printing cost. This income from news constitutes the centre's income. Thirdly, centre operators can compile their own newsletter and email it to the SIBC, the Solomon Star, or Radio New Zealand.

Interestingly, when questioned on suggestions to improve the news service, almost 29% suggested they want more local news; 23% stated that PFnet should be promoted and 19% stated that more pictures should be added for persons who cannot read (Table 14).

Amongst the 'users' the researchers were interested to find out the main reasons why they were not currently using PFnet services. Table 15 shows the result. Multiple responses were re-

Table 14. Suggestions to improve the news service (by news service users only) by centre

How can the news service be improved?	Sigana	Sasamungga	Hutuna	Pirupiru	Silolo	Total	%
Local news	1	6	13	2	8	30	28.6
Promote PFnet	4	7	3	6	4	24	22.9
Add pictures for those who can't read	5	5	5	1	4	20	19.0
More detailed information	3	5	4	0	5	17	16.2
More computers	2	4	3	1	4	14	13.3
Total	10	14	12	2	13	105	100

corded. Two-thirds (66%) of the respondents indicated that they were not aware of the types of services provided and did not know how to use them, 41% indicated that the centre was too far from the village, and another 40% indicated they had no need to use the services.

Throughout the interviews the point that 'people do not know how it works' came out vividly as one of the most important issues. Many people had heard about the email centre — they even attended the opening of the centre — but still did not fully comprehend the system. One villager near the Silolo centre said: "PFnet is new and many people here are not very confident on how to use it".

In Sigana, knowledge of how to use PFnet is also an issue. In the focus group meetings for women and business people, it was noted that most people are aware of the centre, but do not know how it works. This result indicates that more awareness programmes by various stakeholders are needed for greater utilization of PFnet services by the rural people of Sigana.

On the other hand, there is widespread awareness of the Hutuna PFnet services throughout Rennell. Isolation might be driving up need. Another

factor that might have contributed to this is the practice of holding an open day for Honiara-based members of the community where their email centre is deployed. This has produced good results for Hutuna. Honiara residents have only limited means of communicating quickly with their home village, and were therefore very quick to use the operator-assisted services in the Internet Café, or to open web mail accounts and receive training from the PFnet staff. Traffic generated from these people then drives up the usage in the village until a critical mass is reached.

The researchers asked the 'never used' group whether they were likely to use PFnet services in future and around 86% indicated they were, 8% said they were not and the remaining 7% were not sure. Table 16 shows the results. The researchers also asked the 'user' group to throw some light on why some of their fellow villagers were not using PFnet services. Their perceptions are shown in Table 17.

The results show that that around 28% of users indicated that the main reasons their fellow villages were not using PFnet are that they do not have an urgent need to use it, 19% mentioned lack of confidentiality, and 15% indicated that people

Table 15. Reasons for 'users' not currently using PFnet services by centre (multiple responses)

Reason for not using PFnet now	Sigana	Sasamungga	Hutuna	Pirupiru	Silolo	Total	%
Not aware of the types of services provided and do not know how to use it.	24	42	24	18	63	171	65.5
Too far from village	15	8	29	22	34	108	41.4
Do not have the need to use the services	21	19	28	25	11	104	39.8
Too expensive as have limited income	4	3	4	1	1	13	5.0%
I prefer letter-writing		5	3		2	10	3.8
To old to use it	1	1			1	3	1.1
Because I don't know who to contact, also am illiterate	1		1			2	0.8
My contacts do not have email		1				1	0.4
Total	67	79	90	66	112	414	

Table 16. Likelihood of 'never used' using PFnet in future

Are you likely to use PFnet in future?							
	Sigana	**Sasamungga**	**Hutuna**	**Pirupiru**	**Solo**	**Total**	**%**
Yes	45	40	41	50	48	224	85.8
No	4	8	4	0	4	20	7.7
No response	4	2	5		6	17	6.5
to	**53**	**50**	**50**	**50**	**58**	**261**	**100.0%**

did not know how it works. The fear of personal and confidential matters being revealed by operators is one of the factors affecting the uptake of email services. The issue of confidentiality is worth noting and it is discussed at length later in this chapter.

Cost of Using PFnet Services

The results show that 15% thought the service was 'very cheap', 36% indicated 'cheap' and 45% indicated it was 'reasonable'. In total, a very high proportion (97%) of the users indicated that the cost of sending and receiving emails was either 'reasonable', 'cheap' or 'very cheap'. However, amongst the 'never used' group, 19% indicated that cost was a barrier to their use of PFnet services. Furthermore, some respondents (particularly schoolteachers) in a few focus group meetings at one PFnet centre (Sasamungga) commented that the services of 'typing and printing' were expensive. In Sasamungga the problem arose

not because PFnet charges are high, but because the PFnet operator in that centre was ignorantly overcharging clients because she did not fully understand the instructions given by the PFnet management based in Honiara (see Table 18).

Literacy Level and Use of PFnet Services

It must be noted that the way the PFnet system works, does not require people to be literate in English to be able to use PFnet services. Centre operators play a crucial role as intermediaries for the people of the community. They perform all the functions such as typing out-going email messages, opening and printing in-coming messages, etc. However, the usage data shows that most users (71%) have at least ninth year of formal schooling. In Hutuna and Silolo, users with up to ninth year of education constitute the largest group, 86% for Hutuna and 75% for Silolo, whereas in Sigana users with primary education

Table 17. 'User' group's views on why 'never used' group were not using PFnet services

	Sigana	**Sasamungga**	**Hutuna**	**Pirupiru**	**Silolo**	**Total**	**%**
No urgent need to use it	6	25	20	14	3	68	27.5
Lack of confidentiality	16	6	9	8	9	48	19.4
Do not know how it works	6	5	3	4	19	37	15.0
Not aware of it	7	7	5	11	4	34	13.8
Not educated	8	2	6	6	8	30	12.1
No money	10	7	5	7	1	30	12.1
Total	**53**	**52**	**48**	**50**	**44**	**247**	**100.0**

Table 18. View of PFnet service prices by centre

What do you think of the price of PFnet?	Sigana	Sasamungga	Hutuna	Pirupiru	Silolo	Total	%
Very cheap	9	10	6	8	5	38	15.1
Cheap	9	31	27	15	9	91	36.3
Reasonable	32	10	16	27	28	113	45.0
Expensive	0	0	0	0	3	3	1.2
Very expensive	3	1	0	0	0	4	1.6
No Response	0	0	2	0	0	2	0.8
Total	**53**	**52**	**51**	**50**	**45**	**251**	**100.0**

only constitute the largest group. In Sasamungga and Pirupiru, users with senior secondary education (tenth year or higher) constitute the largest group — 65% and 53% respectively. This may be explained by the proximity of large community schools and other institutions such as a major rural hospital (Sasamungga). However, it still means that between one third and a half of all users in Sasamungga and Pirupiru, have not gone beyond ninth year of education.

Use of PFnet Services by Women

The researches findings from the 'user-log data' (recorded over 8 weeks of research) show that on average 31% of users are women. Hutuna has the high percentage of women users (with 42%), followed by Pirupiru with 35%, Sasamungga with 31%, Silolo (19%) and Sigana (16%).

The research findings from the user-log monitoring data (recorded over 15 months) show-

ing details of the number and percentages of emails sent by women in each of the five centres are shown in two tables below. Women's use of PFnet services varies quite significantly, not only across centres but also with time.

Table 21 shows, in Hutuna, women's usage ranged from 0% to 53% with the average of 27%. The female usage is seen to increase towards the end of the reporting period to coincide with the time the user log was being recorded, with a maximum of 53% in February 2004. In other centres, the data shows women's usage was from 15% (Silolo) to 23% (Sasamungga and Pirupiru). The general observation from this and the user log data is that the three best used centres (Hutuna, Pirupiru and Sasamungga) have much greater women's usage than the two less used centres. The reasons for this include logistical and economic reasons, in addition to the cultural ones. There might also be an effect caused by differences in the effectiveness of PFnet awareness and

Table 19 . Use rate by gender by centre

	Male	Female	Total
Sasamungga	83 (69%)	38 (31%)	121
Hutuna	52 (58%)	37 (42%)	89
Pirupiru	70 (65%)	37 (35%)	107
Silolo	64 (81%)	15 (19%)	79
Sigana	36 (83%)	7 (16%)	43

Source: User-log recorded over 8 weeks of research from January to February 2004.

Table 20 . Number of emails sent by women per month by centre

Month	Jan 03	Feb	Mar	Apr	May	Jun	JuL	Aug	Sep	Oct	Nov	Dec	Jan 04	Feb	Mar
Sasam ungga	38	30	25	31	26	37	37	35	35	39	25	21	49	41	33
Pirupiru	13	36	17	31	29	32	39	45	35	18	20	23	33	33	27
Sigana	6	8	8	7	4	6	5	5	6	5	4	2	3	4	7
Silolo	13	2	7	6	13	3	3	12	9	8	2	2	9	15	14
Hutuna	0	0	2	27	36	36	40	28	32	32	38	10	52	46	42

Source: User-log monitoring data recorded over 15 months

Table 21. Percentage of the total of email sent monthly by women (from daily reports)

Month	Jan 03	Feb	Mar	Apr	May	Jun	Jul	Aug	Sep	Oct	Nov	Dec	Jan 04	Feb	Mar	Apr
Sasam unnga	24	20	16	18	16	26	22	22	20	26	27	29	37	29	19	23
Pirupiru	15	27	14	22	24	33	28	30	25	18	22	20	25	26	21	23
Sigana	19	26	24	28	14	32	17	24	16	25	22	9	9	17	18	20
Silolo	30	2	25	13	26	8	11	15	15	11	4	4	14	33	21	15
Hutuna	0	0	0	23	30	34	24	18	16	29	17	7	48	53	31	27

Source: User-log monitoring data recorded over 15 months

Table 22. Reasons women do not use PFnet services (multiple responses)

Reasons	Total	%
Don't know how PFnet works	62	25
Too far from my village	47	19
Do not have the need to use it	46	19
Using other type of communication	20	8
Not aware of PFnet services	9	4
Too expensive	4	2
Don't like it	2	1
Other reasons	54	22
Total	**244**	**100.0%**

training processes, and other management and ownership factors. Women in the 'never used' group' were asked why they do not use PFnet and the results are shown below.

The results show that 25% of the women indicated that they do not know how PFnet services work, around a fifth reported that the centre was too far from their village and another fifth reported that they do not need to use PFnet services.

The survey results from the 'user-group' reveal that women use PFnet services less than men. Users were asked to indicate whether women in their families used PFnet services. The results show that around 36% of users stated that women in their family use PFnet services.

Users were asked to give reasons why women use PFnet less and the results are shown in Table 24.

Table 24 shows the perceptions of PFnet users in each community of women's utilization. 15% of the respondents reported that the main reason for not using the service was that women were too busy with other chores. 12% disagreed with the premise that women use it less than men. Not surprisingly, most of these respondents were from Hutuna, where the user log shows that women's usage is highest (42%) of the five locations. A further 10% indicated that it was considered a male responsibility/activity. If one assumes that this response indicates a cultural explanation, the

table also shows that the traditional role of women in society is a factor in limiting their utilization. Adding the responses 'thought that only males used it' and 'used males to send messages' as a secondary indicator, a total of 26.9% of the overall responses indicates a cultural factor. In a way, 'too busy with other chores' is also a factor associated with women's role, as women are often occupied with childcare and tending gardens that might be quite a distance from their homes.

In terms of differences between women's utilization in the five communities, the table shows that women's role (apart from the fact of their other chores being time-consuming) is least an

Table 23. Percentage of women using PFnet by centre

Women using PFnet	Sigana	Sasamungga	Hutuna	Pirupiru	Silolo	Total	%
Yes	8 (15%)	17 (33%)	29 (57%)	31 (62%)	5 (11%)	90	35.9
No	2	0	5		10	17	6.8
Not sure	43	35	17	19	30	144	57.4
Total	**53**	**52**	**51**	**50**	**45**	**251**	**100**

Table 24. Reasons women are less frequent users than men

Reasons	Centres						
	Sigana	Sasamungga	Hutuna	Pirupiru	Silolo	Total	%
Distance (access) problems	1	2	2	4	4	13	5.4
Don't know how to use PFnet	4	7	2	1	18	32	13.2
Don't have anyone to contact	7	0	0	6	4	17	7.0
Thought only males & educated use it	8	0	1	11	2	22	9.
Shy/afraid to use PFnet	7	7	3	2	7	26	10.7
Too busy with other chores	2	11	20	4	1	38	15.7
Don't like going to offices	0	0	0	1	0	1	0.4
Use males to send messages for them	3	10	0	4	3	20	8.3
Consider it a male activity/responsibility	2	4	0	16	1	23	9.5
Not interested	1	1	0	0	0	2	0.8
There are equal male/female users	13	0	16	0	0	29	12.0
Other reasons	4	7	3	0	5	19	7.9
Total	**52**	**49**	**47**	**49**	**45**	**242**	**100.0**

issue in Hutuna (only 1 out of 47 respondents thought women's role was an issue), and most in Pirupiru (31 out of 49 responses). This difference prompts us to look at these two communities in more detail.

The women's focus group meeting at Sigana, which has the lowest women's utilization (20% average from the daily reports data and 16% from the user log), also reported that the traditional women's role restricted them from using the facility. One lady from Sigana village commented:

Most activities related to communication out from the village are done by the man. Women's role is very limited to domestic activities such as gardening and other household duties.

The other centre where women's usage is low is Silolo (15% average from the daily reports data and 19% from the user log). Strong cultural influences were cited:

Male dominance is very real and tangible in this area, creating an imbalance in gender development and the approach to other development areas.

The committee members in each centre were asked why women use PFnet Services less than men. The results are consistent with the arguments developed above; they suggest cultural reasons, which differ in the five communities according to the strength of the traditional values prevalent there.

In Hutuna, where the women's role is least restrictive, a committee member suggested that the real reason might be lack of training rather than cultural reasons. In other centres the traditional view of women's roles is more apparent.

Education of women also seems to play a part. Although the usage data from the daily reports show that there are users with all standards of education, including no formal education, the survey result shows proportionally more educated women are using the centre. It is known that women are more likely to have a lower education standard and leave school earlier. Therefore, women may use the centres less because they are generally less educated than men. Table 24 shows that 9.1% of

people thought that women use the facility less than men because they thought only males and educated people use it.

Lack of awareness was cited as a reason why women are not using the Sigana centre much. The women's focus group reported that:

Some women in the focus group never visit the centre, they are only aware that a communication system is in the village. Most women do not know what PFnet is and what it does, apart from being a speedy communication system.

It is interesting to note that when Sigana (PFnet's 4th email centre) was deployed, PFnet did not hold special women's awareness meetings during the establishment of the centre, as is the rule now.

Greater participation of women in women's organizations might lead to greater demand for communication and networking. Avis Mamao comments that this is indeed a factor in women's utilization.

Perhaps the lack of promotion and participation of rural women in women's groups and NGOs on the Island and at Provincial levels also has some effect here in terms of fewer female users. The only active groups that use the centre are women's church and youth groupings for emails and typing documents.

In the women's focus group discussions, confidentiality was highlighted as a reason for less use by women. For example, in Hutuna centre, some women respondents indicated being shy, especially because a male operator is in charge of the email centre. They sometimes felt too shy to give the operator their messages to type and for this reason they expressed a strong desire for basic computer training and the provision of extra computers where they could type their messages themselves.

Generally, lower female participation vis-à-vis male participation is understandable because Solomon Islands (like most Pacific Island countries) are a patriarchal society where men play a more dominant role in family and societal affairs. Solomon Islands population is made up of a very diverse ethnic mix, with Polynesians, Micronesians, European, Chinese and other minorities in addition to the majority Melanesian groups. Even amongst each of these groups one finds a great diversity. Not surprisingly, women's roles and expectations of women in these societies are also widely different. These roles may therefore be expected to have some impact on the degree that women are free or willing to embrace ICT.

Having said this, however, some women in the focus group meetings pointed out that women's usage may really be higher than recorded; this has to do with the system of recording used by PFnet operators. They record the gender of the person who comes to send the emails and not the gender of the person who wrote the message or is sending the message. Thus, if a father goes to the centre, it is recorded as a 'male' statistic and if a mother goes to the centre it is recorded as a 'female' statistic, regardless of who wrote or instigated the message. Furthermore, 8% of women respondents in the survey mentioned that they send males in their family to send email messages

Another issue that needs to be taken into consideration is that there is difficulty in defining when a message is distinctively a 'female message' vis-à-vis a 'male message'. Some women in

the focus group interviews mentioned that when the need to send an email arises (e.g. contacting school for their children) this is a 'whole family issue' and not a 'male' or a 'female' issue and hence it does not matter who physically goes to the centre to send the email.

Use of PFnet Services by Age

The research findings from the user-log data show that the biggest group of users (around 20%) was in the 40 – 44 years age bracket. The second biggest group (17%) was in the 35 – 39 years age bracket, followed by 30 – 34 years age group (12%) and 25 – 29 age groups (11%). In Sigana, Sasamungga, Pirupiru and Silolo the biggest group of users were people in their thirties and forties, while in Hutuna centre, the biggest group was in their fifties.

Analysis of Positive Contribution of PFnet Services on The Lives Of Rural People In Solomon Islands

The PFnet services in Solomon Islands have had a number of positive impacts on the lives of rural grass-roots people in small remote islands.

Table 25. Users by age

y	Sigana	Sasamungga	Hutuna	Pirupiru	Silolo	Total	%
10-14	0	0	0	1	0	1	0.4
15-19	1	1	0	6	0	8	3.2
20-24	2	8	7	3	4	24	9.6
25-29	4	4	5	6	8	27	10.8
30-34	9	4	5	5	7	30	12.0
35-39	12	6	4	8	12	42	16.7
40-44	10	8	18	9	4	49	19.5
45-49	6	4	2	3	1	16	6.4
50-54	3	5	5	2	4	19	7.6
55-59	3	2	4	4	3	16	6.4
60+	3	10	1	3	2	19	7.6
Total	53	52	51	50	45	251	100.0

The deployment of PFnet services has definitely brought benefits to the people. If PFnet services were not available then it would be *status quo* for the people. The following are the main positive impacts of PFnet services to rural people in Solomon Islands.

PFnet has Provided an Alternative Means of Communication between Remote Islands to Honiara

PFnet has provided an alternative means of quick communication (*vis-à-vis* radio telephone) for rural people in small remote islands. Prior to the introduction of PFnet services the only means of communication between remote islands and Honiara was via 'radio telephone'. There are a number of disadvantages with the radio telephone system of communication. First, radio telephone is expensive (USD 1 per average call) compared to emails (USD 0.26 cents per email). Second, with radio telephone system there is a need to book a call in advance and hence urgent messages could not be sent immediately. Third, radio telephones do

not work properly during bad weather conditions and hence delayed communication. Fourth, the radio telephone system requires the adult person of the household (father or mother) to physically come to the radio centre and speak on the phone, whilst with the email system of PFnet anybody (children or village boys) can take the message to the PFnet email centre.

PFnet has Assisted in Reducing the Digital Divide

PFnet has helped in reducing digital divide. It provides quick and affordable communications to rural people in small remote islands (to around 85% of the 450,000 population) where no penetration of communication services has yet been possible beyond the nine provincial towns.

The research findings show that a high proportion (87.3%) of respondents indicated they use PFnet services to communicate with family and friends (see Table 26). In addition to the survey findings, the results from respondents in the focus group meetings show that PFnet has greatly

Table 26. Main purpose of using PFnet services (user group)

Main purpose of using PFnet	Sigana	Sasamungga	Hutuna	Pirupiru	Silolo	Total	%
Communication with family and friends	43	44	49	46	37	219	87.3
Education	16	30	16	16	13	91	36.3
Business purposes	13	14	8	8	13	30	22.4
Church/Religious	8	1	7	5	3	24	9.6
Remittance of money	0	14	1	0	4	19	7.6
Project/NGO	2	3	5	1	4	15	6.0
Health/medical	1	14		1	2	18	7.2
Government administration	1	2	3	0	3	9	3.6
Travel	4	1	1	0		6	2.4
Sports	0	3	0	0	1	4	1.6
Police/law and order	0	0	0	0	3	3	1.2
Agriculture	0	2	0	0		2	0.8
Other	1	0	1	0	1	3	1.2

assisted communications of rural people. This point was mentioned by respondents in all the focus group meetings conducted in five PFnet email centres.

In particular, PFnet has established a communication network between the following:

a. Remote villages (on distant islands) and the capital Honiara in Guadalcanal Island,
b. Remote villages and towns in other islands,
c. Remote villages and overseas countries.

These increased communications between places has assisted in reducing the digital divide within and outside Solomon Islands. PFnet has provided the rural population of Solomon Islands with access to easier communication services.

PFnet has Increased Communication in the Education Sector

PFnet has increased communication in the education sector. The survey data show that education is the second major reason why people use PFnet services (see Table 26). It is important to note that the two centres that reported most communications concerning educational use are Sasamungga (where Distance and Flexible Learning education trials were held) and Pirupiru (where the email centre is situated in a school). It is also interesting that in these two locations, the most common educational level of users is college educated.

Most of the people used the PFnet services for education administration rather than for learning. The majority of people use the PFnet for the following issues:

1. Communication between parents and schoolteachers with regard to questions on their children's enrolment issues and to arrange paying school fees.
2. Communication between parents and their high school children who are attending schools in Honiara or towns.

3. Communication between parents and children who are attending colleges or universities in Fiji, PNG, Australia and NZ.
4. School teachers/headmasters/ principals are using email to contact the education authorities (e.g. The Ministry of Education in Honiara and vice versa.), get curriculum for courses and solicit donations. Head teachers also use PFnet to communicate with head teachers and government officials in different remote islands.
5. Schoolteachers use PFnet's typing service to prepare teaching notes and print exam papers. The survey results show that 61% out of the 85 PFnet users who reported using PFnet for secretarial purposes said that they did so to type and print assignments/tests/exam papers.
6. The vocational training sector also uses PFnet services. For example, the 'Rural Teacher Training College' (which is located near Sasamungga PFnet centre) uses the email service to communicate with its Headquarters in Honiara.
7. The University of the South Pacific Distance and Flexible Learning (DFL) students use PFnet to send assignments from Solomon Islands to Suva in Fiji. Also students from Solomon Islands communicate with lecturers in Suva Fiji via email.
8. In 2002, the Solomon Island Ministry of Education used the PFnet email centre at Sasamunga for 'Distance Education Trials' and this was successful. The Solomon Island Ministry of Education plans to use PFnet system for Distance Education on a national scale.

PFnet has Contributed towards the Health Sector

PFnet email centre has greatly assisted the health sector. The survey results show that around 7.2% of people used PFnet's services for health-related issues. The main users of PFnet centres are doctors, nurses, and health workers from different parts of Solomon Islands who use emails to communicate to each other regarding 'medical results' of rural patients, 'diagnoses', 'advice on treatment', 'medicines' to be given to patients, and 'ordering of medicines'. This point was also underscored by participants in the focus group meetings. In the focus group meetings most health workers mentioned that they are using PFnet email services. For example, in one focus group meeting in Sasamungga, one nurse mentioned:

We use emails for our daily work. In the past (before PFnet) it took 3 – 4 weeks to get blood test and X-Ray results for patients by post, which came in boat from Honiara. Now with emails, we can get the results as soon as it is known in the lab in Honiara and we can then give appropriate medicine to patients immediately without waiting for a long period. PFnet centre has helped us a lot.

It is noteworthy, that all the PFnet centres are situated close to Health Centers/Clinics and in one case in Sasamunga, the PFnet centre is located in the health centre building.

PFnet Services have Assisted Farmers in Remote Islands

PFnet has assisted farmers in remote islands in Solomon Islands. Farmers use PFnet email centres for two main purposes. Farmers use emails to contact relevant agricultural authorities and NGOs in Honiara to get information and advice on farming matters, as well as to find customers (markets) for their products in Honiara.

The survey results show that 5% of users stated that PFnet has helped them in their farming activities. Through PFnet email services, farmers in remote islands are able to contact relevant agricultural authorities and NGOs to get information and advice. In the focus group meetings, farmers mentioned that they usually contact the *Kastom Gaden Association*, an NGO which gives all types of advice to farmers. More

specifically, respondents mentioned two examples of how they benefited from the *Kastom Gaden Association*. They are:

- A group of young farmers from Malaita Island were able to obtain technical advice from a specialist on poultry diseases,
- Subsistence farmers on Rennell Island have obtained advice concerning taro diseases affecting their crop. Via the *'TEK-websearch'* facility, one group of farmers was able to access detailed technical information about vanilla farming and to communicate with a specialist from the *Kastom Gaden Association*.

In focus group meeting, farmers in remote islands mentioned that they were able to find customers (markets) for their products in Honiara city. The farmers mentioned that they wrote emails to hotel, restaurants and cafes in Honiara and some of them began to order vegetables and fruits from them.

PFnet Services have Assisted Existing Business Activities and also Helped Create a Few New Businesses

PFnet has assisted people in remote islands to engage in business activities. The survey results show that business activity was one of the major reasons for respondents (22.4%) to use PFnet services (See Table 26). Rural businesspeople use PFnet services to develop business customer contacts in Honiara and other towns, find out the price of goods in Honiara, supply stock, order cargo (e.g. rural shops), get farming/agriculture news, find out shipping schedules, liaise with banks for financial transactions, and liaise with government offices in Honiara. For example, Sasamungga village in Choiseul island has six village stores and all of them use PFnet email services to order stock and make financial payments to their clients via Banks in Honiara. Before the existence of

PFnet, the store-owners ordered goods by letter but now they prefer emails because it reduces the time delay. One store-keeper in Sasamungga had this to say:

"The PFnet centre in our village has greatly helped me in my business and the whole community around here. In the past, I was not able to get all the stock quickly because letter system took time. Now it is easy. I just send them a list of goods I want through email and it saves time. "

Table 27 shows the percentage of all outgoing emails sent for business reasons from usage data collected daily over 15 months.

The level of business activity differs in the five centres. Hutuna has almost no business activity at all, not even a regular store. Farmers have no access to export commodity markets such as copra, cocoa, etc. This is mainly due to the lack of regular shipping. There is a continuous low level of seafood harvesting, mainly beche-de-mer, with local and foreign vessels calling at various locations along the coast. While the user data show a very low usage for business reasons, there may be indirect business benefits not picked up by the data. However, the lack of business application is not hindering the utilization of the centre. Hutuna is the second most utilized of the five centres in terms of communications.

Silolo in populous North Malaita shows the highest business usage in the daily reports data (16.4% of outgoing emails) are concerned with business and investment. Silolo has a very high level of communication with people overseas

(54% of outgoing mails). Malaita has rich mineral and other resources, and there is much interest in exploiting them. Communication with overseas business partners, potential and existing, may be a valuable benefit brought by the email service, one which would otherwise not be available at village level.

Pirupiru recorded 11.9% business reasons for outgoing mails. Avis Mamao of Pirupiru relates how he perceives business usage:

"The business owners quite frequently use the email centre. For instance, it is now easy to contact their business partners directly. "

The point about banking must be highlighted. E-banking and payment systems are a major issue. In Solomon Islands, most rural people have access to banks only in the provincial centers. Through the strong lobbying of the village people themselves, one Honiara bank now allows them to check their bank balances by email. The ability to check bank accounts by email (a discretionary service of the National Bank) saves remote islanders time, money and even their lives as it reduces the need for expensive and dangerous open-sea canoe crossings. This is a major step forward.

Apart from assisting existing business, there is evidence that PFnet has actually helped create two new business firms. Firstly, in 2003, at Pirupiru, a seafood business company named Dream-time Ltd was formed as result of the owner communicating (by email) to hotels and restaurant owners and arranging a contract to provide them with crayfish, crabs, prawns and fish. The service was

Table 27. Percentage of all outgoing emails sent for business reasons

	Sigana	Sasamungga	Hutuna	Pirupiru	Silolo
Business & investment	2.1%	14.5%	0.6%	11.9%	16.4%
Trading	0	0.1%	0.1%	0	0
Ordering cargo	0.2%	0.2%	27.5%	4.9%	0

Source: User-log monitoring data' recorded over 15 months

aimed at the more affluent residents and the hotel market in Honiara. Customers order by email and then deposit their payments in the bank. The company then verifies the payment made before dispatching the order. Secondly, PFnet led to the creation of Solomon Seaweed Company Ltd, a new company which exports seaweed to Japan. Agents for this company are based in each rural seaweed village and they are given private PFnet email accounts and training in communication. This seaweed project is linked to an Online Business Information Service (OBIS), which supplies technical and market information to entrepreneurs and is operated by the Ministry of Commerce. The seaweed project highlights the fact that rural finance is a critical factor connected to the partly subsistence-based economy in rural areas.

In summary, PFnet has led to the emergence of new business in the fisheries and agriculture sectors. Lack of communication for business activities has been one of the main hindrances to the establishment of enterprises in rural areas. Along with poor or no power supply, or sources of credit, PFnet is able to facilitate basic communications access.

PFnet has Helped Development of People's Careers

PFnet has helped people develop their careers. When asked in which way PFnet has helped in their careers, the survey data shows that 19% of the respondents indicated that PFnet has assisted in 'easier and faster communication with working colleagues' in other parts of Solomons Islands, 9% said it 'enhanced their business' and 7% said 'it helped in their teaching of students and getting promotions'.

When we asked PFnet users about information and communications needs for their careers, 8.8% stated that they needed information about how to make business contacts, 7.6% stated that they needed to communicate with business-related contacts such private companies and business

partners, and 4% indicated that they needed to contact overseas buyers and manufacturers. With regard to information and communications needs of PFnet users for 'their private lives', 15.9% said they needed business information and information about business opportunities, 5.2% said they communicated with business partners, 7% said that they needed business-related information but were not able to access it. Some users (1.2%) mentioned the problem with rural finance, recommending that PFnet should set up a system for business people to deposit money when ordering goods.

PFnet has Helped Provide Employment and Capacity Building of Operators at 11 EMail Centres

The PFnet project has led directly to the creation of jobs and capacity building for a number of groups of people. First, in Honiara itself, at the Headquarters, the PFnet project has created employment for seven people (one manager, one technical staff, one Webmaster, one administration officer, two email operators, one secretary, and one mail boy/caretaker). Second, in each of

Table 28. Ways in which PFnet helped in your career/private life

Response	Number	%
Easier and faster communication with family and friends	61	24.3
Easier and faster communication with working colleagues in other parts of Solomons	48	19.1
Enhanced my business	23	9.2
Order construction material quickly	14	5.6
Helped in my teaching and getting promotions	18	7.2
Other	55	21.9
No Response	32	12.7
Total	**251**	**100**

Source: Data from the survey

the eleven email centres in remote islands PFnet has created jobs and capacity building for 26 operators. Without PFnet these people would not be able to find work. The average wages of each email operator is USD120 per month. This has contributed to money for the operator's family and circulation of that money via expenditure in village stores, etc. Operators have learnt skills in the area of computers, typing, printing, internet and websites. Third, with the mere existence of PFnet email centres in their villages, illiterate people of all age group and gender in remote island at the minimum know what emails are, what computers are. Prior to the existence of PFnet, villages did not know the word 'email'. Young people, especially primary school children learn the basics of emails. Also women get to know basic facts about information technology by using the PFnet email centres, learn about computer skills, typing, and printing. Fourth, Committee Members at each of the centre are trained to operate emails, learn how to conduct meetings in their villages and keep records of meetings and finance. Committee members also get the chance to visit Honiara and get trained by PFnet headquarters staff.

PFnet has Assisted Non-Government Organizations (NGOs)

The survey data show that 6% (see Table 10) of the respondents indicated that they use PFnet email services for NGO activities. The local NGO leaders use emails to communicate with their headquarters in Honiara and/or international headquarters. In addition, community organizations and church organizations use emails to communicate with people in Honiara. Focus group interviews revealed that the local church officials use PFnet services quite frequently. For example, the church secretary of the Bible Translation Office in Tanageu, in Sigana, said:

I on behalf of our church frequently use the PFnet centre to communicate with our head office in Honiara for all types of administration jobs.

PFnet Helped Rural People During Period of Natural Disasters

PFnet email services has provided weather news' during cyclones, floods, earthquake, and about disaster management.

PFnet Contribution towards Conflict Prevention, Peace-Building and Reconciliation Process after the Ethnic Conflict

In focus group meetings, respondents mentioned that PFnet has contributed towards security, peace-building and reconciliation. Respondents mentioned that PFnet provided them with objective and accurate information on the facts during and after the ethnic conflict in the Solomon Islands and assisted in reducing the number of false rumors and misinformation. Furthermore, respondents stated that currently PFnet is assisting in the peace-building and reconciliation process by providing objective information through its local news service and access to other independent news sources, both nationally and internationally.

Furthermore, respondents in the focus group meetings said that the PFnet local news service had risen their awareness of what was going on during the ethnic conflict in Solomon Islands and their awareness of issues relating to human rights. One villager in a focus group meeting in Silolo, Malaita Island said:

I did not know about what our rights were. When the fighting began and especially when our rights were abused by fighting factions during the ethnic conflict then I began to have some idea of what human rights were. I got some idea from PFnet news service and also when people in the village began to discuss these issues.

Critical Analysis of Problems Associated with Subsequent Running/ Operations of PFnet Centres

The planning, implementation and subsequent operation of PFnet centres in Solomon Islands has not been perfect. The research findings reveal a number of problems the project has faced and continues to face.

Problems Associated with Committees at PFnet Centres in Remote Islands

According to the research findings, the first problem facing PFnet project is that most of the Committees at the rural email centres are not functioning properly and in two cases it is defunct. This situation is problematic since the PFnet model was founded on the three principles of 'community ownership', 'community participation', and 'community management' of email centres.

The survey results show that on average in all the five email centres only around one-fifth (22%) of the respondents of the users indicated that the Committees were 'doing their work properly' (see Table 29). The remaining 43% of the users mentioned that the Committees were 'not doing their work properly', 26% of the users mentioned that they were 'not sure' about the functioning

of the Committees, and 10% did not give any response. Adding these last three responses together shows that around 79% of the respondents felt that Committees were either 'not doing their work properly' or they were 'not sure' what the Committees were doing.

Further analysis by each centre shows that the worst cases were Pirupiru and Sasamunga centres, where 94% and 56% (respectively) users indicated that the PFnet Committees were not doing their work properly. In fact, focus group meetings and interviews with the operators revealed that in these two cases the Committees were defunct and not operating at all. The RDVA staff, PFnet Management at the Headquarters in Honiara also acknowledged this problem.

Furthermore, the survey results show that 89% of all the respondents reported that they were not aware of any public meeting held by the PFnet committee in their village (see tables 30 and 31). Similarly, in focus groups meetings in three centres, respondent mentioned that the PFnet committees are not functioning. These results indicate that PFnet committees are highly inactive, particularly in Sasamungga, Pirupiru and Silolo centres.

This finding was confirmed by a sample of 20 PFnet committee members themselves. The results show that 90% of them agreed that 'they rarely met'. This view was common in all the five centres studied.

There are two main reasons as to why the Committees at the email centres are not function-

Table 29. Whether PFnet committees are doing their job properly

PFnet committees doing their job properly	Sigana	Sasamungga	Hutuna	Pirupiru	Silolo	Total	%
Yes	20 (38%)	1(2%)	23 (44%)	0 (0%)	10 (22%)	54	21.5
No	14 (27%)	29 (56%)	8 (16%)	47(94%)	9 (20%)	107	42.6
Not sure	9 (17%)	21(40%)	12 (24%)	3 (6%)	20 (44%)	65	25.9
No response	10 (18%)	1(2%)	8 (16%)	0 (0%)	6 (14%)	17	10.0
Total	53 (100%)	52 (100%)	51 (100%)	50 (100%)	45 (100%)	251	100.0

ing well (Interviews with Committee Members). First, Committee Members mentioned that there are no allowances given by PFnet Management to attend the Committee meetings and hence financial initiatives to do work for PFnet. The current system is doing 'voluntary work' and hence members do not want to take out their productive time to come and attend the meetings. Secondly, there exists personality, family and community conflicts between Committee members and this affects the work of PFnet. This problem needs to be tackled by PFnet Management in Honiara for the PFnet to be successful.

Problems Associated with Work of Email Centre Operators

The research findings indicate there were problems with regard to work done by email centre operators. Although, a high proportion (87%) of user-respondents indicated that centre operators were doing their jobs properly, a small proportion (13%) had some complaints. The main complaints were: 'operators were breaking the confidentiality rule' 'operators were not present at the centre during working hours or were late', 'operators

refusing to open the centre after hours in cases of emergencies'; 'operators were slow in forwarding urgent in-coming emails'; and 'operators were not typing the message accurately'. Each of these issues are discussed in detail below.

Operators Revealing Confidential Information about Customers

The research results reveal that one factor affecting the 'usage of emails' is that of 'confidentiality'. The results show that around 19% of users indicated that the main reasons their fellow villages were not using PFnet is the 'lack of confidentiality'. In the focus group meetings and interviews a number of respondents mentioned that at times 'confidential' information was leaked by the operators to the people in the community. The issue of confidentiality is worth noting. The fear of personal and confidential matters being revealed by operators is one of the factors affecting the uptake of email services. Some respondents felt that an operator reads the message because in a few cases confidential matters have been revealed by operators. The research results show that, in a few cases, the operators have revealed confidential

Table 30 . PFnet committee meetings

Does PFnet committee meet regularly	Sigana	Sasamungga	Hutuna	Pirupiru	Silolo	Total	%
Yes	13	0	10	0	1	24	11.2
No	31	52	17	50	40	190	88.8
No response	9	0	24	0	4	37	14.7
Total	53	52	51	50	45	251	100.0

Table 31. Frequency of committee meeting

Frequency of committee meeting	Sigana	Sasamunga	Hutuna	Pirupiru	Silolo	Total	%
Whenever the need arises		1	1			2	10.0%
Rarely	6	2	4	5	1	18	90.0%
Total	6	3	5	5	1	20	100

Table 32. Work done by email centre operators

Operators doing their job properly	Sigana	Sasamunga	Hutuna	Pirupiru	Silolo	Total	%
Yes	43	52	47	47	30	219	87.3
No	1	0	0	0	7	8	3.2
No, delays in forwarding us urgent emails	3	0	0	1	0	4	1.6
No, operator missing during working hours	2	0	0	0	1	3	1.2
Not sure	3	0	0	1	1	5	2.0
Others	0	0	1	1	5	7	2.8
No response	1	0	3	0	1	5	2.0
Total	**53**	**52**	**51**	**50**	**45**	**251**	**100**

material to other people and in closely knit rural communities this has led to embarrassment and resentment. This problem of confidentiality is a result of the system of sending and receiving emails which operates as follows: when a person needs to send a message he/she writes it down either in English or Pidgin and gives it to the operator who then types the message in the laptop and sends it. This is a rule of the PFnet management and not that of an operator. The justification given by the PFnet management is that they do not want many people handling the laptop because it leads to maintenance problems. By typing the message, an operator knows its content and all users are aware of this. Therefore, for confidential issues (such as pregnancy) people prefer to use alternative methods of communication (letter-writing). Some respondents also complained about the confidential issue with regard to the in-coming emails. The procedure for in-coming emails is as follows: when an email message comes in an operator has to print it and pass it to the person concerned by reading only the name of the recipient, not the content.

For example, there was a case where a lady sent an email message to her husband in Honiara that their 18 old daughter was 'pregnant'. This information was leaked by the operator to a few people and this news spread quickly within the village and within days the whole village (50 households) knew about this. This incident caused embarrassment and loss of face to the family concerned. As a result of this people in the village realized that emails were not safe means of passing messages and it did affect 'usage' for a while.

Clients should be made aware that if there is a breach of confidentiality, there is a complaint procedure. The PFnet committee needs to take action when this happens. Procedures should be set up such that a certain number of proven breaches will lead to termination as an operator.

Operators Were not Present at the Centre during Working Hours/Late

The research findings show that since there is no one to supervise the operators, some operators do not open email centres on time, have extended lunch or are absent in working hours and this affects people who want to send urgent emails. One way to solve this problem would be to have at least two operators recruited and rostered to provide service to the people. Operators could be rostered to provide services to prevent the PFnet centre being closed during opening hours.

Operators Refusing to Open the Centre after Hours in Cases of Emergencies

The research findings show that at times operators have refused to open the centre when there is an emergency request for service after 4.30pm in working days or in weekends. This has caused concern from users of email centres

Operators were Slow in Forwarding Urgent In-Coming Emails

The research findings show that on some occasions operators have not forwarded 'urgent in-coming' emails to customers and some people have complained about this issue. Also there were complaints about operators 'not typing the message accurately'.

Lack of Awareness of the Functions of PFnet

The research findings show that respondents who are 'non-users' mentioned that they do not know much about PFnet services. Most of the respondents stated that the email centre Committee and operators should run 'awareness programme'. The PFnet committee members and the operators need to work closely with each other to promote the centre's services. Operators have to be members of the PFnet centre committees in order to be more pro-active in raising awareness, accountability and ownership. Operators should take an active role in promoting awareness programmes in their locality. They should be well versed with PFnet services and hence well placed to conduct the awareness programme.

Problems Associated with Technical Aspects of PFnet Services

Some respondents complained about the technical problems of PFnet services. These include: computer out of order, radio (via which message is sent) not working properly, and delay in receiving the messages.

Suggestions Given by Respondents on How to Improve PFnet Services

The user-respondents were asked to provide some suggestions for improvements and Table 33 shows the results.

More than a third of the respondents indicated that PFnet committees should run awareness programmes. Around 13% of the respondents stated that the PFnet centre should be housed separately and not be part of the health clinic or church. They also wanted the centre to be more spacious and to have a separate room for writing messages. Another 12% stated that more computers were needed, as people often have to wait for a while due to the small number of laptops at the moment. 8% wanted the PFnet committee to run training programmes for the villagers so that they learn how to send and receive mails on their own.

In the focus group meetings, the following suggestions were made:

- there should be more than one operator, with shift hours, so that someone is at email centre all the time;
- office hours to be clearly displayed on the centre door;
- operators should not provide free service to their family and friends;
- operators should have transport to deliver urgent emails;
- operators should always be confidential and send accurate messages;
- there should be more awareness programmes to inform people of PFnet services; and
- operators should be trained on customer service and should train people how to use email.

Table 33. Suggestions to improve PFnet services

How can PFnet services be improved?	Sigana	Sasa mungga	Hutuna	Piru piru	Silolo	Total	%
Run awareness programmes, particularly by PFnet committees	15	21	6	42	11	95	37.8
Have a special place for the email centre, more spacious, a room for emailing	13	4	8	0	7	32	12.7
Additional computers	1	6	20	1	2	30	12.0
Train people how to use email	3	2	7	4	4	20	8.0
Committee to meet on regular basis	0	14	0	1	3	14	7.2
Establish a centre at the other villages	2	3	4	1	7	17	6.8
More radios, have TV, scanner, fast printer and other services	6	0	2	0	3	10	4.0
Have someone deliver emails	6		1	0	1	8	3.2
Install Internet services	2	1	1	0	4	8	3.2
Establish a bank to use for ordering cargo from Honiara	2	0	1	0	0	3	1.2
PFnet committee members should have ID	1	0	0	0	1	2	0.8
Use of PFnet for distance learning must be promoted	0	0	2	0	0	2	0.8
Operator must be confidential	0	1	1	0	0	2	0.8
Change system from HF to digital for faster com-munication	0	1	0	1	0	2	0.8
Provide villagers with mail boxes in the centre	1	0	0	0	0	2	0.8

These results indicate that much more work is needed on the part of the PFnet committees and the operators in order to increase the uptake and utilization of PFnet services.

Lessons to Be Learnt from PFnet

People who are thinking of setting up ICT projects in their countries can learn the following five lessons from the case study of PFnet:

1. Proper holistic strategic planning is needed before any ICT project is to be embarked on. ICT projects should not be established on an ad- hoc manner and it should not be rushed into because some donor agency is giving the money.

2. Country wide feasibility study needs to be conducted before any ICT project is launched and if possible small feasibility studies as pilot projects need to be carried out in rural areas where the ICT project will be established. This is necessary because the socio-ethnic-cultural-economic features may be different from one area to another. A socio-ethnic-cultural-economic profile of each project area should be complied and analysed before any major decision is made.

3. All key stakeholders need to be consulted and involved from day one. It cannot be imposed from the top by government, donor agencies or overseas consultants. Local community, village leaders, religious leaders, health workers must be involved from the beginning. The case study of PFnet shows that an ICT project which involves 'local community participation' works. PFnet is a model whereby the ownership and day-to-

day decision-making process are in the hands of the rural communities and village leaders. It is based on a partnership between the Rural Development Volunteer Association (RDVA) and Village People's Committee. Hence, in this 'community participatory' system the grass root poor people are involved in programmes that affect their life. Without this participation, PFnet would have never worked. It must be people-focused and not donor agency-focused.

4. Local staff must be involved in every stage of the ICT project, from the beginning to the implementation stage. They must be involved starting from the planning stage, feasibility study stage, selection of the email centre site, discussions with local village people prior to and during the setup of the project and implementation stage. Where there is need for overseas consultants to be involved then they should play a facilitating role.

5. Cost of using ICT services must be affordable by rural people. The PFnet case shows that the cost for sending and receiving emails was within the financial means of rural people. ICT services must be 'affordable' by the rural people if it is to succeed.

SUMMARY AND CONCLUSION

This chapter has reviewed and examined how PFnet project in the Solomon Islands has contributed to reducing digital divide in the Solomon Islands. The PFnet programme has increased communication between people in rural areas (in remote islands) and the capital city Honiara. Through the internet café at the Headquarters, PFnet has also increased communication between people in Honiara and overseas countries such as Fiji, PNG, Australia and New Zealand via 'face book' and other web programmes. In particular, this chapter has examined the following issues: Firstly, the

main purposes for use were 'communicating with family members' and 'educational' and 'medical services'. Secondly, the chapter examined the impact of PFnet services on the lives of grass-roots people and in particular the issues such as whether the PFnet project has improved the lives of rural people. The empirical evidence show that PFnet has facilitated in communications for remote and rural villagers, helped farmers through agriculture information, assisted NGOs, enhanced business activities, find out shipping schedules, liaise with banks for financial transactions, liaise with government offices in Honiara, assisted in education and assisted in health-related issues. Although the PFnet has its minor weaknesses at times, it has been a success story and since 2001 it has reduced the digital divide in the Solomon Islands. This ICT model can be replicated in other developing countries in the world.

ACKNOWLEDGMENT

The chapter is based on an empirical research conducted in Solomon Islands between the period 2004-2005 and subsequently updated with interviews and focus group meeting with PFnet staff and users between January-July 2009.

REFERENCES

Badshah, A., & Jha, S. (2002). *Taking the Expansive View: From Access to Outcomes: Utilizing the Knowledge-Based Economy to Empower the Poor in India.* Digital Partners Institute.

Curtain, R. (2003, May 22) *Information and Communication Technologies and Development: help or hindrance?* Retrieved January 2, 2010 from http://www.developmentgateway.com.au/jahia/Jahia/lang/en/pid/247

Fortier, F. (2003). Sustainable Rural Networking, Community Ownership and Appropriate Technologies. Retrieved January 1, 2010 from http://www.ecissurf.org/database/actions/getFile.cfm?DocumentID=2634 or http://www.peoplefirst.net.sb/Downloads/FortierSustainableRuralNet2003-0

Guild, R. (2003). *Digital Review of Asia Pacific 2003: Pacific Islands*. APDIP . In Hammond, A. L., Jenkins, E., Kramer, W. J., & Paul, J. H. (Eds.), *Learning from the Poor: a bottom-up approach to development*. World Resources Institute.

Leeming, D. (2003). *Education through Wireless Networking in Solomon Islands*. Paper presented at the Asia Media Information and Communications Centre AMIC. 12th Annual Meeting, Singapore, November 2003.

Leeming, D. (2003). *Challenges for Sustainable Rural Networking in Solomon Islands*. Round Table on Science for Developing Countries, Abdus Salam Centre (ICTP), Trieste, Italy, Oct 2003.

Leeming, D. (2003). Input Paper for the Solomon Islands People First Network, paper presented at the World Summit on the Information Society, Tokyo Regional Meeting, January 2003.

Leeming, D. (2003). Success *Factors for the Solomon Islands People First Network*. Global Knowledge Partnership AGM, Rome, May 2003, downloadable at www.peoplefirst.net.sb/general/PFnet.htm

Leeming, D., & Baliki, R. (2003). *Final report People First Network, the Solomon Islands' Rural E-mail networks for Peace and Development* (Interim Assistance Project SOI/02/004). Retrieved January 1, 2010 from http://www.undp.org.fj/documents/ICT4DEV/PFnet_Final_Report.pdf

Liloqula, R. (2000). Understanding the conflict in the Solomon Islands as a practical means to peacemaking. *Development Bulletin (Canberra)*, *53*, 41–43.

Mathison, S., Prasetyo, J., & Kemp, M. (2003). *Information and Communication for Development, Guidelines for Practitioners*. The Foundation for Development Cooperation.

Otter, M. (2002). *Solomon Islands Human Development Report: Building a Nation*. Windsor: Government of the Solomon Islands/UNDP.

Patson, P., Taniveke, P., Leeming, D., Agassi, A., & Baliki, R. (2002). *Final Technical Report*. Sasamungga Distance Learning and Research Project, Rural Development Volunteers Association. Retrieved December 30, 2009 from www.peoplefirst.net.sb/General/Distance_Learning.htm#latest

PFnet. (n.d.). Retrieved January 3, 2010 from www.peoplefirst.net.sb/general/PFnet.htm

Stork, E. (2002). *Enhancing People's Participation in the Pacific through the Usage of ICT's*. UNDP. Retrieved from http://www.undp.org.fj/documents/ICT4DEV/EnhancingPeopleParticip.zip.

Stork, E. UNDP (2004). *Formulation Mission Report* UNDP PFnet Replica Project Vanuatu: Port Vila, Tanna, Espiritu Santo, and Malekula. 4th April - 16th April 2004. Retrieved from http://www.undp.org.fj/Strenghtening_Community_Access_to_Information.htm

Stork, E. UNDP (2004). *Formulation Mission Report* UNDP PFnet Replica Project Papua New Guinea: Port Moresby and Bougainville: 24th March 2004 - 1st April 2004. Retrieved December 30, 2009 from http://www.undp.org.fj/Strenghtening_Community_Access_to_Information.htm

UNDP. (2001*). Human Development Report 2001: Making New Technologies work for Human Development*. Retrieved January 1, 2010 from http://hdr.undp.org/reports/global/2001/en

UNDP, Regional Bureau Asia and the Pacific. (2003). *Good practices in Asia and the Pacific - Expanding choices, empowering people: People First: Networking for Peace and development*, (pp. 22-23).

Chapter 11

Stronger Voices?
Experiences in Paraguay
with Interactive ICTs

Claire Buré
The Zoltner Consulting Group, Chile

ABSTRACT

This case study focuses on a civil society organization called Radio Viva in Asunción, Paraguay. It was found that the interactive use of 'traditional' and 'new' technologies in locally innovative ways was able to meet community needs through the creation of two local products. Specifically, when radio and telephony were integrated with telecentre services (including internet access), new physical and virtual communication spaces were opened up for civic participation. Second, ICT interactivity was found to lead to the creation of locally relevant content production, helping Paraguayan communities to gain access to useful and contextualized information while also turning local 'information recipients' into 'knowledge users'.

INTRODUCTION

Community participation has long been recognized as a vital component of all stages of development processes, yet development initiatives often place a higher focus on the 'application' of new information and communication technologies for poverty alleviation through greater access to the 'knowledge economy'. Yet it is not the application of technologies that leads to community change, but the reflexive and democratic uses to which

they are applied in people's lives. This paper aims to move past deterministic discussions of technology access, and instead encourages a greater contextualized focus on the locally creative and innovative uses of communication technologies in ways that can help communities answer their own needs. Democratic communication organizations can play a big part in encouraging greater levels of civic participation through the use of appropriate communication media. This Paraguayan case exemplifies how this is possible when radio communication is combined with 'new' ICTs in telecentre, statically changing according to local

DOI: 10.4018/978-1-61520-997-2.ch011

needs. Community radio is an appropriate technology that is far too often ignored as development enthusiasts instead focus on newer emerging technologies. Yet the community radio movement in Latin America remains strong, where radio is often the only mass medium available in rural areas. When combined with ICTs in telecentres, such as computers with internet access, as well as with other traditional communication media like telephones, a multitude of communication channels is produced, giving rise to plural community engagement.

The research presented here focuses on Radio Viva, a community organization based in the outskirts of Asunción, Paraguay, that combines the use of communication technologies in ways that are locally successful in meeting community needs by facilitating civic participation. The key purpose of the study was to investigate how active community participation and dialogue may lead to community change through the increased media channels that are created when an 'old' technology like the radio is combined with a 'new' community technology service like a telecentre. Case study findings revealed that ICT integration through radio and telecentres leads to the creation of two local products. First, communication through interactive ICTs opens up physical and virtual spaces for community dialogue to occur, allowing for civic participation about local issues and challenges. Second, it opens up opportunities for local content production. This leads to the creation of locally useful and contextualized information, allowing for community members to shift from being information recipients to knowledge producers. The framework of this analysis is a social constructivist approach, recognizing that human interactivity and technologies are mutually influential (MacKenzie & Wajcman, 2002).

This chapter begins by presenting the reader with a contextual background of current literature on ICT and poverty reduction strategies, community radio, telecentres, and interactive technologies. Next, case study background is

provided on Radio Viva; including a brief history of the initiative, and information on basic human resources, technical background, services and current set up. This is followed by a description of the methodology used, after which case study findings are discussed in light of how local creative and innovative activities using ICTs can lead to local social change. A summary is presented advocating for a more contextualized approach to media use, particularly including 'traditional' technologies such as the radio and telephone in meeting community needs. This report emphasizes the need for more concrete research to be conducted about the integration of ICTs, and highlights pertinent areas for further discussion to take place. Given time and resource constraints, the purpose of this paper is to bypass discussions on whether Radio Viva is a successful or unsuccessful development organization, focussing instead on one unique aspect of community development organizations – the integration of ICTs in development processes – which has until now received very little study. By exploring the innovative ways in which different communication technologies are leveraged and applied in ways that are locally relevant, we can derive an incredibly useful picture of the ways in which ICT users can engage in civic dialogue (and thereby community change).

BACKGROUND

In the debate about the potential usefulness of ICTs in poverty reduction strategies it is becoming increasingly recognized that a contextualized approach to media use must be taken (Gumucio-Dagrón, 2001; Gómez & Martínez, 2001; Tacchi, Slater & Lewis, 2003). That is, an appreciation of the context surrounding ICT appropriation and use (including social, economic and political inequalities) is key to a deeper understanding of the ways in which ICTs can be useful in human development processes. One of the major challenges to the success of development strategies using ICTs has been the tendency to place excessive focus on connectivity. Gómez and Martínez (2001) explain how "the Latin American experience teaches us that ICTs *can* contribute to development on the condition that they go beyond connectivity, to ensure equitable access, meaningful use, and social appropriation of ICT resources" (2001: 6). Based on many years of practical experience in Latin America, the authors describe four conditions for the creation of an "enabling environment" that ICT for development strategies need to incorporate in order to be useful for communities (Gómez & Martínez, 2001: 8). These are important conditions to keep in mind throughout this paper, and while considering the 'value' of ICTs in community development projects. First, ICTs should be integrated into existing (rather than new) social activities that promote positive change in the community. Second, information and communication technologies should be used as part of a strategy to achieve clearly defined goals that aid the local community, rather than as an end in themselves. The application of ICTs to achieve specific goals has been aptly referred to as the "effective use" of technologies (Gurstein, 2003: 6). Third, and importantly, democracy and citizen participation should be present as preconditions to change, since ICT use in and of itself will not necessarily lead to a more pluralistic or democratic society. Last, the authors emphasize how processes of human development cannot be diminished to economic growth alone. Instead, ICT appropriation and use in development "should be inscribed in an ethic of solidarity, reciprocity, and enthusiasm, based on deep-seated values that seek to transform individuals and their relationships" (Gómez & Martínez, 2001: 9). Similarly, Zulberti (2003) echoes the need for basic conditions relating to social and cultural concerns: "In order to have a significant impact on development programmes, ICT services must be readily accessible and meaningful to broad segments of rural populations and the information they carry must be adapted and disseminated in formats and languages that they

can comprehend. They must also service people's needs for entertainment, cultural enlightenment, and human contact – needs which, despite being strongly felt by us all, are too often overlooked by development professionals" (2003: iii).

This discussion is critical in development dialogue, since the costs of further excluding some members of society from sharing valuable information and knowledge can be detrimental for many. It is important to move the focus from the technologies themselves – while recognizing that technology infrastructure is obviously important as a precondition to the use of ICTs – to acknowledge and learn about how they are integrated into people's lives. A central theme of this paper therefore focuses on flows of democratic communication and sharing of information through interactive ICTs.

Much hype surrounds the potential of ICTs and communication systems to disseminate information and knowledge to 'the masses' in an effort to bring excluded groups into the so-called 'knowledge society'. Yet an analysis of the way the concept of knowledge is used in development rhetoric reveals that it has become a "major issue", in danger of being oversimplified in its application in development projects and processes (Chataway & Wield, 2000: 803). Knowledge (not just information) is often treated as a commodity to be imparted for human development to take place, yet the danger of treating it as a prescriptive tool for change underestimates the process-based role of knowledge in learning, unlikely to bring about social change in and of itself (Chataway & Wield, 2000). Neither should too much focus be placed on the importance of global knowledge – but rather on stronger integration between local and global knowledge (Chataway & Wield, 2000). Information and knowledge need to be directly applied to local problems, in order to be useful (Nnadi & Gurstein, 2007). Similarly, information and communication processes should be less mechanical and more oriented towards the human development aspect of ICT for development projects (Saravia,

2003). Knowledge is most effectively distributed through human communication, as opposed to the technical systems themselves, through what can be called "community intermediaries" (Heeks, 1999: 18). These individuals are key players in knowledge distribution processes, helping to gather and impart locally relevant information and knowledge to the community via various media channels. Community intermediaries are community members who are locally involved, and can be anything from agricultural workers to teachers to experienced elderly individuals (Girard, 2003). Their typical characteristics include "proximity, trust and knowledge (including the ability to combine 'tech knowledge' about ICT with 'context knowledge' about the environment in which it is used)" (Heeks, 1999: 18). A deeper look needs to be taken at how knowledge can be most effectively created and shared within communities for local development purposes.

Knowledge is gained when an individual is exposed to, and can learn from, relevant and meaningful information in the form of content. Girard (2003) provides examples of how: "Content that explains useful agricultural techniques or the workings of local markets can be transformed into knowledge and contribute to increased production and better prices. Content about locally available traditional medicine or about nutrition can lead to longer and better lives. Content about rights, responsibilities and options can be both a prerequisite and a catalyst for democracy" (2003:6).

The need for more (and better) local content is well recognized by development agencies, yet a common response still tends to be an 'external' content push from the 'outside' for communities to absorb other's knowledge (Chataway & Wield, 2000; González, n.d.). Roman and Colle (2003) explain how this is because "much of the effort to develop content is based on what officials and experts think certain populations need and want, often based on credible demographic and socio-economic data", a practice to which they refer as having 'normative needs' (2003: 90). Yet it is obvious that the cultural relevance of content

is inextricably tied to its local significance and usefulness within that community. Information must be meaningful to the community at large, and the information accessed must be locally relevant, in a language that is easily understood. Roman and Colle (2003) argue that the process of content production should therefore incorporate consumer demand, or the 'expressed needs' of the community (Roman & Colle, 2003: 90). ICTs should be considered less as a set of infrastructural tools that mechanically deliver information, and more as a system of channels and creative tools that can be used to produce and distribute content for positive change (Saravia, 2003; Tacchi, 2006). This information should be relevant to the daily lives of those receiving it, highlighting again the importance of locally relevant content production.

The creation of communication channels to promote open community dialogue is essential for marginalized communities to be given the opportunity to debate, analyze and make decisions about relevant local issues (Fraser & Restrepo-Estrada, 2002). Specifically, "the emergence, health and diversity of civil society depend on access to information on key issues that affect people's lives, and the capacity of people and organizations to have their voices heard in the public and political arena" (Deane et al., 2004: 66). Community engagement and participation is therefore critical to processes of local social change, where community members are given the voice – or voices – needed to affect local decision-making and problem solving. Interestingly, the interactive potential of information and communication technologies is slowly being recognized for leading to greater levels of democratic participation in communities (Girard, 2003; Tacchi, 2006). That is, 'interactive broadcasting' is an emerging and growing phenomenon that can potentially create new opportunities through the use of new and traditional ICTs for educational and entertainment purposes, as well as new business models for more sustainable enterprises (Wortley, 2004: 259).

Very little research exists so far on the effects of interactive technologies, but it is becoming increasingly clear that interactivity between 'old' technologies like radio and 'new' technologies like the internet provide great opportunities for social communication processes – allowing for new ways for people and communities to interact with each other (Girard, 2003). For example, Zulberti (2003) suggests how the convergence of rural radio and ICTs can lead to change, by providing a "powerful support for harnessing and communicating knowledge for development, for ensuring wider access to information, and for permitting local cultural expression and development" (p.iii). Where literature does exist about interactive ICTs, the focus tends to be placed on the radio combined with the internet. The aim of this paper is to focus specifically on the creative ways in which radio can be combined with telecentres – and the public space it provides for community members to gather and share knowledge. First, a brief discussion of both telecentres and community radio is useful here.

Telecentres are public places where people can gain shared access to a range of information and communication technologies and services (usually housing a number of computers with an internet connection) for certain social, educational, economic or personal development purposes (Gómez, Hunt and Lamoureux, 1999). They are intended to provide not just access but also support in order to help people build the capabilities needed to use ICTs. Telecentres are part of a broader, social movement to provide spaces for communities to gather, share experiences, meet new people, learn from each other and build on existing skills. In other words, they are places that hold potential for "expanding local capacity for developing, managing and maintaining ICT capabilities" (Gurstein, 2003, n.p.). Although the telecentre movement is growing around the world (Parkinson, 2005), telecentres are not equally successful at meeting community needs (Benjamin and Dahms, 1999; Gómez & Martínez, 2001) and sustainability is often a challenge (Proenza, 2001).

Community radio helps to facilitate social change by enabling participation in public dialogues. It is one of the most pervasive information and communication technologies, reaching "more people than any other mass medium" since it overrides illiteracy, gender, class, conflict, distance and poverty barriers (Anonymous, 2007: 13). Radio thereby provides a voice – or better yet, a multitude of voices – for the community via this low-cost, easy to operate, grassroots communication channel (Padania & Silvani, 2005). It allows people to express their comments and questions on air about any given topic in the community, allowing them to actively participate in the creation and communication of local content. It also puts pressure on local authorities to take certain actions, such as those related to good governance or transparency (Fraser & Restrepo-Estrada, 2002). The production of radio content is relatively straightforward, in that no special qualifications are needed to record, edit or broadcast information, apart from being able to read and write (Acharya, 2007). The four most important characteristics of radio are therefore said to be: "(1) its pervasiveness, (2) its local nature, (3) the fact that it is an oral medium, and (4) its ability to involve communities and individuals in an interactive social communication process" (Girard, 2003: 8). Community radio is intended to empower citizens by providing them with a 'voice'. This can help to resolve local problems, promote awareness (for example, on political or health-related information) and other ideas and information that are relevant to local communities. Radio (as a pervasive and accessible technology) helps to facilitate social change by providing communities with an opportunity for self-expression. Community radio allows listeners to provide commentary about community issues, whether through a telephone call that is broadcast live on air, or through an email to the radio program hosts themselves, for example. In turn, information drawn from the internet can help to strengthen this communication channel, particularly when radio content is produced by community members (such a local youth) enhancing the relevance of content. This brings attention not just to access of information (by the community via radio or at the telecentre, but also to the process of learning gained through production of content as an important component of social development that should not be overlooked.

The potential social impact of radio converging with other ICTs was recognized as early as 1932, when Bertold Brecht claimed in his famous speech on 'The Radio as an Apparatus of Communication' that "radio could be the most wonderful public communication system imaginable, a gigantic system of channels - could be, that is, if it were capable not only of transmitting but of receiving, of making listeners hear but also speak, not of isolating them but connecting them" (cited in Priestman, 2004: 83). These words still ring true today for the many stations around the world that combine the use of radio with other ICTs in some way, such as UNESCO's Community Multimedia Centers, or Kothmale Radio in Sri Lanka (Pringle & David, 2003). This paper argues for the need for more academic research about the integration of radio and ICTs (and telecentres), particularly given that this process has been seen as holding 'added value' (Creech, 2006). Research by Saravia (2003), based in Peru, finds that rural connectivity structures are most successful when combining telecentres with traditional media such as the radio, its relevancy being greater precisely because it's an "intra-community" technology (2003: 27). Yet where does this added value come from? What happens when radio and the telephone are integrated with internet services based in a telecentre, with the aim of helping marginalized communities?

The radio is sometimes described as a "gateway" to the internet, which affects not just content development, but also new ways of communicating as radio shifts from being a one-way medium to a complex group of communication channels (James, 2004: 53). Steve Buckley (2000) says that "It is radio which remains, today, the world's most pervasive and accessible electronic medium, and

as such it potentially offers a bridge between the vast knowledge resources available through the internet and the millions of people who have access to no other means of electronic communication" (2000: 185). Using the internet, community radio stations can easily transmit programs online since no license is required. Listeners can be either local or global, listening either in real-time, or after the program has aired (if programs are digitally archived and available online). Online programming may nevertheless lack the connection with an audience that radio can achieve, precisely because local relevance and accessibility play a key role in how effectively content is perceived and absorbed by listeners (Priestman, 2004). Radio combined with the internet also changes who has access to, and who can contribute to public dialogue. That is, the internet allows listeners the possibilities to communicate and interact through email, blogs, online forums, or VOIP applications such as Skype.

If radio is a gateway to the internet, when combined with telecentre services (and particularly a network of telecentres), the communication channels created become increasingly complex. The physical location of a telecentre opens up a public space for community members to meet and interact in person (the implications of which will be discussed later), allowing individuals the freedom to explore the internet on their own terms. According to Lamoureux (1999), this is advantageous because it can lead to enhanced communication efficiency: individuals are required to devote more attention to surfing the internet than would be required to listen to the radio, and visual information is more easily retained than aural information. However, further study is required about how the internet is actually used in telecentres, since anecdotal evidence suggests that they are most often used for playing games, messaging friends, email, and sometimes web searches, and thus information retention becomes less relevant to community development. Internet access at a telecentre also offers the independent use of applications like email, chat or online forums providing users with the opportunity to participate in the 'global communication process' (Lamoureux, 1999: 196-197). Again however, individual users may not necessarily be motivated to use the internet for anything other than entertainment or personal communication purposes. Additionally, telecentre use brings its own set of requirements (which may not be accessible to all), including the time, expenses, and transportation needed to access the telecentre. Also required is the ICT capacity and meaning of the technology in order to use it. Additionally, it is important to recognize that the use and convergence of ICTs brings both positive and negative effects, profoundly changing how people use these tools to communicate and interact, and generally rendering communication more complex (Heeks, 1999). For example, in UNESCO's evaluation report of its Community Multimedia Centres (or CMCs), an acknowledgment is made that the introduction of new technologies when leveraged with existing ones has brought challenges and adjustments for those people involved. One such challenge emphasized the increased complexity for managers to make decisions about finances, staff training and technical services (Creech, 2006).

CASE STUDY BACKGROUND

Findings presented here are based on an organization called Radio Viva, located in Trinidad, on the outskirts of the capital city of Asunción, Paraguay. Trinidad is a large, relatively poor neighbourhood encompassing many smaller communities (many of which are built on reclaimed land), with a total population of approximately 65,000 inhabitants. Radio Viva was created in 1995 as a non-profit community radio station, originally called "FM Trinidad 95.5". It was created through a strong grassroots effort in Trinidad, with support from a local NGO called Alter Vida that supports sustainable development, and a number of other local social organizations. After several years of successful

transmission, the community radio was effectively shut down (after several attempts by the state to do so) when a new telecommunications law was passed in 2000 which recategorized community radio stations as "third sector communications", separate from state or commercial radio stations. FM Trinidad 95.1 was finally "silenced" when the creation of the National Radio of Paraguay took over the same frequency of 95.1 at ten times the signal strength. After 18 months of official closure, the radio was re-launched as Radio Viva, legally functioning as a citizen's radio cooperative (in Spanish: "*una radio ciudadana y cooperativa*"). It currently transmits at the frequency of 90.1 on air, and broadcasts online at www.radioviva.com. py. For the purposes of this paper, Radio Viva's essence and functionality therefore remain very similar to that of a community radio, where any differences that may be found are largely legal.

Radio Viva's head office is located in a large, three-floor building in the community of Trinidad, which hosts the radio station (including antennae), spaces for community events (both outside and inside) and offices for program staff and volunteers. It also hosts the national news agency called Jaku'éke Paraguay, which distributes both local and global news content. The radio station contains approximately five computers to generate radio content (using editing software), three telephone connections to receive listeners' calls connected to a studio console, a mixer, input/output speakers, headphones and microphones, studio monitor speakers, a changing CD player, portable audio recorders, and a digital clock. All staff have access to a computer with internet connectivity and phone access, as do journalists working for the news agency. Additionally, Radio Viva owns five mobile radio units (or vans) which travel to any given area throughout central Asunción and surrounding areas to gather news about current topics relevant to the community of Trinidad. The mobile units have the capacity to send live broadcasts using portable audio recording equipment to record content.

Like many radio stations, Radio Viva connected to the internet when it realized the need for the digitization of content, online information searches and online streaming for radio programming. Subsequently, the organization became involved in the monitoring and support of telecentres in the community in order to improve levels of information access for local youth (particularly those living in vulnerable neighbourhoods). Telecentres were intended to help students with school-related tasks, and indeed were initially used to primarily answer questions from local students relating to schoolwork (as part of a project called 'Info-Express' funded by a Canadian NGO). According to the director of Radio Viva, a little over 65% of the population in Paraguay is comprised of people under the age of 30. Radio Viva therefore focuses on answering the information and communication needs for youth, through telecentres.

Radio Viva works closely with nine telecentres that were created independently, in response to community needs, by local community development organizations such as the locally run 'neighbours' association'. Some international funding was also awarded for the creation of the telecentres (such as the Inter-American Bank of Development). The telecentres are spread out within various neighbourhoods of Trinidad, namely: San Blas, Puerto Botánico, Luque, Mbayué de Limpio, Tablada Nueva and Zeballos Cué. A seventh telecentre is based in a women's jail (Cárcel de Mujeres del Buen Pastor) and an eighth in a youth detention centre for juvenile delinquents (Centro Educativo de Itaguá). At the time of writing, a ninth telecentre is currently being built in Vírgen de Fátima, and a tenth is being planned for eventual location in the organization's head office, intended to provide local teachers with the digital skills and resources for pedagogical activities. Although the telecentres vary in size, socio-economic status and mobilization levels of the community in which they are based, services provided are similar. Each telecentre is lead by two or three telecentre managers, with a host of

volunteers who provide monitoring and digital skills support for telecentre users. Each telecentre contains approximately 10 computers with a working internet connection. Most also contain a small library of books, with a shipment of 10,000 more books to arrive from Spain before the end of 2009, for all nine telecentres to share. Regular training workshops include digital training for telecentre users, training for news correspondents based in each neighbourhood (and associated with the telecentre), and training on how to write a curriculum vitae in order to find work. Specific telecentre programs in place include a health service in Tablada Nueva, through an ICTs-Health and Gender program, which runs pap tests and a women's cancer preventative program. Last, training about urban neighbourhood cleanup is provided as part of an ICTs and Environment program in Mbayué de Limpio.

At the time of writing, Radio Viva staff is composed of 37 employees, and 20 volunteers who work at the organization headquarters. According to public opinion and statistics institute IBOPE Paraguay, It is estimated that Radio Viva reaches 800,000 listeners in total. Programming is transmitted 24 hours per day, both on air across greater Asunción (to both urban and rural areas covering 80 square km) and online (which is of particular interest considering that approximately one third of Paraguayan nationals have migrated to other countries). Radio Viva broadcasts in both Spanish and the local language of Guaraní. Listeners tend to be from low, medium-low and medium levels of socioeconomic status; where a slightly higher proportion of listeners are women than men.

Since its inception, Radio Viva maintains its original primary objectives, namely to:

1. Facilitate a "culture of participation" in a neutral communication space, encouraging citizens to act upon their rights and civic duties in support of free expression for community change;

2. Generate new opportunities for improved local relations between various sectors of the community, acting as an important intermediary between the community and local authorities;

3. Bring new topics to the public agenda on behalf of civil society members and organizations.

The organization's values are based on the promotion of solidarity, creativity, social justice, gender equality and cultural identity. This is accomplished through the production and broadcasting of information and awareness campaigns on issues relating to the environment, citizenship rights, child labour, women's rights, transparency and fighting corruption to low-income communities, among other relevant issues. Radio Viva receives 60% of its funding from external (foreign) sources, 30% from internal income, and 10% from the local and national governments, respectively.

METHODOLOGY

This case study is based on qualitative research methods. Data was collected through individual face-to-face interviews and focus groups consisting of a maximum of three individuals at a time. A total of 17 people were interviewed using informal, reflexive, semi-structured interviews. Respondents included: the organization founder and director, funding agency staff, program managers, telecentre operators and leaders from three different telecentres, radio hosts (for both Spanish and Guaraní programs), radio program administrators and content producers, community trainers, journalists, organization administrators, volunteers, and radio and computer technicians. Some findings are also drawn from informal observations and conversations while spending time at each initiative (both at the radio and associated telecentres), as well as through participatory observation at two workshops, which helped to

provide a better understanding of context. The first workshop was organized by Radio Viva with about 20 young voluntary telecentre leaders at a newly established telecentre in Trinidad, and the second was a knowledge exchange workshop between approximately 50 radio producers in Chile and Bolivia organized by a Chilean NGO to share experiences, lessons learned and to plan more coordinated radio production activities. All interviews were audio recorded, with permission from respondents, and all personal information was kept anonymous and confidential. Unless otherwise indicated, all research present in this paper has been updated from research conducted in late 2006 and 2007, including information about the organization and its services.

The social construction of technology (SCOT) perspective informs the analysis and interpretation of case study findings here. The SCOT perspective understands technologies as socially constructed artefacts affected by social, cultural, political and economic contexts (Bijker, Hughes & Pinch, 1987). The use and appropriation of the ICTs in the case studied here are therefore understood within the local context of the community of Trinidad (where the case study organization is located). This includes the surrounding social, cultural, political and economic contexts. The social construction of technology perspective is based on a social shaping approach that challenges the deterministic view of technology development and subsequent use as inherently inevitable, instead recognizing that many social factors influence how technologies are developed and used. Social shaping sees technologies as affecting human activities, and humans in turn influence how these technologies become created and used (MacKenzie & Wajcman, 2002). Findings are placed within a broader scope of ICT for development and communication fields of literature. Given that the findings presented are based on qualitative case study research, it is difficult to draw generalizations relating to broader contexts. Similarly, it is acknowledged that case studies can never be fully objective, and thus the researcher's background can never fully be removed from the analysis of the research findings. It is clear that further research is needed to draw deeper conclusions on issues highlighted here.

DISCUSSION

A deeper look will now be taken at how the human and technical dynamics of Radio Viva's organizational structure can promote community participation through the innovative use of interactive ICTs. By exploring locally creative and innovative approaches to the use of interactive ICTs in everyday life, as well as its implications for community change, we can reconsider where more research is needed on practices relating to ICT use. Innovatory use of ICTs can describe a variety of practices, including new applications of technologies, new practices (such as the production of content), changing the creative design or technology content itself (such as the 'look', or the software), and new patterns of use (Haddon, 2005). Technology users can be seen as innovators in this process, challenging ideas of technological determinism as it becomes obvious that technologies do not just produce impacts, but that technology users are actively involved in outcomes of use (regardless of whether this leads to intended or unintended consequences) (Haddon, 2005). This paper also aims to demonstrate the importance of the collective dimension of user innovation, rather than individual creativity alone. That is, both members of the community and the organization can be seen as creative innovators of how the technology is used, since a complex network of people are involved in radio production, dissemination, and telecentre management, while many others are active and participating listeners or telecentre users. By exploring the case of Radio Viva as an example of local creativity and innovation, we will see how new forms of visibility are created, how new contacts are established in communities, and how local learning, knowledge

sharing and community mobilization can occur. More specifically, it will be seen how new media technologies complement traditional media technologies in creating multiple communication channels that widen the scope for civic dialogue in Paraguayan communities, from community citizens to other nations (due to migration patterns). The interactivity of ICTs opens up both virtual and physical spaces for community participation, while simultaneously raising awareness for other services of the organization. Last, production of content leads to locally relevant knowledge dissemination in communities, with the effect that technology 'users' can also become 'producers' of knowledge.

It is well documented that civil society strongly depends on the freedom of access to information and engagement in inclusive communication and debate in the public arena (Deane et al., 2004). However, in processes for democratic change, Deane and colleagues (2004) describe how people in developing countries are making their voices heard through "the other information revolution", one that actually involves more 'traditional' technologies than new ones. This is in comparison to developed countries that concentrate more heavily on access to new ICTs such as computers and the internet (2004: 66). He explains: "Over the last decade, and the last five years in particular, the media in most developing countries have undergone a revolution in their structure, dynamism, interactivity, reach and accessibility. This has had a profound impact on and for civil society in these countries, and very mixed implications for the inclusiveness and character of public debate, particularly in relation to the exposure of public and political debate to the voices, concerns and perspectives of the poor and marginalized in theses societies." (2004: 67).

Similarly, Scheufele and Nisbet (2002) claim that "traditional mass media maintain a key role in promoting democratic citizenship", while the role of the internet in promoting citizen participation is more limited (2002: 55). Moreover, in the same empirical study the researchers found that "respondents who used the Web frequently for entertainment purposes were less likely to feel efficacious about their potential role in the democratic process and also knew less about facts relevant to current events" (Scheufele & Nisbet, 2002: 55). Similarly, other research contends that the internet plays a complementary role to traditional media in fostering civic dialogue and political debate, which in turn fosters civic participation (Shah et al., 2005). These findings accurately describe the case of Radio Viva, where communication media rely heavily on radio and telephone use, and to a lesser extent on mobile phones and the internet, in ways that are mutually interactive and increasingly complex. In many ways, the radio can be seen as the 'hub' of this infrastructure, inviting commentary from the community using various media. That is, people contact the radio directly via telephone, mobile phone, or the internet (in turn, allowing for communication through VOIP applications such as Skype, chat, email, or blogs, for example). Most interesting is one radio programmer's assertion that "the more communication media available, the more people will speak up… will *say* something!" This points to two observations; first, that media variety, or communication choices available to citizens is significant in promoting participation, and second, it reiterates that not all ICTs are used in the same way, or for the same purposes. A manager of Radio Viva further explains:

"In order to enlarge the information's access and diminish the social breaches, it is important to open multiples entrance points [sic]. In other words, if the objective is good, almost anything could be used as [a] mean[s]. On the other hand, acting in a human network context is indispensable. Every member has information to share with the others, and the exchange is enriches to all us [sic]." (Bregaglio, 2003, n.p.).

The ICTs used by Radio Viva can therefore be seen as a complex infrastructure for the sharing of information and knowledge that changes and adapts as new technology applications become available, and according to local needs.

Radio Viva has always aimed to encourage civic dialogue, their slogan being "*la voz de la gente*", or, 'the voice of the people'. Community engagement and debate is most active on the radio waves, which encourages commentary from anyone, regarding any issue. The radio was consistently described as a useful tool for the promotion of the diversity and plurality of people, opinions and identity. One young radio programmer claimed, "Diversity is a pretext to working together", while another asserted, "We want to include, rather than exclude". Yet another radio producer explained, what is special about radio is "*la libertad que hay por expresarse*", or the freedom for self-expression. Radio Viva always gives high priority to anyone who contacts the radio, many of whom phone directly to the radio production studio to one of the three fixed 'public caller' telephone numbers, or via email, chat or Skype (particularly if calling from abroad). Without fail, a caller is able to go on air immediately. The music is faded out and the issue – regardless of the subject – is discussed, encouraging other listeners to voice their opinions. Email is either read aloud or condensed for listeners (often depending on the writer's preference). While many people call in with comments about community issues, others use it as a way to send out greetings to friends or family members (such as birthday wishes), or to make announcements (such as an upcoming wedding). Still others use the radio to resolve more personal issues, such as to announce a missing child or to ask about a local market for one's goods. It is clear why one respondent described the radio as an "anchor for communication".

Of particular interest is Radio Viva's scope for encouraging community dialogue, not just within the communities of Trinidad, or even Asunción, but spanning other countries. Immigration patterns are slowly changing the shape and location of communities, so radio combined with a community technology such as the internet plays a key role in helping families and communities to maintain ties to one another (Girard, 2003). This is reflected in one of the newest additions to Radio Viva's programming: a weekly program dedicated to Paraguayan migrants living in Argentina, Spain and the United States, a program designed to serve the high number of Paraguayan nationals who have immigrated to other countries. Many of these immigrants are women (both documented and undocumented) who often take on domestic work or care for elderly citizens. This leads to what is being referred to as the 'feminization of migration', where many migrant women have families of their own in Paraguay whom they support through remittances. The main issue, according to the organization director, is that this type of migration is "breaking up families". Radio Viva plays a key role in making bridges between the local and global, allowing listeners in Paraguay and abroad to listen and participate about immigration issues in real-time. This global listenership (and subsequent ability to participate in radio conversations) has enormous implications for migrant populations to maintain links to their own communities, and to share knowledge and expertise about local development issues, given that there are approximately 75 million migrant workers and dependents in the world (Girard, 2003). It is clear that the use of integrated ICTs within migrant communities is an area deserving of more research.

Radio Viva also strives to provide a reliable source for national and local news and information for community members. It must be noted that the ability to produce quality investigative journalism, however, is not easy (or common). With respect to Latin American journalism, Deane and colleagues (2004) describe how:

"The achievements of watchdog journalism in holding authorities accountable [...] are only one side of the reality of the press in the region. Most reporting is superficial, timid and formulaic.

Working conditions in most newsrooms are not conducive to hard-hitting, high-quality reporting. With a few exceptions, reporters are notoriously underpaid and have scarce resources to produce stories. Unwritten rules about subjects and sources limit what is news." (2004: 97).

The point here is to emphasize the difficulty of producing high quality news that can effectively challenge authorities, and to underline the importance of the production of in-depth, objective journalism. Together with the Jaku'éke news agency, Radio Viva undertakes general news collection and also special coverage of events across Paraguay. Subject matters are related to the main interests of listeners, often focusing on social and political processes in the region. Using any one of the five radio vans, audio information can be broadcast live on the spot (and then streamed online). Audio information can also be digitized using recorders to be saved and edited for later use. News collected covers global information (having recently published information about US President Obama's policies, for example); and national, regional and local information (such as renegotiations concerning the planned hydroelectric plant to be built in Paraguay). News is disseminated via a variety of media channels, the most important being the radio since it reaches the largest audience – both within Asunción and surrounding areas, and across the world through online streaming. Recently, Radio Viva has added a feature capable of sending a news feed directly to individual cell phones to which users can subscribe via the website (using WAP functionality). The website provides updated news information in the form of a blog, as well as archived audiovisual materials.

As part of their goal to provide educational material, selected radio programming is prepared in advance, covering topics from health to environmental information. These may take the entire space of a radio program, or in the form of 'micro-programs' that run 25 seconds to one minute long. The objective is to provide a short story about a relevant community issue, with the purpose to inform, but which is also open to sparking debate. Interestingly, one radio content producer claimed how "there is always someone who speaks up". One set of micro-programs, for example, covered an insect plague that destroyed 22 hectares of soy in 2006, describing the most effective chemical solutions that could be used as pesticides. Another set of programs covered sexually transmitted diseases, and still others have focused on tuberculosis and diabetes. Educational programming is supplemented by music played intermittently – and not the other way around – which is chosen by the radio program producer, host, or technician. It is interesting to note that one of Radio Viva's future aspirations (at the time of interviewing) was to hire someone professionally to choose appropriate music, in order to compete for listenership with popular commercial radio stations.

Community radio closely engages with communities, where citizens are encouraged to voice opinions on any issue. Issues are brought to the forefront, discussed, and consequently resolved in some way. ICTs play an important role to "help establish new alliances and to engage in decentralized, collaborative efforts. These uses of ICTs can create conditions that facilitate public advocacy and government accountability" (Gómez & Martínez, 2001: 12). Radio Viva, like many civil organizations, takes action and follow-up with authorities on the issues raised. This type of mediation may take place through everyday press coverage, such as in 2006 when Radio Viva journalists aired information about city plans to turn approximately five hectares of the botanical gardens into a garbage disposal area. A group of approximately 500 local citizens gathered at the entrance of the gardens to protest, and Radio Viva aired the event live on the radio, interviewing many protesters. Local authorities subsequently cancelled the rezoning plans and the area of land in question finally remained a part of the botanical gardens. Public reactions and Radio

Viva's press coverage of the event were named as key factors to the city's eventual decision to retract plans. Additionally, Radio Viva runs a radio program called "Radio Neighbourhood Forums" in which they bring together community leaders, community members and local authorities in a dialogue transmitted directly from the radio studio. Listeners call in to express their opinions and points of view about community problems and possible solutions. Radio Viva thereby plays an informal intermediary role between authorities and the community, and represents a key part of the process to greater democratization and minimization of equalities through communication.

At Radio Viva, the radio as a medium plays an important role in communicating information about the organization's other services, including social events, training workshops, and particularly in highlighting telecentre services. Although it is difficult to measure the extent to which radio publicity may bring new visitors to a community development initiative, it clearly raises awareness for the project, an important precursor to participation and social change. As part of this process, telecentres need to be accepted as legitimate public spaces in order to be used effectively, without leaving out certain segments of the population. At Radio Viva, telecentres were described as "a different world" compared to the radio. Relatively few people used them, and those who did tended to be youth. Some telecentres drew more users others, and all were slowly becoming increasingly recognized spaces for education and learning. Most challenging was the need for communities to accept the telecentre as part of the community, yet Radio Viva realized that telecentres are necessary to keep communities connected, in a way that is "realistic" for the community so that that telecentres are socially accepted. One young and dynamic telecentre leader in Mbayué de Limpio explained how some parents of local youth mistrusted the new telecentre in the community, believing it was an inappropriate space for their children to spend time or money. The need was therefore expressed to promote the telecentre to this older generation of community members who seemed to lack an understanding of the usefulness of the telecentre and its services. This is interesting in light of the fact that local telecentre volunteers (approximately 20 youth in total) commonly agreed that their favourite thing about the telecentre is that it is part of the community, especially because they lacked a 'plaza' (or any public meeting place for that matter) in their neighbourhood. These youth showed visible excitement about having the space to congregate in and make use of, initiating the creation of their own library for example. For them it was a more useful place to go, "instead of hanging around on the street, wasting time, and stuff like that". Social acceptance of telecentres is a common problem in many places around the world (Gómez & Martínez, 2001), and therefore the radio may play a key role in helping to promote a common understanding for telecentres to be accepted as legitimate public spaces.

Knowledge and information, in order to be useful, needs to be locally relevant. Yet the majority of what is available on the internet comes from – and caters to – people in developed countries (Gumucio-Dagrón, 2003). Most information on the World Wide Web is also available only in the English language (Gumucio-Dagrón, 2003), rendering the majority of information as ineffective to Spanish and Guaraní-speaking communities in Asunción, Paraguay. Gumucio-Dagrón therefore claims "the development of local content is the single most important non-negotiable condition for the use of ICTs for social change and material progress in urban or rural communities" (2003: 29). Content development can be described here as "the processing and diffusion of information customized in any suitable format to fit the needs of a specific community" (Roman & Colle, 2003: 86). It must be noted, however, that local content production requires significant human resources (including dedicated individuals), time resources, financial stability of the organization, and strong communication channels between services run by the same development initiative.

Local content production using interactive technologies is currently blurring the distinction between information recipients and knowledge producers (Tacchi, 2006). This is because "new media technologies have the potential to be interactive, rather than one-to-many, and can combine producer and receiver roles rather than separate them. This is particularly interesting in relation to questions of engagement, self-representation and social, political and cultural participation" (Tacchi, 2006, p.3). It also represents a very important shift from imparting information (a fairly isolated property that exists independently of individuals) to knowledge (that which requires "a knowing subject and cannot be conceived of independently from the communication network in which it is both produced and consumed") (Bach & Stark, 2003: 10). Bach and Stark further explain that "This blurring is to some degree a function of digital technologies characteristics: online consumption, for example, blurs with production process by allowing (or forcing) users to engage in an activity formerly relegated to production, such as data entry, or by producing information in the act of consuming that is then sold for profit" (2003, p.10). Information brokers may help to maintain the gap between producers and consumers in an information society, but organizations in a 'knowledge society' function as facilitators between users and producers – emphasizing communication rather than information. That is why the social effect of this amalgamation of roles ultimately depends on how the organization approaches the situation (Bach & Stark, 2003).

Radio Viva actively supports the production of local content through a variety of means using interactive ICTs. First, each telecentre has a local correspondent who contacts the radio station as significant news arises. Each telecentre has a fixed telephone line to call directly to the head radio station, so that correspondents – or any community member – can call Radio Viva. Second, a monthly rotating radio program focuses on each telecentre consecutively. The local community can therefore broadcast its own content, including live and pre-programmed material that is broadcast live via the mobile radio units that visit each telecentre. Most significant is the fact that Radio Viva has helped each telecentre to install its own radio production space, where anyone from the community can create content. In most cases this consists of a small, soundproofed room with at least one computer with an internet connection. Audio can be recorded straight to the computer via a microphone, and saved as a digital file. At least two of the telecentres had their own working radio antennas in the past in order to broadcast directly from the community, but the National Commission of Telecommunications declared this illegal so the antennas have not been used since. Content production, however, is a time-consuming effort, so Radio Viva makes a point of encouraging local youth to become involved. Often the progression to involvement in telecentre activities begins with chatting online with friends, which was found to spark interest in other subjects found online (from sports to schoolwork topics). For some individuals, this lead to further interest in volunteering to monitor the telecentre or to create radio content about topics of personal interest or for specific pockets within their communities. This is important, since community development and social change is "not a matter of just learning to use computers or digital technology. It is a matter of learning to take advantage of the information and that these tools can help access, produce, or process, and of making the work of solving real problems and improving the quality of life more effective" (Gómez and Martínez, 2001:.8). Last, local content is produced at Radio Viva through the transmission of a radio show called "Open Studies" (or '*Estudios Abiertos*'), of which they produce approximately 36 studies annually. Here, the radio picks a place in the community where the telecentre is based, and airs a live discussion about a relevant local topic from one of the mobile radio vans. Direct community participation is encouraged from local citizens. Community members can therefore become directly involved

in ongoing conversations that identify ongoing issues in the community. Content production teams in telecentres can therefore help to retrieve relevant information, and broadcast it live on air and online, vastly widening the audience who has access to the information. It also reinforces the fact that traditional media like the radio still maintains a key role in affecting the type of information that people receive and how they help to transform our world.

Digitization of content allows for easier sharing, redistribution, storage and retrieval of content. This means that popular radio shows can be found online after they have aired, making content much more widely accessible, and can change how information is accessed. An excellent example in content sharing concerns the involvement of Radio Viva in a local project to share content with other stations for the citizens of Asunción and global listeners. In 2006, a number of local radio stations (both commercial and community-oriented) each simultaneously broadcast informational programs via the radio and over the telephone through a call-in number. The purpose was to share simple, more practical treatments for dengue fever than what the Paraguayan Ministry of Health was providing. These alternatives were based on health information drawn from health specialists at the World Health Organization and the Pan-American Health Organization, while a Spanish doctor was on air to encourage people on an international scale to phone in with any questions.

FUTURE TRENDS

Clearly, more research is required to more fully understand the effects of applying interactive ICTs in community development projects. In many cases, we have seen that ICTs can help to encourage civic dialogue and the creation of local content, resulting in the opening up public (and virtual) spaces for people to meet. This provides great potential for decreasing the margin between those who can access locally relevant information and knowledge; and communicate their rights, interests and opinions. In the meantime, it is important to recognize and understand the barriers to the use of ICTs, and telecentres too. We need to comprehend why one citizen may eagerly encourage a family member to attend a telecentre (where they will spend money and time), while another of similar background may not trust the space as a place in the community. Similarly, we need to explore community radio's potential for interactivity with other ICTs (other than the internet) in helping people to get their voices heard. This is imperative for the movement towards democratic communities where civil rights are upheld and local inequalities are diminished. On a higher level, we need to look at the potential barriers to interactive ICTs: are there potential barriers related to social, political, economic or cultural issues? Where can lessons be drawn in order to help other initiatives improve their services in meeting community needs? Last, the role of networks is a theme that was not fully explored here, and deserves greater study. If people in a community can communicate in a functional network of communication technologies, in a sustainable way, we will be better able to see how a 'communicative ecology' is a useful community development tool. Indeed, this is a concept that deserves further analysis in relation to ICT for development initiatives.

The interactivity of ICTs, particularly with radio, influences how communities communicate not just on a local scale, but also on a global scale, changing the way people think, interact and share knowledge within communities, often spanning nations. Changing migration patterns will keep influencing this process. A better understanding is key to how community media and 'interactive broadcasting' is leading to new local and global communication patterns. This is also highly relevant with respect to telecentres, since they provide accessible, in-person contact in communities that are increasingly globalized. Moreover, thousands of telecentres exist across the world. If they are drawn together through more concrete networking processes, they can be places where people can keep in touch – say migrant families – via video-conferencing tools for example. In looking at how telecentres can interact with more traditional media like radio and telephony, it is clear there remains enormous potential for new, interactive tools to strengthen personal and democratic ties between people and civic organizations. The telecentre movement itself represents enormous potential for new communicative media and channels.

CONCLUSION

Although they are often seen as a panacea for development, ICTs cannot replace the development priorities of any community. Rather, they are tools that can be used to achieve a group or individual's goals, stemming from the need to share knowledge and information, and to make more informed choices about ideas and activities. Using interactive technologies is no guarantee of a positive outcome, but if used in ways that *can* contribute to local development, they can be a highly useful – and indeed critical – way to promote democratic community dialogue. From the case study presented here, we can see that Radio Viva is ultimately focused on strengthening neighbourhoods, enabling people to have a say about the decisions and issues that affect their lives, ultimately improving their living standards. Moreover, as Radio Viva is growing and expanding, it continues to find ways to innovatively bridge the radio and telecentre services it supports, to communicate effectively and efficiently in ways that support local social development. Traditional media combined with new media, via telecentres and with the support of a strong civil organization, opens up an incredible number of opportunities for access to locally relevant information and communication channels leading to the sharing – and eventual follow-up – of personal and community issues. Additionally, the strength and importance of community radio, as an appropriate technology, and as one of the most effective mass media available, must not be ignored. This is what the potential for interactive ICTs (including the public spaces offered by telecentres) can offer. Development dialogues about ICTs should focus less on the application of ICTs as transformative technologies that can diminish digital inequalities, and more on the innovative social uses of these technologies to communicate about how to achieve local change. More focus should be placed on the need to endorse the creation of a communication environment that can easily adapt to local community's needs in terms of accessibility, proving locally relevant information, and encouragement of dialogue.

REFERENCES

Acharya, M. (2007). Serving tool for the farming communities. *Information for Development*, 5(4), 10–12.

Anonymous,. (2007). Developing Countries Farm Radio Network. *Information for Development*, 5(4), 13–14.

Bach, J., & Stark, D. (2003). *Technology and transformation: Facilitating knowledge networks in Eastern Europe. Technology, Business and Society Programme Paper Number 10*. Geneva: UNRSID.

Benjamin, P., & Dahms, M. (1999). Socialise the modem of production: The role of telecentres in development. In Gómez, R., & Hunt, P. (Eds.), *Telecentre Evaluation: A global perspective* (pp. 49–67). Ottawa: International Development Research Centre.

Bijker, W. E., Hughes, T. P., & Pinch, T. (1987). *The social construction of technological systems*. Cambridge, MA: MIT Press.

Bregaglio, A. (2003, September 25). *Info Express.* Retrieved January 10, 2009 from http://www.iconnect-online.org/Stories/Story.import5130

Buckley, S. (2000). Radio's new horizons: Democracy and popular communication in the digital age. *International Journal of Cultural Studies*, 3(2), 180–187. doi:10.1177/136787790000300206

Chataway, J., & Wield, D. (2000). Industrialization, Innovation and Development: What does knowledge management change? *Journal of International Development*, 12, 803–824. doi:10.1002/1099-1328(200008)12:6<803::AID-JID714>3.0.CO;2-H

Creech, H. (2006). *Evaluation of UNESCO's Community Multimedia Centres: Final report.* Winnipeg: IISD.

Deane, J., Dixit, K., Mue, N., Banda, F., & Waisbord, S. (2004). The Other Information Revolution: Media and empowerment in developing countries. In Osiochru, S., & Girard, B. (Eds.), *Communication in the Information Society* (pp. 65–100). Geneva: United Nations Research Institute for Social Development.

Fraser, C., & Restrepo-Estrada, S. (2002). Community Radio for Change and Development. *Development*, 45(4), 69–73. doi:10.1057/palgrave.development.1110408

Girard, B. (2003). Radio and the Internet: Mixing media to bridge the divide. In Girard, B. (Ed.), *The One to Watch: Radio, new ICTs and interactivity* (pp. 2–20). Rome: FAO.

Gómez, R., Hunt, P., & Lamoureux, E. (1999). Telecentre Evaluation and Research: A global perspective. In Gómez, R., & Hunt, P. (Eds.), *Telecentre Evaluation: A global perspective* (pp. 15–29). Ottawa: International Development Research Centre.

Gómez, R., & Martínez, J. (2001). *The Internet... Why? And what for? Thoughts on information and communication technologies for development in Latin America and the Caribbean.* San José, Costa Rica: International Development Research Centre and Fundación Acceso.

González, R. (n.d). *The need for Local Content. Paris: UNESCO Communication and Information Portal.* Retrieved April 14, 2007, from http://portal. unesco.org/ci/en/ev.php-URL_ID=5463&URL_ DO=DO_TOPIC&URL_SECTION=201.html

Gumucio-Dagrón, A. (2001). *Making Waves: Stories of Participatory Communication for Social Change.* New York: Rockefeller Foundation.

Gumucio-Dagrón, A. (2003). Take Five: A handful of essentials for ICTs in development. In Girard, B. (Ed.), *The One to Watch: Radio, new ICTs and interactivity* (pp. 21–38). Rome: FAO.

Gurstein, M. (2003). Effective Use: A community informatics strategy beyond the digital divide. *First Monday, 8*(12). Retrieved February 3, 2009, from http://firstmonday.org/htbin/cgiwrap/bin/ ojs/ index.php/fm/article/viewArticle/1107/1027

Haddon, L. (2005). Introduction. In Haddon, L. (Ed.), *Everyday Innovators* (pp. 1–16). Dordrecht: Springer. doi:10.1007/1-4020-3872-0_1

Heeks, R. (1999). *Information and Communication Technologies, Poverty and Development. Development Informatics: Working Papers, Institute for Development Policy and Management, University of Manchester.* Retrieved December 12, 2008, from http://www.sed.manchester.ac.uk/i dpm/research/publications/wp/di/

James, J. (2004). *Information Technology and Development: A new paradigm for delivering the Internet to rural areas in developing countries.* London: Routledge. doi:10.4324/9780203325506

Lamoureux, E. (1999). RadioNet: Community Radio, Telecentres and Local Development. In R. Gómez, R. & P. Hunt (Eds.), *Telecentre Evaluation: A Global Perspective* (pp. 195-202). Ottawa: International Development Research Centre.

MacKenzie, D., & Wajcman, J. (1985/2002). Introductory essay: The social shaping of technology. In MacKenzie, D., & Wajcman, J. (Eds.), *The social shaping of technology* (pp. 3–27). Buckingham: Open University Press.

Nnadi, N., & Gurstein, M. (2007). Towards Supporting Community Information Seeking and Use. *Journal of Community Informatics, 3*(1). Retrieved January 25, 2009, from http://ci-journal. net/index.php/ciej/article /viewDownloadInterstitial/325/325.

Padania, S., & Silvani, F. (2005). Local radio in the Information Society: Technology, participation and content in Africa. In Warnock, K., & Wickremasinghe, R. (Eds.), *Information and Communication Technologies and large-scale poverty reduction: Lessons from Asia, Africa, Latin America and the Caribbean* (pp. 33–36). London: Panos.

Parkinson, S. (2005). *Telecentres, Access and Development: Experience and lessons from Uganda and South Africa.* Ottawa: International Development Research Centre.

Priestman, C. (2004). Narrowcasting and the dream of radio's great global conversation. *The Radio Journal: International Studies in Broadcast and Audio Media, 2*(2), 77–88. doi:10.1386/ rajo.2.2.77/1

Pringle, I., & David, M. J. R. (2003). Using radio to make the internet visible. In Girard, B. (Ed.), *The One to Watch: Radio, new ICTs and interactivity* (pp. 2–20). Rome: FAO.

Proenza, F. (2001). *Telecentre Sustainability: Myths and opportunities*. Rome: FAO. Retrieved April 11, 2007, from http://www.t-forum.org/staat_privat /dokumente/myths.pdf

Roman, R., & Colle, R. D. (2003). Content creation for ICT development projects: Integrating normative approaches and community demand. *Information Technology for Development*, *10*, 85–94. doi:10.1002/itdj.1590100204

Saravia, M. (2003). Ideas para Repensar la Conectividad en Áreas Rurales [Ideas to Rethink Connectivity in Rural Areas]. *Otro Lado de la Brecha: Perspectivas Latinoamericanas y del Caribe ante la CMSI* (pp. 29-33). Caracas, RedISTIC.

Scheufele, D. A., & Nisbet, M. C. (2002). Being a citizen online: New opportunities and dead ends. *The Harvard International Journal of Press/Politics*, *7*(3), 55–75.

Sein, M. K., & Harindranath, G. (2004). Conceptualizing the ICT Artifact: Toward Understanding the Role of ICT in National Development. *The Information Society*, *20*(1), 15–24. doi:10.1080/01972240490269942

Shah, D. V., Cho, J., Eveland, W. P., & Kwak, N. (2005). Information expression in a digital age: Modeling internet effects on civic participation. *Communication Research*, *32*(5), 531–565. doi:10.1177/0093650205279209

Tacchi, J. (2006) New Forms of Community Access. In *UNESCO IPDC/IFAP Joint Thematic debate: Giving Voice to Local Communities: From community radio to blogs. Paris: UNESCO*. Retrieved February 3, 2009, from http://eprints.qut.edu.au/archive/ 00003860/02/3860.pdf.

Tacchi, J., Slater, D., & Lewis, P. (2003, May*). Evaluating Community Based Media Initiatives: An ethnographic action research approach*. Paper presented at OUR Media III conference, Baranquilla, Colombia. Retrieved February 21, 2007, from http://pcmlp.socleg.ox.ac.uk/it 4d/thinkpieces/tacchi.pdf.

Tuomi, I. (2005). Beyond User-Centric Models of Product Creation. In Haddon, L. (Ed.), *Everyday Innovators* (pp. 21–38). Dordrecht: Springer. doi:10.1007/1-4020-3872-0_2

Wortley, D. J. (2004). Interactive Broadcasting and Community Informatics. In Khalid, H. M., Helander, M. G., & Yeo, A. W. (Eds.), *Work with Computing Systems* (pp. 259–260). Kuala Lumpur: Damai Sciences.

Zulberti, E. (2003). Foreword. In Girard, B. (Ed.), *The One to Watch: Radio, new ICTs and interactivity* (pp. iii–iv). Rome: FAO.

Section 4
Managing ICT4D

Chapter 12
Donor Project Funded ICT Initiatives in the Vocational and Technical Education (VTE) Sector of Asian Developing Countries:
A Systems Approach to Managing Project Intervention Processes

Channa Wimal Gunawardena
Lancaster University, UK

David H. Brown
Lancaster University, UK

ABSTRACT

This chapter is set against a background of national ICT initiatives implemented in the Vocational and Technical Education (VTE) sectors of developing Asian countries through donor agency funded projects. This research is based on a ten year research study of ICT initiatives implemented in nine VTE sector donor funded projects covering Laos, Sri Lanka and Vietnam. The empirical data was gathered through contextual observations, action research and a review of project documentation. The ICT initiatives studied focussed on MIS (management information systems) aiding strategy formulation and management in the VTE sector and computer based training (CBT). The research reveals that the projects studied were designed by host governments and donor agencies in response to perceived problems in the VTE sector. The research also reveals that process of managing donor projects, which is largely based on hard approaches, is problematic. Soft Systems Methodology (SSM) is based on a learning and enquiring cycle. The research uses SSM to learn about the nature and scope of the selected donor projects in VTE, which can be conceptualised as Project Intervention Processes (PIPs).

DOI: 10.4018/978-1-61520-997-2.ch012

INTRODUCTION

This chapter aims to contribute to the gap in theory and practice by investigating the management issues of ICT initiatives implemented through donor funded projects in the VTE sector of selected Asian developing economies. The countries studied in the research are Vietnam, Laos and Sri Lanka. At the outset, the broad research goal was:

Using a soft systems approach to explore strategy and management issues of project based ICT initiatives in the VTE sector of particular South and South East Asian Developing Economies with a view to help establish good practice and contribute to the literature.

This broad research goal will be addressed through the following research sub-questions:

1.   What is the nature and scope of donor funded projects with ICT initiatives in the VTE sector of developing Asian countries studied?
2.   How can SSM contribute to the managing of donor funded projects with ICT initiatives in the VTE sector of Asian developing countries?
3.   What are the generic lessons from the application of SSM to project based ICT initiatives in the VTE sector which help inform donor project management practice and theory?

The research studied nine projects, three each in Laos, Sri Lanka and Vietnam. Each project was initiated by a sponsor domain (donor agency) for a host domain (Government. Access to these VTE donor funded projects was made possible through the authors' positioning as a formal project team member in the projects studied. Each project studied targeted a multi-organisational VTE sector spanning central government institutions, provincial government institutions and VTE schools. Each project had a number of ICT initiatives, each of which could be seen a sub-intervention. Each of these ICT initiatives had a number of 'Activities'

with 'Expectations' in terms of a 'Response' from the VTE sector actors and a set of 'Outcomes'.

The observations from the research revealed that the process of managing projects was problematic and that projects were not being managed appropriately to generate desirable outcomes from the ICT initiatives to improve perceived VTE problems. This research contributes to the theory of project management by applying SSM as an approach to the management of donor based ICT projects in developing countries.

The presentation and interpretation of this research is structured into five major parts. Firstly the current state of the area of concern, VTE in Asian developing countries, is reviewed in terms of the nature of VTE, emerging issues and ICT initiatives in VTE. These provide the contextual setting for the implementation of IS initiatives through donor projects. The second part of the paper positions the research theoretically. In addition to the central concern of donor project management the research framework explicitly considers the use of SSM in managing donor project based ICT initiatives as it provides an intellectual device for learning and enquiry. Part three details the research approach and the empirical design. Part four presents the research outcomes and the interpretation of these. Finally, part 5 provides conclusions to the research.

VTE TRENDS IN ASIAN DEVELOPING COUNTRIES

VTE Nature and Emerging Issues

In the context of Asian developing economies, the vocational and technical education (VTE) sector plays a pivotal role in meeting the human resource requirements of national economic development (ILO, 2002). The broad aim of VTE is to equip work-forces, in particular school leavers, for job opportunities across a range of 'labour markets' brought about by industry needs (Middleton *et al* 1993). VTE comprises 'vocational training' and 'technical education'. Vocational training broadly focuses on the preparation of 'practical work skills' and competencies to be used for the development of skilled and semi-skilled workers. On the other hand technical education focuses on 'technical skills' which are required by technicians (ILO, 2008).

Since the late 1990s many Asian developing countries have critical skills gaps in their labour markets (ADB, 1999b). In many instances the need for skilled workers has not been met and industry has lagged behind as a consequence. Studies indicate tremendous pressure on the VTE sectors to increase the number of people who receive employable skills. Examples can be drawn from studies conducted by the Asian Development Bank (ADB) in Laos (ADB, 1996), Sri Lanka (ADB, 1999a) and Vietnam (ADB, 1998). These conclude that the VTE sectors are: (i) supply driven and not market driven; (ii) without labour and education management information systems (LMIS and EMIS respectively); (iii) have little or no program or institutional accreditation, or skill standards and testing certification (SSTC) mechanism; (iv) faced with poorly trained instructors and educational managers; and (v) have VTE infrastructure, capital resources, learning materials and instructors' guides i.e. teaching and learning resources (TLRs) which are generally out-dated, and not related to the emerging needs of local and national–level employer expectations.

ICT Initiatives in VTE

Faced with perceived problem situations outlined above, many Asian developing countries have embarked on national initiatives to modernise their VTE systems to meet industry needs. These initiatives have been designed and funded by donor agencies such as the Asian Development Bank (ADB), European Commission (EC) and the World Bank and been implemented through projects. These projects have provided the main technical and financial impetus for modernising

the VTE sectors in Asian developing countries including the introduction of ICT. These projects are implemented by a multi-organisational 'host' domain involving Education and Training Ministries, VTE agencies, Industrial sector Ministries, Provincial bodies, VTE Schools and private sector organisations. The projects range in timescale from between six months to six years and are major imperatives due to their financial scale, with projects sometimes over 100 million US dollars in size. At the time of starting this research in 1998, the usage of ICT in VTE sector of developing Asian countries was limited and most it was fragmented. However, ICT initiatives have been important components of these donor funded projects. Typically these initiatives included Labour Market Information Systems (LMIS), Education Management Information Systems (EMIS), Financial Management Information Systems (FMIS) and Benefit Monitoring and Evaluation (BME) systems.

In terms of ICT initiatives in VTE of developing countries there is a body of literature dealing with specific IS initiatives such as LMIS (dealt with by authors such as Sparreboom, 2001; ILO, 2002; Hopkins, 1999) and computer based training (dealt with by authors such as Ledgerwood and Kernaghan, 1998; Commonwealth of Learning, 2002; World Resource Institute, 2002). However this literature focuses on the objectives and specifications of such ICT initiatives as opposed to managing these ICT initiatives within project based interventions which is the focus of this particular research. The lack of relevant literature has meant that there is only a small body of knowledge to inform the practice of initiating and implementing ICT initiatives through projects in developing countries. The ADB which is the biggest donor agency in the VTE sectors of South and South East Asia has recognised the limited success of implementing ICT initiatives through projects (ADB, 1999b; ADB, 2005). This research paper contributes to the literature gap by investigating the design and implementation of ICT initiatives implemented through projects in the VTE sectors of selected Asian developing economies.

SELECTED LITERATURE REVIEW

Donor Project Management

The vast majority of changes and innovations to VTE are implemented in developing Asian countries through a project based process. Consequently the theory surrounding projects and project management is of significance to this research. Much project management theory is based on a 'hard systems' orientation. The projects involving IS initiatives in the VTE sectors of Asian countries are predominantly 'soft' oriented driven by a messy social context and donor agencies as important stakeholders. An appropriate definition of a 'soft' project as applied to the context of international donor projects is provided as:

...an engagement of limited duration, negotiated amongst people representing varied programme strands in agent [consultant], host and sponsor domains by (Friend, 1998: 2).

According to Crawford and Bryce (2003) key distinguishing features between donor projects and construction/manufacturing projects which are the major focus in the project management body of knowledge (PMBOK) of the Project Management Institute (PMI) include (emphasis added):

- Project goals deal with *social transformation/human development* as opposed to "hard" implementations. Even aid projects with hard components are often a means to achieve some form of developmental end. This makes aid project performance measurement notionally complex

- Aid projects are *inherently political* as they create social, economic and environmental impacts. Thus they have a wide range of

stakeholders with high levels of accountability which requires complex reporting
- The operating environment of aid projects is often *contextualized by issues* which make traditional project management tools and approaches less appropriate. These issues include wide geographic distances between project actors (recipient country, contractors and funding agency), cultural differences between project actors, competing agendas between project stakeholders, challenging operating conditions and unpredictable socio-political environments.

The limited relevance of existing project management theory to the practice of managing complex, social projects has previously been noted such as Morris (1994) and Koskela and Howell (2002). According to Winter (2002) much current project management theory, including the body of knowledge from major institutes such as the global Project Management Institute (PMI) and the UK's Association of Project Management (APM), focus on project activity carried out through a predefined sequence of stages typically defined by a project lifecycle. This in turn would involve application of hard project management techniques and suggests that project management would focus on managing specific 'technical' processes such as engineering, development, training and so on. The use of 'hard' systems approaches are even more pronounced in IS projects which draws heavily upon hard approaches such as the waterfall method, PRINCE, SSADM, critical path analysis and work breakdown structures.

The relevance of traditional project management theory to *managing donor projects* is even more inadequate according to authors such as Morris (1994) and Friend (1998). Donor projects are characterised by a heavy bias towards 'soft' or 'social' development (ADB, 1999b and 2005, World Bank, 1998). They are often even more complex than soft projects implemented in developed countries as they have added stake-holder pressures brought about by international donors and expectations from a multitude of local stakeholders.

Against this background of limitations in traditional project management theory and the complex 'soft' characteristics of donor projects has been the interest to apply soft approaches such as SSM to provide insights into project management. There has been a gradual shift in project management approaches and increasing interest in using 'soft' approaches to deal with:

"...soft, poorly structured problem situations, especially those involving human behavioural factors." (Yeo, 1993: 111).

The 1990s have seen a number of publications in the area of applying SSM to project management such as Yeo (1993) and Neal (1995). However, these studies have largely been driven by theoretical discussions with limited real world empirical data to support the debate. Winter's work (2002) was the first major contribution to the literature, whereby SSM application for managing projects was supported by real world empirical data. Recent arguments for strengthening the application of SSM in project management with empirical data include:

"...we need more empirical work that focuses on, and learns from, the use of SSM in real project situations." (Winter, 2006: 803).

This research addresses this gap in the application of SSM to project management literature, by basing its findings on empirical data from nine real world donor projects.

Soft Systems Methodology (SSM)

Many authors feel that soft systems approaches are better suited for project management specially when dealing with social or people based project

situations (Morris, 1994; Winter, 2002; Checkland and Winter, 2006). According to Winter (2002) the 'soft systems' view of managing projects focuses on the social process of 'managing' in complex situations and trying to cope with an ever-changing flux of messy situations and complex issues. In these messy project situations, the aims and objectives are generally the main problem as opposed to how to achieve them. Here SSM has gained credibility amongst project management theorists due to its emphasis on 'learning' what needs to be done rather than trying to solve a particular problem (Morris, 2002; Winter, 2006). SSM is particularly well suited to messy project situations with its emphasis on problem situations rather than well defined problems, different worldviews, models as devices for learning rather than prediction and consciously organized inquiry.

Soft Systems Methodology (SSM) is particularly well suited to messy project situations with its emphasis on problem situations rather than well defined problems, different worldviews, models as devices for learning rather than prediction and consciously organised inquiry. Theories based on a hard or functionalist stance, such as many traditional project management approaches, view the world as systemic, which can be engineered. According to Checkland and Scholes the key theoretical difference between hard and soft thinking is the shift in systemicity. According to Checkland (1986: 24) SSM differs from hard systems thinking by 'shifting systemicity' from the world to a process of thinking about the world. It is this basic distinction that often results in the misinterpretation of SSM in the secondary literature emerging from outside the work of Lancaster University. A more detailed distinction between hard and soft systems thinking is provided by Holwell (1997: 126) who presents 8 different ways to distinguish 'hard' and 'soft' systems.

The differences between hard and soft systems thinking has major implications for studying the area of concern. Firstly, as discussed earlier, the problems facing VTE sectors in developing countries are decidedly soft as they are unstructured in nature and are characterised by activities with uncertain decision making and poorly defined measures of performance. Secondly there are major implications for addressing sectoral issues in VTE through ICT, which in developing Asian countries is typically done through donor funded projects. The desirable aims and objectives of such projects are difficult to define, however they are designed and implemented using traditional project management approaches which are hard in nature.

SSM emerged in the 1970s from an action research programme of Lancaster University driven by Peter Checkland and Brian Wilson. Their approaches to SSM are however assumed by many in the secondary literature to be part of the same body of SSM work. However, a critical review of the SSM accounts by Checkland and Wilson paints a different picture. Wilson's approach (Wilson, 2001) to SSM differs to Checkland's current approach (Checkland and Scholes, 2005) in a number of ways. Firstly the use of SSM as a learning cycle is less explicit in Wilson's approach. Secondly Wilson's focus of SSM is particularly targeted at real world problem situations within an organisation or unit. Wilson focuses on the logical aspects of organisations, which can be expressed in a primary task model, and his conceptualisation of organisations is in terms of a collection of resources organised to achieve a particular purpose. Checkland on the other hand views the real world as a complexity of relationships with organisations being viewed as an abstraction of relationship managing. Thirdly Wilson's problem solving approach focuses on the logic based stream of analysis of SSM and to thus establish a logic based process to using SSM. The reasoning behinds Wilson's approach is purportedly to facilitate the use of SSM by organisational analysts, with limited prior knowledge of SSM, leading to logical derivation of relevant models which can be used to compare with the real world and achieve a solution in terms of an

accommodation of views. This focus of SSM on the logic based stream of analysis would laudably enable the analyst to internalise SSM in terms of logic based systems thinking (Wilson, 2001: xvii) much more rapidly. Checkland's problem solving approach focuses on a learning process involving both a cultural stream of analysis and a logical stream of analysis leading to debate about change.

Checkland's view of the real world makes his form of SSM far more applicable to a problem situation arising out of a process (i.e. a project intervention process such as a donor funded project) which affects a number of organisations and stakeholders each with different purposes or objectives, such as those organisations and stakeholders affected by a VTE project intervention with ICT initiatives. Having reviewed a wide range of literature on SSM, the enquiry/learning cycle behind SSM as per the work of Checkland and Scholes (2005) was applied to interpreting the research findings in terms of understanding the 'problem situation' surrounding donor project based ICT initiatives, and inquiring into such a situation. According to Checkland and Scholes (2005: 7) the current version of SSM is a 'four activities model' consisting of the following activities:

1. Finding out about a problem situation, including culturally/politically;

2. Formulating some relevant purposeful activity models;

3. Debating the situation, using the models, seeking from that debate both

   ◦ changes which would improve the situation and are regarded as both desirable and (culturally) feasible, and

   ◦ the accommodations between conflicting interests which will enable action-to-improve to be taken;

4. Taking action in the situation to bring about improvement

These four activities model of SSM were applied to the research as part of the learning and enquiry cycle. As this research focussed on projects, which are process based, as opposed to organisations, which are content based, the form of SSM used in this research was SSMp as per the distinction recently made in the literature by Checkland and Winter (2006). The specific SSM concepts and devices applied to the research and the manner in which they were applied are described further under the Research Approach.

RESEARCH APPROACH

Overall Approach

This research is concerned with investigating management issues of IS initiatives in the VTE sectors of developing Asian countries – an extremely complex social process that unfolds within each country's context. In researching this area of concern, it is acknowledged that formal/rational and subjective/social aspects are important as this would reveal a rich perspective of the situation. The setting for this Chapter was the belief that the research questions must dictate the philosophical underpinnings of the research. Therefore, due to the need to abstract richness and the focus on social aspects, this research is underpinned through a phenomenological philosophy supported through the use of qualitative research methods. The engagement of such an approach is discussed in more detail below.

Checkland's (1985) FMA model of research was adapted and used as the research approach to inform and guide the authors' interventions. The GRM provides an organised intellectual approach to learn about an area of concern (A), using a methodology (M) and Framework of ideas (F). This is shown in Figure 1.

Each research 'intervention' was essentially a case study of a project intervention, with a view to understanding problematic areas and making recommendations for improvement. In using the FMA model, it is essential, as Checkland and Holwell (1998) point out, to declare *in advance of the action*, the elements F, M and A. By doing so the researcher has two hopes: that the declared-in-advance methodology (with the framework of ideas) will provide practical help in the situation; and that experiences of using the methodology will enable new insights and lessons to be learnt. In this research, these elements were:

- the **area of concern A** which was 'ICT initiatives in the VTE sector of developing Asian countries' with a particular focus on Project Intervention Processes as a vehicle for IS implementation
- the **methodology M** which was based on: the learning cycle of SSM as illustrated in Figure 2 and live and retrospective case studies of projects in Laos, Sri Lanka and Vietnam
- the **framework of ideas F** which was the application of concepts embodied in SSM to project management theory, especially the concept of structuring the enquiry process as a learning system, the use of purposeful activity models as devices to structure discussion on managing project processes relevant to ICT initiatives and to propose feasible 'changes' to overcome such issues.

Empirical Design

The main issue in the design of the research was access to project actors and project literature due to the political sensitivity from donor agencies, host governments and consultants. Much of the access was facilitated through a consultancy company involved in development work in Asia, which employed one of the authors. Case studies were used as the main empirical tool and were designed based on the approach of Yin (2003). Nine case studies were identified based on access opportunities, three each in Vietnam, Laos and Sri Lanka. These case studies were on nine real world project intervention processes with IS initiatives undertaken in Vietnam, Laos and Sri Lanka. As part of a longitudinal process the cases involved a combination of retrospective and live studies of real world projects.

The retrospective case studies were on projects that had been completed at the time of undertaking the research. These case studies were developed through semi-structured interviews with key project actors and through access to secondary data in the form of the extensive project documentation. The live case studies were on projects that were ongoing at the time of undertaking the research. These live case studies were developed through the project documentation, interviews with all the project actors and the contextual observations of the author involved as part of the project team.

Each country studied involved one retrospective case study, and two live case studies of projects. The interviews were conducted with key actors in each project from the sponsor domain, host domain and agent (consultant) domain. Each

case study typically involved an interview sample of about 50 actors from the government host domain (including central government, provincial government and VTE schools), between 5 to 20 actors from the agent domain and 1 to 2 actors from the donor domain (ADB or the European Commission). The nine projects studied in this research are listed below for each country.

Vietnam:

- V1, a retrospective study on an ADB funded advisory Technical Assistance (**TA**) project: *"ADB TA 3063: Capacity Building in Vocational and Technical Education"*, implemented from September 1998 to September 1999.
- V2, a live study on an ADB funded **Loan** Project: *"Vocational and Technical Education Loan Project"*, implemented from September 2001 to September 2005.
- V3, a live study on an EC funded advisory Technical Assistance (**TA**) project: *"Project EDIT: strengthening ICT initiatives in VTE through EU Distributed Multimedia and Communications Technologies"*, implemented from December 2002 to May 2004.

Figure 1. Conceptual road map of research (based on organised use of rational thought, Checkland, 1985)

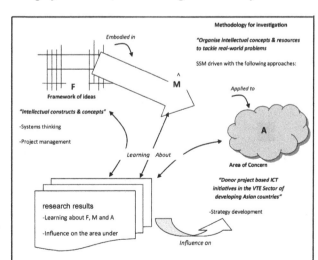

Laos:

- L1, a retrospective study on an ADB funded Project Preparatory Technical Assistance (**PPTA**) project: *"ADB TA 2326: Employment Promotion & Training project"*, implemented from October 1995 to January 1997.
- L2, a live study on an ADB funded advisory Technical Assistance (**TA**) project: *"ADB TA 2925: Capacity Building for Employment Promotion project"*, implemented from May 1998 to February 1999.
- L3, a live study on an EC funded advisory Technical Assistance (**TA**) project: *"Project EQUIT: Education Quality Improvement through Information Technology"*, implemented from March 2002 to May 2004.

Sri Lanka:

- S1, a live study on an ADB funded **Loan** Project: *"Skills development loan project 1707"*, implemented from December 2001 to December 2006.
- S2, a live study on an EC funded advisory Technical Assistance (**TA**) project: *"Project EQUIT: Education Quality Improvement through Information Technology"*, implemented from March 2002 to May 2004.
- S3, a retrospective study on an ADB funded Project Preparatory Technical Assistance (**PPTA**) project: *"Human Resources Investment Project, ADB TA 4090 SRI"*, implemented from September 2003 to March 2004.

Approach to Case Study Analyses and Findings

The approach and logic to the case study analyses and the resulting findings consisted of 4 main steps which can be visualised in Figure 2. These four steps are summarised further below.

Step 1. Finding Out about Each Project

This step dealt with the 'finding out' phase as part SSM to understand the real world problem situation surrounding each project process. Each case study was narrated as part of the 'finding out' process implied by SSM using project documentation and interviews with key project actors. Following the narration SSM based analyses were undertaken to gain insight into the "problem process" using the concepts of Wilson (2001) and Checkland and Scholes (2005). These analyses include:

1. a 'rich picture' based analysis of the 'situation' surrounding each project intervention,
2. an analysis of the 'project intervention process' itself, which is historic, and takes the form of a modified Analysis One,
3. an analysis of the social background of each project studied in the form of an Analysis Two and
4. a political analysis to understand the disposition of power in each project situation in the form of an Analysis Three.

In addition to these four SSM bases analyses, a further analysis framework an 'Intervention Analysis' was developed by the authors to engage in more detailed learning about each project process studied. A major outcome of the 'finding out' step of each project was conceptualising the project as a project intervention process (PIP).

Step 2. Purposeful Activity Models of Each Project (SSMp1)

The second step to the problem structuring of project processes dealt with the development of a relevant purposeful activity model and undertaking a comparison to generate structured debate by the author about the problematical situation surrounding each project intervention studied. For each project a number of issue based models were considered and the one proving to be the most accessible to the project actors was selected. This latter point was crucial to involving the actors in the SSM modelling activities, due to the political and resource dynamics of each project. The emphasis of the project was to meet specific outputs which were reported through quarterly reporting mechanisms. Each member of the project team had a specific Terms of Reference

(TOR) to undertake their relevant activity. The emphasis of each member and the project team as a whole was one of conformance, meeting specific criteria specified in the project design. Thus the type of the model could not be imposed by the researchers due to these real world constraints. The preferred models of the project team were then formulated via Root Definitions (RDs) and

Figure 2. Approach & logic to case study analyses and findings

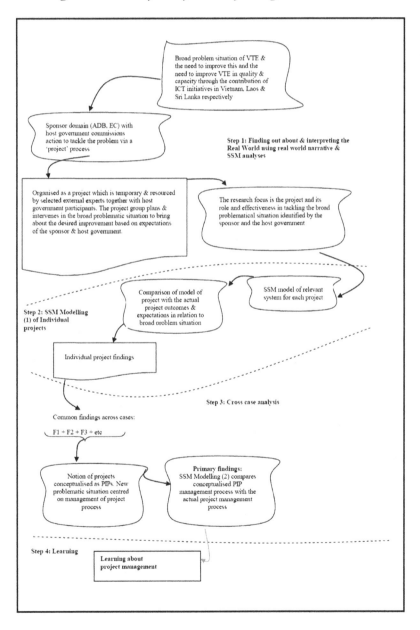

Conceptual Models (CMs) of activities. A debate was then generated by comparing the most relevant model for each project with the actual project activities, expectations and achievements. This led to identifying purposeful action that could be done to improve each project studied.

Step 3. Purposeful Models of Conceptualised Project (SSMp2)

The third step to the problem structuring of project processes dealt with a comparison of findings across cases both within each country and across countries for a generalisation of findings. The cross case analysis concluded that based on a perceived problem in the VTE sector the sponsor (which in the cases studied was either the ADB or the EC), together with the host government, designed and commissioned action to address the perceived problem situation. The action was organised as a set of initiatives in a 'project' which was temporary and staffed by local and international experts and officials from relevant Government agencies to effect the desired changes to VTE. The project was financed by the donor in the form of a Grant or Loan Project. The project team planned and intervened in the problem situation to bring about desired improvements based on the expectations of the sponsor. This action and overall process was conceptualised by the researcher as a "Project Intervention Process" (PIP). The findings revealed that managing this project process was a problematic situation, leading to poorly designed and performing projects. Relevant SSM models (RDs and CMs) were developed of the conceptualised process of managing a project. A debate was then generated by comparing the models of the conceptualised 'process of managing projects' with the actual project managing processes that took place. This debate led to recommendations for managing projects which were politically and socially feasible.

Step 4. Learning

The fourth step of the approach deals with the learning that emerged from the findings which are presented in the findings section. This learning is from both the case findings and cross case findings and focuses on the process of project initiation and managing. This learning emerged as a result of the debate from the cross case findings, comparing the model of the conceptualised project managing process with the actual process that took place.

CASE STUDY EXAMPLE: VIETNAM CASE V1

This section provides an example of one out of the nine case studies developed during the research. This case study provides insights into the nature and issues of a typical donor project studied. This particular case study focussed on a VTE project in Vietnam.

Vietnam: Country Profile of VTE

Vietnam has a population nearly 80 million people and about 80 percent of the people live in rural areas with approximately half the population less than 20 years of age (ADB, 1998). According to the ADB (1998) per capita income in 1997 was 360 US Dollars per year. In an effort to improve its economy, Vietnam adopted a social and economic reform program called *'Doi Moi'*. This promoted a shift from a supply-driven economy to an economy that responds to market demands. The policy was adopted in 1986 and given stronger endorsement in 1991. The country's industrial and service sectors had developed rapidly in the 1990s with average growth rates of 13% and 9% in these sectors respectively and new technologies were being introduced in the agricultural sector (ADB, 1999d).

The economic developments in Vietnam resulting from 'Doi Moi' created demands for skilled workers and technicians, demands that the vocational and technical education (VTE) sector were unable to meet as of 1998. According to studies sponsored by the ADB (ADB, 1999d and ADB, 1998) the VTE sector had a number of deficiencies, which are highlighted below.

- The VTE sector lacked a clear, consistent, comprehensive policy framework to support demand driven VTE programmes.
- Management at the national, provincial, district and school levels was poorly co-ordinated and inefficient, partly due the lack of management information systems and labour market information systems (Hopkins, 1999).
- By the early 1990s VTE training programs were out-of-date and poorly related to the emerging needs of the labour force. Curriculum guides, textbooks and other teaching and learning resources (TLRs) were virtually unavailable (ADB, 1999d).
- Workshop and laboratory equipment was so obsolete that it was unsafe and irrelevant to student needs and many buildings needed refurbishing.
- Teachers and administrators lacked appropriate technical, pedagogical and management knowledge, skills and attitudes.
- There were no provisions for accrediting programs and VTE institutions, nor was there any mechanism for issuing meaningful certificates to students (ADB, 1998).

The VTE sector deteriorated just as the need for trained workers accelerated. By 1997 of the nation's 36 million workers, 70 percent worked in mainly low-technology jobs in the agricultural sector (ADB, 1998). The remaining 30 percent were in the industrial and service sectors. Some 87 percent of the labour force was classed as unskilled (untrained). Only 10 percent of workers had technical or vocational training, and fewer than three percent were university graduates. Estimations were that the labour force would grow from 36 million in 1997 to 44.2 million in 2005 (ADB, 1998). As of 2002 the labour force had increased to 41 Million (ADB, 2006).

In 1997 a project preparatory TA (PPTA) was financed by the ADB to review the VTE arrangements in Vietnam and reform its policy orientation and management to suit the market driven employment requirements. The PPTA was implemented by a team of consultants with the Ministry of Education and Training (MOET) as the host domain. Based on this PPTA the ADB in 1998 approved a Loan project to reform the VTE sector in Vietnam to meet the needs of its labour market. Following the Loan project approval the government of Vietnam handed over the responsibility of role of coordinating and monitoring of all vocational training activities from MOET to the Ministry of Labour, Invalids and Social Affairs (MOLISA). This was a significant management shift and was done to ensure the VTE reforms met the needs of the labour market. The coordination of Technical Education was entrusted to MOET who operated 4 technical teacher training colleges and a university department for teacher training (ADB, 1999d).

With the new responsibility for planning and managing the VTE sector MOLISA established a General Department of Vocational and Technical Education (GDVT) on 1st July 1998 to oversee policy formulation and management of the VTE sector. By early 1999 the GDVT had 48 staff members most of whom had not directly participated in management of vocational training. The GDVT's mandate is to:

- identify labour market demands,
- specify the training programs that must be offered in order to meet those demands,
- ensure that appropriate training programs are delivered by the VTE sector.

At the time of starting the case studies in 1999 the VTE sector in Vietnam was characterised by multiple training providers (institutions) at central and local levels of government. Developed as a supply-driven system it served a variety of sector specific ministries, or 'line ministries'. The personnel and training divisions of these line-ministries were responsible for the organisation and management of VTE programs to meet the specific needs of their sectors (ADB, 1999d). In addition, companies operating under line ministries also administered VTE delivery. At the provincial level, the Department of Education (DOE) was responsible for the provision of services for secondary technical education and the Department of Labour, War Invalids and Social Affairs (DOLISA) was in charge of vocational training (Hopkins, 1999). There were also VTE institutions at the district level, managed by the District People's Committees together with institutions operated by trusts, associations and unions. Furthermore, there were private vocational schools and centres which also provide short-term training courses.

Background of Project Intervention

This case is a retrospective study of an ADB TA (Technical Assistance) project titled: TA 3063 Capacity building for VTE Project, which was initiated in September 1998 and completed in September 1999.

As described above the ADB approved a Loan project to reform the VTE sector in Vietnam to meet the needs of its labour market in 1998. Following the Loan project approval the government of Vietnam handed over the responsibility of VTE from MOET to the Ministry of Labour, Invalids & Social Affairs (MOLISA) who set up the General Department of Vocational and Technical Education (GDVT) with a specific mandate as described in section 5.1. With the approval of the VTE Loan project, the ADB recognised the need to strengthen the capacity of key VTE sector stakeholders, in particular the GDVT, to implement reform by ad-

dressing certain perceived weaknesses. To address this perceived problem situation project TA 3063 Capacity building for VTE was designed by the ADB with a number of ICT based and non-ICT based initiatives. The perceived problem situation and the project initiatives to address this situation are summarised in the intervention profile given in section 5.2.2.

The TA project was implemented by a consultancy firm recruited by the ADB and the host domain from the government was coordinated by the GDVT. The major activities of the TA were carried out by the project team with the help of three task forces established amongst actors from the GDVT, MOLISA, key schools and provincial departments so that they would be exposed to the technical know-how available to the project team. By involving these task forces the ADB expected that the TA activities and outputs will be more sensitised to the local context and promote strong local ownership amongst the VTE actors. Numerous project actors were interviewed to gather data for this case study and the key project actors interviewed are listed in Table 1.

Intervention Profile for Case V1

Based on the documentation and interviews carried out with the ADB project officer, the team leader from the consultancy firm and Project director from GDVT an intervention profile of the project was developed. This profile summarises the *problem situation* in terms of key problem areas and factors contributing to these areas as perceived by the donor agency which led to the design of the project. The specific project *initiatives* that attempt to address the problem situation are also summarised with a focus on the ICT based initiatives. The non-ICT based initiatives are not treated in the case study.

The *problem situation* perceived by the ADB and accepted by the host government focussed on three key problem areas each with specific contributing factors.

Table 1. list of interviewees case study V1

	Position and Organisation
	Donor domain: ADB
1.	ADB project officer: education programme specialist for South East Asia
	Government domain
	Central Government interviewees
2.	Project Director, and Director General GDVT
3.	Project Manager from GDVT
4.	Project task force A Chairman, and head of financial and planning unit, GDVT
5.	Project task force B Chairman, and head of skills standards unit, GDVT
6.	Project task force C Chairman, and head of organization and personnel unit, GDVT
7.	Head of vocational teacher training unit, GDVT
8.	Chief Inspector, school inspection unit, GDVT
9.	Head of administration unit
10.	Deputy director, GDVT
	Provincial Government interviewees
11.	Head vocational training unit Hanoi DOLISA
12.	Head vocational training unit Haiphong DOLISA
13.	Head vocational training unit Danang DOLISA
14.	Head vocational training unit Hanoi DOLISA
	Key school interviewees
15.	Principal from Hanoi Key school
16.	Principal from Danang Key school
17.	Principal from Hai Phong Key school
18.	Principal from Ho Chi Minh Key school
	Consultant (agent) domain
19.	Team leader and vocational and technical education policy expert
20.	Deputy team leader and institutional capacity building expert
21.	Labour market information and analysis expert
22.	Multimedia instructional materials development expert
23.	Local VTE program development expert
24.	Instructional materials development expert

- Firstly the VTE sector in Vietnam was supply driven due to its historic command driven ideology. Perceived factors contributing to this included absence of information to identify labour market needs for VTE activity, insufficient training needs analysis to identify more relevant to training for employment needs, chronic under-funding in the VTE sector, poor capital resources in terms of buildings, training equipment, workshop facilities and poor coordination and a fragmented VTE structure amongst stakeholders across all 3 VTE functions. Low salary levels amongst officials and other VTE sector staff was also identified as contributing factor.

- Secondly there was a major mismatch between training provided and job opportunities. Perceived factors contributing to this included absence of short-term skills and job-training programmes to equip the labour force with employable skills, limited quantity and quality of administrative and teaching personnel for schools, inappropriate programme offerings, absence of curriculum guides, shortage of TLRs, inadequate, unsafe and out-dated workshop equipment, overly passive teaching and learning methods, poor evaluation of student achievement, and absence of accreditation standards, procedures and systems for certifying skills standards.

- Thirdly the GDVT has limited capacity to manage and implement the forthcoming VTE loan project to implement VTE reform. Perceived factors contributing to this included limited experience in implementing reforms in the VTE sector, absence of management information from schools, absence of relevant data and monitoring on internal and external efficiencies of VTE sector.

- In response to the above perceived problem situation, the ADB designed a number of ICT and non-ICT *initiatives*. The *ICT initiatives* included:

- Strengthening GDVT capacity in labour market (LM) monitoring and training needs analysis using information systems
- Promoting computer based training (CBT) instructional materials
- Capacity building of GDVT for management of the VTE sector and development of a masterplan for computerisation of VTE

These ICT initiatives were the focus of this case study. The non-ICT initiatives were not researched in the case study. However, examples of these non-ICT initiatives included promoting instructional materials development (e.g. textbooks, teaching guides etc), developing frameworks and procedures for VTE sector policy development, study tours to regional countries for govern officials, fees for key officials and other resources as part of the above initiatives.

Rich Picture of the Project

Having gathered data for the project and completed a real world narrative, a rich picture of the problematical situation surrounding the project and the stakeholder expectations was produced. This is presented in Figure 3.

Analysis One of V1

The nature the project studied was then interpreted in terms of a role profile of those involved by undertaking an SSM based Analysis One of each project process as described in the research approach. The Analysis One undertaken for case V1 is described further below. The traditional role analysis is provided in points i to iii and these are supplemented by additional analysis of the original perceived problem content in the VTE sector and the perceived solution in the form of the project.

Analysis of Client Role

The client role is that which causes the project to happen. In the case of V1 the clients are the director general of the GDVT and the project officer of the ADB. The aspirations of the clients in initiating the project are to strengthen the capacities of the GDVT and the fifteen Key Schools enabling them to handle the prospective Loan Project.

Analysis of Problem Solver Roles

The problem solvers or practitioners identified were the project manager from the GDVT, GDVT project staff, counterpart staff from the key schools and the international and local consultant team hired by the ADB. The resources available to the problem solvers included the professional expertise of the consultants, decision making powers of GDVT/Key School staff, seven months of project time, the terms of reference (TORs) given by the ADB to undertake the intervention, and a grant given by the ADB to purchase equipment, software, conduct workshops and implement project activities. The constraints on the problem solvers included the twelve month project timeframe, ADB and government procedures, the TORs, limited capacity and availability of staff from the GDVT and key schools.

Analysis of Problem Owner Roles

The problem owners identified were the ADB and the Government of Vietnam represented by the GDVT. There significant real world implications of the problem owners chosen. Firstly the ADB signed a Memorandum of Understanding (MOU) with the Government of Vietnam (GOV) to implement the project through the GDVT and selected key schools. Secondly the ADB signed a service contract with the consultants providing them with obligations for carrying out specific initiatives in the intervention process according to the given TORs. The GDVT accepted the TA

3063 project MOU and made necessary decisions and functional arrangements to conduct the project process, monitor its progress continuously and to make use of the outputs for capacity building of staff from the GDVT and key schools.

In terms of the *broad VTE problem situation*, the ADB and Government of Vietnam signed an agreement in mid 1998 for a major five year Loan project that was to start in late 1999. This Loan project was to be implemented by the newly formed GDVT in association with 15 key VTE schools in different provinces. The problem owners felt that *the GDVT and key Schools had limited capacity to implement the activities of this forthcoming Loan Project efficiently and effectively*. This problematic situation needed priority attention and was to be addressed by the TA 3063 project (V1). In terms of the value of the project, the problem owners felt that capacity building of the GDVT and key schools would enable the GDVT and key schools to receive and implement the proposed Loan Project quickly. Similarly it would be of value to the ADB so they could process the Loan Project which is an important measure for their performance.

An appreciation of the real world *constraints* on the perceived problem content and solution is also important in order to develop relevant primary task models of the project. The role analysis revealed that the GDVT had been established only shortly before the implementation of the project. The GDVT had only a basic operational structure and had limitations to support the TA project adequately. At the same time the GDVT could not absorb the full capacity building benefits from the TA project as it did not have a full cadre of staff in operation. The role analysis also revealed that the key schools were at different levels of functional efficiency in terms of the areas covered in the capacity building activity. Hence some key schools benefited more than others in terms of improving their capacities for operation in the VTE sector.

Intervention Analysis

Analyses 1 provides insights into the nature of relevant human activity systems for the TA project. These insights relate in turn to the wider problem situation in VTE perceived by stakeholders from the sponsor domain and host domain. As described in the research approach, in order to capture detailed learning about each project, an 'intervention analysis' was developed by the author. This focuses on capturing the detailed essence of the perceived solution, in the form of project TA 3063, designed by the Client role players. The solution focussed on an ADB funded TA based project to strengthen the capacity of GDVT and key schools covering three main ICT initiatives for VTE namely:

- **Initiative 1.** labour market monitoring and training needs analysis,
- **Initiative 2.** promotion of computer based training materials and
- **Initiative 3.** strengthening VTE management through Information Systems (IS) to improve planning, coordination and administration.

As mentioned earlier the solution also included non-ICT initiatives which are not treated in the case study.

The production of the rich picture and undertaking of Analysis one provided insights into the manner in which each of the three key ICT initiatives were implemented by the project. Each initiative is described in this section in the terms of the 'intervention analysis' developed covering key 'activities', the 'expectation' from the sponsor domain for each activity, the actual 'response' from the government side of the project team to each activity and the 'outcome' from each activity on the VTE sector. The intervention analysis for initiative 1 of case V1, dealing with labour market monitoring and training needs analysis, is provided in Table 2.

The intervention analysis for initiative 2, dealing with computer based training (CBT) materials is provided in Table 3.

The intervention analysis for initiative 3, dealing with strengthening of management for the VTE sector through IS is described in Table 4.

The above 'intervention analysis' together with the role analysis from 5.2.4 provide useful perceptions on the *adequacy of the project solution*. The Loan Project which was to be implemented, and which gave rise to this TA project, involved a wide range of fields such as Labour market information systems (LMIS), job placement services, instructional materials development, multimedia instructional materials, education management information systems (EMIS), mobile training, benefit monitoring and evaluation (BME) and financial management. According to the perceptions of the problem solvers the project solution was too narrow in its design and did not cover all key areas needed to adequately implement the forthcoming Loan project. The project

solution was also inadequate in terms of meeting the perceived 'expectations' and 'outcomes' set out by the sponsor for each of the ICT initiatives.

Analysis Two: Social Analysis for Vietnam Case Studies

Following the Analysis One and the Intervention Analysis, each project was interpreted using Analysis Two of SSM to provide a social system analysis. The Analysis Two undertaken for all three cases within each country was found to have common issues. Thus generalised Analysis Two were produced for all three cases within each country. The generalised Analysis Two for Vietnam, applicable to case V1, is described below.

Functions of GDVT and Key Schools

Since 1998 the role of coordinating and monitoring of all Vocational Training activities was transferred to MOLISA of which the GDVT was

Table 2. Intervention Analysis for initiative 1, labour market (LM) monitoring and training needs analysis

	Activity	Expectation	Actual Response & Outcome
1.	Undertook 3 types of surveys across 3 schools.	The GDVT would initiate surveys across the remaining 11 key schools. Surveys would provide data to LMIS to determine training needs.	**Response**: Activities for 11 remaining key schools not initiated. **Outcome**: Training needs of remaining 11 key schools not known. No data was gathered to help feed LMIS and determine training needs. Capacities of for training needs analysis in 3 schools, who undertook surveys, increased.
2.	Designed a labour market information system (LMIS) making use of data from the surveys and labour market signalling techniques	That GDVT would implement a basic LMIS with labour market signalling to identify skills that are of strategic importance to economic development	**Response**: The GDVT did not implement any LMIS recommendations. However, interviews indicate that TA initiatives enhanced the understanding of LMIS and its relevance amongst key staff of the GDVT. **Outcome**: The GDVT did not determine training needs post-project thus giving limited scope to make VTE programmes more relevant.
3.	Provided training to GDVT staff & stakeholders (key schools and DOLISAs) in undertaking surveys, development of LMIS and training needs analysis	That the GDVT staff would undertake training needs assessment in all 14 key schools and improve capabilities of its provincial structures (DOLISAs) to determine short-term training needs	**Response**: Activities amongst DOLISAs and remaining 11 key schools not replicated. Post-project interviews revealed that some key schools which participated in the TA based training workshops took their own initiative. They implemented their own LMIS to better determine their own training needs. **Outcome**: GDVT did not use new skills to replicate assessment of training needs amongst key schools and provincial DOLISAs. This led to poor information in the design of loan project inputs. Some key schools took their own initiative to implement in-house systems to determine training needs.

the responsible department. The role corresponding coordinating and monitoring of Technical Education activities was with the Department of Technical Education (DTE) of the Ministry of Education and Training (MOET). In all three Vietnam projects studied the project execution role was played by the GDVT even though each project had Technical Education components.

In each of the three Vietnam projects studied the GDVT played the roles of Client, Problem Solver

Table 3. Intervention analysis for initiative 2: computer based training (CBT) materials

	Activity	Expectation	Actual Response & Outcome
1.	Produced sample courseware materials and provided training to GDVT staff	That the GDVT would pilot the sample materials in key schools in order to demonstrate & promote the role of ICT based courseware in VTE programs	**Response**: Following project completion, the sample materials were kept in storage & not piloted **Outcome**: Thus schools were not exposed to courseware through piloting and were not able to make use of sample materials
2.	Conducted workshops on how to develop programs, curricula and computer based training materials	Improve capacities of GDVT and key schools for developing CBT materials. The TA expected GDVT to facilitate key schools to adopt CBT materials in some of their programmes.	**Response**: There was no institutional action by GDVT to promote CBT in key schools. CBT adoption was done in some schools using their own initiative. **Outcome**: No concerted implementation of CBT. Ho Chi Minh, Danang and Hanoi key schools introduced some CBT materials using their own initiative.
3.	Prepared a manual on how to develop courseware instructional packages	TA expectation was for GDVT to develop some VTE programmes using CBT material with the involvement of key schools & to disseminate the manual amongst the key schools	**Response**: No follow up action was undertaken to develop new curricula or CBT packages. Following project completion, the manual was kept in storage & not distributed. **Outcome**: Key schools and VTE programmes did not benefit from development of innovative CBT materials. Some staff members from GDVT claimed that their understanding and technical skills in this area were improved.

Table 4. Intervention analysis for initiative 3: strengthening of management for the VTE sector through IS

	Activity	Expectation	Actual Response & Outcome
1.	A number of improved alternative organisational structures were designed by the TA team and task force and discussed with senior GDVT staff.	The expectation of this activity was for the GDVT to implement improved structural changes immediately	**Response**: Post-TA interviews revealed that no structural changes were made by the GDVT. **Outcome**: GDVT was not restructured more suitably. Limited changes were implemented within the VTE sector. However, GDVT recognised the importance of these changes and were keen to implement certain structural changes once the Loan project had commenced.
2.	A master plan for computerisation of the VTE sector was developed with BME and EMIS components.	Plan developed with strong GDVT participation involving all 3 task forces. The expectation was for GDVT to develop a basic education EMIS linking the GDVT and some of the key schools to aid VTE sector management	**Response**: No computerisation activity was carried out by the GDVT post-project. GDVT revealed that the main constraint was availability of capital resources for this activity. **Outcome**: Poor linkages with key schools and poor management of VTE sector. Interviews revealed that Ho Chi Minh, Danang and Hanoi Key schools implemented some computerisation on their own initiative.
3.	Develop linkages amongst key VTE organisations within Vietnam and outside	The expectation was that the GDVT would exchange information and best practices with other schools within Vietnam at least via email.	**Response**: No information exchange was initiated by the GDVT. The GDVT lacked an organised research unit which could manage and conduct this activity. **Outcome**: No information exchange, leading to lack of exposure to best practices.

and Problem Owner. For project implementation purposes, the GDVT project staff included a project director who was also the director general of GDVT and a full-time project manager managing day to day activities of the Projects. Each project involved other agencies including 15 key schools operated by different ministries. These key schools played the role of training provider to students and as a demonstration school to other VTE schools.

The GDVT's official mandate was to: (i) identify labour market demands, (ii) specify the training programmes that must be offered in Vietnam in order to meet such demands and (iii) ensure that such appropriate training programmes are delivered by the VTE sector. Based on this mandate, GDVT had a functional relationship with the key schools. The GDVT's role included functional responsibilities for the areas of LMIS (labour market information systems), job placement services, TLRs (teaching and learning resources), BME (benefit monitoring and evaluation), financial management, administration, construction supervision and procurement. Hence there were specific staff within GDVT to cover each of the areas in each project studied.

Norms

The expected behaviour or norms of GDVT and key school staff was typified by their very bureaucratic nature which was focussed on strong conformance to rules and regulations resulting in too much attention to technical planning in each project activity which was the domain of the consultants. This strong emphasis on conformance meant that there was limited feasibility by the project to introduce new approaches and stimulate changes in the VTE sector. There was a strong lack of ownership amongst the government sector staff and where ever possible responsibilities were passed onto to other role players in the project.

Values

The senior Vietnamese role players exhibited affinity towards demonstrating authority and for other staff to recognize such authority. They looked upon project team members largely in hierarchical terms, preferring to act as supervisors rather than team players making improvements to the VTE sector. They *liked to work in donor funded projects as the projects involved large sums of money which provided them with power and status*. The senior Vietnamese role players liked to be rewarded for their efforts in the project but had no norms to reward other project actors who performed well.

Analysis Three: Political Analysis Relevant to Vietnam Case Studies

Each project intervention was analysed using Analysis Three of SSM to provide a political system analysis. The Analysis Three undertaken for all three cases within each country was found to have similar issues. Thus a generalised Analysis Three was produced which covered the political issues of all three projects within each country. The generalised Analysis Three for Vietnam, as applicable to case V1, is described below.

Disposition of Power

Power was largely exercised by role players from the sponsor and the host domain. The sponsor domain, which financed the project, exercised power in designing and initiating the project based on their perceptions of the problem situation and likely solutions. However once the project was commissioned, the donor played a more distant role in implementing project activities due to the intervals of the review process. The power exercised by the government project actors was driven hierarchy terms. Most of the time senior decision makers would insist that they were correct and did not like their decisions to be challenged by differing perceptions from other members in the project team. The position of the director general of the GDVT was equivalent to a vice minister and hence the key schools respected this seniority of the director general of the GDVT.

Nature of Power

The nature of power held by the director general of the GDVT centred around the ability to influence and persuade other project staff from within the GDVT and from Key schools. This was strongly dominated by the ability to demonstrate power in terms of hierarchy within the government service. In the project implementation the nature of centralised power was reinforced through contractual provisions for the hiring of government project staff which were linked into executive decision making by the director general of the GDVT. This further imposed a centralised power structure. These project mechanisms enabled the director general to direct other staff and to demand deliverables irrespective of whether there contrasting perceptions from other team members in the project.

Processes Associated with Power

The process by which power was obtained by host domain role players and actors within each project related to the hierarchical position held by each project member. The hierarchical position enabled the gaining of respect and command over junior staff.

The process by which power was executed in each project was threefold. Firstly was through regular project review meetings and project communications in the form of circulars or notices. Secondly power was also executed by ordering junior staff to perform activities. Thirdly power was executed by monitoring and recording performance of junior staff.

Power was preserved within each project by utilizing the hierarchical position of each role

within the host domain. Power was also preserved by demonstrating authority to government sector project staff through the different processes of executing power as described above. In case where there were major variations in perceptions amongst the role players, especially from the consultants, government power was preserved by seeking confirmation and assistance from other senior government officials, such as the vie minister at the ministry.

There was limited passing on of power and devolving of responsibilities amongst the government project team members. In a few instances limited amounts of power was passed onto other project actors from within the GDVT, especially those who ensured loyalty and dependability towards the director general of the GDVT, and who provided confidence based on their performance in undertaking tasks given by the director general.

Root Definition and Conceptual Model

Based on the rich picture developed and the analyses carried out, the broad problematic situation leading to the project, referred to in SSM as the Problem Content System or PCS, and the nature of the project solution, referred to in SSM as the Problem Solving System or PSS were identified. In trying to describe relevant human activity systems for the TA project a few Root Definitions (RDs) were developed. The most relevant RD, based on its accessibility by the project actors, is given below:

A VTE sector owned and ADB funded system, operated by project staff, to instigate GDVT action for improving VTE project implementation and system delivery capabilities by using ICT-based initiatives for training needs assessment and labour market monitoring, instructional programme enhancement and management strengthening of VTE whilst generating GDVT and other stakeholder response and within TA project constraints.

- The CATWOE test of this Root Definition is summarised below.
- C: GDVT and ADB
- A: Project staff
- T: Instigate GDVT action for improving VTE project implementation & system delivery capabilities
- W: Use ICT-based interventions for training needs assessment and labour market monitoring, instructional programme enhancement and management strengthening of VTE
- O: VTE sector of Vietnam
- E: Generate GDVT and other stakeholder response and operate within TA project constraints

The root definition developed describes a purposeful project HAS relevant to the broad problem situation. They are not descriptions of what the project is or was doing but they capture the purpose of a relevant HAS.

The RD provided above describes a system to *'instigate GDVT action'* which appears to be the purpose of a very relevant HAS for the TA project. In fact the ability to improve VTE project implementation and systems delivery capabilities depends on GDVT action and the TA could only *instigate* this process via the project. This RD also clearly captures the point that the *TA intervention is not an end in itself but it is to instigate GDVT action to improve VTE system.* Although the TA project covered many areas the particular HAS referred to in the RD is a system which focuses only the ICT initiatives.

A conceptual model (CM) of a relevant purposeful human activity system implied by the RD was developed by applying the concepts specified by Checkland (1981) and Wilson (2001). In trying to develop the CM using SSM concepts verbs expressed in the imperative were identified whilst recognising the transformation process *'instigate GDVT action'* to *'improve VTE project implementation and system delivery capabilities'* implied by the selected RD. The basic conceptual model with key activities is presented in Figure 4.

A more detailed conceptual model, describing purposeful human activities for each of the ICT initiatives is presented in Figure 5. The abbreviations used in the diagram are:

- KSs: key schools
- LMS: labour monitoring system

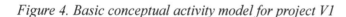

Figure 4. Basic conceptual activity model for project V1

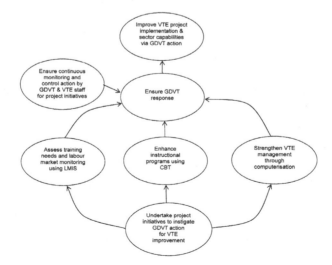

Issues Emerging from Debate

This section summarises the issues emerging from the debate and comparison of the conceptual activity model of the project, shown in diagram

5.3, with the real world activities that took place in the project. The purpose of this debate and comparison was to learn about the nature of the project and problematic issues it faced. There were four notable issues.

Figure 5. Detailed conceptual model for project V1

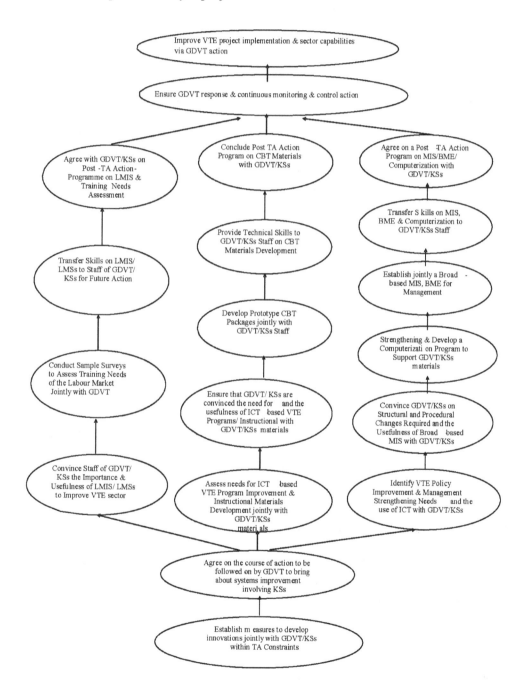

1.   Poor engagement by government officials.

The main purpose of the TA project examined in case study V1 was to strengthen the capacity of the GDVT and key schools to implement the forthcoming Loan project. In order to achieve this, the GDVT and key schools had to undertake necessary action, as per the expectations of the intervention analysis. The TA project could only 'initiate' some ICT and non-ICT activities which in turn was expected to '*instigate*' GDVT action. In reality the TA project only provided the know-how and skills that could improve GDVT capacity but this was undertaken in a non-collaborative manner without full participation from the govern project staff. The government project staff did not make use of the know-how and skills provided to them in a structured manner. The TA project brief expected the development of innovations jointly with the staff of GDVT and key schools through the three task forces. However, there was no emphasis to monitor such efforts and the TA did not include any terms of reference (TOR) to agree on some course of action to be followed on by the GDVT to bring about systems improvement. The TA brief assumed that implementation of the project activities and technology transfer to government project staff by the consultancy team would be followed by GDVT and key school action.

2.   Poor follow-up action.

According to the post-TA analysis undertaken by the consultancy team, of which the author was a member, the task forces did not produce any specific post-TA follow up action programs in the key areas of LMIS, training needs assessments, CBT materials development, MIS and computerization. The TA did not make explicit attempts to ensure GDVT and key school follow up action for VTE sector improvement. The TA expected the task forces to continue their role after the TA completion but these task forces disappeared immediately after the TA project completion. Hence there was no follow up action in any of the project initiative areas by the government actors. The debate revealed that the TA interventions and its overall design as an intervention process were not rigorous enough in terms of achieving the desired project objectives with efficiency, effectiveness and efficacy.

3.   Inadequate TA Project design

There were additional deficiencies in the design of the TA project. For example, in the area of improving managing in VTE using ICT, the focus of the TA was on establishing a computerization master plan. According to the post-TA analysis team, the initiative would have been far more effective if the emphasis was placed on improvement of managing using a MIS and developing a computerization master plan as a support to the MIS rather than a means to an end. According to the post-TA analysis such a MIS should have been linked to a Benefit Monitoring and Evaluation (BME) System for the GDVT to monitor the impact of project activities on the VTE sector and undertake corrective action.

4.   Poor project outcomes.

The post-project interviews by the author revealed that the impact of the technical outputs of the TA had been limited to a set of reports and monographs literally stored in the bookshelves of the GDVT with no application in GDVT nor key school operations. However, the training provided by the TA had a positive impact among staff of the GDVT/keys schools to be involved in the Loan Project. As the TA was a grant from the ADB, according to some officials of the GDVT the only benefits and improvements that the TA project provided were the equipment and furniture procured under the project.

RESEARCH FINDINGS

The contributions from this research work consist of four themes as summarised below.

- Firstly is defining the nature and scope of a donor funded project in the VTE sector of developing countries and the conceptualisation of such projects as a Project Intervention Process (PIP) which contributes to the developing country project management literature.
- Secondly is the use of SSM for managing donor funded projects in the VTE sector of developing countries, including a relevant generalised conceptual activity model, which also contributes to the developing country project management literature.
- Thirdly the research recommends the procedures which need to be accompanied by each activity in the conceptual model for managing donor project based ICT initiatives. These recommended procedures accommodate the different interests and requests from the different stakeholder domains involved in a donor project to facilitate the implementation of ICT initiatives in developing countries through donor funded projects.
- Fourthly the research provides recommendations which develop the 'finding out' phase of SSM as applied to ICT initiatives implemented through donor funded projects. These SSM developments can be applied to other, process, based ICT interventions in developing countries.

These four research themes are discussed further below.

Theme 1. Nature, Scope and Conceptualisation of Donor Projects as PIPs

An important contribution from this research is conceptualising the nature and scope of donor projects, in the VTE sector of developing countries, in SSM terms. The setting for each project was a broad-multi organisational VTE sector, with a messy social context and an evolving flux of events, which had specific situations that were perceived to be problematical by donor agencies and host governments. The donor agencies designed projects to bring about 'improvement' to such VTE problem situations with the involvement of the host government and financed by the donor either in the form of a TA grant or loan project.

Each project was organised as a set of activities in an intervention process, which was temporary and staffed by selected local and international experts together with officials from relevant Government agencies, to effect desired improvements to VTE based on the expectations of the sponsor and government host.

This action and overall process was conceptualised by the researcher as a *Project Intervention Process or PIP*.

The sponsor and government host who designed and initiated each project had consideration through 'whose eyes' the improvement to the corresponding VTE problem 'content' was to be 'judged'. In these terms the project situations studied met the conditions of an 'intervention process' defined by SSM (Checkland & Scholes, 2005).

Each project process itself was identified to be a problem situation in terms of SSM (Checkland and Scholes, 2005). The projects were situations in everyday life which were regarded by actors involved in the interventions as problematical and requiring improvement. Hence the projects studied, though intervention processes introduced to improve some perceived VTE problems were themselves problematical, leading to a new problem situation. This project based intervention process, and its effectiveness in tackling the broad problematical situation identified by the sponsor and the host government, became the focus of the research which can be visualised in Figure 6.

Theme 2. Using SSM for Managing the Project Process

The inadequacy of traditional project management theory as endorsed by Morris (1994) and Koskela and Howell (2002) was summarised in the selected literature review section. The need for SSM based approaches to project management backed by real world empirical research was also discussed, as articulated by Winter (2006). This section presents a SSM based generalised Root Definition and Conceptual Model for managing of donor funded project based ICT initiatives in the VTE sector of developing countries.

In trying to reflect on ways of improving projects with ICT initiatives in the VTE sector SSM based thinking was used to understand each project situation studied. This included using SSM based analyses to find out about each project situation and developing conceptual models of purposeful

activity to debate improvements to each project based on the concepts of Checkland and Scholes (2005). The application of SSM to each project studied, revealed that the main factor resulting in the problematic nature of each project was the *process* of *initiating and managing* the projects. Consequently the researcher attempted to conceptually model the process of *initiating and managing* such donor funded projects with ICT initiatives in the VTE sector in order to debate and propose defensible action to improve such processes.

The author's project observations and interviews with key project actors revealed that the process of managing a donor funded project with ICT initiatives in the VTE sector involves four major tasks. These tasks are: firstly the identification of a project, secondly managing initiatives of the project (including ICT initiatives), thirdly facilitating project implementation through 'administrative support' and fourthly ensuring project 'terminating action' at the end of the project. The task of initiating a project was recognised to be outside the project process itself in all the real world projects studied. However the cases revealed that

Figure 6. Conceptualisation of a donor funded project in VTE in SSM terms

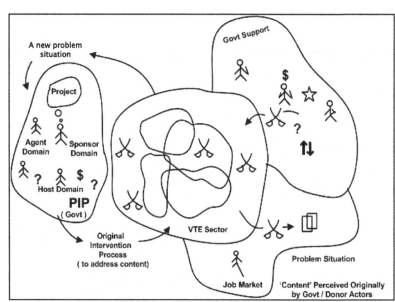

the task of 'initiating' which defines the project interventions, stakeholders and resources was largely problematical. Hence*:*

in improving project interventions project initiation needs to be taken as part of the overall process of 'managing'.

A number of Root Definitions of donor Project Intervention Processes were developed from different perspectives and view points to accommodate these four main tasks. Finally a 'root definition' capturing more than one such view was crafted as given below:

a sponsor domain funded, government host domain and agent domain staffed collaborative system to instigate Government action to improve efficiency, effectiveness and efficacy of the VTE sector by initiating and managing an intervention process with ICT initiatives, with relevant agent action, administrative support and terminating action.

For the purpose of generating a debate, which could improve the situation of project processes, a purposeful human activity system capturing the notion implied by the root definition was developed. The Conceptual Model as shown in Figure 7 was developed for this debate.

This general conceptual model of managing a PIP with ICT initiatives was compared with the actual situation that existed in the nine projects studied in the cases. The comparison revealed that the activities exist only in some rudimentary form. In the projects studied the initiating phase is highly dominated by the donor agency who designs the project in a prescriptive manner. 'Managing' a project is not taken adequately as a joint collaboration between the host and agent domains. The agent (consultant) undertakes their components according to their TORs (terms of reference) whilst expecting the government host domain to contribute in terms of effecting necessary change within the VTE sector. The sponsor reviews

progress in a 'detached' manner through annual or bi-annual missions. Currently collaboration and participation is missing at all levels. The absence of these key activities in a vigorous form can be attributed as a major reason for the problematical nature of these project processes with ICT initiatives.

Theme 3. Procedures for Managing Donor Projects with ICT Initiatives

As discussed in Theme 2 of the research findings, a project intervention process or PIP should be defined as an effort involving collaboration by host, sponsor and the hired agent instigating host action to improve efficiency, effectiveness and efficacy of the VTE sector within the scope of the most suitable initiatives and resources available. Managing a PIP is thus the process of 'ensuring such collaborative effort amongst these tripartite domains (sponsor, host government and agent consultant) to improve the perceived problem situation of a VTE sector utilising the best suited initiatives within available resources'. This implies that the initiatives to be included in a PIP should be determined carefully from the outset having learnt the nature and scope of the problem situation with active participation and collaboration of all stakeholders.

In trying to formulate some changes or improvements to the managing of donor projects with ICT initiatives, the observations from the comparison were reviewed in the light of the findings gathered from the Social Analyses and Political Analyses corresponding to each case. Having considered the social and political sensitivity some contributions could be made to improve the managing of donor projects in the VTE sector. These changes could be used in the real world as they present an 'accommodation' between different interests of role players in the projects. The activities of the proposed conceptual model for managing a donor PIP with ICT initiatives, discussed in theme 2, were thus further developed by

Figure 7. Generalised Conceptual Model (CM) of managing a donor funded project intervention process (PIP)

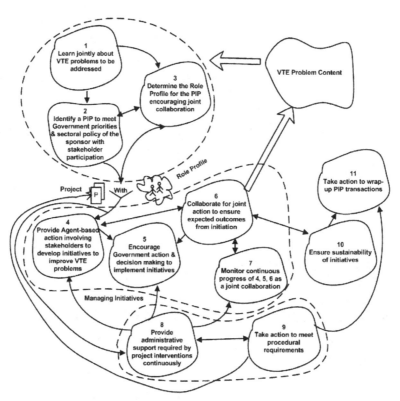

SSM concepts. These activities were developed to indicate procedures which need to be accompanied by each activity. These recommended procedures accommodate the interests and requests from the three main domains involved in the donor funded projects, namely the sponsor (donor agency), the host government implementing the project and the agent (or consultant). The suggested procedures for each activity with necessary 'accommodations' are presented in Table 5.

Theme 4. Developing the 'Finding Out' Phase of SSM for Donor Project and other Process Based ICT Interventions

This research provides a rich learning experience from the use of SSMp to learn about problematic donor funded project processes whilst contributing

to the literature on the use of SSM for managing of donor projects. One of the methodological outcomes from this research is the general contribution to the sparse literature on SSMp by using SSM in this explicit form to find out about nine project processes, as discussed earlier. Of specific contribution to the SSMp literature is the particular approach to SSMp used by the author to 'find out' about the nine project processes. Due to the lack of literature on applying SSM for a 'multi-organisational' 'process', a debate was undertaken to understand the way in which the 'finding out' phase could be undertaken. This led to five analyses being adopted by the author to 'find out' about each project intervention as described in the research approach section. These analyses were firstly a 'rich picture' of the problematic project domain, secondly a modified 'Analysis One', thirdly a specific 'Intervention Analysis', fourthly

Table 5. suggested accommodations and changes for improving the managing of donor projects with ICT initiatives

Activity of the Suggested Process	Procedure with suggested changes
1. Learn jointly about VTE Problems of priority	VTE problems need to be understood with a learning process involving open investigation of the VTE situation by the stakeholders of the host domain together with the Project Officer. A participatory approach taking different values, views and interests is suggested. This learning process should be detached from possible initiatives to be used.
2. Identify a PIP and initiatives most Appropriate	It is suggested that the PIP most appropriate to suit the problem situation understood from the earlier mentioned learning process should be identified by a working team of the donor staff and Government Officials (GOs). This could be done whilst considering priorities of the Government and sectoral policy of the donor agency so that the different interests of both parties are accounted. Initiatives to be included in a PIP should be determined once jointly with some agent guidance. This should be only after the Government agrees to the scope of the proposed PIP and its justification (what and why).
3. Define Role Profile for Collaborative Action	To implement a PIP and generate desirable outcomes to address VTE problems would require a major role to be played by the Government Officials (GOs) who need to feel that the innovations based on initiatives are developed with their close participation using technical guidance of the agent domain. The GOs also need to play the key role of decision makers. The Role Profile should give priority to these needs. This requires a great deal of accommodation emphasising the importance of the role of GOs and modifying TORs to insist that the role of the agent domain is to provide technical guidance and facilitate government action.
4. Provide Agent guided Action with Stakeholder Participation	Agent guided action to develop and introduce various innovations utilising initiatives (including ICT) is critical for the success of a PIP due to lack of technical capacity of GOs. But this development work should not take place in isolation of GOs and other stakeholders. As some subsequent work is to be undertaken by the GOs, they should be closely and continuously involved. Both the host domain and the sponsor domain must ensure that these interests are accommodated to both project guidelines and their real-world practice.
5. Encourage Government Action and Decision Making	For PIP and its initiatives to bear desirable outcome GOs must play their role of decision making and action appropriately. Hence agents should clearly demonstrate action and decision making expected from the Gos and both the Agents and Government Project Managers/Directors need to ensure that the Action & decision making by the GOs are done as required.
6. Collaborate action to ensure expected outcomes	Collaborative efforts to ensure expected outcomes should be encouraged by total coordination of efforts of technical guidance of the agent domain with decision making and action of the GOs. This should be seen as one well integrated process of teamwork between Agent and host domains.
7. Monitor continuous progress as a joint collaboration	Monitoring should be directed towards achieving desirable outcomes of the PIP with various initiatives as a joint venture involving different domains rather than finding weaknesses of each party. The Agent domain should monitor the progress of action and decision making of GOs by assessing their response continuously. Similarly the Government should monitor the progress of the agent domain to ensure collaborative joint efforts are taking place to improve VTE problems rather than merely preparing reports. Sponsor domain needs to accommodate these requirements into PIP management procedures and ensure they are practiced in the real-world.
8. Provide Administrative Support for Initiatives	Administrative support should facilitate initiatives to develop their innovations and to implement them on schedule. Especially long delays in commencing a PIP should be avoided to ensure the consultants are available at the time of requirement as originally planned and scheduled. Support function also should facilitate coordination of different consultants whose inputs and outputs are closely interconnected.
9. Take Procedural Action	The contractual obligations between host, sponsor and agent domains require efficient procedural action. This also should be considered as a process for transparency in project management. These procedures should be based on the requirements specified by the Government and the donor. Accommodation is required to minimise delays due to conflicting procedures of the Government and donor and to reduce bureaucracy.
10. Ensure Sustainability of initiatives	The Agent domain needs to incorporate measures for sustainability as part of the action. Also transfer of skills, competencies and technology by the agent domain by working closely with the GOs should be encouraged to ensure sustainability of initiatives brought in by a PIP once the consultants leave.
11. Take action to wrap-up PIP	This procedural requirement should involve smooth handing over of reports, databases, software, equipment etc and should be undertaken jointly by the GOs and Agent domain with the guidance of the sponsor domain. Adequate documentation from the part of the agent domain is required for the usage of innovations including databases by the host domain.

an 'Analysis Two' and fifthly an 'Analysis Three'. The specific contribution to the SSMp literature as applied to 'finding out' about donor project processes includes two innovations developed by the authors:

- firstly a modified application of 'Analysis One' and
- secondly the development of an 'Intervention Analysis' as part of the 'finding out' process.

These five analyses, including the two innovations, are reflected upon further below.

Following the observations of each project's problem situation provided by the rich picture, an 'Analysis One' or role analysis was found a useful starting point to learn out about the projects. The process in which this 'Analysis One' was adopted is summarised herewith. Some of these projects (studied in cases V3, S1 and S3) had ad-hoc entities named Project Implementation Units (PIUs) within the main government department handling each respective project. These PIUs were not fully responsible for project implementation as the PIUs did not have total control over the respective project. The PIUs at best only coordinated the project efforts of the main VTE agencies from the host domain, the donor and the consultants. The actual implementation of the project involved many VTE actors and stakeholders who were not coordinated by the PIU. Under these circumstances the researcher recognised that it was not feasible and reasonable to consider 'a project', involving an intervention process handled by multi organisational actors, to be a process managed by the PIU. Therefore even in the few cases where there were PIUs the researcher was reluctant to consider this ad-hoc unit as the focus on which the case study could be centred on. Rather the studies were undertaken by considering the project as an intervention process involving a multi-organisational setup and responsibilities executed by *role players* who are themselves multi-organisational. It

was found useful to visualise the role players of each project process in Analysis One terms. This enabled conceptual insights into the role players of each VTE sector project in terms of:

- the 'client': the persons who caused the project to take place, which were typically the donor agencies like the ADB or EC,
- the 'problem solvers': those who are involved and willing to do something about the situation, typically this was the project team made up of staff from the relevant government agencies and consultants engaged to provide expertise for each project,
- the 'problem owners': the persons who are entrusted with addressing the problem through a project process together with the client and problem solvers. In fact these projects came into being with contractual agreements signed between governments and donors. Thus formally there were such problem owners who took the main ownership.

Therefore it was recognised that a 'role analysis' of each project known as Analysis One in SSM could be a useful concept to finding out about these projects. This involved the use of Analysis One in a modified manner, by focussing on the real world *project process* as opposed to an SSM process of investigation which is the usual domain for Analysis One. Such an Analysis One was complemented by both Social Analysis (Analysis Two) and Political Analysis (Analysis Three) as it was quite apparent about the existence of these project situations as 'social systems' and 'political systems' as implied by SSM.

A role analysis together with social and political analyses although useful, was recognised to be insufficient to understand the essence of a project process in a rigorous form. The review of project documents and interviews with the project actors helped to recognise certain basic elements involved in a project process. The researcher recognised that the projects had a set of real world actions undertaken by the host domain with the help of an agent domain (consultants). These 'activities' were undertaken with certain 'expectations' from the actors and stakeholders of the host domain. According to the many actors of the sponsor domain and the agent domain interviewed a major problem area of the project processes studied was that these 'expectations' were never met. In other words the 'response' of the actors and stakeholders of the host domain was not as expected. Based on these real-world observations a hypothesis was developed to include these three basic elements embodied in the project namely 'activities', 'expectations' and 'response' as part of the analytical framework to 'find out' about the projects. The first two cases were studied with this analytical framework which enabled the hypothesis to be tested. Further review of the observations emerging from the two case studies recognised that the actions within a project process were undertaken by the agent domain

guided by the sponsor domain with some specific expectations. These expectations were partly in the form of some action to be taken by the actors/stakeholders of the host domain which could be observed via 'response' as mentioned earlier. The expectations also included an expected impact or 'outcomes' addressing the wider VTE problem situation. This became quite clear after some interviews with key project actors and reviews of the project documentation. Hence the analytical framework, referred to as an 'Intervention Analysis' was updated with 'activities, 'expectations' (in terms of both expected response from the host domain and expected effect on the VTE problem situation), 'response' (of the host domain) and the 'outcomes' on the VTE sector. This revised framework was used in all cases including in the first two cases as a second attempt. The observations were quite encouraging and the framework was recognised to greatly enrich the 'finding out' approach to the projects studied and provide many of the insights gained.

Figure 8. Recommended approach for 'Finding Out' about donor funded project processes with ICT initiatives

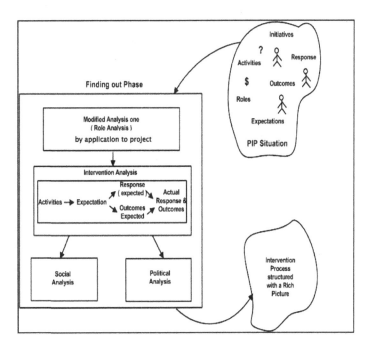

It was recognised that the modified 'Analysis One' or role analysis of a project provides something similar to the 'structure' element corresponding to an organisational situation as implied by the original idea of SSM. The 'intervention analysis' with four elements (Action, Expectations, Response and Effect) was found to be something similar to the 'process' and 'climate' of the original SSM concept. On the other hand the Analysis Two and Analysis Three were found useful as complementary concepts to understand the social and political elements. Hence the researcher considers that the framework that has emerged from this research would be a useful contribution for those who are using SSM for finding out donor funded project intervention processes. This analytical framework to be used for the finding out phase of projects could be referred to as the 'intervention process' framework and could be visualised from Figure 8.

CONCLUSION

Since donor funded project based ICT initiatives are aiming to address some problem situations of VTE sectors, this SSM based study not only facilitated understanding their problematical nature in terms of managing but found the concept of Project Intervention Processes (PIPs) as a worthwhile vehicle to comprehend the problems faced by donor funded project based ICT initiatives applied to VTE sectors in developing countries.

The application of a universal hypothesis for administrative science has been endorsed by major development agencies such as the ADB, World Bank and IMF by applying traditional project management theory in the management of IS projects in developing countries. However, as Lubatkin et al (1997) demonstrate the application of this universal hypothesis can have very limited roles in the management activity of ICT initiatives in developing countries. The research

undertaken demonstrated the complexity of VTE sectors in developing countries with their complex organisational context and 'extra-soft' problem content involving difficult to structure problem situations. The research revealed that it is an extremely difficult task to manage project based ICT initiatives by applying the traditional hard approaches of project management used in developed countries. A softer approach to managing donor funded ICT projects is proposed by the authors using the enquiring/learning cycle of SSM. A conceptual model of the process of managing PIPs was developed. The recommended activities in the model accommodate the different interests and requests from the different stakeholders involved in the projects themselves and are socially and politically feasible.

REFERENCES

Asian Development Bank. *(1996)*. Final Report: TA 2326 Employment Promotion & Training Project for the Ministry of Labor and Social Welfare (MOLSW) of Lao PDR, Manila, Philippines.

Asian Development Bank. *(1998)*. Report and recommendation of the president to the board of directors on a proposed loan to the Republic of Vietnam for the Vocational and Technical Education Project, Manila, Philippines.

Asian Development Bank. *(1999a)*. Report and recommendation of the president to the board of directors on a proposed loan to the Republic of Sri Lanka for the Skills Development Project, Manila, Philippines.

Asian Development Bank. (1999b). *Impact evaluation study of Regional technical and vocational education projects, Manila, Philippines.*

Asian Development Bank. (2005). *Technical Assistance for Selected Evaluation Studies for 2005: Operations Evaluation Department, Manila, Philippines.*

Checkland, P. (1985). From optimising to learning: a development of thinking for the 1990s. *The Journal of the Operational Research Society, 36*(9), 757–767.

Checkland, P., & Holwell, S. (1998). *Information, Systems and Information Systems: Making Sense of the Field.* UK: John Wiley and Sons.

Checkland, P. B. (1986). The application of systems thinking in real world problem solving: the emergence of soft systems methodology. In Jackson, M. C., & Keys, P. (Eds.), *New Directions in Management Science* (pp. 87–96). London: Gower.

Checkland, P. B., & Scholes, J. (2005). *Soft Systems Methodology in Action - Includes a 30 year Retrospective.* Chichester, UK: John Wiley and Sons.

Checkland, P. B., & Winter, M. (2006). Process and content: two ways of using SSM. *Journal of the Operational Research Society* (Special Issue: Problem Structuring Methods - New Direction in a Problematic World). doi: 10.1057.

Commonwealth of Learning. (2002). *Perspectives on Distance Education: Skills Development through Distance Education.* Vancouver: Commonwealth of Learning.

Crawford, P., & Bryce, P. (2003). Project Monitoring and Evaluation: a Method for Enhancing the Efficiency and Effectiveness of Aid Project Implementation. *International Journal of Project Management, 21,* 363–373. doi:10.1016/S0263-7863(02)00060-1

Friend, J. (1998). Managing Development Projects and Programmes: Fresh Perspectives towards an Action Research Agenda, Working Paper. No. 21, School of Management, University of Lincolnshire and Humberside.

Holwell, S. E. (1997). *Soft systems methodology and its Role in Information Systems.* Unpublished PhD thesis, Lancaster University, Lancaster.

Hopkins, M. (1999). Training Needs in Vietnam with Related Labour Market and Methodological Issues, Monograph prepared for Ashton Brown Associates, ADB TA 3063-VIE: Capacity Building in Vocational and Technical Education Project.

ILO (International Labour Organisation). (2002). Labour Market policies and poverty reduction strategies in recovery from the Asian Crisis: Report of the ILO – Japan – Government of Indonesia sub-regional seminar, Jakarta, Indonesia 29 April to 1st May 2002.

ILO (International Labour Organisation). (2008). *Vocational training and productivity.* Montevideo: ILO/Cinterfor.

Koskela, L., & Howell, G. (2002). The underlying theory of project management is obsolete. *Conference Proceedings of the 2002 PMI Conference, Seattle,* Project Management Institute.

Lamoureux, M. (1999). Monograph: National policies for VTE in Lao PDR, ADB TA 2925 LAO.

Ledgerwood, D., & Kernaghan, T. (1998). Monograph: Developing training materials for short term skills development, ADB TA 2925 LAO.

Lubatkin, M., Ndiaye, M., & Vengroff, R. (1997). The nature of managerial work in developing countries: a limited test of the universalist hypothesis, *Journal of International Business, 28.*

Middleton, J., Ziderman, A., & Van Adams, A. (1993). *Skills for Productivity: vocational education and training in developing countries*. New York: Oxford University Press.

Morris, P. (1994). *The Management of Projects*. London: Thomas Telford.

Morris, P. (2002). Science, objective knowledge and the theory of project management. *Civil Engineering Proceedings of ICE*, 150, 82-90.

Neal, R. A. (1995). Project definition: the soft-systems approach. *International Journal of Project Management*, *13*(1), 5–9. doi:10.1016/0263-7863(95)95697-C

Project Management Institute. (2000). *A Guide to the Project Management Body of Knowledge*. Newton Square, PA: Project Management Institute.

Sparreboom, T. (2001). An Assessment of Labour Market Information Systems in South Africa. *Africa Development. Afrique et Developpement*, *XXVI*(3 & 4), 149–181.

Wilson, B. (2001). *Soft Systems Methodology: Conceptual Model Building and its Contribution*. Chichester, UK: John Wiley and Sons.

Winter, M. (2002). *Management, Managing and Managing Projects: Towards An Extended Soft Systems Methodology*. PhD thesis, Department of Management Science, Lancaster University, UK.

Winter, M. (2006). Problem structuring in project management: an application of soft systems methodology (SSM). *The Journal of the Operational Research Society*, *57*(7), 802–812. doi:10.1057/palgrave.jors.2602050

World Bank. (1998). *Education and Training in the East Asia and Pacific Region, Education Sector Unit*. Washington: World Bank.

World Bank. (2002). *Skills and Literacy Training for Better Livelihoods: A Review of Approaches and Experiences*. Washington: World Bank.

World Resource Institute (2002). *Jhai Foundation's Internet Learning Centres and the Remote IT Village Initiative*.

Yeo, K. T. (1993). Systems thinking and project management - time to reunite'. *International Journal of Project Management*, *11*(2), 111–117. doi:10.1016/0263-7863(93)90019-J

Yin, R. K. (2003). *Applications of case study research*. Thousand Oaks, CA: Sage Publications.

KEY TERMS AND DEFINITIONS

ADB: Asian Development Bank
BME: Benefit Monitoring and Evaluation
CBT: Computer Based Training
CM: Conceptual Model
CG: Channa Gunawardena
CM: Conceptual Model
CBT: Computer Based Training
DB: David Brown
EC: European Commission
EMIS: Education Management Information System
FMIS: Financial Management Information System
ICT: Information and Communication Technology
IS: Information System
LM: Labour Market
LMI: Labour Market Information
LMIS: Labour Market Information Systems
LS: Labour Statistics
MIS: Management Information System
NGO: Non-Governmental Organisation
PIP: Project Intervention Process
PIU: Project Implementation Unit
PPTA: Project Preparatory Technical Assistance

RD: Root Definition
SSM: Soft Systems Methodology
TA: Technical Assistance
VTE: Vocational and Technical Education

Chapter 13

iREACH:
Lessons from a Community Owned ICT Network in Cambodia

Helena Grunfeld
Victoria University, Australia

Seán Ó Siochrú
NEXUS Research, Ireland

Brian Unger
University of Calgary, Canada

Sarun Im
iREACH project, Cambodia

ABSTRACT

Cambodia is for various reasons a challenging environment for ICT development. This did not deter IDRC (Canada) from funding an ambitious and ground-breaking project designed ultimately to influence ICT policy in Cambodia but initially to establish two pilot community-owned networks in poor rural areas. Each comprises both a cluster of local telecentres (10 in each area), and a mini telecoms enterprise run by the communities. Begun in May 2006, with initial funding of USD1.3 million the project runs to May 2010 when the question of sustainability comes to the fore. Additional support is likely to be needed. iREACH' experiences are being fully documented and lessons are emerging around community capacity building and empowerment; technical challenges in a rural environment; developing relevant and appropriate services; creating a community based enterprise; deploying a range of participatory monitoring and evaluation approaches; and working within a centralised and fluid political context.

INTRODUCTION

The Informatics for Rural Empowerment and Community Health (iREACH) project in Cambodia takes a holistic view of ICT. Rather than treating users as consumers of ICT, it has invited community members to become active participants in the production of the ICT environment, including the physical infrastructure, management structures and processes, training, capacity building, content development and use.

DOI: 10.4018/978-1-61520-997-2.ch013

This chapter sets out the paradigm within which iREACH has been established and moves on to describe, analyse, and interpret the project by addressing its objectives and processes, and the issues faced. It concludes with a consideration of what lies ahead for this unique approach to using ICT for rural development.

BACKGROUND AND CONCEPTUAL FRAMEWORK

The traditional way of deploying telecommunications networks is to build hierarchical, centrally controlled structures (Davies, 1994, Noam, 1987;), starting at the 'centre', and gradually expanding the network outwards towards the 'periphery' (Souter, 2008). The centre is normally in densely populated urban areas and network growth would continue as far as is considered commercially viable. As telecommunications became integral to the social and economic development, most western governments in the developed world introduced some form of subsidy system, usually involving universal service obligations (USOs), to encourage extension of networks to geographic areas and user communities that would not be sufficiently profitable for commercial operators.

Many countries in the developing world have embraced the concept of a universal service policy (or universal access policy), and a variety of mechanisms have been developed to implement it (Gillwald, 2005; Ó Siochrú 2009). But the resources available and the approaches adopted are rarely equal to the scale of the challenge. The access gap between urban and rural areas remains extremely high. This is particularly the case for internet-based and broadband services, which in many countries are in any case not included under universal service policy.

In response to the limited reach of market-driven services, and as an alternative to top-down, centralised approaches to network deployments, some communities have taken matters into their own hands and established small operators designed to service their local areas. Deployments of this nature, referred to as community–driven operators, or micro-telcos, represent alternative and innovative business models and strategies to service markets that are normally not considered profitable by other operators (Galperin & Bar, 2006; Galperin & Gerard, 2005; Ó Siochrú & Girard, 2005). Rather than building from the centre to the 'periphery' using top-down design methods, these networks start with the users and build towards the centre through various interconnection arrangements with the major operators that control national backbone networks. In addition to the benefits of the actual services coming available through this process these alternative networks incorporate the specifics of local contexts, which the top-down approach may be unwilling or unable to do (Harris, 2004).

Ó Siochrú & Girard (2005) identified three types of community driven ICT models: user/community-owned cooperatives, local authority owned networks, and hybrid entrepreneur/community driven approaches. The cooperative structure has, they noted, been recognised by the UN as conducive to combining commercial and development activity and accordingly it has adopted guidelines to assist governments in formulating legislative environments that facilitate the establishment of cooperatives.

There are combinations and permutations of these, for instance where a community-owned utility, e.g. in the power sector, expands into telecommunications, but through a separate subsidiary; or the Tamil Nadu SARI project, where a majority of the kiosks are locally owned and operated by self-employed entrepreneurs, while some are operated by self-help groups of a local nongovernmental organisation (Kumar, 2007).

Small-scale operators can also be at the initiative of a government seeking to pursue several objectives simultaneously, with more or less community participation. This was the case with the Akshaya project in Kerala, a state government initiated project with social objectives but operated by private entrepreneurs (Kuriyan, Ray & Toyama, 2008) under local community guidance; and South Africa's Under-Serviced Area Licensing (USAL). While the USAL model has the potential to deliver both affordable telecommunications to previously underserviced areas, and innovative business models, stimulation of growth and job creation, it has so far been less than successful. According to Gillwald (2005), government regulatory action, or rather inaction, was responsible for the unsatisfactory outcomes of the first round of this project. Regulatory issues not adequately addressed included lack of timely access to incumbent facilities at reasonable interconnection terms, high license fees, and lack of co-ordination among USALs that would have enabled them to gain economies of scale through aggregation. Any success of subsequent rounds would be despite, rather than because of, a conducive policy environment.

A community based operation can also form part of a franchising structure. It has been suggested that franchising could be a means to deploy large numbers of small operators quickly, either by governments or corporations, while at the same time balancing the commercial and development aspects of these facilities (Harris, 2007). There are several examples of more commercially oriented franchise operations, without a development agenda, in developing countries, established either by the incumbent, as in Senegal and Indonesia, or by local entrepreneurs, as in Ghana (Falch & Anyimadu, 2003). One model that combines both objectives is the Brazilian Committee for the Democratisation of Information (CDI), which has adopted a model referred to as 'social franchising' for scaling its activities. The expansion programme, which is affected by funding and local demand, is to a large extent funded through extensive international and national fundraising (Ferraz, et al., 2004).

The economies of scale inherent in franchising, including bulk purchases of equipment,

network monitoring and management, product development, training, and marketing hold some attractions for this structure. Franchising on the basis of replication of exactly the same "menu" in all local operations, in the McDonald's way, would forfeit the benefits associated with being community based, whereas franchising with a high degree of autonomy and flexibility at the local level could be a promising approach.

Corporate bodies can also anchor projects in communities and the e-Choupal initiative in India illustrates how corporate involvement can incorporate local specifics. Owned by ITC, a major Indian conglomerate, the project has appropriated some symbols from a community-based approach and combined these with methods used in franchising. Even the choice of name for the initiative, 'choupal' which means 'meeting place' in Hindi, signifies a community based positioning. All the infrastructure is owned by ITC and each choupal is managed by a local farmer, in whose house the equipment is often located. This farmer is required to take an oath to service the entire community at a public ceremony, bestowing the aura of a public official to that person. The deployment programme is managed by ITC's head office, which has adopted a modular approach with incremental deployment, based on expected revenue streams (Annamalai & Rao, 2003; Bowander, Gupta & Singh, 2003). The MS Swaminathan Research Foundation (MSSRF) in India has taken the opposite approach to the location and management of village knowledge centres (VKCs) and mandates that these be located in public buildings. Subject to meeting its basic principles, MSSRF is encouraging decentralisation of decision making to local communities and acts as a facilitator and coordinator of information gathering and training (Arunachalam, 2002; Rao, 2004).

In addition to providing much needed infrastructure, Ó Siochrú & Girard (2005) argued that a key advantage of community owned and managed networks is that they have a stake in the development of communities. An examples they used to illustrate such dual purpose is the telecommunications co-operatives established in Poland in the early 1990s. These constituted a mechanism through which communities involved in servicing previously underserved areas with telecommunications have also spawned new projects, such as environment friendly production, recreation centres, and other services that are socially important.

It was with the expectation that community-based ICT operators in Cambodia could deliver similar benefits that the International Development Research Centre (IDRC) supported the iREACH project as a pilot in 2006.

But the IDRC brings its own agenda, and can be seen as an actor in the structure and outcomes of iREACH. IDRC is a Canadian Crown corporation collaborating with researchers in the developing world in their endeavour to build healthier, more equitable, and prosperous societies. It supports research on practical, long-term solutions to the social, economic, and environmental problems, with a particular focus on building local capabilities and enabling local researchers to engage with the wider national and global research communities. The fact that a research organisation, rather than an aid agency, initiated and funded iREACH means that iREACH has a strong focus on research. iREACH was designed to comply with IDRC's three key research areas for its Asia ICT 2006-2011 programme. These are:

- building evidence and promoting dialogue to inform policies that enable knowledge societies in Asia,
- applied research and piloting of innovative ICT applications for development,
- researching and building capacity for understanding the socio-economic effects of ICTs on Asian communities.

A number of factors prompted IDRC to work in partnership with the Ministry of Commerce (MoC) on iREACH, and channel funding through them. An ongoing successful project on localisation of Khmer Language for software had built a level of trust with the senior official and manager involved; and the MoC responsibilities for enterprise development, including small and medium-sized enterprises in rural areas was also a factor. From the outset, the project was thus not seen as centrally about ICTs or telecommunications in isolation but about building enterprise and providing services locally.

THE IREACH PROJECT

The interdependence between the various components of any rural telecommunications system, and of iREACH in particular, demonstrate that all aspects of a community based operator have to be considered as a system with strong interdependencies, not only between the different parts of the system, but also with stakeholders beyond the system (Andrew & Petkov, 2000; Ramirez, 2003). In the case of iREACH the technical, training, management, adequate products and services and associated marketing, staffing, community involvement, and partnerships are just some of the components of this system, none of which operate in isolation. It is an open system and as such is part of a wider context, the features of which are to a large extent determined by government policies and actions.

In this section, the main body of the chapter, we describe and analyse the multi-faceted aspects of the iREACH project. To set the scene, the context of the wider system within which iREACH operates, we start with an overview of the policy and regulatory environments in Cambodia

Policy, Regulatory and Institutional Environment Cambodia

Cambodia finds itself at the lower end of international indicators measuring countries in terms of access to ICT. Table 1 shows a very low ICT

Table 1. ICT Development Index for Cambodia (Source: ITU, 2009)

	2007		2002		
	Rank	IDI	Rank	IDI	% change
ICT Development Index (IDI)	121	1.53	126	1.07	43%
Average in all countries		3.40		2.48	37%
Average in low IDI groups		1.30		1.00	31%
IDI access sub-index	149	0.02	142	0.01	100%
IDI skills sub-index	123	4.00	131	3.15	27%
(A total of 154 countries were ranked)					

Development Index (IDI) for Cambodia. This is a composite index, based on indicators relating to ICT infrastructure and access, ICT use primarily by individuals, intensity of use, and ICT skills (ITU, 2009).

Most fixed telephone services making up the 0.3% penetration rate, as shown in Table 2, are located in the capital city Phnom Penh.

According to the National Institute of Statistics, about 28% of urban households owned a mobile phone in 2006, compared to just 5.8% of rural households (World Bank, 2008, p. 7). Cambodia did not fare much better in the e-readiness index developed by the United Nations (UN, 2008) and is based on sub-indices on website assessment,

Table 2. Access and use indicators for Cambodia (Source: ITU, 2009)

Access indicators	2007	2002
Fixed telephone lines/100 inhabitants	0.3	0.3
Mobile cellular subs/100 inhabitants	10.9	0.9
International internet bandwidth per Internet user (bit/s)	3,751	400
% of households with computers	4.1	0.5
% of households with Internet	2.4	0.1
Use indicators		
Internet users/100 inhabitants	0.5	0.2
Fixed broadband subscribers/100 inhabitants	0.1	-

telecommunication infrastructure, and human resource endowment. Cambodia occupied the 139th place (out of 182 countries) in 2008, having dropped from 128th place in 2005.

Responsibility for ICTs is dispersed among three ministries and several agencies involved in regulating, coordinating and promoting ICT in Cambodia. The Ministry of Post and Telecommunications (MPTC) is responsible for both policy and the regulation of telecommunications and ICT policy, whereas the prime role of the Ministry of Information (MoI) is the development and regulation of media and publications.

The use of ICT in education as a teaching and training tool is handled by the Ministry of Education, Youth and Sport (MoEYS) and the Ministry of Labour and Vocational Training (MLVT). Judging by the skills indicators in the ITU's IDI index, these departments face considerable challenges but have also made much progress over the past few years.

In December 2004, the Cambodian government adopted a policy entitled 'Policy and Strategies: Information and Communication Technology in Education in Cambodia', with ambitious goals. In his analysis of reasons for the limited achievement of objectives in that plan, Richardson (2008) found that the implementation process had been ad hoc, rather than properly planned. He attributed this to lack of transparency and equity in the distribution and support of the ICT infrastructure, and insufficient risk taking in trialling different

Table 3. Skills indicators in the ICT Development Index (Source: ITU, 2009)

Skills indicators	2007	2002
Gross enrolment ratio secondary education	42.0	22.7
Gross enrolment ratio tertiary education	5.4	2.5
Adult literacy rate	72.7	69.4

Table 4. Price baskets and ranks compared to 150 countries. Source: ITU (2009)

Telecommunications pricing	Rank	USD	% of GNI/ capita
Fixed telephone sub-basket	133	8.0	17.9
Mobile cellular sub-basket	121	5.0	11.2
Fixed broadband Internet sub-basket	125	90.6	201.2

technologies. He also suggested that MoEYS should involve itself in information and education campaigns and advocacy at the community level.

Others with roles in the ICT sector are Telecommunications Cambodia (TC), the government owned fixed line telecommunications operator, and National ICT Development Agency (NiDA). The objectives of NiDA are to develop ICT policy for short, medium and long term development as well as promoting ICT and it is responsible, for instance, for the e-government programme.

The incumbent operator, the government owned carrier Telecommunications Cambodia (TC), is one of a number of operators involved in developing backbone infrastructure, including fixed lines, regional backbone network and international connections. The Chinese owned CFOC Network is building an optical fibre ring; and most recently the Vietnamese company Viettel has connected in a short period of 15 months all twenty four provincial capitals in Cambodia in an optical fibre network, to service its nationwide mobile telephony service, top level government videoconferencing, ISPs and other customers.

There are eight mobile operators in Cambodia, with three more licences to be issued (Hab, 2009). Chuan Wei (Cambodia) is the only carrier licensed to operate a nationwide WiMAX mobility network. Despite strong competition in the mobile and ISP markets, with some 37 ISPs, 10 of which are major (Green, 2009), prices for these services are very high by international standards. This is shown in Table 4, which ranks services in 150

countries in actual terms and as a proportion of the gross national income (GNI).

The policy and regulatory environments are not fully transparent, as evidenced by licensing of mobile carriers without an open legal framework (Unger & Robinson, 2008). A policy on community radio, of direct relevance to the iREACH project, has not yet been formulated; and a universal service policy was drafted by the MPTC in mid-2006 but is still awaiting approval by the government.

This lack of transparency is further complicated by the government's involvement in joint ventures in the sector. There was no independent regulator at the time of writing, but as some investments may be conditional on greater transparency, e.g. a soft loan from the Japanese government to fund an optical fibre backbone, it may be a matter of time until a regulatory authority is established. Such an authority would also be required to investigate the relatively high telecommunications prices, including bandwidth for Internet use, currently acting as a constraint to promoting a knowledge society (Unger & Robinson, 2008).

A summary of the geographic institutional structure provides a useful context for future cooperation between iREACH and decentralised authorities, as described later in this chapter.

Cambodia is administered through 24 provinces. These fall under the Ministry of the Interior, which appoints administrators at that level. The provinces are responsible for issuing land titles and business licenses for smaller businesses and also participate in the development of the budget. Similar to regulation of telecommunications, the responsibilities of the provinces and the central government are not totally transparent (World Bank, 2002). The provinces are further subdivided into districts, communes, and villages.

Consideration is currently being given to allocating more responsibilities to district and commune levels. There are in excess of 1,600 communes, each of which comprises four to seven villages, and has its own directly elected Council with a 5-year mandate. The number of elected councilors varies from five to eleven, depending on demography and geography. The second commune elections took place in 2007. Articles 30 and 31 of the Law on Commune (Kingdom of Cambodia, 2001) govern the relationship between commune councils and village chiefs, who are appointed by the councils, but lack decision-making power. They serve primarily as an interface between villagers and the councils

Objectives, Resources, Budget, Structure

Inspired by the UNDP publication on community based networks (Ó Siochrú & Girard, 2005) and in an endeavour to explore the potential for community based operators to improve the ICT situation in rural Cambodia, IDRC awarded the Ministry of Commerce (MoC) a grant of USD 1.3 million to conduct a 3-year (1 May 2006 – 31 April 2009 – subsequently extended to 2010) pilot project based on the principles advocated in that publication.

The overall objective of iREACH is to build evidence and capacities to help inform Cambodia's rural ICT and telecommunications policies and, subject to proving the suitability of this type of operation in the Cambodian environment, to mainstream this type of ICT project to all provinces throughout Cambodia. The project and its associated research activities are also useful for furthering general understanding of principles and practical issues involved in community based networks. The specific objectives are to:

1. establish and nurture the pilot e-communities in the rural locality of Kep and Kamchai Mear,
2. pilot-test a community-driven system of blended technologies as contributing to social, economic and cultural development by deploying wireless technology, solar energy, wind power and community radio,
3. facilitate community capacity-building by training in ICT use, developing service content and enterprise, and
4. document in detail the activities and processes for research purposes. Documents and research findings would also be useful for policy makers and other practitioners.

Kamchai Mear and Kep were chosen as pilot sites for a number of reasons: their higher than average level of poverty; their reasonable proximity (daytrip distance) to, but different directions from, Phnom Penh; diverse livelihoods (Kep is a coastal fishing and farming area in the south and Kamchai Mear an agricultural district of Prey Veng province); and expressions of support from local administrative institutions and Cambodian partners interested in participating in the project. Concrete support from the local government authorities and other local partners included the provision of HQ premises in each pilot at no charge.

Despite a relatively small population of about 34,000, Kep was recently designated as a province in its own right, having formerly held the political status of a municipality. (All four municipalities in Cambodia were similarly redesignated.) It comprises just two districts, one of which is Kep town, and five communes. Located 176 km from Phnom Penh, Kep, the main town and capital, has a dispersed population of approximately 4,000. Fishing and small-scale agriculture are the main sources of livelihood sources in the area. The iREACH project covers the more rural district of Damnak Chang Eur, with a population of approximately 20,000 spread among three rural communes: Pong Tuek, Ang Koal and Ou Krasar.

One of 12 districts of Prey Veng province, Kamchai Mear (KCM) consists of eight decentralised administrative communes, which in turn are divided into a total of 129 villages. The district capital, Kamchai Mear is approximately 45 km (1 hour by car) east of the provincial capital of Prey Veng. The population of the district of KCM was approximately 85,000 in 2005. The catchment area for the pilot project covers 56 villages within the three communes of Smoang Choeung, Smoang Tbaung and Kranhoung, all of which are adjacent to the district capital. Their composite poverty indices were below the national average in 2005. The population within the catchment area represents 45% of the total population of the KCM Mear district.

A number of important characteristics distinguish iREACH from most ICT4D pilot initiatives piloted over the past decade or so, including the strong focus on research and policy input and the attention to capacity building on all aspects associated with operating a telecommunications business. An emphasis on gender equality, livelihood matters, and governance issues also characterise this project. As is the case with all IDRC funded projects, gender equality and empowerment of women in the context of overall community development plays an important role and this is reflected in the management committee, staff and users.

One of the initial tasks was to, in conjunction with respective communities, establish a governance framework for the development of the initiative.

iREACH offers a 'learning by doing' environment, in which participants, whether staff, management committee members, or other villagers can learn and practice governance and democratic processes. Rather than just assuming that new technologies can facilitate democratic processes, the very foundation of iREACH is based on democratic principles, through its elected local management committees. Activities are in place to encourage policy input from villagers. It was expected that skills and experience gained from being invited to express their views would equip villagers with capabilities to use ICT facilities for democratic processes as well as other purposes. The only evidence so far of iREACH being used for democratic governance processes is its use by commune council members.

One of the guiding principles behind the design of the network was the recognition of externalities, i. e. that the value of the service increases with the aggregate number of users (Best & MacLay, 2002; Estache, Gomez-Lobo & Leipziger, 2001). In this case, the value would increase with the ability to communicate between different villages within the same or adjacent communes. So, rather than adopting the single site model so common for pilots, the iREACH design focused on building a network that has the potential to facilitate integration of the dispersed villages, thereby strengthening their capacity for improving their livelihoods.

This is reflected in the architecture of each pilot site, which is designed as a mini rural network, consisting of a headquarters (HQ) and village hubs, located in publicly accessible buildings, such as commune offices, health centres, pagodas and schools, within a radial distance of up to 20 kilometres from the headquarters. Each hub, which has one computer, is staffed by a local community facilitator. The hubs and the HQ are linked via wireless connections. All hubs in both pilots are connected to the Internet via a satellite connection at the HQ. The participatory research conducted in February 2009 confirmed the value of the inter-village connectivity, which has led to more co-operation between villages.

A central office was established in Phnom Penh to co-ordinate the iREACH project. After a preparatory phase of almost nine months, which included recruitment of key staff, the project began in mid-2006 with baseline studies on community livelihoods, ICT service access and other community issues of importance for the project. This was followed by the physical development of the two pilot sites, in KCM and Kep, respectively. Each pilot site consists of an HQ and nine village hubs. The elected local management committees at each site are responsible for the strategic direction of the respective pilot site.

As noted, gender empowerment and equality are integral parts of the iREACH project. Consistent with this philosophy, iREACH has encouraged women to become active participants at all levels of the operation, as members of the management committee, staff members, and users. The promotion of female management committee members and employment has been an effective and important part of creating awareness of gender equality and the visibility of women in the community has increased. By participating in the different processes of the project, it was envisaged that the women involved would develop their confidence, learning and information skills, improve their ability to control various aspects of their lives and community issues, including their ability to influence public policies. Both men and women who participated in the participatory research have noted a significant improvement in gender equity and empowerment. Men were also positive about women being involved in iREACH, even their wives, as long as that was not at the expense of home duties.

The greatest success has so far been achieved in the management committees, where women represent over 50% of members. They have become active in most aspects of the operations and women have accepted responsibility for organising the monthly meetings of the management committee. This is a major achievement for someone who may not previously have attended a meeting. Another approach involves the preparation of content, targeting women in their various roles, whether as farmers, business operators, mothers, wives, or household operators.

Setting up the Team

Although currently run as a 'project' under the Ministry of Commerce, it has been anticipated from the start that iREACH will evolve into an independent legal entity in its own right.

The central office in Phnom Penh is headed by a Project Manager ultimately reporting to a Project Director in the Ministry. Other staff at the central office include an accountant, a webmaster, technical staff, and a research manager, who works in close cooperation with external advisors and research co-ordinators at the pilot sites.

Each pilot site is overseen by a non-governmental partner and managed by a pilot co-ordinator. Other staff at each HQ include a research coordinator, a media coordinator, three content developers, and one technical support person responsible for systems and network administration. The pilots also have an administration/financial support person and security people. There is also one community facilitator (CF) at each HQ and at each of the hubs, a total of nine at each pilot site.

The pilot sites have a high degree of autonomy within the overall framework and financial accountability of the whole project. This arrangement has the benefit of enabling each to evolve in a culturally appropriate way in their respective communities. During the initial phase, there was little cooperation between the pilot sites, but since May 2008 cooperation and coordination between them has grown. Rather than being imposed by the central office, this coordination has been initiated by staff at the pilot sites including for instance on service promotional activities.

CFs play a key role in supporting their communities as intermediaries between users and the technologies, thus enabling inexperienced users to benefit from the services provided. Community members are gradually gaining the skills required to make meaningful use of the equipment and services on their own. Key MC members have been trained and mentored to become CFs.

With Cambodia's severe shortages of relevant skills, staff recruitment was a major challenge. It was impossible to find qualified staff within villages and they were difficult to recruit from major cities, as few are willing to work in rural areas. Recruitment continued well into 2007. Capacity building of all staff is a high priority, in functional areas such as computer literacy, the English language, media production, project management, community survey and research skills, service delivery, enterprise development and performance monitoring, as well as generic skills such as leadership and teamwork capabilities.

Capacity building programmes have also been conducted for MC members and other community members, with an initial focus on key staff and other members of local organisations and agencies. iREACH has built capacity both through formal courses and 'learning by doing', a method embraced by the CFs rather than formal training. This external capacity development includes training on how to mainstream ICT into community institutions.

As iREACH approaches the end of the initial funding period in April 2010, its transformation into an independent organisation, formally registered with local and national authorities, is being pursued. This will enable iREACH to evolve towards a community-owned enterprise in each area, continuing current activities and expanding into related areas.

Setting up the Technologies and Infrastructure

Having specified the ICT and power requirements, iREACH engaged in a lengthy process of negotiating with suppliers of the different components: building renovation, equipment, installation, and connectivity. District councils provided the premises for each HQ and iREACH renovated and equipped the buildings with the appropriate infrastructure, including power supply and cabling, since only the HQ in Kep was provided with mains power.

Hardware

Each of the pilot HQ is connected via satellite (IPstar) to the Internet at 1024/512 Kb/s. Hubs are connected to the HQ via wireless networks in both the Kep and KCM pilots. The wireless connection between an HQ and its hubs is a mixture of point-to-point and omni-directional links. Omni connectivity is provided using Securelink equipment within the unlicensed 2.4 GHz band at a rate of 54 Mb/s using the 802.11g protocol. The point-to-point links are via Trango equipment using the unlicensed 5.8 GHz band that supports a 10Mb/s data transfer rate with a proprietary protocol similar to WiMax.

These local ICT networks were designed and installed by a Cambodian-based IT company. The tender was issued in November 2006 but contracts were signed only in May 2007 due to inadequate initial specifications, limited technical capabilities of suppliers in Cambodia, and the generally slow pace of contract development. The final design, specification and deployment of the infrastructure also took much longer than expected. Difficult topography at Kep created problems for Gateway, the successful bidder, with line of sight propagation, requiring a complicated wireless transmission structure with one repeater station. The complete ICT infrastructure was finally in place at both sites in April 2008.

Each HQ has a desktop computer used as a server and the Pilot Coordinator, Research Coordinator, Multi-media coordinator and Content Developers each have a laptop computer. There is also one desktop with an LCD display at each hub, managed by the hub's CF.

In all but three centres in Kep - the HQ and two hubs which are connected to the grid - electrical power is supplied by solar panel/battery systems. The KCM HQ has sixteen solar panels and a battery supported system, while all hubs have solar power. Both HQs have petrol powered backup generators. Each hub has one or more solar panels, with a battery, capable of supplying between 300 and 600 watts of power, enough for the single computer and networking equipment.

Software

From the outset staff laptop computers and servers located at the central office in Phnom Penh and HQ pilots were running the pre-installed Windows Vista or XP operating system. This proprietary operating system was chosen mainly because only the Microsoft Office suite of user applications was fully localised into the Khmer language at the time of the iREACH launch. Further, what prior experience staff had was entirely based on Windows. Initial application level software that was selected to run on this base was: Skype, Active Webcam, and Netop School. The servers also ran Kerio Winroute firewall.

During the initial period of operation network management was performed in an ad-hoc manner, without any operational processes or documentation. There was no software for IT systems management and no security assessment was done during the installation and initial operation of the system. At least one incident resulting in service downtime for the entire network was due to unauthorised access to the network. An intruder was able to log in and change all the configurations.

As a result of this and subsequent unsatisfactory technical performance of some aspects of the network, iREACH commissioned a technical review of the whole system in May 2008. A key recommendations of the report resulting from this review was to install a network management system based on open source software, including the OpenNMS network management platform. This has subsequently been implemented.

An extract from the report described some aspects of the systems management:

There is 1 technical staff [TS] at each HQ responsible for Systems and Network Adminis-

tration. The [TS] at KCM HQ is more familiar with systems while the [TS] at Kep HQ is more familiar with networks. [Neither TS is familiar with the others' work and would not be capable of switching roles].

Due to the lack of documentation and inconsistent [approach to] deployment, the loss of either [TS] will have an impact on the provision of support services, resulting in potential downtime, service unavailability and longer periods of recovery. The impact is higher if the passwords that provide access to systems and network were not [shared]. In addition, the entire infrastructure could be held hostage by a disgruntled staff. Unauthorized access to the network can occur if the access rights of ex-staff are not removed.

In the longer term, there will be a lack of knowledge institutionalised within the project. There are no processes established or root cause analysis. [Neither TS] are familiar with open source OS and [applications] programs.

The report put forward several suggestions regarding IT management systems, including software tools that would enable centralised monitoring of all systems and network operation from the Phnom Penh office. Such tools could also support remote recovery from some field computer problems. Several of these network management recommendations have been implemented and there is now significant centralised management of the network. However, there still is much room for more comprehensive monitoring and efficient management of the ICT infrastructure.

A number of the other recommendations from this technical assistance report have also been implemented with a recent considerable movement toward use of open source software. Ubuntu (Linux) is now used on Phnom Penh servers and some laptops; Apache at both HQs; Makala, a Khmer version of Firefox and Mozilla's browser, is widely used; Mayura, a Khmer email client (an Outlook look alike); and several other open source applications.

The technical support staff person in Phnom Penh has given three one day workshops on Open Office with Khmer Unicode and MySQL to all staff at the central office and at both pilots. However, the pilot CFs, located at the hubs still need more training and experience with Linux and open office before they can move to open source.

Creating Partnership with the Community

Building partnerships was from the outset a central goal of iREACH. Establishing occasional as well as enduring relationships with organisations at every level - community based organisations, service providing NGOs, commune, provincial and national government entities and agencies, donors and private sector – is seen as critical to sustainability. Partnerships are a way of embedding iREACH within the immediate community and the broader environment, developing interdependencies and synergies, extending the breadth of potential upstream and downstream ICT users and services provided.

A first step in extending stakeholders was to ensure that each pilot, although under the Minister of Commerce, was managed by independent Cambodian bodies. The Center for Social Development (CSD), an independent Cambodian NGOn active in several provinces, agreed to oversee the pilot in Kep; and Maharishi Vedic University (MVU – the university has since been renamed Chea Sim Kamchai Mear University), at the time Cambodia's only rural university and based in Kamchai Mear itself, agreed to oversee the pilot there.

Perhaps the most interesting and successful of the partnerships developed is with the community itself. The elected pilot management committees (MCs) provide effective guidance to the pilots, as well as engendering a sense of ownership and commitment among the wider community. Their success is critical to iREACH since these are the kernel of a community owned enterprise, evolving over time to develop the various skills and

capabilities needed to run an autonomous and sustainable business. The process of establishing the management committees was therefore carefully planned with the maximum level of participation from the community. The challenge was to design and implement a process that is initiated and overseen from the outside, yet could quickly earn legitimacy and acceptance among the local community.

In a country lacking a long tradition of democracy, the process of electing the management committees using transparent, democratic and widespread (if not universal) suffrage was certainly a new experience for the communities involved. All management committee members are directly elected local villagers.

Designed and managed by the pilot teams, an interim pilot committee was first formed through secret ballots at the communes involved in each pilot. Based on the selection criteria, a total of 12 Interim Committee members were elected from three communes of KCM (four elected in each commune) and another 12 Interim Committee members were elected in three communes of Kep (four in each commune). These Interim Committees selected the locations for hubs, established the guidelines for the election of the Management Committees and established the bylaws.

Management Committees were then elected through a process in principle similar to that of the interim committees, in each pilot, organized by the Interim Committee with support from the project staff. Based on the selection criteria, a committee of 12 was elected from the three KCM communes (including six women) and a Committee of 13 from the three Kep communes (including five women). With four candidates in each commune, the inclusion of at least one of each gender on the list of four was mandatory. During the election process candidates were permitted to speak for two to three minutes in support of their case, introducing themselves, stating what they could offer and what they wanted to do to assist the community.

iREACH has thus been successful in achieving its gender balance objective for the management committees. Almost half of members are women, and have been given key management roles as chair, deputy chair and secretary.

The main tasks of the committees are to provide advice and direction to the project, maintain and manage all hubs, including setting prices of ICT service, conduct management meetings, coordinate project activities and represent the community. Management committee members represent a diverse group of local villagers. They do not receive a salary but get a small allowance for attending meetings and working with the community. Other community members have gradually become involved in day-to-day management of the hubs in their villages as well as taking charge of the various activities involved in arranging committee meetings, such as preparing the agenda, which regularly includes items dealing with future activities required to improve the sustainability of iREACH. Committee members are also involved in the whole process of preparing audio programmes, from the selection of topics, to collection of material, preparation of scripts, and recording. The level of participation is subject to external influences: for instance, farming cycles mean that most community members are busy during the rice season and national elections during June/July 2008 diverted attention from active participation in hub activities.

Other partnerships have also been developed at the national and local levels. Both pilots have strengthened their collaboration with local authorities, including commune and district councils and have good relationships with local institutions, such as pagodas and schools. These institutions assist with the promotion of iREACH. The KCM pilot has strong links with the district agricultural office; SEILA, a UNDP supported local government capacity building programme; and IFAD (International Fund for Agricultural Development) projects in the locality. The Kep pilot site is in the process of establishing partnerships Bridges

Across Borders (BAB), a Cambodian NGO. Both Pilots are developing a partnership with CAMIP, a donor funded agricultural project, to provide market related market information to farmers.

While maintaining the independence of iREACH and the future community enterprises, and with the approval of the Ministry of the Interior, iREACH pilots are in the process of exploring the means by which formal institutional links and even governance links could be established with local authorities and the iREACH model adopted within the strategic plans of commune councils.

Putting it All Together: The Services

An early and serious disappointment for the team and the communities related to community radio. The original plans included a community radio station, managed by the community and broadcasting at each pilot site. This was to comprise a central part of the pilots, in terms of reaching out to the more remote parts and marginalised groups in the community, providing key services, and generating income. Despite early assurances, however, obtaining a license proved impossible. Audio content has been communicated over village loudspeakers in the hubs which, though popular, is no substitute for broadcast radio.

The Internet and local broadband network carry most iREACH services. But rather than being a telecentre, iREACH services focus on economic and social development. Standard web and email access is available at all the hubs, but content produced by iREACH, with user feedback facilities, and other specifically developed services such 'Family-Link-Up' and 'Village-to-Village' are also available to community members at all village hubs.

Education

Recognising that formal and informal distance learning has the potential to contribute to economic and social development (UNDP, 2004), building of human capacity through education is a critical activity for iREACH. Baseline surveys conducted at the start of the project revealed some disturbing facts about education. Despite free primary education and free school breakfasts provided by UNICEF, participants in a baseline survey consultation workshop in Kep in 2007 estimated that approximately 10% of children in the 6-12 age group were not enrolled in primary schools. The estimate in the KCM baseline study was 7-10%. There is no official discrimination against girls, but most of the children who do not attend school are girls. No females were enrolled at university, not even at the local state-supported university in KCM. The drop-out rate for both boys and girls was high in both primary and secondary school, at 32% in secondary school. Reasons for dropping-out of school included poverty, children having to work, parents not realising the importance of education, failing the exams, distance between the school and home, and concern about the safety of children on the way between home and school.

Most learning activities at iREACH have been of an informal nature, addressing local issues, including agriculture, animal husbandry, and human health. In order to address a lack of knowledge in these areas, the content developers at iREACH have produced locally and culturally appropriate audio and video training material and made it available through different media. In the absence of the radio license, the pilot sites have displayed their creativity by narrowcasting through loudspeakers, mobile video, and conducting training over their networks, through the 'Village–to-Village' service (see below). Experts on different agricultural topics have been invited to give lectures over the networks. Community members can participate in these lectures by going to the nearest hub. Thematic video and audio conferences and conversations over Skype have also been used for educational purposes. Programme material primarily covers child rearing, health, education, agriculture, (for example appropriate fertilisers for rice production, gourd planting using natural

methods, animal husbandry) and fishing. iREACH also provides on-demand informational services on these and other topics on which villagers are seeking knowledge. As an encouragement for villagers to send their children to school, iREACH has produced a video on school enrolment, which has been shown in some villages.

More formal distance education is also planned in conjunction with potential partners. The ability of students to use the hubs for their homework is another way in which iREACH is contributing to education in the local area. In collaboration with Pandora, another IDRC funded project focusing on distance education and operating in several Asian countries, the Kep facilities will be used in a trial for teacher training.

Product Development Process

A number of services have been developed along a more conventional 'product development' path, an approach that deliberately introduces business practices to the pilot teams and the local committees. Each service is intended ultimately to generate income and introduce a set of practices that can be replicated in the future.

The product development process includes market research, product definition, operational processes, launch and other implementation details. The Family-Link-Up service for overseas calls, using VOIP via Skype, was the first product to be subject to this form of planning. A modest income is generated from this service, which enables villagers to stay in contact with family members who have moved away from the villages.

Another service developed in this way is the 'Village–to-Village' portfolio. As the name suggests, this service is based on audio and visual communication between different villages, an embodiment of positive externalities, i.e. the greater the coverage of the system and the more villagers that become involved in iREACH, the greater the value of iREACH to each user. It is a tool for interactive learning and other interaction involving two or more hubs. Village-to-Village applications use a combination of Skype and Netop School (proprietary training software). Examples of initiatives offered under the Village-to-Village service include the following:

- Using skype between villages for interaction, communication and education purposes
- Talk by a young female user of the benefits she has derived from using iREACH. She explained how she, in addition to being able to search for information and using e-mail to communicate with friends and relatives overseas, had learned to type Khmer script and was using this skill to design invitations for weddings and promotional material for festivals and ceremonies.
- English courses, operated so far on a trial basis, and run by iREACH staff. Consideration is now given to offering them as accredited courses through an English school, generating revenue for iREACH.
- Videoconferences on the various aspects of rice production (soil types, worm and insect protection), chicken raising, dengue fever and on benefits of using iREACH.
- A Buddhist ceremony followed by questions and answers
- Two regular daily narrowcasting programmes at KCM, consisting of material produced elsewhere, e.g. material downloaded from the Internet, and excerpts from radio stations and from daily newspapers covering news and topics such as health, education, agriculture.

In addition there are daily thematic narrowcasts from the Kep HQ using loudspeakers, with over 300 topics covered, ranging from latest news and information on agriculture, education and health issues. Most topics are from the daily newspapers. The narrowcasts are extended to the village hubs, where the content can be re-narrowcast by connecting the PCs with loudspeakers.

During the second half of 2008, the pilot sites began charging for some services, including Family-Link-Up. Learning how to administer revenue from an accounting perspective is another important capacity being developed at iREACH.

Users

Attendance at the hubs was slower to develop than had been hoped, but strong growth has been recorded into 2009 as more services became available.

During the 18 month period September 2007 to the end of April 2009, the total number of unique visitors using all hub services in the Kep pilots amounted to 3,553, 43% of them female and amounting in total to about 10% of the population. These included 2,369 students, 782 community members, 210 school teachers and civil servants, 33 NGO staff, 96 monks and 63 business people/traders. However, users made multiple visits to the hubs so that the total number of *visits* to all hubs in the Kep pilot came to 36,967 (14,888 by women) for the period. This yields an average monthly visit count of over 2,053, but this had grown to over 3,100 by March 2009.

In the case of the KCM pilot, the total number of unique visitors using all hub services from August 2007 April 2009 came to 10,687 – nearly 13% of the population – and a total of 4,107 (38%) of them women. These comprised 8,539 students, 2,009 community members, 123 school teachers and civil servants, and 16 NGO staff. The total number of *visits* to all hubs in KCM amounted to 96,183, of which 36,963 were by women. Overall, the higher absolute numbers in KCM are accounted for by the larger population and the location of the university in KCM adjacent to the iREACH HQ hub facilitating the use of iREACH services by university students. But the predominance of students leads to significant variations during term time and holiday periods.

Usage levels might have risen earlier were it not for some initial disappointment with the lack of a telephony service. Villagers were under the impression that cheap overseas calls would be available from the hubs and some of them became disillusioned when regulatory obstacles blocked the development of this service. A compromise, in the form of the Family-Link-Up service, was introduced in September 2008 and with less than two months availability in that reporting period, its full effect has not yet been felt in the usage statistics.

Taking a wider perspective of the term 'users', it should include villagers who attend mobile video shows screened by iREACH in villages. These shows combine education with entertainment. Although statistics for attendance at these shows are not available, the total number of villagers exposed iREACH in this way are likely to far exceed the number attending the village hubs.

Evaluating the Processes and Outputs

To some extent, iREACH may be seen as a grand experimental platform for ICTs in poor rural areas, covering technologies, capacity building and empowerment, service development and use, and enterprise creation. Given also the interests of the IDRC, a systematic and comprehensive approach is taken to monitoring, evaluating and documenting every aspect of the pilots and other activities. This is particularly challenging in Cambodia given the limited experience and capacity in these activities.

As a donor funded project, six-monthly administrative reports are prepared covering past activities, comparing them to plans, addressing challenges, and outlining priorities for the next six months. These encourage staff to regularly review their activities and think about how iREACH can be improved to better service communities, and offer ongoing insights into the development of the project. Reports are available on the iREACH website.

But more formal monitoring and evaluation is also deployed across a number of areas.

Baseline Surveys

At an early stage of the project, between November 2006 and July 2007, baseline surveys were conducted at both pilot sites to assess the current circumstances of the community and to provide a set of benchmarks against which progress could be measured.

Approximately 100 randomly selected households at each pilot site were surveyed. The surveys were complemented with participatory rural appraisal (PRA) activities, both of which were led by external advisors and overseen by the research manager and pilot co-ordinators. The research findings confirmed the critical role of education in building human capacity and supporting development goals and also yielded important data that enabled the project team to construct an information and communications profile of the area, depicting ICT usage in different community sectors. Table 5 summarises ownership of ICT equipment in KCM and Kep. The study also revealed that none of the local population was familiar with the Internet or VoIP and only 1% could use a computer.

The most common way to communicate and disseminate information for social and work/business purposes was through house-to-house visits, community billboards, and community events. Mobile phones were used only to a limited extent, and there were no public phone booths in the villages. There is no functioning postal system.

Table 5. Ownership of ICT equipment

Ownership of ICT equipment	KCM	Kep
Television	77%	20%
VCR/DVD player	34%	20%
Radio receiver	18%	15%
Mobile phone	20%	7%

Needs Assessment using Participatory Development Communication

The participatory development communication (PDC) approach was deployed to assess community needs and as a capacity building exercise in itself, both for the pilot team and the people participating. Using a series of intensive workshops at local community level, the needs of each of the two pilots were explored through various mapping techniques. Beginning with general needs, these narrowed in on the area of communication.

The PDC process was in itself a positive experience for the local communities in terms of generating awareness of the value of their own knowledge, and publicising the iREACH project. The local community showed a keen awareness of their needs and of the potential role of communication, and their eagerness to participate was seen as a positive sign for iREACH.

OM/SPEAK

Monitoring and ongoing evaluation is undertaken using a combination of two participatory methodologies.

Outcome Mapping (OM) is a tool for project management and ongoing monitoring (www.outcomemapping.ca) originating with International Development Research Centre (IDRC) in Canada and now widely used in development projects. In iREACH, OM has been uniquely combined with SPEAK (Strategic Planning, Evaluation and Knowledge system), a software supported participatory monitoring and evaluation tool developed in Ireland by NEXUS Research Cooperative.

Together, the two offer a methodology that enables systematic reflection on the use of resources to achieve ongoing goals, a means to record and capture ongoing resources use, outputs and impacts, and to keep the pilots focused on their main goals (Ó Siochrú, Hak & Long, 2009).

Recognising that development is about the interaction between people and their environments, OM/SPEAK focuses on changes in behaviour, relationships, actions, and activities in the people,

groups, and organisations it works with directly. These are referred to as boundary partners. All staff members are required to input data on their activities and achievements in the programme's database, enabling the compilation of a resource audit. This is related to outputs, and workshops are combined with evidence to collectively examine outcomes, including the participation of the pilot committees. OM/SPEAK is implemented on an annual cycle, which then feeds back into goals and objectives.

Miscellaneous Research

The Pilots also conduct other regular as well as ad-hoc research, for instance market research for new services. The role of the pilot research co-ordinators extends beyond research for the actual 'project', where the project is defined in a narrow sense. The intention is that they will spearhead local research teams that can initiate and respond to various needs of the community and in order to accomplish this, the starting point was to include training in basic research capabilities in capacity development activities.

For example, a survey was conducted prior to the introduction of the Family-Link-Up service in August 2008 and the research co-ordinators are following up with a post-implementation survey through a user information form.

Finally, an impact assessment project has begun, building on the data provided above. The results of its initial set of research activities, are presented below in a section devoted to considering the impact of iREACH.

THE IMPACT OF IREACH ON THE LOCAL COMMUNITY

This section is an edited extract from a report on the research (Grunfeld et al., 2009). iREACH staff, together with an external researcher, conducted a participatory impact evaluation assessment in February 2009 involving 22 focus group sessions,

10 in Kep, and 12 in KCM. The results offer a first opportunity to assess how iREACH has impacted on the daily lives of the two communities. The research was the first wave of a planned three part longitudinal study over a two to three year period.

Of the 149 participants, 42% were women. Slightly less than half of all participants had used computers and/or the Internet. A few participants had used iREACH since its inception and other users were relative newcomers, most having first visited less than a year before. The frequency of iREACH attendance among participants varied considerably, from daily to irregular visits and from a few minutes to an hour per visit.

Separate focus group sessions were held for different interest groups: teachers, NGO and government staff, fishing and farming communities, village and commune leaders, women, youth, business owners, and management committee members. Nobody participated in more than one group, despite the obvious overlap in categories e.g. village leaders may also be farmers and women. Users and non-users were in separate groups in KCM, but not in Kep.

Staff at iREACH arranged invitations to the sessions in cooperation with the management committees. All sessions were at the iREACH HQ and hubs across the coverage area. iREACH staff facilitated the sessions and interpreted for the external researcher.

The findings are not necessarily representative of the population in the coverage area as the sampling technique was not probabilistic. They nevertheless give an insight into the views of broad cross-sections of the communities.

The involvement of staff and an external researcher may have influenced responses. However, the high degree of consistency in views across the focus groups indicates a reasonable level of reliability, i.e. that participants were sincere and accurate in their responses.

A common framework guided all sessions, which were semi-structured. Questions included general views about communities and the role of iREACH, ICT usage, reasons for non-use, views about iREACH and participants' perception of iREACH's impact. The emphasis here is on how those who participated in the focus groups perceived the contribution made by iREACH to their livelihoods and other aspects of well-being. Relevant questions for that purpose were:

- most significant changes resulting from iREACH
- main benefit(s) of iREACH
- new and useful knowledge and how this had been applied
- whether participants were able to do anything they did not realise they could do,
- the influence on equality, especially gender equality, and
- the impact on relationships between parents and children.

No responses were mutually exclusive, e.g. there was no limit to how many items participants could include as most significant changes or benefits.

Most Significant Change and Main Benefit of iREACH

Responses to questions about the most significant change and the main benefits of iREACH almost mirrored each other. In both cases, participants overwhelmingly referred to access to information and newly gained understanding of and ability to use computers and other ICT facilities. They often mentioned the children's opportunity to learn and ability to use ICTs: 'it is important for the children to understand ICT', and 'it is good to see them learn computers and other skills, such as English and Khmer typing instead of playing in the streets'. Some participants noted the benefits of children teaching other children and adults as well as volunteering in other ways at the hubs, and of them finding new friends overseas.

The ability to learn new farming methods also ranked highly in response to both questions, with ten groups mentioning this.

IREACH was frequently associated with improved communication facilities. Participants referred to better communication in different ways, including: maintaining contacts with family and access to improved communication systems for communities. Some participants made specific reference to Family-Link-Up and others just used 'access to communication'. The fact that Family-Link-Up is cheap compared to the most convenient alternative i.e. to use their own or a time-shared mobile service, was an important consideration. Participants in several groups identified as a key benefit, savings resulting from not having to travel to other ICT facilities and the free or low-cost nature of iREACH's services

Six groups, four of which were non-users in KCM, attached great importance to local and overseas news, and four groups referred to positive changes in livelihoods, poverty reduction, and higher incomes.

The only group in which the majority could not identify any discernible change was the business group in Kep; but at least one of the participants in that group identified better ICT knowledge and better information on agriculture market prices as a key benefit.

New and Useful Knowledge and Application of that Knowledge

A series of questions was designed to explore the extent to which participants have found new and useful knowledge; how they applied what they learned; and whether iREACH has enabled them to do anything they did not realise they were capable of. As they yielded similar data, responses are combined in this section.

The most frequent response related to knowledge of and ability to use computers and the Internet. For some, the mere exposure to computers and the Internet was a revelation. Many participants

perceived their ability to find information as a major achievement. For children, ICT had greater instrumental value. The youth and older participants, on behalf of the younger generations, were eager for them to learn ICTs as they associated this capability with income-earning opportunities.

Several users have applied their new ICT skills to typing and communicating beyond the village level, using email and Skype. Participants in five of the groups specifically referred to typing, which they explained is a difficult task with the large number of signs in the Khmer script. They considered the ease with which many can now communicate externally another achievement. Audio editing by a young man volunteering with preparation of broadcasts in Kep is another example of a new ICT skill with a practical application.

The second most common response related to the application of new farming techniques. Participants attributed better living conditions to improved practices and higher yields resulting from this knowledge. One woman remarked how she has a much healthier pig after learning about feeding, watering, and cleaning it. Using knowledge obtained through the Internet, some participants in the farming community group in KCM have established an experimental mushroom growing plot. This is a community project at one of the hub sites. Chea Sim Kamchai Mear University supplied the spawn culture and supervised the project. Villagers primarily learned about new farm practices through Village-to-Village lectures and training and other forms of information mediation, rather than from accessing the Internet by themselves.

Knowledge about computers and improved livelihoods through agriculture information were also common responses in the non-user group at KCM. As they were non-users of iREACH, they would have learnt this from others. Participants in four of the six non-user groups in KCM considered iREACH had been useful for community development. Only two groups among the users in KCM, and none in Kep, referred to community development. The views of non-users indicate that iREACH has spillover effects, beyond its actual users.

Participants in several groups thought that iREACH has provided useful knowledge on health. One of the outcomes mentioned was an increase in the number of women availing themselves of pre-natal care at the clinics.

The younger participants gained confidence in job applications with their computer skills and thought they would be able to find vacancies more easily on the Internet. They knew of someone who had gained employment with an NGO after finding the vacancy on the Internet.

Community management members, who have received special training, e.g. in script writing, minute taking, and project management, referred to their new skills as something they had not expected they would be able to learn.

Impact on Equality and Gender Empowerment

A question relating to the impact of iREACH on equality, explored the perception of iREACH with respect to improving the conditions of the most disadvantaged and other aspects of equality. Rather than addressing impact most participants instead pointed to iREACH's policies and practices. Despite an absence of a specific gender analytical dimension in this research, the discussion on equality focused almost exclusively on gender equality.

The initial response to the question on equality in nearly every group was that iREACH is 'transparent', which meant that iREACH does not discriminate against anyone. Some of the groups went further and expressed the view that iREACH has encouraged women to participate actively in its activities, through gender awareness that has been promoted throughout the project's history. Someone in the Kep NGO group gave the example of a community facilitator visiting homes, specifically inviting women to attend regular training. As

a result, in that hub, five women were attending a typing course on Saturdays. They considered typing a useful skill for women, e.g. for employment in NGOs and for typing job applications.

Participants in the farming group in Kep referred to the election process for the management committee as having led to greater gender awareness. However, members of the management committee in Kep did not highlight any gender equality improvements in their communities. Participants in other groups had noticed that women had become more active in the community, but did not attribute this solely to iREACH, and commented that other NGOs also promote gender equality.

One of the outcomes pointed out by two groups in KCM was that previously women had nowhere to go outside their homes and therefore rarely ventured out other than to attend to necessities. Using iREACH as a meeting place, in combination with the information and communication opportunities at the hubs, they noted that the lives of female users have become easier and more enjoyable. Many women have developed skills in using computers, including typing and finding information by themselves, skills they never thought they would be able to acquire.

Several participants considered women's ability to use ICT a sign of improved equality. Some women in the farming group aspired to use their ICT skills in working with NGOs and for teaching computers to others. A few outspoken female students in the youth group in KCM explained how the resources of iREACH had helped them in their studies. A female student in KCM had become somewhat of a legend when she managed to find an explanation to a mathematical formula on the Internet after the teacher had been unable to explain it to the satisfaction of some of the students. In addition to the youth group, participants in the village and commune leader group mentioned this incident.

Three groups in KCM (commune and village leaders, women, and farmers) talked about what men think about women's participation in iREACH. Despite being sometimes worried about the security of women leaving their homes, the consensus was that men were supportive of their wives attending iREACH and the opportunity for learning this represents, as long as home duties were not neglected. Participants in the KCM women's group added a different perspective. They colourfully illustrated how, equipped at the iREACH centre with knowledge about domestic violence, they had lectured their intoxicated husbands.

Where women do not have time to attend, many of them benefit from their children or others attending, as someone in the KCM women's group commented: 'we delegate to our children to learn and bring home knowledge'.

No socio-cultural issues emerged that would prevent women from making use of iREACH per se. The only exception could be the reluctance of women to sit close to monks. According to the business group in Kep, with increasing number of monks attending hubs at pagodas, many women shy away. However, user statistics did not indicate a lower proportion of women in pagoda hubs, compared to other hubs in Kep.

Impact on Family Relationships

The impact of iREACH on family relationships was explored by a question on whether parents had any concern about their children attending iREACH. By contrast, many parents encouraged their children to use iREACH and were proud of their ICT skills. Participants illustrated how iREACH has improved family relationships.

Firstly, it has made it easier to be in contact with family members living overseas. The Family-Link-Up service and, to a lesser extent e-mail and skype, have facilitated links with overseas family members. Secondly, relationships between parents and children have strengthened, by children passing on knowledge and news to their parents. Many adults learned new agricultural skills and obtained international, national, and local news, e.g. security

alerts, in this way. Some parents found out about Family-Link-Up from their children, who often encouraged their parents to attend.

Reasons for not Participating in iREACH

Most of those who do not use iREACH responded that they are too busy, whether with home duties, income generating work, or schoolwork. Participants in two groups saw no need for and/or benefits of using iREACH. Other reasons included: 'did not know about iREACH', 'afraid to damage computers', 'insufficient literacy and other skills and knowledge', 'cannot speak English', and 'want to give opportunities to children'. A few considered that they lived too far from the hub, but not everyone living in the proximity of a hub was a user. For example, someone in the women's group in Kep had never visited the hub located just across the road from her house.

Key Findings of Participatory Research

The findings of the study indicate that iREACH has made significant progress in adapting ICT to local needs of different population segments in Kep and KCM. This has resulted in many positive outcomes. Most participants could attribute improvements in their livelihoods and well-being, particularly from better agriculture and heath knowledge to iREACH and some participants have used iREACH facilities in innovative ways. Participants have also noticed benefits on children's education and their interest in learning. There were high expectations that iREACH will be useful in finding employment and increasing the employability of the youth.

However, iREACH has so far not led to any new enterprises and there was only limited reference by commune council members of iREACH having been used for governance applications.

Throughout the sessions, participants indicated, often by implication rather than directly, that their exposure to iREACH was empowering, particularly for women. Many of the individual and community capacities and capabilities participants attributed to iREACH have created conditions for further empowerment. Through its community engagement and community centred activities, iREACH has gained the trust of participants. This was evidenced by recurring appeals for iREACH to continue.

FUTURE PERSPECTIVES

iREACH was initially funded until April 2009 and then granted an extension until April 2010. The initial delays had led to underspending so that no additional funding was required for this extension.

The objective of transforming the project into sustainable community enterprises, however, is likely to need additional time beyond 2010 and additional external resources. Community members require considerable exposure to and experience of new technologies before acceptance (Musa 2006), and before the benefits are evident and sufficiently widespread among the community.

Extending the model to other rural areas will also require a successful process of policy mainstreaming.

Sustainability and Viability

Sustainability problems have plagued many community based ICT initiatives in developed and developing countries alike. Revenues generated from the local population rarely suffice to sustain their operation. There are different arguments. Equating self-funding and commercial viability with sustainability of community based operators can clash with their community and social objectives. Just as universal service obligations are accepted as a policy instrument to bring services to remote locations in the developed world, so

it may make policy sense for community based operators to be subsidised. The arguments, ranging from economic to social, used in favour of universal service mechanisms are equally valid for community based operators: externalities, social inclusion, and equity. Although possibly not fully realisable until a critical mass emerges to support more applications, there are also potential cost savings associated with providing health, education, and other government services. It is ironic that where the greatest savings can be made in the provision of government services, i.e. in remote areas, is also where obtaining funding for sustainability of adequate infrastructure faces its greatest challenge.

Future sustainability is likely to require a number of elements. Ongoing voluntary contributions of time and some resources from the community will be critical, and self generated income will over time increase, but iREACH is unlikely in the foreseeable future to become entirely self-funded. Rather than having to rely on grants of a short term nature, it must therefore seek regular and committed funding from public sources, linked to the services it delivers to the community. This requires a policy environment that shifts perceptions of community based operators as organisations that must become self-funding to a recognition of the contribution they can make to the welfare of communities and to achieving public policy objectives

Policy Influencing

A key objective of iREACH is to 'mainstream' the experiences and lessons into ICT policy in a manner that will enable the concept to be incorporated into government policy at different levels.

To this end, staff is documenting their experiences in the project, has analysed relevant national policy and regulatory documentation and is engaged with communities on policy input. Discussions are underway at the district and community levels about various barriers of existing ICT policy and difficulties in obtaining relevant information. The outcome of this community engagement, together with ongoing findings from the pilots, will provide essential feed-back from the micro-level to national-level policymakers, particularly regarding its impact and benefits. The knowledge produced can contribute to further development of the conceptual framework within which iREACH is operating and influence the government in its formulation of ICT policies. Such a framework would take social, as well as technical, legal, economic and market factors into account. It is envisaged that the policy input will incorporate views on how information and knowledge through a project such as iREACH can be used to improve sustainable livelihoods, capabilities, social capital, and equality. iREACH can use its experiences at the local level to inform the government on how its policies are affecting people.

Both the local and the national level of policy and government are relevant. Indeed, local level policy could be particularly important. Each pilot covers three communes, each of which has an elected commune council. Cambodia, with strong support from international donors and agencies, is undergoing a sustained process of decentralisation under which the commune level will receive increased budgets but also the power to collect revenues through taxation and other means. The two pilots are exploring mechanisms to link commune councils to local pilot committees at the level of governance, perhaps through the incorporation of some elected council members onto the committee. The goal here is to integrate the iREACH model or specific services as part of the Commune Development Plans regularly drawn up by the communes. Such plans can then draw on funding from various sources.

At the same time, iREACH is preparing policy input aimed at influencing government policy in a direction that will enable the replication of the iREACH model. This might be timely since, as noted earlier, a universal service policy has been drafted and is awaiting (for some time) govern-ment approval. Although universal telephony is the immediate focus of the draft policy, more advanced communications including telecentres are also specifically mentioned. There are also moves to create an independent regulator. And pilots are planned to provide e-government service at commune level. The iREACH objective is to influence such policies in a direction favourable to poor communities and to women, building on the experience of iREACH in community-driven ICT enterprises and incorporating best practice from international experience.

When governments undertake policy analyses, various options are usually compared against a checklist in which financial indicators play an important role. In addition to the documented benefits, the iREACH policy input also requires a reasonable assessment of the costs associated with establishing and running a community based operator. The accounting information and experi-ence gained by iREACH can contribute to this analysis. Future projects can learn from iREACH and avoid some of the expenses incurred. At the same time a focus on financial information should not obscure the social value of the model, and special attention must be given to resolving any conflict between financial viability and social goals. As demonstrated in the Akshaya case study (Kuriyan, Ray & Toyama, 2008), clarity in these objectives and their interrelationships is essential to achieving social development objectives.

New Initiatives

Regardless of how favourable the policy environ-ment turns out to be, iREACH must nevertheless constantly innovate and evolve, to enhance its local impact and remain relevant to the needs of its constituencies. Some initiatives currently being planned or underway are primarily in the areas of additional partnerships and the introduction of new products and services.

Further partnerships are being sought among government agencies and NGOs such that these institutions will use iREACH facilities. This can take several forms. For example, the government can use iREACH to trial e-government applications and general services. In addition to education, health is an area where iREACH could play a useful role. The baseline surveys pointed to a lack of public medical facilities and, where they exist, villagers are not attending them due to unsatisfactory service. iREACH may consider using its facilities for remote consultation and treatment, involving specialists located in Phnom Penh.

Business partnerships is another area for further development. iREACH could be used as some form of business incubator for local businesses or individuals with business ideas. The skills developed by staff are useful in different areas of business development, e.g. market research, administration, and design of promotional material. Businesses can also use iREACH to promote their products and services.

On the product side, the next major initiative is involvement in the one laptop per child (OLPC) scheme. iREACH has been offered 400 XO laptops and is preparing a plan on how to make best use of these. One option is to deploy them at the hubs to increase the number of villagers that could make use of these. There is sufficient capacity at the hubs to take on a greater number of access points. The technical consultant's report referred to above suggested a move towards the use of low cost portable devices at the hubs, which have 'hotspot' capabilities, i.e. the reach would be beyond the actual hub itself. This would enable greater access to iREACH applications, encourage and empower users to experiment and use the applications, attract a larger user base.

Existing mobile phones that support wifi access (such as Nokia N series and iPhone) can also be used. Software programs such as Fring can be installed on standard mobile devices to leverage the hub's wifi capabilities to access functions such as voice calls, instant messaging and file transfers. Fring is compatible with Symbian 8, 9.1, 9.2, Windows Mobile 5 & 6 and UIQ handsets.

CONCLUDING REMARKS

iREACH has been successful in overcoming initial obstacles to deployment of its physical infrastructure and has developed a team of enthusiastic and skilled staff. In particular, it has been effective in engaging the local community in management and other project activities and in extending access to knowledge through the production and exchange of information. With the adoption of proper network management tools and a professional approach to product management, iREACH is gradually adopting enterprise practices without compromising its community development objectives.

More time is needed for conclusive evidence of the merits of the community based operator model as a means to deploy ICTs in rural areas in Cambodia. It is not overly optimistic to discern promising signs that the model can deliver both ICT-based services and desirable social outcomes in rural Cambodia. But the key issue comes back to sustainability and the form that this might take. Financial viability can only to some degree come from user revenues, and volunteer and community support reduces costs significantly. But local communities are poor, and the model is likely to require additional sources of income. A number of possibilities exist. For instance the delivery of e-government services, such as health and education, can lead to revenue streams from central sources. Other users can also be targeted such as tourism in the Kep area (which has a past history of tourism and is designated as a growth centre).

Sustainability may also emerge from the Cambodian government policies and a regulatory framework conducive to operators with this commercial and social function dual function.

A universal service scheme, already existing in developed and developing countries to provide services in areas unprofitable for commercial operators, lends itself to this type of operation. It makes sense that such a scheme should be implemented not solely by agencies involved in ICT policies. Government entities with mandates and obligations to provide services to the public must also be part of developing the scheme, capable of aggregating the benefits accruing from using a network of this nature for health, education and other services. And it is only when these applications are available on the network, that the true benefits become apparent to users.

The next couple of years will be critical in terms of whether the government can introduce a universal service scheme that will encourage the spread of community based networks across rural areas of Cambodia. This time would be used to deepen the benefits of the iREACH pilots, documenting them thoroughly, feeding into a business model for such rural community driven networks.

REFERENCES

Andrew, T. N., & Petkov, D. (2003). The need for a systems thinking approach to the planning of rural telecommunications infrastructure. *Telecommunications Policy, 27*(1-2), 75–93. doi:10.1016/S0308-5961(02)00095-2

Annamalai, K., & Sachin, R. (2003). *What works: ITC's E-Choupal and profitable rural transformation web-based information and procurement tools for Indian farmers*. Washington, DC: World Resources Institute.

Arunachalam, S. (2002). Reaching the unreached: How can we use information and communication technologies to empower the rural poor in the developing world through enhanced access to relevant information? *Journal of Information Science, 28*(6), 513–522. doi:10.1177/016555150202800607

Best, M., & Maclay, C. (2002). Community Internet access in rural areas: solving the economic sustainability puzzle. In Kirkman, G. (Ed.), *The global information technology report 2001-2002: readiness for the networked world*.

Bowonder, B. Gupta., V., & Singh, A. (2003). Developing a rural market e-hub: The case study of e-Choupal experience of ITC. Planning Commission of India. Retrieved April 6, 2009, from http://planningcommission.nic.in/reports/sereport/ser/stdy_ict/4_e-choupal%20.pdf

Davies, A. (1994). *Telecommunications and politics: the decentralised alternative*. London: Pinter Publishers.

Estache, A., Gomez-Lobo, A., & Leipziger, D. (2001). Utilities privatization and the poor: lessons and evidence from Latin America. *World Development, 29*(7), 1179–1198. doi:10.1016/S0305-750X(01)00034-1

Falch, M., & Anyimadu, A. (2003). Tele-centres as a way of achieving universal access: the case of Ghana. *Telecommunications Policy, 27*(1-2), 21–39. doi:10.1016/S0308-5961(02)00092-7

Ferraz, C., Fonseca, R., Pal, J., & Shah, M. (2004). Computing for social inclusion in Brazil: a study of the CDI and other initiatives. Berkeley: University of California, Berkeley. Retrieved on March 23, 2008, from http://bridge.berkeley.edu/2005_Pages/pdfs/cdi_Brazil_report.pdf

Galperin, H., & Bar, F. (2006). The microtelco opportunity: evidence from Latin America. *Information Technologies and International Development, 3*(2), 73–86. doi:10.1162/itid.2007.3.2.73

Galperin, H., & Girard, B. (2005). Digital poverty: Latin American and Caribbean perspectives. In H. Galperin & J. Mariscal (Eds.). *Digital poverty: Latin American and Caribbean perspectives* (pp. 93-115). Ottawa: IDRC, 93-115.

Gillwald, A. (2005). A closing window of opportunity: Under-Serviced Area Licensing in South Africa. *Information Technologies and International Development, 2*(4), 1–19. doi:10.1162/154475205775249364

Green, N. (2009, March 31). Govt key to lower internet prices. *The Phnom Penh Post*. Retrieved on April 1, 2009, from http://www.phnompenhpost.com/index.php/ Special-Supplements/Govt-key-to-lower-internet-prices.html

Grunfeld, H., Hak, S., Long, D., Tara, P., Dara, S., Chanda, P., et al. (2009, April). What Villagers think of iREACH, Report on participatory evaluation conducted in February 2009. Retrieved on April 29, 2009 from http://www.idrc.ca/uploads/user-S/12410151941 What_villagers_think_of_iREACH_-_Report_on_participatory_evaluation_conducted_in_February_2009l.pdf

Hab, H. (2009, March 24). More mobile firms due to enter market. *The Phnom Penh Post*. Retrieved on March 25, 2009, from:http://www.phnompenhpost.com/index. php/2009032424958/Business/More-mobile-firms-due-to-enter-market.html

Harris, R. (2007). Telecentre sustainability: financing ICTs for the poor. *APDIP e-Note 15*, Retrieved September 9, 2007, from http://www.apdip.net/apdipenote/

Harris, R. W. (2004). *Information and communications technologies for poverty alleviation*. Kuala Lumpur: UNDP-APDIP.

ITU – International Telecommunication Union. (2007). Retrieved on January 16, 2008, from http://www.itu.int/ITU-D/ict/publications/ict-oi/2007/material/table1.html#low

ITU – International Telecommunication Union. (2009). *Measuring the information society: the ICT Development Index*. Geneva: International Telecommunications Union.

Kingdom of Cambodia. Law on Commune. (2001). Retrieved on April 7, 2009, from http://www.interior.gov.kh/other_ doc.asp?id_doc=1

Kumar, R. (2007). Making e-government projects in developing countries more successful and sustainable: lessons from two case studies from India. *Information technology in developing countries, 17*(3). (IFIP Working Group 9.4).

Kuriyan, R., Ray, I., & Toyama, K. (2008). Information and communication technologies for development: the bottom of the pyramid model in practice. *The Information Society, 24*(2), 93–104. doi:10.1080/01972240701883948

Musa, P. F. (2006). Making a case for modifying the technology acceptance model to account for limited accessibility in developing countries. *Information Technology for Development, 12*(3), 213–224. doi:10.1002/itdj.20043

Noam, E. (1997). The public telecommunications network: a concept in transition. *The Journal of Communication, 37*(1), 30–48. doi:10.1111/j.1460-2466.1987.tb00966.x

Ramirez, R. (2003). Bridging disciplines: the natural resource management kaleidoscope for understanding ICTs. *The Journal of Development Communication, 1*(14), 51–64.

Rao, S. S. (2004). Role of ICTs in India's rural community information systems. *info, 6*(4), 261-269.

Richardson, J. W. (2008). ICT in education reform in Cambodia: problems, politics, and policies impacting implementation. *Information Technologies and International Development, 4*(4), 67–82. doi:10.1162/itid.2008.00027

Ó Siochrú, S., & Girard, B. (2005). *Community-based networks and innovative technologies: new models to serve and empower the poor*. UNDP.

Siochrú, Ó. S. (2009). *Pro-Poor ICT Access toolkit: Policy and Regulatory Module Overview. APC*. Retrieved on July 29, 2009, from http://access.apc.org/index.php/Pro-Poor_ICT_Access_toolkit_documents#Policy_and_Regulatory_Issues_Module:_Overview

Siochrú, Ó., & Hak, S. S., & Long, D. (2009). Cambodia's iREACH integrates OM and SPEAK. *Outcome Mapping Learning Community Newsletter, 2009*(1). Retrieved July 29, 2009, from http://outcomemapping.ca/resource/ resource. php?id=223

Souter, D. (2008). Equitable access: people, networks and capabilities. Association for Progressive Communications. Retrieved December 25, 2008 from http://www.apc.org/en/system/files/ APC_ EquitableAccess_PeopleNetworksCapabilities_IssuePaper_20080730.pdf

UN – United Nations. (2008). *United Nations e-Government survey 2008: from e-Government to Connected Governance. Department of Economic and Social Affairs, Division for Public Administration and Development Management*. New York: United Nations.

UNDP – United Nations Development Programme. (2004). *Promoting ICT for Human Development in Asia: realizing the Millennium Development Goals*. New Delhi: Elsevier.

Unger, B.W., & Robinson, N.T. (2007). Information & communication technology (ICT) in Cambodia. *Digital Review of the Asia Pacific*, invited chapter, 122-130.

World Bank (2002). *Private Solutions for Infrastructure in Cambodia: A Country Framework Report.*

World Bank. (2008). *Improved Access to Communications in Rural Cambodia*. Cambodia: GPOBA Commitment Document.

Section 5
Informed Planning and Cooperation

Chapter 14
Why Institutional Partnerships Matter:
A Regional Innovation Systems Approach to Making the ICT for Development Projects More Successful and Sustainable

Rajendra Kumar
Ministry of Communications and Information Technology, India

ABSTRACT

This chapter examines the role of institutional partnerships in making the ICT for development projects more successful and sustainable in developing countries. Employing a regional innovation systems (RIS) perspective, I examine this issue in the context of lessons drawn from the failure of telecenters in Melur taluka of Tamil Nadu under the Sustainable Access in Rural India (SARI) project. These telecenters aimed at delivering a host of services such as email, voice chat, health, e-government, and agricultural and veterinary services to the rural community. They were operated by two sets of operators: self-employed local entrepreneurs and a local NGO. After operating for nearly three years, most of the kiosks run by the self-employed entrepreneurs had closed down by mid-2005, whereas those run by the NGO were still operating. Using primary data from interviews with the kiosk owners and operators, I argue that the failure of the kiosks to sustain themselves was due to weak institutional linkages and networking among actors in the local and regional innovation systems, and the inability of the RIS to evolve and respond effectively and quickly to the changing preferences and needs of the rural community. I conclude that ensuring a project's success and sustainability requires the presence of an effective regional innovation system with strong but flexible and dynamic linkages among the relevant actors such as the state, universities, private sector, civil society organizations, the user community, and the funding organizations.

INTRODUCTION

Information and communications technologies (ICTs) have assumed great importance during the past nearly two decades as the primary tools to foster social, economic, and political development in developing countries. They have fundamentally changed the way we communicate and access information. Scholars have claimed that they have the potential to cause impact on human society on

DOI: 10.4018/978-1-61520-997-2.ch014

a scale comparable to that of the industrial revolution (Alberts and Papp 1997) and they can deeply impact democratic institutions and democratic governance (King and Kraemer 1997). In the context of developing countries, ICTs have been acknowledged as major instruments of development in a variety of areas: empowering communities by increasing their access to information and widening the opportunities available to them; e-governance; delivering services such as health; education; etc. Information and knowledge lie at the heart of economic and social development and ICTs are perceived to be the key to harnessing these for achieving international development goals (The World Bank 1998; Chataway and Wield 2000; UNDP 2001; Velden 2002). Several major international initiatives such as The Digital Opportunity Task Force constituted by the G-8 in 2000; the Global Digital Opportunity Initiative, a global public-private initiative of UNDP and some other organizations; and the Global Development Gateway (2001), an initiative of the World Bank, have all acknowledged the great potential of ICTs in bridging the international knowledge and information divide.

Encouraged by the huge potential of ICTs in enabling development, almost all developing countries have launched ICT for development projects aimed at bringing the benefits of ICTs to the rural and poor communities, which typically have low individual ownership of ICTs. However, though these projects have been in existence for well over a decade now, scholars have noted that most of these projects have either failed completely or have succeeded only partially in achieving their objectives (Heeks 2003a). Heeks (2003a) has noted that only 15% of the e-government projects in developing countries can be classified as successes, while 50% have been partial failures and 35% have failed completely.

Analysts have attempted to analyze the reasons for failures of specific projects in developing countries. Cecchini and Raina (2003) studied one such project on e-governance in rural India and found that usage of the services was low and the poorest people were seldom using the services. In a study of a community-based e-government initiative in South Africa, Benjamin (2001) found that lack of regularly updated content and interactivity led to the failure of the project. Heeks (2002) has noted several more cases of total or partial failure of ICT initiatives in developing countries. Researchers have also found that lack of government support, flaws in the design of the projects, and low market demand for these services have led to limited success or partial failure of these projects in developing countries (Dagron 2001; Proenza 2001; McNamara 2003).

Analytically, researchers have tried to explain the failures of these projects in terms of critical success and critical failure factors (CSF and CFF) (Heeks and Bhatnagar 1999), 'design-actuality' (Heeks 2002) or 'design-reality' gaps (2003a), poor economic sustainability of rural ICT projects (2002), or political and institutional factors due to lack of commitment on the part of political leadership and public managers (2000). A sustainability failure model has also been advanced to examine projects that succeed initially but fail to meet their objectives in the long-term (2006).

Though the approaches noted above help us in understanding the reasons for success or failure of these projects, they fail to adequately take into account the institutional factors behind the failure of such projects. In the context of ICTs as innovations, these factors include the institutional processes and linkages among various institutions and actors, both public and private, that lead to innovation and its diffusion among the users. In this chapter, I examine the institutional factors behind the failure of one such project using a regional innovation systems (RIS) perspective.

Specifically, I examine the sustainability failure of the privately owned and operated telecenters under the Sustainable Access in Rural India (SARI) project in Melur taluka in Tamil Nadu in India. Aiming at rural social, economic, and political development, this project had established 78 computer and internet kiosks in rural communities by June 2004. These kiosks offered a number of services including basic computer education, e-mail, web browsing, e-government, health, and agricultural and veterinary services mostly on a fee-for-service basis. Thirty-six of the 78 kiosks were run by rural self-employed entrepreneurs while the remaining 42 were run by a local NGO, called the Dhan Foundation. After over three years of operation, most of the self-employed entrepreneurs had closed down their kiosks. By July 2005, 32 of the 36 kiosks run by the local entrepreneurs had closed down. At the same time, the Dhan kiosks continued to operate. Based on a comparative analysis of the performance of the two sets of kiosks and employing a RIS perspective, I examine the institutional factors responsible for the sustainability failure of the kiosks owned by the self-employed entrepreneurs. Examining sustainability failures of such projects is important as lessons drawn from them can help us in improving the long-term sustainability of such projects in developing countries.

Figure 1 shows the location of Melur where this project was implemented.

The rest of the chapter is organized as follows: first, I present a brief review of the relevant literature on regional innovation systems and discuss why institutional factors are important for ensuring the long-term success of ICT for development projects; then I briefly describe the overall project and discuss how it succeeded initially in meeting the objectives of its stakeholders by forging institutional partnerships with the government and other agencies (both public and private) for delivery of services; next, I discuss the research methods employed for this study; then I present the results and analyze the institutional factors responsible for the closure of the kiosks; and finally, I discuss the implications of the findings of this study for ensuring the sustainability of such projects in developing countries. I conclude by presenting this as an alternative framework for analyzing the long-term sustainability of such projects. In presenting the materials in this chapter, I draw partly from Best and Kumar (2008) as the source of data is same for both the studies.

Figure 1. Location of Melur in India (Source http://gis.nic.in/cen/; modifications by the author)

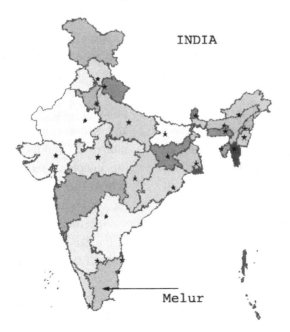

LITERATURE REVIEW

Before discussing the relevant literature on regional innovation systems, it is helpful to specify the meaning and the context in which I use the term "institutions" in this paper. Scholars have defined institutions in two principal ways. Many scholars view them as long standing social rules and norms that influence behavioral patterns among people and organizations. Others have defined them in a more formal way, meaning specific and identifiable organizations or organizational systems that have been established to perform specific tasks. The innovation systems literature has usually treated institutions in a more formal way, meaning the tangible and identifiable organizations such as universities, R&D institutions and agencies, firms, government agencies dealing with the industries, etc. In this paper, I use a more inclusive concept of institutions that encompasses both the "social norms and rules" that influence behavior and the physical organizations designed to perform specific tasks. The reason for focusing on an inclusive meaning of the term is to help us in understanding how the complex interplay between the social rules and norms and the tangible and identifiable organizations affects the institutional behavior and the long-term outcome of ICT for development projects.

The main literature on innovation systems is very large. This body of research focuses on the role of institutions in the innovation process in an economy. Understood mainly as the complex network of institutions, both public and private, that support and foster the innovation process in an economy, the innovation systems focus on the role of interaction and networking among these institutions and the institutional peculiarities that offer distinct incentives for learning and innovation (Lundvall 1993; Lall 2000; Amsden and Chu 2003; Segal 2003; Yusuf 2003). This literature treats innovation as an evolutionary and social process that is influenced by several actors (Edquist 2004). It is viewed as a cumulative and interactive process that is influenced by several actors at each stage (David 1975; Rogers 2003). Scholars have also emphasized the importance of "learning by doing" in the process of innovations by the producers (Arrow 1962) and "learning by using" by the users (Von Hippel 1976; Rosenberg 1982). They have also noted the importance of learning through interactions among the various actors involved in the process of innovations (Lundvall 1989) and the interconnectedness of the institutions to create, store, and transfer the knowledge generated (Metcalfe 1997). The actors involved in the process of innovations can be both internal and external to the firm. The innovation process is influenced by the collective and collaborative learning through interactions with the other institutions in the innovation system. It is this collective and interactive learning process that lies at the heart of the innovation system and places great emphasis on the role of the interacting institutions in creating and sustaining innovations.

The innovation system discussed above is usually referred to in the context of a national economy and is generally termed as a national innovation system. In the context of use and diffusion of ICTs and ICT based interventions, such a system would consist of the basic infrastructure for ICTs, research and development by the public and the private sectors, and creating the necessary human and organizational capacities in a complex network of interacting institutions to support and foster innovations. However, innovation systems can also be rooted or locally embedded within specific regions to take advantage of the specific regional and local capabilities or resources (Storper 1997; Kirat and Lung 1999). Scholars have generally referred to these innovations systems as regional innovation systems (RIS). This body of literature views innovation as a regionalized and localized process that emerges out of interactions among the regional and local institutions, such as universities, government agencies, firms, civil society organizations, etc. These institutions and actors derive advantages from proximity and localization economies and the region-specific norms, rules, and conventions that help in knowledge creation and dissemination (Doloreux and Parto 2004). The interacting knowledge generation and diffusion systems at the regional or local level can also be linked to other regional, national, and global systems of innovation for creation, transfer, and commercialization of knowledge (Cooke, Heidenreich et al. 2004).

A recent variant of the regional innovation systems in the context of innovations in knowledge-based economies is the triple helix model which places emphasis on the central role of universities in fostering the innovation process (Etzkowitz and Leydesdorff 1997; Benner and Sandstrom 2000; Leydesdorff 2000; Edquist 2001). This model views networking and interactions among government, academia, and industry as the keys to creating and sustaining innovations. Though this model is helpful in understanding the systemic dimensions of the innovation process, it largely ignores the role of other actors such as civil society organizations and users and the complex feedback mechanisms that underlie the interactions among various actors (Sreekumar 2003). Scholars have argued that the role of civil society organizations in fostering ICT based innovations for development has largely been ignored in the innovation systems literature (Sreekumar 2003). They have also argued that this literature does not adequately consider the role of social processes in feedback mechanisms that help in creating and sustaining innovations (Khan 1998). This literature is relevant in this research as it was a civil society organization (SARI) that was primarily responsible for introducing and sustaining the ICT intervention in a rural area.

Another body of literature that is relevant here in understanding the process of ICT-based innovations is that of international geography of innovations. This body of literature places emphasis on the role of international or cross-border knowledge flows through global value chains in creating and sustaining innovations (Gereffi and Korzeniewicz 1994; Gereffi 1999; Gereffi and Kaplinsky 2001). Though this research tradition mainly refers to global production systems for goods and services, insights derived from this literature on the role of international linkages in knowledge flows in generating and sustaining innovations can help us in understanding their importance even for ICT for development projects in developing countries where the major collaborators or funding agencies are generally from the developed nations. This body of literature is also relevant here as the emphasis in this literature on knowledge flows through cross-border linkages is in contrast to the innovations systems literature, which emphasizes these linkages among firms and public and private institutions mainly within the context of national, regional, or local economies.

The concept of RIS is relevant in this study as it focuses on the role of interactions among the regional and the local institutions in sustaining the ICT based intervention in rural communities. In the specific context of telecenter projects, scholars have pointed out the importance of networking and linkages among the telecenters in pooling resources and developing new and locally relevant content and services, sharing best practices, developing capacity, and in creating partnerships (Fillip and Foote 2007; UNCTAD 2007). They have also noted the importance of continuously upgrading the content and services in sustaining the demand from the users and ensuring their involvement in the project (Cecchini 2002). Importance of understanding the local social, economic, and political context within which the projects operate and designing appropriate services and content is also very important in ensuring the success of telecenter projects (Fillip and Foote 2007).

Discussion in the preceding paragraphs suggests that the presence of an effective innovation system within the region with efficient and effective networking and interactions among the relevant public and private institutions and actors is extremely important for creating and sustaining innovations. This is all the more important in the context of ICT for development projects in developing countries where the innovation systems may be characterized by weak linkages among the relevant institutions or even the absence of some key institutions. This chapter focuses on analyzing one such project, where weak institutional linkages among various institutions and actors within the regional innovation system were the major reasons for the sustainability failure of the project.

DESCRIPTION OF THE PROJECT

Institutional collaborations have been a key feature of the SARI project right from the outset. The project is a collaborative venture of several organizations: the Indian Institute of Technology, Madras; Berkman Center for Internet and Society, Harvard Law School; Georgia Institute of Technology; I-Gyan Foundation; and n-Logue Communications Pvt. Ltd. In the initial stages, the Massachusetts Institute of Technology was also a partner. It uses a Wireless-in-Local Loop (WLL) technology developed at IIT, Madras to provide Internet connectivity to rural villages.

The Internet connectivity is offered to the local community at kiosks which are run as self-sustained businesses with cost recovery through service charges. As noted before, the kiosks are operated by two sets of operators. A local NGO, called the Dhan Foundation, operated 42 such kiosks at the time of this study in July 2005. The remaining 36 were owned and operated by local self-employed entrepreneurs. These kiosks were called as 'Chirag kiosks' while those operated by the NGO were known as 'Dhan kiosks'. Technical support for all the kiosks was provided by n-Logue Communications. n-Logue Communications also provided maintenance services to the Chirag kiosks.

Kiosk Services

The kiosks provide a host of applications and services to the rural people. These include computer education; email/voice mail/voice chat; e-government services such as obtaining birth and death certificates from government offices; agricultural, veterinary, and health services; web browsing, etc. They provide internet content in the local language in these areas. The services are based on a self-sustaining commercial model with the charges ranging from Rs. 10 (approx. US $0.22) for sending an email to Rs. 100 (approx. US $2.2) for one hour of basic computer education everyday for one month. The various services offered and charges levied are given in the Table 1.

The initial bouquet of services at the kiosks was designed keeping in mind a number of studies conducted in the project area. These studies assessed the community networking and information needs of the rural communities and proposed suitable applications for these kiosks (Sinan, Marcela et al. 2001; Blattman, Jensen et al. 2003). Sinan et al (2001) proposed applications in agriculture, labor market and employment, health care, government services, and education that could be useful to the rural users. These services could drive demand for these kiosks and make them financially self-sustainable. However, the kiosks were unable to become financially self-sustainable in the long-run despite showing promise in the first 18 months of operation when 10 Chirag kiosks had achieved commercial viability (Kumar 2004).

Usage of Kiosk Services

The kiosks mostly attract young male users, either school or college students. Kiosks are mainly used by this group who visit them to get computer education. Computer training is the most frequently used service, followed by computer games, email, browsing, and voice mail/voice chat. In a study of diffusion of the SARI kiosks

Table 1. Services offered and charges levied at the SARI kiosks

Service	Unit of Charge	Rate (Rs.)
Web Browsing	Per Hour 1-15 min. 16-30 min. 31-60 min.	25 10 15 25
E-mail/Voice mail/Photo mail/Video mail	Per email	10
E-Post (Inter Village email Service)*	Per email	5
Online Chat	Internet time per hour	25
Video Conferencing	Internet time per hour	25
E-government Services	Per application	10
Message to a Private Eye Hospital	Per message	10
Agricultural and Veterinary Services	Per message	10
Computer course – Beginner's level	Per month	50/75**
Computer course- Intermediate level	Per month	100
Astrology	One full set of printouts	140
Studio	One set of 5 photos	50

* Offered by the Dhan Kiosks only
** Dhan Kiosks usually charge Rs. 50 while n-Logue kiosks usually charge Rs. 75.
(Note: 1 US $ = Approx. Rs. 47 in Aug. 2003)
Source: Kumar (2004)

(both Chirag and Dhan) and within their communities, Kumar and Best (2006) found that only around 5% of the village population had used the kiosks and that the users were more likely to be male, below the age of 30 years, from relatively higher income households, and relatively better educated compared to the village population. The users were also less likely to be from the religious minorities and socially and economically disadvantaged castes within the rural communities. Thus, despite being in operation for a considerable length of time, the kiosks had failed to diffuse wisely among their communities in terms of usage of the kiosks. However, the Dhan kiosks had succeeded in introducing new and locally relevant services to attract more users that had helped them to remain operational even after the Chirag kiosks had closed down (Kumar and Best 2006). The Chirag kiosks failed to upgrade their content to make it more relevant to a wider section of the village population.

Institutional Partnerships for Delivery of Services

The project had developed partnerships with other institutions and agencies – both public and private – for delivering various services to the users. This was one of the key features of the project. The partnerships included tie-ups with the state government to provide e-government services, with the state owned Tamil Nadu Agricultural and Veterinary University for providing agricultural and veterinary services, and with a private eye hospital for providing tele-medicine eye check-ups. The state government supported the project from the beginning by offering e-government services through the kiosks for issuance of birth and death certificates, and by receiving petitions through email for a number of other services and benefits, such as income certification, copies of land and cultivation records, complaints regarding civic services, and general petitions on other issues.

Figure 2. SARI Project Partnerships for Delivery of Services

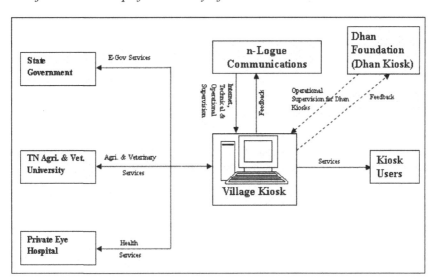

It is important to note here that the scope of these tie-ups or partnerships for the partner organizations were limited to receiving petitions from the kiosks and responding to them. It didn't cover providing funding or other material support to the kiosks. It is also relevant to mention here the partnerships were not one-way, i.e., they were not meant to support only the kiosks. The partner organizations also expected to benefit in two ways: gaining additional clientele in the case of the private hospital, and providing an additional mode of sending petitions and reducing delays in providing government services to citizens in the case of the government.

Figure 2 explains the role of these partnerships in the delivery of services.

The partner organizations provided their services by replying to the requests of the villagers sent through kiosks through email. Follow-up face-to-face meetings were also arranged when found necessary. As I discuss later in the paper, failure of these partnerships to sustain themselves over a long term period was one of the major reasons for the closure of the kiosks.

Institutional Framework for Operation of the Kiosks

The project was launched within the broad institutional and legal framework as laid out through an executive order of the Tamil Nadu state government in Feb. 2001. This order permitted the sponsors of the SARI project to launch in Madurai district of the state. The order mentioned that the rural kiosks would aim at providing a host of services, such as agriculture, health, telemedicine, and e-government, for the benefit of the rural population. In order to ensure smooth implementation of the e-government component of the project within the district, the Madurai District Collector, the chief government administrator of the district, was asked to play a lead role.

Scope of Partnership with the Government

The scope of the partnership with the government was limited to two aspects: first, it allowed the kiosks to send applications electronically to the Melur Taluk office for various e-government services, and, second, it established a coordinating mechanism for monitoring the processing of such applications. This coordination and monitoring was to be executed by the District Collector through regular meetings with the SARI project officials. While these coordination meetings were conducted regularly till the end of 2002, they virtually stopped after the incumbent District Collector was transferred out of the district in Feb. 2003. At around the same time, the administrative head of the Melur Taluk office was also transferred out. The transfer of these two key officials was one of the major reasons for the collapse of the e-government services at the Taluk office (Kumar and Best 2006).

Implementation of the Project

In the case of the Chirag kiosks, the entire equipment is loaned to the operator by n-Logue Communications through a tie-up with a public sector bank. Under an existing government subsidy scheme, the entrepreneur gets a subsidy of 15% on the principal loan amount. For the Dhan kiosks, the entire costs of setting up the kiosks are borne by the NGO and it also appoints its own operators. All operators are trained by n-Logue in technical and operational aspects. In a study of the SARI kiosks in Melur, Kumar (2004) found that Dhan Foundation had also appointed more women as operators in its kiosks compared to those in the Chirag kiosks. While slightly less than half (46.3%) of the operators in all the SARI kiosks were women, 63.2% of the operators in Dhan kiosks and 31.8% in Chirag kiosks were women (Kumar 2004). Women operators were instrumental in attracting more women users to the kiosks (Kumar 2004).

In addition to appointing more women operators, Dhan has also adopted a specific policy of reaching the poor and the SC/ST households in the villages. Discussions with the Dhan officials revealed that operators were specifically asked to canvass among the poor and the SC/ST households regarding the kiosk services offered. Dhan kiosks

also offer two additional services: e-Post, an inter-village postal service through which printed copies of emails are delivered to any person in a village having a Dhan kiosk; and e-Commerce, which allows a user to put any household item for sale online among the Dhan kiosk villages.

Interviews with the kiosk operators revealed some important differences in the operation of the kiosks by the two sets of operators. The first difference was in the overall objectives with which the kiosks were established by the two operators. While the Dhan Foundation operated the kiosks with the specific goal of reaching the most socially and economically disadvantaged communities in rural areas, the self-employed entrepreneurs aimed at attracting the relatively well-off sections of the rural community with the goal of achieving financial sustainability quickly. The second difference was in the financial support that the two groups of kiosks received. While the Chirag kiosks received no financial support for operating expenses and were expected to become financially self-sustainable on their own, the Dhan kiosks received substantial financial support for operating expenses from the Dhan Foundation. As I discuss subsequently in the paper, this aspect crucially affected the long-term financial sustainability of the two sets of kiosks.

Achieving long-term financial and operational sustainability was one of the major goals of the project. However, after over three years of operation, most of the self-employed entrepreneurs had closed down their kiosks. By July 2005, 32 of the 36 Chirag kiosks had closed down. At the same time, most of the kiosks run by the Dhan Foundation were still operating.

RESEARCH METHODS

I use a combination of qualitative and quantitative methods for this research. The most important source of data was a structured survey of 27 Chirag kiosk owners who had closed down their kiosks after operating them for periods ranging from six months to three years. This survey was conducted during August and September 2005. These surveys were conducted in the local language by two trained interviewers. I also collected quantitative longitudinal data from the records maintained by SARI project officials on the performance of the kiosks. The period for which data were collected was from December 2001 to May 2005. I also conducted structured interviews with two Dhan kiosk operators. Finally, I conducted semi-structured interviews with other stakeholders of the project, such as SARI project officials, n-Logue officials, government officials, and Dhan Foundation managers. The officials interviewed included the then Secretary of the Information Technology Department, Tamil Nadu Government in Chennai; n-Logue officials in Melur; the District Collector and the head of the National Informatics Center (NIC) in Madurai; and the Executive Director and other officials of the Dhan Foundation in Madurai. I conducted a total of 10 such interviews. These interviews were conducted in English during July and August 2005.

DATA ANALYSIS

Active and Inactive Kiosks

A comparative analysis of the performance of the Chirag and the Dhan kiosks reveals some important differences. While most of the Dhan kiosks remained active during the period of operation of the project from December 2001 to May 2005, Chirag kiosks failed to show the same level of activity. Defining a kiosk as "active" if it had used at least one hour of internet time during the month under study, (Best and Kumar 2008) find that the activity levels of the Chirag kiosks started declining progressively from September 2002 and the percentage of active Chirag kiosks declined to only 11.1% during May 2005. Figure 3 shows the percentage of Chirag kiosks that remained

active during the month for the duration of the project. The number of these kiosks had reached a peak of 36 during March 2004 after proliferating rapidly during the first two and a half years of operation. The number of total and the active Chirag kiosks during their duration of operation are shown in Figure 4.

A similar analysis for the Dhan kiosks presents a different picture. The total cumulative number of Dhan kiosks was 42 in May 2005, while the number of active kiosks was 30. As a proportion of the total cumulative number of kiosks, the percentage of active Dhan kiosks was 71.4% in May 2005 (Figure 5). It is relevant to note here that the absence of active Dhan kiosks from March to May 2003 is due to suspension of the Internet connections during this period by n-Logue over a payment dispute. Figure 6 presents the number of total and the active Dhan kiosks during the same period.

The above analysis indicates that the Dhan kiosks remained more active when compared to the Chirag kiosks during the research period. This is evident from the fact that while the proportion of active Chirag kiosks was just over 10% in May 2005, over 70% of the Dhan kiosks remained active during the same month. This holds true even if we consider the entire period of operation of the kiosks (from December 2001 to May 2005). While the mean of the monthly percentages of active Chirag kiosks for the entire period was 53.7%, it was 78.1% for the Dhan kiosks.

Factors Associated with the Length of Time a Kiosk Operated

As noted before, only 4 out of 36 Chirag kiosks had remained active as of July 2005. The remaining 32 kiosks had either closed down or had become idle after remaining functional for varying lengths of time. Data collected on 27 of these closed or idle kiosks showed that 52% of these kiosks closed down within 12 months of starting operations, while 22% closed within 24

Figure 3. Percentage of active Chirag kiosks in Melur (Source Best and Kumar (2008))

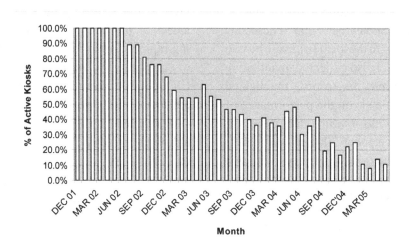

months and an equal percentage closed after 24 months but before 36 months of opening. Only one kiosk managed to operate for more than 36 months (Best & Kumar, 2008).

It is relevant to examine the factors that might be associated with the differences in the periods of operation of the Chirag kiosks. Based on the qualitative evidence collected during interviews with the kiosk owners, (Best and Kumar 2008) found that the performance of the kiosks depended on a number of factors. First, the kiosks that reported receiving relatively better technical and operational support from n-Logue performed better and remained open for more days. Second, the kiosks which were operated by a different person than the owner remained open for more days. Prior training of the owners in computers and support from the elected representatives in the village were other factors that could be associated positively with the duration that the kiosks functioned. Using multivariate linear regression analysis, we found that the duration of functioning of the kiosks was significantly positively associated with three key variables: technical and operational support from

Figure 4. Total and active Chirag kiosks in Melur

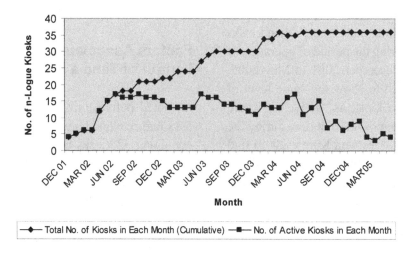

Figure 5. Percentage of active Dhan kiosks in Melur (Source Best and Kumar (2008))

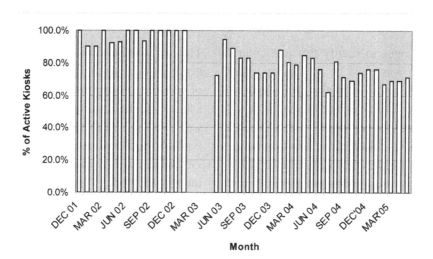

n-Logue, owner and operator being two differ-ent persons, and owners having prior training in computers. Support from n-Logue was the most significant variable.

The results of the statistical analysis above were confirmed by qualitative evidence obtained during interviews with the kiosk owners. All kiosk owners stated that technical and operational sup-port for delivery of services from n-Logue was

crucial for the successful operation of the kiosks. Lack of support from n-Logue was a major reason for the closure of the kiosks. As one of the kiosk owners stated:

"The relay base station for transmitting wireless signals had failed and n-Logue took over six months to rectify the problem. As there was no

Figure 6. No. of total and active Dhan kiosks in Melur

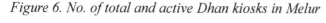

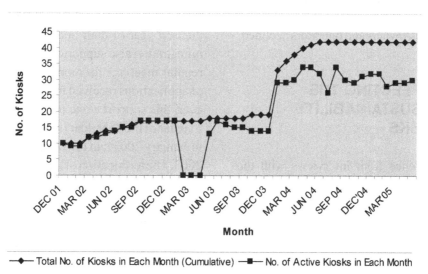

connectivity during this period, no services could be provided and I had to close down the kiosk."

Failure of n-Logue to rectify this particular relay base station was cited by owners of four kiosks as the main reason for closing their kiosks.

The finding that kiosks having different owners and operators lasted longer was also confirmed during the interviews. Most of the kiosk owners stated that having a different operator facilitated the task of coordinating with the public and private agencies for delivery of services. It also made following up for technical and operational support with n-Logue personnel in Melur easier. This point was particularly emphasized by one of the owners who stated that *"having a operator at the kiosk to handle the day-to-day operations frees me up and allows me to spend more time with the n-Logue people for support and expanding my kiosk services"*.

It is relevant to examine why the support from n-Logue was not uniform for all the kiosks. A vast majority of the Chirag kiosks reported receiving no or little sustained support. I found that while all kiosk owners reported good technical and operational support till the end of 2003, the support declined significantly after that. The quality of support deteriorated for both technical and operational aspects. Operational support also declined significantly as the number of support staff was reduced and the frequency of coordination meetings with the kiosk owners and operators declined.

FACTORS AFFECTING THE FINANCIAL SUSTAINABILITY OF THE KIOSKS

Qualitative evidence from interviews with the government and n-Logue officials at Melur and kiosk owners revealed several factors that affected the operational and financial sustainability of the kiosks (both Dhan and Chirag) in Melur. I discuss these factors below.

Lack of Adequate Institutional Partnerships for Delivery of Services

Though SARI and n-Logue had developed partnerships with several organizations for delivery of services, these partnerships did not sustain for a long time. For example, partnerships with a private eye hospital at Madurai and with the Tamil Nadu Agricultural and Veterinary University had virtually ended by the end of 2004 and most of the kiosks (both Chirag and Dhan) had stopped using these partnerships for delivery of services. Interviews with the SARI project officials and kiosk operators indicated that the main reason for the failure of these partnerships was lack of incentives for these organizations to continue these partnerships. For example, the additional clientele that the private eye hospital had hoped to gain did not materialize as there was no regular follow up by the kiosks on the patients identified. There was no regular follow up by the SARI project officials with these organizations on the services provided by them. This indicates that the partnerships need to work for the mutual benefit of both sides for them to be successful in the long-term.

Lack of Institutional Support for e-Government Services

The Taluk office at Melur provided good support for e-government services at the kiosks during the first year of their operation. The district administration also supported this initiative through regular meetings for monitoring the prosecution of applications received in the Taluk office. However, this support came to a virtual end with the transfer of the Tahsildar (head of the Taluk office) in January 2003 and the District Collector in Feb. 2003. The termination of this support deprived the kiosks of a vital source of revenue. The primary reason for the termination of the partnership with the government was lack of institutionalization of the initiative and opposition from the lower ranked officials due to reduction in rent-seeking opportunities. A complete analysis of these factors can be found in Kumar and Best (2006).

Lack of Adequate Technical Support for the Kiosks

As noted before, technical support for the kiosks was provided by n-Logue. This included maintenance of a relay base station (RBS) which delivered wireless connectivity to some more remote kiosks. Four Chirag kiosks reported lack of connectivity for over six months due to failure of the RBS and these kiosks reported this as the major reason for closing down. During July 2005, six Dhan kiosks also had no connectivity due to failure of the RBS.

Lack of New and Relevant Content

The Chirag kiosks had to mostly limit themselves to offering the same basket of services during their entire period of operation. There was no real success in developing new and relevant content or services for the kiosks. This was primarily due to lack of adequate organizational efforts in this direction on the part of SARI, despite continuous feedback on the need for new content and services by the kiosk operators. However, the Dhan kiosks were able to offer some new services due to the efforts of the Dhan Foundation in this direction. One example was the new weekly online video-conferencing facility offered to the farmers through which they could talk directly with the agricultural experts instead of sending an email. According to the Dhan officials, this new service proved quite successful in some villages.

COMPARATIVE ANALYSIS OF THE PERFORMANCE OF DHAN AND CHIRAG KIOSKS

It is relevant to examine as to why the Dhan kiosks out-lived the Chirag kiosks. Detailed interviews with the Dhan and n-Logue officials and two

Dhan kiosk operators revealed two main reasons for this. I discuss these reasons below.

Additional Financial Support for Dhan Kiosks

Interviews with the Dhan officials in Madurai revealed that the Dhan kiosks remained functional due to the additional financial support given to them by the Dhan Foundation and the provision of new services by the kiosks to attract more users. However, despite provision of new services, the Dhan kiosks were unable to become financially self-sustainable. The average monthly total revenue for Dhan kiosks was approximately Rs. 1200 (approx. US $24) per kiosk, whereas the average total cost per kiosk (including the fixed and variable costs) was approximately Rs. 3000 (approx. US $60) per month. Hence these kiosks were able to recover only around 40% of their monthly costs. The balance was met through financial support by the Dhan Foundation. In contrast to this, the Chirag kiosks received no similar support.

Better Institutional Support

Dhan Foundation also provided better institutional support to its kiosks in two forms: appointing kiosk operators centrally and developing its own locally relevant content for the kiosk services. The operators were then appointed to the various kiosks as per need. The operators were paid their monthly salaries irrespective of the revenues from their kiosks. This helped the operators in focusing on delivering services to the disadvantaged sections of the community rather than on generating additional revenue alone.

Dhan also focused on developing content for the kiosk services independent of the services supported institutionally by n-Logue. As mentioned earlier, one such service provided by the Dhan kiosks was the weekly online video-conferencing facility offered to the local farmers with the agricultural experts at Melur.

SUSTAINABILITY FAILURE OF THE CHIRAG KIOSKS

Before analyzing the sustainability failure of the Chirag kiosks, it is important to examine the multiple dimensions of sustainability that are relevant here. Kumar and Best (2006) describe five principal dimensions of sustainability of telecenter projects: financial or economic sustainability where the telecenters achieve commercial sustainability through user fees for the services provided; cultural or social sustainability where all social groups within the community get benefited from the project and no group is disproportionately hurt; technological sustainability where the sponsor organization ensures that hardware and software are upgraded continuously and the content is continuously revised and updated based on user feedback; political or institutional sustainability where the larger institutional structures are in place to ensure that the project runs smoothly even when initial leaders or champions leave the organization; and environmental sustainability where the project has plans in place for reuse or recycling of used hardware. A project can suffer a sustainability failure along any of these dimensions.

Comparative analysis of the performance of the Chirag and Dhan kiosks reveals a number of factors that were responsible for the sustainability failure of the Chirag kiosks. Principal among these were failure of institutional partnerships with the partner organizations to sustain themselves in the long-run, failure of the e-government services at the kiosks after a relatively successful start, lack of technical and institutional support for these kiosks from n-Logue, and lack of new and relevant content. At the same time, the Dhan kiosks performed better due to better institutional and financial support from the parent organization. Their ability to continuously respond to the changing needs of the customer and provide new content and services in collaboration with their partner organizations was also an important reason for their sustainability.

We can summarize the performance of the Chirag and Dhan kiosks along the five principal dimensions of sustainability as shown in the Table 2.

Thus, the Chirag kiosks suffered from sustainability failure along multiple dimensions: financial, technological, and institutional.

How best can we understand the sustainability failure of the Chirag kiosks analytically? The analysis in the preceding sections points to the importance of institutional linkages and networking among the various stakeholders and actors in ensuring the success and sustainability of such projects. In this particular case, the Chirag kiosks failed due to weak institutional and technical support from the sponsor organization and the failure of the institutional linkages and partnerships with the supporting and partner institutions to sustain themselves in the long-run. This adversely impacted the financial sustainability of these kiosks. These kiosks also failed to provide new and relevant content in response to the changing needs and preferences of the rural users over time.

Table 2. Comparative analysis of the Chirag and Dhan kiosks on sustainability

Sustainability Dimension	Chirag Kiosk	Dhan Kiosk
Financial Sustainability	No	Yes (with additional funding from the NGO)
Cultural/Social sustainability	Limited	Yes
Technological sustainability	No	Yes
Institutional Sustainability	No	Yes
Environmental Sustainability	Yes	Yes

A regional innovation systems approach provides an excellent analytical framework to examine the failure of the Chirag kiosks. The local and the regional innovation system for the two sets of kiosks consisted of the network of institutions supporting them in their operation and performance. The kiosks were introduced as innovations in their rural communities and were expected to sustain themselves operationally and financially in the long-term. However, the Chirag kiosks suffered a sustainability failure along multiple dimensions due to weak institutional linkages and networking among actors in the local and regional innovation system and the inability of the RIS to evolve and respond effectively and quickly to the changing preferences and needs of the rural community. At the same time, the Dhan kiosks continued to sustain themselves due to better financial and institutional support from their parent organization and the ability of the collaborating institutions to respond effectively to the changing needs of the users.

It is also relevant to discuss further the differences in the institutions involved in running the two sets of kiosks to rule out any plausible rival explanations. Was additional funding for the Dhan kiosks the main reason for their comparatively better longevity? Would the Chirag kiosks have remained functional if they had received additional financial support at the same level as that received by the Dhan kiosks? It is important to keep in mind that the failure of the institutional partnerships in the delivery of services and weak institutional and technical support from n-Logue affected both sets of kiosks equally. However, the Dhan Foundation responded to this situation by providing technical support to its kiosks and responded to the changing needs of the users by developing new and locally relevant content. They also succeeded in forming new institutional partnerships to provide the new services. The institutional support, forging new partnerships, and networking for developing and delivering new content were completely lacking for the Chirag kiosks. Therefore, additional fund-

ing for the Dhan kiosks alone does not explain their comparatively much better longevity.

It is also relevant to examine whether the Dhan kiosks could have survived without the institutional and financial support of their parent organization. Based on the experience of the Chirag kiosks, which lacked this support from their sponsor organization, I think the Dhan kiosks would also have experienced similar problems in continuing their services if they had not been supported by the Dhan Foundation. The relevant aspect to keep in mind here is that the support from the parent organization helped the kiosks in forging new partnerships and delivering new and better content and services. This could not have been achieved by the individual kiosks on heir own.

Does the analysis above suggest that only a civil society organization can provide a sustainable model for ICT for development projects in rural communities? I think the answer lies in the belief of the SARI project officials that the self-employed entrepreneurs could become financially self-sustaining relatively quickly in a relatively small market where the potential user base was low. This did not happen. The Chirag kiosks needed the institutional partnerships for delivery of services to continue for a much longer time to continue to attract the users and needed the technical and institutional support from the sponsor organization in developing new content and forging new partnerships. They also needed additional financial support for some more time to sustain themselves. Unlike the Dhan kiosks, none of these happened in their case.

However, this raises a further question as to whether private sector initiatives for such projects can ever be made financially self-sustainable. I believe the answer lies in the lessons learnt from the Dhan experience, though the two projects are not directly comparable: institutional and financial support and forging successful and sustainable partnerships with other organizations for developing and providing new and locally relevant content and services. The Chirag kiosks, acting mostly as individual entities, lacked effective technical and institutional support from their parent organization in developing new content and the institutional partnerships had failed.

It is relevant here to examine how the lessons from this study compare with those from similar projects elsewhere. Researchers have pointed out the need for forging effective partnerships both among the telecenters and with outside organizations for developing new content and services, technical and organizational support, and learning and experience sharing (Roman and Colle 2002; Bank 2003; Fillip and Foote 2007). Telecenters that aim at achieving social and economic development objectives need to continually evolve and cater to the changing needs of their communities (Gurstein 2001; Van Belle and Trusler 2005). Networking and being part of a larger organization may also provide benefits due to network and scale economies, maintaining quality standards, and help in recruitment and training (Bank 2003). Proactive role of the telecenter operators in reaching out and engaging their communities to understand their changing needs and preferences has also been noted (Harris and Rajora 2006). In the context of this study, these aspects underscore the importance of the presence of a robust regional innovation system in the region that can help the telecenters in effectively responding to the changing needs of the user communities.

IMPLICATIONS FOR ICT FOR DEVELOPMENT PROJECTS

What lessons can be drawn from this study for the success of ICT for development projects in developing countries? This research highlights some important differences between the dominant thinking in the literature and the conclusions from this study on ensuring sustainability of such projects. I discuss these differences below and discuss how best such projects can be made successful and sustainable.

Scholars have noted the importance of institutional linkages and networking among the relevant actors in the local and regional innovation system in creating and sustaining innovations. The collective and collaborative learning through interactions with the other institutions in the innovation system greatly influences the innovation process and lies at the heart of the innovation system. This study shows that that the effectiveness of the local and the regional innovation system was the key to the success and sustainability of this project. As discussed before, weak institutional support and linkages among the collaborating institutions and their inability to respond effectively to the emerging challenges for the continued success of the project were the principal reasons for the failure of the Chirag kiosks. At the same time, the Dhan kiosks enjoyed relatively better success due to better institutional support and their ability to form new institutional partnerships for delivering new content and services. The Dhan operators also had much better linkages with the local community and responded quickly to the changing needs and preferences of the community.

The literature on the importance of knowledge transfer through international collaborations and cross-border linkages in global value chains in generating and sustaining innovations is also relevant for this study as some of the major funding and collaborating organizations for this project were located in the west. However, as this research shows, the key to the failure of the Chirag kiosks and the success of the Dhan kiosks was the effectiveness of the local and regional institutional linkages. The external linkages for this project continued to be intact throughout the duration of the project.

With specific reference to ICT or knowledge based innovations, scholars have noted the central role of universities and/or research organizations in sustaining innovations through interactions with the industry and the state. However, this framework is also unable to explain the sustainability failure of the kiosks in this project as the state did not play a significant role in the success of the Dhan kiosks, though failure of the state to support e-governance services was a major reason for the failure of the Chirag kiosks. Role of a university was also not significant in ensuring the sustainability of the Dhan kiosks though the technology was initially developed by an academic institution (IIT Madras) and the project had collaborations with major research universities in the US.

Discussion in the preceding paragraphs suggests the broad contours of a regional innovation system that may prove effective in ensuring the success and sustainability of such projects in developing countries. As this research suggests, the networking and the collaborating institutions in such an RIS need to include all the relevant stakeholders and actors. In the case of the Dhan kiosks, major role was played by the NGO itself in ensuring the sustainability of the kiosks. The role of funding organizations in continuing financial support in case the kiosks are not financially sustainable on their own is also very important. This is especially relevant for projects that aim at achieving social and economic development goals, as such projects may not be able to achieve commercial self-sustainability quickly. Thus, an effective regional innovation system for ensuring the sustainability of such projects should include not only the academic institutions, the state, and the industry, but also other stakeholders such as civil society organizations, the user community, the funding organizations, etc. These networking institutions and actors need to develop strong but flexible and dynamic linkages among themselves and need to have strong feedback mechanisms at every stage to sustain their innovations. This is all the more important in rural communities in developing countries where the individual affordability for such innovations may be low and the needs and preferences of the users may be changing relatively fast.

CONCLUSION

This research clearly shows the importance of an effective regional innovation system in ensuring the success of ICT for development projects in developing countries. Using a comparative framework for analyzing the performance of two sets of kiosks under the same project, it highlights the importance of strong but flexible institutional linkages and networking among the partner institutions in ensuring the success and sustainability of such projects. The collaborating institutions within such an RIS include not only the academic institutions, the industry, and the state, but also other stakeholders such as civil society organizations, the user community, the funding organizations, etc. For telecenters with development objectives, they need to create collaborations or networks among themselves and become part of the larger regional innovation system to be able to respond effectively to the changing needs of their user communities and offer new content and services.

REFERENCES

Alberts, D. S., & Papp, D. S. (Eds.). (1997). *The Information Age: An Anthology on Its Impact and Consequences*. Washington, D.C.: CCRP Publication Series, Office of the Assistant Secretary of Defense.

Amsden, A. H., & Chu, W. W. (2003). *Beyond Late Development: Taiwan's Upgrading Policies*. Cambridge, MA: MIT Press.

Arrow, K. J. (1962). The Economic Implications of Learning by Doing. *The Review of Economic Studies, 29*, 155–173. doi:10.2307/2295952

Benjamin, P. (2001). Community development and democratisation through information technology: building the new South Africa. In Heeks, R. B. (Ed.), *Reinventing Government in the Information Age* (pp. 194–210). London: Routledge.

Benner, M., & Sandstrom, U. (2000). Institutionalizing the Triple Helix: Research Finding and Norms in the Academic System. *Research Policy*, 29(2), 291–302. doi:10.1016/S0048-7333(99)00067-0

Best, M. L., & Kumar, R. (2008). Sustainability Failures of Rural Telecenters: Challenges from the Sustainable Access in Rural India (SARI) Project. *Information Technologies and International Development*, 4(4), 31–45. doi:10.1162/itid.2008.00025

Best, M. L., & Maclay, C. M. (2002). Community Internet Access in Rural Areas: Solving the Economic Sustainability Puzzle. In Kirkman, G., Sachs, J. D., & Cornelius, P. K. (Eds.), *The Global Information Technology Report 2001-2002: Readiness for the Networked World*. Oxford: Oxford University Press.

Bhatnagar, S. (2000). Social Implications of Information and Communication Technology in Developing Countries: Lessons from Asian Success Stories. *The Electronic Journal of Information Systems in Developing Countries*, 1(4), 1–9.

Blattman, C., & Jensen, R. (2003). Assessing the Need and Potential of Community Networking for Development in Rural India. *The Information Society*, 19(5), 349–365. doi:10.1080/714044683

Cecchini, S. (2002). Information and Communications Technology for Poverty Reduction. Lessons from Rural India. In *Technology and Society 2002. (ISTAS'02). 2002) International Symposium on* (pp. 93-99). Raleigh, NC, USA, IEEE.

Cecchini, S., & Raina, M. (2003). Electronic Government and the Rural Poor: The Case of Gyandoot. *Information Technologies and International Development*, 2(2), 65–75. doi:10.1162/1544752044193434

Chataway, J., & Wield, D. (2000). Industrialization, innovation, and development: What does knowledge management change? *Journal of International Development*, 12(6), 803–824. doi:10.1002/1099-1328(200008)12:6<803::AID-JID714>3.0.CO;2-H

Cooke, P., Heidenreich, M., & Braczyk, H. J. (Eds.). (2004). *Regional Innovation Systems* (2nd ed.). London: Routledge.

Dagron, G. (2001). Prometheus Riding a Cadillac? Telecentres as the promised flame of knowledge. *Journal of Development Communication: Special Issue on Telecentres*, 12(2), 85–93.

David, P. A. (1975). *Technical Choice, Innovation and Economic Growth*. Cambridge, England: Cambridge University Press.

Doloreux, D., & Parto, P. (2004). Regional Innovation Systems: A Critical Synthesis (Discussion Paper no. 2004-17). UNU-INTECH.

Edquist, C. (2001, June). *The Systems of Innovation Approach and Innovation Policy: An Account of the State of the Art*. Paper presented at the Nelson Winter Conference, DRUID, Aalborg.

Edquist, C. (2004). Systems of Innovation - A Critical Review of The State of the Art. In Fagerberg, J., Mowery, D., & Nelson, R. (Eds.), *Handbook of Innovation* (pp. 181–208). Oxford: Oxford University Press.

Etzkowitz, H., & Leydesdorff, L. (Eds.). (1997). *Universities and the Global Knowledge Economy: A Triple Helix of University-Industry-Government Relations*. London: Cassell Academic.

Fillip, B., & Foote, D. (2007). *Making the Connection: Scaling Telecenters for Development*. Washington, D.C.: Academy for Education Development.

Gereffi, G. (1999). International Trade and Industrial Upgrading in the Apparel Commodity Chain. *Journal of International Economics, 48*(1), 37–70. doi:10.1016/S0022-1996(98)00075-0

Gereffi, G., & Kaplinsky, R. (Eds.). (2001). The Value of Value Chains. *IDS Bulletin, 32*(3), 1–136. doi:10.1111/j.1759-5436.2001.mp32003001.x

Gereffi, G., & Korzeniewicz, M. (Eds.). (1994). *Commodity Chains and Global Capitalism*. Westport, CT: Praeger.

Gurstein, M. (2001). Rural Development and Food Security, A "Community Informatics" Based Conceptual Framework. In *Proceedings of the 34th Hawaii International Conference on System Sciences.* Hawaii: IEEE Computer Society.

Harris, R., & Rajora, R. (2006). Empowering the Poor: Information and Communications Technology for Governance and Poverty Reduction - A Study of Rural Development Projects in India. UNDP-APDIP: Elsevier.

Heeks, R. (2002). Information systems and developing countries: Failure, success, and local improvisations. *The Information Society, 18,* 101–112. doi:10.1080/01972240290075039

Heeks, R. (2003a). Most eGovernment-for-Development Projects Fail: How can Risks be Reduced? (I-Government Working Paper No. 14) Manchester, UK: University of Manchester: Institute for Development Policy and Management.

Heeks, R., & Bhatnagar, S. C. (1999). Understanding Success and Failure in Information Age Reform. In Heeks, R. (Ed.), *Reinventing Government in the Information Age: International Practice in IT enabled public sector reform.* London: Routledge. doi:10.4324/9780203204962

Khan, H. A. (1998). *Technology, Development and Democracy: Limits of National Innovation Systems in the Age of Post-Modernism.* Cheltenham, UK & Northampton, USA: Edward Elgar.

King, J. J., & Kraemer, K. L. (1997). Computer and communication technologies: Impacts on the organization of enterprise and the establishment and maintenance of civil society. In *National Research Council, Computer Science and Telecommunications Board, Fostering Research on the Economic and Social Impacts of Information Technology* (pp. 188–210). USA: National Academy Press.

Kirat, T., & Lung, Y. (1999). Innovation and proximity: territories as loci of collective learning processes. *European Urban and Regional Studies, 6*(1), 27–38. doi:10.1177/096977649900600103

Kumar, R. (2004). *Social, Governance, and Economic Impact Assessment of Information and Communication Technology Interventions in Rural India.* Unpublished MCP Thesis, Massachusetts Institute of Technology, Cambridge, MA.

Kumar, R., & Best, M. L. (2006). Impact and Sustainability of E-Government Services in Developing Countries: Lessons Learned from Tamil Nadu, India. *The Information Society, 22*(1), 1–12. doi:10.1080/01972240500388149

Lall, S. (2000). Technological Change and Industrialization in the Asian Newly Industrializing Economies: Achievements and Challenges. In Kim, L., & Nelson, R. R. (Eds.), *Technology, learning, and Innovation. Experiences of Newly Industrializing Economies* (pp. 13–68). Cambridge: Cambridge University Press.

Leydesdorff, L. (2000). The Triple Helix: An Evolutionary Model of Innovations. *Research Policy, 29*(2), 243–255. doi:10.1016/S0048-7333(99)00063-3

Lundvall, B.-A. (1989). Innovation as an Inter-active Process: User-producer Relations. Technical Change and Economic Theory. In Dosi, G., Freeman, C., Nelson, R., Silverberg, G., & Soete, L. (Eds.), *Technical Change and Economic Theory* (pp. 349–369). London, New York: Pinter.

Lundvall, B.-A. (1993). Explaining Inter-Firm Cooperation and Innovation: Limits of the Transaction Cost Approach. In Grabher, G. (Ed.), *The Embedded Firm: On the Socio-Economics of Industrial Networks* (pp. 52–64). London: Routledge.

McNamara, K. S. (2003). *Information and Communication Technologies, Poverty and Development: Learning from Experience* (A Background paper for the infoDev Annual Symposium). Washington, D.C.: The World Bank.

Metcalfe, J. S. (1997). Technology Systems and Technology Policy in an Evolutionary Framework. Technology, Globalization and Economic Performance. In Archibugi, D., & Michie, J. (Eds.), *Technology, Globalization and Economic Performance* (pp. 268–296). Cambridge: Cambridge University Press.

Proenza, F. J. (2001). Telecenter Sustainability: Myths and Opportunities. *The Journal of Development Communication, 12*(2), 94–109.

Rogers, E. M. (2003). *Diffusion of innovations.* New York: Free Press.

Roman, R., & Colle, R. (2002). *Themes and issues in telecentre sustainability* (Development Informatics Working Paper Series Paper No. 10). Manchester, UK: University of Manchester, Institute of Development Policy and Management.

Rosenberg, N. (1982). *Inside the Black Box: Technology and Economics.* Cambridge: Cambridge University Press.

Segal, A. (2003). *Digital Dragon: High Technology Enterprises in China.* Ithaca, London: Cornell University Press.

Sinan, A., Marcela, E., & Randal, N. (2001). *Assessing network applications for Economic Development* (Pilot Phase Assessment Report). Cambridge, MA: Harvard University, JFK School of Government.

Sreekumar, T. T. (2003). De-hyping ICTs: ICT Innovations by Civil Society Organizations in. Rural India. *i4d-Information for Development, 1*(1), 22-27.

Storper, M. (1997). *The Regional World.* New York: The Guilford Press.

The World Bank. (1998). *Knowledge for Development. World Development Report.* Washington, D.C.: The World Bank.

The World Bank. (2003). *Sustainable Telecenters: A Guide for Government Policy.* Washington, DC: The World Bank.

UNCTAD. (2007). Promoting Livelihoods through Telecentres. In UNCTAD, *Information Economy Report 2007-2008, Science and Technology for Development: The New Paradigm of ICT* (pp. 269-320). Geneva: UNCTAD.

UNDP. (2001). *Human Development Report 2001: Making new technologies work for human development.* New York: United Nations Development Programme.

Van Belle, J.-P., & Trusler, J. (2005). An Interpretivist Case Study of a South African Rural Multi-Purpose Community Centre. *The Journal of Community Informatics, 1*(2), 140–157.

Velden, M. V. D. (2002). Knowledge Facts, Knowledge Fiction: The Role of ICTs in Knowledge Management and Development. *Journal of International Development, 14*(1), 25–37. doi:10.1002/jid.862

Von Hippel, E. (1976). The Dominant Role of Users in the Scientific Instrument Innovation Process. *Research Policy, 5,* 212–239. doi:10.1016/0048-7333(76)90028-7

Yusuf, S. (2003). *Innovative East Asia: The Future of Growth.* Washington, D.C.: The World Bank. doi:10.1596/0-8213-5356-X

Chapter 15

"Developed in the South:"
An Evolutionary and Prototyping Approach to Developing Scalable and Sustainable Health Information Systems

Vincent Shaw
University of Oslo, Norway & Health Information Systems Program, South Africa

Jorn Braa
University of Oslo, Norway

ABSTRACT

The expansion of ICT across Africa is influenced by many factors including political imperatives, donor priorities, private sector and NGO needs, and economic interests and as a result takes place in a haphazard and largely uncontrolled fashion. The health sector is no exception. The challenge, as in many developing countries, is to provide a robust and reliable health information system while effecting a transition between paper-based systems and computerized systems. The transition involves not only the introduction of new ICT, and the accompanying social and educational transformations of people and processes that accompany the introduction of ICT, but also the development of scalable health information systems that can facilitate a smooth transition as ICT expansion and development takes place. This chapter draws on 10 years of experience of the Health Information Systems Programme (HISP), an action research orientated network of public health practitioners and academics who initiated a pilot project in health information systems development in the post-apartheid transformation of South Africa, and which has subsequently had a profound effect on the development of health information systems in Africa and Asia. Through an exploration of health information systems development in numerous countries in Africa, we highlight insights into approaches and methodologies that contribute to successful and sustainable health information systems in resource constrained settings.

DOI: 10.4018/978-1-61520-997-2.ch015

INTRODUCTION

The expansion of ICT across Africa is proceeding at a rapid rate. Not only is access to computers becoming more pervasive, internet access is also increasing. The expansion of information and communication technology (ICT) networks is influenced by many factors including political imperatives (see for instance Sahay, Monteiro and Aanestad (2009)), private sector and NGO needs (Odedra, 1994), and economic interests (for instance Madon, Reinhard, Roode and Walsham (2009)). The result is that the expansion of ICT networks takes place in a haphazard and largely uncontrolled fashion (Braa, Hanseth, Heywood, Mohammed, & Shaw, 2007; Odedra, 1992). The health sector is no exception. The challenge, as in many developing countries, is to take advantage of the opportunities presented by increased access to ICT, to provide a robust and reliable health information system while effecting a transition between paper based systems and computerized systems (Boerma, 2005; Shibuya, Scheele, & Boerma, 2005; The Lancet Editorial, 2009). This chapter draws on 10 years of experience of the Health Information Systems Programme (HISP) network in health information systems development (HISD) in Africa to describe an evolutionary and prototyping approach to the development of scalable health information systems (HIS).

The transition from paper-based to computerized systems involves not only the introduction of new ICT, and the accompanying social and educational transformations of people and processes that accompany the introduction of ICT, but also the development of scalable health information systems that can facilitate a smooth transition as ICT expansion and development takes place. HISD is complicated by a number of factors, namely:

1. In traditional business processes, information systems development (ISD) is expected to take place in a uniform and controlled manner. This is seldom possible in an environ-ment where ICT development takes place at an uneven pace. For instance, in resource constrained contexts, access to computers and the internet does not become universally available at the same time – rather they are distributed from the centre to the periphery in a haphazard manner that reflects socio-political imperatives and economic realities. Not only is the expansion process uneven from a geographical perspective, but the access to technology is also uneven in the sense that a range of technologies may be simultaneously available from the very so-phisticated to the very outdated. HISD must be able it to respond to the unevenness by ensuring that HIS can be easily scaled from paper to computerized systems as access to ICT improves in an uneven manner;

2. A second major challenge is having to ac-commodate the low level of resources and infrastructure as reflected by the inadequate or absent power supplies, absence of paper on which to print reports, and restricted finances to purchase supplies;

3. The third, and perhaps most significant challenge, is related to human resource is-sues – from low staffing levels, to dealing with staff who have a very poor educational background and who have not been exposed to ICT;

4. Fourthly, but not least important, the influ-ence of social and political practices, which often reflect vested interests and decision making processes unrelated to health infor-mation systems development, may have a profound effect on the outcome of develop-ment projects.

The traditional health information systems literature describes the development and imple-mentation of health information systems as being a fairly uniform and deterministic process (Pan American Health Organization, 1999). The process is described as being the typical waterfall approach of planning, preparing, procuring, testing and implementation. In addition, it is claimed that the process is usually initiated in the financial and administrative area. Following this clinical systems should be added, and through the combination of financial and clinical data an assessment can be made of health improvements and best clinical practices. As additional pieces of information are added, the system will enable the institution to "focus its efforts on prevention of disease, rather than treatment, wellness instead of illness, and integration of continuum of care, rather than isolated practices"(Pan American Health Organization, 1999, Section B.1.2.2). Unfortunately, HISD is never as easy as this. The large majority of health information systems in sub-Saharan Africa are not flexible, but specifically designed to mainly cater for the needs of (sub-) national managers and international stakeholders. It has been asserted that most systems are also developed by either international consultants working locally or international companies (Odedra, 1993; Siika et al., 2005), making modifications and improvements difficult and often costly. However, as will be demonstrated more fully in the theory section of this chapter, several authors (Ciborra, 2000; Hanseth & Braa, 2000) have alluded to the need for different, more flexible approaches to information systems development. This is particularly supported by the literature on complex systems (Benbya & McKelvey, 2006; Jacucci, Hanseth, & Lyytinen, 2006), and on information systems development in developing country contexts (Jayasuriya, 1999; Silva, 2007; Walsham & Sahay, 1999). Given the need to be able to accommodate change on a regular basis, information systems in complex systems cannot be developed in a "waterfall" type approach – rather an iterative, participative prototyping approach is required where systems are developed as loosely coupled systems which can be integrated and which can evolve over time (Ramanathan, 2005; Tan, Wen, & Awad, 2005).

As a result, HISP adopted a multi-dimensional perspective to health information systems development (HISD), acknowledging the complex interplay between individuals as social beings, and technology as a dynamic and rapidly changing field influenced by a huge range of factors, many of which are beyond the control of any single individual. Given this understanding, the challenge in many developing countries is not only to develop an appropriate HIS, but also to be able to scale the system and sustain it in a context which is rapidly changing. The health sector demands are rapidly changing, especially with the spread of HIV/AIDS and the changing patterns of care and treatment, while access to technology is increasing. The aim of this chapter is to analyze the approaches that have been used by the HISP network to scale health information systems (HIS) across Africa, as well as the factors that may contribute to the development of sustainable HIS.

The chapter is structured as follows. The next section provides some contextual background to the HISP network, and a review of relevant literature. In the main section of this chapter we describe three aspects of the development of HIS in Africa, namely the evolutionary and iterative nature of the district health information software (DHIS) development, the development of capacity and support networks to underpin HISD and lastly, approaches to the scaling of the system in Africa. In the analysis and discussion section we first discuss the scaling process, and elaborate on what exactly has been scaled, and then explore how this understanding, and the creation of support networks contributes to sustainable HIS.

BACKGROUND AND LITERATURE REVIEW

This section begins with a description of the HISP network, and is then followed by an exploration of the literature on two main issues, namely the evolutionary and participatory prototyping approach to software systems development, and the current thinking on scaling of health information systems.

Background to the HISP Program

The Health Information Systems Programme (HISP) network was initiated by the University of Oslo in 1994 (Braa, Monteiro, & Sahay, 2004). It includes academic staff and health information systems developers and implementers in South Africa, Mozambique, Ethiopia, Tanzania (including Zanzibar), Botswana, Malawi, Nigeria, Zambia, India and Vietnam. The HISP network seeks to strengthen HIS within these countries through five key mechanisms.

The first is to design, develop, and implement free and open source software (FOSS). Secondly, the network works directly with the health services in the respective countries to deploy health information systems (HIS) within their health services to strengthen the informational basis for public health care delivery. Third, the network provides large scale and intensive capacity building for health staff at all levels of the health system with a key focus on "using information to support local action", and also through formalized professional masters and doctoral programs in HIS. Fourthly, the network supports institutional development at the national and state levels around monitoring and evaluation activities for the millennium development goals (MDG's) and lastly, the international sharing of best practices by drawing upon and contributing to HIS related knowledge across developing countries.

HISP South Africa (HISP-SA) was launched with Norwegian funding in 1994 as a joint collaboration between the Norwegian Computer Centre and University of Cape Town's Department of Community Health and University of Western Cape's School of Public Health (Braa & Hedberg, 2000). The approach and software developed by this project and piloted in the Western Cape is now adopted as the standard for monitoring primary health care and hospital services in all nine provinces in South Africa. HISP-SA, constituted as a not for profit non-governmental organisation now supports the development of HIS in South Africa, Malawi, Botswana, Nigeria, Zambia, Liberia and Namibia. It has been instrumental in the development of the district health information software (DHISv1.3 and DHISv1.4) (see below) which is used extensively in these countries, in both primary health care (PHC) and hospital settings, to support the process of making health information available to improve service delivery.

Located at the Department of Informatics, University of Oslo, the HISP-Oslo component provides expertise in the field of information systems (IS) analysis, design and development; data warehouse design and development; systems integration and standardization within complex organisational settings and FOSS development. The group has 15 years of experience in applying these areas of expertise from the general IS field in the particular context of HIS in low and mid-income countries. Since 1999 the Oslo group has coordinated the growing international "HISP-network" for HIS strengthening and taken part in concrete development in a number of countries such as Mozambique, India, Tanzania, Cuba, Mongolia, Ethiopia and Vietnam.

In their description of the HISP network as a "network of action", Braa, et al (2004) suggest that sustainable HIS requires a "network" approach rather than implementation in single sites. Sustainable systems are created through balancing vertical flows (local appropriation of systems and processes) with horizontal (diffusion) of experiences through the use standards for HIS (for example standard datasets and associated processes), education and training, and software development.

The Rationale for Participatory and Evolutionary Design

We address the design and development of information systems from an action research perspective as carried out in the HISP network (Braa, Monteiro, & Sahay, 2004)). Action research was introduced in the 1940's as a way of generating knowledge about a social system while, at the same time, attempting to change it (Elden & Chisholm, 1993). Our approach to action research and information systems design was initially influenced by a number of union based action research projects in Scandinavia in the 70's and 80's. The focus in the earlier participatory design projects was on empowering workers who were affected by or threatened by new technology, exploring ways in which their influence over technological solutions could be ensured (Bjerknes, Ehn, & Kyng, 1987; Sandberg, 1979). The later projects shifted toward producing technological alternatives by involving workers in cooperative design at the workplace (Greenbaum & Kyng, 1991). Adaptation of information systems to the local context, empowerment through practical learning, and the creation of local ownership through participative processes are central issues in the Scandinavian projects which, despite the differences in context, offer important lessons for third world IS design (Braa, Monteiro, Reinert, 1995).

Because there is a lack of experience of information technology and information systems design in African user organisations (see for instance an analysis on the difficulties of introducing IT in Africa in Odedra, 1992), designers have a high level of uncertainty regarding both the goals of the system and the context of its development and future use (Davis, 1982). In these situations Davis (1982) suggests experimental approaches (incorporating user involvement through participatory prototyping) are appropriate as compared to more structured approaches. Similar recommendations are made by other authors (Korpela et al., 1998; Mash & Mohammed, 2000; Sandiford, Annett, & Cibulskis, 1992).

It also follows that IS design under such conditions needs to follow an evolutionary approach starting with the basic needs and gradually building on these to expand the use of the system as the users learn more about the technology and its potential (Braa, Hanseth, Heywood, Mohammed, Shaw, 2007; Korpela et al., 1998).

In summary then, the rationale for using participatory design approaches is based on three important priorities (Greenbaum, Madsen, 1993):

- as a means to increase productivity;
- as a strategy to overcome the problem of lack of shared understanding between developers and users;
- from a political perspective, participatory approaches are a democratic strategy to give people the means to influence their own work places.

In the case descriptions which follow, we will show how these principles have contributed to the development of significant capacity for HISD and sustainable HIS in a number of countries. However, in the health sector, the challenge is not only to develop HIS, but also to scale them (Braa, Monteiro, Sahay, 2004). This is important because in the health sector, it is not only important to know how many children have been immunized. Health workers must also be able to compute the coverage achieved in a given area. Unless data is obtained from all health services in the area, this information cannot be calculated. This is the "all or nothing" imperative (ibid, p 341). For this reason, it is appropriate to reflect on the difficulties and approaches to scaling of health information systems.

Scaling of HIS

In this chapter we ascribe to the view suggested by Sahay and Walsham (2005) that scaling is the process by which the system is expanded in scope and size. Drawing on the information infrastructure perspective, they suggest that scaling of health information systems is a complex process that requires the spread of "heterogeneous networks around the technology" (ibid, pg 43). The heterogeneous networks consist of people, processes, software, infrastructure, technical support and political support. They describe scaling a health information system from an initial coverage of 9 PHC facilities to 49 and then up to 1500 health facilities over a vast geographical area in India, what is scaled, who is involved in the scaling process and how it is scaled. The authors allude to the inherent drive to effect scaling that characterizes health information systems that must have complete data coverage to be meaningful (Braa, Monteiro, & Sahay, 2004). Similarly, Eoyang (1996) suggests that complex systems have an ability to self-replicate. She describes scaling as the property of complex systems in which one part of the system reproduces the same structure and patterns that appear in other parts of the system (Eoyang 1996: 36).

But scaling does not occur without some support and intervention. Numerous authors advocate for a cultivation approach (Bergqvist, Dahlberg, Ljungberg, 2002; Rolland, Monteiro, 2002) to the scaling process. Sahay and Walsham (2005) extend this concept to include scaling the HISP-India team, as well as scaling capacity within the government bureaucracy. They argue that the main challenge experienced is the scaling of complexity, particularly associated with having to manage the increased political exposure that goes with scaling efforts, and the frequent changes that are embedded characteristics of the health sector (influenced not only by changing disease patterns, but also changing demands and methods of providing care, especially in the face of the HIV/AIDS epidemic).

Using case studies from the Health Information Systems Programme in Nigeria and Ethiopia, interdependencies between human capacity, access to structural issues like technology and hardware and software, and data processing capacity are identified as important factors to be considered in scaling health information systems (Shaw, Mengiste, & Braa, 2007). The authors suggest that given the imbalances that exist between human capacity, and access to technology for instance, homogenous scaling across all levels of the health system may be impractical – rather the approach should be to scale to areas which have the capacity to absorb training and technology even if this means proceeding in an uneven manner. They advocate for a cultivation process – which would allow the implementation process to be responsive to local nuances and variations from the norm.

Given the heterogeneous environment within which scaling has to be accommodated, technical standards for the health information infrastructure can be used to support the scaling process (Braa, Hanseth, Heywood, Mohammed, Shaw, 2007). Data standards (namely defining a minimum dataset) are essential as a component of the scaling process especially where heterogeneous systems (for instance different computer systems, or paper-based and computerized processes that need to interface with one another to ensure the seamless flow of data) need to be taken into consideration. By establishing a set of standards for the handling and transmission of data through the health hierarchy, heterogeneity can be overcome by using gateways to address the incompatibility between heterogeneous systems while maintaining the flow of data.

Despite these descriptions, and guidelines very little has been written about the process of HIS development in Africa, how the challenges around resource allocation and low education levels have been addressed. In particular, how do choices get made and how do they contribute or detract from sustainable systems development, especially given the need to be flexible so as to respond to ad hoc requests or opportunities. In the next section we describe HISD in South Africa, Malawi, and Nigeria over a five to ten year period, and draw on the case studies to suggest a comprehensive approach to sustainable HISD.

HEALTH INFORMATION SYSTEMS DEVELOPMENT USING THE HISP APPROACH

In this section we describe HISD in four countries (South Africa, Malawi, Nigeria, and Zambia, and allude briefly to our experience in Liberia) by examining three aspects of the HISP approach, namely the incremental development of software in response to users needs, approaches to HR capacity building and the emergence of a new cadre of health worker skilled in HISD, and lastly, HISD and HIS implementation through three approaches to scaling HIS, namely the standard approach, the prioritized sample approach, and the hierarchical cluster approach.

HISD in South Africa as Incremental Software Development

DHIS as a Tool to Empower Health Workers to Improve Health Services

While HISD in South Africa has been described more comprehensively in a number of other publications (Rohde et al., 2008), this section focuses on the contribution to HISD in Africa through the development of the DHIS. The DHIS has been developed through a participatory prototyping approach (Braa, Hedberg, 2002). The software has gone through numerous iterations (for instance DHISv1.3 is the version that was distributed outside of South Africa from 1998 onwards, and was preceded by earlier versions. DHIS1.4 is the latest version developed in South Africa, while DHISv2.0 has been developed by the Indian and Norwegian teams largely in response to a request to develop a system free of user licence fees) in response to inputs received from users in the health sector in many developing countries (Braa, Monteiro, & Sahay, 2004), and has been developed as a generic database system that requires customization to reflect the context in which it is used. Most of the initial DHIS design and development

has taken place in South Africa, using MS Access as the underlying technological platform. While coding was initially in VB, increasingly Java based code is being used. Through the links within the network, together with masters and PhD students, the DHIS2.0 system has been developed which is a web-based, platform independent, and database independent version of the DHIS database. While the development of DHIS2.0 so far is coordinated from and for a significant part also carried out in Norway/Europe, the "drive' behind the system is the requirements on the ground in India for a system that is "license-free" and FOSS. The aim is to distribute more of the development to the South, and increasingly designers and programmers in Ethiopia, India, Vietnam, and Nigeria are being incorporated into the network. In this chapter the focus is on the development of DHISv1.3 and DHISv1.4, and its use across Africa.

The DHIS (versions 1.3 and v1.4) provide the tools to capture, and validate anonymized, aggregated data, and to process it into indicators. It enables the data to be presented as both raw and processed data using either Excel pivot tables, a report generator function or a GIS interface. While the software is described as FOSS (in the sense that the code is freely available and the software is freeware), the system does require MS Access and MS Excel and a Windows environment to function. This arrangement began as a pragmatic compromise to "hardcore" FOSS principles based on the almost universal availability of Windows and MS Office in the public sector in South Africa (Braa, Hedberg, 2002).

The main philosophical standpoints that have driven the software development are:

- The software should empower health workers at facilities and district levels to use information to improve health services, and there is therefore a strong focus to allow users at a local level to adapt the software system to suite their needs.

- The software is an aide to use of information.
- That users at all levels should be given feedback on the data that is entered into the system. Reporting must therefore be integrated with data capture and should include access to geographic information system (GIS) reports.
- Reporting on routine monthly data should be restricted to small data sets to avoid overloading health workers with unnecessarily burdensome reporting responsibilities, but is complemented by survey data.
- The DHIS is developed as a Data Warehouse which can incorporate data from a variety of different software systems and integrate them for use by managers.

Central to the DHIS success has been its ability to be customized by health workers to the local context. Customization is required in two main areas, (see Figure 1):

a)   The organisational hierarchy – each reporting unit belongs to a parent organisation and each of these parents can belong to a higher level parent – creating a hierarchy which then usually spreads upwards towards the district health office, provincial and national ministries of health, and could include a sub-regional level. In a typical primary health care setting health facilities are grouped in a geographical area (a local municipality, or ward, or zone), and these are grouped by health district. This is important because it enables data and indicators to be aggregated to higher levels (for example out-patient attendances of individual reporting units can be aggregated to reflect all out-patient attendances in the hospital, and these can be aggregated to reflect out-patient attendances in a district or region, etc).

b)   For each reporting unit, data can be collected against three phenomenologically different data elements. Data elements represent the services that are measured, for example children weighed or children fully immunized, etc. Routine data represents data that is collected on a routine basis (daily, weekly, monthly, annually). Survey data is

Figure 1. Aspects of the DHIS which require customization

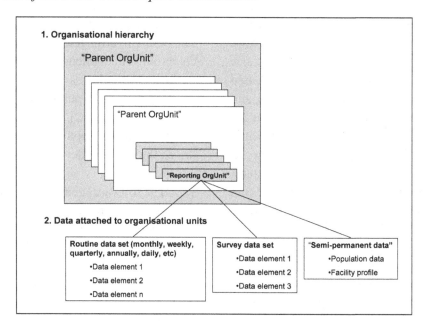

data that presents a "snapshot in time" view of a specific service, collected on an ad-hoc, or infrequent basis, and usually has validity for a specific period. Semi-permanent data represents data that does not change frequently. For each of these data types, the software can be customized to represent the specific data collection needs of the user.

Evolution of the DHIS in Response to User Needs

Figure 2 details the development of the DHIS software (functionality expansion). The process of developing the DHIS software has happened in parallel to the geographic scaling of the system across South Africa and a number of other countries (the process of some of these implementations are discussed below and in Chilundo, 2004; Chilundo, Aanestad, 2004; Mavimbe, Braa, Bjune, 2005), and as an iterative process fed by the expansion of users as the scope of the system (the incorporation of additional program data into the DHIS) was scaled. The improvements in software capacity (e.g. improvements in the ability of MS Excel pivot tables to handle increasing volumes of data between versions 2000 and 2003, and similar improvements in MS Access functionality) have fortuitously paralleled the expansion in the volume of data in the DHIS database.

It is interesting to reflect on the iterative nature of the feedback loops and interchanges that has accompanied the DHIS development. For instance, enabling survey and audit functionality in the software allowed the addition of data from a paper-based client satisfaction tool in the DHIS.

Figure 2. Three domains of health information systems development

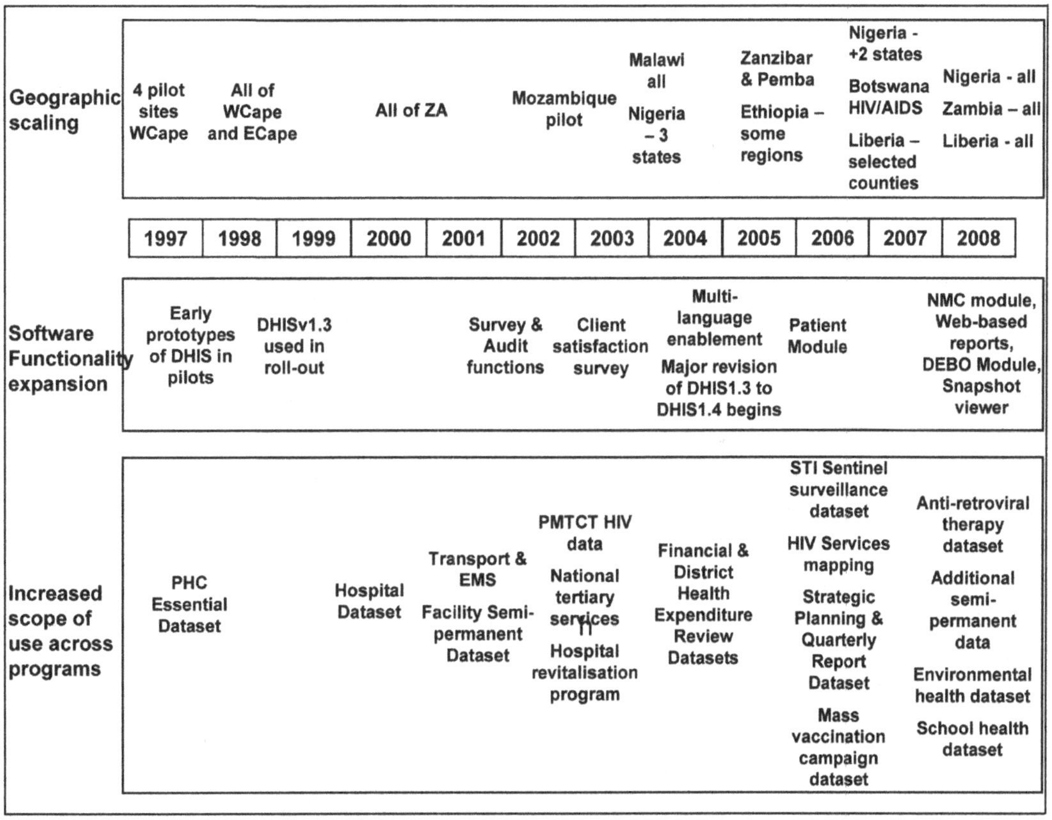

Similarly, the addition of the patient module (the result of a specific request from a hospital department in Malawi – see later), resulted in the expansion of scope of program data in the DHIS to include notifiable medical conditions module in South Africa, and the Integrated Disease Surveillance Reporting System in Zambia.

While in general the use of the software in South Africa has driven the demand for additional functionality, there are notable instances when additional functionality has been added to address demands for use of the DHIS software outside of South Africa, namely:

- The Mozambiquean team tired of rewriting new releases of the program in Portuguese and pushed for the creation of a "multi-language conversion" table that would effect the translation of key terms into languages other than English – this is triggered by a change in the Windows ® language settings. Currently, supported languages include Spanish (Cuba), Portuguese (Mozambique), Mongolian, Russian, and Chinese. Efforts are underway to complete the translation into Swahili (Tanzania), Telugu (Andra Pradesh, India), Kannada (Karnataka, India).

- The use of the DHIS in Ethiopia resulted in some University of Oslo students developing the DEBO Software for tracking patients receiving HIV/AIDS Anti-Retroviral Therapy. Subsequently, this has been further developed and refined by a team of developers in South Africa, and has recently been released as a module of the DHIS.

- In 2007, the HISP-SA team was requested to assist in revising the software for the HMIS in Zambia. The installed system had a useful functionality which tracked the data completeness for certain data elements. This functionality was at the time not available in the DHIS, but was sub-

sequently added as the "snapshot viewer" functionality to address this need.

- In Kenya, a team at the International Organisation for Migration (IOM) adapted the system to enable their centers to capture the specificities of HIV care and counseling as well as pre-departure medical examinations. They did this without any face to face meetings, only email guidance and support from the software development team in South Africa. Their requests for support helped to improve the functional integration between the patient module and the core module of the DHIS.

In South Africa, an important factor that has contributed to the drive for the seamless integration of datasets (for example primary health care (PHC) data, hospital data, environmental health data, financial data and survey data) has come from the National Department of Health (DoH) who implemented a system of quarterly reporting (the QRS) on selected indicators. Initially, the process of reporting for this was a manual process of collating data from different sources, including various DHISv1.3 databases, and legacy systems such as the human resource and financial management systems (Phase 1 of Figure 3). With the development of DHISv1.4, it was possible to integrate various separate DHISv1.3 databases into a single database in version DHISv1.4 (Phase 2 of Figure 3), and to create a dataset that represented the elements of the QRS report (Phase 3 of Figure 3).

While the DHIS was always envisaged as a data warehouse, its efficiency in fulfilling this role has improved through the functionality introduced in DHISv1.4. In this version, data elements are grouped in datasets. A dataset is a data input construct which usually represents a form that contains data to be captured. Data elements may belong to more than one dataset. For example, the data element "Total Live Births" can belong to the PHC Dataset that captures data

Figure 3. The evolution of an integrated HIS in a phased manner

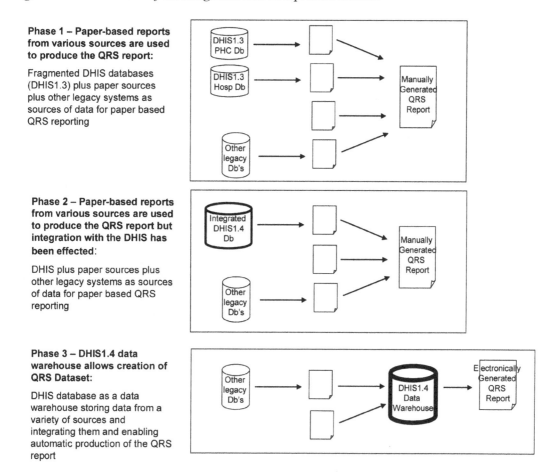

Phase 1 – Paper-based reports from various sources are used to produce the QRS report:

Fragmented DHIS databases (DHIS1.3) plus paper sources plus other legacy systems as sources of data for paper based QRS reporting

Phase 2 – Paper-based reports from various sources are used to produce the QRS report but integration with the DHIS has been effected:

DHIS plus paper sources plus other legacy systems as sources of data for paper based QRS reporting

Phase 3 – DHIS1.4 data warehouse allows creation of QRS Dataset:

DHIS database as a data warehouse storing data from a variety of sources and integrating them and enabling automatic production of the QRS report

related to PHC services, as well as the Hospital dataset being a dataset that reflects the services provided in a hospital. A hospital might have to provide a report to the PHC management on the PHC services it provides, as well as a report for Hospital Management. While the data for these two reports might be sourced from different units within a hospital, the reports contain the same data elements. The integration of hospital and PHC databases has resulted in improved data accuracy because only a single value can be stored against the common data elements, thus ensuring that reporting through two different forms is coherent. In South Africa this degree of integration, and the demand for the QRS report, has forced an evaluation of the overlap between different data sources and data element definitions. It was found that various reports used different data element names for essentially the same data, reported different values, and generally led to confusion when planning and budgeting for services. A re-alignment of naming conventions for data elements and reporting formats has resulted. Changes in the DHIS have therefore resulted in a simplification of processes through the integration of various data sources, but in another sense it represents an increase in complexity from the point of view of a complex database which integrates and manages data from various sources to produce a single report. As the complexity of the underlying database grows, if the additional functionality is to be utilized, users are required to have a deeper understanding of the system. The implications of this are discussed in the next section.

An important feature of the DHIS development process has been the evolutionary development of the software, fed by an iterative cycle fed by the geographic scaling and expansion of scope of use of the software over a 10 year period. This is the "bazaar" style of development that Raymond (1999) describes in his description of the FOSS movement, and which is sharply contrasted to that of the typical "cathedral" development style of most proprietary health software. The success in one geographic area, and with a limited scope, has resulted in a drive for additional functionality, and so the bazaar gradually grows into a bigger assembly of more closely integrated bazaars, thereby strengthening its role.

The development of the "bazaar" can be partly attributed to the software acting as an "attractor"(Braa, Hanseth, Heywood, Mohammed, Shaw, 2007). The attractor consisted of two related components, and these allowed the scaling of HIS across the two domains (the geographic domain,

and the functional scope). One component of the "attractor" was the identification of a minimal dataset (i.e. a limited scope of program data). The DHIS as a coherent software application that easily supported data capture, analysis and reporting, while also being flexible to accommodate changes over time was the second component. Together, these created a strong "attractor". The "attractor" was appealing to use, and encouraged others to also utilize the same standards. As more data came to be incorporated, and integrated (with the transition from DHISv1.3 to DHISv1.4), the system became even more attractive to managers who were required to report on a wide range of data. Figure 4 illustrates the increase in activities measured (data records in the database) while the number of patient encounters leveled off after the initial scaling (1999-2002).

Human Resource Capacity Building

We address the challenge of building capacity in health workers through first describing how skills were developed in the anesthetic department of a

Figure 4. DHIS database expansion over 10 years

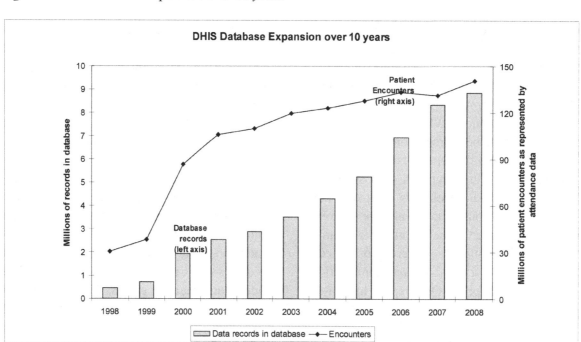

large, academic hospital in Malawi. The department developed a simple form for the collection of anesthetic related data and utilized anesthesia clinical assistants (CA's) to capture the data in the DHIS. This process was important because it not only developed computer skills in the staff, it also expanded their understanding about information systems and allowed the department to gather data specifically related to their services. This enabled them to also assess the quality of care being provided, and in fact to effect changes to improve the quality of care. We then use this example to describe the emergence of a new cadre of health worker, the health information systems practitioner. Lastly, mechanisms for support of this cadre, and for ongoing human resource development are discussed.

Developing Capacity to Manage the DHIS in Africa

During one of the early co-ordination meetings for the development of a hospital management information system in a large hospital in Malawi in 2005, a representative from the anesthesia department was asked whether they had been "effectively using" the computer which had been donated to them. The reply was that they had been capturing data, but were having trouble analyzing it. A review of their data revealed a MS Excel worksheet, with multiple columns, some of which contained mixed data (e.g. age and sex combined (e.g. 40M as representing a 40 year old male patient), or diagnosis and outcome were combined in complicated ways). The spreadsheet was reformatted into columns containing uniform data by using advanced MS Excel commands, and a pivot table was developed for data analysis.

This led to a discussion about the data needs for the anesthesia department, and the process by which they collected data. The result was the development of a simple form for collecting the data (it went through a number of iterations as additional data types were added), and in combina-

tion with the help of a software programmer (also a member of the HISP team), a "patient module" linked to the DHIS was developed which could capture specific patient data (the request for this type of database opportunistically coincided with the development of DHIS14 Patient Module, aspects of which incorporated some early thinking around systems for collecting patient specific data related to the tuberculosis and ARV programs). This was not an electronic patient record (EPR) in the true sense of the word. Rather, by building on the "local customization" concept of the DHIS, it allowed a person who did not have programming skills (as in the case of the principle author), but who knew the basics of database use, to set up a simple database in which the units providing services, and data elements could be customized. The "patient module" expanded the standard DHIS data collection of aggregated anonomised data to include patient specific data and text values. An export function into MS Excel created a pivot table, and both the numeric and text data could be analyzed. In this way, the department had the functionality of being able to access patient specific data (e.g. to get a complete record of the anesthetic process in a patient who died while receiving anesthesia), or numeric data. For instance, after two months of data collection an analysis of theatre utilization revealed that more than 50% of caesarian sections were being done in a facility which had less staff and less equipment than the "main" facility.

However, getting to this stage was not without its own problems. The computer that was used was outdated, and could only read a CD or a diskette. It had USB ports, but as it operated on Windows 98 getting the computer to read from a flash disk was problematic. We limped through this phase improvising, and after some months were able to upgrade it to Windows 2000, at which point it became easier to load and extract data from the computer. Experience has taught the HISP team that this is the norm in developing country contexts, and for this reason the DHIS software has had to be maintained as a system that can function on MS Office 97, 98, and 2000 (only recently has support for MS Office 97 been dropped). If this had not been the strategy, it would not have been able to retain its relevance as a suitable system in these settings. But even despite this strategy, there was a delicate balance that had to be achieved between the software, and the capacity of the hardware. Because the software is "relatively simple" and unsophisticated in its demands from the system, it could be accommodated on a "fragile" computer, a situation that is not uncommon in Africa.

Emergence of a New Cadre of Hybrid Health Workers

As suggested by Braa et al. (2002) people (the staff) have been central in initiating the development of the IS. This is an important aspect of the implementation process. The IS requires people to drive it, maintain it, and continue to develop it. Their motivation for involvement is based on the returns that they get from the investment that they make.

The staff that captured the data in the anesthetic department were the clinical assistants (CA's), and they became computer literate through the process of capturing data. The clinical head of

department facilitated tremendously by ensuring that at all times during the period, there was at least one CA who took the lead in maintaining the system. Even the clinical head of department, while clearly understanding her information needs, was not very computer literate, and had to be taught how to utilize the pivot tables – in fact, in order to reduce her frustration levels, the pivot tables were placed on a CD Rom, so that she could manipulate and adjust them, but would never be able to overwrite the CD, thus ensuring that she could abort and restart from the familiar beginning!

This case description highlights a few important issues related to building human capacity for computerized health information systems. In the case description, we see the development of a system as an interaction between the system developers (in this case the HISP-SA team), and the users. The developers of the system are not a uniform group (see Table 1) – in this case they are a heterogeneous collection of people who work together in a unique way, contributing their various skills in order to develop a functional system. Users contributed to the development of the system by saying "but can you change this so that we can do ….", and when that was accomplished, they in fact became sponsors because the system now served

Table 1. The health information systems development team

Origin of team member	Team member	Skills base
External development team (this is the HISP implementing team)	Professional Software Developer and Head of Software Development Team	Able to envisage software development, and listens extremely well to needs of health workers, and has been able to translate this into a user friendly software program.
	Professional Software Developer	Skilled software developer, while also having good inter-personal skills, the technology orientated focus dominates.
	Medical doctor	Due to a deep understanding of DHIS and data base conceptualization, and information needs of managers, is able to bridge the medical, and informatics world, and see opportunities in both.
Internal hospital staff (Internal to the Health Department)	Head of department, and "Executive sponsor"	Medical specialist, with deep understanding of medical issues, and a vision for using data. But little understanding of how to translate medical related data to management information. Poor database management and computer literacy skills
	Clinical assistants	Medical knowledge, and growing computer literacy

their purpose. Had this team not been available (as is commonly the case in developed countries), the solution would have been very different – a paper based register could have taken the place of the electronic register. But, because there were a variety of skills available, an innovative solution was developed.

The transfer of skills has not only been in terms of computer literacy. In many instances, the users have developed a more detailed understanding of the database and its functions, and how the system is arranged in the 'back-end". The transfer of skills can be depicted by viewing a spectrum with the "Pure User" at one end and the "Pure Developer" at the other. The degree of sophistication of the use of the DHIS system will depend on the degree of interaction and skills transfer that takes place between the people at the two extremes – the extent to which they shift closer towards each other through the skills transfer process. A "pure user" with little knowledge of HIS's will not be able to reprogram the DHIS, but one with a little understanding can customize the system. Someone with a greater degree of skill in the use of the DHIS can customize it for use in a variety of settings (example from Kenya IOM), and someone with far greater skills in database manipulation can effect internal structural changes. This scenario represents the new cadre of health worker that is developing – a person who is computer literate and has sufficient skills to effect changes in the computerized information system. We call this emerging cadre the health information systems practitioner (HIS practitioner). Other authors have referred to this person as an implementer (Seebregts et al., 2009), although in our assessment the implementer is closer in the spectrum to the developer than the HIS practitioner.

Creating Local and Regional Networks of HIS Practitioners

One of the strengths of the scaling process adopted in South Africa, Zambia (Shaw, Simoonga, Kalinda, & Muyambo, 2008), India (Sahay & Walsham, 2005) and Nigeria has been the creation of local NGO's to support and help develop HIS practitioners. The HISP-SA team has maintained a team of 8 full-time HIS practitioners since it was constituted as not-for-profit non-governmental organisation, and has recently expanded its membership to 20 full-time practitioners, in addition to up to 10 part-time consultants that are drawn in from time to time. Team membership is varied, and comprises developers, medical practitioners, nurses, environmental health practitioners, and educators. Recently younger staff with no formal post schooling education have been enrolled as part of an initiative to help develop young South Africans from disadvantaged backgrounds. Most team members are adept at least at the "simple" software customization responsibilities. However, the transfer of skills and development of capacity has not happened overnight, and is increasingly challenging as the competency of staff in the government service has increased significantly over the years, and they are therefore demanding increasingly sophisticated support. HISP-SA has to constantly weigh the odds on whether to draw new recruits from the public service (which is where a large pool of expertise lies) or to seek it outside the public service, where the pool is much smaller. A fair balance has prevailed where of the five staff that left HISP-SA since 2003, three have been employed in senior positions in the public service while of the 11 staff employed in the last year, only 2 came from the public service, and 2 from local government.

In Nigeria, since 2003 a team of six to eight HIS practitioners have been identified as "national consultants" and they have been supported by the "regional consultants" from HISP-SA who visit Nigeria on a regular basis. The capacity within these local teams varies across the spectrum from "pure user" to HIS practitioner – seldom have pure developers been identified in these countries.

In Zambia the lead national consultant (who is a programmer running a software development company) very quickly developed advanced DHIS skills, and together with his thorough understanding of the health system, has made him an invaluable support to the Ministry of Health. He has also been contracted as a regional consultant to Nigeria to translate an Excel spreadsheet used by the WHO Epi program into a dataset within the DHIS. We see therefore the beginnings of a process of cross-fertilization occurring between "second generation" HIS practitioners on the continent who are sharing skills and experiences amongst themselves – this is likely to escalate as communication between these teams expands, and as capacity develops.

The networks are maintained through the use of email and interactive wiki websites, sharing of publications and reports, and opportunities to study masters and PhD programs in Oslo and at universities in Africa (South Africa- University of Western cape and University of Pretoria; Mozambique – Universidade Eduardo Mondlane; Tanzania – University of Dar es Salaam; Ethiopia – University of Gondar and University of Addis Ababa). An interesting series of developments related to this has taken place in Nigeria. A young Nigerian medical doctor who is also a self-taught programmer has enrolled for a PhD with the University of Oslo. His interests lie in mobile technology and the potential use of the DHIS2 in Nigeria. He has also participated in the OpenMRS Internship program and Google "Summer of Code" initiative, and this provides some interesting possibilities for strengthening networks around HISD in Nigeria. The agreement with the HISP-Nigeria team is that while he completes his studies he would be "bonded "to the team, and would provide support to the various initiatives in Nigeria as part of his fieldwork. Similarly, a PhD student from LSE asked to be able to do some field work in the country of his birth, and has also been supporting HIS in the Northern Nigerian states, and will hopefully upon the completion of his studies continue to be involved with HISD being effected by the HISP-Nigeria team. Through these

academic and institutional linkages and networks, synergistic opportunities arise for strengthening individuals and HISD in an evolutionary manner as described in the "networks of action" approach (Braa, Monteiro, Sahay, 2004).

HIS Development and DHIS Implementation

Over the years, different approaches have been adopted for strengthening the health information systems in various countries. In South Africa, the approach has been to develop a small data set for monthly reporting, and the data collection tools to support this. These systems are all paper based, and data in the monthly reports was computerized at the district level. The "standard approach" to scaling has been to begin small in selected sites, scale to district or provincial level, and then scale across provinces to achieve national coverage. In South Africa the pilot began in 1997 and was eventually effected across the whole country by 2001 (Braa & Hedberg, 2002). Data submission rates are high (above 70% within 1 month of end of reporting period and above 90% within 3 months after end of reporting period). A similar approach was adopted in Zambia, except that the implementation began as a Provincial-wide process in one province. The implementation process was utilized as an opportunity to develop capacity in a team of trainers (comprised of provincial and district information officers, and representatives from nursing colleges who were requested by the National MoH to include the concepts of HISD in their under-graduate curricula) who then took responsibility for the implementation across the other provinces. The process was initiated in October 2007, and all provinces were using the system by November 2008. Although it is still to early to say with certainty, it appears as if data submission rates are reasonably high, but with a longer time lag from the end of reporting period. As in South Africa, the monthly reports are paper-based, and computerization generally takes place at the district level. In Liberia, a similar approach has been adopted, with government employees scaling the system beyond the initial pilot in 15 counties.

In Nigeria, the process has been significantly different, and continues to evolve. Initially, all facilities within a few local government authorities (LGA's) (typically between 15-20% of all LGA's in a state) were selected as pilot sites. Staff in facilities were trained, and monthly reports were sent from facilities to LGA level – in the past they were collated and aggregated at this level before onward transmission, but with the revision of the HIS, it was deemed important to have data disaggregated at facility level, and so the facility reports were sent onwards to the state level. It was at this level where computerization took place, mainly because computers were not available at the LGA level. Power supply at the LGA level was extremely unreliable, and it was impossible to identify a secure environment in which to store a computer. As a result between 4-6 data capturers were utilized at the state level to capture data for the whole state (Shaw, Mengiste, & Braa, 2007). After a period of 18 months, the system was expanded to include the remainder of the LGA's. While the aim was to gradually decentralize data capture to the LGA level, after 2 years of no progress it was decided to rather cluster data capture sites around a group of LGA's (called a zone), and to locate the computers in hospitals which were more likely to have staff to capture the data, to have a reliable power supply, and a reasonably secure room for the computer.

However, reporting rates remained low, and as data for an extended period of time became available, it revealed that a relatively small number of facilities actually provide health care. For instance, a review of data from Jigawa State reveals that the two busiest facilities in each LGA provide 52% of all immunization services in the state, and the 4 busiest facilities, represented 72% of all the immunization services provided[1]. Similarly, when analyzing maternity data for 2006 across 5 states, 1.6% of facilities are responsible for 52.5% of all deliveries. Given the resource constraints experienced in the Nigerian health sector, the limited support that could be provided by donors, and the low base from which health services are being developed, it became apparent that it was more effective to focus on selected facilities than on all facilities.

One approach is to focus on the busiest hospital and the busiest primary health care facility in all LGA's. Over time, implementation would then adopt the layer of "next busiest" facilities in each LGA, and so on. This is called the "prioritized sample" approach to scaling of HIS. An alternative approach is to select a cluster of facilities that are linked in a hierarchy of service provision, for example in the provision of maternal and child health services (see Figure 5). Some facilities (for example health facilities that are open 24 hours a day, 7 days a week) may provide basic ante-natal care, but not offer maternity services. Maternity services are instead provided at Basic Emergency Obstetric Care (BEOC) facilities, but these facilities would only deal with uncomplicated deliveries. Complicated deliveries requiring more specialized care would be provided at Comprehensive Emergency Obstetric Care (CEOC) facilities. The "hierarchical cluster" model provides an alternative approach to focus HIS strengthening initiatives. The intention of the existing project is to expand from one cluster to three clusters per state over a 9 month period, and to effect HISD in these clusters over the 5 year project duration. The effectiveness of this approach will only become apparent as the project unfolds.

These two approaches are not a deviation from the "all or nothing imperative" described by Braa et al 2004, p 340), but rather an experiment in approaches to scaling. Both the "prioritized sample" method, and the "hierarchical cluster" method will expand the implementation to other sites over time, and as capacity develops, so that eventually all health facilities are incorporated in the initiatives. The time taken to effect scaling is

Figure 5. The Hierarchical Cluster Approach

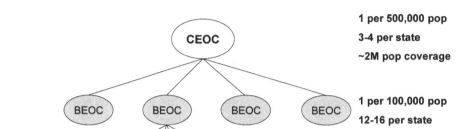

a function of the level of investment, the success in building capacity, the allocation of local resources to support the scaling efforts, and perhaps most importantly, the level of sophistication in information use that is desired.

The critique of these approaches is that it they do not immediately address equity issues which are so important in health service delivery. However, our experience suggests that these approaches should be viewed as a mechanism for effectively scaling health information system development, and that equity issues can be addressed through alternative approaches, such as the use of population of facility surveys that target a broader range of health facilities or communities, and identification of sentinel sites that collect additional data to unearth inequities that require attention.

ANALYSIS AND DISCUSSION

Our analysis first focuses on the geographic scaling of HIS and the scaling of the scope of use of the software. We explore the way in which the scaling across these domains influence and interact with one another, and how scaling in one area affects scaling in the other. Thereafter we analyze the factors that have contributed to sustainable HISD in Africa.

Software Development in Support of Scaling across Two Domains

This chapter has described the scaling process across two "domains". The most obvious is the scaling across the geographic domain. Different approaches have been used to accommodate local circumstances and resource availability. Scaling across the geographic domain is probably the most complex scaling process because it must take into consideration the structural requirements for the effective functioning of the HIS (including the software component), and access to resources must be considered – like power supply and internet access, secure and safe storage space for hardware, access to computers, paper, and printers). Because the pace at which access to ICT (for example the internet, or computers) is gained is erratic and relatively unpredictable a wide range of tools (from paper based systems to simple computerized systems, more complex computerized systems and an emergent internet based system) continues to be maintained so that HIS can be easily (and seamlessly) scaled from paper-based systems to computerized systems over time.

Other factors like human resource capacity of staff to absorb the revised HIS (capacity both in terms of numbers and level of education) must also be considered. These are the factors that will ultimately influence the process that will be used to effect the scaling of the system. This is clearly reflected in the unique approach to scaling the HIS adopted in Nigeria with the "hierarchical cluster" approach. It suggests an interesting balance between the imperative to cover all health facilities while also prioritizing selected facilities as a first phase to scaling across the rest of the geographic area.

The second domain in which we have seen scaling occur has been in relation to the scaling of the scope of use of the software across health domains (PHC, hospital data, survey data, disease surveillance, etc). The scaling across the geographic dimension has taken place at the same time as the scaling in scope, but in reality, while geographic scaling is being implemented, the scope of the version that is being scaled has been held static. In other words, the focus during geographic scaling has been on data for a specific domain, and even if the scope was extended as new software modules became available, these were only really introduced and utilized once the geographic scaling process had stabilized to some extent. For example, in Zambia the scaling across the whole country involved the use of the DHISv1.4 for data capture and data analysis, and

even these two components were introduced and taught separately as part of a phased approach to the scaling across the country (Figure 6 shows how different aspects of the revised HMIS system were scaled in a phased approach). While the scaling process was being undertaken, we were customizing the notifiable medical conditions module in the Zambian database, with the intention that this would be introduced at a later stage as an additional module. Once the system has been introduced, and basic training has been completed, it is much easier to introduce additional modules (expand the scope) because the users are already familiar with the basic configuration.

The HISP approach to development and scaling integrated information systems (in the sense of systems that support a broad base of data across a wide scope (or range of programs)) is in stark contrast to the single-disease systems (single program systems) being advocated across Africa for HIV/AIDS information systems. While this could be considered as a first step to scaling of HIS, these systems often become an end in themselves, which result in fragmented and duplicative reporting systems and which detract from the capacity to focus resources on a single integrated system.

Figure 6. Integrated HMIS roll-out in Zambia as a phased process

Months/Weeks	Dec-07	Jan-08	Feb-08	Mar-08	Apr-08	May-08			
						5	12	19	26
1. Rollout of tools				1. Ea, So, +Ce	1. Lu, No, + Lus				
2. Data returned using new tools ready for capture in revised HMIS	2. NW + West								
3. DHIS Foundation course			3. NW + West			3. Ea + Ce	3. So + Lus		
4. DHIS Advanced								4. Copper	4. NW + Ce
5. Use of information								5. Copper	5. NW + Ce

Developing Sustainable Systems in Africa

While our experience over the last 10 years is relatively short, we believe that there is sufficient evidence to suggest that the HISD that has taken place has not only been the result of the availability of software or information processing capacity. A better way of describing the development of sustainable information systems would be as a continuously evolving balance between information systems development, human capacity development and scaling approaches. The "glue" holding these components together is the information system and its use. Building on Braa, et al (2007) we have described the information system as flexible, in a variety of ways. Combining paper-based systems, with computerized systems and internet systems through common standards provides a flexibility to seamlessly integrate information from the periphery (where often computers do not exist) to the centre (where internet access may be available). The modularization of these components allows them to respond dynamically to the changing access to ICT that characterizes development in Africa. The information systems are also flexible in the sense that they can accommodate change (minor changes that might take place with the health system in response to new diseases and threats), and can be adapted in significant ways to be utilized outside of the traditional health care sector, such as its use in by IOM in Kenya. The availability of a range of software tools is another important aspect of the systems flexibility and ability to accommodate the range of contexts found in Africa.

A factor in making the system an "attractor" has been its ability to effect integration between fragmented systems. While initially it did this by bringing PHC program data together in a single database, along with survey and "semi-permanent data", this was later expanded by the increased internal functionality available in DHISv1.4. Ironically, the more information systems are fragmented by single-disease reporting systems, the more attractive the concept of the DHIS as a data warehouse becomes to managers who are required to report on a range of services drawn from different reports.

Lastly, but perhaps most important, is the incremental "bazaar" type development of the system in response to user demands. This has ensured that the system is rooted in the needs of workers in the "South", rather than being a "cathedral" that is designed and developed in the "North" and transposed and implanted on users in the south. It has also been a practical way of developing software where funding has had to be secured through small projects, each of which could only fund a small component of the system, not dissimilar from the growth of a bazaar in a typical down-town African village. Software development costs are reduced because the users are also the "testers", and they help to find and communicate bugs through internet links, thus increasing ownership, albeit also accompanied by frustration at the existence of bugs.

Utilizing the FOSS philosophy of freely sharing not only software products, but also training materials, and manuals has probably also contributed significantly to the spread of the software in Africa. Maybe not because of the significantly lower costs associated with this type of technology, but rather because the philosophy resonates with the spirit of "ubuntu"[2] that is so prevalent in Africa. Within the HISP network this approach is increasingly becoming a selling point, especially as it denotes an approach that does not seek to create dependence on outside support.

The prototyping approach that has as its aim the empowerment of local users is important in converting users to become advocates for the system. The result has been that the HISP network has seldom initiated a HISD project on the basis of the systems specifications and what it portends to do – rather it has been through a process of small-scale, bottom-up start-up, which has scaled because the processes and procedures that have been developed have spoken for themselves. This is where the systems development process has interacted with the scaling process in an iterative manner. The initial scaling of a system across one area (Copperbelt province in Zambia for instance) has been followed by repeated waves of increasingly sophisticated additions to the system. This 'developmental' approach to ISD recognizes that capacity to absorb new processes and procedures, and to institutionalize them takes time. If the new systems are too complex or radical, then it is likely that they will be rejected as inappropriate, but small changes that build towards a bigger vision has a much better chance of being accepted. As discussed earlier, recognizing that the scaling process is encapsulated within a bigger developmental process, allows certain aspects of the HIS to be held static, while the scaling takes effect. There is no need to "implement everything all at once" (as is so often the call by eager donors or officials), when the capacity to absorb and institutionalize it all at once is limited. Hence, it is acceptable to incrementally increase the range of programs that are incorporated by the system, or to expand the modules of the system, once the initial scaling has been effected. This allows the systems and processes to grow in synch with the increased capacity of users.

Utilizing the "hierarchical cluster" approach to scaling of HIS is perhaps the most interesting aspect to monitor over time. It is interesting because HISD is being effected in tandem with other health systems strengthening initiatives. Together they may create a critical mass that is more successful at producing quality information for program monitoring than HIS strengthening efforts on their own have done. In this example the network approach to development of HIS (Braa, Monteiro, & Sahay, 2004) is further expanded to include program managers. This is not an insignificant issue, especially as the referral patterns within the cluster run parallel to and will hopefully support the vertical and horizontal diffusion of HIS strengthening efforts. In addition, the expanded

network of users is an important factor in countering the political impulsiveness and vested interests of decision makers in much of Africa.

While the HIS may be the glue around which the systems and procedures are developed, it is the people that make the information system work. The recognition of a special cadre of health worker called the HIS practitioner, who has a range of IT skills to complement knowledge of the health sector is important because it helps to define the specific skills that need to be developed to help these individuals address their daily tasks. Since the publication of the article by Braa et al (2004), a number of developments have taken place. The HISP-SA node has become significantly stronger, and has extended its influence through longitudinal support to HIS development in Nigeria, Liberia, Zambia and Namibia. The model developed by the HISP-SA team of a three pronged partnership with academia, local non-governmental organisations and government continues to be tested and developed in Nigeria and Zambia. The 'networks of action" are therefore shifting from being Oslo-centric to a more Afro-centric pattern, made increasingly interesting by the sharing of HIS-practitioners amongst themselves.

CONCLUDING REMARKS

Over the 10 years of HIS development we have seen a range of responses to the development of HIS. In some countries the take-up has been slow, and probably related to the low base from which systems are being developed, the insecure funding environment that is reflected by low levels of commitment and erratic government spending, and the general lack of access to resources. This is in contrast to the situation in Zambia where there has been a long history of HIS development, and where a revision of the software and accompanying processes was able to be effected in a relatively short space of time. Public health officials actively supported the process, and contributed from their own resources to compliment donor funding. Similarly, in Liberia there has been active involvement by public health officials and a commitment to scale the system beyond the initial pilot in 4 counties. In South Africa the HISD effort has been funded by national and increasingly provincial and local government and is largely independent of donor funding. Ongoing research is needed to explore how different approaches can scale more quickly while still being effective in terms of their outcomes.

In addition, while we have acknowledged the existence of systems and processes focused on a narrow disease priority which result in fragmented information systems, further research is needed to explore how these systems can be merged with existing information flows to strengthen the overall HIS.

To conclude, perhaps the best way to summarize the experience of the HISP network to date is to suggest that developing scalable and sustainable health information systems requires adherence to five key approaches, namely:

- Health information systems (not only the software) should be flexible so as to be able to adapt to the constantly changing environment;
- The utilization of a participatory prototyping approach to HISD helps to secure adoption and use of the system while also reducing development costs;
- Adherence to the FOSS philosophy of sharing and sharing alike is easily internalized in the African culture of 'ubuntu';
- Health information systems should seek to integrate systems and procedures rather than fragment them;
- The utilization of broad-based "networks of action" incorporating local non-governmental organisations, government, and academia both locally and abroad appear

to be succeeding especially in the creation of a cadre of HIS practitioner.

These approaches appear to lay the building blocks for sustainable HISD in complex contexts which are beyond the control of any single individual.

REFERENCES

Benbya, H., & McKelvey, B. (2006). Toward a Complexity Theory of Information Systems Development. *Information Technology & People*, *19*(1), 12–34. doi:10.1108/09593840610649952

Bergqvist, J., Dahlberg, P., & Ljungberg, F. (2002). Scalability through Cultivation - designing IT support for co-ordination work. Retrieved November 13, 2006, from http://citeseerx.ist.psu.edu/viewdoc/ summary?doi=10.1.1.22.1564

Bjerknes, G., Ehn, P., & Kyng, M. (Eds.). (1987). *Computers and Democracy - A Scandinavian Challenge*. Aldershot: Avebury.

Boerma, T. (2005). WHO News - Getting the numbers right. *Bulletin of the World Health Organization*, *83*(8), 567–568.

Braa, J., Hanseth, O., Heywood, A., Mohammed, W., & Shaw, V. (2007). Developing Health Information Systems in Developing Countries - the flexible standards strategy. *Management Information Systems Quarterly*, *31*(Special Issue).

Braa, J., & Hedberg, C. (2000). *Developing District-based Health Care Information Systems: The South African Experience*. Paper presented at the IRIS 23.

Braa, J., & Hedberg, C. (2002). The Struggle for District Based Health Information Systems in South Africa. *The Information Society*, *18*, 113–127. doi:10.1080/01972240290075048

Braa, J., Monteiro, E., & Reinert, E. S. (1995). Technology Transfer vs. Technological Learning: IT infrastructure and health care in developing countries. *Information Technology for Development*, *6*(1), 15–23. doi:10.1080/02681102.1995.9525252

Braa, J., Monteiro, E., & Sahay, S. (2004). Networks of Action: Sustainable Health Information Systems Across Developing Countries. *Management Information Systems Quarterly*, *28*(3), 337–362.

Chilundo, B. (2004). *Integrating Information Systems of Disease-Specific Health Programmes in Low Income Countries*. Oslo, Norway: University of Oslo.

Chilundo, B., & Aanestad, M. (2004). Negotiating Multiple Rationalities in the Process of Integrating the Information Systems of Disease-Specific Health Programmes. *Electronic Journal on Information Systems in Developing Countries*, *20*(2), 1–28.

Ciborra, C. (2000). *From Control to Drift - the Dynamics of Corporate Information Infrastructures*. Oxford University Press.

Davis, G. B. (1982). Strategies for Information Requirements Determination. *IBM Systems Journal*, *21*(1), 4–31. doi:10.1147/sj.211.0004

Elden, M., & Chisholm, R. F. (1993). Emerging Varieties of Action Research - Introduction to the Special Issue. *Human Relations*, *46*(2), 121–142. doi:10.1177/001872679304600201

Eoyang, G. (1996). Complex? Yes! Adaptive? Well, maybe.... *Interaction*, *3*(1), 31–37. doi:10.1145/223500.223509

Greenbaum, J., & Kyng, M. (Eds.). (1991). *Design at Work: Cooperative design of computer systems*. Hillsdale, NJ: Lawrence Erlbaum Associates.

Greenbaum, J., & Madsen, K. (1993). Small Changes: Starting a Participatory Design Process by Giving Participants a Voice. In Schuler, D., & Namioka, A. (Eds.), *Participatory Design: Principles and Practices*. Hillside, N.J.: Lawrence Erlbaum Associates.

Hanseth, O., & Braa, K. (2000). Globalization and "Risk Society". In Ciborra, C. (Ed.), *From Control to Drift - the Dynamics of Corporate Information Infrastructures* (pp. 41–55). Oxford: Oxford University Press.

Jacucci, E., Hanseth, O., & Lyytinen, K. (2006). Introduction - taking complexity seriously in IS research. *Information Technology & People*, *19*(1), 5–11. doi:10.1108/09593840610649943

Jayasuriya, R. (1999). Managing Health Information Systems for Health Services in a Developing Country: a case study using a contextualist framework. *International Journal of Information Management*, *19*, 335–349. doi:10.1016/S0268-4012(99)00031-6

Korpela, M., Soriyan, H. A., Olufokunbi, K. C., Onayade, A. A., Davies-Adetugbo, A., & Adesanmi, D. (1998). Community Participation in Health Informatics in Africa: An Experiment in Tripartite Partnership in Ile-Ife, Nigeria. [CSCW]. *Computer Supported Cooperative Work*, *7*(3-4), 339–358. doi:10.1023/A:1008695307062

Madon, S., Reinhard, N., Roode, D., & Walsham, G. (2009). Digital inclusion projects in developing countries: Processes of institutionalization. *Information Technology for Development*, *15*(2), 95–107. doi:10.1002/itdj.20108

Mash, B., & Mohammed, H. (2000). Participatory development of a minimum dataset for the Khayelitsha District. *South African Medical Journal*, *90*(10), 1024–1030.

Mavimbe, J. C., Braa, J., & Bjune, G. (2005). Assessing immunization data quality from routine reports in Mozambique. *BMC Public Health, 5*(108).

Odedra, M. (1992). Is Information Technology Really Being Transferred to the African Countries? In Bhatnagar, S., & Cyranek, G. (Eds.), *Technology Transfer for Development: The prospects and Limits of Information Technology* (pp. 47–58). New Delhi: Tata MC Graw Hill.

Odedra, M. (1993). Sub-Saharan Africa: A Technological Desert. *Communications of the ACM, 36*(2). doi:10.1145/151220.151222

Odedra, M. (1994). The Role of International Organisations in Technology Transfer. *Journal of Third World Science, Technology and Development Forum,* 12.

Pan American Health Organization. (1999). *Setting up Healthcare Services Information Systems: A Guide for Requirement Analysis, Application Specification, and Procurement.* Washington, D.C.: Pan American Health Organization.

Ramanathan, J. (2005). Fractal Architecture for the Adaptive Complex Enterprise. *Communications of the ACM, 48*(5), 51–57. doi:10.1145/1060710.1060739

Raymond, E. S. (1999). *The Cathedral and the Bazaar.* Sebastopol, California: O'Reilly.

Rohde, J., Shaw, V., Hedberg, C., Stoops, N., Venter, S., & Venter, K. (2008). Information for Primary Health Care. In Barron, P., & Roma-Reardon, J. (Eds.), *South African Health Review 2008* (p. 423). Durban: Health Systems Trust.

Rolland, K., & Monteiro, E. (2002). Balancing the Local and the Global in Infrastructural Information System. *The Information Society, 18,* 87–100. doi:10.1080/01972240290075020

Sahay, S., Monteiro, E., & Aanestad, M. (2009). Configurable Politics and Asymmetric Integration: Health e-Infrastructures in India. *Journal of the Association for Information Systems, 10*(5), 399–414.

Sahay, S., & Walsham, G. (2005, 26-28 May). *Scaling of Health Information Systems in India: Challenges and Approaches.* Paper presented at the International Federation for Information Processing Working Group 9.4 Conference, Abuja, Nigeria.

Sandberg, A. (Ed.). (1979). *Computers Dividing Man and Work.* Stockholm, Sweden: Arbeitslivcentrum.

Sandiford, P., Annett, H., & Cibulskis, R. E. (1992). What can Information Systems do for Primary Health Care? An International Perspective. *Social Science & Medicine, 34*(10), 1077–1087. doi:10.1016/0277-9536(92)90281-T

Seebregts, C., Mamlin, B., Biondich, P., Fraser, H., & Wolfe, B., Jazayeri, d., et al. (2009). (Forthcoming). The OpenMRS Implementers Network. *International Journal of Medical Informatics,* 10.

Shaw, V., Mengiste, S., & Braa, J. (2007). *Scaling of health information systems in Nigeria and Ethiopia - Considering the options.* Paper presented at the IFIP 9.4 9th International Conference on Social Implications of Computers in Developing Countries, Sao Paulo, Brazil.

Shaw, V., Simoonga, C., Kalinda, P., & Muyambo, S. (2008, 7-9 May 2008). *Using Communities of Practice as a Lens for Understanding Adoption of ICT.* Paper presented at the IST-Africa Conference 2008 Windhoek, Namibia.

Shibuya, K., Scheele, S., & Boerma, T. (2005). Health statistics: time to get serious. *Bulletin of the World Health Organization, 83*(10), 722.

Siika, A. M., Rotich, J. K., Simiyu, C. J., Kigotho, E. M., Smith, F. E., & Sidle, J. E. (2005). An electronic medical record system for ambulatory care of HIV-infected patients in Kenya. *International Journal of Medical Informatics*, *74*(5), 345–355. doi:10.1016/j.ijmedinf.2005.03.002

Silva, L. (2007). Institutionalization does not occur by decree: Institutional obstacles in implementing a land administration system in a developing country. *Information Technology for Development*, *13*(1), 27–48. doi:10.1002/itdj.20056

Tan, J., Wen, H. J., & Awad, N. (2005). Health Care and Services Delivery Systems as Complex Adaptive Systems. *Communications of the ACM*, *48*(5), 36–44. doi:10.1145/1060710.1060737

The Lancet Editorial. (2009). Europe's aid to sub-saharan Africa: better results needed. *Lancet*, *373*(9662), 434. doi:10.1016/S0140-6736(09)60113-6

Walsham, G., & Sahay, S. (1999). GIS for District-Level Administration in India: Problems and Opportunities. *Management Information Systems Quarterly*, *23*(1), 39–66. doi:10.2307/249409

ENDNOTES

[1]   Source: DHIS data for Jigawa as at Nov 2008.

[2]   "Ubuntu" means "a person is a person through (other) persons" (umuntu ngumuntu ngabantu)

Chapter 16
The Role of Statistics in Development Informatics

Jacques Steyn
Monash University, South Africa

ABSTRACT

ICT4D and Development Informatics literature and media reports often use statistics offered by the World Bank, ITU or CIA to make a case for the introduction of ICTs in developing contexts. Arguably the most widely used statistic is the claim of World Bank statistics that a very large proportion of the global population live on less than USD2 per day. When scrutinized, such claims are not based on solid methodology or logic. Such overgeneralized statistics seem to ride on media hype, and appeal to empathy rather than good science. Yet ICT4D evangelists, who present ICT as the holy grail to transform underdeveloped regions into global economic powerhouses, appeal to such statistics for justification of their cases. Here a brief analysis of some problems with statistics, such as ICT4D data, is presented. Claims and policy-making based on such data should be approached critically and interpreted with a large dose of skepticism. A consolidated table of CIA Yearbook data on the global penetration of landline phones, internet access and mobile phones is presented as an appendix.

INTRODUCTION

Statistics is a tool for collecting, calculating and displaying sets of data that are categorized according to pre-selected attributes. That the attributes are pre-selected suggests that the slice made would show bias, and will influence the data, as any pre-selection depends on a subjec-

tive decision-making process. Statistics may be useful, but we need to acknowledge that it is not objective. It is only objective within a framework - which is constructed subjectively. It can tell us only what we force it to say, and what we want to hear. The process of data selection or reporting will also influence the data, and so will the interpretation and presentation of the data. And finally, statistical results could be used to justify just about any position.

DOI: 10.4018/978-1-61520-997-2.ch016

DATA INTERPRETATION

A recent popular science book by Wilkinson and Picket (2010) is a prime example. The subtitle of the book states that equality is better for everyone, and the book offers numerous statistics and graphs in support of this statement. To address the inequalities among the global human population, their remedy boils down to a redistribution of wealth, a socialist position regarded by John Gray (2010) presently as existing only in the United States as an intellectual movement. Several of the remedies proposed by Wilkinson and Picket will be good from any ideological perspective - except of course for neo-classical corporate-minded economists. They argue amongst other things, for closing tax loopholes, to limit 'business expenses', some form of democratic employee-ownership, and more - which, given the abuse by many corporates, may be good, regardless of one's economic ideology. The foundation of their argument is what they perceive as a lack of democracy in economics, assuming that economics should be democratic, and further based on the assumption that equality is a basic human right. Such ideas are sweet music to the ears of social activists, but the framework within which they are presented assumes a monocultural americo-eurocentric view of humankind, a simplistic view of democracy and human liberty, as well as clinging to the ideal of progressivism. As Gray points out, these liberal and positivistic ideals of the Enlightenment, with its origin in the Judaeo-Christian view of the world, disregard the multiplicity and plurality of human behaviors, cultures, desires and endeavors.

Note that statistics itself is not used to make these claims. The argument in Wilkinson and Picket runs as follows. Among people with a lower income, there are statistically more health problems, social problems, and psychological problems than among people with higher income. Therefore the discrepancy in income is the cause of these problems. Social and even health problems must be due to the fact that lower-income individuals do not earn enough to live in the dream. They argue that all social evils, ranging from homicides, bullying and crime to poor aspirations of young people are due to financial inequality among people. If your income is not as high as other people, you are bound to have such problems. The remedy to fix this is to take away income from the higher income group, give it to the lower income group, and these problems will disappear. This is the result of the most surprising aspect of Wilkinson and Picket's argument: the confusion between correlation and cause, and moreover, an oversimplified view of causality. Human behavior is much more complex than to be reduced to singularities. In any complex system linear, monoplanar causality theory does not work. For more than half a century the feedback loop, for instance, was required to make cybernetic systems work. And humans are far more complex than mechanical cybernetic systems. Since the 1960s the "butterfly effect" has been used in climatology to explain complex non-human behavior. Causality in chaos theory proposes that there is no simple correlation between the input and output of a system. Causal theory has come a long way over the past half a century. Wilkinson and Picket's presentation on the causes of human problems is just too simplistic to be taken seriously. Also, social ills cannot be fixed with the simple medicine of money. As the fundamental cause in the case of their book is contributed to the lack of living in the American dream, it is assumed that cultures all over the globe want to live that dream.

Equality and Equity

Another problem with the position of Wilkinson and Picket is a confusion between equality (which I take to mean being equal) and equity (as the quality of being fair and impartial, which operates in the context of equal opportunities). Equality, a member of the French trinity (*liberté, égalité, fraternité*) during the era of being enlightened, originated in the late 1700s with reference to politics, not primarily to economics, and neither to any of the many other domains of human activity. Even in politics there was then no true democracy during or immediately after the Enlightenment, as women voting rights were implemented in Europe more than a century after the French Revolution, so equality has always been a limited equality, not a universal one. The proclaimed liberal human right of supposed equality is based on a myth, reflecting a conceptual framework that suffers form its own peculiar biases. As Gray (2010) points out, a system of idealized rights contains rights that are conflicting among one another, as there is no universal consensus about the contents of these rights. Equal distribution, for example, is a dream, not even accomplished by Marxist social experiments. The history of humankind shows equality to be a Platonic ideal, seldom found in the real world. Of course, for Plato rule in democracy is for the privileged philosophers, while the general population, women and slaves remain serfs. Yet equality is a dominant theme among liberal thinkers who argue that information access should be a basic right, and consequently the tools to access that information.

Nature shows that equality is a dream. If we take evolutionary theory seriously, by nature the weak are bound to become extinct. It is a misplaced dream of the Enlightenment that social progress can overcome the constraints of natural evolution. Neurologically the brains of males and females differ. Physically, based on normal distribution statistic, males have more muscular power than females, while females typically have more emotional intelligence than males. The geographical context also plays a role in inequalities. It allows some cultures to develop certain technologies, while others do not have access to the same minerals to develop such technologies, or natural vegetation to develop large-scale agriculture to feed large populations. Such cases demonstrate that life is not equal for all people. Today ICT technologies are concentrated in densely populated areas with higher income, resulting in activists

complaining about the digital divide. Due to biological and geographical constraints we start off unequal. From this it does not follow that a nation, living in a region where mass agriculture is impossible, has a right to the food sources of another more fortunate nation. The same goes for oil. It does not give the right to military powerful nations to colonize other nations because of their geographical advantage of access to minerals or oil, such as the immoral interference of the USA in the affairs of oil rich nations with lesser military technologies.

Wilkinson and Picket spend only three pages on technology as the interest of their book is more on social and political inequality. Nevertheless, their use of statistics is typical of its application in ICT4D literature, especially in mass media claims. I use their book as an example as it offers a broad use of statistics over a wide range of topics for similar purposes than in ICT4D literature. In ICT4D the argument runs as follows. Large institutions today cannot compete in the global economy without the use of ICT. The most successful global companies are well-connected and ICT devices are important tools not only for communication, but as a technological extension of the human brain. Therefore ICT access is essential to become global economic players. Remote villages need to be connected to join in the global frenzy. Just as in the case of Wilkinson and Picket, this line of argument confuses causes. It is impossible in principle to quantitatively determine the effect of ICT on economic output. ICT is also not the only determinant of higher economic output. A very wide range of other factors also play a role, including historical advantage (the riches stolen from the colonies by European nations, such as Portugal, Spain, the Netherlands, and England, were used to gain a competitive advantage) and cultural ways of doing business. It is a false view to assume that only one economic model fits all cultures, and hints at neo-colonialism - the attempt to convert all cultures to adopt the neo-classic western model of economics. The culprit for reaching such a view of ICT4D is statistics. Richer nations have more computer units, more phones, more internet access. Therefore, it is concluded, we need to give more ICT to poorer nations so that they could join the capitalist dream. The silent argument underlying this more or less runs as follows: "We already have the advantage, and we can expand our markets further if we get the presently under-developed regions onto the consumer bandwagon". This view may be silent among many philanthrocapitalists, but some make it explicit, as Gates does (2008).

Aid

Traditionally the development of infrastructure for ICT (the telegraph, telephone, radio, etc.) has been the domain predominantly of governments, and more recently also of business and social organizations. For most part of the twentieth century the Keynesian economic model of government regulation dominated policies. Since around the 1980s neo-classical economic models began to dominate, and which assume that markets regulate themselves. There should be no interference on markets by governments. In fact, many government enterprises (ranging from energy and water supplies to telecommunications) were privatized so that they could be run as private businesses. Infrastructures for such services, which were previously paid by taxes, are now run on business models that require financial return on investment, while social or psychological return is ignored. Governments began to neglect their social duty of looking after the return of well-being of their citizens.

In the developed world infrastructures introduced with tax money over the past century are well-established. In the developing world money generated was often (and often still is) channeled back to the developed country. Populations of developing countries are also relatively poor, which results in a lower tax-base, making it virtually impossible for those governments to develop infrastructures, even if they wanted to. Concerning infrastructure development, there is a huge backlog among developing countries.

Within the framework of globalization the answer to this dilemma is financial aid. Models for aid have changed over the past half a century, but they share a commitment to economic development. The basic assumption is that humans are an economical species, and if we turn out enough profit, we reach nirvana where equality reigns, and neo-classical economics rules. In practice, socially conscious activists play this game by appealing to statistics by quantifying social needs in order to make a case for funding and in a language business-biased institutions will understand.

The problem with such an approach is that the development of infrastructure is now measured with reference to return on investment. The prohibitive cost of ICT infrastructure prevents business from investing in remote areas where network coverage costs can never be recovered from the sparse populations. Such regions are not high on the list of political priorities. This is the case not only in the developing world, but even in highly developed regions, such as Australia, Canada and the USA. The Australian Outback is not connected. Reservation areas in Canada have poor connectivity (Adria *et al* 2006). Rural areas in the USA do not have broadband access (Pigg 2010). The dream of a global economy based on a network of global ICT in which everyone is equal seems to be an impossible dream.

GDP (Gross Domestic Product)

To justify aid, in addition to social conscience, appeal is made to statistics to indicate the dire economic situation in which poorer countries find themselves. Such statistics are calculated on the basis of some or other set of indicators or indexes. Business planning, developing government policies and guidelines for implementing ICT are based on statistics, measuring some or other property of a population that is considered to be an important indicator. Until about a decade ago GDP was the preferred indicator to measure the economic status of countries. Economic growth was, and still is, the mantra, and an individual's worth is calculated on the basis of his or her position within the nebulous abstraction of statistical means. Growth is typically based on economic progress (not psychological or social growth, or increase in happiness), which in turn is measured on the basis of the neo-classic capitalist model of economic theory.

Among globalists and philanthrocapitalists such as Sachs (2005, 2008) it is assumed that poverty can be quantified, measured and alleviated. To qualify to be regarded as poor requires that standard of living must be measured by money available for spending, and the underlying guideline is GDP (Gross Domestic Product). With some statistical trickery the magical USD1 and USD2 daily living cost is conjured from the development marketing slogan hat (e.g. Sachs 2005, 2008). Projects that appeal to alleviate the supposed poverty of those living on USD1 and USD2 per day are misdirected, despite this kind of statement reaching mythical status. GDP is calculated as the sum of

GDP = Consumer Spending

+ Investment made by industry

+ Excess of Exports over Imports

+ Government Spending

Note that spending money is only one item in the formula, and also based on a particular economic ideology - not on a deeper understanding of the relative quality of the notion "standard of living", which is expressed differently in different societies. For example, a small-scale farmer in any part of the world, who can provide enough food for his family and a place of living, might have a higher standard of living with reference to health

or food (yet has no cash to spend at all), than a homeless person in New York who perhaps begs and "earns" more than the mythical USD2 per day while sleeping under a pile of newspapers and cardboard boxes. The New York beggar might prefer to spend his consumer money on drinks or drugs, or both. "Standard of living" is a relative concept. From a neo-capitalist point of view spending means getting hooked on consumerism. The more consumer goods a household has, the better standard of living. But that is the assumption of a specific economic ideology. There are many cultures with different sets of values. As I have mentioned elsewhere, take the case of African workers on a guest farm who do not wish to work overtime over weekends as their basic salary is enough for their needs, as they perceive them. They would rather spend their weekends socializing with friends than to earn extra money. By some western metric their standard of living may be very poor - they don't have much spending money. By their own standards, they are rich enough and perfectly happy with the way in which they live. Consumer spending data is not a useful metric in such cases as it is based on a monistic view of global cultures, and neglects to account for pluralism.

For deep rural communities some items in the GDP formula, such as *investment by industry* and *export-import ratios*, are also meaningless. Village economies are based on cottage industries and predominantly local agriculture. In addition, some such informal economies depend on the exchange of goods (a dozen eggs for a pot of honey), without any money exchanging hands. Such economies are not typically included in figures for industry investment. The "import-export" activities are mainly between villages, not across national borders to other countries, which is what GDP measures. Finally, *government spending* in deep rural areas pales in comparison to spending in urban areas, which results in unequal opportunities with reference to economics. But GDP is calculated nationally, not locally, so it does not indicate the unequal spread of government spending among regions.

A higher-level problem with the GDP formula when used for developing regions is that measured GDP growth typically shows only the local growth of the middle class. The middle class (only as households, not as individual income within households) and the rich have more spending money, chasing the consumer spending index upwards, resulting in an illusionary better economic situation for households along a longitudinal axis. Growth statistics, based on comparative household incomes over the past half a century very seldom makes clear that the make-up of the contributors to household income has changed. Before the Second World War households typically had a single breadwinner. Today, in middle class households there are typically at least two sources of income, and often more, such as in cases when young members who have left school still live at home, but have jobs and contribute to household income. Household income with single breadwinners has actually continuously declined since the 1970s (Saul, 2009). Middle class households today are thus in fact poorer than they were decades ago, contrary to the optimistic claims by philanthrocapitalists. More members are now economically active to contribute to the household income, resulting in the illusion that households are better off. The lack of considering any social stratification shows that GDP cannot be a good measure of success.

Apart from this problem, global statistics with figures showing supposed growth in the developing world are contaminated and skewed by the exceptional growth of the middle class in India and in China - but Asian growth is not experienced in other regions, especially not in Africa. Fernandes (2006) claims a new Indian middle class of 250 million people, which is about the same size as a quarter of the population of the entire African continent. Such a very large number of people in one country only skews the global development statistics, and gives the impression that globally

there is an economic improvement, while in reality in many regions, particularly Africa, poor people actually become poorer (Easterly, 2006, Saul, 2009). Even in Asia the poor remain poor, as it is only the educated middle class that now have more spending money, skewing the statistics on supposed Indian growth even further. Growth is unequal among different groups of citizens. The "success" of globalization for developing countries, as promoted by philanthrocapitalists, such as Sachs, is suspect, to say the least. GDP figures are totally useless as a tool to measure poverty.

HDI (HUMAN DEVELOPMENT INDEX) AND MPI (MULTIDIMENSIONAL POVERTY INDEX)

One of the goals of the United Nations' Millennium Development Goals (MDGs), declared in 2000, is to eradicate extreme poverty by 2015 (MDG 2000). At the time of writing the present text, that date is a handful of years away. As early as 2004 the UN acknowledged that this target will not be reached: "Hunger is receding in all regions of the world since 1990, although not everywhere at a rate currently sufficient to reach the 2015 target of reduction by half." (UN Press Release, 2004). The MDG's goals are formulated on the basis of statistics, and the framework within which this was conceptualized is a system of indicators.

Thinkers and critics in the developing world found the GDP approach unsatisfactory, but lacked an alternative approach until around 1990 when Mahbub ul Haq and his team at the United Nations tried to deliberately move from development economics to people centered policies. Anand and Sen offered the first framework and new philosophical basis for this approach which lead to the Human Development Index (HDI) as a practical tool for measurement that policy makers could use. The dimensions of HDI cover health (life-expectancy), knowledge (education, literacy) and economics (standard of living, instead of consumer spending) none of which is measured by GDP (Anand & Sen 1994). It is claimed that a high living standard, as measured by HDI, may show a low living standard by GDP for the simple reason that market mechanisms do not deal well with public goods. Another available index, GNH (Gross National Happiness - Saul 2009: 23; Blanchflower and Oswald 2005) has not been taken seriously except in Bhutan. More recently, a Multidimensional Poverty Index (MPI) was developed at Oxford University (Alkire and Santos 2010).

Interestingly enough, the individual indexes used as component statistics in the current HDI and MPI models are highly correlated. HDI and MPI show relative weights bias, which implies that the results could be tweaked to favor a particular aspect of development. The weighting schemes of both HDI and MPI are subjective. On HDI Cahill concludes, and I would add the same comment as applying to MPI:

"The statistics used in the HDI are so closely correlated with one another that indistinguishable alternative indexes can be created from the same statistics with very different weights." (Cahill 2005:4).

Cahill ends his paper in the words of McGillivray

"...the UNDP's index is yet another redundant composite intercountry development indicator." (quoted in Cahill 2005:5).

The main weakness of HDI and MPI is that because different units cannot be compared statistically, it introduces an interpretative layer that translates units into the same weighted scheme. The weighted scheme, however, is highly suspect as it is subjective and biased, turning results into meaningless figures. For example, in HDI literacy is given a weight of two-thirds and enrollment in school one-third. In MPI education is assigned a

weight of 1/6, and the six standard of living indicators, each 1/18. But there is no clear basis for this choice. Any other ratio could have been picked at random. After all, how can one compare abstract notions such as education and standard of living on a quantitative scale? And if this were indeed possible, who decides the value of importance to drinking water as opposed to the number of years of schooling? Comparing apples and bananas in this manner results in a fruit salad...

Not only is weighting a problem, but so is the content of the indicators. Consider this. What is the curriculum of "education"? The MDG five years of education assumes reading and writing, but the question is then, what relevance this knowledge has for a very remote community where local knowledge about clean water is more important for survival than the ability to read. In this particular hypothetical community, the MPI weighting of 1/6 for a "global" educational curriculum compared to 1/16 for access to water is wrong. MPI also does not consider access to clean drinkable water as opposed to access to any water, while seemingly preferring access to any water, as long as it is within the MDG's 30 minutes of walking time - assuming further that that particular community uses clocks to keep precise time. Walking 29 minutes to water is acceptable, but not 31 minutes. So 2 minutes difference puts one community into one category, and another community into another. Such an approach to indicators assumes that the same standard must apply globally to all communities, and that that standard should be the western enlightened, humanist model of life. There is no room for pluralism and diversity.

Systems of indicators are also further suspect, as there is no consensus about what social development entails. Social development is "driven by good intentions rather than well-defined theoretical principles." (Midgley 2003: 832). Midgley explains that social development originated within a framework that was non-reflectively based on the biases of modernist, Keynesian and populist approaches. This boat was rocked somewhat in

1971 when André Gunder Frank pointed out the ideological biases of social development, that they are contaminated by a neo-Marxist point of view. Apart from the implicit neo-Marxist ideological assumption that societies can be engineered toward whatever the prevalent ideology regards as the goal, there is also the problem of the use of statistics to argue the case for development. Paradoxically, although ICT4D projects typically function within the framework of neo-classical capitalism, the underlying philosophy is neo-Marxist social engineering! That is because Marxism is also based on the ideals of the Enlightenment, specifically assuming that progress can and must be attained, while progress is defined economically. In this respect Marxism is just a different economic model reaching for the same goal as liberal capitalism. It is only the methodology that differs. Both Marxism and classic capitalism embrace progressivism.

The notion that phenomena can be measured and quantified is rooted deeply in the western way of thinking. The success of physics and chemistry, using statistics, was a major reason for the reign of positivism, and as the other sciences (or academic "arts") attempted to follow the king and queen of the sciences in their methodologies, it became fashionable to quantify human behavior. Probability theory was introduced around the 1800s by Pierre-Simon Laplace (1749-1827) and contemporaries. It was particularly Ludwig Boltzmann (1844-1906) who laid the foundation for statistical mechanics, based on probability theory, which in turn is based on the theory that the properties of matter obey the laws of physics, even if this "obedience" is by pure chance (Ulanowicz 2009). Statistical mechanics assumes an ideal state and that the system is in equilibrium, but accounts poorly for systems not in equilibrium, or non-linear systems. This tool, used for interpreting mindless matter, was later applied to complex human behavior.

The notion that human behavior can be quantified is the hallmark of positivism. To Auguste Comte (1798-1857) mathematics is the model for science, including the social sciences. If it cannot be quantified, it cannot be known. Gray proposes that this notion "helped spawn the idea of a global free market" (2010:271). He further states:

"Without realizing it - for few of them know anything of the history of thought, least of all their own subject - the majority of economists have inherited their way of thinking from the positivists. Working their way into the discipline via Logical Positivism, Saint-Simonian and Comtean ideas have become the standard methodology of economics." (2010:271)

One very simple reason why human behavior cannot be reduced to simple physical cause and effect is the human property of agency, which enables humans to change their minds and to deliberately resist causes. In a closed system of chemical gases, the billions of particles all follow the same rules on an arrow of time. The six billion humans on this planet may share many traits, but their behavior is not predetermined. Humans have the ability to deliberately override a causal event, which leads to a totally different outcome than had they just gone with the flow of the event. Humans have, among others, different likes, personalities, preferred behavior patterns, social interests, and cultures that impact on their decisions and actions. In short, for humans pluralism reigns, while in the ideal state of mechanics, relatively simple patterns of molecular and sub-atomic behavior can be detected, constituting a mono-culture. To the extent to which it may be determined, an agent continuously updates its behavior with feedback loops, which means the causal path is not linear, not necessarily followed, and often not transparent, leading to the possibility of infinite patterns of human behavior. Attempts at quantifying human behavior should thus be approached with a good deal of skepticism. ICT is a tool used by humans to facilitate their behavior and actions. Counting tools does not really inform much about the use

Table 1. Demographics of South Africa. CIA Yearbook (2009)

0-14 years: 32.1%	14.34 million
(male 7.17 million/female 7.21 million)	
15-64 years: 63%	32.74 million
(male 18.00 million/female 14.74 million)	
65 years and over: 4.9%	2.19 million
(male 0.8 million/female 1.39 million)	
Total population:	49.27 million

Table 2. Mobile phone subscribers in South Africa

Vodacom	26.5m subscribers	(Stones 2009)
MTN	17.2m subscribers	(Mochiko 2009)
Cell C	6.5m subscribers	(Klein 2009)
Total:	50.2m subscribers	

of tools or their effects on the myriad possibilities of human behavior.

Given the complexity of human behavior, it is actually impossible to determine the causes of success (whichever way success is defined). Different individuals, different cultures may reach the same outcome, but by different paths, and perhaps by different motivations. Goals would be perceived differently, and content of success will be defined not only culturally, but also individually. Even in apparent homogenous cultures there is diversity. Almost half a century after the hippie movement, today in the age of brand names, there are still individuals who prefer that style of living. They are still selling beads and smoking dope, wearing real faded and torn no-name brand jeans. It is their choice. Why should the lifestyle preferred by philanthrocapitalists be enforced on developing cultures? Surely it is their choice how to live.

MOBILE PHONE DATA

In ICT literature, data collecting methodologies are not always clear, sometimes dubious, and often suspect. The exact metrics used are often not obtainable. Counting phonelines informs how many lines have been installed, but makes no statement about the number of users per phoneline, nor the frequency of use by those users, or the purposes of using the phones. The most dubious of all the

data is cell phone usage. To explain this, I will use data from South Africa as an example.

According to the *CIA Yearbook* (2009) the age demographics of South Africa is presented in Table 1.

The 2009 released numbers of mobile phone subscribers are presented in Table 2, as claimed by mobile phone operators in South Africa.

The *CIA Yearbook* (2009) states that 45,000,000 South Africans have mobile phones - a 5 million (or 10%) difference from the numbers claimed by mobile phone companies. Using the mobile phone companies data, in a country with a population of 49.27m people, there are 50.2m mobile phone subscribers. How does this make sense? There are more claimed mobile phone subscribers than the total South African population. We can state with certainty that babies and toddlers will not be cellphone subscribers. If generally people begin to own their own phones by their teens, the following can be deduced. There are 34.93 million South Africans 15 years and older, i.e. 70.8% of the South African population, and if there is a 100% penetration of cellphones from this group upwards, a potential of 34.93 million national cellphone subscribers. The statistics offered by the cellphone companies thus overstate subscribers by 15.27 million, a 43.716% error*! Such an error margin, based on the assumption that in a population cell phones are used by teenagers and older, is so ridiculously high, it renders any statements based on such data totally useless. Of course many pre-teen kids in affluent homes also have cell phones. But not 100% of the South African population have cell phones, so perhaps this offsets the number of affluent pre-teen kids. Regardless of the value of such statistical gymnastics, the bottom line is that the statistics on offer in the media, and even formal reports on the use of ICT, cannot be trusted.

There is a fourth operator in South Africa, Virgin Mobile for which I could not find data. In media reports I could find only claims such as that by 2010 Virgin Mobile would have 1% of the South African market (Mochiko 2009). If their data were added to the above calculations an even larger error would obviously show up. The only useful purpose of such statistics is to keep shareholders under the happy illusion of growing profits. For planning purposes, one might as well throw the dice to get some numbers.

Cellphone companies are very vague on how they gather their statistics, and my attempts to obtain clarity have not been successful as they do not seem to wish to share that information. Some possibilities to account for the discrepancies between populations and claimed mobile phone subscriptions are: they count the number of SIM cards sold, or count the number of cellphone devices sold, or the number of phone numbers (although there is typically a unique phone number per SIM card). A significant proportion of the South African population have more than one SIM card, some because they have lost phones over the years, or had to get new phone cards. As calls between different service providers are expensive in South Africa, and SIM cards relatively cheap, many people (more specifically my students) have SIM cards from different service providers and if they need to phone someone on a different network, they slot in the card for that service provider. Each person in my social circle, including myself, presently have several phones and SIM cards. There is no one-to-one correlation between subscribers and individuals.

Collecting data about the number of SIM cards sold as a measure of individual connectivity is thus totally unreliable to determine actual penetration and use. The period which the data would cover

also results in a problem. Over what period would the number of SIM cards be counted? Since my first cellphone in the early 1990s, I must have had at least ten different numbers and cellphones - I have not kept an explicit record. Is the entire history of SIM cards counted? If not, over what period are they counted? There is no clear record of active or inactive SIM cards or phone numbers, and neither is it clear how many SIM cards are in circulation owned by a specific individual. The number of devices sold is just as problematic, simply because a single person may have acquired several devices over a period.

Perhaps the only usable statistic would be one that measures how many phones were used to make or receive calls over a specific period. The distinction between calls made and calls received is important, as many people have phones that are not used for making calls, only for receiving them. In South Africa the caller pays for the call, the receiver only pays to be connected to the network. Those who cannot afford it have phones that enable others to phone them, but they do not make calls at all.

To compound the problem, mobile phones have become icons of social prestige. Johanson and Denison (this volume) refer to Fladrich reporting that among Chinese migrants working and living in Prato, Italy, there is a desire to own two or more phones for the sake of prestige and status.

Counting phones (or SIM cards) thus offer unreliable data that cannot be used for any useful planning purposes. A landline phone could be in a public place, used by thousands of people. A household needs one phone line to serve an entire family. In some countries cell phones are shared or rented per call, and in this respect are similar to public landline phones. One device serves many people, but this is not reflected in the data. In affluent countries the cell phone is extremely personal to such an extent that others may not use one's own phone, and allowing this to happen only reluctantly. One person may have several points of device access (several mobile phones, or several places from where to make landline calls). Statistics supplied by the ITU, World Bank, or *CIA Yearbook* merely count items, and the counted items are technologies - mainly access points and devices. Then the numbers are correlated with populations. Such an exercise does not have much value for the actual use of ICT, nor for the purposes of use. Such data also makes sensible planning impossible. It is not known what the distribution of phones is through an entire population. It is unknown from these statistic how many phones (including mobiles) are available in rural areas; how many phones are available across social strata (between rich and poor); what proportion of a population uses a phone to make calls (either by renting one or borrowing one), or only receive calls, what the nature of calls are (e.g. social - to keep in touch; or business - to order goods); for what purposes phones are used: for private communication, for business purposes; what services are used by individual users: only to receive calls; can they receive or read text messages?; do they use it to generate income? The data does not offer answers to such questions.

So what can ICT data from the World Bank, ITU and *CIA Yearbook* tell us about how many individuals have access to landline phones, mobile phones and the internet? The answer seems to be: Nothing! As stated above, statistics can tell us only what we force it to say, and what we want to hear.

The lack of valid and relevant data offers a great opportunity for well-designed ICT4D research to determine the actual state of affairs. Elsewhere I have complained about the lack of ICT4D theory. But if the basics (such as valid data collection) are not solid, it would be difficult to construct good theory. It seems that on the basis of the current status of ICT4D data, at best we could construct vague notions of understanding the state of affairs.

USING STATISTICS FOR DEVELOPMENT PLANS

Finally, what is the point of all these statistics? What does it mean to state, for example, that Chad has 13,000 landline phone users, 1,809,000 mobile phone users, and 130,000 internet users. What does it mean to compare access to ICT in different countries? What can be learned from this? Typical appeals to statistics may state that in a highly developed region such as the United States 75.19% of the population have access to the internet, and 87.89% have access to mobile phones, while in a lesser developed region such as Swaziland, 3.6% of the population have internet access and 34.18% have access to mobile phones. Such statistics imply that internet and mobile phone penetration are correlated with the degree of development.

The first problem with such a comparison is that of implied technological determinism, i.e. that having greater penetration of ICT impacts on the degree of development. Secondly, one finds causal oversimplification. The USA was economically more highly developed than Swaziland long before the era of ICT. So it cannot be argued that ICT played a role in one region being more highly developed than another. Even if ICT does indeed play a role in development, one cannot argue that it causes development, which would be a gross oversimplification of the complexity of causes in any human behaviors and endeavors. It is more likely that in a highly developed region there is more money available to spend on hi-tech than in a developing region. Of course, having more money does not cause the implementation of more ICT. The money may be spent on other endeavours.

Having said that, there is nevertheless, generally speaking, a correlation between the degree of economic development, political will and the implementation of ICT infrastructure, bearing in mind that correlation is not to be confused with cause. Countries with a higher tax-base do indeed have better government sponsored infrastructure (although today ICT is more often privatized, but historically developed by governments), and densely populated regions, such as urban areas, have better business initiated ICT infrastructure. It can thus be concluded that without a good tax-base, and/or without an opportunity for business to get a return on their investment, ICT infrastructure will not be developed. As there is presently no known technology to make possible cheaper ICT infrastructure, we are forced to conclude that remote and rural regions will not be connected in the near future, if ever.

From a comparison between the quantity of the use of three different media (landline phone access, mobile phone access and internet access) in the table in the appendix, we may conclude that in most regions more people have access to mobile phones than to landline phones, although no statement can be deduced about what the uses are. For example, it is possible that mobile phones are not used for economic activity, but predominantly for social communication (to keep in touch with friends and family), and it is also possible that landlines are used mainly for business and internet access. We don't know. Given a context where this might be true, we might conclude that landlines are used more by business, while mobile phones are used more for personal use. This speculative context would impact on policy, as governments attempt to cover their tax-base, and consequently would favor the use of landlines - assuming that business could be stimulated by landlines, generating potentially more tax income - which would be an indirect result. Bland statistics make no statements about the impact of technology, whether social, economic or psychological.

With reference to media penetration, the question of *When is enough enough?* should also be addressed. No media has ever reached 100% of any population. Data from World Bank reports indicate that even in the highly developed USA in the 1990s 2% of households did not have TV, that the developed world has six times as many newspapers and four times as many radio sets as

developing nations (Steyn 1999). Norris (2003) shows that there is a correlation between the penetration of old media and new media:

"... the proportion of those online in each country was mostly related to the distribution of hosts, telephones, and PCs, but it was also significantly and strongly related to the distribution of radios, TV sets, and newspaper readership in each nation. (Norris 2003:53).

Accessing information thus seems to depend on the cultural uptake and acceptance of ICT, which in turn depends on availability - as an absent technology cannot be adopted. A culture in which there is not much reading is not suddenly going to start reading web pages, even if such services are freely available. Broad statistics of quantitative ICT use without considering the functions for which technology is used is not particularly useful.

The presented statistics of ICT use make no statements about actual use, the causes of particular uptakes, nor the cultural and psychological aspects for adopting or using ICT. Present sets of statistics are superficial, presenting head counts of people, devices and access points. Statistics that include actual use, and the purpose of use would be more useful. But such statistics should not drive singular global goals. They should allow for diversity and pluralism, while the implementation of ICT4D should meet local needs.

CONCLUSION

ICT4D statistics as offered by institutions such as the World Bank, the *CIA Yearbook*, and in media and NGO reports, as well as by promoters of development plans (philanthrocapitalists and globalists), are based on vague categories and suspect methodologies of data collection and presentation. Arguments for the development of communities are based on such data sets.

Data for the uptake of ICT, particularly such as the claimed number of mobile phones in a specific country is void of useful meaning, as mere numbers of devices or access points or SIM cards and so on do not include statements of function, and are highly inflated due to poor, non-scientific methodologies and sampling techniques.

Data results provided by indicators, whether GDP, HDI or MPI, are suspect. GDP does not consider the complexities of human culture or behavior, while HDI and MPI weights are chosen haphazardly and do not offer objective measurements.

Despite the reservations expressed about such data, what is nevertheless useful is that one may get a very broad (and vague) brushstroke of general trends from such data. While it is wise to ignore paying any significance to precise numbers or percentages, the data in the enclosed table can nevertheless point to general trends, such as that for a particular country there seems to be more uptake of a certain technology than another. It may also be safe to conclude that the uptake in certain countries is higher than in others. That's about all. No conclusions can be reached about causes for the uptake, the functions technology is used for, its impact on a variety of topics ranging from economic benefit to psychological well-being merely because the user is socially connected. Not even the well-ridden slogan of living under USD2 per day is particularly meaningful -- it is a myth. Theoreticians and practitioners in the arena of ICT4D and Development Informatics have a lot of work to do before any meaningful conclusions could be reached from data collection on the use of ICT.

ACKNOWLEDGMENT

Thanks to my colleague Neil Manson for the number crunching. Error = (50.2 - 34.93) / 34.93 = 43.716%. Also thanks to him for the calculations in the table. Thanks to the following friends and colleagues for comments on an early draft: Larry Stillman, Paul Plantinga, Tom Denison, Graeme Johanson, and Jean-Paul van Belle.

REFERENCES

Adria, M., Bakardjieva, M., Poitras Pratt, Y., & Mitchell, D. (2006). *The Constructive Role of Researchers in the Social Shaping of Technology in Communities*. Paper presented at 3rd Prato International Community Informatics Conference. Retrieved December 2006 from http://www.ccnr. net/?q=node/123.

Anand, S., & Sen, A. (1994). *Sustainable human development: concepts and priorities*. New York: United Nations Development Programme.

Biswas, B., & Caliendo, F. (2004). A multivariate analysis of the Human Development Index. *The Indian Economic Journal, 49*(4), 96-100. Retrieved March 2010 from http://unpan1.un.org/ intradoc/groups/public/documents/APCITY/ UNPAN019757.pdf.

Blanchflower, D. G., & Oswald, A. J. (2005). *Happiness and the Human Development Index: The paradox of Australia*. Cambridge, MA: National Bureau of Economic Research.

Cahill, M. B. (2005). Is the Human Development Index redundant? *Eastern Economic Journal, 31*(1), 1–5.

Easterly, W. (2006). *The white man's burden. Why the west's efforts to aid the rest have done so much ill and so little good*. Oxford: Oxford Univ Press.

Fernandes, L. (2006). *India's New Middle Class: Democratic Politics in an Era of Economic Reform*. Minneapolis, USA: Univ. of Minnesota Press.

Gates, B. (2008). How to fix capitalism. *Time, 172*(6), 24–29.

Gray, J. (2010). *Gray's anatomy. Selected writings.* London: Penguin Books.

http://www.nber.org/papers/w11416.pdf, last accessed March 2010

International Telecommunications Union (ITU). (2006). Telecommunication Development Report: ICT Statistics. Retrieved July 2006 from http://www.itu.org/statistics

Klein, M. (2009, March 15). Cell C and Telkom to join forces? *Business Times.* Retrieved December 2009 from http://mybroadband.co.za/news/Telecoms/7320.html.

Lakire, S., & Santos, M. E. (2010). *Acute Multi-dimensional poverty: A new index for developing countries. OPHI Working Paper 38.* Oxford University. Retrieved August 2010 from http://www.ophi.org.uk/wp-content/uploads/ophi-wp38.pdf.

MDG. (2000). *United Nations Millennium Development Goals.* Retrieved October 2007 from http://www.un.org/millenniumgoals/

Midgley, J. (2003). Social development: the intellectual heritage. *Journal of International Development, 15*(7), 831–844. doi:10.1002/jid.1038

Mochiko, T. (2009). *Merger talks delay MTN issue.* Business Report August 28, 2009. Retrieved December 2009 from http://www.busrep.co.za/index.php?fSectionId=563&fArticleId=5142081.

Norris, P. (2003). *Digital divide. Civic engagement, information poverty, and the internet worldwide.* Cambridge: Cambridge University Press.

Pigg, K. (2010). Information Communication Technology and Its Impact on Rural Community Economic Development. In Steyn, J., & Johanson, G. (Eds.), *ICTs and Sustainable Solutions for the Digital Divide: Theoretical Issues.* Hershey, PA: IGI Global.

Sachs, J. (2005). *The end of poverty. How we can make it in our lifetime.* London: Penguin Books.

Sachs, J. (2008). *Common wealth. Economics for a crowded planet.* London: Penguin Books.

Saul, J. R. (2009). *The collapse of globalism and the reinvention of the world.* London: Atlantic Books. (Original work published 2005)

Sen, A. (2001). *Development as freedom.* Oxford: University Press.

Steyn, J. (1999). *The Info era: evolution, revolution or solution?* Conference Paper: New Media Conference, Poitiers, France. Retrieved December 2009 from http://www.steyn.pro/papers/infoera/.

Stones, L. (2009, January 28). South Africa: Subscriber Surge Lifts Vodacom's Revenue. *Business Day.* Retrieved December 2009 from http://allafrica.com/stories/200901280049.html.

Ulanowicz, R. E. (2009). *A third window.* West Conshohocken, PA: Templteton Foundation Press.

UN Press Release. (2004, September 7). UN finds progress on world anti-poverty goals, but crisis areas remain. *United Nations Press Release.* Retrieved October 2007 from http://www.un.org/millenniumgoals/mdg_pr_09_2004.pdf.

Wilkinson, R., & Picket, K. (2010). *The spirit level. Why equality is better for everyone.* London: Penguin Books.

World Factbook, C. I. A. (2009). Retrieved September 2009 from https://www.cia.gov/library/publications/the-world-factbook/.

APPENDIX

The data in this appendix reflects estimates by the CIA. Population estimates were made July 2009, while the data for technology is predominantly from 2008, with isolated cases going as far back as 2004 (e.g. Jersey, Netherlands Antilles) and even 1999 (Cocos - Keeling Islands). Thanks to Neil Manson for the calculations.

Table 3. Populations by countries, and claimed use of landline phones, internet and mobile phones

	Population			Mobile phones				Internet				Phones			
		Rank	% of World		Rank #	% of Pop	Rank %		Rank #	% of Pop	Rank %		Rank #	% of Pop	Rank %
WORLD	6,790,062,216			4,017,294,000		59.16		1,604,000,000		23.6		1,268,000,000		18.67	
Africa															
Algeria	34,178,188	35	0.50	31,871,000	30	93.25	76	4,100,000	50	12.00	129	3,314,000	45	9.70	137
Angola	12,799,293	70	0.19	6,773,000	74	52.92	136	550,000	103	4.30	164	114,300	140	0.89	192
Benin	8,791,832	90	0.13	3,435,000	99	39.07	156	60,000	163	0.68	198	159,000	130	1.81	175
Botswana	1,990,876	146	0.03	1,486,000	133	74.64	105	120,000	142	6.03	155	142,300	134	7.15	146
Burkina Faso	15,746,232	61	0.23	2,553,000	113	16.21	191	140,000	140	0.89	196	144,000	132	0.91	191
Burundi	9,511,330	87	0.14	480,600	156	5.05	205	65,000	161	0.68	197	30,400	176	0.32	208
Cameroon	18,879,301	58	0.28	6,161,000	79	32.63	165	725,000	97	3.84	168	198,300	123	1.05	188
Cape Verde	429,474	172	0.01	277,700	169	64.66	121	102,800	149	23.94	97	72,000	154	16.76	107
Central African Republic	4,511,488	120	0.07	154,000	176	3.41	207	19,000	187	0.42	205	12,000	198	0.27	211
Chad	10,329,208	79	0.15	1,809,000	124	17.51	188	130,000	141	1.26	192	13,000	197	0.13	215
Comoros	752,438	162	0.01	42,000	198	5.58	204	23,000	183	3.06	174	23,300	185	3.10	168
Congo, Democratic Republic of	68,692,542	18	1.01	9,263,000	63	13.48	196	290,000	127	0.42	204	37,300	172	0.05	217
Congo, Republic of the	4,012,809	127	0.06	1,807,000	125	45.03	150	155,000	139	3.86	167	22,200	189	0.55	203
Cote d'Ivoire	20,617,068	57	0.30	10,449,000	60	50.68	142	660,000	99	3.20	172	356,500	106	1.73	178
Djibouti	724,622	164	0.01	44,100	196	6.09	203	13,000	193	1.79	180	10,800	199	1.49	183
Egypt	78,866,635	16	1.16	41,272,000	28	52.33	138	11,414,000	26	14.47	119	12,011,000	21	15.23	115
Equatorial Guinea	633,441	167	0.01	346,000	165	54.62	135	12,000	194	1.89	179	10,000	201	1.58	181
Eritrea	5,647,168	108	0.08	108,600	180	1.92	211	200,000	133	3.54	170	40,400	167	0.72	198
Ethiopia	85,237,338	14	1.26	3,168,000	106	3.72	206	360,000	114	0.42	203	908,900	83	1.07	187
Gabon	1,514,993	151	0.02	1,300,000	137	85.81	89	90,000	151	5.94	156	26,500	181	1.75	176
Gambia, The	1,778,081	148	0.03	1,166,000	138	65.58	118	114,200	144	6.42	154	48,900	162	2.75	171
Ghana	23,887,812	47	0.35	11,570,000	53	48.43	145	997,000	89	4.17	165	143,900	133	0.60	202
Guinea	10,057,975	81	0.15	2,600,000	112	25.85	178	90,000	151	0.89	195	50,000	161	0.50	205
Guinea-Bissau	1,533,964	150	0.02	500,200	155	32.61	166	37,100	172	2.42	176	4,600	209	0.30	210

	Population			Mobile phones				Internet				Phones			
		Rank	% of World		Rank #	% of Pop	Rank %		Rank #	% of Pop	Rank %		Rank #	% of Pop	Rank %
Kenya	39,002,772	33	0.57	16,234,000	41	41.62	154	3,360,000	55	8.61	142	252,300	118	0.65	199
Lesotho	2,130,819	142	0.03	581,000	153	27.27	174	73,300	158	3.44	171	65,200	155	3.06	169
Liberia	3,441,790	132	0.05	732,000	148	21.27	185	20,000	186	0.58	199	2,000	215	0.06	216
Libya	6,324,357	103	0.09	4,828,000	89	76.34	102	323,000	121	5.11	163	1,033,000	78	16.33	111
Madagascar	20,653,556	56	0.30	4,835,000	87	23.41	181	316,100	122	1.53	188	164,900	129	0.80	196
Malawi	15,028,757	64	0.22	1,781,000	127	11.85	198	316,100	122	2.10	177	236,000	121	1.57	182
Mali	13,443,225	68	0.20	3,267,000	102	24.30	180	200,000	133	1.49	189	82,800	147	0.62	200
Mauritania	3,129,486	135	0.05	2,092,000	119	66.85	115	45,000	169	1.44	190	76,400	151	2.44	173
Mauritius	1,284,264	154	0.02	1,033,000	142	80.44	95	380,000	112	29.59	82	364,500	102	28.38	75
Mayotte	223,765	184	?	48,100	195	21.50	184	10,000	210	?	210	10,000	201	4.47	159
Morocco	31,285,174	38	0.46	22,816,000	35	72.93	108	10,300,000	30	32.92	72	2,991,000	49	9.56	139
Mozambique	21,669,278	53	0.32	4,405,000	91	20.33	186	350,000	117	1.62	186	78,300	149	0.36	207
Namibia	2,108,665	143	0.03	1,052,000	141	49.89	143	113,500	145	5.38	162	140,000	136	6.64	149
Niger	15,306,252	63	0.23	1,677,000	129	10.96	199	80,000	155	0.52	200	24,000	183	0.16	213
Nigeria	149,229,090	8	2.20	62,988,000	16	42.21	152	11,000,000	28	7.37	150	1,308,000	68	0.88	194
Rwanda	10,746,311	74	0.16	1,323,000	136	12.31	197	300,000	124	2.79	175	16,800	196	0.16	214
Saint Helena, Ascension, and Tristan da Cunha	7,637	225	?		214	?	214	1,100	209	14.40	121	2,300	214	30.12	72
Sao Tome and Principe	212,679	187	?	49,000	194	23.04	182	24,800	180	11.66	130	7,700	205	3.62	163
Senegal	13,711,597	67	0.20	5,389,000	82	39.30	155	1,020,000	84	7.44	149	237,800	120	1.73	177
Seychelles	87,476	197	?	85,300	183	97.51	64	32,000	175	36.58	67	23,200	186	26.52	79
Sierra Leone	5,132,138	113	0.08	1,009,000	144	19.66	187	13,900	192	0.27	207	31,500	174	0.61	201
Somalia	9,832,017	83	0.14	627,000	150	6.38	202	102,000	150	1.04	193	100,000	143	1.02	189
South Africa	49,052,489	24	0.72	45,000,000	24	91.74	78	4,187,000	48	8.54	143	4,425,000	34	9.02	141
Sudan	41,087,825	29	0.61	11,186,000	55	27.22	175	4,200,000	47	10.22	139	356,100	107	0.87	195
Swaziland	1,337,186	152	0.02	457,000	157	34.18	164	48,200	167	3.60	169	44,000	165	3.29	165
Tanzania	41,048,532	30	0.60	14,723,000	46	35.87	161	520,000	104	1.27	191	179,849	125	0.44	206
Togo	6,031,808	105	0.09	1,547,000	131	25.65	179	350,000	117	5.80	158	140,900	135	2.34	174
Tunisia	10,486,339	77	0.15	8,569,000	67	81.72	94	2,800,000	61	26.70	92	1,239,000	69	11.82	128
Uganda	32,369,558	37	0.48	8,555,000	68	26.43	177	2,500,000	63	7.72	148	168,500	127	0.52	204

	Population			Mobile phones				Internet				Phones			
		Rank	% of World		Rank #	% of Pop	Rank %		Rank #	% of Pop	Rank %		Rank #	% of Pop	Rank %
Western Sahara	405,210	173	0.01	?	214	?	214		210	?	210		?	?	218
Zambia	11,862,740	71	0.17	3,539,000	96	29.83	170	700,000	98	5.90	157	90,600	145	0.76	197
Zimbabwe	11,392,629	73	0.17	1,655,000	130	14.53	195	1,421,000	76	12.47	128	354,000	108	3.11	167
	943,212,048														
North America															
Canada	33,487,208	36	0.49	21,455,000	37	64.07	122		210	?	210	18,250,000	17	54.50	23
Saint Pierre and Miquelon		?	?		214	?	214		210		210		?	?	218
United States	307,212,123	3	4.52	270,000,000	3	87.89	84	231,000,000	2	75.19	14	150,000,000	2	48.83	32
Asia															
Afghanistan	28,395,716	43	0.42	8,450,000	69	29.76	171	500,000	105	1.76	182	460,000	99	1.62	180
Albania	3,639,453	129	0.05	3,141,000	107	86.30	88	471,000	107	12.94	124	316,400	112	8.69	142
Bangladesh	156,050,883	7	2.30	45,750,000	22	29.32	172	556,000	102	0.36	206	1,390,000	66	0.89	193
Bhutan	691,141	165	0.01	251,000	170	36.32	160	40,000	170	5.79	159	27,500	180	3.98	161
Brunei	388,190	176	0.01	376,000	162	96.86	66	217,000	131	55.90	43	76,600	150	19.73	102
Burma / Myanmar	48,137,741	26	0.71	375,800	163	0.78	213	108,900	146	0.23	208	829,000	84	1.72	179
Cambodia	14,494,293	66	0.21	4,237,000	92	29.23	173	74,000	157	0.51	201	45,100	163	0.31	209
China	1,338,612,968	1	19.71	634,000,000	1	47.36	147	298,000,000	1	22.26	105	365,600,000	1	27.31	78
Hong Kong	7,055,071	100	0.10	11,374,000	54	161.22	8	4,124,000	49	58.45	39	4,108,000	37	58.23	17
India	1,156,897,766	2	17.04	427,300,000	2	36.93	159	81,000,000	4	7.00	151	37,540,000	7	3.24	166
Indonesia	240,271,522	4	3.54	140,578,000	6	58.51	131	30,000,000	11	12.49	127	30,378,000	10	12.64	126
Japan	127,078,679	10	1.87	110,395,000	7	86.87	85	90,910,000	3	71.54	19	47,579,000	4	37.44	56
Kazakhstan	15,399,437	62	0.23	14,911,000	43	96.83	67	2,300,000	65	14.94	116	3,410,000	44	22.14	92
Korea, North	22,665,345	50	0.33		214	?	214		210	?	210	1,180,000	70	5.21	153
Korea, South	48,508,972	25	0.71	45,607,000	23	94.02	73	37,476,000	10	77.26	9	21,325,000	13	43.96	38
Kyrgyzstan	5,431,747	111	0.08	3,394,000	100	62.48	125	850,000	93	15.65	115	494,500	98	9.10	140
Laos	6,834,345	102	0.10	1,822,000	123	26.66	176	30,000	176	0.44	202	97,600	144	1.43	184
Macau	559,846	169	0.01	993,545	145	177.47	7	259,000	128	46.26	51	173,533	126	31.00	70

	Population			Mobile phones				Internet				Phones			
	Rank		% of World		Rank #	% of Pop	Rank %		Rank #	% of Pop	Rank %		Rank #	% of Pop	Rank %
Malaysia	46	25,715,819	0.38	27,125,000	31	105.48	57	16,903,000	21	65.73	31	4,292,000	35	16.69	109
Maldives	175	396,334	0.01	450,500	158	113.67	44	71,700	159	18.09	111	50,396	160	12.72	125
Mongolia	136	3,041,142	0.04	1,796,000	126	59.06	128	330,000	120	10.85	135	165,000	128	5.43	151
Nepal	42	28,563,377	0.42	4,200,000	93	14.70	194	499,000	106	1.75	183	805,100	86	2.82	170
Pakistan	6	174,578,558	2.57	91,440,000	9	52.38	137	18,500,000	19	10.60	136	4,546,000	32	2.60	172
Philippines	12	97,976,603	1.44	68,102,000	14	69.51	110	5,618,000	41	5.73	160	3,905,000	39	3.99	160
Singapore	117	4,657,542	0.07	6,375,000	77	136.87	17	3,370,000	54	72.36	16	1,857,000	58	39.87	49
Sri Lanka	54	21,324,791	0.31	11,082,000	56	51.97	139	1,164,000	81	5.46	161	3,446,000	43	16.16	112
Taiwan	48	22,974,347	0.34	25,412,000	33	110.61	51	15,143,000	24	65.91	30	14,273,000	19	62.13	13
Tajikistan	96	7,349,145	0.11	3,500,000	98	47.62	146	600,000	101	8.16	145	360,000	105	4.90	156
Thailand	20	65,998,436	0.97	62,000,000	17	93.94	74	16,100,000	22	24.39	95	7,024,000	25	10.64	131
Turkmenistan	114	4,884,887	0.07	810,000	146	16.58	189	75,000	156	1.54	187	495,000	97	10.13	134
Ukraine	27	45,700,395	0.67	55,695,000	19	121.87	33	10,354,000	29	22.66	103	13,177,000	20	28.83	74
Uzbekistan	44	27,606,007	0.41	12,734,000	49	46.13	149	2,469,000	64	8.94	141	1,850,000	60	6.70	148
Vietnam	13	88,576,758	1.30	70,000,000	13	79.03	99	20,834,000	17	23.52	100	29,591,000	11	33.41	62
		3,840,457,256													
Asia / Europe															
Moldova	122	4,320,748	0.06	2,423,000	116	56.08	134	850,000	93	19.67	109	1,115,000	72	25.81	81
Russia	9	140,041,247	2.06	187,500,000	4	133.89	19	45,250,000	8	32.31	75	44,200,000	5	31.56	64
Europe															
Akrotiri	218	15,700	?		214	?	214		210	?	210		?	?	218
Andorra	199	83,888	?	64,200	189	76.53	101	59,100	164	70.45	21	37,400	171	44.58	35
Austria	92	8,210,281	0.12	10,816,000	58	131.74	21	5,937,000	38	72.31	18	3,285,000	46	40.01	48
Belarus	86	9,648,533	0.14	8,693,000	66	90.10	81	3,107,000	56	32.20	76	3,718,000	40	38.53	52
Belgium	78	10,414,336	0.15	11,822,000	51	113.52	45	7,292,000	33	70.02	23	4,457,000	33	42.80	42
Bosnia and Herzegovina	119	4,613,414	0.07	3,179,000	105	68.91	112	1,308,000	79	28.35	84	1,031,000	79	22.35	90
Bulgaria	98	7,204,687	0.11	10,633,000	59	147.58	11	2,647,000	62	36.74	66	2,258,000	54	31.34	68

	Population			Mobile phones				Internet				Phones			
		Rank	% of World		Rank #	% of Pop	Rank %		Rank #	% of Pop	Rank %		Rank #	% of Pop	Rank %
Croatia	4,489,409	121	0.07	5,924,000	80	131.96	20	1,880,000	70	41.88	55	1,851,000	59	41.23	45
Cyprus	1,084,748	158	0.02	1,017,000	143	93.75	75	334,400	119	30.83	81	413,300	101	38.10	55
Czech Republic	10,211,904	80	0.15	13,780,000	48	134.94	18	6,028,000	37	59.03	38	2,278,000	53	22.31	91
Denmark	5,500,510	109	0.08	6,551,000	75	119.10	38	4,579,000	43	83.25	5	2,487,000	52	45.21	33
Dhekelia	15,700	218	?		214	?	214		210	?	210		?	?	218
Estonia	1,299,371	153	0.02	2,525,000	114	194.32	5	888,100	92	68.35	24	498,100	95	38.33	54
Faroe Islands	48,856	208	?	54,900	192	112.37	49	37,500	171	76.76	10	21,800	190	44.62	34
Finland	5,250,275	112	0.08	6,830,000	73	130.09	24	4,383,000	45	83.48	4	1,650,000	62	31.43	66
France	64,057,792	21	0.94	59,259,000	18	92.51	77	42,912,000	9	66.99	26	35,909,000	8	56.06	20
Georgia	4,615,807	118	0.07	2,755,000	110	59.69	127	1,024,000	83	22.18	107	618,000	92	13.39	121
Germany	82,329,758	15	1.21	107,245,000	8	130.26	23	61,973,000	6	75.27	13	51,500,000	3	62.55	12
Gibraltar	28,796	214	?	18,400	204	63.90	123	6,500	199	22.57	104	24,000	183	83.34	4
Greenland	57,600	205	?	55,800	191	96.88	65	36,000	173	62.50	34	22,800	187	39.58	50
Greece	10,737,428	75	0.16	13,799,000	47	128.51	25	4,253,000	46	39.61	60	5,975,000	28	55.65	21
Grenada	90,739	196	?	60,000	190	66.12	117	24,000	181	26.45	93	28,600	179	31.52	65
Guernsey	65,484	204	?	43,800	197	66.89	114	46,100	168	70.40	22	45,100	163	68.87	9
Hungary	9,905,596	82	0.15	12,224,000	50	123.40	28	5,873,000	39	59.29	37	3,094,000	47	31.23	69
Iceland	306,694	179	?	342,000	166	111.51	50	250,000	129	81.51	6	187,000	124	60.97	14
Ireland	4,203,200	125	0.06	5,048,000	85	120.10	36	2,830,000	60	67.33	25	2,202,000	55	52.39	28
Isle of Man	76,512	200	?		214	?	214		210	?	210		?	?	218
Italy	58,126,212	23	0.86	88,580,000	10	152.39	10	24,992,000	13	43.00	53	20,031,000	16	34.46	60
Jersey	91,626	195	?	83,900	184	91.57	79	29,000	178	31.65	78	74,000	153	80.76	5
Kosovo	1,804,838	147	0.03	562,000	154	31.14	169		210	?	210	106,300	142	5.89	150
Latvia	2,231,503	141	0.03	2,234,000	118	100.11	62	1,254,000	80	56.20	41	644,000	91	28.86	73
Liechtenstein	34,761	210	?	34,000	200	97.81	63	23,000	183	66.17	28	19,600	193	56.39	19
Lithuania	3,555,179	130	0.05	5,023,000	86	141.29	14	1,777,000	71	49.98	47	784,900	87	22.08	94
Luxembourg	491,775	170	0.01	707,000	149	143.76	12	387,000	111	78.69	8	260,600	117	52.99	26
Macedonia	2,066,718	144	0.03	2,502,000	115	121.06	35	847,900	95	41.03	57	457,100	100	22.12	93
Malta	405,165	174	0.01	385,600	161	95.17	70	198,800	135	49.07	48	241,100	119	59.51	15

	Population			Mobile phones				Internet				Phones			
	Rank	% of World			Rank #	% of Pop	Rank %		Rank #	% of Pop	Rank %		Rank #	% of Pop	Rank %
Monaco	211	?	32,965	22,000	203	66.74	116	22,000	185	66.74	27	35,000	173	106.17	1
Montenegro	166	0.01	672,180	735,000	147	109.35	54	294,000	126	43.74	52	362,000	104	53.85	25
Netherlands	59	0.25	16,715,999	19,927,000	39	119.21	37	14,273,000	25	85.39	2	7,324,000	24	43.81	40
Norway	116	0.07	4,660,539	5,287,000	84	113.44	46	3,935,000	51	84.43	3	?	?	?	218
Poland	34	0.57	38,482,919	44,004,000	25	114.35	42	18,679,000	18	48.54	50	1,928,000	56	5.01	155
Portugal	76	0.16	10,707,924	14,910,000	44	139.24	15	4,476,000	44	41.80	56	4,121,000	36	38.49	53
Romania	51	0.33	22,215,421	24,467,000	34	110.14	52	6,132,000	36	27.60	86	5,036,000	30	22.67	88
San Marino	212	?	30,167	17,700	205	58.67	130	17,000	188	56.35	40	21,300	191	70.61	8
Serbia	95	0.11	7,379,339	9,619,000	61	130.35	22	2,936,000	58	39.79	59	3,085,000	48	41.81	43
Slovakia	110	0.08	5,463,046	2,055,000	120	37.62	157	3,566,000	52	65.27	32	1,098,000	74	20.10	100
Slovenia	145	0.03	2,005,692	2,055,000	120	102.46	59	1,126,000	82	56.14	42	1,010,000	80	50.36	30
Spain	32	0.60	40,525,002	49,682,000	20	122.60	31	25,240,000	12	62.28	35	20,200,000	15	49.85	31
Sweden	88	0.13	9,059,651	10,988,000	57	121.29	34	8,100,000	31	89.41	1	5,323,000	29	58.76	16
Switzerland	94	0.11	7,604,467	8,780,000	65	115.46	41	5,739,000	40	75.47	12	4,820,000	31	63.38	11
United Kingdom	22	0.90	61,113,205	75,565,000	11	123.65	27	48,755,000	7	79.78	7	33,209,000	9	54.34	24
			540,043,311												
Latin America															
Anguilla	221	?	14,436	13,100	207	90.75	80	4,500	201	31.17	80	5,800	208	40.18	46
Antigua and Barbuda	198	?	85,632	136,600	177	159.52	9	65,000	161	75.91	11	38,000	169	44.38	36
Argentina	31	0.60	40,913,584	46,509,000	21	113.68	43	11,212,000	27	27.40	87	9,631,000	22	23.54	85
Aruba	194	?	103,065	127,100	178	123.32	29	24,000	181	23.29	101	38,500	168	37.36	57
Bahamas	178	?	307,552	358,000	164	116.40	40	106,500	147	34.63	68	133,000	137	43.24	41
Barbados	181	?	284,589	406,000	160	142.66	13	188,000	137	66.06	29	150,000	131	52.71	27
Belize	177	?	307,899	160,000	175	51.97	140	34,000	174	11.04	133	31,100	175	10.10	135
Bermuda	202	?	67,837	79,000	188	116.46	39	51,000	165	75.18	15	57,600	158	84.91	3
Bolivia	84	0.14	9,775,246	4,830,000	88	49.41	144	1,000,000	85	10.23	138	690,000	89	7.06	147
Brazil	5	2.93	198,739,269	150,641,000	5	75.80	103	64,948,000	5	32.68	74	41,141,000	6	20.70	99
British Virgin Islands	215	?	24,491	80,300	185	327.88	1	4,000	203	16.33	114	18,900	194	77.17	7

	Population		Mobile phones				Internet				Phones			
	Rank	% of World		Rank #	% of Pop	Rank %		Rank #	% of Pop	Rank %		Rank #	% of Pop	Rank %
Cayman Islands	49,035	?	33,800	202	68.93	111		210	?	210	38,000	169	77.50	6
Chile	16,601,707	0.24	14,797,000	45	89.13	82	5,456,000	42	32.86	73	3,526,000	42	21.24	97
Colombia	43,677,372	0.64	41,365,000	27	94.71	71	17,117,000	20	39.19	61	6,820,000	26	15.61	114
Costa Rica	4,253,877	0.06	1,887,000	122	44.36	151	1,460,000	74	34.32	70	1,438,000	65	33.80	61
Cuba	11,451,652	0.17	331,700	167	2.90	209	1,450,000	75	12.66	126	1,104,000	73	9.64	138
Dominica	72,660	?	100,000	182	137.63	16	27,500	179	37.85	63	17,500	195	24.08	84
Dominican Republic	9,650,054	0.14	7,210,000	70	74.71	104	2,147,000	67	22.25	106	985,700	81	10.21	133
Ecuador	14,573,101	0.21	11,595,000	52	79.56	96	1,310,000	78	8.99	140	1,910,000	57	13.11	122
El Salvador	7,185,218	0.11	6,951,000	72	96.74	68	826,000	96	11.50	131	1,077,000	76	14.99	116
Guatemala	13,276,517	0.20	14,949,000	42	112.60	48	1,960,000	69	14.76	118	1,449,000	64	10.91	130
Guyana	752,940	0.01	281,400	168	37.37	158	205,000	132	27.23	89	125,000	139	16.60	110
Haiti	9,035,536	0.13	3,200,000	104	35.42	163	1,000,000	85	11.07	132	108,000	141	1.20	186
Honduras	7,833,696	0.12	6,211,000	78	79.29	98	658,500	100	8.41	144	825,800	85	10.54	132
Jamaica	2,825,928	0.04	2,723,000	111	96.36	69	0	210	?	210	316,600	111	11.20	129
Mexico	111,211,789	1.64	75,304,000	12	67.71	113	23,260,000	15	20.92	108	20,539,000	14	18.47	104
Montserrat	5,097	?	3,000	209	58.86	129	1,200	207	23.54	99	2,800	212	54.93	22
Netherlands Antilles	227,049	?	200,000	171	88.09	83		210	?	210	88,000	146	38.76	51
Nicaragua	5,891,199	0.09	3,039,000	108	51.59	141	185,000	138	3.14	173	312,000	113	5.30	152
Panama	3,360,474	0.05	3,805,000	94	113.23	47	934,500	90	27.81	85	495,800	96	14.75	117
Paraguay	6,995,655	0.10	5,791,000	81	82.78	93	894,200	91	12.78	125	363,000	103	5.19	154
Peru	29,546,963	0.44	20,952,000	38	70.91	109	7,128,000	35	24.12	96	2,878,000	51	9.74	136
Puerto Rico	3,966,213	0.06	3,354,000	101	84.56	92	1,000,000	85	25.21	94	1,038,000	77	26.17	80
Saint Barthelemy	7,448	?		214	?	214		210	?	210		?	?	218
St. Kitts and Nevis	40,131	?	80,000	187	199.35	3	16,000	190	39.87	58	20,400	192	50.83	29
St. Lucia	160,267	?	169,600	174	105.82	56		210	?	210	40,900	166	25.52	82
Saint Martin	29,820	?		214	?	214		210	?	210		?	?	218
St. Vincent and the Grenadines	104,574	?	0	214	?	214	66,000	160	63.11	33	22,800	187	21.80	96
Suriname	481,267	0.01	416,000	159	86.44	86	50,000	166	10.39	137	81,500	148	16.93	106
Trinidad and Tobago	1,229,953	0.02	1,505,000	132	122.36	32	227,000	130	18.46	110	307,000	114	24.96	83

	Population			Mobile phones				Internet				Phones			
		Rank	% of World		Rank #	% of Pop	Rank %		Rank #	% of Pop	Rank %		Rank #	% of Pop	Rank %
Turks and Caicos Islands	22,942	216	?		214	?	214		210	?	210		?	?	218
Uruguay	3,494,382	131	0.05	3,508,000	97	100.39	61	1,340,000	77	38.35	62	959,300	82	27.45	77
Venezuela	26,814,843	45	0.39	27,084,000	32	101.00	60	7,167,000	34	26.73	91	6,304,000	27	23.51	86
Virgin Islands	109,825	191	?	80,300	185	73.12	107	30,000	176	27.32	88	74,200	152	67.56	10
	585,562,784														
Pacific Ocean															
American Samoa	65,628	203	?	2,200	210	3.35	208	9,000	196	13.71	122	28,800	177	43.88	39
Australia	21,262,641	55	0.31	22,120,000	36	104.03	58	15,170,000	23	71.35	20	9,370,000	23	44.07	37
Cook Islands	11,870	224	?	6,700	208	56.44	132	5,000	200	42.12	54	6,700	207	56.44	18
East Timor / Timor-Leste	1,131,612	156	0.02	101,000	181	8.93	201	1,800	206	0.16	209	2,400	213	0.21	212
Fiji	944,720	159	0.01	600,000	151	63.51	124	103,000	148	10.90	134	129,100	138	13.67	120
French Polynesia	287,032	180	?	187,100	173	65.18	119	90,000	151	31.36	79	54,600	159	19.02	103
Kiribati	112,850	190	?	1,000	212	0.89	212	2,000	205	1.77	181	4,000	211	3.54	164
Marshall Islands	4,522	228	?	1,000	212	22.11	183	2,200	204	48.65	49	4,400	210	97.30	2
Micronesia	107,434	192	?	34,000	200	31.65	168	16,000	190	14.89	117	8,700	203	8.10	144
Nauru	14,019	222	?		214	?	214		210	?	210	1,800	216	12.84	124
New Caledonia	227,436	182	?	196,500	172	86.40	87	85,000	154	37.37	64	63,000	156	27.70	76
New Zealand	4,213,418	124	0.06	4,620,000	90	109.65	53	3,047,000	57	72.32	17	1,750,000	61	41.53	44
Northern Mariana Islands	51,484	206	?		214	?	214		210	?	210		?	?	218
Palau	20,796	217	?		214	?	214		210	?	210	7,500	206	36.06	59
Papua New Guinea	5,940,775	106	0.09	600,000	151	10.10	200	120,000	142	2.02	178	60,000	157	1.01	190
Samoa	219,998	185	?	124,000	179	56.36	133	9,000	196	4.09	166	28,800	177	13.09	123
Solomon Islands	595,613	168	0.01	14,000	206	2.35	210	10,000	195	1.68	184	8,000	204	1.34	185
Timor-Leste / East Timor	1,131,612	156	0.02		214	?	214		210	?	210		?	?	218
Tonga	120,898	189	?	50,500	193	41.77	153	8,400	198	6.95	152	25,500	182	21.09	98
Tuvalu	12,373	223	?	2,000	211	16.16	193	4,200	202	33.94	71	1,500	217	12.12	127
Vanuatu	218,519	186	?	36,000	199	16.47	190	17,000	188	7.78	147	10,400	200	4.76	158
Wallis and Futuna	15,289	220	?		214	?	214	1,200	207	7.85	146		?	?	218

	Population			Mobile phones				Internet				Phones			
		Rank	% of World		Rank #	% of Pop	Rank %		Rank #	% of Pop	Rank %		Rank #	% of Pop	Rank %
	36,710,539														
Western Asia															
Armenia	2,967,004	137	0.04	2,336,000	117	78.73	100	191,000	136	6.44	153	650,000	90	21.91	95
Azerbaijan	8,238,672	91	0.12	6,548,000	76	79.48	97	1,485,000	73	18.02	112	1,311,000	67	15.91	113
Bahrain	728,709	163	0.01	1,400,000	135	192.12	6	402,900	110	55.29	44	220,000	122	30.19	71
Gaza Strip	1,551,859	149	0.02	1,153,000	139	74.30	106	356,000	115	22.94	102	348,000	109	22.42	89
Iran	66,429,284	19	0.98	43,000,000	26	64.73	120	23,000,000	16	34.62	69	24,800,000	12	37.33	58
Iraq	28,945,569	40	0.43	17,529,000	40	60.56	126	300,000	124	1.04	194	1,082,000	75	3.74	162
Israel	7,233,701	97	0.11	8,902,000	64	123.06	30	2,106,000	68	29.11	83	2,900,000	50	40.09	47
Jordan	6,269,285	104	0.09	5,314,000	83	84.76	91	1,500,000	72	23.93	98	519,000	94	8.28	143
Kuwait	2,692,526	139	0.04	2,907,000	109	107.97	55	1,000,000	85	37.14	65	541,000	93	20.09	101
Lebanon	4,017,095	126	0.06	1,430,000	134	35.60	162	2,190,000	66	54.52	45	714,000	88	17.77	105
Oman	3,418,085	133	0.05	3,219,000	103	94.18	72	465,000	108	13.60	123	274,200	115	8.02	145
Palestinian State		?	?		214	?	214		210		210		?		218
Qatar	833,285	160	0.01	1,683,000	128	201.97	2	436,000	109	52.32	46	263,400	116	31.61	63
Saudi Arabia	28,686,633	41	0.42	36,000,000	29	125.49	26	7,700,000	32	26.84	90	4,100,000	38	14.29	118
Syria	21,762,978	52	0.32	7,056,000	71	32.42	167	3,565,000	53	16.38	113	3,633,000	41	16.69	108
Turkey	76,805,524	17	1.13	65,824,000	15	85.70	90	24,483,000	14	31.88	77	17,502,000	18	22.79	87
United Arab Emirates	4,798,491	115	0.07	9,358,000	62	195.02	4	2,922,000	59	60.89	36	1,508,000	63	31.43	67
West Bank	2,461,267	140	0.04	1,153,000	139	46.85	148	356,000	115	14.46	120	348,000	109	14.14	119
Yemen	22,858,238	49	0.34	3,700,000	95	16.19	192	370,000	113	1.62	185	1,117,000	71	4.89	157
	290,698,205														

Compilation of References

Abram, S. (1998). Introduction: anthropological perspectives on local development. In Abram, S., & Waldren, J. (Eds.), *Anthropological Perspectives on Local Development: Knowledge and Sentiments in Conflict. The European Association of Social Anthropologist*. London, New York: Routledge. doi:10.4324/9780203451021_chapter_1

Acharya, M. (2007). Serving tool for the farming communities. *Information for Development, 5*(4), 10–12.

Adler, P. S., & Kwon, S.-W. (2002). Social Capital: Prospects for a New Concept. *Academy of Management Review, 27*(1), 17–40. doi:10.2307/4134367

Adria, M., Bakardjieva, M., Poitras Pratt, Y., & Mitchell, D. (2006*). The Constructive Role of Researchers in the Social Shaping of Technology in Communities*. Paper presented at 3rd Prato International Community Informatics Conference. Retrieved December 2006 from http://www.ccnr.net/?q=node/123.

Agarwal, A. (Ed.). (2007). *eGovernance Case Studies*. Hyderabad: Universities Press.

Alberts, D. S., & Papp, D. S. (Eds.). (1997). *The Information Age: An Anthology on Its Impact and Consequences*. Washington, D.C.: CCRP Publication Series, Office of the Assistant Secretary of Defense.

Alessi, S. M., & Trollip, S. R. (2001). *Multimedia For Learning* (3rd ed.). Allyn & Bacon.

Aluko, B. T. (2005). Building Urban Local Governance Fiscal Autonomy through Property Taxation Financing Option. *International Journal of Strategic Property Management, 9*, 201–214.

Amsden, A. H., & Chu, W. W. (2003). *Beyond Late Development: Taiwan's Upgrading Policies*. Cambridge, MA: MIT Press.

Anand, S., & Sen, A. (2000). Human Development and Economic Sustainability. *World Development, 28*(12), 2029–2049. doi:10.1016/S0305-750X(00)00071-1

Anand, S., & Sen, A. (1994). *Sustainable human development: concepts and priorities*. New York: United Nations Development Programme.

Anderson, G. T. (1994). Dimensions, Context and Freedom: The Library in the Social Creation of Knowledge. In Barrett, E. (Ed.), *Sociomedia: multimedia, hypermedia and the social construction of knowledge* (pp. 107–124). London: MIR Press.

Anderson, L., Crowder, L. V., Dion, D., & Truelove, W. (1998). Applying the lessons of participatory communication and training to rural telecentres. In *The first mile of connectivity*. Rome, Italy: Food and Agriculture Organisation of the United Nations. Retrieved May 2007 from http://www.fao.org/WAICENT/FAOINFO/SUSTDEV/Cddirect/Cdre0029.html

Andrew, T. N., & Petkov, D. (2003). The need for a systems thinking approach to the planning of rural telecommunications infrastructure. *Telecommunications Policy, 27*(1-2), 75–93. doi:10.1016/S0308-5961(02)00095-2

Annamalai, K., & Sachin, R. (2003). *What works: ITC's E-Choupal and profitable rural transformation web-based information and procurement tools for Indian farmers*. Washington, DC: World Resources Institute.

Anonymous,. (2007). Developing Countries Farm Radio Network. *Information for Development, 5*(4), 13–14.

Arrow, K. J. (1962). The Economic Implications of Learning by Doing. *The Review of Economic Studies, 29*, 155–173. doi:10.2307/2295952

Arunachalam, S. (2002). Reaching the unreached: How can we use information and communication technologies to empower the rural poor in the developing world through enhanced access to relevant information? *Journal of Information Science, 28*(6), 513–522. doi:10.1177/016555150202800607

Asian Development Bank. *(1996).* Final Report: TA 2326 Employment Promotion & Training Project for the Ministry of Labor and Social Welfare (MOLSW) of Lao PDR, Manila, Philippines.

Asian Development Bank. *(1998).* Report and recommendation of the president to the board of directors on a proposed loan to the Republic of Vietnam for the Vocational and Technical Education Project, Manila, Philippines.

Asian Development Bank. *(1999a).* Report and recommendation of the president to the board of directors on a proposed loan to the Republic of Sri Lanka for the Skills Development Project, Manila, Philippines.

Asian Development Bank. (1999b). *Impact evaluation study of Regional technical and vocational education projects, Manila, Philippines.*

Asian Development Bank. (2005). *Technical Assistance for Selected Evaluation Studies for 2005: Operations Evaluation Department, Manila, Philippines.*

Australia Institute of Aboriginal and Torres Strait Islander Studies. (2005). *The National Indigenous Languages Survey Report. Report submitted to the Department of Communications, Information Technology and the Arts by the Australian Institute of Aboriginal and Torres Strait Islander Studies in association with the Federation of Aboriginal and Torres Strait Islander Languages.* Canberra: Department of Communications, Information Technology and the Arts.

Australian Bureau of Statistics. (2006). *Population Characteristics, Aboriginal and Torres Strait Islander Australians.* (No. 4713.7.55.001). Canberra.

Avgerou, C. (1998). How Can IT Enable Economic Growth in Developing Countries? *Information Technology for Development, 8*(1), 15–28. doi:10.1080/02681102.1998.9525288

Avgerou, C., & Walsham, G. (2000). Introduction: IT in Developing Countries. In Avgerou, C., & Walsham, G. (Eds.), *Information Technology in Context: Studies from the Perspective of Developing Countries* (pp. 1–8). Aldershot: Ashgate.

Avgerou, C., & Madon, S. (2005). Information Society and the Digital Divide Problem in Developing Countries. In Berleur, J., & Avgerou, C. (Eds.), *Perspectives and Policies on ICT in Society* (pp. 205–217). New York: Springer. doi:10.1007/0-387-25588-5_15

Avison, D. E., Lau, F., Myers, M. D., & Nielsen, P. A. (1999). Action research. *Communications of the ACM, 42*(1), 94–97. doi:10.1145/291469.291479

Bach, J., & Stark, D. (2003). *Technology and transformation: Facilitating knowledge networks in Eastern Europe. Technology, Business and Society Programme Paper Number 10.* Geneva: UNRSID.

Badshah, A., & Jha, S. (2002). *Taking the Expansive View: From Access to Outcomes: Utilizing the Knowledge-Based Economy to Empower the Poor in India.* Digital Partners Institute.

Bahl, R. W., & Linn, J. F. (1992). *Urban Public Finance in Developing Countries.* New York: Oxford University Press.

Bala, P. (2008). *Desire for progress: The Kelabit experience with information communication technologies (ICTs) for RURAL DEVELOPMENT in Sarawak, East Malaysia.* Unpublished doctoral Dissertation, Cambridge: Christ's College, Cambridge University.

Bala, P., Egay, E., & Datan, E. (2003). *Dynamic Of Cultural Diversity In Everchanging Environment*. Paper Presented at the Simposium Budaya Sarawak IV, 2003 sempena Perayaan Sambutan Jubli Delima Sarawak Merdeka d/a Majlis Adat Istiadat Sarawak, Jabatan Ketua Menteri, Sarawak. Ogos 2-3, 2003.

Bala, P., Harris, R. W., & Songan, P. (2003). E Bario Project: In Search of a Methodology to Provide Access to Information Communication Technologies for Rural Communities in Malaysia. In Marshall, S., Taylor, W., Xinghuo Yu (eds), *Using Community Informatics to Transform Regions*. Hershey, PA: Idea Group.

Balaji, V., & Harris, R. W. (2002). Information Technology Reaching the Unreached - Village Knowledge Centers in Southern India, Second Global Knowledge Conference (GkII), Kuala Lumpur, Malaysia, March 7-10, 2002.

Baldassar, L., Baldock, C. V., & Wilding, R. (2007). *Families Caring Across Borders; Migration, Ageing, and Transnational Caregiving*. Basingstoke, UK: Palgrave Macmillan.

Balkcom, S. (1992). Cooperative learning [Online]. *The Education Research Consumer Guide*. Retrieved January 2004 from http://www.ed.gov/pubs/OR/Consumer-Guides/cooplear.html

Bangalore Mahanagara Palike. (2000). *Property Tax Self-Assessment Scheme Handbook: Golden Jubilee Year 2000*. Bangalore: BBMP.

Bangalore Mahanagara Palike. (2007). *Assessment and Calculation of Property Tax Under the Capital Value System (New SAS): 2007- 2008*. Unpublished Handbook.

Barab, S. A., & Squire, K. (2004). Design-based Research: Putting a Stake in the Ground. *The Journal of the Learning Sciences.*

Baron, N. S. (2008). Text, Talk, or View: How Much of Ourselves do We Reveal? In *The Role of New Technologies in Global Societies; Theoretical Reflections, Practical Concerns, and Its Implications for China. Conference Proceedings 30–31 July 2008 Department of Applied Social Sciences, Hong Kong Polytechnic University* (pp. 330-347).

Barr, D. F. (1998). Integrated rural development through telecommunications. In *The first mile of connectivity*. Rome, Italy: Food and Agriculture Organisation of the United Nations. Retrieved December 2002 from http://www.fao.org/WAICENT/FAOINFO/SUSTDEV/Cd-direct/Cdre0029.html

Bartholomew, D. J. (1987). *Latent Variable Model and Factor Analysis*. Charles Griffin and Company Limited.

Baskerville, R. L., & Wood-Harper, A. T. (1996). A critical perspective on action research as a method for information systems research. *Journal of Information Technology, 11*, 235–246. doi:10.1080/026839696345289

Batchelor, S., & Norrish, P. (2003). Sustainable Information Communication Technologies (ICT): Sustainability. Retrieved February 7, 2009, from http://www.sustainable-icts.org /Sustainable.htm

Batty, P. (2005). White Redemption Rituals: Reflections on the Repatriation of Aboriginal Secret-Sacred Objects. In Lea, T., Kowal, E., & Cowlishaw, G. (Eds.), *Moving Anthropology: Critical Indigenous Studies*. Darwin: Darwin University Press.

Baxter, J., & Eyles, J. (1997). Evaluating qualitative research in social geography: Establishing 'rigour' in interview analysis. *Transactions of the Institute of British Geographers, 22*, 505–552. doi:10.1111/j.0020-2754.1997.00505.x

Beamish, A. (1999). Approaches to Community Computing: Bringing Technology to Low-Income Groups. In Schon, D. A., Sanyal, B., & Mitchell, W. J. (Eds.), *High Technology and Low-Income Communities: Prospects for the Positive Use of Advanced Information Technology*. MIT Press.

Beamish, A. (1995). *Community On-line: Computer-Base Community Networks*. Master of City Planning Thesis, Massachusetts Institute of Technology. Retrieved August 5, 2008 from http://sap.mit.edu/anneb/cn-thesis/

Benbya, H., & McKelvey, B. (2006). Toward a Complexity Theory of Information Systems Development. *Information Technology & People, 19*(1), 12–34. doi:10.1108/09593840610649952

Benjamin, P., & Dahms, M. (1999). Socialise the modem of production: The role of telecentres in development. In Gómez, R., & Hunt, P. (Eds.), *Telecentre Evaluation: A global perspective* (pp. 49–67). Ottawa: International Development Research Centre.

Benjamin, P. (2001). Community development and democratisation through information technology: building the new South Africa. In Heeks, R. B. (Ed.), *Reinventing Government in the Information Age* (pp. 194–210). London: Routledge.

Benner, M., & Sandstrom, U. (2000). Institutionalizing the Triple Helix: Research Finding and Norms in the Academic System. *Research Policy*, *29*(2), 291–302. doi:10.1016/S0048-7333(99)00067-0

Bergqvist, J., Dahlberg, P., & Ljungberg, F. (2002). Scalability through Cultivation - designing IT support for co-ordination work. Retrieved November 13, 2006, from http://citeseerx.ist.psu.edu/viewdoc/summary?doi=10.1.1.22.1564

Besser, H. (2003). *The Next Digital Divide*. Retrieved July 6, 2003 from http://tcla. gseis.ucla.edu/ divide/politics/besser.html

Best, M. L., & Kumar, R. (2008). Sustainability Failures of Rural Telecenters: Challenges from the Sustainable Access in Rural India (SARI) Project. *Information Technologies and International Development*, *4*(4), 31–45. doi:10.1162/itid.2008.00025

Best, M. L., & Maclay, C. M. (2002). Community Internet Access in Rural Areas: Solving the Economic Sustainability Puzzle. In Kirkman, G. S., Cornelius, P. K., Sachs, J. D., & Schawb, K. (Eds.), *The Global Information Technology Report 2001-2002: Readiness for the Networked World* (pp. 76–89). Oxford, UK: Oxford University Press.

Best, M. L., & Maclay, C. M. (2002). Community Internet Access in Rural Areas: Solving the Economic Sustainability Puzzle. In Kirkman, G., Sachs, J. D., & Cornelius, P. K. (Eds.), *The Global Information Technology Report 2001-2002: Readiness for the Networked World*. Oxford: Oxford University Press.

Bhagat, R. B. (2005). Rural-Urban Classification and Municipal Governance in India. *Singapore Journal of Tropical Geography*, *26*(1), 61–73. doi:10.1111/j.0129-7619.2005.00204.x

Bhagwan, J. (1983). *Municipal Finance in the Metropolitan Cities of India: A Case Study of Delhi Municipal Corporation*. New Delhi: Concept Publishing.

Bhatnagar, S. (2004). *E-Government: From Vision to Implementation*. New Delhi: Sage Publications.

Bhatnagar, S. (2000). Social Implications of Information and Communication Technology in Developing Countries: Lessons from Asian Success Stories. *The Electronic Journal of Information Systems in Developing Countries*, *1*(4), 1–9.

Bhatnagar, S. (2003). Development and Telecommunications Access: Cases from South Asia. In Avgerou, C., & Rovere, R. L. L. (Eds.), *Information Systems and the Economics of Innovation* (pp. 33–52). Northampton, MA: Edward Elgar Pub.

Bhatnagar, S. (2003a). E-Government: Building a SMART Administration for India's States. In Howes, S., Lahiri, A., & Stern, N. (Eds.), *State-level Reform in India: Towards More Effective Government* (pp. 257–267). New Delhi: Macmillan India Ltd.

Bhatnagar, S. (2003b). Public Service Delivery: Does E-Government Help? In S. Ahmed & S. Bery (Eds.), *The Annual Bank Conference on Development Economics 2003* (pp. 11-20). New Delhi: The World Bank and National Conference of Applied Economic Research.

Bhatnagar, S. (2003c). *Transparency and Corruption: Does E-Government Help?* Draft paper for the compilation of the Commonwealth Human Rights Initiative 2003 Report 'Open Sesame: looking for the Right to Information in the Commonwealth.

Bhatnagar, S. (2005). *E-Government: Opportunities and Challenges*. World Bank Presentation Retrieved June 22, 2005 from http://siteresources.worldbank.org/ INTEDEVELOPMENT/ Resources/ 559323-1114798035525/1055531-1114798256329/10555556-1114798371392/Bhatnagar1.ppt

Bijker, W. E., Hughes, T. P., & Pinch, T. (1987). *The social construction of technological systems*. Cambridge, MA: MIT Press.

Bill and Melinda Gates Foundation. Remote Australian Library System Receives Award for Teaching Technology Literacy Skills Through Preservation of Culture. (2007) Retrieved December 12, 2008, from http://www.gatesfoundation.org/press-releases/Pages/northern-mn territory-library-atla-winner-070820.aspx

Biswas, B., & Caliendo, F. (2004). A multivariate analysis of the Human Development Index. *The Indian Economic Journal, 49*(4), 96-100. Retrieved March 2010 from http://unpan1.un.org/intradoc/groups/public/documents/APCITY/UNPAN019757.pdf.

Bjerknes, G., Ehn, P., & Kyng, M. (Eds.). (1987). *Computers and Democracy - A Scandinavian Challenge*. Aldershot: Avebury.

Blackburn, J., & Holland, J. (Eds.). (1998). *Who Changes? Institutionalizing participation in development*. London: Intermediate Technology Publication.

Blanchflower, D. G., & Oswald, A. J. (2005). *Happiness and the Human Development Index: The paradox of Australia*. Cambridge, MA: National Bureau of Economic Research.

Blattman, C., & Jensen, R. (2003). Assessing the Need and Potential of Community Networking for Development in Rural India. *The Information Society, 19*(5), 349–365. doi:10.1080/714044683

Bloor, D. (1997). *Wittgenstein, Rules and Institutions*. London, UK: Routledge.

Boerma, T. (2005). WHO News - Getting the numbers right. *Bulletin of the World Health Organization, 83*(8), 567–568.

Boud, D., Cohen, R., & Sampson, J. (1999). Peer Learning and Assessment. *Assessment & Evaluation in Higher Education, 24*(4), 413–426. doi:10.1080/0260293990240405

Bourdieu, P. (1986). The Forms of Capital. In Richardson, J. G. (Ed.), *Handbook for Theory and Research for the Sociology of Education* (pp. 241–258). Wesport, CT: Greenwood Press.

Bowonder, B. Gupta., V., & Singh, A. (2003). Developing a rural market e-hub: The case study of e-Choupal experience of ITC. Planning Commission of India. Retrieved April 6, 2009, from http://planningcommission.nic.in/reports/sereport/ser/stdy_ict/4_e-choupal%20.pdf

Braa, J., Hanseth, O., Heywood, A., Mohammed, W., & Shaw, V. (2007). Developing Health Information Systems in Developing Countries - the flexible standards strategy. *Management Information Systems Quarterly, 31*(Special Issue).

Braa, J., & Hedberg, C. (2002). The Struggle for District Based Health Information Systems in South Africa. *The Information Society, 18*, 113–127. doi:10.1080/01972240290075048

Braa, J., Monteiro, E., & Reinert, E. S. (1995). Technology Transfer vs. Technological Learning: IT infrastructure and health care in developing countries. *Information Technology for Development, 6*(1), 15–23. doi:10.1080/02681102.1995.9525252

Braa, J., Monteiro, E., & Sahay, S. (2004). Networks of Action: Sustainable Health Information Systems Across Developing Countries. *Management Information Systems Quarterly, 28*(3), 337–362.

Braa, J., & Hedberg, C. (2000). *Developing District-based Health Care Information Systems: The South African Experience.* Paper presented at the IRIS 23.

Bregaglio, A. (2003, September 25). *Info Express.* Retrieved January 10, 2009 from http://www.iconnect-online.org/Stories/Story.import5130

Breiter, A. (2003). Public Internet Usage Points in Schools for the Local Community – Concept, Implementation and Evaluation of a Project in Bremen, Germany. *Education and Information Technologies, 8*(2), 109–2003. doi:10.1023/A:1024550229787

Brenner, N. (1999). Beyond state-centrism?: Space, Territoriality, and Geographical Scale in Globalization Studies. *Theory and Society*, *28*, 39–78. doi:10.1023/A:1006996806674

Bresciani, P., Donzelli, P., & Forte, A. (2003). Requirements Engineering for Knowledge Management in eGovernment (LNAI 2645, pp. 48-59).

British Educational Communications and Technology Agency. (2002). *Digital Divide*. ICT Research Network, A Collection of Papers from the Toshiba/Becta Digital Divide Seminar: 19th February 2002. Retrieved on November 23, 2003 from www.becta.org.uk/research

Brown, A. L. (1992). Design experiments: Theoretical and methodological challenges in creating complex interventions in classroom settings. *Journal of the Learning Sciences*, *2*(2), 141–178. doi:10.1207/s15327809jls0202_2

Buckley, S. (2000). Radio's new horizons: Democracy and popular communication in the digital age. *International Journal of Cultural Studies*, *3*(2), 180–187. doi:10.1177/136787790000300206

Budhiraja, R. (2003) *Electronic Governance: a Key Issue in the 21st Century*. Additional Director, Electronic Governance Division, Ministry of Information Technology, Government of India. Retrieved June 14, 2008 from http://www.mit.gov.in/eg/ article2.htm

Buré, C. (2007). *Grounding Gender Evaluation Methodology for Telecentres: The Experiences of Ecuador and the Phillipines*. Ottawa: Telecentre.Org, International Development Research Centre (IDRC).

Burt, R. S. (2001). *Bridge Decay*. Retrieved November 6 2003 from http://gsbuwn.uchicago.edu/fac/ronald.burt/research/BD.pdf

Butler, T. (2002). Bridging the Digital Divide Through Educational Initiatives: Problems and Solutions. Special Series on the Digital Divide. *Informing Science*, *5*(3).

Cademártori, J. (2001). *Chile - El Modelo Neoliberal*. Santiago: Ediciones ChileAmérica CESOC.

Cahill, M. B. (2005). Is the Human Development Index redundant? *Eastern Economic Journal*, *31*(1), 1–5.

Cairncross, F. (1997). *The Death of Distance. How the Communications Revolution will Change our Lives*. London: Orion Publishing.

Carr, N. G. (2003, May). IT Doesn't Matter. *Harvard Business Review*, 41–49.

CASEN. (2000). Encuesta de Caracterización Socioeconómica Nacional. Retrieved August 26, 2006, from http://www.mideplan.cl/casen/ modulo_demografia.html.

Castells, M. (2000a). *End of Millennium - The Information Age: Economy, Society and Culture* (2nd ed., *Vol. 3*). Malden, MA: Blackwell Publishers.

Castells, M. (2000b). *The Rise of the Network Society - The Information Age: Economy, Society and Culture* (2nd ed., *Vol. 1*). Malden, MA: Blackwell Publishers.

Castells, M. (2008). Afterword. In Katz, J. E. (Ed.), *Handbook of Mobile Communication Studies* (pp. 447–451). Cambridge, MA: MIT Press.

Ceccagno, A. (2008). Chinese Migrants as Apparel Manufacturers in an Era of Perishable Global Fashion: New Fashion Scenarios in Prato, Italy. In Johanson, G., Smyth, R., & French, R. (Eds.), *Living Outside the Walls: The Chinese in Prato* (pp. 42–74). Newcastle upon Tyne: Cambridge Scholars Publishing.

Cecchini, S., & Raina, M. (2003). Electronic Government and the Rural Poor: The Case of Gyandoot. *Information Technologies and International Development*, *2*(2), 65–75. doi:10.1162/1544752044193434

Cecchini, S. (2002). Information and Communications Technology for Poverty Reduction. Lessons from Rural India. In *Technology and Society 2002. (ISTAS'02). 2002 International Symposium on* (pp. 93-99). Raleigh, NC, USA, IEEE.

CENSO. (2002). *Instituto National de Estadísticas. Censo 2002*. Retrieved May 5, 2006, from http://alerce.ine.cl/ine/canales/chile_estadistico /demografia_y_vitales/indicecenso02.php.

Centre for Policy Research (2001, June). *The Future of Urbanisation: Spread and Shape in Selected States*. New Delhi: Centre for Policy Research.

Chambers, R. (1993). *Rural development: Putting the last first*. Essex, England: Longman Group Limited.

Chambers, R. (1997). *Whose Reality Counts? Putting the Last First*. London: Intermediate Technology Publications.

Charmaz, K. (2006). *Constructing Grounded Theory: A Practical Guide through Qualitative Analysis*. London, UK: Sage Publications.

Charp, S. (2001). Bridging the Digital Divide. [Technological Horizons in Education]. *T.H.E. Journal, 28*.

Chataway, J., & Wield, D. (2000). Industrialization, Innovation and Development: What does knowledge management change? *Journal of International Development, 12*, 803–824. doi:10.1002/1099-1328(200008)12:6<803::AID-JID714>3.0.CO;2-H

Chataway, J., & Wield, D. (2000). Industrialization, innovation, and development: What does knowledge management change? *Journal of International Development, 12*(6), 803–824. doi:10.1002/1099-1328(200008)12:6<803::AID-JID714>3.0.CO;2-H

Checkland, P. (1985). From optimising to learning: a development of thinking for the 1990s. *The Journal of the Operational Research Society, 36*(9), 757–767.

Checkland, P., & Holwell, S. (1998). *Information, Systems and Information Systems: Making Sense of the Field*. UK: John Wiley and Sons.

Checkland, P. B., & Scholes, J. (2005). *Soft Systems Methodology in Action - Includes a 30 year Retrospective*. Chichester, UK: John Wiley and Sons.

Checkland, P. B. (1986). The application of systems thinking in real world problem solving: the emergence of soft systems methodology. In Jackson, M. C., & Keys, P. (Eds.), *New Directions in Management Science* (pp. 87–96). London: Gower.

Checkland, P. B., & Winter, M. (2006). Process and content: two ways of using SSM. *Journal of the Operational Research Society* (Special Issue: Problem Structuring Methods - New Direction in a Problematic World). doi:10.1057.

Cheema, G. S. (2005). *Building Democratic Institutions: Governance Reform in Developing Countries*. Bloomfield: Kumarian Press, Inc.

Chen, W., & Wellman, B. (2003). E-Commerce Development: Charting and Bridging the Digital Divide. *I-Ways. Digest of Electronic Commerce Policy and Regulation, 26*, 155–161.

Chilundo, B. (2004). *Integrating Information Systems of Disease-Specific Health Programmes in Low Income Countries*. Oslo, Norway: University of Oslo.

Chilundo, B., & Aanestad, M. (2004). Negotiating Multiple Rationalities in the Process of Integrating the Information Systems of Disease-Specific Health Programmes. *Electronic Journal on Information Systems in Developing Countries, 20*(2), 1–28.

Christen, K. (2005). Gone Digital: Culture as Interface in Aboriginal Collaborations. *International Journal of Cultural Property, 12*(3), 315–345.

Christen, K. (2007) The Politics of Search: Archival Accountability in Aboriginal Australia. Presented at the MIT5: Media in Transition 5 Conference Technological Translations and Digital Dilemmas Panel. April 28th, 2007. Retrieved January 12, 2008 http://web.mit.edu/comm-forum /mit5/papers/Christen.pdf

Christie, M. (2003). Computer Databases and Aboriginal Knowledge. Learning Communities. Retrieved December 13, 2008, from: http://www.cdu.edu.au/centres/ik/pdf / CompDatAbKnow.pdf

Christie, M. (2004) Words, Ontologies and Aboriginal databases. Retrieved December 13, 2008, from: http://www.cdu.edu.au/centres/ik/pdf/ WordsOntologiesAbDB.pdf

Chu, W.-C., & Yang, S. (2006). Mobile phones and new migrant workers in a South China village: an initial analysis of the interplay between the 'social' and the 'technological. In Law, P., Fortunati, L., & Yang, S. (Eds.), *New Technologies in Global Societies. Part 3* (pp. 221–244). doi:10.1142/9789812773555_0010

Ciborra, C. (2000). *From Control to Drift - the Dynamics of Corporate Information Infrastructures.* Oxford University Press.

Cisler, S. (2002). Schools Online Planning for Sustainability: How to keep your ICT project running. *Community Technology Centers' Network.* Retrieved February 7, 2009, from http://www2.ctcnet.org/ctc/Cisler/sustain.doc

Cobb, P., Confrey, J., Disessa, A., Lehrer, R., & Schauble, L. (2003). Design experiments in educational research. *Educational Researcher, 32*(1), 9–13. doi:10.3102/0013189X032001009

Coelen, S. P. (1980). *Regression Analysis of Regional Quality of Life. Dordect, Holland & Boston.* MA: D. Reidel Publishing Co.

COFISA. (2008). *COFISA Project Plan, Dwesa Living Lab: Village Connection Component.* Pretoria: COFISA.

Cohen, H. (2005). The visual mediation of a complex narrative: T.G.H. Strehlow's Journey to Horseshoe Bend. *Media International Australia, 116,* 36–51.

Colby, S.-S. (2001). *Anti-Corruption and ICT for Good Governance.* Deputy Secretary-General, OECD in Anti-Corruption Symposium 2001: The Role of Online Procedures in Promoting and Good Governance.

Coleman, J. S. (1988). Social Capital in the Creation of Human Capital. *American Journal of Sociology, 94,* 95–120. doi:10.1086/228943

Collins, A., Joseph, D., & Bielaczyc, K. (2004). Design research: Theoretical and methodological issues. *Journal of the Learning Sciences, 13*(1), 15–42. doi:10.1207/s15327809jls1301_2

Collins, A. (1992). Toward a design science of Education. In Scanlon, E., & O'Shea, T. (Eds.), *New Directions in Educational Technology.* Berlin: Springer-Verlag.

Collis, J., & Hussey, R. (2003). *Business Research: A Practical Guide for Undergraduate and Postgraduate Students* (2nd ed.). Basinstoke, Hampshire, UK: Palgrave Macmillan.

Commonwealth of Australia. (2008a). Australia 2020: Initial Summit Report. Retrieved May 1, 2008 http://www.australia2020.gov.au/docs/ 2020_Summit_initial_report.pdf.

Commonwealth of Australia. (2008b). *Australia 2020 Summit Final Report.* Canberra: Department of Prime Minister and Cabinet.

Commonwealth of Learning. (2002). *Perspectives on Distance Education: Skills Development through Distance Education.* Vancouver: Commonwealth of Learning.

Comune di Prato. (2008). Stranieri residenti a Prato divisi per cittadinanza. Retrieved April 20, 2010 from http://www.comune.prato.it/prato/ htm/strwrld.htm

Cooke, B., & Kothari, U. (2001). *Participation: The New Tyranny?* London, New York: Zed Books.

Cooke, P., Heidenreich, M., & Braczyk, H. J. (Eds.). (2004). *Regional Innovation Systems* (2nd ed.). London: Routledge.

Costello, A. B., & Osborne, J. W. (2005). Best Practices in Exploratory Factor Analysis: Four Recommendations or Getting the Most from Your Analysis. *Practical Assessment Research and Evaluation, 10*(7), 1–9.

Crawford, P., & Bryce, P. (2003). Project Monitoring and Evaluation: a Method for Enhancing the Efficiency and Effectiveness of Aid Project Implementation. *International Journal of Project Management, 21,* 363–373. doi:10.1016/S0263-7863(02)00060-1

Creech, H. (2006). *Evaluation of UNESCO's Community Multimedia Centres: Final report.* Winnipeg: IISD.

Cui, Y., Chipchase, J., & Ichikawa, F. (2007). A Cross Culture Study on Phone Carrying and Physical Personalisation. In Aykin, N. (Ed.), *Usability and Internationalisation, Part I, HCII 2007* (LNCS 4559, pp. 483-492).

Cullen, R. (2001). Addressing the Digital Divide. *Online Information Review, 25*(5). doi:10.1108/14684520110410517

Curtain, R. (2003, May 22) *Information and Communication Technologies and Development: help or hindrance?* Retrieved January 2, 2010 from http://www.developmentgateway.com.au/jahia/Jahia/lang/en/pid/247

Dagron, G. (2001). Prometheus Riding a Cadillac? Telecentres as the promised flame of knowledge. *Journal of Development Communication: Special Issue on Telecentres, 12*(2), 85–93.

Dalvit, L., Thinyane, M., Muyingi, H., & Terzoli, A. (2007). The Deployment of an e-Commerce Platform and Related Projects in a Rural Area in South Africa. *International Journal of Computing and ICT Research, 1*(1), 9–18.

Dalvit, L., Isabiriye, N., Thinyane, M., & Terzoli, A. (2006, July). *A case study on the teaching of computer literacy in a marginalized community.* Paper presented at the Comparative Education Society of Europe Conference, Granada, Spain.

Daniel, B., Schwler, R. A., & McCalla, G. (2003). Social Capital in Virtual Learning Communities and Distributed Communities of Practice. *Canadian Journal of Learning and Technology, 29*(3).

Datta, A. (1984). *Municipal Finances in India.* New Delhi: Indian Institute of Public Administration.

Datta, A. (1999). Institutional Aspects of Urban Governance in India. In S.N. Jha & P.C. Mathur (Eds.), *Decentralization and Local Politics* (pp. 191-211). New Delhi: Sage Publications.

David, P. A. (1975). *Technical Choice, Innovation and Economic Growth.* Cambridge, England: Cambridge University Press.

Davies, A. (1994). *Telecommunications and politics: the decentralised alternative.* London: Pinter Publishers.

Davies, S., Schwartz, A. W., Pinkett, R. D., & Servon, L. J. (2003). *A Report to the Ford Foundation: Community Technology Centres as Catalyst for Community Change.* A Report to the Ford Foundation, New School University Retrieved October 25, 2003 from www.bctpartners.com/resources/ CTCs as Catalysts.pdf.

Davis, G. B. (1982). Strategies for Information Requirements Determination. *IBM Systems Journal, 21*(1), 4–31. doi:10.1147/sj.211.0004

De Haan, J. (2003). IT and Social Inequality in the Netherlands. *IT&Society, 1*(4), 27–45.

de Villiers, MR (Ruth). (2007). Interpretive research models for Informatics: action research, grounded theory, and the family of design- and development research *Alternation, 12*(2), 10-52. (Dated 2005, appeared 2007).

De'. R. (2007). *Antecedents of Corruption and the Role of E-Government Systems in Developing Countries.* Paper presented at the Electronic Government 6th International Conference, EGOV 2007, Proceedings of Ongoing Research, Regensburg, Germany, September 3-7, 2007.

Deane, J., Dixit, K., Mue, N., Banda, F., & Waisbord, S. (2004). The Other Information Revolution: Media and empowerment in developing countries. In Osiochru, S., & Girard, B. (Eds.), *Communication in the Information Society* (pp. 65–100). Geneva: United Nations Research Institute for Social Development.

Dede, C. (2005). Why design-based research is both important and difficult. *Educational Technology, 45*(1), 5–8.

Degenne, A., & Forse, M. (1994). *Introducing Social Networks (I. Borges, Trans. 1999).* Sage Publications.

Denison, T., Arunachalam, D., Johanson, G., & Smyth, R. (2009). The Chinese Community in Prato. In Johanson, G., Smyth, R., & French, R. (Eds.), *Living Outside the Walls: The Chinese in Prato* (pp. 2–24). Newcastle upon Tyne: Cambridge Scholars Publishing.

Denison, T., Stillman, L., Johanson, G., & Schauder, D. (2003). Theory, Practice, Social Capital, and Information and Communication Technologies in Australia. *Many Voices, Many Places – Electronically Enabling Communities for and Information Society: A Colloquium Proceedings*. Monash Prato, Italy, 15-16 September, 2003. Retrieved October 25, 2006 from http://www.ccnr.net/?q=node/234

Denzin, N. K. (1989). *The Research Act*. Englewood Cliffs, NJ: Prentice Hall.

Department of Corporate and Information Services. (2005). *Telecommunications in Remote NT Indigenous Communities: assessing the economic and social impact of upgraded telecommunications services in remote Indigenous communities in the NT*. Darwin: ACIL Tasman.

Department of Statistic. Malaysia (2006). *Key Statistics*. Retrieved June 16, 2007 from http://www.statistics.gov.my/english/ frameset_keystats.php

Díaz Andrade, A. (2009). Interpretive Research Aiming at Theory Building: Adopting and Adapting the Case Study Design. *The Qualitative Report, 14*(1), 42-60. Retrieved on April 7, 2009 from http://www.nova.edu/ssss/QR/QR-14-1/diaz-andrade.pdf

Díaz, À., & Rivas, G. (2005). Innovación tecnológica y desarrollo digital: el aporte de los gobiernos de la Concertación. In Meller, P. (Ed.), *La Paradoja Aparente - Equidad y Eficiencia: Resolviendo el Dilema* (pp. 473–528). Santiago: Aguilar Chilena de Ediciones.

Digital Divide Council. *Digital Divide and Underserved Groups*. Retrieved on April 25, 2005 from http://www.digitaldividecouncil. com / digitaldivide/progress_date.html

Dillinger, W. (1988). *Urban Property Taxation in Developing Countries*. World Bank Policy Research Working Paper Series, Number 41.

Dinmore, G. (2010). Tuscan town turns against Chinese migrants. Financial Times. Retrieved April 20, 2010 from http://www.ft.com/cms/s/0/a2ff28f6-1 4df-11df-8f1d-00144feab49a.html

Dipartimento per le Liberta Civili e l'Immigrazione Organizzazione Internazionale per le Migranzioni (2008). Analisi ed Elaborazione Date Sull'Immigrazione Cinese in Italia. Dipartimento per le Liberta Civili e l'Immigrazione Organizzazione Internazionale per le Migranzioni.

Directorate of Municipal Administration. (2007). Retrieved from http://municipaladmn.kar. nic.in

Directorate of Municipal Administration. (2008). The Intention of Self Assessment of Property Tax: Part 1. Retrieved November 10, 2008 from http://municipaladmn. kar. nic.in/SASe1.htm

Doloreux, D., & Parto, P. (2004). Regional Innovation Systems: A Critical Synthesis (Discussion Paper no. 2004-17). UNU-INTECH.

Donner, J. (2008). Research Approaches to Mobile Use in the Developing World: A Review of the Literature. *The Information Society, 24*(3), 140–159. doi:10.1080/01972240802019970

Donnermeyer, J. F., & Hollifield, C. A. (2003). Digital Divide Evidence in Four Rural Towns. *IT&Society, 1*(4), 107–117.

Doorman, F. (1995). Participation, efficiency and the common good: an essay on participation in development. In Ferks, G., & den Ouden, J. H. B. (Eds.), *In Search of the Middle Ground: Essays on the Sociology of Planned Development*. Wageningen: Agricultural University.

Drezner, D. W. (2004). The Global Governance of the Internet: Bringing the State Back In. *Political Science Quarterly, 119*(3), 477–498. doi:10.2307/20202392

Dutton, W. H. (1999). *Society on the Line: Information Politics in the Digital Age*. Oxford: Oxford University Press.

Easterly, W. (2006). *The white man's burden. Why the west's efforts to aid the rest have done so much ill and so little good*. Oxford: Oxford Univ Press.

Economic and Social Council, United Nations (2000). Development and international cooperation in the twenty-first century: the role of information technology in the context of a knowledge-based global economy.

Economic Planning Unit. (1999). *Malaysian Quality of Life 1999*. Malaysia: Economic Planning Unit, Prime Minister's Department.

Economic Planning Unit. (2002). *Malaysia Quality of Life 2002*. Prime Minister's Department, Malaysia. Retrieved May 25, 2004 from http://www.epu.jpm.my/ Bi/publi/mqli2002/content.pdf

Edelman, M., & Hangerud, A. (2005). Introduction: The Anthropology of Development and Globalization. In Edelman, M., & Haugerud, A. (Eds.), *The Anthropology of Development and Globalization: From classical Political Economy to Contemporary Neoliberalism*. Blackwell Publishing.

Edquist, C. (2004). Systems of Innovation - A Critical Review of The State of the Art. In Fagerberg, J., Mowery, D., & Nelson, R. (Eds.), *Handbook of Innovation* (pp. 181–208). Oxford: Oxford University Press.

Edquist, C. (2001, June). *The Systems of Innovation Approach and Innovation Policy: An Account of the State of the Art*. Paper presented at the Nelson Winter Conference, DRUID, Aalborg.

Eisenhardt, K. M. (1989). Building Theories from Case Study Research. *Academy of Management Review, 14*(4), 532–550. doi:10.2307/258557

Eisenhardt, K. M., & Graebner, M. E. (2007). Theory Building from Cases: Opportunities and Challenges. *Academy of Management Journal, 50*(1), 25–32.

Elden, M., & Chisholm, R. F. (1993). Emerging Varieties of Action Research - Introduction to the Special Issue. *Human Relations, 46*(2), 121–142. doi:10.1177/001872679304600201

Ellen, D. (2000). *Telecentres and the Provision of Community Based Access to Electronic Information in Everyday Life*. PhD. Thesis, Manchester Metropolitan University, United Kingdom. Retrieved May 11, 2003 from http://www.mmu.ac.uk/h-ss/dic/research /ellen/contents.html

Ellen, D. (2003). Telecentres and the Provision of Community Based Access to Electronic Information in Everyday Life in the UK. *Information Research, 8*(2), paper number 146. Retrieved May 11, 2003 from http://informationr.net/ir/8-2/paper146.html

Elliott, J., & Elliott, J. (1993). *Action research for educational change*. Philadelphia: Open University Press.

Emory, C. W., & Cooper, D. R. (1991). *Business Research Methods* (4th ed.). Richard D. Irwin, Inc.

Eoyang, G. (1996). Complex? Yes! Adaptive? Well, maybe.... *Interaction, 3*(1), 31–37. doi:10.1145/223500.223509

Ernberg, J. (1998). *Integrated Rural Development and Universal Access towards a Framework for Evaluation of Multipurpose Telecentres: Pilot Projects Implemented In ITU and Its Partners*. Retrieved August 28, 2004 from http://www.itu.int/ITU-D/univ_access/ telecentres/papers/guelph.html

Estache, A., Gomez-Lobo, A., & Leipziger, D. (2001). Utilities privatization and the poor: lessons and evidence from Latin America. *World Development, 29*(7), 1179–1198. doi:10.1016/S0305-750X(01)00034-1

Esteva, G. (1987). Regenerating people's space. *Alternatives, 10*(3), 125–152.

Etta, F., & Wamahiu, S. P. (Eds.). (2003). *Information and Communication Technologies for Development in Africa* (Vol. 2). Jointly published by Ottawa, ON: IDRC and Dakar: Council for the Development of Social Science Research in Africa (CODESRIA).

Etzkowitz, H., & Leydesdorff, L. (Eds.). (1997). *Universities and the Global Knowledge Economy: A Triple Helix of University-Industry-Government Relations*. London: Cassell Academic.

Falch, M., & Anyimadu, A. (2003). Tele-centres as a way of achieving universal access: the case of Ghana. *Telecommunications Policy*, *27*(1-2), 21–39. doi:10.1016/S0308-5961(02)00092-7

Fals Borda, O. (1988). *Knowledge and People's Power*. Delhi: Indian Social Institute.

Ferlander, S. (2003). *The Internet, Social Capital and Local Community*. PhD Thesis, University of Sterling. Retrieved July 23, 2004 from http://www.crdlt.stir.ac.uk/Docs/ SaraFerlanderPhD.pdf

Fernandes, L. (2006). *India's New Middle Class: Democratic Politics in an Era of Economic Reform*. Minneapolis, USA: Univ. of Minnesota Press.

Ferraz, C., Fonseca, R., Pal, J., & Shah, M. (2004). Computing for social inclusion in Brazil: a study of the CDI and other initiatives. Berkeley: University of California, Berkeley. Retrieved on March 23, 2008, from http://bridge.berkeley.edu/2005_Pages/ pdfs/cdi_Brazil_report.pdf

Field, J. (2003). *Social Capital*. London, UK: Routledge.

Fillip, B., & Foote, D. (2007). *Making the Connection: Scaling Telecenters for Development*. Washington, D.C.: Academy for Education Development.

Finfacts; Ireland's Business and Financial Portal (2009). Pay in Europe in 2006 – The Gap in European Pay. Retrieved April 20, 2010 from http://www.finfacts.ie/Private/isl/Payin Europe.htm

Fitzgerald, J. (2007). *Big White Lie. Chinese Australians in White Australia*. Sydney: University of New South Wales Press.

Fladrich, A. (2009). The Chinese Labour Market and Job Mobility in Prato. In Johanson, G., Smyth, R., & French, R. (Eds.), *Living Outside the Walls: The Chinese in Prato* (pp. 96–128). Newcastle upon Tyne: Cambridge Scholars Publishing.

Fladrich, A. (2010). Email communication with G. Johanson. 26 March.

Flatters, F., & MacLeod, W. B. (1995). Administrative Corruption and Taxation. *International Tax and Public Finance*, *2*, 397–417. doi:10.1007/BF00872774

Flick, U. (2006). *An Introduction to Qualitative Research*. London: Sage.

Forrest, R., & Kearns, A. (2001). Social Cohesion, Social Capital and the Neighbourhood. *Urban Studies (Edinburgh, Scotland)*, *38*(12), 2125–2143. doi:10.1080/00420980120087081

Fortier, F. (2003). Sustainable Rural Networking, Community Ownership and Appropriate Technologies. Retrieved January 1, 2010 from http://www.ecissurf.org/database/actions/getFile.cfm?DocumentID=2634 or http://www.peoplefirst.net.sb/Downloads/FortierSustainableRural-Net2003-0

Fortunati, L., Manganelli, A. M., & Law, P. L. (2008). Beijing Calling… Mobile Communication in Contemporary China. *Knowledge Technology and Policy*, *21*, 19–27. doi:10.1007/s12130-008-9040-1

Fox, N. (1998). How to use observation in a research project [Online]. *Trend Focus Group*. Retrieved November 2003 from http://www.trentfocus.org.uk/resources/how%20to%20use%20observations.pdf

Fraser, C., & Restrepo-Estrada, S. (2002). Community Radio for Change and Development. *Development*, *45*(4), 69–73. doi:10.1057/palgrave.development.1110408

French, W.L., & Bell Jr, C.H. (1978). Action research and organization development. *Organizational Diagnosis: A Workbook of Theory and Practice*, 69.

Friend, J. (1998). Managing Development Projects and Programmes: Fresh Perspectives towards an Action Research Agenda, Working Paper. No. 21, School of Management, University of Lincolnshire and Humberside.

Fullilove, M. (2008) *World wide webs: diasporas and the international system*. Lowy Institute Paper 22. Retrieved April 20, 2010 from http://www.lowyinstitute.org/ Publication.asp?pid=753

G8. (2000). Okinawa Charter on Global Information Society. Retrieved on the 5th of August 2004 from http://www.mofa.go.jp/policy/economy /summit/2000/documents/charter.html.

Gabe, T. M., & Abel, J. R. (2002). Deployment of Advanced Telecommunications Infrastructure in Rural America: Measuring the Digital Divide. *American Journal of Agricultural Economics*, *84*(5), 1246–1252. doi:10.1111/1467-8276.00385

Galperin, H., & Bar, F. (2006). The microtelco opportunity: evidence from Latin America. *Information Technologies and International Development*, *3*(2), 73–86. doi:10.1162/itid.2007.3.2.73

Galperin, H., & Girard, B. (2005). Digital poverty: Latin American and Caribbean perspectives. In H. Galperin & J. Mariscal (Eds.). *Digital poverty: Latin American and Caribbean perspectives* (pp. 93-115). Ottawa: IDRC, 93-115.

Garcia, D. L., & Gorenflo, N. R. (1998). Rural networking cooperatives: lessons for international development and aid strategies. In *The first mile of connectivity*. Rome, Italy: Food and Agriculture Organisation of the United Nations. http://www.fao.org/WAICENT/FAOINFO/SUSTDEV/Cddirect/Cdre0033.html Last accessed in April 2000

Gardner, K., & Lewis, D. (1996). *Anthropology, Development and the Post-Modern Challenge*. London: Pluto.

Gardner, K., & Lewis, D. (2005). Beyond Development? In Edelman, M., & Haugerud, A. (Eds.), *The Anthropology of Development and Globalization: From classical Political Economy to Contemporary Neoliberalism*. Blackwell Publishing.

Gasco, M. (2003). New Technologies and Institutional Change in Public Administration. *Social Science Computer Review*, *21*(1), 6–14. doi:10.1177/0894439302238967

Gates, B. (2008). How to fix capitalism. *Time*, *172*(6), 24–29.

Geertz, C. (1973). *Description of Cultures*. New York: Springer.

Gereffi, G. (1999). International Trade and Industrial Upgrading in the Apparel Commodity Chain. *Journal of International Economics*, *48*(1), 37–70. doi:10.1016/S0022-1996(98)00075-0

Gereffi, G., & Kaplinsky, R. (Eds.). (2001). The Value of Value Chains. *IDS Bulletin*, *32*(3), 1–136. doi:10.1111/j.1759-5436.2001.mp32003001.x

Gereffi, G., & Korzeniewicz, M. (Eds.). (1994). *Commodity Chains and Global Capitalism*. Westport, CT: Praeger.

Gergen, K. J. (2001). *Social construction in context*. London: Sage Publications.

Gerster, R., & Zimmermann, S. (2003). *Information and communication technologies (ICTs) for poverty reduction?* Bern: Swiss Agency for Development Cooperation.

Gerster, R., & Zimmermann, S. (2003). *Information and Communication Technologies and Poverty Reduction in Sub-Saharan Africa*. Richterswil: Gerster Consulting.

Giddens, A. (1984). *The Constitution of Society: Outline of the Theory of Structuration*. Cambridgeshire, UK: Polity Press.

Giddens, A. (1987). *Social theory and modern sociology*. Stanford University Press.

Gillwald, A. (2005). A closing window of opportunity: Under-Serviced Area Licensing in South Africa. *Information Technologies and International Development*, *2*(4), 1–19. doi:10.1162/154475205775249364

Girard, B. (2003). Radio and the Internet: Mixing media to bridge the divide. In Girard, B. (Ed.), *The One to Watch: Radio, new ICTs and interactivity* (pp. 2–20). Rome: FAO.

Glaser, B. G. (1992). *Basics of Grounded Theory Analysis*. Mill Valley, CA: Sociology Press.

Glaser, B. G., & Strauss, A. L. (1967). *The Discovery of Grounded Theory: Strategies for Qualitative Research*. Chicago, IL: Aldine Pub.

Goggan, G. (2008). Cultural Studies of mobile Communication. In Katz, J. E. (Ed.), *Handbook of Mobile Communication Studies* (pp. 353–366). Cambridge, MA: MIT Press.

Goh, B. L. (2002). Rethinking Modernity: State, Ethnicity, and class in the Forging of a Modern Urban Malaysia. In in C.J.W.-L. Wee (Ed.), *Local Cultures and the New Asia. The Society, Culture and Capitalism in Southeast Asia*. Singapore: Institute of Southeast Asian Studies.

Gómez, R., & Martínez, J. (2001). *The Internet... Why? And what for? Thoughts on information and communication technologies for development in Latin America and the Caribbean*. San José, Costa Rica: International Development Research Centre and Fundación Acceso.

Gómez, R., Hunt, P., & Lamoureux, E. (1999). Telecentre Evaluation and Research: A global perspective. In Gómez, R., & Hunt, P. (Eds.), *Telecentre Evaluation: A global perspective* (pp. 15–29). Ottawa: International Development Research Centre.

González, R. (n.d). *The need for Local Content. Paris: UNESCO Communication and Information Portal*. Retrieved April 14, 2007, from http://portal.unesco.org/ci/en/ev.php-URL_ID=5463&URL_DO=DO_TOPIC&URL_SECTION=201.html

Government of Malaysia. (1997). *Digital Signature Act 1997 (Act 562)*. Kuala Lumpur, Malaysia: Percetakan Nasional Malaysia Berhad.

Government of Malaysia. (1998). *Communications and Multimedia Act 1998 (Act 588)*. Kuala Lumpur, Malaysia: Percetakan Nasional Malaysia Berhad.

Government of Malaysia. (2001b). *The Third Outline Perspective Plan 2001-2010*. Retrieved May 20, 2004 from www.epu.jpm.my/Bi/dev_plan/opp3.htm

Government of Malaysia. (2006). *The Ninth Malaysia Plan 2006-2010*. Kuala Lumpur, Malaysia: Percetakan Nasional Malaysia Berhad.

Graham, S. (2002). Bridging Urban Divides? Urban Polarisation and Information and Communications Technologies (ICTs). *Urban Studies (Edinburgh, Scotland)*, *39*(1), 33–56. doi:10.1080/00420980220099050

Granovetter, M. S. (1973). The Strength of Weak Ties. *American Journal of Sociology*, *78*(6), 1360–1380. doi:10.1086/225469

Gray, J. (2010). *Gray's anatomy. Selected writings*. London: Penguin Books.

Green, N. (2009, March 31). Govt key to lower internet prices. *The Phnom Penh Post*. Retrieved on April 1, 2009, from http://www.phnompenhpost.com/index.php/Special-Supplements/Govt-key-to-lower-internet-prices.html

Greenbaum, J., & Kyng, M. (Eds.). (1991). *Design at Work: Cooperative design of computer systems*. Hillsdale, NJ: Lawrence Erlbaum Associates.

Greenbaum, J., & Madsen, K. (1993). Small Changes: Starting a Participatory Design Process by Giving Participants a Voice. In Schuler, D., & Namioka, A. (Eds.), *Participatory Design: Principles and Practices*. Hillside, N.J.: Lawrence Erlbaum Associates.

Greenhill, K. (2009). Why Learning about Emerging Technologies is Part of Every Librarian's Job. Peer reviewed paper presented at Educause Australiasia. Retrieved 22 August 2008 from http://librariansmatter.com/published/EducauseAustralia09/ GreenhillEmergingTechReasonsRevised.doc.

Grillo, R. D. (1997). Discourses of Development: The View from Anthropology. In Grillo, R.D & R.L. Stirrat (Eds.), *Discourses of Development: Anthropological Perspectives* (pp. 1-33). New York: Berg.

Grootaert, C., Narayanan, D., Jones, V. N., & Woolcock, M. (2003). *Measuring Social Capital: An Integated Questionnaire*. World Bank Working Paper No. 18.

Grunfeld, H., Hak, S., Long, D., Tara, P., Dara, S., Chanda, P., et al. (2009, April). What Villagers think of iREACH, Report on participatory evaluation conducted in February 2009. Retrieved on April 29, 2009 from http://www.idrc.ca/uploads/user-S/12410151941 What_villagers_think_of_iREACH_-_Report_on_participatory_evaluation_conducted_in_February_2009l.pdf

Grupo de Accíon Digital. (2004). *Agenda Digital - Chile 2004-2006. Te Acerca el Futuro*. Santiago: Report by the Grupo de Acción Digital.

Guijt, I., & Shah, M. K. (Eds.). (1998). *The Myth of Community: Gender Issues in Participatory Development.* London: Intermediate Technology Publications.

Guild, R. (2003). *Digital Review of Asia Pacific 2003: Pacific Islands.* APDIP. In Hammond, A. L., Jenkins, E., Kramer, W. J., & Paul, J. H. (Eds.), *Learning from the Poor: a bottom-up approach to development.* World Resources Institute.

Gumucio-Dagrón, A. (2001). *Making Waves: Stories of Participatory Communication for Social Change.* New York: Rockefeller Foundation.

Gumucio-Dagrón, A. (2003). Take Five: A handful of essentials for ICTs in development. In Girard, B. (Ed.), *The One to Watch: Radio, new ICTs and interactivity* (pp. 21–38). Rome: FAO.

Gupta, P., & Bagga, R. K. (Eds.). (2008). *Compendium of eGovernance Initiatives in India.* Hyderabad: Universities Press.

Gurstein, M. (1999). *Community Informatics: Enabling the Community Use of Information and Communications Technologies.* Hershey, PA: Idea Group Publishing.

Gurstein, M. (2000). Community Informatics: Enabling Community Use of Information and Communication Technology. In Gurstein, M. (Ed.), *Community Informatics: Enabling Communities with Information and Communications Technologies* (pp. 1–32). Idea Group Publishing.

Gurstein, M. (2001). Rural Development and Food Security, A "Community Informatics" Based Conceptual Framework. In *Proceedings of the 34th Hawaii International Conference on System Sciences.* Hawaii: IEEE Computer Society.

Gurstein, M. (2003). Effective Use: A community informatics strategy beyond the digital divide. *First Monday, 8*(12). Retrieved February 3, 2009, from http://firstmonday.org/htbin/cgiwrap/bin/ojs/ index.php/fm/article/viewArticle/1107/1027

Gush, K. (2004). *Open Source and the Digital Doorway.* Paper presented at the Idlelo Conference, Cape Town, January 2004.

Gush, K. (2008). Towards a more personalised user experience and better demographic data on the Digital Doorway public computer terminals. *5th Prato Community Informatics & Development Informatics Conference 2008: ICTs for Social Inclusion: What is the Reality?* Conference CD. 27 October-30 October, Monash Centre, Prato Italy. December 2008. Editors: Larry Stillman, Graeme Johanson

Gush, K., Smith, R., & Cambridge, G. (2004). *The Digital Doorway, Minimally Invasive Education in Africa.* Paper presented at the ICT In Education Conference, Cape Town, March 2004.

Hab, H. (2009, March 24). More mobile firms due to enter market. *The Phnom Penh Post.* Retrieved on March 25, 2009, from:http://www.phnompenhpost.com/index.php/2009032424958/Business/More-mobile-firms-due-to-enter-market.html

Habing, B. (2003). *Exploratory Factor Analysis.* Retrieved January 12, 2006 from www.stat.sc.edu/~habing/courses/530EFA.pdf

Hacker, K. L. (2000). *Divide Facts and Fictions Digital.* Retrieved July 6, 2003 from http://khacker2. freeyellow. com/ddnow6.htm

Haddon, L. (2005). Introduction. In Haddon, L. (Ed.), *Everyday Innovators* (pp. 1–16). Dordrecht: Springer. doi:10.1007/1-4020-3872-0_1

Hair, J. F., Anderson, R. E., Tatham, R. L., & Black, W. C. (1998). *Multivariate Data Analysis* (5th Ed.). Prentice Hall. Hampton, K.N., & Wellman, B. (2000). Examining Community in the Digital Neighborhood: Early Results from Canada's Wired Suburb. In T. Ishida & K. Isbister (Eds.), *Digital Cities: Technologies, Experiences, and Future Perspectives* (LNCS 1765, pp. 194-208).

Hammond, A. L. (2001). Digitally Empowered Development. *Foreign Affairs (Council on Foreign Relations), 80*(2), 96–106.

Hanseth, O., & Braa, K. (2000). Globalization and "Risk Society". In Ciborra, C. (Ed.), *From Control to Drift - the Dynamics of Corporate Information Infrastructures* (pp. 41–55). Oxford: Oxford University Press.

Harper, R., & Kelly, M. (2003). *Measuring Social Capital in the United Kingdom*. Retrieved January 19, 2005 from www.statistics.gov.uk/socialcapital/ downloads/ harmonisation_stere_5.pdf

Harris, R. W. (1999). Rural Information Technology for Sarawak's Development. *Sarawak Development Journal*, *2*(1), 72–84.

Harris, R. W., Bala, P., Songan, P., & Khoo, G. L. (2001). Challenges and Opportunities in Introducing Information and Communication Technologies to the Kelabit Community of North Central Borneo. *New Media & Society*, *3*(3), 271–296. doi:10.1177/14614440122226092

Harris, R. W. (2004). *Information and communications technologies for poverty alleviation*. Kuala Lumpur: UNDP-APDIP.

Harris, R. (2001). Telecentres in Rural Asia: Towards a Success Model. *Conference Proceedings of International Conference on Information Technology, Communications and Development* (ITCD 2001), November 23-3-, Katmandu, Nepal. Retrieved May 24, 2006 from http://unpanl.un.org/introdoc/groups/ public/documents/APC-ITY/UNPA C006304.pdf

Harris, R. (2007). Telecentre sustainability: financing ICTs for the poor. *APDIP e-Note 15*, Retrieved September 9, 2007, from http://www.apdip.net/apdipenote/

Harris, R., & Rajora, R. (2006). Empowering the Poor: Information and Communications Technology for Governance and Poverty Reduction - A Study of Rural Development Projects in India. UNDP-APDIP: Elsevier.

Harrisson, T. (1959). *World Within: A Borneo Story*. Singapore: Oxford University Press.

Harvey, D. (2005). *A Brief History of Neoliberalism*. Oxford: Oxford University Press.

Heeks, R. (2002). i-Development not e-Development: Special Issue on ICTs and Development. *Journal of International Development*, *14*, 1–11. doi:10.1002/jid.861

Heeks, R. (2000). The Approach of Senior Public Officials to Information Technology Related Reform: Lessons from India. *Public Administration and Development*, *20*(3), 197–205. doi:10.1002/1099-162X(200008)20:3<197::AID-PAD109>3.0.CO;2-6

Heeks, R. (2002a). i-Development not e-Development: Special Issue on ICTs and Development. *Journal of International Development*, *14*(1), 1–11. doi:10.1002/jid.861

Heeks, R. (2002b). Information Systems and Developing Countries: Failure, Success and Local Improvisations. *The Information Society*, *18*, 101–112. doi:10.1080/01972240290075039

Heeks, R. (2005). eGovernment as a Carrier of Context. *Journal of Public Policy*, *25*(1), 51–74. doi:10.1017/S0143814X05000206

Heeks, R. (2006). *Implementing and Managing eGovernment – An International Text*. New Delhi: Vistar Publications.

Heeks, R. (2002). Information systems and developing countries: Failure, success, and local improvisations. *The Information Society*, *18*, 101–112. doi:10.1080/01972240290075039

Heeks, R., & Bhatnagar, S. C. (1999). Understanding Success and Failure in Information Age Reform. In Heeks, R. (Ed.), *Reinventing Government in the Information Age: International Practice in IT enabled public sector reform*. London: Routledge. doi:10.4324/9780203204962

Heeks, R. (1998a). *Information Technology and Public Sector Corruption* (Working Paper 4). Institute for Development Policy Management, University of Manchester.

Heeks, R. (1998b). *Information Age Reform of the Public Sector: The Potential and Problems of IT for India* (Information Systems for Public Sector Management Working Paper Series Paper No. 6). IDPM, University of Manchester.

Heeks, R. (1999). *Information and Communication Technologies, Poverty and Development. Development Informatics: Working Papers, Institute for Development Policy and Management, University of Manchester*. Retrieved December 12, 2008, from http://www.sed. manchester.ac.uk/i dpm/research/publications/wp/di/

Heeks, R. (2002). Failure, Success and Improvisation of Information Systems Projects in Developing Countries. *Development Informatics, Working Paper Series - No 11*. Retrieved Feb 2, 2009, from http://www.sed.manchester. ac.uk/id pm/research/publications/ wp/di/di_wp11.htm

Heeks, R. (2003). *Most eGovernment-for-Development Projects Fail: How Can the Risks be Reduced?* (iGovernment Working Paper Series – Paper No. 14), University of Manchester.

Heeks, R. (2003a). Most eGovernment-for-Development Projects Fail: How can Risks be Reduced? (I-Government Working Paper No. 14) Manchester, UK: University of Manchester: Institute for Development Policy and Management.

Heeks, R. (2005). *Sustainability and the Future of eDevelopment*. Retrieved February 7, 2008, from http://www. sed.manchester. ac.uk/idpm/publications /wp/di/short/ DIGBriefing10Sustain.doc.

Hendry, J. (2005). *Reclaiming Culture: Indigenous People and Self-Representation*. New York: Palgrave MacMillan.

Herron, R. E., & Sutton-Smith, B. (Eds.). (1971). *Child's Play*. New York: John Wiley and Sons.

Hietanen, O. (2002). Indicators of Sustainable Development. Finnish Society for Future Studies. *Futura, 21*(2), 6-7.

Hindriks, J., Keen, M., & Muthoo, A. (1999). Corruption, Extortion and Evasion. *Journal of Public Economics, 74*, 395–430. doi:10.1016/S0047-2727(99)00030-4

Holvast, J., Duquenoy, P., & Whitehouse, D. (2005). The Information Society and its Consequences: Lessons from the Past. In Berleur, J., & Avgerou, C. (Eds.), *Perspectives and Policies on ICT in Society* (pp. 135–152). New York: Springer. doi:10.1007/0-387-25588-5_10

Holwell, S. E. (1997). *Soft systems methodology and its Role in Information Systems*. Unpublished PhD thesis, Lancaster University, Lancaster.

Homer-Dixon, T. (2000). *The ingenuity gap*. New York: Knopf.

Hopkins, D. (1985). *A teacher's guide to classroom research*. Philadelphia: Open University Press.

Hopkins, M. (1999). Training Needs in Vietnam with Related Labour Market and Methodological Issues, Monograph prepared for Ashton Brown Associates, ADB TA 3063-VIE: Capacity Building in Vocational and Technical Education Project.

Hoskins, J. (1987). The headhunter as hero: local traditions and their reinterpretation in national history. *American Ethnologist, 14*(4), 605–622. doi:10.1525/ ae.1987.14.4.02a00010

http://www.nber.org/papers/w11416.pdf, last accessed March 2010

Hudson, E., & Kenyon, A. T. (2005). *Copyright and Cultural Institutions: Short Guidelines for Digitisation*. Melbourne: Centre for Media and Communications Law, University of Melbourne Faculty of Law and the Intellectual Property Research Institute of Australia.

Hudson, E. (2006). Cultural Institutions, Law and Indigenous Knowledge: A Legal Primer on the Management of Australian Indigenous Collections. Intellectual Property Research Institute of Australia, the University of Melbourne, Melbourne.

Hughes, M., & Dallwitz, J. (2007). Towards Culturally Appropriate IT Best Practice in Remote Indigenous Australia. In Dyson, Henriks, & Grant, (Eds.), *Information technology and Indigenous people*. University of Technology Sydney, Sydney.

Huque, A. S. (1994). Public Administration in India: Evolution, Change and Reform. *Asian Journal of Public Administration, 16*(2), 249–259.

Hurworth, R. (2003). *Photo-interviewing for research. Social Research Update, 40*. Department of Sociology University of Surrey.

IAD. (2002). *Central Australian Aboriginal Languages – current distribution. Map produced by the Institute for Aboriginal Development Press*. Alice Springs.

IDC Market Research. (n.d.). *Malaysia Internet Market*. Retrieved August 12, 2003 from http://www.idc.com.my/

ILO (International Labour Organisation). (2002). Labour Market policies and poverty reduction strategies in recovery from the Asian Crisis: Report of the ILO – Japan – Government of Indonesia sub-regional seminar, Jakarta, Indonesia 29 April to 1st May 2002.

ILO (International Labour Organisation). (2008). *Vocational training and productivity*. Montevideo: ILO/ Cinterfor.

INEI. (2006a). Banco de Información Distrital. Retrieved June 30, 2006 from http://www.inei.gob.pe

INEI. (2006b). Perú en Cifras. Retrieved on June 20, 2006 from http://www.inei.gob.pe.

InfoDev Survey of ICT Education in Africa. (2006). Retrieved January 2009 from http://www.infodev.org/ en/Project.7.html

Institute for Rural Advancement. (1995). *Philosophy and Strategy of Rural Development towards the Year 2020*. Institute for Rural Advancement.

Institute of Strategic and International Studies (ISIS). (2002). *Knowledge-Based Economy Master Plan*. ISIS Malaysia.

Intel Teach Program – South Africa Case Study, (2006). Retrieved January 2009 from http://download.intel.com/ pressroom/kits/education/teach/SouthAfrica-IntelTeach-Program.pdf

International Development Research Centre (IDRC) (2003). *Opportunities and Challenges for Community Development: Information and Communication Technologies for Development in Africa* (Vol. 1). Jointly published by Ottawa: IDRC and Dakar: Council for the Development of Social Science Research in Africa (CODESRIA).

International Development Research Centre (IDRC). (2005). Learning from IDRC-Supported Rural ICT Projects in Asia. *International Development Research Centre*. Retrieved Mar 14, 2005, from http://web.idrc. ca/en/ev-67344-201 -1 -DO_TOPIC.html

International Institute for Management Development (IMD). (2003). *The World Competitiveness Scoreboard 2003*. Retrieved July 21, 2003 from http://www01.imd. ch/documents/ wcy/ content/ ranking.pdf

International Telecommunication Union (ITU). (2003). *World Telecommunication Development Report 2003: Access Indicators for Information Society*. Geneva: World Summit on the Information Society.

International Telecommunications Union (ITU). (2006). Telecommunication Development Report: ICT Statistics. Retrieved July 2006 from http://www.itu.org/statistics

IOM (International Office of Migration). (2008). *Developing Migration Policy; Diaspora and Development*. Retrieved April 20, 2010 from http://www.iom.int/jahia/ Jahia/pid/539.

Ismawati, N.J., & Ainin, S. (2003). Bridging the Digital Divide in Malaysia: A Review of ICT Programs and Initiatives. *The International Journal of Knowledge, Culture and Change Management, 3*.

ITU – International Telecommunication Union. (2007). Retrieved on January 16, 2008, from http://www.itu. int/ITU-D/ict /publications/ict-oi/2007/material/table1. html#low

ITU – International Telecommunication Union. (2009). *Measuring the information society: the ICT Development Index*. Geneva: International Telecommunications Union.

Jackson, L. A., Barbatsis, G., von Eye, A., Biocca, F., Zhao, Y., & Fitzgerald, H. (2003). Internet Use in Low-Income Families: Implications for the Digital Divide. *IT&Society, 1*(5), 141–165.

Jacucci, E., Hanseth, O., & Lyytinen, K. (2006). Introduction - taking complexity seriously in IS research. *Information Technology & People, 19*(1), 5–11. doi:10.1108/09593840610649943

Jaeger, P.T., Bertot, J.C., McClure, C., & Rodriguez, M. (2007). Public Libraries and Internet Access across the United States: A Comparison by State, 2004-2006. *Information technology and Libraries, 26*(2), 4-14.

Jalal, J. (2005). Good Practices in Public Sector Reform: A Few Examples from Two Indian Cities. In Singh, A. (Ed.), *Administrative Reforms: Towards Sustainable Practices* (pp. 96–116). New Delhi: Sage Publications.

James, J. (2004). *Information Technology and Development: A new paradigm for delivering the Internet to rural areas in developing countries*. London: Routledge. doi:10.4324/9780203325506

Jaramillo, O., & Castellon, L. (2002). *Telecentros, Usuarios y Apropiación de las TICs*. Santiago: Universidad Diego Portales.

Jarus, O. (2010). 'Ambassador or slave? Researchers Mystified by East Asian Skeleton Discovered in Vagnari Cemetery'. *The Independent*. Retrieved April 20, 2010 from http://www.independent.co.uk/news/ science/archaeology/news/ambassador-or-slave-east-asian-skeleton-discovered-in-vagnari-roman-cemetery-1879551.htm.

Jayasuriya, R. (1999). Managing Health Information Systems for Health Services in a Developing Country: a case study using a contextualist framework. *International Journal of Information Management, 19*, 335–349. doi:10.1016/S0268-4012(99)00031-6

Johanson, G. (2008). Flicking the Switch: Social Networks and the Role of Information and Communications Technologies in Social Cohesion among Chinese and Italians in Melbourne, Australia. In The *Role of New Technologies in Global Societies; Theoretical Reflections, Practical Concerns, and Its Implications for China. Conference Proceedings 30–31 July 2008* (pp. 118-127). Department of Applied Social Sciences, Hong Kong Polytechnic University.

Kane, T., Holmes, K. R., & O'Grady, M. A. (2007). *2007 Index of Economic Freedom*. Washington, D.C.: The Heritage Foundation.

Katz, J. E. (2006). *Magic in the Air: Mobile Communication and the Transformation of Social Life*. New Brunswick, NJ: Transaction Publishers.

Katz, J. E. (2008). Mainstreamed Mobiles in Daily Life: Perspective and Prospects. In Katz, J. E. (Ed.), *Handbook of Mobile Communication Studies* (pp. 433–445). Cambridge, MA: MIT Press.

Katz, J. E., & Aakhus, M. A. (2002). Conclusion: making meaning of mobiles – a theory of Apparatgeist. In Katz, J. E., & Aaakhus, M. A. (Eds.), *Perpetual Contact: Mobile Communication, Private Talk, Public Performance* (pp. 301–318). New York: Cambridge University Press. doi:10.1017/CBO9780511489471.023

Keeble, L., & Loader, B. D. (2001). *Challenging the Digital Divide? A Preliminary Review of Online Community Support*. CIRA, University of Teesside. Retrieved October 31, 2003 from www.cira.org.uk/downloads/ Rowntrees %20Report.shtml

Kelly, A. E. (2003). Research as design. *Educational Researcher, 32*(1), 3–5, 35–37. doi:10.3102/0013189X032001003

Keniston, K. (2002). *IT for the Common Man. Lessons from India. The Second M N Srinivas Memorial Lecture. NIAS Special Publication SP 7 – 02*. Bangalore: National Institute of Advanced Studies.

Kenny, C. (2003). The Internet and Economic Growth in Less-Developed Countries: A Case of Managing Expectations? *Oxford Development Studies, 31*(1), 99–113. doi:10.1080/1360081032000047212

Keohane, R. O., & Nye, J. S. (2002). Power and Interdependence in the Information Age. In Kamarck, E. C., & Nye, J. S. Jr., (Eds.), *Governance.com: Democracy in the Information Age* (pp. 161–177). Washington, D.C.: Brookings Institution Press.

Khan, H. A. (1998). *Technology, Development and Democracy: Limits of National Innovation Systems in the Age of Post-Modernism*. Cheltenham, UK & Northampton, USA: Edward Elgar.

King, V. (1999). *Anthropology and Development in Southeast Asia: Theory and Practice*. Kuala Lumpur: Oxford University Press.

King, J. J., & Kraemer, K. L. (1997). Computer and communication technologies: Impacts on the organization of enterprise and the establishment and maintenance of civil society. In *National Research Council, Computer Science and Telecommunications Board, Fostering Research on the Economic and Social Impacts of Information Technology* (pp. 188–210). USA: National Academy Press.

Kingdom of Cambodia. Law on Commune. (2001). Retrieved on April 7, 2009, from http://www.interior.gov.kh/other_doc.asp?id_doc=1

Kirat, T., & Lung, Y. (1999). Innovation and proximity: territories as loci of collective learning processes. *European Urban and Regional Studies*, *6*(1), 27–38. doi:10.1177/096977649900600103

Kirby, J. R., Knapper, C. K., Maki, S. A., Egnatoff, W. J., & Van Melle, E. (2002). Computers and Students' Conceptions of Learning: The Transition from Post-Secondary Education to the Workplace. *Journal of Educational Technology & Society*, *5*(5), 47–55.

Klein, H. K., & Myers, M. D. (1999). A Set of Principles for Conducting and Evaluating Interpretive Field Studies in Information Systems. *Management Information Systems Quarterly*, *23*(1), 67–88. doi:10.2307/249410

Klein, M. (2009, March 15). Cell C and Telkom to join forces? *Business Times*. Retrieved December 2009 from http://mybroadband.co.za/news/Telecoms/7320.html.

Kleine, D. (2007). *Empowerment and the Limits of Choice: Microentrepreneurs, Information and Communication Technologies and State Policies in Chile*. Unpublished PhD thesis, Department of Geography and Environment. London: London School of Economics and Political Science.

Kling, R. (2000). Learning about information technologies and social change: The contribution of social informatics. *The Information Society*, *16*(3), 217–232. doi:10.1080/01972240050133661

Kootstra, G. J. (2004). *Exploratory Factor Analysis: Theory and Application. Retrieved January 12, 2006 from odur.let.rug.nl/~nerbonne/teach/rema_stats_meth-seminar/Factor_analysis_kootrstra_04*. PDF.

Korpela, M., Soriyan, H. A., Olufokunbi, K. C., Onayade, A. A., Davies-Adetugbo, A., & Adesanmi, D. (1998). Community Participation in Health Informatics in Africa: An Experiment in Tripartite Partnership in Ile-Ife, Nigeria. [CSCW]. *Computer Supported Cooperative Work*, *7*(3-4), 339–358. doi:10.1023/A:1008695307062

Koskela, L., & Howell, G. (2002). The underlying theory of project management is obsolete. *Conference Proceedings of the 2002 PMI Conference, Seattle,* Project Management Institute.

Kral, I. (2008, November). *Literacy and remote Indigenous youth: Why social practice matters*. Presented at ANU seminar, Canberra.

Kumar, R., & Best, M. L. (2006). Impact and Sustainability of E-Government Services in Developing Countries: Lessons Learned from Tamil Nadu, India. *The Information Society*, *22*, 1–12. doi:10.1080/01972240500388149

Kumar, R. (2004). *Social, Governance, and Economic Impact Assessment of Information and Communication Technology Interventions in Rural India*. Unpublished MCP Thesis, Massachusetts Institute of Technology, Cambridge, MA.

Kumar, R. (2007). Making e-government projects in developing countries more successful and sustainable: lessons from two case studies from India. *Information technology in developing countries, 17*(3). (IFIP Working Group 9.4).

Kuriyan, R., Ray, I., & Toyama, K. (2008). Information and communication technologies for development: the bottom of the pyramid model in practice. *The Information Society*, *24*(2), 93–104. doi:10.1080/01972240701883948

Kynge, J. (2006). *China Shakes the World; the Rise of a Hungry Nation*. London: Weidenfeld & Nicolson.

Lakire, S., & Santos, M. E. (2010). *Acute Multidimensional poverty: A new index for developing countries. OPHI Working Paper 38*. Oxford University. Retrieved August 2010 from http://www.ophi.org.uk/wp-content/uploads/ophi-wp38.pdf.

Lall, S. (2000). Technological Change and Industrialization in the Asian Newly Industrializing Economies: Achievements and Challenges. In Kim, L., & Nelson, R. R. (Eds.), *Technology, learning, and Innovation. Experiences of Newly Industrializing Economies* (pp. 13–68). Cambridge: Cambridge University Press.

Lamoureux, E. (1999). RadioNet: Community Radio, Telecentres and Local Development. In R. Gómez, R. & P. Hunt (Eds.), *Telecentre Evaluation: A Global Perspective* (pp. 195-202). Ottawa: International Development Research Centre.

Lamoureux, M. (1999). Monograph: National policies for VTE in Lao PDR, ADB TA 2925 LAO.

Langton, M., & Ma Rhea, Z. (2003). *Traditional lifestyles and biodiversity use regional report: Australia, Asia and the middle east. Composite report on the status and trends regarding the knowledge, innovations and practices of indigenous and local communities relevant to the conservation and sustainable use of biodiversity. Prepared for the secretariat of the convention on biological diversity.* Geneva: UNEP.

Larsen, K. L. (1998). Discourses on development in Malaysia. In Abram, S., & Waldren, J. (Eds.), *Anthropological Perspectives on Local Development: Knowledge and Sentiments in Conflict. The European Association of Social Anthropologist.* London, New York: Routledge. doi:10.4324/9780203451021_chapter_2

Laudon, K. C., & Laudon, J. P. (2004). *Management Information Systems: Managing the Digital Firm* (8th ed.). Prentice Hall.

Law, P., & Peng, Y. (2006). The Use of Mobile Phones among Migrant Workers in Southern China. In Law, P., Fortunati, L., & Yang, S. (Eds.), *New technologies in global societies* (pp. 245–258). Singapore: World Scientific. doi:10.1142/9789812773555_0011

Lawley, D. N., & Maxwell, A. E. (1971). *Factor Analysis as a Statistical Method.* London: Butterworths.

Ledgerwood, D., & Kernaghan, T. (1998). Monograph: Developing training materials for short term skills development, ADB TA 2925 LAO.

Lee, J.-W. (2001). Education for Technology Readiness: Prospects for Developing Countries. *Journal of Human Development, 2*(1), 115–151. doi:10.1080/14649880120050

Lee, P. S. N., Leung, L., Lo, V., & Xiong, C. (2007). The Perceived Role of ICTs in Quality of Life in Three Chinese Cities. *Social Indicators Research, 88*(3), 457–476. doi:10.1007/s11205-007-9214-3

Leeming, D. (2003). *Challenges for Sustainable Rural Networking in Solomon Islands.* Round Table on Science for Developing Countries, Abdus Salam Centre (ICTP), Trieste, Italy, Oct 2003.

Leeming, D. (2003). *Education through Wireless Networking in Solomon Islands.* Paper presented at the Asia Media Information and Communications Centre AMIC. 12th Annual Meeting, Singapore, November 2003.

Leeming, D. (2003). Input Paper for the Solomon Islands People First Network, paper presented at the World Summit on the Information Society, Tokyo Regional Meeting, January 2003.

Leeming, D. (2003). Success *Factors for the Solomon Islands People First Network.* Global Knowledge Partnership AGM, Rome, May 2003, downloadable at www.peoplefirst.net.sb/general/PFnet.htm

Leeming, D., & Baliki, R. (2003). *Final report People First Network, the Solomon Islands' Rural E-mail networks for Peace and Development* (Interim Assistance Project SOI/02/004). Retrieved January 1, 2010 from http://www.undp.org.fj/documents/ICT4DEV/PFnet_Final_Report.pdf

Legrain, P. (2002). *Open World: The Truth About Globalisation.* London: Abacus.

Lenhart, A., & Horrigan, J. B. (2003). Re-Visualizing the Digital Divide as a Digital Spectrum. *IT&Society*, *1*(5), 23–39.

Lewin, K. (2004). Action research and minority problems. *Fundamentals of Action Research*, *2*, 19.

Lewin, K. M. (2000). New Technologies and Knowledge Acquisition and Use in Developing Countries. *Compare*, *30*(3), 313–321. doi:10.1080/713657464

Lewis, A. (1982). *The Psychology of Taxation*. Oxford: Martin Robertson & Company.

Leydesdorff, L. (2000). The Triple Helix: An Evolutionary Model of Innovations. *Research Policy*, *29*(2), 243–255. doi:10.1016/S0048-7333(99)00063-3

Liloqula, R. (2000). Understanding the conflict in the Solomon Islands as a practical means to peacemaking. *Development Bulletin (Canberra)*, *53*, 41–43.

Lin, A., & Tong, A. (2008). Mobile cultures of migrant workers in southern China: informal literacies in the negotiation of (new) social relations of the new working women'. *Knowledge. Technology and Policy*, *21*(2), 73–81. doi:10.1007/s12130-008-9045-9

Lincoln, Y. S., & Guba, E. (1985). *Naturalistic Enquiry*. London: Sage.

Long, N. (2001). *Development Sociology: Actor Perspectives*. London: Routledge. doi:10.4324/9780203398531

Lubatkin, M., Ndiaye, M., & Vengroff, R. (1997). The nature of managerial work in developing countries: a limited test of the universalist hypothesis, *Journal of International Business*, *28*.

Lundvall, B.-A. (1989). Innovation as an Inter-active Process: User-producer Relations. Technical Change and Economic Theory. In Dosi, G., Freeman, C., Nelson, R., Silverberg, G., & Soete, L. (Eds.), *Technical Change and Economic Theory* (pp. 349–369). London, New York: Pinter.

Lundvall, B.-A. (1993). Explaining Inter-Firm Cooperation and Innovation: Limits of the Transaction Cost Approach. In Grabher, G. (Ed.), *The Embedded Firm: On the Socio-Economics of Industrial Networks* (pp. 52–64). London: Routledge.

MacKenzie, D., & Wajcman, J. (1985/2002). Introductory essay: The social shaping of technology. In MacKenzie, D., & Wajcman, J. (Eds.), *The social shaping of technology* (pp. 3–27). Buckingham: Open University Press.

Madon, S. (1993). Introducing Administrative Reform through the Application of Computer-Based Information Systems: A Case Study in India. *Public Administration and Development*, *13*, 37–48. doi:10.1002/pad.4230130104

Madon, S. (2004). Evaluating the Developmental Impact of E-Governance Initiatives: An Exploratory Framework. *Electronic Journal of Information Systems in Developing Countries*, *20*(5), 1–13.

Madon, S., & Bhatnagar, B. (2000). Institutional Decentralised Information Systems for Local Level Planning: Comparing Approaches Across Two States in India. *Journal of Global Information Technology Management*, *3*(4), 45–59.

Madon, S., Sahay, S., & Sahay, J. (2004). Implementing Property Tax Reforms in Bangalore: An Actor-Network Perspective. *Information and Organization*, *14*, 269–295. doi:10.1016/j.infoandorg.2004.07.002

Madon, S., Reinhard, N., Roode, D., & Walsham, G. (2009). Digital inclusion projects in developing countries: Processes of institutionalization. *Information Technology for Development*, *15*(2), 95–107. doi:10.1002/itdj.20108

Maheswari, S. R. (1993). *Administrative Reform in India*. New Delhi: Jawahar Publishers and Distributors.

Mair, J., & Marti, I. (2005). Social Entrepreneurship Research: A Source of Explanation, Prediction and Delight. *Journal of World Business*, *41*, 36–44. doi:10.1016/j.jwb.2005.09.002

Malaysia Communication and Multimedia Commission (MCMC). (2006). *Facts and Figure – Internet Subsriber 2006*. Retrieved September 26, 2006 from www.mcmc. gov.my /facts_figures/ stats/index.asp

Malaysia Communication and Multimedia Commission (MCMC). (2008). *Facts and Figure 2007*. Retrieved November 10, 2008 from www.mcmc.gov. my/facts_figures/ stats/index.asp

Malaysia Communication and Multimedia Commission (MCMC). (2009). *Facts and Figure – Internet Subsriber 2009*. Retrieved September 14, 2009 from http://www. skmm.gov.my/facts_f igures/stats/index.asp

Malaysia Communications and Multimedia Commission ((MCMC) (2002a). *Communication and Multimedia in Malaysia: Looking Back and Planning Ahead*. Malaysia Communication and Multimedia Commission (2002).

Malaysia Debt Ventures Berhad. (2005). *Perak Launches ICT Blue Print to Become K-State by 2020*. Retrieved June 26, 2006 from http://www.debtventures.com/page. cfm? name=Perak

Malaysian Communication and Multimedia Commission (MCMC). (2001). *Communications and Multimedia Act 1998: Commission Determination on Universal Service Provision – Determination No.2 of 2001*. Retrieved May 26, 2004 from www.mcmc.gov.my

Malaysian Communication and Multimedia Commission (MCMC). (2002b). *Communications and Multimedia Act 1998: Commission Determination on Universal Service Provision (Determination No.6 of 2002) – Variation No.1 of 2003*. Retrieved May 26, 2004 from www.mcmc.gov.my

Malaysian Communication and Multimedia Commission (MCMC). (2004). *Universal Service Provision (USP): Notification of Universal Service Targets (NT/USP/1/04)*. Retrieved May 26, 2004 from www.mcmc.gov.my

Mansell, R., & Wehn, U. (1998). *Knowledge Societies: Information Technology for Sustainable Development*. New York: Oxford University Press.

Margetts, H. (1998). *Information Technology in Government: Britain and America*. London: Routledge.

Margetts, H. (2006). Transparency and Digital Government. In Hood, C., & Heald, D. (Eds.), *Transparency: the Key to Better Governance?* (pp. 197–210). London: The British Academy.

Marsden, T. (2004). The quest for ecological modernisation: re-spacing rural development and agri-food studies. *Sociologia Ruralis*, *44*(2), 129–148. doi:10.1111/j.1467-9523.2004.00267.x

Mash, B., & Mohammed, H. (2000). Participatory development of a minimum dataset for the Khayelitsha District. *South African Medical Journal*, *90*(10), 1024–1030.

Maslow, A. H. (1943). A Theory of Human Motivation. *Psychological Review*, *50*, 370–396. doi:10.1037/h0054346

Mason, S. M., & Hacker, K. L. (2003). Applying Communication Theory to Digital Divide Research. *IT&Society*, *1*(5), 40–55.

Mathew, G. (2006). A New Deal for Municipalities. In *Proceedings of the National Seminar on Urban Governance in the Context of the Jawaharlal Nehru National Urban Renewal Mission* (pp. 102-116). India Habitat Centre, New Delhi 24th – 25th November 2006.

Mathison, S., Prasetyo, J., & Kemp, M. (2003). *Information and Communication for Development, Guidelines for Practitioners*. The Foundation for Development Cooperation.

Mavimbe, J. C., Braa, J., & Bjune, G. (2005). Assessing immunization data quality from routine reports in Mozambique. *BMC Public Health*, *5*(108).

Maya-Jariego, I., & Armitage, N. (2007). Multiple senses of community in migration and commuting. *International Sociology*, *22*(6), 743–766. doi:10.1177/0268580907082259

Mbeki, T. (2002). State of the nation address. Retrieved 2008 from http://www.info.gov.za/speeches /2002/0202281146a1001.htm

Mchombu, K. J. (2004). Sharing Knowledge for Community Development and Transformation: A Handbook. Retrieved on September 12, 2004 from http://www.oxfam.ca/publications/ downloads/Sharing%20Knowledge%20 2%20Inside%20Pages.pdf

McNamara, K. S. (2003). Information and Communication technologies, Poverty and Development: Learning from Experience. *A Background Paper for the InfoDev Annual Symposium, December 9-10, 2003, Geneva, Switzerland.* Washington DC: The World Bank.

McNamara, K. S. (2003). *Information and Communication Technologies, Poverty and Development: Learning from Experience* (A Background paper for the infoDev Annual Symposium). Washington, D.C.: The World Bank.

MDG. (2000). *United Nations Millennium Development Goals*. Retrieved October 2007 from http://www.un.org/millenniumgoals/

Mechling, J. (2002). Information Age Governance. In Kamarck, E., & Nye, J. S. Jr., (Eds.), *Governance.com: Democracy in the Information Age* (pp. 171–189). New York: Brookings Institution.

Meijer, A. (2002). Geographical Information Systems and Public Accountability. *Information Policy, 7*, 39–47.

Menou, M.J. (2001). The Global Digital Divide: Beyond HICTeri. *Aslib Proceeding: The New Information Perspectives, 53*(4).

Metcalfe, J. S. (1997). Technology Systems and Technology Policy in an Evolutionary Framework. Technology, Globalization and Economic Performance. In Archibugi, D., & Michie, J. (Eds.), *Technology, Globalization and Economic Performance* (pp. 268–296). Cambridge: Cambridge University Press.

Michaels, E. (1985). Constraints on Knowledge in an Economy of Oral Information. *Current Anthropology, 26*(4), 505–510. doi:10.1086/203312

Middleton, J., Ziderman, A., & Van Adams, A. (1993). *Skills for Productivity: vocational education and training in developing countries*. New York: Oxford University Press.

Midgley, J. (2003). Social development: the intellectual heritage. *Journal of International Development, 15*(7), 831–844. doi:10.1002/jid.1038

Ministry of Energy, Water and Communications (MEWC). (2006). *Industry Introduction: Institutional Arrangement.* Retrieved November 29, 2006 from http://www.ktak.gov.my/bm/ template01.asp? contentid=42

Ministry of Finance. (2003). *Malaysia Budget 2004.* Retrieved May 28, 2004 from http://www.treasury.gov.my/ englishversionbaru/index.htm

Minogue, M. (2002). Power to the People? Good Governance and the Reshaping of the State. In Kothari, U., & Minogue, M. (Eds.), *Development Theory and Practice* (pp. 117–135). Basingstoke: Palgrave.

Misra, S. (2005). eGovernance: Responsive and Transparent Service Delivery Mechanism. In A. Singh (Ed.), *Administrative Reforms: Towards Sustainable Practices* (pp. 283-302), New Delhi: Sage Publications.

Mitra, R. (2000). Emerging State-level ICT Development Strategies. In Bhatnagar, S., & Schware, R. (Eds.), *Information and Communication Technology in Development: Cases from India* (pp. 195–205). New Delhi: Sage Publications.

Mitra, S. (2000). *Minimally Invasive Education for mass computer literacy*. Paper presented at the CRIDALA 2000 Conference, 21-25 June 2000, Hong Kong.

Mitra, S. (2002). Experiments in Bangalore, Karnataka. Retrieved November 2003 from http://niitholeinthewall.com/home

Mochiko, T. (2009). *Merger talks delay MTN issue.* Business Report August 28, 2009. Retrieved December 2009 from http://www.busrep.co.za/index.php?fSectionId=563&fArticleId=5142081.

Molina, A. (2003). The Digital Divide: The Need of a Global e-Inclusion Movement. *Technology Analysis and Strategic Management, 15*(1). doi:10.1080/0953732032000046105

Molyneux, M. (1985). Mobilisation without emancipation? Women's interests, states and revolution in Nicaragua. *Feminist Studies, 11*(2), 227–254. doi:10.2307/3177922

Moodley, S (2005). The Promise of E-Development? A Critical Assessment of the State of ICT for Poverty Reduction Discourse in South Africa. *Perspectives on Global Development, 4*(1).

Morino Institute. (2001). *From Access to Outcomes: Raising the Aspirations for Technology Initiatives in Low-Income Communities*. A Morino Institute Working Paper.

Morris, P. (1994). *The Management of Projects*. London: Thomas Telford.

Morris, P. (2002). Science, objective knowledge and the theory of project management. *Civil Engineering Proceedings of ICE, 150*, 82-90.

Mosse, D. (2003). *Good Policy is Unimplementable? Reflections on the Ethnography of Aid Policy and Practice*. Paper presented at the EIDOS Workshop on 'Order and Disjuncture: the Organisation of Aid and Development', SOAS, London 26-28th September 2003.

Mulder, I., Bohle, W., Boshomane, S., Morris, C., Tempelman, H., & Velthausz, D. (2008). Real World Innovation in Rural South Africa. *The Electronic Journal for Virtual Organisations and Networks, 10*, 8–20.

Municipio (2005). *Informe de Patentes Industriales, Patentes Comerciales, Patentes Profesionales, Patentes Alcohólicas*, Municipio de [Algun].

Munyua, H. (2000). Information and Communication Technologies for Rural Development and Food Security: Lessons from Field Experiences in Developing Countries. *Sustainable Development Department, Food and Agriculture Organization of the United Nations*. Retrieved Feb 2, 2009, from http://www.fao.org/sd/CDdirect / CDre0055b.htm

Musa, P. F. (2006). Making a case for modifying the technology acceptance model to account for limited accessibility in developing countries. *Information Technology for Development, 12*(3), 213–224. doi:10.1002/itdj.20043

Myerson, G. (2001). *Heidegger, Habermas and the Mobile Phone*. Cambridge, UK: Icon Books.

Nakata, M., Gibson, J., Nakata, V., Byrne, A., & McKeough, J. (2008). Indigenous digital collections: an early look at the organisation and culture interface. *Australian Academic & Research Libraries, 39*(4), 223–236.

Nakata, M., Nakata, V., Anderson, J., Hart, V., Hunter, J., Smallacombe, S., et al. (2006). Evaluation of the Northern Territory Library's Libraries and Knowledge Centres Model Darwin Northern Territory Library. Retrieved January 1, 2009 from http://www.ntl.nt.gov.au/_data/ assets/pdf_ file/0018/4680/nakata_finalreport.pdf

Nakata, M., Nakata, V., Anderson, J., Hunter, J., Hart, V., Smallacombe, S., McGill, J., Lloyd, B., Richmond, C., & Maynard, G. (2007). Libraries and Knowledge Centres: Implementing public library services in remote Indigenous communities in the Northern Territory of Australia. *Australian Academic & Research Libraries, 38*(3).

National Information Technology Council. (2000). *Access, Empowerment and Government in the Information Age*. NITC Publication.

National Information Technology Council. *ICT in Malaysia*. Retrieved September, 2003 from www.nitc.org. my/ press/ speeches_ 8jun00.html

National Institute of Urban Affairs (NIUA). (2004). *Reforming the Property Tax System. Research Study Series No. 94*. New Delhi: NIUA Press.

National Telecommunication and Information Administration (NTIA). (1999). *Falling Through the Net: Defining the Digital Divide*. Retrieved March 26, 2004 from http:// www.ntia.doc.gov/ntiahome /fttn99/contents.html

Neal, R. A. (1995). Project definition: the soft-systems approach. *International Journal of Project Management, 13*(1), 5–9. doi:10.1016/0263-7863(95)95697-C

Negroponte, N., Bender, W., Battro, A., & Cavallo, D. (2006). One Laptop per Child. Retrieved August 2009 from http://olpcnews.com/presentations/ olpc-nov-2006t.pdf

Newman, J. (Ed.). (2005). *Remaking Governance: Peoples Politics and the Public Sphere*. Bristol: The Policy Press.

Nilekani, N. (2004, October 25). Redemption in this World, this Land. *The Economic Times*. Retrieved June 31, 2008 from http://economictimes.indiatimes. com / articleshow/897648.cms

Nnadi, N., & Gurstein, M. (2007). Towards Supporting Community Information Seeking and Use. *Journal of Community Informatics, 3*(1). Retrieved January 25, 2009, from http://ci-journal.net/index.php/ciej/article / viewDownloadInterstitial/325/325.

Noam, E. (1997). The public telecommunications network: a concept in transition. *The Journal of Communication, 37*(1), 30–48. doi:10.1111/j.1460-2466.1987.tb00966.x

Norris, P. (2002). *Civic Engagement, Information Poverty, and the Internet Worldwide*. Cambridge: Cambridge University Press.

Norris, P. (2003). *Digital divide. Civic engagement, information poverty, and the internet worldwide*. Cambridge: Cambridge University Press.

North, D. C. (1990). *Institutions, Institutional Change, and Economic Performance*. Cambridge, NY: Cambridge University Press.

Northern Territory Library. (2005). Comprehensive Review of the 'Readiness' of Communities in the West MacDonnell's Region for the Libraries and Knowledge Centre's Program. Unpublished report. Northern Territory Government, Darwin: Jason Gibson.

Northern Territory Library. (2008). *The Walk to School: an indigenous early years literacy strategy for northern territory public libraries and knowledge centres. Northern Territory Library*. Darwin: Cate Richmond.

Ó Siochrú, S., & Girard, B. (2005). *Community-based networks and innovative technologies: new models to serve and empower the poor*. UNDP.

O'Neil, D. (2001). *Merging Theory with Practice: Toward an Evaluation Framework for Community Technology*. Paper presented at Internet Research 2.0: INTERconnections: The Second International Conference of the Association of Internet Researchers, October 10-14, 2001 at University of Minnesota, Minneapolis-St. Paul, Minnesota, USA.

O'Neill, M. (1992). Community Participation in Quebec. *International Journal of Health Services, 22*(2), 287–301.

Odedra, M. (1993). Sub-Saharan Africa: A Technoligical Desert. *Communications of the ACM, 36*(2). doi:10.1145/151220.151222

Odedra, M. (1992). Is Information Technology Really Being Transferred to the African Countries? In Bhatnagar, S., & Cyranek, G. (Eds.), *Technology Transfer for Development: The prospects and Limits of Information Technology* (pp. 47–58). New Delhi: Tata MC Graw Hill.

Odedra, M. (1994). The Role of International Organisations in Technology Transfer. *Journal of Third World Science, Technology and Development Forum, 12*.

Odendaal, N. (2002). ICTs *In* Development – Who Benefits? Use of Geographic Information Systems on the Cato Manor Development Project, South Africa. *Journal of International Development, 14*, 89–100. doi:10.1002/jid.867

Olowu, D. (2004). Property Taxation and Democratic Decentralisation in Developing Countries (Working Paper Series No. 401). Institute of Social Studies, The Hague.

Omar Abdul Rahman. (1993). Industrial targets of Vision 2020: The science and technology perspective. In Ahmad Sarji Abdul hamid (Ed.), *Malaysia's Vision 2020: Understanding the concept, implications and challenges*. Petaling Jaya: Pelanduk Publications.

Organisation for Economic Co-operation and Development. (2001). *Understanding the Digital Divide*. OECD Publications.

Orlikowski, W. J., & Baroudi, J. J. (1991). Studying Information Technology in Organizations: Research Approaches and Assumptions. *Information Systems Research, 2*(1), 1–28. doi:10.1287/isre.2.1.1

Otter, M. (2002). *Solomon Islands Human Development Report: Building a Nation*. Windsor: Government of the Solomon Islands/UNDP.

Owen, W. J., & Darkwa, O. (1999). Role of Multipurpose Community Telecentres in Accelerating National Development in Ghana. *First Monday*. Retrieved August 28, 2004 from http://www.firstmonday.dk/issues/issue5_1/owen/.

Padania, S., & Silvani, F. (2005). Local radio in the Information Society: Technology, participation and content in Africa. In Warnock, K., & Wickremasinghe, R. (Eds.), *Information and Communication Technologies and large-scale poverty reduction: Lessons from Asia, Africa, Latin America and the Caribbean* (pp. 33–36). London: Panos.

Pade, C., Mallinson, B., & Sewry, D. (2008). An Elaboration of Critical Success Factors for Rural ICT Project Sustainability in Developing Countries: Exploring the Dwesa Case. [JITCAR]. *Journal of Information Technology Case and Application Research, 10*(4), 32–55.

Pade, C. (2006). *An Investigation of ICT Project Management Techniques for Sustainable ICT Projects in Rural Development*. Unpublished Masters thesis, Rhodes University, Grahamstown.

Pade, C., Mallinson, B., & Sewry, D. (2006, October). *An Exploration of the Categories Associated with ICT Project Sustainability in Rural Areas of Developing Countries: A Case Study of the Dwesa Project*. Paper presented at the Annual Conference of the South African Institute of Computer Scientists and Information Technologists (SAICSIT). Gordon's Bay, South Africa.

Page, M., & Scott, A. (2001). Change Agency and Women's Learning: New Practices in Community Informatics. *Information Communication and Society, 4*(4), 528–559. doi:10.1080/13691180110097003

Page, J., & Plaza, S. (2005). *Migration Remittances and Development: A Review of Global Evidence*. World Bank.

Paisley, D., & Richardson, D. (1998). Why the first mile and not the last? In The first mile of connectivity. Rome, Italy: Food and Agriculture Organisation of the United Nations. Retrieved January 2004 from http://www.fao.org/WAICENT/FAOINFO/SUSTDEV/Cddirect/Cdre0026.html

Palmer, R., Timmermans, H., & Fay, D. (2002). *From Conflict to Negotiation: Nature-based Development on South Africa's Wild Coast*. Pretoria: Human Sciences Research Council.

Pan American Health Organization. (1999). *Setting up Healthcare Services Information Systems: A Guide for Requirement Analysis, Application Specification, and Procurement*. Washington, D.C.: Pan American Health Organization.

Papandrea, F., Daly, A., & McCallum, K. (2006). *Telephone and Internet Use in Remote Indigenous Communities*. Canberra: University of Canberra, Communication and Media Policy Institute.

Parkinson, S. (2005). *Telecentres, Access and Development: Experience and lessons from Uganda and South Africa*. Ottawa: International Development Research Centre.

Parks, T. (2005). A Few Misconceptions about eGovernment. Retrieved November 10, 2008 from http://www.asiafoundation.org/pdf/ICT_eGov.pdf

Pathak, R. D., & Prasad, R. S. (2005). The Role of eGovernment in Tackling Corruption: the Indian Experience. In R. Ahmad (Ed.) *The Role of Public Administration in Building a Harmonious Society, Selected Proceedings from the Annual Conference of the Network of Asia-Pacific Schools and Institutes of Public Administration and Governance (NAPSIPAG)*, December 5-7, 2005 (pp. 343-463).

Patson, P., Taniveke, P., Leeming, D., Agassi, A., & Baliki, R. (2002). *Final Technical Report*. Sasamungga Distance Learning and Research Project, Rural Development Volunteers Association. Retrieved December 30, 2009 from www.peoplefirst.net.sb/General/Distance_Learning.htm#latest

Paul, S., & Shah, M. (1997). Corruption in Public Service Delivery. In Guhan, S., & Paul, S. (Eds.), *Corruption in India: Agenda for Action*. New Delhi: Vision Books.

Pejabat Daerah dan Tanah Manjung (2004). *KedaiKom*. Retrieved April 26, 2004 from http://pdt.manjung.perak. gov.my/BM/ dotcom.html

Pereyra Romo, A. (2002). *Sistematización Fase Piloto: Proyecto Sistema de Información Rural Urbano (SIRU) - Socializando Nuestra Experiencia*. Cajamarca, Perú: ITDG.

PFnet. (n.d.). Retrieved January 3, 2010 from www. peoplefirst.net.sb/general/PFnet.htm

Pigato, M. A. (2001). Information and Communication Technology, Poverty, and Development in Sub-Saharan Africa and South Asia. *African Region Working Paper Series No. 20. August 2001. The World Bank*. Retrieved February 16, 2009 from http://www.worldbank.org /afr/ wps/wp20.pdf

Pigg, K. E. (2003). Applications of Community Informatics for Building Community and Enhancing Civic Society. *Information Communication and Society*, *4*(4), 507–527. doi:10.1080/13691180110096996

Pigg, K. E., & Crank, L. D. (2004). Building Community Social Capital: The Potential and Promise of information and Communications Technologies. *The Journal of Community Informatics*, *1*(1), 58–73.

Pigg, K. (2010). Information Communication Technology and Its Impact on Rural Community Economic Development. In Steyn, J., & Johanson, G. (Eds.), *ICTs and Sustainable Solutions for the Digital Divide: Theoretical Issues*. Hershey, PA: IGI Global.

Pinkett, R. D. (2001). *Integrating Community Technology and Community Building: Early Results form the Camfield Estates-MIT Creating Community Connection Project*. 43rd Annual Conference of the Association of Collegiate Schools of Planning (ACSP), Cleveland, Ohio, Nov. 8-11. Retrieved July 25, 2003 from http://web.media. mit.edu/~rpinkett/ papers/ index.html

Pitkin, B. (2001). Community Informatics: Hope or Hype? In *Proceedings of the 34th Hawaii International Conference on System Sciences, January 3-6, 2001* (pp. 2860-2867).

PNUD. (2002). *Informe sobre Desarrollo Humano - Perú 2002: Aprovechando las Potencialidades*. Lima, Perú: Programa de las Naciones Unidas para el Desarrollo - Oficina del Perú.

Pollack, M. (2003). Más y mejor capacitación para una economía competitiva. In Gomá, O. M. (Ed.), *Hacia un Chile Competitivo: Instituciones y Políticas* (pp. 193–238). Santiago: Editorial Universitaria.

Porter, D., Allen, B., & Thompson. G. (1991). *Development in Practice: Paved with Good Intentions*. London: Routlege.

Portus, L. M. (2008). How the Urban Poor Acquire and Give Meaning to the Mobile Phone. In Katz, J. E. (Ed.), *Handbook of Mobile Communication Studies* (pp. 106–118). Cambridge, MA: MIT Press.

Pratchett, L. (1999). New Technologies and the Modernization of Local Government: An Analysis of Biases and Constraints. *Public Administration*, *77*(4), 731–750. doi:10.1111/1467-9299.00177

PRC (People's Republic of China), National Bureau of Statistics. (2009). Chinese Migrant Workers Totaled [sic] 225.42 Million at the End of 2008. China News, 25 March. Retrieved April 20, 2010 from http://www.boxun.us/ news/publish/chinanews/ Chinese_Peasant_Workers_Totaled_225_42_Million_at_the_End_of_2008.shtml

Preston, P. W. (1986). *Making Sense of Development: An Introduction to classical and contemporary theories of Development and their application in Southeast Asia*. London, New York: Routledge & Kegan Paul.

Preston, P. (2001). *Knowledge or 'Know-less Societies'?* Retrieved January 28, 2007 from www.lirne.net/resources/ netknowledge/ preston.pdf

Priestman, C. (2004). Narrowcasting and the dream of radio's great global conversation. *The Radio Journal: International Studies in Broadcast and Audio Media*, *2*(2), 77–88. doi:10.1386/rajo.2.2.77/1

Pringle, I., & David, M. J. R. (2003). Using radio to make the internet visible. In Girard, B. (Ed.), *The One to Watch: Radio, new ICTs and interactivity* (pp. 2–20). Rome: FAO.

Proenza, F. J., Bastidas-Buch, R., & Montero, G. P. (2001). *Telecentres for Socioeconomics and Rural Development in Latin America and the Caribbean: Investment Opportunities and Design Recommendations, with Special Reference to Central America. FAO, ITU*. Washington, DC: IADB.

Proenza, F. J. (2001). Telecenter Sustainability: Myths and Opportunities. *The Journal of Development Communication, 12*(2), 94–109.

Proenza, F. (2001). *Telecentre Sustainability: Myths and opportunities*. Rome: FAO. Retrieved April 11, 2007, from http://www.t-forum.org/staat_privat /dokumente/ myths.pdf

Project Management Institute. (2000). *A Guide to the Project Management Body of Knowledge*. Newton Square, PA: Project Management Institute.

Pruett, D., & Deane, J. (1998). The Internet and Poverty: Real Help or Real Hype? *Panos Briefing*. Retrieved on June 3, 2006 from http://www.panos.org.uk/resources / reportdetails.asp

Purdue, D. (2001). Neighbourhood Governance: Leadership, Trust and Social Capital. *Urban Studies (Edinburgh, Scotland), 38*(12), 2211–2224. doi:10.1080/00420980120087135

Putnam, R. D., Leonardi, R., & Nonetti, R. Y. (1993). *Making Democracy Work: Civic Traditions in Modern Italy*. Princeton, NJ: Princeton University Press.

Radoll, P. (2006). Information Communication Technology. In Hunter, B. H. (Ed.), *Assessing the evidence on Indigenous socioeconomic outcomes: A focus on the 2002 NATSISS Research Monograph 26* (pp. 197–212). Canberra: Australian National University, Centre For Aboriginal Economic Policy Research.

Ramanathan, J. (2005). Fractal Architecture for the Adaptive Complex Enterprise. *Communications of the ACM, 48*(5), 51–57. doi:10.1145/1060710.1060739

Ramirez, R. (2003). Bridging disciplines: the natural resource management kaleidoscope for understanding ICTs. *The Journal of Development Communication, 1*(14), 51–64.

Ramsey, G. (2003). Future Directions for Secondary Education in the Northern Territory. Report submitted to the Northern Territory Government. Northern Territory Government, Darwin. Retrieved December 12, 2008 from http://www.betterschools.nt.gov.au/history/ sec_ed_report.shtml.

Rao, N. R. (1986). *Municipal Finances in India (Theory and Practice)*. New Delhi: Inter-India Publications.

Rao, S. S. (2004). Role of ICTs in India's rural community information systems. *info, 6*(4), 261-269.

Rao, V. (2003). *Property Tax Reforms in Bangalore*. Paper presented to the Innovations in Local Revenue Mobilisation Seminar. Retrieved December 10, 2008 from http:// www1.worldbank.org/publicsector/ decentralization/ June2003 SeminarPresentations/VasanthRao.ppt

Rathswohl, E. J. (2003). Introduction to Special Series on Community Informatics. *Informing Science Journal, 6*, 101–102.

Raymond, E. S. (1999). *The Cathedral and the Bazaar*. Sebastopol, California: O'Reilly.

Reeves, T. C. (2000). Socially Responsible Educational Technology Research. *Educational Technology, 40*(6), 19–28.

Revised Tshwane Integrated Development Plan 2020 (2009). Retrieved Julyk 2009 from http://www.tshwane. gov.za/ documents/idp2020/

Reyes, J. C. (2005, 12 September). Siete Millones sin Electricidad. *La República*, p. 9.

Reyment, R., & Jöreskog, K. G. (1993). *Applied Factor Analysis in the Natural Science*. Cambridge University Press. doi:10.1017/CBO9780511524882

Rhodes, R. A. W. (1996). The New Governance: Governing without Government. *Political Studies, 44*, 652–667. doi:10.1111/j.1467-9248.1996.tb01747.x

Ribeiro, E. F. N. (2006). Urban Growth and Transformations in India: Issues and Challenges. In *Proceedings of the National Seminar on Urban Governance in the Context of the Jawaharlal Nehru National Urban Renewal Mission, India Habitat Centre, New Delhi 24ᵗʰ – 25ᵗʰ November 2006* (pp. 1-11).

Richardson, J. W. (2008). ICT in education reform in Cambodia: problems, politics, and policies impacting implementation. *Information Technologies and International Development, 4*(4), 67–82. doi:10.1162/itid.2008.00027

Richey, R. C., Klein, J., & Nelson, W. (2004). Developmental research: Studies of instructional design and development. In Jonassen, D. (Ed.), *Handbook of Research for Educational Communications and Technology* (2nd ed., pp. 1099–1130). Mahwah, NJ: Lawrence Erlbaum Associates, Inc.

Robison, L. J., & Flora, J. L. (2003). The Social Capital Paradigm: Bridging Across Disciplines. *American Journal of Agricultural Economics, 5*, 1187–1193. doi:10.1111/j.0092-5853.2003.00528.x

Rogers, E. M. (2003). *Diffusion of Innovations* (5th ed.). New York: Free Press.

Rohde, J., Shaw, V., Hedberg, C., Stoops, N., Venter, S., & Venter, K. (2008). Information for Primary Health Care. In Barron, P., & Roma-Reardon, J. (Eds.), *South African Health Review 2008* (p. 423). Durban: Health Systems Trust.

Rolland, K., & Monteiro, E. (2002). Balancing the Local and the Global in Infrastructural Information System. *The Information Society, 18*, 87–100. doi:10.1080/01972240290075020

Roman, R., & Colle, R. D. (2003). Content creation for ICT development projects: Integrating normative approaches and community demand. *Information Technology for Development, 10*, 85–94. doi:10.1002/itdj.1590100204

Roman, R., & Colle, R.D. (2003). Content creation for ICT development projects: Integrating normative approaches and community demand. *Information technology for Development, 10*(2), 85-94.

Roman, R., & Colle, R. (2002). *Themes and issues in telecentre sustainability* (Development Informatics Working Paper Series Paper No. 10). Manchester, UK: University of Manchester, Institute of Development Policy and Management.

Ronaghan, S. A. (2002). *Benchmarking E-Government: A Global Perspective*. The United Nations Division for Public Economics and Public Administration (DPEPA) Report.

Rosenberg, N. (1982). *Inside the Black Box: Technology and Economics*. Cambridge: Cambridge University Press.

Rosengard, J. K. (1998). *Property Tax Reform in Developing Countries*. Boston: Kluwer Academic Publications.

Roy, S. (2005). *Globalisation, ICT and Developing Nations: Challenges in the Information Age*. New Delhi: Sage Publications.

Rozner, E. (1998). *Haves, Have-Nots, and Have-to-Haves: Net Effects on the Digital Divide*. Retrieved July 6, 2003 from http://cyber.laws.harvard.edu/ fallsem98/final_papers/Rozner.html

Russel, D. (2003). *Minimally Invasive Education pilot project: Cwili Village. Interim evaluation report on the Digital Doorway pilot site in Cwili Village* (pp. 1–12). Eastern Cape.

Russell, N. (2000). *Evaluating and Enhancing the Impact of Community Telecentre: A Companion Project of the InforCauca Initiative to Foster Sustainable Development in Marginalized Regions*. Submitted to the Rockefeller Foundation by the International Center for Tropical Agriculture (CIAT).

Rysavy, S. D. M. & Sales, G. C. (1991). *Cooperative Learning in Computer-based Instruction Educational Technology Research and Development*. Lecture notes distributed in 'The teacher as a competent professional educator' at Southeast Missouri State University, Spring 1998.

Sachdeva, P. (1993). *Urban Local Government and Administration in India*. Allahabad: Kitab Mahal.

Sachs, J. (2005). *The end of poverty. How we can make it in our lifetime*. London: Penguin Books.

Sachs, J. (2008). *Common wealth. Economics for a crowded planet*. London: Penguin Books.

Saguaro Seminar. (2000). *Social Capital Community Benchmark Survey*. Retrieved August 10, 2003 from http://www.ksg.harvard.edu/saguaro/ measurement.htm

Sahay, S., Monteiro, E., & Aanestad, M. (2009). Configurable Politics and Asymmetric Integration: Health e-Infrastructures in India. *Journal of the Association for Information Systems, 10*(5), 399–414.

Sahay, S., & Walsham, G. (2005, 26-28 May). *Scaling of Health Information Systems in India: Challenges and Approaches*. Paper presented at the International Federation for Information Processing Working Group 9.4 Conference, Abuja, Nigeria.

Sampson, D., Karagiannidis, C., Schenone, A., & Cardinali, F. (2002). Knowledge-on-Demand in e-Learning and e-Working Settings. *Journal of Educational Technology & Society, 5*(5), 107–112.

Sandberg, A. (Ed.). (1979). *Computers Dividing Man and Work*. Stockholm, Sweden: Arbeitslivcentrum.

Sandiford, P., Annett, H., & Cibulskis, R. E. (1992). What can Information Systems do for Primary Health Care? An International Perspective. *Social Science & Medicine, 34*(10), 1077–1087. doi:10.1016/0277-9536(92)90281-T

Sarangamath, S. (2007). BangaloreOne: Integrated Citizen Service Centre. In Agarwal, A. (Ed.), *eGovernance Case Studies* (pp. 148–152). Hyderabad: Universities Press.

Saravia, M. (2003). Ideas para Repensar la Conectividad en Áreas Rurales [Ideas to Rethink Connectivity in Rural Areas]. *Otro Lado de la Brecha: Perspectivas Latinoamericanas y del Caribe ante la CMSI* (pp. 29-33). Caracas, RedISTIC.

Saul, J. R. (2009). *The collapse of globalism and the reinvention of the world*. London: Atlantic Books. (Original work published 2005)

Schätzl, L. H. (Ed.). (1988). *Growth ad Spatial Equity in West Malaysia*. Singapore: Institute of Southeast Asian Studies.

Scheh, S., & Haggis, J. (2000). *Culture, and development: A Critical Introduction*. Oxford: Blackwell.

Scheufele, D. A., & Nisbet, M. C. (2002). Being a citizen online: New opportunities and dead ends. *The Harvard International Journal of Press/Politics, 7*(3), 55–75.

Schmitz, H., & Musyck, B. (1993). Industrial districts in Europe: policy lessons for developing countries. *Institute of Development Studies, Discussion Paper No. 324*. Brighton: University of Sussex.

Schware, R. (2000). Useful Starting Points for Future Projects. In Bhatnagar, S., & Schware, R. (Eds.), *Information and Communication Technology in Development: Cases from India* (pp. 206–213). Delhi: Sage Publications.

Schwarz, M., & Thompson, M. (1990). *Divided We Stand: Redefining politics, technology and social choice*. New York: Harvester Wheatsheaf.

SearchEnterpriseLinux.com. TechTarget (2008). Retrieved January 2009 from http://searchenterpriselinux.techtarget.com /sDefinition/0,sid39_gci212709,00.html

Seebregts, C., Mamlin, B., Biondich, P., Fraser, H., & Wolfe, B., Jazayeri, d., et al. (2009). (Forthcoming). The OpenMRS Implementers Network. *International Journal of Medical Informatics, 10*.

Segal, A. (2003). *Digital Dragon: High Technology Enterprises in China*. Ithaca, London: Cornell University Press.

Sein, M. K., & Harindranath, G. (2004). Conceptualizing the ICT Artifact: Toward Understanding the Role of ICT in National Development. *The Information Society, 20*(1), 15–24. doi:10.1080/01972240490269942

Sekaran, U. (2003). *Research Methods for Business*. New York: Wiley & Sons, Inc.

Selwyn, N. (2003). *Defining the 'Digital Divide': Developing a Theoretical Understanding of Inequalities in the Information Age*. Occasional Paper 49, 'Adults Learning@ Home' – An ESRC Funded Research Project. Retrieved March 23, 2004 from www.cardiff.ac.uk/socsi/ict

Sen, A. (1998). *On Ethics and Economic*. Oxford: Blackwell. (Original work published 1987)

Sen, A. K. (1999). *Development as Freedom*. New York: Alfred A. Knopf.

Sen, A. (2001). *Development as freedom*. Oxford: University Press.

Shah, D. V., Cho, J., Eveland, W. P., & Kwak, N. (2005). Information expression in a digital age: Modeling internet effects on civic participation. *Communication Research*, *32*(5), 531–565. doi:10.1177/0093650205279209

Shaw, V., Mengiste, S., & Braa, J. (2007). *Scaling of health information systems in Nigeria and Ethiopia - Considering the options*. Paper presented at the IFIP 9.4 9th International Conference on Social Implications of Computers in Developing Countries, Sao Paulo, Brazil.

Shaw, V., Simoonga, C., Kalinda, P., & Muyambo, S. (2008, 7-9 May 2008). *Using Communities of Practice as a Lens for Understanding Adoption of ICT*. Paper presented at the IST-Africa Conference 2008 Windhoek, Namibia.

Shet, D. L. (1987). Alternative development as political practice. *Alternatives*, *12*(2), 155–171.

Shibuya, K., Scheele, S., & Boerma, T. (2005). Health statistics: time to get serious. *Bulletin of the World Health Organization*, *83*(10), 722.

Sidorenko, A., & Findlay, C. (2001). The Digital Divide in East Asia. *Asian-Pacific Economic Literature*, *8*, 18–30. doi:10.1111/1467-8411.00103

Sieborger, I., Terzoli, A., & Hodgkinson-Williams, C. (2008). *The development of ICT networks for South African schools: Two pilot studies in disadvantaged areas. Learning to live in the knowledge society*. Boston: Springer.

Siika, A. M., Rotich, J. K., Simiyu, C. J., Kigotho, E. M., Smith, F. E., & Sidle, J. E. (2005). An electronic medical record system for ambulatory care of HIV-infected patients in Kenya. *International Journal of Medical Informatics*, *74*(5), 345–355. doi:10.1016/j.ijmedinf.2005.03.002

Silva, L. (2007). Institutionalization does not occur by decree: Institutional obstacles in implementing a land administration system in a developing country. *Information Technology for Development*, *13*(1), 27–48. doi:10.1002/itdj.20056

Simon, H. A. (1981). *The sciences of the artificial* (2nd ed.). Cambridge, MA: MIT Press.

Simpson, L. (2005). Community Informatics and Sustainability: Why Social Capital Matters. *The Journal of Community Informatics*, *1*(2), 79–96.

Sinan, A., Marcela, E., & Randal, N. (2001). *Assessing network applications for Economic Development* (Pilot Phase Assessment Report). Cambridge, MA: Harvard University, JFK School of Government.

Singh, A. (1990). Computerisation of the Indian Income Tax Department. *Information Technology for Development*, *5*(3), 235–251. doi:10.1080/02681102.1990.9627198

Singh, S. S., & Misra, S. (1993). *Legislative Framework of Panchayati Raj in India*. New Delhi: Intellectual Publishing House.

Singh, N. (1996). *Governance and Reform in India*. Paper presented at Indian National Economic Policy in an Era of Global Reform: An Assessment, Cornell University, March 29-30 1996

Siochrú, Ó. S. (2009). *Pro-Poor ICT Access toolkit: Policy and Regulatory Module Overview. APC*. Retrieved on July 29, 2009, from http://access.apc.org/index.php/Pro-Poor_ICT_Access_toolkit_documents#Policy_and_Regulatory_Issues_Module:_Overview

Siochrú, Ó., & Hak, S. S., & Long, D. (2009). Cambodia's iREACH integrates OM and SPEAK. *Outcome Mapping Learning Community Newsletter, 2009*(1). Retrieved July 29, 2009, from http://outcomemapping.ca/resource/resource.php?id=223

Slater, D., & Tacchi, J. (2004). ICT's at Works in the Hands of the Poor: Innovation and Research in South Asia. *i4d online*. Retrieved on July 6, 2004, from http://www.i4donline.net/issue/may04/innovation_research_full.htm

Slay, H., Thinyane, M., Terzoli, A., & Clayton, P. (2006). *A preliminary investigation into the implementation of ICTs in marginalized communities.* Paper presented at the Southern African Telecommunications Networks and Applications Conference (SAICSIT), Spier - Western Cape, South Africa.

Smith, R., Cambridge, G., & Gush, K. (2003). *Curiosity cures the knowledge gap - Cwili township Digital Doorway project: a case study.* CSIR.

Smith, R., Cambridge, G., & Gush, K. (2005). *Unassisted Learning – Promoting Computer Literacy in Previously Disadvantaged areas of South Africa.* Paper presented at the WSIS Conference, 2005.

Smith, T. (2004, February 19). Crisis in Tuscany's Chinatown. *BBC News.* Retrieved from http://news.bbc.co.uk/2/hi/europe/ 3500285.stm.

Souter, D. (2008). Equitable access: people, networks and capabilities. Association for Progressive Communications. Retrieved December 25, 2008 from http://www.apc.org/en/system/files/APC_EquitableAccess_PeopleNetworksCapabilities_IssuePaper_20080730.pdf

Sparreboom, T. (2001). An Assessment of Labour Market Information Systems in South Africa. *Africa Development. Afrique et Developpement, XXVI*(3 & 4), 149–181.

Sreekumar, T. T. (2003). De-hyping ICTs: ICT Innovations by Civil Society Organizations in. Rural India. *i4d-Information for Development, 1*(1), 22-27.

Statistics South Africa. (2001). Census 2001: Investigation into appropriate definitions of urban and rural areas for South Africa. Discussion document. Report no. 03-03-20 (2001), 2001, Retrieved February 26, 2009, from http://www.statssa.gov.za/ census01 /html/UrbanRural.pdf

Steyn, J. (1999). *The Info era: evolution, revolution or solution?* Conference Paper: New Media Conference, Poitiers, France. Retrieved December 2009 from http://www.steyn.pro/papers/infoera/.

Stillman, L., & Linger, H. (2009). Community Informatics and Information Systems: Can They Be Better Connected? *The Information Society: An International Journal, 25*(4), 255–264.

Stockholm Challenge. (2006). Biblioredes: Nosotros en Internet (us on the Internet), a window to local culture. Retrieved October 3, 2006, from http://www.stockholmchallenge.se/ projectdata.asp?id=1&projectid=1134.

Stoker, G. (1998). Governance as Theory: Five Propositions. *International Social Science Journal, 50*(155), 17–28. doi:10.1111/1468-2451.00106

Stoll, K. (2005). Basic Principles of Community Public Internet Access Point's Sustainability. In Badshah, A., Khan, S., & Garrido, M. (Eds.), *Connected for Development: Information Kiosks and Sustainability* (pp. 61–66). New York: United Nations Publications.

Stoll, K. (2003). Telecentres sustainability: What does it mean? *ICT for development, Development Gateway.* Retrieved February 14, 2006, from http://topics.developmentgateway.org /ict /sdm/previewDocument. do~activeDocumentId=442773

Stones, L. (2009, January 28). South Africa: Subscriber Surge Lifts Vodacom's Revenue. *Business Day.* Retrieved December 2009 from http://allafrica.com/stories/200901280049.html.

Stones, W. (2001). *Measuring Social Capital: Towards a Theoretically Informed Measurement Framework for Researching Social Capital in Family and Community Life.* Research Paper No. 24, February 2001. Australian Institute of Family Studies.

Stork, E. (2002). *Enhancing People's Participation in the Pacific through the Usage of ICT's.* UNDP. Retrieved from http://www.undp.org.fj/documents/ICT4DEV/EnhancingPeopleParticip.zip.

Stork, E. UNDP (2004). *Formulation Mission Report UNDP PFnet Replica Project Vanuatu: Port Vila, Tanna, Espiritu Santo, and Malekula. 4th April -16th April 2004.* Retrieved from http://www.undp.org.fj/Strenghtening_Community_Access_to_Information.htm

Stork, E. UNDP (2004). *Formulation Mission Report UNDP PFnet Replica Project Papua New Guinea: Port Moresby and Bougainville: 24th March 2004 - 1st April 2004.* Retrieved December 30, 2009 from http://www.undp.org.fj/Strenghtening_Community_Access_to_Information.htm

Storper, M. (1997). *The Regional World.* New York: The Guilford Press.

Strauss, A. L., & Corbin, J. (1990). *Basics of Qualitative Research: Grounded Theory Procedures and Techniques.* London: Sage.

Strover, S. (2003). Remapping the Digital Divide. *The Information Society, 19,* 275–277. doi:10.1080/01972240309481

Tacchi, J. (2006) New Forms of Community Access. In *UNESCO IPDC/IFAP Joint Thematic debate: Giving Voice to Local Communities: From community radio to blogs. Paris: UNESCO.* Retrieved February 3, 2009, from http://eprints.qut.edu.au/archive/00003860/02/3860.pdf.

Tacchi, J., Slater, D., & Hearn, G. (2003). Ethnographic Action Research. Retrieved on May 19, 2004 from http://unescodelhi.nic.in/ publications/ear.pdf.

Tacchi, J., Slater, D., & Lewis, P. (2003, May). *Evaluating Community Based Media Initiatives: An ethnographic action research approach.* Paper presented at OUR Media III conference, Baranquilla, Colombia. Retrieved February 21, 2007, from http://pcmlp.socleg.ox.ac.uk/it4d/thinkpieces/tacchi.pdf.

Talyarkhan, S. (2004). Connecting the first mile: a framework for best practice in ICT projects for knowledge sharing in development. *Intermediate Technology Development Group (ITDG).* Retrieved February 16, 2009 from http://www.itdg.org/ docs/icts/ ict_best_practice_framework.pdf.

Talyarkhan, S., Grimshaw, D. J., & Lowe, L. (2005). *Connecting the First Mile. Investigating Best Practice for ICTs and Information Sharing for Development.* Rugby: ITDG.

Tan, J., Wen, H. J., & Awad, N. (2005). Health Care and Services Delivery Systems as Complex Adaptive Systems. *Communications of the ACM, 48*(5), 36–44. doi:10.1145/1060710.1060737

Tapscott, D. (2003). *Future Leaders.* McGraw-Hill. Retrieved February 2004 from http://www.growingupdigital.com

Taylor, M. (2003). *Public Policy in the Community.* Palgrave MacMillan.

Taylor, J. (2006). Population Diversity: Policy Implications of Emerging Indigenous Demographic Trends. (CAEPR Discussion Paper No.283/2006). Canberra: Australian National University, Centre For Aboriginal Economic Policy Research.

Taylor, J., & Williams, H. (1988). *Information and Communication Technologies and the Transformation of Local Government* (Working Paper 9), Centre for Urban and Regional Development Studies (Newcastle).

Taylor, S. (2004). Indigenous knowledge centres - the Queensland experience. ALIA Biennial Conference, Challenging Ideas. Gold Coast, QLD. Retrieved August 2, 2008 from http://conferences.alia.org.au/alia2004/pdfs/taylor.s.paper.pdf.

Taylor, W., & Marshall, S. (2003). Community Informatics Systems: A Construct for Addressing the Digital Divide. In *Proceedings of the 3rd International Conference on Information Technology in Asia* (CITA '03), Kuching, Sarawak, Malaysia, 17-18 July. Retrieved May 24, 2006 from http://inforcom.cqu.edu/Research/Research_Groups/CIS/Group_Site/CONTENT/ CIS%20a%20construct%20fa%20DD_WTSM.pdf.

Telecommons Development Group. (2000). Rural Access to Information and Communication Technologies (ICTs): The Challenge of Africa. *Prepared for African Connection Initiative of the African Connection Secretariat. Department for International Development (DFID), The World Bank, InfoDev.* Retrieved March 18, 2006 from http://www.unbotswana.org.bw/ undp/docs/bhdr2002/rural%20access%20to%20ICT%20the%20challenge%20of%20Africa.pdf

The Design-Based Research Collective. (2003). Design-based research: An emerging paradigm for educational inquiry. *Educational Researcher, 32*(1), 5–8. doi:10.3102/0013189X032001005

The Economic Times. (2008). Urban India Gets Under the Digital Mapping Radar. 8ᵗʰ June (p. 14).

The eGovernments Foundation (2003). *Street Naming and Property Numbering Guide*. The eGovernments Foundation, Bangalore, India.

The eGovernments Foundation (2004). *The Property Tax Information System with GIS*. Presentation document.

The Government of India. (2003) Electronic Governance – A Concept Paper. Retrieved November 12, 2008 from http://egov.mit.gov.in

The Government of Karnataka. (2005, Unpublished). A Note on the Process of Implementation of Computerisation etc – Guidance Notes.

The Lancet Editorial. (2009). Europe's aid to sub-saharan Africa: better results needed. *Lancet, 373*(9662), 434. doi:10.1016/S0140-6736(09)60113-6

The Times of India. (2006, July 22). E-governance, GIS: New Face of BMP (p.1).

The Times of India. (2008, December 15). Hiding Property Tax Info? Face Checks, Pay Fine: Revenue Officials Can Now Come Calling (p.1).

The Times of India. (2009a, January 8). Popular Debut for Online Tax Calculator: Applicable for Residential Properties, Citizens Rue Increase in Net Amount (p. 2).

The Times of India. (2009b, January 10). E-Calculator Spreads its Wings (p. 2)./

The World Bank (2004). *Building Blocks of eGovernment: Lessons from Developing Countries* (PREM Notes No. 91), August 2004.

The World Bank. (1998). *Knowledge for Development. World Development Report*. Washington, D.C.: The World Bank.

The World Bank. (2003). *Sustainable Telecenters: A Guide for Government Policy*. Washington, DC: The World Bank.

Third State Finance Commission (Government of Karnataka) (2007) *Decentralisation in Karnataka: A Status Report*, October 2007.

Thorley, P. (2002). Current Realities, Idealized Pasts: Archaeology, Values and Indigenous Heritage Management in Central Australia. *Oceania, 73*, 110–124.

Tipton, F. B. (2002). Bridging the Digital Divide in Southeast Asia: Pilot Agencies and Policy Implementation in Thailand, Malaysia, Vietnam, and the Philippines. *ASEAN Economic Bulletin, 19*(1), 83–99. doi:10.1355/AE19-1F

Tsing, A. L. (1999). Becoming Tribal Leader, and other Green Development Fantasies. In Li, T. M. (Ed.), *Agrarian Transformations in Upland Indonesia* (pp. 159–202). London: Harwood Academic Publications.

Tung, X., Sebastian, I. M., Jones, W., & Naklada, S. (2002). *E-Commerce Readiness in East Asian APEC Economies – A Precursor to Determine HRD Requirements and Capacity Building*. Bangkok, Thailand: Asia-Pacific Economic Cooperation, Telecommunications and Information Working Group, Business Facilitation Steering Group, National Electronic and Computer Technology Centre.

Tuomi, I. (2005). Beyond User-Centric Models of Product Creation. In Haddon, L. (Ed.), *Everyday Innovators* (pp. 21–38). Dordrecht: Springer. doi:10.1007/1-4020-3872-0_2

Ufford, P. Q. V. (1993). Knowledge and Ignorance in the practices of development. In Hobart, M. (Ed.), *An Anthropological Critique of Development, The Growth of Ignorance* (pp. 135–160). London, New York: Routledge.

Ulanowicz, R. E. (2009). *A third window*. West Conshohocken, PA: Templteton Foundation Press.

UN – United Nations. (2008). *United Nations e-Government survey 2008: from e-Government to Connected Governance. Department of Economic and Social Affairs, Division for Public Administration and Development Management*. New York: United Nations.

UN Press Release. (2004, September 7). UN finds progress on world anti-poverty goals, but crisis areas remain. *United Nations Press Release*. Retrieved October 2007 from http://www.un.org/millenniumgoals/mdg_pr_09_2004.pdf.

UNCTAD. (2007). Promoting Livelihoods through Telecentres. In UNCTAD, *Information Economy Report 2007-2008, Science and Technology for Development: The New Paradigm of ICT* (pp. 269-320). Geneva: UNCTAD.

UNDP – United Nations Development Programme. (2004). *Promoting ICT for Human Development in Asia: realizing the Millennium Development Goals*. New Delhi: Elsevier.

UNDP. (2001). *Human Development Report 2001: Making New Technologies Work for Human Development*. New York: United Nations Development Programme.

UNDP, Regional Bureau Asia and the Pacific. (2003). *Good practices in Asia and the Pacific - Expanding choices, empowering people: People First: Networking for Peace and development,* (pp. 22-23).

Unger, B.W., & Robinson, N.T. (2007). Information & communication technology (ICT) in Cambodia. *Digital Review of the Asia Pacific*, invited chapter, 122-130.

United Nation Development Programme. (2003). *MalaysiaICT4D Road Map: Malaysian ICT4D Programmes and the Eight Malaysia Plan (2001-2005)*. Retrieved May 26, 2004 from www.undp.org.my/factsheet/docs/ICT4D Roadmap_18Nov03.pdf

United Nation Global E-Government Readiness Report 2005 (2005). *From e-Government to e-Inclusion.* Retrieved April 10, 2009 from http://www.unpan.org/dpepa-egovernment%20report.asp

United Nations Development Programme (UNDP). (2001) Essentials: Information Communication Technology for Development. Synthesis of Lessons Learnt, *Evaluation Office No.5, September 2001.* New York: United Nations Development Program. Retrieved February 16, 2009 from http://www.undp.org/eo/documents /essentials_5.PDF.

United Nations Development Programme (UNDP). (1997). *Corruption and Good Governance: Discussion Paper 3*. New York: UNDP

Van Belle, J.-P., & Trusler, J. (2005). An Interpretivist Case Study of a South African Rural Multi-Purpose Community Centre. *The Journal of Community Informatics*, *1*(2), 140–157.

Van den Akker, J. (1999). Principles & Methods of Development Research. In van den Akker, J., Branch, R. M., Gustafson, K. L., Nieveen, N., & Plomp, T. (Eds.), *Design Approaches and Tools in Education and Training*. Dordrecht: Kluwer Academic Publishers.

Van den Akker, J. (2002). The Added Value of Development Research for Educational Development in Developing Countries. In K. Osaki, W. Ottevanger C. Uiso & J. van den Akker (Eds), *Science Education Research and Teacher Development in Tanzania*. Amsterdam: Vrije Universiteit, International Cooperation Center.

Van Dijk, J., & Hacker, K. (2003). The Digital Divide as a Complex and Dynamic Phenomenon. *The Information Society*, *19*, 315–326. doi:10.1080/01972240309487

Velden, M. V. D. (2002). Knowledge Facts, Knowledge Fiction: The Role of ICTs in Knowledge Management and Development. *Journal of International Development*, *14*(1), 25–37. doi:10.1002/jid.862

Vijayadev, V. (2008). 'SAS 02-03 to 06-07 Excel Spreadsheet', State Nodal Officer, Municipal Reforms Cell, Directorate of Municipal Administration; Private Communication.

Vincent, S. (2004). A New Property Map for Karnataka, *IndiaTogether.org*. Retrieved September 12, 2008 from http://www.indiatogether.org/2004/mar/gov-karmapgis.htm

Von Hippel, E. (1976). The Dominant Role of Users in the Scientific Instrument Innovation Process. *Research Policy*, *5*, 212–239. doi:10.1016/0048-7333(76)90028-7

Wade, R. H. (1985). The Market for Public Office: Why the Indian State Is Not Better at Development. *World Development, 13*(4), 467–497. doi:10.1016/0305-750X(85)90052-X

Wagner, D. A., Day, B., James, T., Kozma, R. B., Miller, J., & Unwin, T. (2005). *Monitoring and Evaluation of ICT in Education Projects: A Handbook for Developing Countries.* Washington DC: The World Bank (InfoDev).

Wajcman, J. (2004). *Technofeminism.* Oxford: Polity Press.

Wallis, C. (2007). *Techno-mobility and Translocal Migration: Mobile Phone Use among Female Migrant Workers in Beijing.* Paper presented at Female Labor Migration in Globalising Asia: Translocal/Transnational Identities and Agencies, 13-14 September, Asia Research Institute. Retrieved April 20, 2010 from http://arnic.info/Papers/Techno-Mobility%20and%20Translocal %20Migration_CaraWallis.pdf

Walsham, G. (1995). Interpretive Case Studies in IS Research: Nature and Method. *European Journal of Information Systems, 4*(2), 74–81. doi:10.1057/ejis.1995.9

Walsham, G. (2001). *Making a World of Difference: IT in a Global Context.* Chichester, UK: Wiley.

Walsham, G., Robey, D., & Sahay, S. (2007). Foreword: Special Issue on Information Systems in Developing Countries. *Management Information Systems Quarterly, 31*(2), 317–326.

Walsham, G. (1995). The emergence of interpretivism in IS research. *Information Systems Research, 6*(4), 376–394. doi:10.1287/isre.6.4.376

Walsham, G., & Sahay, S. (1999). GIS for District-Level Administration in India: Problems and Opportunities. *Management Information Systems Quarterly, 23*(1), 39–66. doi:10.2307/249409

Wang, F., & Hannafin, M. J. (2005). Design-based research and technology-enhanced learning environments. *Educational Technology Research and Development, 53*(4), 5–23. doi:10.1007/BF02504682

Warschauer, M. (2003). Dissecting the "Digital Divide": A Case Study in Egypt. *The Information Society, 19,* 297–304. doi:10.1080/01972240309490

Warschauer, M. (2003). *Technology and Social Inclusion: Rethinking the Digital Divide.* Cambridge, MA: The MIT Press.

Warschauer, M. (2002). Reconceptualizing the Digital Divide. *First Monday.* Retrieved October, 16 2003 from www.firstmonday.dk/issues/ issue7_ 7/warschauer

Warschauer, M. (2002). Reconceptualizing the Digital Divide. [Online]. Retrieved July 2009 from http://firstmonday.org/htbin/cgiwrap/bin /ojs/index.php/fm/article/view/967/888

Warschauer, M. (2003). *Technology and Social Inclusion: Rethinking the Digital Divide.* Cambridge: Massachusetts Institute of Technology (MIT). Endnote [1] For more information on the Meraka Institute website, their website is http://www.meraka.org.za/. The CSIR website is http://www.csir.co.za/

Weigel, G., & Waldburger, D. (Eds.). (2004). ICT4D: Connecting People for a Better World. Berne: Swiss Agency of Development and Cooperation and the Global Knowledge Partnership.

Wilkinson, R., & Picket, K. (2010). *The spirit level. Why equality is better for everyone.* London: Penguin Books.

Wilson, B. (2001). *Soft Systems Methodology: Conceptual Model Building and its Contribution.* Chichester, UK: John Wiley and Sons.

Winter, M. (2006). Problem structuring in project management: an application of soft systems methodology (SSM). *The Journal of the Operational Research Society, 57*(7), 802–812. doi:10.1057/palgrave.jors.2602050

Winter, M. (2002). *Management, Managing and Managing Projects: Towards An Extended Soft Systems Methodology.* PhD thesis, Department of Management Science, Lancaster University, UK.

Woolcock, M., & Narayan, D. (2000). Social capital: implications for development theory, research and policy. *The World Bank Research Observer, 15*(2), 225–249.

World Bank (2002). *Private Solutions for Infrastructure in Cambodia: A Country Framework Report.*

World Bank. (1998). *World Bank Development Report, Knowledge for Development*. Washington, DC, USA: The World Bank.

World Bank. (1998). *Education and Training in the East Asia and Pacific Region, Education Sector Unit*. Washington: World Bank.

World Bank. (2002). *Skills and Literacy Training for Better Livelihoods: A Review of Approaches and Experiences.* Washington: World Bank.

World Bank. (2008). *Improved Access to Communications in Rural Cambodia*. Cambodia: GPOBA Commitment Document.

World Bank. (1998). Knowledge for Development. *World Development Report*. Retrieved on November 15, 2001 from http://www.worldbank.org/wdr/wdr98/contents.htm

World Bank. (2004). *Country Data: Malaysia*. Retrieved April 26, 2004 from http://www. worldbank.org/cgi-bin/sendoff.cgi?page=%2 Fdata%2Fcountrydata%2Fict% 2Fmys_ict.pdf&submit=Go

World Factbook, C. I. A. (2009). Retrieved September 2009 from https://www.cia.gov/library/publications/the-world-factbook/.

World Resource Institute (2002). *Jhai Foundation's Internet Learning Centres and the Remote IT Village Initiative.*

Wortley, D. J. (2004). Interactive Broadcasting and Community Informatics. In Khalid, H. M., Helander, M. G., & Yeo, A. W. (Eds.), *Work with Computing Systems* (pp. 259–260). Kuala Lumpur: Damai Sciences.

Wright, S. (1995). Anthropology: still the uncomfortable discipline? In Ahmed, A. S., & Shore, C. N. (Eds.), *The future of Anthropology: Its Relevance to the Contemporary World*. London: Athlone.

Wu, B. (2009). International Migration and Wenzhou's Development. In Johanson, G., Smyth, R., & French, R. (Eds.), *Living Outside the Walls: The Chinese in Prato* (pp. 238–260). Newcastle upon Tyne: Cambridge Scholars Publishing.

Xiao, C., & Ochsmann, R. (2009). Lost in Alien Surroundings: the Identity Crises Among Chinese Labourers in Prato. In Johanson, G., Smyth, R., & French, R. (Eds.), *Living Outside the Walls: The Chinese in Prato* (pp. 192–201). Newcastle upon Tyne: Cambridge Scholars Publishing.

Xiaolv, Z., Yi, C., & Smyth, R. (2009). The contribution of donations of overseas Chinese to Wenzhou development. In G. Johanson, R. Smyth, & R. French (Eds.), *Living Outside the Walls: The Chinese in Prato* (pp. 261-273). Newcastle upon Tyne, Cambridge Scholars Publishing. 261-273.

Yang, X-Y., & Hua-bing, X. (2010). Collecting survey responses in Prato in October 2008. In e-mail communication to the first-named author on 13 March 2010.

Yeo, K. T. (1993). Systems thinking and project management - time to reunite'. *International Journal of Project Management, 11*(2), 111–117. doi:10.1016/0263-7863(93)90019-J

Yin, R. K. (2003). *Case Study Research: Design and Methods* (3rd ed., *Vol. 5*). Thousand Oaks, CA: Sage Publications.

Yin, R. K. (2003). *Applications of case study research*. Thousand Oaks, CA: Sage Publications.

Yusuf, S. (2003). *Innovative East Asia: The Future of Growth*. Washington, D.C.: The World Bank. doi:10.1596/0-8213-5356-X

Zulberti, E. (2003). Foreword. In Girard, B. (Ed.), *The One to Watch: Radio, new ICTs and interactivity* (pp. iii–iv). Rome: FAO.

About the Contributors

Jacques Steyn holds a PhD in language and complex systems, and he received an award for excellence in science from the South African Association for the Advancement of Science (S2A3) for his Masters Degree. In 1999 he developed the first XML-based general music markup language (http://www.musicmarkup.info). He was member of the international ISO/MPEG-7 standards workgroup on metadata for interactive-TV and Multimedia. He was also member of the ISO/MPEG-4 extension workgroup for music notation (i.e. symbolic music representation). In 1999 and 2000 he was Associate Professor of Multimedia at the University of Pretoria. Since February 2005 he served as Head of the School of IT at Monash University's South African campus. Prior to that, for close to a decade, he was a private consultant in the field of new media, web technologies and multimedia. His interest in ICT4D began in 1999. In 2006 he established the International Development Informatics Association, which at the time of writing had its 3rd annual conference. The idea of this book was born from frustration with the scarcity of well-founded academic research in the field of ICT4D, where media hype seems to reign.

Jean-Paul Van Belle joined the Department of Information Systems of UCT in 1997 and became an associate professor in 2006. He is currently Head of the Department. He obtained a licentiate in 1983 (Rijksuniversiteit Gent, Belgium), an MBA in 1988 (GSB, Stellenbosch University, South Africa) and his PhD in 2004 (UCT, South Africa). In the last 8 years, he has authored or co-authored about 15 books/chapters, 15 journal articles and more than 60 peer-reviewed published conference papers. His key research area is the social and organisational adoption of emerging information technologies in a developing world context. The key technologies researched include e-commerce, M-commerce, e-government and, more recently, open source software. He has considerable experience with both quantitative survey approaches as well as qualitative case study research. His main research focus for the near future will be on small organisations i.e. small and micro-businesses as well as NGOs.

Eduardo Villanueva Mansilla holds a B.A. in Library Science and a M.A. in Communication Studies both by PUCP. After working as systems librarian and webmaster of his University, since 2005 is a full-time faculty member at the Communications department where he conducts research and teaches on subjects related with ICT and communications, including information society, media and new media policy. From 1994 to 1997 he was a member of the International Federation of Library Associations and Institutions (IFLA) Latin American and Caribbean standing committee, as well as a corresponding member of the information technology committee; in 2002 he acted as Senior Policy Advisor for the vice minister of communications of Peru, as well as advisor to the President of Peru's National Science,

Technology and Innovation Council. His multiple publications, in Spanish and English, led to his current position as associate editor of the Journal of Community Informatics (ci-journal.net).

* * *

Antonio Díaz Andrade is a Senior Lecturer in Business Information Systems at Auckland University of Technology (AUT), New Zealand. Antonio has accumulated more than 13,000 hours of work in projects and became a Project Management Professional (PMP) in 2009. He obtained his doctoral degree (PhD) in Management Science and Information Systems from The University of Auckland in 2007, under the sponsorship of The University of Auckland Doctoral Scholarship. His main research interest is in the transmission of computer-mediated information, especially in underserved communities, through existing face-to-face networks. His work has been published in the Information Technology for Development journal, The Qualitative Report, the Electronic Journal of Information Systems in Developing Countries and a number of book chapters. Antonio has also presented at the International Conference on Information Systems (ICIS), the International Federation for Information Processing (IFIP) Working Group 9.4 "Computers in Developing Countries", among other prestigious forums.

Poline Bala is a Senior Lecturer at the Faculty of Social Sciences, University Malaysia Sarawak (UNIMAS). She is also the Deputy Director of Centre of Excellence in Rural Informatics at University Malaysia Sarawak. Her area of interest and research includes examining the impacts of political boundary lines on the formation of cultural, political and economic units at the border regions of Borneo. Most recently her research explores the role of Information Communication Technologies (ICT) on development activities in rural Sarawak. Looking specifically at the e-Bario project which she and a team of researchers initiated in the Kelabit Highlands of Sarawak in 1998, she examines social change that is connected to the use of ICT in Bario of Central Borneo.

Zulkefli bin Ibrahim is the Director at Management Development Division, Malaysian Administrative Modernisation & Management Planning Unit, Kuala Lumpur.

Jørn Braa is associate professor at the Department of Informatics, University of Oslo, Norway. Since 1993 he has worked extensively with national and local health authorities on assessing and developing HIS and human and institutional capacity in a number of countries. He has been heavily involved in the establishment and expansion of the HISP project for over 10 years. His research interests focus on strategies and conditions for action research, Open Source Software development and application and health information systems in developing countries. He is currently engaged in collaboration with WHO & Health Metrics Network on the development of Open Source "public health country toolkit" an integrated data warehouse application for country HIS including DHISv2 and the new web based WHO application Open HealthMapper.

David Brown is Professor of Strategy and Information Systems at the Department of Management Science and Director of the Lancaster China Management Centre at Lancaster University Management School. His research interests have two separate but linked strands. Firstly, strategic studies including strategic information systems and e-business, and secondly the application of these strands internationally, especially in transitional economies. Current research includes: SMEs and e-business, e-business policy in developing economies and strategic information systems. He has authored over 40 research articles, and has co-authored and edited three books on management transition in China. In 1998 he was appointed Fellow Professor in Management Science at Renmin University of China, and in 2008 he received the Greater China Recognition Award from UKTI (UK Trade and Investment Department) for his personal contribution in building partnerships and fostering Sino-UK relationships.

Claire Buré is a program coordinator with the Zoltner Consulting Group in Santiago, Chile, where she is currently leading a project that uses SMS messaging for low-income people working in the agricultural industry. Prior to this position, Claire worked as a researcher both at telecentre.org at the International Development Research Centre (IDRC) in Ottawa, Canada; and at the Institute for the Study of Science, Technology and Innovation (ISSTI) at the University of Edinburgh. Her key research interests concentrate on the local use and appropriation of mobile phones, community radio and the internet, as well as on gender perspectives in science and technology. Claire holds a Master's degree in Science and Technology Studies from the University of Edinburgh, UK.

Grant Cambridge has been working as a researcher at the Counsel for Scientific and Industrial Research (CSIR) since 1997. He has been involved in the Digital Doorway 'Unassisted Learning' project since 2002. He is involved in the system design, manufacturing process and deployment of the Digital Doorways.

Anand Chand is a Senior Lecturer in the Department of Management and Public Administration in the Faculty of Business and Economics at University of the South Pacific in Fiji. He has a BA (Tasmania, Australia), Post-Graduate Diploma in HRM and Industrial Relations (USP), Post-Graduate Diploma in Business Studies (Canterbury, NZ), MA in Industrial Relations/ HRM (USP), MA in Social Science Research Methods (Manchester, UK), PhD (Wales, UK). He has been teaching and researching at USP for the last 24 years and also whilst in UK, he taught at Cardiff University for six month. Furthermore, Anand has extensive experience in conducting primary large-scale base-line surveys for national and international agencies in Fiji and other South Pacific Islands. For example he has conducted research for the United Nations Development Program (UNDP), United Nations Fund for Population Activities (UNFPA), International Labour Organisation (ILO) in Suva and Bangkok offices, Japanese Institute of Labour (JIL), Japanese International Cooperation Agency (JICA), International Planned Parenthood Federation (IPPF-UK), New Zealand Save the Children Fund (NZSCF), Fiji Save the Children Fund (FSCF), and for the EU/USP Employment and Labour Market Programme. He has visited and taught in a number of South Pacific Islands countries. Anand has presented 30 papers at international conferences and published 25 articles and few book chapters. He teachers and does research in the area of Employment Relations, Industrial Relations, HRM and Global Supply Chains.

Lorenzo Dalvit holds a Laurea in Sociology from the University of Trento (Italy), an MA in Linguistics and Applied Language Studies from Rhodes University (South Africa) and a PhD in ICT Education from Rhodes University (South Africa). He is a Lecturer in ICT Education in the Education Department at Rhodes University. He is also the Research and ICT coordinator of the South Africa – Norway Tertiary Education Development (SANTED) programme within the African Studies Section of the School of Languages at Rhodes University. He has been a researcher in Multilingualism and ICT for many years within the Telkom Centre of Excellence in the Computer Science Department at Rhodes University and at the University of Fort Hare (South Africa). Dr Dalvit has published extensively across disciplines on issues related to ICT, language and cultural issues and their impact on social development and access to education. His contributions range from edited collections, textbooks and book chapters to articles in peer-reviewed academic journals. He has organised and presented at a local and international conferences, and presented work at institutions in South Africa and overseas. Dr Dalvit has initiated and contributed to various ICT for development projects. He conducts and supervises research within the Siyakhula project in rural South Africa. He initiated a stream of accredited ICT qualifications in Dwesa, a rural area in the marginalised and economically impoverished region of Transkei. His vision is to turn the area in a centre for ICT education, capable of attracting students from the whole of Transkei. Dr Dalvit is also involved in outreach ICT for development projects in marginalised suburbs of Grahamstown, where Rhodes University is based. He is an associate of Translate.org.za, and NGO committed to making open-source software accessible in all 11 South African languages.

Ruth de Villiers is a professor in the School of Computing at the University of South Africa (UNISA), one of the world's mega-universities. UNISA is a distance-teaching institution, which emphasizes the role of research into open distance learning and educational technology. Ruth has a PhD and also holds masters degrees in the domains of Information Systems and Computer-integrated Education, respectively. For more than twenty five years, she has taught Computer Science and Informatics. Her major current research interests and teaching areas are Human-Computer Interaction and e-Learning. She has combined these areas by undertaking research and development in the usability and usability evaluation of a broad variety of e-learning applications and environments, including systems targeting users across the Digital Divide. She has also published in the focus area of meta-research, involving work on various research designs and methodologies. Ruth supervises masters and doctoral students in the fields mentioned above.

Tom Denison is a Research Associate with the Centre for Community Networking Research (CCNR) within Monash University's Faculty of Information Technology. His main research focus is in the areas of social and community informatics, focusing on the take-up and sustainable use of information and communications technologies (ICTs) by non-profit organisations, and the use of ICTs by migrants and migrant support organisations. With a background in library automation and electronic publishing, Tom has also consulted widely in Australia and Vietnam.

Tengku Mohamed Faziharudean obtained his doctorate from Global Information & Telecommunication Studies, Waseda University, Japan. He is currently attached to the Operations and Management Information Systems Department, Faculty of Business and Accountancy, University of Malaya, Kuala Lumpur, Malaysia. His research interest includes the issues related to digital divide, technology adoption and diffusion and in area of Internet banking.

Jay Gibson collaboratively with Aboriginal people in Central Australia. For the past three years, he has assisted a number of remote Aboriginal communities to establish digital archives of cultural and historical materials as a part of the Northern Territory Library's Libraries and Knowledge Centres Program. Jason's work history includes research consultancies with both the University and government sectors regarding the design of cultural heritage services for Indigenous communities, the management of Indigenous knowledge in digital environments, and the indexing the field diaries of the seminal anthropologist and linguist TGH Strehlow. He has also been periodically engaged as a specialist documenter of Indigenous cultural knowledge, mythology and social histories in the Arandic language region. Jason holds a Masters degree from Swinburne University of Technology. His thesis investigated Indigenous uses of online technologies following the popularisation of the Internet and other digital technologies in the late 1990s. He has published a number writings on the interface between digital media technologies and Indigenous culture for both a scholarly and popular audience. He is currently a researcher with the Australian National Universities 'Reconstructing the Spencer and Gillen Collection: Museums, Indigenous Perspectives and Production of Cultural Knowledge' ARC Linkage project and is based at Museum Victoria.

Helena Grunfeld has over 30 years experience in the ICT sector in Australia, working for the incumbent telecommunications operator Telstra, and participating in the establishment of a new carrier, Uecomm. She has also completed numerous consulting assignments for various organisations, including co-authoring a book on number portability with Ovum and developing a costing and pricing model for ARCOM, the regulatory authority in Timor-Leste, through an assignment with the International Telecommunication Union. Helena has an undergraduate degree from the School for Social Work and Public Administration in Lund, Sweden and completed a Master of Business Administration at the Royal Melbourne Institute of Technology in 1989. She is now a research scholar at the Centre for Strategic Economic Studies at Victoria University, Melbourne, Australia.

Channa Gunawardena is a Project Management and Management Systems specialist, with over 12 years experience in international development consulting focusing on Information Society and ICT measures for sustainable development. He is currently Director at Megaskills Limited an UK based development consulting company focused on Emerging Markets. He has worked on consultancy assignments across over 25 countries covering much of Europe, South Asia and South-East Asia. He has worked in over 30 major projects funded by International Funding Agencies (IFAs) including the European Commission (EC), Asian Development Bank (ADB), World Bank and UN agencies providing expertise in project management, management systems, benefit monitoring & evaluation (BME), sustainability measures, multiplier effects, value chain analysis and information systems. He recently completed a part-time PhD in "Donor project funded ICT Initiatives in the Vocational and Technical Education (VTE) Sector of Asian Developing Countries: A Systems Study" focussed on his area of practice at the Lancaster University Management School, UK.

Kim Gush studied electronic engineering and computer science at UCT, completing his Bsc Eng in 1996. He has been working in development and research at the Counsel for Scientific and Industrial Research (CSIR), South Africa since 1998. He has been involved in the Digital Doorway 'Unassisted Learning' project since 2002. He is involved with system design and open source software implementation on the Digital Doorway systems.

Im Sarun graduated from Cambodia's University of Health Science as Medical Doctor in 1996 and obtained a Master Degree of Public Health in 2004 from St. Louis University, Missouri, USA, specializing in International Community Health Education under William J. Fulbright scholarship. He has been a public health professional for more than ten years with government and non-governmental organizations in Cambodia and USA in the area of reproductive and child health, HIV/AIDS and Malaria. His professional skills include project design, planning, management, monitoring & evaluation, research and communication. He is now Research Manager for iREACH. He is also a vice president of Board of Directors of PSP non-governmental organization.

Graeme Johanson has extensive experience of research into and the application of information and communications technologies for the purposes of development. As Associate Dean Research Training, Faculty of Information Technology, Monash University, he participates in research projects on all of Monash's overseas campuses. He attended both of the World Summits on the Information Society, being a member of the official Australian delegation in Geneva at the second (2005) Summit. His work on the Chinese diaspora extends from Wenzhou and Chengdu in China, to Australia, South Africa and northern Italy. Information and Communications Technologies are shown to be extremely important for migration experiences overall, and the personal well-being and financial welfare of migrant families. Other projects involve knowledge management and development in Vietnam, the role of the Digital Doorway from the Meraka Institute in southern Africa, government policy for third sector development in Australia, online donations for NGOs in Australia, research agendas for the Asia-Pacific region, capacity-building by mobile phones for small businesses as drivers of development in Indonesia, and mobile banking in poor townships in South Africa.

Dorothea Kleine is Lecturer in Human Geography at Royal Holloway, University of London and a member of the ICT4D Collective/UNESCO Chair in ICT4D. Her research interests include: theoretical approaches to ICT4D; the capability approach; globalisation and trade; Fair Trade; ethical consumption; gender; and local economic development. She has published widely in peer-reviewed journals and is author of Surfen in Birkenstocks (Oekom, 2005). From 2004-2007 she was Managing Editor of the journal Information Technologies and International Development (MIT Press). She served as Project Manager of the EPSRC FairTracing Project (2006-2009, www.fairtracing.org), seeking to empower UK ethical consumers as well as producers in India and Chile. She is a Fellow of the Royal Geographical Society (with the IBG) and has worked as a consultant/advisor to EuropeAid, GTZ, InWent and to NGOs. Before joining Royal Holloway, she was a Research Associate at Cambridge University. She holds a Staatsexamen from Munich University (LMU) and a PhD from the London School of Economics and Political Science.

Rajendra Kumar, I.A.S., is a senior officer in the Indian Administrative Service (I.A.S.) and is currently working as a Director in the office of the Union Minister of Shipping in the Government of India in New Delhi. His current research interests are in examining how the potential of modern information and communication technologies (ICTs) can be harnessed for greater social, economic, and political development in developing countries. His focus is on examining how science, technology, and innovation policies can help in achieving this goal. He has conducted research on assessing the social, economic, and governance impacts of ICT for development projects in India and has examined how these projects can help in social and economic development of poor rural communities. At a macro level, he has focused his research on the role of the state in promoting innovations in the ICT industries to make them globally competitive. Specifically, he has examined the role of the state in three southern states in India in attracting and making their software and software services industries internationally competitive. Dr. Kumar holds a PhD in international economic development and regional planning and

443

an MCP from Massachusetts Institute of Technology, an MTech from the Indian Institute of Technology in Delhi, and a BTech from the Indian Institute of Technology in Kanpur. He has published a book and several articles in international journals.

Brian Lloyd has been a professional writer / researcher for the past five years. He currently works at Australian Parliament House, Canberra. Before this he held research, teaching and information roles in universities and, for a time, with a software company. He holds a Ph.D. in English and a Masters in Business Information Technology. Brian has written on a variety of subjects, including: nuclear policy; Indigenous affairs; alcohol and other drugs; Defence; trade; ICTs; libraries; and the literary avant-garde.

Seán Ó Siochrú has twenty five years experience in programme design, evaluation and implementation in over fifty countries and for a variety of international organisations. His main themes are community empowerment and communication rights, as well as media, and information and communication technologies (ICTs). He has worked extensively with UNDP (headquarters, as well as with a dozen or so County Offices), leading the final evaluation of the Sustainable Development Networking Programme (SDNP) that had been implemented over a decade in dozens of countries; and evaluating, designing and supporting the implementation of projects at national level in Albania, Bangladesh, Belarus, Bosnia & Herzegovina, Guyana, India, Kenya, Kyrgyzstan, Mozambique, Pakistan, Rwanda, Tanzania, Turkmenistan and Uganda. He has also worked for UNECA, IDRC, IFAD, World Bank Institute, ITU, UNESCO and the European Union on a variety of missions and locations. He collaborates closely with NGOs, and was on the Civil Society Bureau of the World Summit on the Information Society (WSIS), where he played an active part in mobilising civil society. He has had a leading role in various NGOs, including the MacBride Round Table and CRIS (Communication Rights in the Information Society), and was member of a pre-WSIS Human Rights mission to Tunis in 2003. He is Research Director at NEXUS Research in Dublin, a non-profit research institutions, and founder and Chair of Dublin Community Television.

Caroline Pade Khene is a PhD research candidate in the Department of Information Systems at Rhodes University, South Africa. She also holds a Masters in Information Systems (2005-2006), and a Bachelor of Business Science in Information Systems and Mathematical Statistics (2001-2004) from Rhodes University. Her current research is on the development and implementation of an evaluation framework for rural ICT projects in developing countries. This research was inspired by her Masters research on an investigation of ICT project management techniques for sustainable ICT projects in rural development. Her involvement in the Siyakhula Living Lab since inception has provided her with the opportunity to experience and research the realities and context of rural ICT projects. She has participated as a Baseline Study researcher for the Siyakhula Living Lab from 2008-2009; to assess the existing socio-economic and readiness status of the community the ICT project aims to support. In 2008, she acted as a Baseline Study collaborator between the Siyakhula Living Lab and the Moutse Living Lab of the Meraka Institute. She continues to evaluate other key aspects of rural ICT projects. Her research interests include ICT for development, project management, requirements elicitation, and project evaluation.

Cate Richmond is Assistant Director, Public Libraries and Knowledge Centres, Northern Territory Library. Cate has held this position since 2004 and has overseen the implementation of the Libraries

444

and Knowledge Centres Program: a new model for library services to remote Indigenous communities in the Territory. Cate has more than 30 years of library experience and has worked in the academic, government and public library sectors. Cate has a Bachelor of Arts from Flinders University and a Graduate Diploma of Librarianship from Riverina-Murray Institute of Higher Education. Since joining Northern Territory Library, Cate has published several papers on Indigenous library services and is the Northern Territory representative on the National and State Libraries of Australasia (NSLA) Indigenous Library Services and Collections Working Group. She is committed to ensuring that all Territorians, no matter where they live, have access to relevant library services, with opportunities to preserve and access their cultural heritage.

Vincent Shaw is a medical doctor with a Masters in Family Medicine and a PhD in Information Management. He has extensive experience in health management having served in the Eastern Cape Province of South Africa at facility, district, regional and provincial levels for many years. He has been involved in the development of hospital information systems, and has led the revamping of the HMIS in Zambia. He has over the last 4 years worked extensively in northern Nigeria, developing health information systems in contexts characterized by low levels of access to technology and power, and low computer literacy. His research interests relate to the development of HIS in resource constrained settings, and to the development of organizations such as HISP to provide ongoing support to the public sector in Africa. He has published numerous articles and book chapters related to health information systems development in resource constrained contexts.

Ingrid Siebörger has a Masters degree in Computer Science from Rhodes University (2006 with Distinction), where she investigated Models of Internet connectivity for secondary schools. She is currently working towards a PhD in Computer Science focusing on ICT architectures that are pedagogically suitable and cost effective for secondary schools in South Africa. She has been the research assistant for the Telkom Centre of Excellence (an industry sponsored research group) in the Computer Science Department at Rhodes University since 2006 and is involved in a number of ICT4D projects within the Centre of Excellence, focusing on network provision in rural or peri-urban green field environments and the use of technology in and for education.

Ronel Smith is a project manager at the Counsel for Scientific and Industrial Research (CSIR). She has been closely involved with the Digital Doorway project since 2002.

Ainin Sulaiman obtained her PhD from University of Birmingham, United Kingdom. She is currently attached to the Operations and Management Information Systems Department, Faculty of Business and Accountancy, University of Malaya, Kuala Lumpur, Malaysia. Her research interest includes technology adoption and diffusion, digital divide, electronic commerce and performance evaluation.

Hannah Thinyane has a PhD in Computer Science from University of South Australia, where she investigated human computer interaction techniques in ubiquitous computing environments. She is currently employed as a lecturer in Computer Science at Rhodes University. Her field of research is in human computer interaction, particularly within a development context. She is involved in a number of ICT4D projects within the Telkom Centre of Excellence at Rhodes University, including the Siyakhula Living Lab.

Brian Unger is currently Interim President and CEO of Cybera Inc. (www.cybera.ca). He is also Professor Emeritus and the Executive Director of the Grid Research Centre (grid.ucalgary.ca) at the University of Calgary, and is the Special Advisor for iREACH ("informatics for rural empowerment and community health"), a research project supported by the International Development Research Centre of Canada (IDRC), and by the Cambodian Ministry of Commerce (ireach.org.kh). He was the founding President of the Netera Alliance which is now Cybera Inc. and the founding President of iCORE (the "informatics circle of research excellence") from 1999 through 2004 (www.icore.ca). Cybera Inc. is a not-for-profit consortium that builds cyberinfrastructure (advanced networking, computing and data management) in support of industry and academic research in Alberta and iCORE is a not-for-profit corporation aimed at recruiting exceptional ICT researchers to Alberta universities. In its first five years iCORE invested $43 million in 17 research chairs and professorships that now support over 500 faculty, graduate students and research staff. Dr Unger was the founding board chair of C3.ca Inc. (www.c3.ca), a national consortium aimed at building Canada's infrastructure in high performance computation. C3.ca was one of the originators of the current Compute Canada initiative. He was a Co-Principal Investigator of WestGrid (www.westgrid.ca), 2002-2008, which raised $48 million to provide research infrastructure for Western Canada universities; and was the founding president and CEO of a for-profit startup company, Jade Simulations, that developed and marketed parallel simulation software products from 1988 through 1993. Dr. Unger was named a Canada Pioneer of Computing at the IBM CASCON conference, Toronto, October, 2005, and received the IWAY Public Leadership award for outstanding contributions to Canada's information society in 2004, and the 1993 ASTech award for "Innovation in Alberta Technology" for research in parallel simulation and distributed computation.

Shefali Virkar is research student at the University of Oxford, U K, currently reading for a D.Phil. in Politics. Her doctoral research seeks to explore the growing use of Information and Communication Technologies (ICTs) to promote better governance in the developing world, with special focus on the political and institutional impacts of ICTs on local public administration reform in India. Shefali holds an MA in Globalisation, Governance and Development from the University of Warwick, UK. Her Master's thesis analysed the concept of the Digital Divide in a globalising world, its impact developing countries and the ensuing policy implications. At Oxford, Shefali is a member of Keble College.

Index

A

B

C

D